COOK'S

ILLUSTRATED

~ 1996 ~

$29.95

Published by
Boston Common Press Limited Partnership
17 Station Street
Brookline, MA 02445

ISBN: 0-9640179-5-4
ISSN: 1068-2821

To get home delivery of future issues of *Cook's Illustrated*, call 800-526-8442 inside the U.S., or 515-247-7571 if calling from outside the U.S.

In addition to the Annual Hardbound editions, *Cook's Illustrated* offers the following publications:

The *How to Cook* series of single topic cookbooks
Titles include *How to Make A Pie, How to Make An American Layer Cake, How to Stir-Fry, How to Make Ice Cream, How to Make Pizza, How to Make Holiday Desserts, How to Make Pasta Sauces, How to Make Salad, How to Grill, How to Make Simple Fruit Desserts, How to Make Cookie Jar Favorites, How to Cook Holiday Roasts & Birds, How to Make Stew, How to Cook Shrimp & Other Shellfish, How to Barbecue & Roast On The Grill, How to Cook Garden Vegetables, How to Make Pot Pies & Casseroles, How to Make Soup, How to Sauté, How to Cook Potatoes,* and *How to Make Quick Appetizers.* A boxed set of the first 11 titles in the series is available in an attractive, protective slip case. New releases are published every two months, so give us a call for our complete list of available titles.

The Best Recipe
This 560-page book is a collection of over 700 recipes and 200 illustrations from the past seven years of *Cook's*. We've included basics, such as how to make chicken stock, as well as recipes for quick weeknight meals and special entertaining. Let *The Best Recipe* become your indispensable kitchen companion.

Multi-Year Master Index
Quickly find every article and recipe *Cook's Illustrated* has published from the Charter Issue in 1992 through the most recent year-end issue. Recipe names, authors, article titles, subject matter, equipment testings, food tastings, cookbook reviews, wine tastings, and ingredients are all now instantly at your fingertips.

The Cook's Bible **and** *The Yellow Farmhouse Cookbook*
Written by Christopher Kimball and published by Little, Brown and Company.

To order any of the books listed above, call 800-611-0759 inside the U.S., or 515-246-6911 if calling from outside the U.S.

You can order subscriptions, gift subscriptions, and any of our books by visiting our online store at
www.cooksillustrated.com

BC=Back Cover

COOK'S ILLUSTRATED INDEX 1996

COOK'S
ILLUSTRATED

Roasting Chicken 14 Ways

Don't Baste, Don't Truss, and Don't Start Breast Up

Chewy Chocolate Chip Cookies

Melted Butter Makes the Difference

Best Brewed Coffee

Basic Drip Method Outperforms All Others

Great Beef Stew

Always Use Chuck, Never Use Round

PERFECT PANCAKES

RATING DIJON MUSTARDS

BEST BORDEAUX UNDER $20

BRAISING WINTER VEGETABLES

STEP-BY-STEP KNIFE TECHNIQUES

$4.00 U.S./$4.95 CANADA

"Winter Vegetables"
See page 26 for braised winter vegetable recipes.

ILLUSTRATION BY
BRENT WATKINSON

Braised Carrots with Sour Cream–Cilantro Sauce, adapted from *Southwest the Beautiful Cookbook*, by Fenzl and Kolpas (Collins, 1994)

ILLUSTRATION BY
CAROL FORTUNATO

COOK'S
ILLUSTRATED

Publisher and Editor CHRISTOPHER KIMBALL

Consulting Editor MARK BITTMAN

Senior Editor JOHN WILLOUGHBY

Food Editor PAM ANDERSON

Senior Writer JACK BISHOP

Articles Editor ANNE TUOMEY

Editorial Production Director MAURA LYONS

Editorial Prod. Coordinator KARIN L. KANEPS

Assistant Editor ADAM RIED

Copy Editor GARY PFITZER

Test Cook MELISSA HAMILTON

....

Art Director MEG BIRNBAUM

Food Stylist MARIE PIRAINO

Special Projects Designer DEBBIE WOLFE

....

Marketing Director ADRIENNE KIMBALL

Circulation Director ELAINE REPUCCI

Ass't Circulation Manager JENNIFER L. KEENE

Circulation Coordinator JONATHAN VENIER

Circulation Assistant C. MARIA PANNOZZO

Production Director JAMES MCCORMACK

Project Coordinator SHEILA DATZ

Production Coordinator PAMELA SLATTERY

Systems Administrator MATTHEW FRIGO

Production Artist KEVIN MOELLER

....

Vice President JEFFREY FEINGOLD

Controller LISA A. CARULLO

Accounting Assistant MANDY SHITO

Office Manager TONYA ESTEY

Special Projects FERN BERMAN

Cook's Illustrated (ISSN 1068-2821) is published bimonthly by Boston Common Press Limited Partnership, 17 Station Street, P.O. Box 569, Brookline, MA 02147-0569. Copyright 1995 Boston Common Press Limited Partnership. Second-class postage paid at Boston, MA, and additional mailing offices, USPS #012487. For list rental information, please contact Direct Media, 200 Pemberwick Road, Greenwich, CT 06830; (203) 532-1000. Editorial office: 17 Station Street, P.O. Box 569, Brookline, MA 02147-0569; (617) 232-1000, FAX (617) 232-1572, E-mail: cooksill@aol.com. Editorial contributions should be sent or E-mailed to: Editor, Cook's Illustrated. We cannot assume responsibility for manuscripts submitted to us. Submissions will be returned only if accompanied by a large self-addressed stamped envelope. Subscription rates: $24.95 for one year; $45 for two years; $65 for three years. (Canada: add $3 per year; all other countries: add $12 per year.) Postmaster: Send all new orders, subscription inquiries, and change of address notices to Cook's Illustrated, P.O. Box 7444, Red Oak, IA 51591-0444. Single copies: $4 in U.S., $4.95 in Canada and other countries. Back issues available for $5 each. PRINTED IN THE U.S.A.

EDITORIAL

LABORS OF LOVE

We tend a small garden each summer on our Vermont farm, and I am fond of growing Red Sun potatoes. Although the potato bugs usually show up in early July and destroy the plants by the end of the month, I am still left with a splendid crop of moist, creamy "new" potatoes, some as small as marbles and others almost full-size. Once or twice a week, I head for the garden, shovel in hand, and call for my two daughters, who quickly abandon their swing set for a chance to help dig. We steam the potatoes for dinner, served with fresh Jersey butter and a handful of snipped chives from the herb garden out next to the stone wall. Unlike most potatoes sold in supermarkets, they have a fresh, loamy taste—alive and sharp with flavor.

CHRISTOPHER KIMBALL

During my childhood and now with my own kids, I have noticed that life on a farm has a peculiar charm. Work becomes pleasurable. Even young children find more excitement in feeding goats or planting seeds than they do in store-bought games. Unlike most of my friends, I spent my summers milking, haying, shoveling manure, and mending fences, and found it vastly more satisfying than summers at camp or the beach. As a Maine farmer and writer, Henry Beston, once put it, there is something fine about family labor. It builds reserves of intimacy and cooperation, which get us through leaner times when the sounds of the whole family at work are only sustaining memories.

For most of us these days, cooking is perhaps our last opportunity to work together as a family, each member doing his or her own vital part. I watch my kids shucking corn, snapping beans, or whisking eggs, and I see little human beings discovering how far their skills can take them—and discovering the joy of labor, a lesson that, once learned, pays rich dividends for a lifetime. They are also wide-eyed with the discovery of beginnings, being witness, for example, to how flour, water, salt, and yeast rise into a thick, country loaf or an elegant twist of dinner roll. The origins of things advertise their essential mysteries without explaining them. The action of yeast is never fully understood, but once made from scratch, a loaf of bread is no longer just a product; it is a bit of the enigma of life right in our own breadbox.

These beginnings, these links to the cycle of life, are as essential to the cook as to the farmer. Just as a good farmer must know about birthing and planting, so a good cook must know how to cut up a chicken or make a starter for bread. To eat the stew without knowing how it was put together thins the full measure of experience. And to cook or farm by oneself is to ignore the great blessings bestowed by community of purpose. Working together is the essence of farm life but has little currency today, when we are each cursed with maximizing personal potential.

In 1963, I spent most of a hot July day at Carl Hess's gas station at the bottom of the road that led up into our mountain town. The farmer I worked for, Junior Bentley, had a Farmall tractor that needed a new clutch, and he and I set out to do the job. Since I was just twelve, I fit easily under that tractor, doing a man's work—slow, often painful, and full of false starts. It finally got done (the tractor and clutch are both still in operation), and we celebrated with a cream soda out of the battered vending machine. There wasn't a breath of air that day, and the goldenrod and thistle by the garage didn't show up any breeze, but it was fine work, a day that is still in my memory over thirty years later. Other days spent tubing down the Battenkill, watching horse draws at local fairs, or partridge hunting up on Southeast Corners Road are not as deeply fixed in my past, lacking the mortar of common purpose and essential work.

As my own children's past starts to form and take shape, my wife and I hope to help them build their own solid foundation. Standing side by side early Sunday morning in the dead of a dark Vermont winter, rolling out the wet dough, flouring the cutter, carefully dropping the rounds into the squat iron kettle, our family makes two dozen buttermilk spice doughnuts for church coffee hour. It is my conviction that the mystery of simple ingredients turned into puffed rounds, the ripe smell of fresh-ground nutmeg, and the sizzle of frying dough will be with them long after their childhood toys are gone. So many of us today avoid cooking because it is difficult and time-consuming, requiring skill and planning. But it is the blessing of common labor—transforming simple beginnings into rich harvests—that is the great joy of cooking and of any life well lived. And it is a joy that reaffirms our faith in the human spirit when it is shared with others, side by side, many hands busy with shared purpose. ■

DEFROSTING FROZEN FOODS

Several brands of "natural defrosting trays" have appeared recently in television commercials and cookware stores. The pitch is that the tray will automatically thaw frozen food in record time without using any electricity or batteries. It supposedly works by "taking heat directly out of the air." But what it really excels at is taking money directly out of your pocket. This hoax got some of my money (temporarily) because I thought I knew what was going on and wanted to confirm my suspicions. I later returned my defrosting tray and got my money back.

By chemical and density tests, I quickly determined that this "remarkable," "high-tech," "space-age miracle device" is nothing more than a thick slab of aluminum. Aluminum is worth about 20¢ per pound, but you'll pay from $17 to $20 for two pounds of aluminum in the form of a "natural" defrosting tray. The idea is that you put frozen food on the slab, and it thaws faster than you can say "plus shipping and handling." But after you buy one and read the instructions, you find out that you should "condition" the metal by running hot water over it for a minute or so before using it and again halfway through the thawing process. Sure sounds like cheating to me.

But what has hooked many people are the astounding demonstrations that the slab makers show on television and challenge you to try at home: Put one ice cube on the miracle slab and another one on the kitchen counter. Lo and behold, the cube on the slab melts quickly before your eyes while the one on the counter just sits there looking embarrassed. I tried this "test" at home and got the same results.

What's going on? Metals are the best conductors of heat among all materials. If you put an ice cube on a thick plate of metal, the metal will conduct heat from the warm room air into the cold ice. Kitchen counters are made of plastic laminate, tile, or wood—such terrible heat conductors they're actually heat insulators. So, naturally, ice on a counter won't melt as fast as ice on metal, any kind of metal. To check this, I placed one cube on the slab and another on a heavy aluminum frying pan. The cubes melted in exactly the same amount of time.

The moral of the story is that unless you're willing to risk heating it in a microwave oven, the fastest and cheapest way to thaw frozen food is to unwrap it and place it on an unheated, heavy frying pan. (Try this with an ice cube; you'll be amazed at how fast it melts.) Except for cast-iron pans, all frying pans are deliberately made to be good conductors of heat.

ROBERT WOLKE
Professor Emeritus of Chemistry
University of Pittsburgh
Pittsburgh, PA

OTHER IDEAS FOR COOKING CORN

On such a sacred ritual as cooking corn on the cob, there's bound to be disagreement, so let me disagree with three points in your article on boiling and grilling fresh corn on the cob (July/August 1995).

1. Silking: If you boil or grill corn in their husks, the silks will come right off with the husks, so you don't need that extra preliminary step of removing the silks.

2. Timing: Most recipes simply haven't caught up with the radical changes in corn breeding in the last decade. Most of the seasonal corn you get in markets in summer and all of the commercial corn you get at other times of the year are hybrid types bred for high sugar. These are of two types: technically termed "sugar-enhanced" and "supersweets." Old-fashioned corn types (such as Golden Cross Bantam) contain 5 to 10 percent sugar, sugar-enhanced types (such as Kandy Korn and Honey and Cream) contain 15 to 18 percent sugar, and supersweets (such as Honey 'N Pearl and How Sweet It Is) contain 25 to 30 percent sugar. Sugar-enhanced varieties have a tenderness that supersweets do not since supersweets are bred to delay conversion of sugar to starch for one to two weeks, time enough for winter corn from Florida to be shipped around the country and still stay sweet.

Sugar content is important because the longer you expose high sugar content to heat, the more sugar turns to starch, destroying that fresh creamy sweetness. The suggested cooking time in your article of five to seven minutes is the way you would cook Golden Bantam, not today's sweet corns. Chefs around the country whom I've consulted all suggest radically shorter cooking times even for corn in the husk, ranging from a thirty-second hot dip in a big pot of boiling water (my preference for truly fresh corn) to one to two minutes for not quite as fresh corn. Think of cooking corn the same way you would cook pasta—al dente, not mushy.

3. Grilling: I've experimented widely with different ways of grilling and smoking corn and have found soaking corn in the husks to be wholly unnecessary. What is necessary is a really hot grill that can "barbecue" your ears instead of steaming them. You can grill them with or without the husks (again, silking is unnecessary). With husks, corn will take six to eight minutes on the grill, and without, just three minutes. My preference is to grill the ears naked to caramelize the sugar in the kernels. I even grill them over an open gas flame on the stove, the way you'd char a pepper.

BETTY FUSSELL
New York, NY

After receiving this letter (the author has written the definitive books on corn), we went back into the kitchen. We found that the silk does come off with the husks after boiling or grilling and that a preliminary step of removing the silks before cooking is unnecessary.

As for the cooking times, when boiling corn in the husks, we still feel that anything less than five minutes will leave corn undercooked and crunchy. Our original cooking times of five to seven minutes leave the corn al dente, and people who like corn fully softened might want to let the corn go another minute or two. When cooking husked corn, cooking times should be lower. Five to seven minutes gets the corn fairly soft. As little as three minutes may be enough for people who like corn fairly crisp. However, cooking times under three minutes leave the corn too crunchy for our tastes.

As for grilling corn, we also found that soaking was not necessary. If the husks were left on, we liked six to eight minutes just fine. Without the husks, we left the corn on the grill for four to five minutes.

Finally, we should note that freshness will affect all cooking times. If you are preparing corn picked that day, you may be able to shave a minute or two off these times. Personal preference is also key. If you like your vegetables al dente, shorter cooking times for corn will be appealing.

MICROWAVING CORN

I was a little surprised to see the discussion of microwaving corn on the cob in your article. The method given seems like a lot more work than what I routinely do. At the store, I check the corn by feel without disturbing the husk. I remove only the loosest, outermost leaves and feel for soft spots or irregular kernels.

At home, I place the corn in the microwave, uncovered, unhusked, and unsilked. One ear cooks in about three minutes, but times, of course, will vary with the microwave and size and number of ears. When the corn is done, I put it on a cutting board, and with a chef's knife I cut off the base of the stalk, about one-half inch up from the bottom, so that the husk leaves are separated from where they grow out of the corn. I stick a corn holder through the bottom, and using a towel or pot holder, I grab the top of the husk and twist it off. The silk all slides off as if it has been greased, and the flavor is the best I've ever had with fresh corn. I rarely put butter and salt on corn since I started cooking it this way.

DAN SCHWARCZ
Hyattsville, MD

We tried microwaving corn as suggested and found that most of the silk will come off with the husk. However, there were some stragglers that had to be picked off. All in all, though, this method works nicely.

POTATO STARCH IN PIES

Y ou mentioned only four thickeners in your article "How to Thicken Fruit Pies" (July/August 1995). You say that tapioca is the best of the four, beating out flour, corn starch, and arrowroot. But there are other thickeners that you did not test. In particular, I wonder why you did not mention potato starch. I think it is the very best thickener and have used it all my life. I make hundreds of pies a year for bake sales, bazaars, friends, and family. Everybody loves the clear, beautiful fruit fillings. Potato starch is available in many stores, especially where kosher foods are purchased.

AINA BLAKE
Universal City, TX

For our article on thickeners for pie fillings, we decided to limit our testing to the four most common thickeners found in supermarkets. Potato starch is rarely sold in supermarkets (we found it in health food stores), so we chose not to include it. However, your letter intrigued us, so we tested our peach pie recipe with three tablespoons of potato starch in place of the tapioca. The results were excellent. The filling was clear and very clean-tasting with no discernible starch or potato flavor. If you can find potato starch, do use it as a pie thickener. Tapioca, because it is sold in supermarkets, remains an excellent as well as a convenient choice.

BACTERIA IN BEEF

I 'm concerned by what I consider a serious flaw in your piece "A Better Burger" (July/August 1995). Your recipe includes timing instructions for cooking burgers "rare" and "medium rare." Of course, you have every right to do that. But I think you also have an obligation to inform your readers about the dangers of eating ground meat that is not cooked well done.
In the early 1990s, hundreds of people on the West Coast were taken ill and two children died because of an invisible pathogen known as

Escherichia coli 0157:H7 (E. coli, for short). The tragedy was traced to some fast-food restaurants that had served undercooked hamburgers. Unfortunately, it's almost impossible to be certain that meat is not contaminated by E. coli.
Because E. coli remains on the surface of the meat, it is eradicated during cooking, even the minimal cooking needed to prepare a rare steak. Hamburger, on the other hand, is different. When you mix contaminated cuts of meat and grind them together, the E. coli mixes throughout the meat. Thorough cooking kills the bacteria in ground beef. There should be no sign of pinkness in the hamburger, and the juices should not be pink either.

CLEM HALLQUIST
Huntingdon Valley, PA

PROTEIN CONTENT OF FLOUR

J ust when I "mastered" the selections of my flour by the percentage of protein, labeling changes mean that protein is now listed in grams. In the past, I have considered flour with a protein content of 8 percent to 9 percent best for cakes and biscuits. An average protein content of 10 percent to 11 percent (most all-purpose flour falls in this range) is best for most general baking needs. Bread and pasta need a high protein flour in the 13 percent to 15 percent range. Can you translate this for me according to the new labels in grams?

BILL MORAN
San Diego, TX

As part of the new labeling law, protein content is now listed in grams of protein per serving. The cake flour in our pantry has two grams of protein per serving, the all-purpose flour has three grams, and the bread flour has four grams. Two grams of protein (this is how it would appear on the label) translates to 6.66 percent protein. Three grams translates to 10 percent protein, and four grams to 13.33 percent protein. However, since the USDA allows manufacturers to round numbers off, 3 grams could actually be as low as 2.50 grams (8.33 percent protein) or as high as 3.49 grams (11.63 percent), a very wide range. Unfortunately, the savvy label reader can only spot the

very low (those under 8.33 percent) protein flours (look for 2 grams of protein per serving) and the high protein flours (look for 4 grams of protein per serving).

SLOW-ROAST SAFETY

Y our editorial "Easy Does It" in the May/June 1995 issue might well be retitled "Queasy Does It." The slow-roast method for turkey and pork could cause consumers to become ill. The editorial states that Adelle Davis advocates cooking "at the final temperature that you want the meat (if you want a turkey cooked to 165 degrees, for example, cook it at that temperature)."
According to U.S. Department of Agriculture microbiologists, oven temperatures of no lower than 325 degrees must be used when roasting raw poultry as well as meat and fish. Cooking these perishable foods at a lower temperature can be dangerous.
At low cooking temperatures, food lingers too long between 40 and 140 degrees, in the "danger zone" where bacteria multiply and may produce toxins or poisons. It can take too many hours of low temperature roasting for poultry to reach a final internal temperature of 160 to 180 degrees.
Poultry that has reached a final internal temperature of 160 to 180 degrees is recognized by food microbiologists as being "safe" when combined with proper handling and cooking. However, low temperature overnight cooking may cause food-borne illness even when the food eventually reaches a final internal temperature of 160 to 180 degrees.

SUSAN CONLEY
USDA Food Safety and Inspection Service
Washington, DC

The Editor Responds: In the interest of safety, I have modified our slow-roasting techniques for poultry for an article in this issue (see "Roasting Chicken 14 Ways," page 9). I start the bird off at 375 degrees for half an hour and then reduce the temperature to 200 degrees for one hour, raising it back up to 400 degrees to finish. During the first half hour of roasting, the internal temperature of the chicken rises to 140 degrees, the point at which any harmful bacteria that is present will be destroyed. ∎

WHAT IS IT?

I found this tool at the back of a drawer in my kitchen and was wondering if you have any idea how to use it.

BOB HARBERTS
Washington, DC

You own a coring hook for use on pears. While the core in an apple is the same thickness from top to bottom, the core in a pear is narrow at the stem end and wider at the base. To use this handy tool, first slice the pear in half lengthwise. Use the narrow end of the hook to scoop out and remove the woody stem section in each half. When you get to the base of the pear halves, flip the hook over to the wide end and continue scooping and scraping to remove the pithy area at the blossom end of the pear. The edges of the hook are beveled to make this switch-over especially smooth and easy. A coring hook can also be used to remove the liquid and seeds in a large beefsteak tomato. La Cuisine Kitchenware sells coring hooks with metal loops and plastic handles for $4.50. To order one, call 800-521-1176.

Quick Tips

CORING APPLE QUARTERS

Mrs. Pat Knox Flower of Round Mountain, California, sent this tip for quartering and coring apples without breaking the quarters.

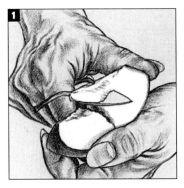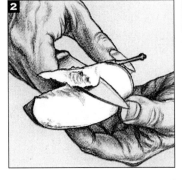

1. When apple quarters are cored starting at the stem end, the quarters tend to break.

2. This problem does not occur if you core the quarters starting at the blossom end.

PORTIONING TOMATO PASTE

Recipes often call for only a tablespoon or two of tomato paste. Unfortunately, the rest of the can often ends up turning brown in the refrigerator and then being discarded. Arthur Okazaki of New Orleans, Paula Fougeray of Lehighton, Pennsylvania, and Laurie Walls of Titusville, Florida, all sent us versions of this useful suggestion.

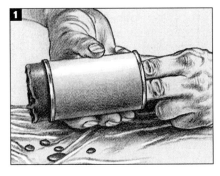

1. Open both ends of the tomato paste can. Remove the lid from one end and use the lid at the other end to push the paste out onto a sheet of plastic wrap. (This method also works as a neat way of getting other solid ingredients, such as frozen juice and almond paste, out of cans.)

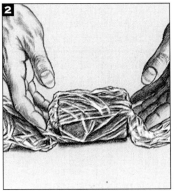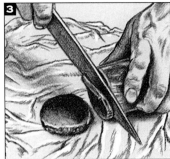

2. Wrap the tomato paste in plastic wrap and place it in the freezer.

3. When the paste has frozen, you can cut off only as much as you need for a particular recipe, then return the frozen log to the freezer.

MORE USES FOR THE EGG SLICER

Egg slicers are handy not only for slicing hard-cooked eggs, but also for slicing any number of other items. These are the best uses suggested to us by readers over the past several months.

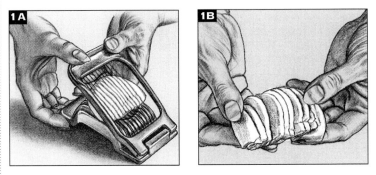

1. Thespi Mortimer of Atlanta finds fresh mozzarella very difficult to slice evenly, either with a knife or with cheese slicers, which are designed for harder cheeses. But the egg slicer does it quickly and perfectly. For julienned mozzarella, simply turn the cheese 45 degrees and slice again.

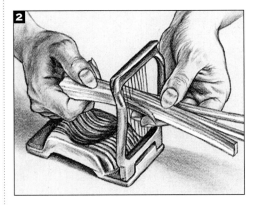

2. Jenny Heath of Emmetsburg, Iowa, makes quick work of slicing celery by pushing stalks lengthwise through the egg slicer. For a finer chop, she suggests running the celery through the slicer a second time.

DRAFT-FREE RISING LOCATION

Lena Menegus of Belvidere, New Jersey, has devised a simple way to create a draft-free environment for the final rising of yeast bread dough.

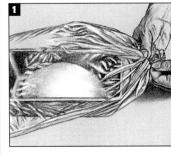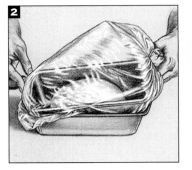

1. After forming the dough and placing it in a loaf pan, slip the pan into an empty plastic bag. Blow air into the bag to inflate it, then tie it securely with a twist tie.

2. Place this loaf pan into another loaf pan so that the air inside the bag is pushed up, providing room for the dough to expand.

ILLUSTRATIONS BY ALAN WITSCHONKE

MAKING SPAETZLE

Spaetzle, the thin, pastalike dumplings common to Alsace, southern Germany, and Switzerland, are ordinarily formed by a device designed specifically for the purpose (*see* Notes from Readers, May/June 1993). Since most American cooks don't have a spaetzle maker, however, the following method, which uses a perforated pizza pan, is a good way of approximating the shape of spaetzle.

1. Set a perforated pizza pan over a soup kettle of barely simmering water. Place a portion of spaetzle dough on the pan.

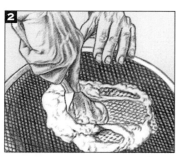

2. Use a spatula to push the dough through the pan; you will have nicely formed spaetzle.

CUTTING UP DRIED FRUIT

Dried fruit very often sticks to the knife when you try to chop it up for use in muffins, breads, and so on. Mary Kendall of Middlebury, Indiana, provides this way to prevent that problem.

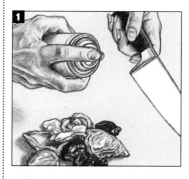

1. Spray a thin film of vegetable spray onto the blade of your knife just before you begin chopping the dried fruit.

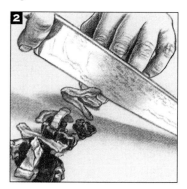

2. The chopped fruit doesn't cling to the knife blade, and the knife stays relatively clean.

SETTING UP A SIMPLE STEAMER

After reading "Steaming Fish Fillets and Steaks" in the March/April 1995 issue of *Cook's Illustrated,* Susan Leshing of Newton, Massachusetts, wrote to share her simple steaming method.

1. Set four sturdy chopsticks, two running lengthwise and two running crosswise, in a wok.

2. Place the food to be steamed in a Pyrex pie plate. Set the pan on the platform created by the chopsticks, cover the wok, and steam.

ROLLING OUT PERFECT COOKIE (OR PIE) DOUGH

Peter Fahrendorf of West Bend, Wisconsin, sent us this tip for rolling out cookie or pie dough to just the proper height.

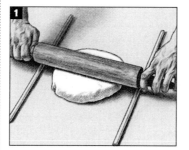

1. Place dowels of the appropriate diameter on the rolling surface just at the outer ends of the rolling pin.

2. Roll out the dough, stopping when the rolling pin hits the top of the dowels—no more low, scorched edges on your cookies.

MAKING SMALLER BREAD LOAVES

Julie Salsman of New Braunfels, Texas, finds that her friends and neighbors often can't eat a full loaf of bread before it dries out. To solve this problem, she has come up with this tip.

1. Divide a two-pound batch of dough into two one-pound balls, place them side by side in a standard loaf pan, let them rise, and bake them as usual.

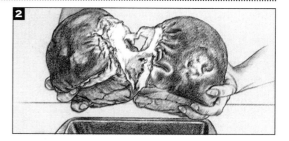

2. Each of the two resulting loaves will be small enough to use before it goes stale but will still have the same cross-sectional dimension as a regular two-pound loaf, perfect for sandwiches.

Thanks to our readers for Quick Tips: The editors of *Cook's Illustrated* would like to thank all of the readers who have sent us their quick tips. We have enjoyed reading every one of them, and have learned a lot. Keep them coming. We will provide a one-year complimentary subscription for each quick tip that we print. Send a description of your special technique to *Cook's Illustrated,* P.O. Box 569, Brookline Village, MA 02147-0569. Please write "Attention: Quick Tips" on the envelope and include your name, address, and daytime phone number. You can also E-mail us at cooksill@aol.com. Unfortunately, we can only acknowledge receipt of tips that will be printed in the magazine. In case the same tip is received from two readers, the one postmarked first will be selected. Also, be sure to let us know what particular cooking problems you would like us to investigate in upcoming issues.

Perfect Pancakes

For the best flavor and texture, cut back on the leavening and use buttermilk thinned with regular milk.

~ BY PAM ANDERSON WITH KAREN TACK ~

Pancakes are fast and simple, but if they are also to be good, there are a few things you have to get right. First, the batter has to be the right texture. Runny batters cook into crepes; thick batters—particularly those made with buttermilk—can cook up wet and heavy. Second, the griddle needs to be the right temperature. An overly hot skillet delivers a cake with a scorched exterior and raw interior while a cool skillet gives the cake a hard, thick crust and a dry interior. But one of the most crucial issues with pancakes—all quick breads, really—is getting the leavening right. Too much baking powder or soda in a batter can result in metallic- or soapy-flavored pancakes—the taste equivalent of fingernails scraping across a blackboard.

Before working on this pancake story, we found chemical leavenings to be a bit of a mystery. Although we understood baking powder and soda in a general way, we did not fully understand how to manipulate them in a recipe to achieve particular results. After performing extensive tests, we're beginning to understand their role in baking. One thing that we are certain of at this point: Many recipes call for far more leavening than is actually needed.

Variations on a Formula

When developing a recipe, we often start by putting together a simple composite formula from our research. We test the original formula, then change, increase, or decrease key ingredients to determine their role in the recipe. We thought this plan made good sense in our search for a light, fluffy, moist, and flavorful pancake. Our simple pancake formula started out with the following ingredients:

1	cup all-purpose flour
1	tablespoon sugar
1	teaspoon baking powder (if using milk)
½	teaspoon baking soda (if using buttermilk)
½	teaspoon salt
1	cup milk or buttermilk
1	egg
2	tablespoons melted butter

After numerous tests the recipe evolved into this formula:

1	cup all-purpose flour
2	teaspoons sugar (optional)
½	teaspoon baking powder
¼	teaspoon baking soda
½	teaspoon salt
¾	cup buttermilk
¼	cup milk (plus a tablespoon or so extra if necessary)
1	large egg
2	tablespoons melted butter

Although the ingredients in the two formulas are the same and the quantity changes may look insignificant, the flavor and textural differences in pancakes made from the original and final formulas are dramatic.

Taking it from the top, we started with flour. We tested the original formula (using milk and baking powder) with all-purpose flour, cake flour, and a combination of the two. We knew a higher-gluten product, such as bread flour, would not deliver the tender pancakes we sought.

We noted immediately that the batters made with cake flour were significantly thinner than those made from regular all-purpose. Although neither batch rose nearly as high as it should have (we were not yet using enough baking powder; *see* "Leavening Lessons," below), the cake flour pancakes were particularly crepelike. The cake flour didn't appear to be strong enough to support the pancake's weighty structure. Although the all-purpose pancakes looked and tasted flat at this point as well, their higher gluten content made them more substantial, yet still tender. The combination cake and all-purpose flour pancakes offered no advantages that would warrant pulling two boxes of flour down from the cupboard.

Thinking that perhaps our original formula caused the cake flour's poor performance, we continued trying cake flour as our formula evolved. But never once did we feel that it outperformed good old all-purpose.

With the flour issue resolved, we decided to work on the pancake's flavor and texture. From past experience, we were certain that buttermilk was the quickest way to boost flavor, so we made the original formula with buttermilk and baking soda rather than milk and baking powder. We were amazed at the textural difference in the batter. Substituting an equal amount of buttermilk for the milk gave us a batter so thick that it had to be spooned, rather than poured, onto the griddle. We thinned the batter with a little milk, but the cooked cakes were too wet and, to our disappointment, lacked that flavor depth and dairy tang we thought we'd get from the buttermilk.

Leavening Lessons

We had simply traded problems with buttermilk. Milk had given us thin batter and thin cakes. Buttermilk gave us thicker batter, but leaden cakes. Although we thought the flour/buttermilk ratio was partially responsible for the pancake's heaviness, we knew it was time to deal with baking powder and soda. We were certain that these leavenings were at least partially responsible for

For flavorful pancakes that are fluffy enough to spring back when you cut into them, use a combination of baking powder and baking soda.

the cake's wet, heavy texture, and were fully responsible for the buttermilk's unimpressive flavor performance. At this point, we knew it was time for us to hit the books.

We turned to works by food scientist Harold McGee (*On Food and Cooking;* Scribner, 1984) and master baker Rose Levy Beranbaum (*The Cake Bible;* Morrow, 1988), both of whom have done extensive leavening testing. From their books we either learned or were reminded of a lot of leavening lore.

As we knew, chemical leavenings such as baking soda and baking powder react with acids to produce carbon dioxide, the gas that causes quick breads to rise. Baking soda relies on an acid within the recipe, such as buttermilk or molasses. Use more baking soda than can be neutralized by the acidic ingredient, and you'll end up with a metallic-tasting, coarse-crumbed quick bread or cake. According to both Beranbaum and McGee, one cup of buttermilk is needed to neutralize one-half teaspoon of baking soda.

Baking powder is simply baking soda mixed with dry acid or acid salt (a built-in acid for the soda to react with) and a touch of dry starch to absorb moisture and prevent premature reactions. Most commercial baking powders are "double-acting." In other words, they contain two kinds of acids—one that produces a carbon dioxide reaction at room temperature, the other responding only to heat. Homemade or single-acting baking powder contains only one acid, cream of tartar, which reacts at room temperature. (You can make a homemade single-acting baking powder by mixing one-quarter teaspoon of baking soda, one-half teaspoon of cream of tartar, and one-quarter teaspoon of cornstarch. You can even skip the cornstarch—the moisture absorber—if making baking powder for a single recipe.)

Since baking powder is nothing more than baking soda and acid, it's easy to convert a recipe from baking powder and milk to baking soda and buttermilk. Just divide the amount of baking powder by four to determine how much baking soda you should use and substitute buttermilk. For example, in a recipe calling for two teaspoons of baking powder and one cup of milk, you could substitute one-half teaspoon of baking soda and one cup of buttermilk. There would be taste and textural differences, it is true, but the leavening action would be about the same.

One final note about baking soda: You may not want it to neutralize all the buttermilk's acidity. If you want to taste the buttermilk, according to Beranbaum, you can substitute baking powder for some or all of the baking soda. Since baking powder has its own built-in acid to react with, the acidity of the buttermilk is allowed to come through. For example, in a recipe that calls for one-half teaspoon of baking soda and one cup of buttermilk, the baking soda could be replaced with two teaspoons of baking powder.

Applying these principles to our pancake recipe, we needed one-half teaspoon of baking soda to neutralize our one cup of buttermilk. But since, prior to our leavening research, we had been unimpressed with the flavor of our pancakes

Although some say that the egg and milk in pancakes need to be brought to room temperature before making the batter, we found our pancakes made from eggs and milk just out of the refrigerator were fine. The only problem we ran into was trying to whisk the melted butter into these cold ingredients. The cold milk and egg caused the butter to reharden and turned the mixture lumpy. While these lumps do dissolve when the pancakes are cooked, we think that the butter is more evenly distributed when stirred into the batter if it does not lump up.

Instead of stirring the whole egg into the milk, we separated the egg, added the white to the milk, but whisked the yolk into the melted butter (*see* illustration below) before stirring it into the milk. (For this technique we are indebted to a *Cook's Illustrated* reader who sent in this tip.)

For an explanation of why this worked, I checked with cookbook author and food scientist Shirley Corriher. The yolk, she explained, is made up of lipoproteins, or fat proteins. The fat in the yolk mixes easily with the butter. The proteins, which are water soluble, help the fat disperse easily into the liquid. So, to avoid butter lumps, mix the butter with the egg yolk first.

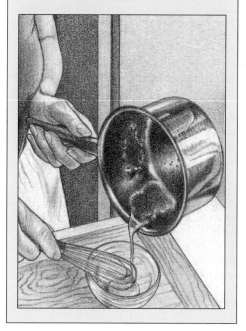

made with one-half teaspoon of baking soda and one cup of buttermilk, we thought Beranbaum might be right; if baking powder and buttermilk were used in a batter, the baking powder would react with its own acid, allowing the full flavor of the buttermilk to come through. We had our next set of tests.

To determine just which leavening, or what combination of leavenings, worked best with the

buttermilk, we made three batches of batter: one with two teaspoons of baking powder, another with one-half teaspoon of baking soda, and a final batch with one-quarter teaspoon of baking soda and one teaspoon of baking powder.

Pancakes made from all three batters rose beautifully on the griddle. The all-baking powder pancakes were pale-colored and very finely textured—almost gummy. Compared to the other two varieties of pancakes, they were tougher. They tasted salty (which we attributed to the acid salt in the baking powder), and they had a tinny, metallic aftertaste. The buttermilk/dairy flavor really came through, but almost too much. Rather than tasting mildly tangy, these pancakes were almost sour.

The all-baking soda pancakes were more yellow in color. They were tender with a coarser crumb, and they weren't too salty like the baking powder pancakes. Although pleasant enough on their own, when compared to the other two varieties, they lacked flavor.

The combination baking powder/baking soda pancakes offered a good balance. They displayed the good qualities of the other two types of pancakes, without any of the negative side effects. The small amount of baking soda (one-quarter teaspoon) gave the cakes a coarser crumb and made them light and tender. Since some of the buttermilk's remaining acid was not neutralized, the pancakes also had a pleasant dairy tang. The baking powder helped with the rise, but since it was busy reacting with its own acid, it had allowed the buttermilk flavor to pass through.

Further Refinements
We were getting close. Although our pancakes were relatively light, they weren't exactly fluffy. Although ideal for waffles (*see* "The Mystery of the Ideal Waffle," November/December 1994), our batter was too thick for pancakes; they came out slightly wet. We wanted our pancakes to look like the ones on the Bisquick box—the kind that spring back into shape when cut. At this point ours didn't—the tops stuck to the bottoms when cut with a fork.

We tried fixing the problem by thinning the batter with milk. To our one cup of buttermilk, we added enough milk to make a semipourable batter. But adding more liquid to the batter wasn't the answer. The pancakes just became wetter. What ultimately worked for us was not adding, but substituting, one-quarter cup of milk for one-quarter cup of the buttermilk. Using three-quarters cup of buttermilk and one-quarter cup of milk lightened the batter and gave us fluffy pancakes.

As I discussed the results of these leavening and liquid tests with a cooking colleague, she suggested that we could perhaps get away with even less baking powder. As someone who is extremely sensitive to baking powder's metallic aftertaste, she said she often used less than recipes call for with good results.

Good advice. We made a batch of pancake batter with one-quarter teaspoon of baking soda, reducing the baking powder to one-half teaspoon, along with the three-quarters cup of buttermilk and one-quarter cup of milk. The pancakes rose as beautifully as if they had been made with the full teaspoon, they looked light and fluffy, and they tasted great.

Another bit of advice proved interesting. Publisher Chris Kimball suggested another potential way for some of the buttermilk's acidity to come through. Instead of reducing the baking soda and compensating with baking powder as we had done, he suggested we might try the formula using the full one-half teaspoon of baking soda, and adding one-quarter teaspoon of cream of tartar (an acid) for the baking soda to react with, which would still leave some of the buttermilk's acid to shine through.

We followed his suggestion and found that pancakes made from our formula and the ones made with baking soda and cream of tartar tasted

fairly similar, the cream of tartar pancake's texture a little coarser and its flavor more salty. Although these minor differences were obvious when tasting the pancakes unadorned, butter and syrup would have surely masked them.

We ultimately stuck with the baking powder/baking soda formula for other reasons. Since baking powder reacts twice—once at room temperature and once at 120 degrees—we found that the baking powder/baking soda batter held up longer than the one made with baking soda only. The single-acting baking soda batter started foaming and bubbling as soon as it came in contact with the liquid, but after twenty minutes or so, the batter started to resemble overrisen bread dough, ready to deflate. The pancakes cooked from this fully risen batter developed noticeable center humps. Although the baking soda pancakes initially looked thicker on the griddle, the baking powder/baking soda pancakes caught up quickly in height once flipped, with the baking powder activated by the griddle heat.

Finishing Touches

Though we were pleased at this point, we wanted to run a final few tests with the secondary ingredients—eggs and butter—and to determine the fastest way to mix up a lumpless batter.

A number of pancake recipes called for separating the egg and mixing the yolk into the batter. The white was whipped, then folded into the already mixed batter. We noticed right off that the batter made by this method was stiff, requiring us to spoon it onto the griddle. The resulting pancakes, though, were airy and tender. We liked this style of pancake enough to make it a variation, but found it a little too delicate for a cake with the nickname "flapjack."

Since we were happy with our pancake's flavor and texture, we knew we didn't want to increase the butter in the recipe, but it's always worth trying to reduce fat these days. So we made the batter with only one tablespoon of butter, only to find the cooked pancakes a bit tougher than those made with two tablespoons of butter.

Dump and Whisk

Enough experiments have been done in this magazine to prove the importance of getting in and out of the mixing phase as quickly as possible. For those who may need reminding, the more you mix a quick-bread batter, the more you develop the flour's gluten, and the tougher the resulting cake or bread. We found the quickest way to incorporate the wet ingredients into the dry ingredients was to dump the milk mixture all at once into the flour mixture, then quickly mix it with a whisk. This method guaranteed us a virtually lumpless batter within seconds every time.

LIGHT AND FLUFFY PANCAKES
Serves 3 to 4 (makes about eight 3-inch pancakes)

This batter serves four perfectly for a light weekday breakfast. You may want to double the recipe for weekend pancake making, when appetites are larger. If you happen to be using salted butter or

buttermilk, you may want to cut back a bit on the salt. If you don't have any buttermilk, mix three-quarters cup of room temperature milk with one tablespoon of lemon juice and let it stand for five minutes. Substitute this "clabbered milk" for the three-quarters cup of buttermilk and one-quarter cup of milk in this recipe. Since this milk mixture is not as thick as buttermilk, the batter and resulting pancakes will not be as thick.

 1 cup all-purpose flour
 2 teaspoons sugar
 ½ teaspoon salt
 ½ teaspoon baking powder
 ¼ teaspoon baking soda
 ¾ cup buttermilk
 ¼ cup milk (plus a tablespoon or so extra
   if batter is too thick)
 1 large egg, separated
 2 tablespoons unsalted butter, melted
   Vegetable oil for brushing griddle

1. Mix dry ingredients in medium bowl. Pour buttermilk and milk into 2-cup Pyrex measuring cup. Whisk in egg white; mix yolk with melted butter, then stir into milk mixture. Dump wet ingredients into dry ingredients all at once; whisk until just mixed.

2. Meanwhile, heat griddle or large skillet over strong medium-high heat. Brush griddle generously with oil. When water splashed on surface confidently sizzles, pour batter, about ¼ cup at a time, onto griddle, making sure not to overcrowd. When pancake bottoms are brown and top surface starts to bubble, 2 to 3 minutes, flip cakes and cook until remaining side has browned, 1 to 2 minutes longer. Re-oil the skillet and repeat for the next batch of pancakes.

Blueberry Pancakes. Follow recipe for Light and Fluffy Pancakes, pouring a little less than ¼ cup batter at a time onto griddle. Starting with ½ cup blueberries, drop about seven blueberries onto top of each cooking pancake. Continue cooking in accordance with above recipe.

Whole Wheat Pancakes. Follow recipe for Light and Fluffy Pancakes, substituting ½ cup whole wheat flour for ½ cup of the all-purpose flour.

Toasted Pecan Pancakes. Heat griddle pan over medium heat. Add ¼ cup pecans, chopped fairly fine; toast, shaking pan frequently, until nuts are fragrant, 3 to 5 minutes. Follow recipe for Light and Fluffy Pancakes, stirring pecans into batter.

Featherweight Pancakes. Follow recipe for Light and Fluffy Pancakes, whisking egg white in large bowl to stiff peaks. (Don't bother with a hand mixer for beating one egg white. By the time you've assembled the mixer, you could be folding the hand-whipped egg into the batter. Don't make the mistake of using too small a bowl either. The egg needs space to aerate, so use a whisk and a large metal bowl.) Quickly fold egg white into batter and continue with recipe, spooning rather than pouring batter onto griddle. ∎

There's no getting around it. Pancakes are best right off the griddle. I'd rather dole them out, one per customer, than to try to hold them so they can be served all at once. But sometimes—whether you're cooking for a crowd or you can't get people to the table—it's just unavoidable. We found that wrapping the cakes in a clean kitchen towel and placing them in a warm oven, as some books suggest, works fairly well. But since the pancakes pick up the towel scent, do not use one that smells of scented laundry detergent or dryer sheets. To wrap the pancakes, line a large baking pan with the towel. Place the cooked pancakes in the pan in a single layer and cover them over (*see* illustration below). Repeat, making sure that each layer of pancakes is covered with toweling. Place them in a 200-degree oven. They should hold for about fifteen minutes.

Roasting Chicken 14 Ways

After roasting fourteen different birds, we offer our two favorite methods.

～ BY CHRISTOPHER KIMBALL ～

For evenly cooked meat and crispy skin, roast the chicken untrussed on a V-rack set in a shallow pan.

Cooking chicken appears to be a simple task at first. The meat is not tough by nature. The dark meat is relatively forgiving in terms of cooking time. The breast meat is not particularly thick, which means that the outer layers are less likely to dry out while you are attempting to properly cook the center of the cut.

Yet, when I am served a perfectly roasted chicken, the experience is not only unusual, it is extraordinary. The skin is perfectly crisp and well seasoned. The white meat is juicy and tender, but with a hint of chew. The dark meat is fully cooked all the way to the bone. There is clearly more to chicken cookery than I at first imagined because most home-cooked chickens are either grossly overcooked or so underdone that they resemble an avian version of steak tartare.

To solve this problem once and for all, I decided to devise a series of tests based on a few simple observations. The first observation is that chicken is made up of two totally different types of meat: white and dark. The white meat is inevitably overcooked and dry even as the dark meat is still little more than raw next to the bone. The second observation is that chicken, unlike beef, has skin, which should be nicely browned and crispy. As I found during the testing process, crisp skin is not always consistent with perfectly cooked meat. Finally, chicken is an odd amalgam of meat and bones. The drumsticks and wings stick out, the thigh meat is on the side of the bird, and the breast meat is on the top (at least when the chicken roasted). The home cook is dealing with a complex three-dimensional structure, quite different than a brisket or a pot roast. These anatomical realities may require a more complex set of cooking instructions. In search of these instruc-

tions, I ended up roasting chickens fourteen different ways.

Structuring the Tests

I began my research by rereading an article by Harold McGee in the charter issue of *Cook's Illustrated* entitled "The Way to Roast Chicken." He started his birds at 500 degrees, reducing the oven temperature to 325 degrees about halfway through cooking; he found that butter is better for basting than oil; he discouraged tightly trussing a chicken as that slows down proper cooking of the thigh and leg meat; he advocated turning the bird once during roasting, finishing with the breast up; and finally, he suggested that the breast be cooked to 150 degrees internal temperature.

Having prepared a number of chickens according to McGee, I still had questions. What about temperatures below 325 degrees? After all, I had enjoyed success with slow-roasting turkeys at 200 degrees. Also, I had found that an internal temperature of 150 degrees for the breast was underdone to my taste—I'd rather err on the side of overcooking chicken than undercooking. Although breast meat cooked to 150 degrees is juicy, to my taste the meat has an unpleasant rawness to it, with a loose and fleshy texture. (I also had some concerns about safety, given that chicken is more prone to bacterial infection than other types of meat. The USDA [United States Department of Agriculture] feels that a final temperature under 160 degrees is high risk.) I also wanted to try some other methods. Does cooking in a clay roaster make a better chicken? Does one turn really do the trick or are

two turns better? Does a vertical roaster expose the bird more evenly to the oven's heat?

Finding the Right Temperature

I started my tests with the most pertinent question: What is the best oven temperature for roasting a chicken? My bias for roasting red meat is slow roasting in a very low oven. I also knew that, for a nice, juicy, evenly cooked bird, my Thanksgiving turkey is best slow-cooked in a 200-degree oven (although the bird is started at a much higher temperature for safety reasons). However, a three-pound chicken is small, and I reasoned that a high-heat roast might work fine as the outer layers would probably not have time to overcook before the inside was done. I decided to test both high- and low-heat cooking.

My first test bird went into a 450-degree oven and cooked for forty-four minutes. When it came out, the skin was dark and crispy, but I encountered the classic problem with high-heat meat cookery: While the dark meat was fine, the outer portion of the white meat was overcooked and on the tough side even as the internal thigh temperature registered 160 degrees.

I then went to the other extreme and tested a bird in a 275-degree oven for one hour and thirty-five minutes and then raised the heat to 425 degrees for the last ten minutes to crisp up the skin. The white meat was not quite as juicy as the dark, but not dry either. The skin, however, was a light gold, not a rich sienna, and it was chewy and not very tasty– obviously, not browned enough.

Finally, I tried a simple, classic approach: I roasted the bird at 375 degrees for one hour. The skin was golden and slightly crispy. At 160 degrees internal temperature, the juices ran clear, but the dark meat was still not properly cooked

---

REMOVING THE WISHBONE BEFORE ROASTING

Wishbone removal makes carving the breast meat easier.

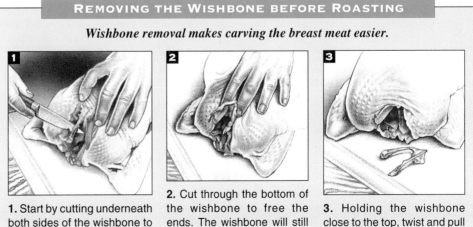

1. Start by cutting underneath both sides of the wishbone to free it from the flesh.

2. Cut through the bottom of the wishbone to free the ends. The wishbone will still be attached at the top.

3. Holding the wishbone close to the top, twist and pull until it comes free.

---

near the bone. I continued cooking to an internal temperature of about 170 degrees (thigh meat), and the white meat was still juicy (the breast meat was close to 180 degrees). This was an interesting discovery. While the breast meat of chicken roasted at 450 degrees was a bit dry when the thigh registered 160 degrees, the bird roasted at 375 degrees still had juicy breast meat when the thigh registered close to 170 degrees. I also found that "until the juices run clear" is an imprecise measure of doneness—the white meat will be cooked, but the dark meat can still be a little bloody at the bone, a sight that I would prefer to leave to B movies rather than my dinner plate.

I then tried starting the oven out at a higher temperature (450 degrees), putting in the chicken, and then immediately turning the oven down to 350 degrees. The bird cooked in fifty-three min-utes, and the skin was a pale gold and slightly chewy—not much difference from the chicken roasted at 375 degrees and not quite as good over-all. So the winner was the simpler method, a constant 375 degrees. By now I felt that I had arrived at a better method than McGee's and one that, while not quite as good as slow roasting (*see* "Slow-Roasting the Bird," below), was certainly more practical in terms of time and effort.

Must You Baste? Truss? Turn the Bird?
Using the 375-degree method, I set out to determine if basting is a good idea or just another one of those hand-me-down cookbook directions that make no sense. I started with butter and basted every fifteen minutes. The results were appalling. Despite a nice brown color, the skin was chewy and greasy. The next bird was basted with oil, which turned out a crispier skin, but the color was off—a pale gold. I then brushed a bird before roasting with butter and shoved it in the oven without any further basting. This was the best method. Great color and great crispy texture.

Basting may have made sense when cooking a large piece of meat on a spit over an open fire. The outer layers would get easily overcooked, and the basting may have prevented burning or scorching. However, a three-pound chicken in a 375-degree oven is a different matter entirely. The skin will not scorch or burn (in fact, if you leave it alone, it will cook rather nicely on its own), and the basting liquid is not going to penetrate the meat, making it more tender. Juiciness has nothing to do with the external application of liquid. In fact, even stew meat does not absorb liquid, nor does braised meat. (An in-depth article on braising will appear later this year.) The only reason, therefore, to brush a chicken with butter is to advance the color of the skin. The oven heat turns the milk solids brown and, in the process, also provides added flavor.

I also noted that some cooks suggest placing a piece of cheesecloth soaked in melted butter over the bird during roasting. Just like frequent basting, this will produce skin that is not at all crispy. Save your cheesecloth for straining stock.

Next I turned to trussing. I must confess that I have often felt a lack of basic motor skills when confronted with those terribly serious step-by-step photos that demonstrate how to truss a chicken or turkey. You start with a long piece of twine, loop it under the tail, cross over, twist around the wings, and on and on. By this time you've either figured out that your string is too short or that the photographs weren't taken from the cook's perspective so that you've done the whole thing backwards! So, what if you decided not to bother trussing at all?

This was easy to test. I trussed a bird according to the best French method and cooked it for what seemed a long time, one and one-half hours (this was a larger bird weighing in at 3.42 pounds). The white meat was overcooked at this point, but the dark meat was just right. It was also interesting to note that the cooking time was so long. I concluded that trussing makes it more difficult to properly cook the inner part of the thigh—it is less exposed to heat and therefore the oven time needs to be longer. Voilà! Overcooked white meat. A 3.11-pound bird took only one hour at 375 degrees without trussing, and the white and dark meat were both nicely cooked.

Incidentally, I also made an odd discovery after I had roasted a half dozen birds with the basic 375-degree method. The thigh that was facing up during the second twenty minutes of roasting ended up lower in temperature than the thigh that started off facing up. At first I thought this was just a random measurement, but after four or five birds, it was clear this was a trend. After thinking about it for a few days, I hit on the problem. The thigh that starts off facing the roasting pan was facing a cold pan that reflected little heat. When the other thigh was turned face down, the pan was now hot and was radiating plenty of heat. So, to

---

SLOW-ROASTING THE BIRD

Given my tenacious devotion to low-heat roasting because of its ability to guarantee even cooking, I decided to have a go with a chicken. By low heat, I mean starting the bird at 300 degrees and then reducing the heat to 200 after thirty minutes. This notion is not original—I borrowed it from Adelle Davis, the sixties health guru and author of *Let's Eat Right to Keep Fit* (Harcourt, Brace).

To test this particular method, I started with a 3.2-pound bird and roasted it for a whopping two hours and fifteen minutes. With the chicken cooked to 160 degrees, I was surprised to discover that the dark meat was not cooked at the bone. An additional twenty minutes finished the cooking satisfactorily. The white and dark meat were perfectly cooked, very juicy and very tender.

The trouble, however, was the skin. It was an unpleasant golden yellow, chewy and soft. So, I went back and did it again, increasing the oven temperature to 400 degrees after two hours and fifteen minutes and then cooking the bird for an additional fifteen minutes. Although the internal temperature was 180 degrees, which means overcooked, dry meat under normal conditions, both the white and dark meat were still juicy and tender. The skin was also improved, with more crisp and snap. A very good and forgiving method overall, although time-consuming—and not United States Department of Agriculture (USDA) approved!

In fact, if you ask USDA personnel, they will advise you never to cook any meat at 200 degrees. Of course, they will also tell you never to cook a hamburger medium-rare, which may be good advice strictly from a safety point of view but makes the meat inedible. However, chicken is particularly prone to bacterial problems *because it is sold with the skin on*. The skin of an animal is the primary source of contamination, and with beef, pork, lamb, and veal, this is less of a problem, as the skin is separated from the meat during processing. For example, pork sold in a supermarket may carry only a few hundred bacteria per square centimeter, while chicken may have thousands. So, chicken does have to be handled carefully.

But, it also pays to use common sense. The problem arises when a contaminated chicken, or any other meat, is subjected to temperatures between 40 and 140 degrees. Bacteria multiply rapidly in this zone, especially on the higher end of the range. In fact, bacteria can double every twenty minutes at these temperatures, which can turn ten thousand of those critters into about forty million in just four hours.

While my original recipe started the low-roasted chickens at 300 degrees, after discussions with USDA hot line experts and a few microbiologists, I decided this was a bit risky. So, I increased the initial oven temperature to 375 degrees and left it there for thirty minutes, long enough to raise the surface temperature to the 140-degree mark, at which any bacteria would be killed.

I then started to wonder about the long cooking time at 200 degrees, which sometimes exceeds two hours with a larger bird (over three and one-half pounds). Not only is this an inconvenient cooking method, but I wanted to get the bird in and out of the oven more quickly for safety reasons. So I did two last tests, starting both of the chickens at 375 degrees for half an hour, turning the oven down to 200 degrees and then cooking one bird for half an hour and the other one for a full hour before ratcheting up the oven to 400 degrees for the final browning stage.

The bird that cooked for only half an hour at 200 degrees had chewy breast meat, but the bird that stayed for the full hour was excellent: juicy, tender, and perfectly cooked. Finally, the perfect slow-roasted bird!—*C.K.*

even things out, preheat the roasting pan.

Having figured out that continuous basting and trussing were both unnecessary, I was hoping to find that the bird need not be turned either. After all, it has always seemed to me that turning a roast in the oven was overdoing it a bit—just leave it alone and enjoy the cocktail hour. But even cooking is crucial to chicken cookery, and a couple of tests were in order.

First, I roasted a bird for twenty minutes on each side and then put it on its back. This was a 3.21-pound chicken and took just fifty minutes. The skin was golden and crunchy, the white and dark meat perfectly cooked, and the overall presentation superb. To make this process a bit easier, I tried roasting another bird breast side down for twenty minutes and then turned it breast side up (the McGee method). This chicken was good, but the skin was less crispy and, at the point at which the white meat was perfect, the dark meat was a bit undercooked. Thus, unfortunately, two turns proved crucial.

Testing Clay and Vertical Roasters

I had heard a lot of good things about clay roasters and had tried "La Cloche," a bell-shaped clay cooker for bread that works well with other recipes. I followed the directions and roasted the bird in a 425-degree oven enclosed in the clay cooker. The directions suggested cooking for ninety minutes (with no specification of how large a bird to use), which seemed absurd—the bird was done in just an hour (the internal temperature of the thigh registering 168 degrees), and this was a 3.4-pound chicken. The good news was that the white and dark meat cooked equally, and the meat was quite juicy. The bad news was that the skin was pale and, although moist, chewy rather than crispy. A good method for even cooking but if you are a skin fanatic, not a first choice.

I had also heard good things about the vertical roaster. A very inexpensive but poorly made item, it consists of a small, round, metal tray with two vertical loops of stainless steel that fit inside the bird's cavity, holding it in a vertical position during roasting. A three-pound bird took about forty-five minutes in a 375-degree oven. The results were pretty good. The white meat was not dry (although not real juicy either), and the skin was somewhere between crispy and chewy. However, the inside of the oven ended up a mess—a major drawback.

When Is It Really Done?

As I have discovered when cooking red meat, internal temperatures are relative, not absolute. That is, 160 degrees means one thing when the food being measured has been roasted at 375 degrees and something quite different when that food has been roasted at 200 degrees. In other words, it's how you get there that matters. Many experts advise cooking the dark meat to 160 degrees, the premise I used for my testing. Forget it. The dark meat

A vertical roaster

just isn't going to be fully cooked at the bone. You need the dark meat (don't measure the breast meat, since the dark meat has to be cooked properly or it is inedible) between 165 and 170 degrees (I vote for the latter). However, if you slow-cook at 200 degrees, you can cook the dark meat up to 175 to 180 degrees without a problem (*see* "Slow-Roasting the Bird," page 10). I also found that in a clay cooker, the chicken can withstand an internal thigh temperature of 175 degrees.

Why the difference? Because at higher oven temperatures, the outer layers of meat will end up at much higher internal temperatures. That is, while the middle of the chicken breast may register 160 degrees whether slow- or fast-roasted, the outer layer of meat may reach 200 degrees if roasted at a high temperature but only 170 degrees if roasted at a low temperature. So, although the exact center of the meat may be the same with both methods, a serving of chicken breast will also contain overcooked meat when roasted at high temperatures. Slow-roasting guarantees even cooking as well as more consistent internal temperatures.

I also tested the notion of the internal temperature rising after the chicken is removed from the oven, as it does with a beef roast. This simply does not happen. I removed a chicken from the oven and inserted an instant-read thermometer into the breast. It started out at 155 degrees and immediately started to fall, ending at 140 degrees after fifteen minutes. Although resting for twenty minutes makes the meat juicier, the bird will not continue to cook.

So, fourteen chickens later, I had finally arrived at the best method: Roast the chicken on its side untrussed at 375 degrees in a preheated pan, turning it on its other side after twenty minutes, then breast side up after another twenty minutes, and cooking until the thigh has reached an internal temperature of 165 to 170 degrees. Easy, straightforward, and guaranteed (or as guaranteed as cooking methods can be) to produce a truly satisfying roast chicken.

EASY ROAST CHICKEN
Serves 4
A three-and-one-half-pound bird should roast in fifty-five to sixty minutes while a four- to four-and-one-half-pound bird requires sixty to sixty-five minutes (*see* "How Much Do Roasting Times Vary Based on Weight?" above). If using a V-rack, be sure to grease it so the chicken does not stick to it. If you don't have a V-rack, set the bird on a regular rack

and use balls of aluminum foil to keep the roasting chicken propped up on its side.

- 1 roasting chicken (about 3 pounds), giblets removed and reserved for another use, chicken rinsed and patted dry with paper towels
- 2 tablespoons butter, melted
  Salt and ground black pepper
  Oil for V-rack

1. Place shallow roasting pan in oven and heat oven to 375 degrees. Brush chicken with butter and sprinkle liberally with salt and pepper.
2. Remove heated pan from oven and set oiled V rack in it. Place chicken on rack, wing side up. Roast 20 minutes, then rotate chicken, other wing side up. Roast 20 minutes, then rotate chicken, breast side up. Roast until instant-read thermometer inserted in breast registers 160 and in thigh registers between 165 and 170, 10 to 15 minutes longer. Transfer chicken to cutting board; let rest 20 minutes. Carve and serve.

SLOW-ROASTED CHICKEN
Serves 4
Larger chickens will obviously require longer roasting time. I suggest adding five minutes of cooking time at 375 degrees for every additional quarter pound of weight over three and one-half pounds (a four-pound bird, for example, would roast for a total of forty minutes at 375 degrees). If the bird is still not cooked after fifteen minutes at 400 degrees, keep the bird in the oven until the thigh meat comes up to temperature. Do not stuff or truss a slow-roasted chicken.

- 1 roasting chicken (3 to 3½ pounds), giblets removed and reserved for another use, chicken rinsed and patted dry with paper towels
- 2 tablespoons butter, melted
  Salt and ground black pepper
  Oil for V-rack

1. Heat oven to 375 degrees. Brush chicken with butter and sprinkle liberally with salt and pepper.
2. Place chicken, breast side up, on oiled V-rack set in shallow roasting pan. Roast 30 minutes, then reduce oven temperature to 200 degrees. Roast 1 hour. Increase temperature to 400 degrees and roast until instant-read thermometer inserted in thigh registers 170 to 175 degrees, about 15 minutes longer. Transfer chicken to cutting board; let rest 20 minutes. Carve and serve. ■

Gravlax Made Easy

Chef Rick Moonen demonstrates an easy method for wet-brining salmon fillets that ensures even, never salty curing.

~ BY JACK BISHOP ~

Americans generally purchase gravlax, thinly sliced cured salmon, at gourmet stores or order it in restaurants as a first course. However, this Scandinavian preparation has its roots in the home kitchen; unlike smoked salmon, which requires the use of a smokehouse, gravlax is salt-cured in the refrigerator. At this time of the year, when you may be hosting a buffet or cocktail party, making your own gravlax is an economical way to serve an elegant appetizer or hors d'oeuvre.

To make gravlax, you usually rub salmon fillets with a mixture of salt (to draw liquid from the fish and cure it), sugar (to counter the harshness of the salt), dill, white pepper, and maybe a few tablespoons of gin or vodka (all of which add flavor). The fish is weighted—a pan is put over the fillet and covered with heavy cans—in order to help extract moisture. After a day or less under weights in the refrigerator, the salmon has lost its raw quality, and the salt has done its work. The side is then sliced, and the creamy, rich fish is served with toast points, sour cream, and lemon wedges.

There is, however, a common problem with gravlax: Because the traditional cure has little or no liquid, the fish often develops what Rick Moonen, executive chef at Oceana, a top seafood restaurant in New York City, calls "hot spots." In these places, the fish has actually been oversalted and has become too dry and even a bit tough.

However, Moonen has developed an easy wet-brining method that avoids this problem, ensuring optimal results for the home cook who wants to make this salmon preparation.

By brining the fish in red onion juice, Moonen ensures that the salt (as well as the other nonliquid curing ingredients) is evenly distributed throughout the fillet. In addition, Moonen says that salmon brined in onion juice is creamier and moister than dry-cured gravlax. "This method gives the gravlax a great mouth-feel," he boasts.

Moonen's technique is somewhat controversial because wet-brining is usually associated with inferior processing, especially when making smoked salmon (*see* "Smoked Salmon Tasting," November/December 1995). However, Moonen does not drop his salmon fillets into a vat of salted water, as is the case with some commercial smoked salmon. Perhaps more important, Moonen heavily weights the salmon for gravlax. This pressure draws liquid out from the fish, causing the texture to change from soft and fluffy to firm and dense. "Using just enough liquid to cover the fish, and not any more, makes the gravlax

Rick Moonen uses red onion juice as a brining liquid, which produces creamy, moist gravlax with no "hot spots."

moist," says Moonen. But if you use too much liquid, he cautions, the fish will become too soft.

Moonen's choice of liquid is also essential. "Red onion juice imparts a lovely sweetness to the salmon so that I can add less sugar," explains this leading seafood chef. "Some traditional recipes call for shallots in the dry cure. That made me think that some sort of sweet onion juice could be used as the liquid in a wet cure."

New Technique

In addition to an original brining recipe, Moonen has made some refinements to the classic salmon preparation technique. In most recipes, sides of boned salmon with the skin still on are covered with the dry cure. Moonen finds that the skin can inhibit penetration of the brine, so he removes it. He uses a simple "shavinglike" technique to separate the skin and flesh. After cutting down to, but not through, the skin (*see* illustration 1), he holds the tail end of the skin taut as he slides a slicing knife parallel to the work surface to lift the flesh from the skin below (illustration 2).

Also, because the wet brine guarantees even coverage and penetration of the salt, there is no need to turn or flip the salmon during the curing process, as is usually the case. Simply mix the onion juice, salt, sugar, dill, and white pepper together, place the fillet in a zipper-lock bag, and then pour enough liquid into the bag to barely cover the fillet inside. The sealed fillet is then weighted down with another pan. The weighted salmon is put in the refrigerator, and the next day—without having to disassemble the setup and flip the fish—the gravlax is ready for slicing.

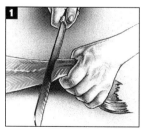

1. With the tail of the salmon pointing perpendicularly to your body, make a small cut just above the tail end. Cut down through the meat but stop just before you get to the skin.

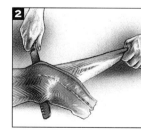

2. Holding onto the tail end by the skin, run a long, flexible slicing knife between the flesh and the skin. Keeping the skin taut and checking the edges of the fillet to make sure the knife

is just above the skin, slide the blade toward the head end until the skin is completely removed.

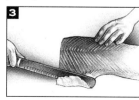

3. Use the slicing knife to trim any excess white fat from the fillet. Fat is most concentrated along the edges of the fillet.

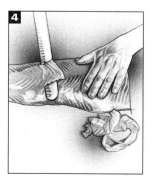

4. Turn the fillet over and trim off any brownish flesh or white fat. Fillets should be uniformly orange.

5. Pin bones run from the head end about halfway back along the fillet. Feel for these bones and pull them toward the head end with small tweezers to remove.

In other respects, Moonen sticks with tradition. For optimal freshness, he starts with a whole salmon that has been scaled and gutted. He uses Atlantic salmon because of its high fat content, wide availability, and relatively low cost. He then removes the head, bones, and tail himself. You will probably want your fishmonger to do this preparation for you, but Moonen relies on a long, flexible slicing knife that is especially made for working with salmon (*see* "What Is It?" November/December 1995).

Once the salmon has been filleted and skinned, Moonen removes any excess fat (it is white in color) as well as any dark, brownish meat, which is often present on the underside (illustrations 3 and 4). Gravlax should be made with a perfectly orange fillet. Pin bones, tiny bones that run in a line down the belly, should also be removed (illustration 5) before applying the wet brine. Don't worry if you make any nicks during the trimming and boning. "It's not the end of the world," remarks Moonen. "Salmon is very forgiving, and the nicks will close up during brining."

To see if the fish has marinated long enough, Moonen looks at the color (the fish should no longer be translucent) and, more importantly, the texture (the fish should be firm, almost rubbery, with no give). For the home cook, a total of three to four pounds of salmon is probably plenty although Moonen's recipe can also be used on larger fish for parties. For the restaurant, Moonen often starts with a ten- to twelve-pound whole fish. Just be sure to make enough marinade to cover the fish in the pan and to increase the marinating time. An eight- to nine-pound fish needs about one and one-half days in the wet brine; a ten- to twelve-pound fish requires a full two days of marinating.

Serving Ideas

Gravlax is perfect for cocktail or holiday parties because it can be made up to one week in advance. Just wrap the whole sides in parchment and then plastic and refrigerate them until ready to slice. Although gravlax should be sliced thin (illustrations 9 and 10), it does not need to be paper-thin like smoked salmon.

Gravlax is fairly rich, so Moonen likes to serve the fish with several accompaniments. A simple onion relish adds some sweetness and a little heat. Crème fraîche flavored with cilantro adds a lemony, herbal note, and toasted rye bread provides a crunchy, savory base on which to enjoy these other flavors.

GRAVLAX
Makes 1 side of cured salmon

Chef Rick Moonen uses a centrifugal juicer to separate the onion pulp from the liquid in seconds. Although a little more time-consuming, onion juice can also be made by grinding onions in a food processor until liquefied, about four minutes. Strain the onions through a double thickness of cheesecloth, squeezing to extract the juice. Serve sliced gravlax with lightly toasted rye bread, Onion Relish, and Cilantro Cream (*see* recipes below).

- 3 medium-large red onions, peeled, quartered, juiced, and foam skimmed to yield about 2 cups juice (*see* note above)
- 1 cup kosher salt
- ¾ cup sugar
- 1 teaspoon ground white pepper
- 2 cups coarsely chopped fresh dill leaves and stems, plus 1 cup minced fresh dill leaves
- 1 whole salmon fillet, 3 to 4 pounds, skinned, excess fat and brown flesh removed, and bones removed with tweezers (*see* illustrations 1 through 5)

1. Pour onion juice into 4-cup glass measure. Add salt and sugar; stir to dissolve. Stir in pepper and the coarsely chopped dill.

2. Place salmon in 2-gallon zipper-lock bag. Pour in marinade, seal bag, and place on jelly roll pan (illustration 6). Marinade should barely cover fish. Place second jelly roll pan over fish and set about 7 pounds of weight (heavy cans or bricks work well) on top pan (illustration 7). Refrigerate weighted fish until very firm, 12 to 18 hours, depending on thickness of fish.

3. Remove salmon fillet from bag and dry with paper towels. Evenly distribute the minced dill over belly side of the fillet, then press dill into flesh (illustration 8). (Gravlax can be wrapped in parchment paper then plastic wrap and refrigerated up to 1 week.)

4. Just before serving, place fillet, belly side up, on work surface. Following illustrations 9 and 10, slice desired amount of gravlax. Rewrap and refrigerate unsliced gravlax for later use.

ONION RELISH
Makes 2 cups

The onions are cooked slowly to bring out their sweetness while the sugar and vinegar temper the heat of the jalapeños. Do not use too much of the relish, or it will overwhelm the delicate, subtle flavors of the fish.

- 2 tablespoons olive oil
- 3 medium white onions (about 1 pound), peeled and diced fine
- 2 medium serrano or jalapeño chile peppers, seeded and minced
- 1 medium red bell pepper, cored, seeded, and diced fine
- ¼ cup sugar
- ¼ cup white wine vinegar

Heat oil in large sauté pan. Add onions; cook over medium heat until soft but not colored, 7 to 9 minutes. Stir in chile and bell peppers; continue to cook until all vegetables have softened, about 5 minutes longer. Stir in sugar and vinegar and cook until pan is almost dry, about 5 minutes. Transfer mixture to airtight container. (Relish can be refrigerated up to 1 week.) Bring to room temperature before serving.

CILANTRO CREAM
Makes about 1 cup

The lemony notes in cilantro are a perfect contrast to the rich gravlax and sweet onion relish. Serve the cream in a small bowl along with the sliced gravlax.

- 1 cup crème fraîche or sour cream
- 4 teaspoons minced fresh cilantro leaves

Mix crème fraîche and cilantro in small bowl. Cover and refrigerate until ready to serve. (Cream can be made 1 day in advance.) ■

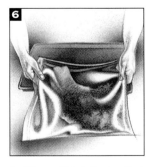

6. Place the salmon in a 2-gallon zipper-lock bag, add the marinade, seal the bag, and place it on a jelly roll pan.

7. Place a second jelly roll pan over the fish and set about 7 pounds of weight (heavy cans or bricks work well) on the top pan.

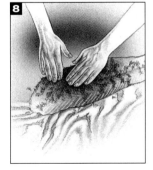

8. Evenly distribute minced dill over the belly side of the fish, then press the dill into the flesh.

9. Starting at the tail end, make a cut on the bias back toward the tail. Hold the knife at about a 20-degree angle and make a slice about ⅛ inch thick.

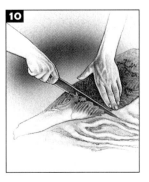

10. Continue making cuts, moving ⅛ inch up toward the head end each time, slicing desired amount.

ILLUSTRATIONS BY HARRY DAVIS

How to Make Tarte Tatin

The trick to perfect caramelization is standing apple quarters on edge.

~ BY STEPHEN SCHMIDT ~

Tarte Tatin, a French dessert said to have been invented by the Tatin sisters at their hotel in the Loire Valley, is basically an apple tart. The apples, however, are caramelized, and the tart is served upside-down; therefore, the dessert looks and tastes much more special.

The first step in the making of tarte Tatin takes place on the stove, not in the oven. The apples, neatly arranged in a tarte Tatin pan or a skillet, are boiled in a buttery caramel sauce over ferociously high heat until they absorb the syrup and become virtually candied. These syrup-soaked apples are then covered with a circle of pastry, and the tart is baked. After baking the tart is flipped over, revealing concentric circles of apples glazed with a golden caramel. It can be served with whipped cream or vanilla ice cream or with a tangy topping that offsets the sweetness of the caramel, such as crème fraîche or a mixture of cream and sour cream whipped together. A good tarte Tatin is one that tastes like caramelized apples, not like apples coated with caramel or, worse, an unidentifiable caramel glop.

When tarte Tatin first came to this country, all sorts of different recipes for it appeared. Some were based on traditional French formulas, but others were highly Americanized. The latter, generally speaking, simply did not work. The unsuccessful recipes varied, but most of them exhibited one of two serious flaws. One of these mistakes was using sliced or chopped apples, which make a wet, loose tart that sprawls and collapses when inverted. The second common error in Americanized recipes was the decision to caramelize the apples on top of the stove only after the tart had been completely baked. Caramelizing a fully baked tart is simply impossible. If the tart turns out juicy, it will not caramelize at all, and if it bakes up dry, it will burn. And you won't even know which disaster is about to befall you because you cannot see what the apples are doing underneath the crust. Having learned all this the hard way a long time ago, I went on to try some new experiments.

Refining the Technique

I have always made tarte Tatin with apple quarters, which is, I believe, the traditional French way. Some recipes, however, call for apple halves, and I found this idea intriguing. When made with apple quarters, tarte Tatin can sometimes seem a little light on fruit because the apples lose juice and shrink when caramelized. When I tried using halved apples, though, I encountered a new set of problems. In my first experiments, I had trouble getting the caramel to penetrate all the way through such large pieces of apple. While I eventually resolved this problem simply by cooking the apples longer, I still was not enthralled by the results. My tarte Tatin now struck me as pulpy and mushy, and there seemed to be too much fruit in relation to crust. Worse, I found that if the skillet was just a tad too small—or the apples unusually juicy—the caramel overflowed the pan during the caramelization process, making a real mess.

In the end, I abandoned the apple halves, but these experiments nonetheless proved useful since they gave me an idea of how to refine my original method using quarters. When you make a tarte Tatin with halved apples, the apples rest on the outer peeled surface so that the full cut side faces up. Apple quarters, by contrast, tend to flop over onto a cut side, but I reasoned that if I tipped each apple quarter onto its cut edge and held it there while I laid the next quarter in place, I could fit more fruit in the skillet. It turned out that I was able to cram an entire extra apple into the skillet this way, with very good results. The tart looked fuller and tasted fruitier, but it did not suffer from apple overload or overflow onto the stove.

The only problem now was that the apples, because they were almost perpendicular to the skillet, caramelized only on the skillet side, leaving the other side pale and sour. One recipe I clipped solved this problem by flipping the apples over during the caramelization process. This maneuver sounded tricky to me, but, as the clipped recipe promised, it was easily accomplished by spearing the quarters with a table fork or the tip of a paring knife. Even though the caramelized side of the apples is very soft, the side facing up remains firm enough not to tear when the apples are speared and flipped. Furthermore, even if the skillet is not nonstick-coated, the apple quarters never stick.

In traditional French recipes for tarte Tatin, the apples, sugar, and butter are all combined at the outset and caramelized in a single step. Many contemporary American recipes, however, call for caramelizing the sugar with the butter before putting the apples in the skillet. I have never understood the purpose of this two-step method, and after trying it several times, I still don't. It is true that the caramel, when prepared on its own, can be cooked to a high temperature and made very dark; after all, there are no apples in the skillet to worry about charring. But if this is the purpose, I think it is a wrong-headed one. When I made several highly caramelized tartes Tatin using the two-step method, the caramel tasted bitter and overwhelmed the apples. And certainly the two-step method offers no advantages when it comes to convenience. It takes more time than the traditional method, and it strikes me as rather dangerous because it entails arranging raw apples in a slithery, slippery, boiling hot caramel.

I have always used Granny Smith apples for tarte Tatin, but many recipes recommend Golden Delicious, and one recipe that I had on hand specified, of all things, Red Delicious, which, it was claimed, gave the tart a pretty look because of the elongated shape. I tested both Golden and Red Delicious as well as Gala and Fuji apples.

The results surprised me. I had expected most of the apples—certainly the Red Delicious—to fall apart, but all held their shape quite well. Flavor, however, was another story. The Golden Delicious apples were acceptable, if barely, but the rest were tasteless. I tried adding lemon juice to augment the flavor of the insipid apples, but I did not find this to be an effective remedy. Lemon juice did cut the sweetness of the caramel, but it did nothing to boost apple flavor. You need to start with apples that are flavorful to begin with, and if supermarket apples are your only option, I think it is safest to stick with Granny Smiths.

Finally, there is the matter of the crust. A crust for tarte Tatin needs extra durability and strength, and so bakers of tarte Tatin usually make the crust with an egg. Egg pastry does not have to be sweetened, but it is indisputably more delicious when it is, and therein lies the problem. Sugar makes pastry dough sticky, crumbly, and generally difficult to handle, and it also tends to fuse the spacers—the little bits of butter that make pastry flaky—leaving the baked crust crunchy, cookielike, and a little hard. After struggling with these problems for years, I finally discovered that the solution was to use confectioners' sugar rather than regular granulated. Granulated sugar is too coarse to dissolve well in dough. It remains in individual grains, then melts into tiny droplets of sticky

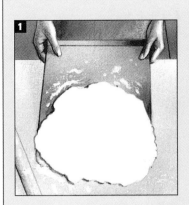

1. Slide a lightly floured rimless cookie sheet or pizza peel under dough that has been rolled into a 12-inch disk. Refrigerate it while caramelizing the apples.

2. Arrange the first apple quarter, thin side down and with an end touching the skillet wall. As you continue to arrange apples, lift each quarter on its edge while placing the next apple quarter on its edge, so that the apple quarters stand straight up.

3. Fill the skillet middle with the remaining quarters.

4. Remove the skillet from the heat, flip the apples, then return the skillet to the heat.

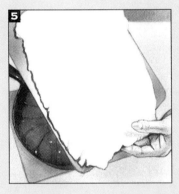

5. Slide the prepared dough over the cooked apples.

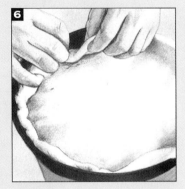

6. Tuck the dough edges gently against the skillet wall.

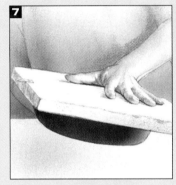

7. Place a serving platter over the skillet and hold tightly against it.

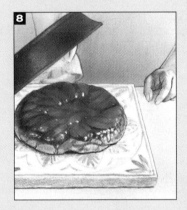

8. Invert the tart onto the platter.

---

syrup that wreak havoc. Confectioners' sugar, by contrast, simply disappears, sweetening the dough without causing any problems. It makes a superbly flaky egg pastry, worthy of the dessert masterpiece called tarte Tatin.

TARTE TATIN
Serves 8
If the caramel isn't cooked to a rich amber color, the apples will look pale and dull rather than shiny and appealingly caramelized.

Flaky Egg Pastry
1⅓ cups all-purpose flour, measured by dip-and-sweep, plus extra for surfaces
¼ cup confectioners' sugar
½ teaspoon salt
8 tablespoons (1 stick) unsalted butter, chilled and cut into ¼-inch pats
1 large cold egg, beaten

Caramelized Apples
8 tablespoons (1 stick) unsalted butter
¾ cup plus 1 tablespoon granulated sugar
3 pounds Granny Smith apples (six large 8-ounce apples or five extra large 10-ounce apples), peeled, quartered, and cored

Tangy Cream Topping
1 cup heavy cream, cold
½ cup sour cream, cold

1. *For the pastry:* Mix flour, sugar, and salt in food processor fitted with steel blade. Scatter butter over dry ingredients; process until mixture resembles cornmeal, 7 to 12 seconds. Turn mixture into medium bowl; add egg and stir with fork until little balls form. Press balls together with back of fork, then gather dough into ball with hands. Wrap in plastic, then flatten into 4-inch disk. Refrigerate at least 30 minutes. (Can be refrigerated overnight; let stand at room temperature to warm slightly before further use.)

2. Unwrap dough and turn out onto well-floured work surface. Sprinkle with additional flour. Starting from disk center outward, roll dough into 12-inch circle, strewing flour underneath to prevent sticking. Slide lightly floured, rimless cookie sheet or pizza peel under crust (*see* illustration 1), cover with plastic, and refrigerate while preparing apples. Adjust oven rack to upper-middle position; heat oven to 375 degrees.

3. *For the filling:* Melt butter in 9-inch skillet or tarte Tatin pan; remove from heat and sprinkle evenly with sugar. Following illustrations 2 through 3, arrange apples in skillet.

4. Return skillet to high heat; cook until juices turn from butterscotch to rich amber color, 10 to 12 minutes. Remove skillet from heat and, using fork or tip of paring knife, turn apples onto uncaramelized sides (illustration 4). Return skillet to highest heat; boil to cook uncaramelized sides of apples, about 5 minutes longer.

5. Remove skillet from heat. Slide prepared dough over skillet (illustration 5), and, taking care not to burn fingers, tuck dough edges gently against skillet wall (illustration 6).

6. Bake until crust is golden brown, 25 to 30 minutes. Set skillet on wire rack; let cool about 20 minutes. Loosen edges with knife, place serving plate over top of skillet (illustration 7), turn tart upside-down, then remove skillet (illustration 8). Scrape out any apples that stick to skillet and put them back into place. (Tart can be kept for several hours at room temperature, but unmold it onto dish that can withstand mild heat. Before serving, warm tart for 10 minutes in 200-degree oven.)

7. *For the topping:* With electric mixer, beat heavy cream and sour cream at medium-high speed until mixture thickens and holds soft but definite peaks. (Topping can be made a day ahead; cover and refrigerate.) Accompany each wedge of tart with generous dollop of topping. ∎

Stephen Schmidt is the author of the forthcoming *Dessert America* (William Morrow).

Basic Knife Techniques

HANDLE GRIP

The handle grip is often favored by cooks with smaller hands. This grip also causes fewer calluses for cooks who spend a lot of time working with knives.

1. Letting the knife rest in your open hand, hold your four fingers together perpendicular to the knife. Your thumb should be relaxed and positioned parallel to the knife.

2. Fold your fingers over the handle and, at the same time, tighten the grasp of your palm. Your thumb should remain in its relaxed position.

3. Turn the knife so that it is now at a right angle to the cutting surface. Then rest your thumb on the side of the handle, opposite the index finger, and you are ready to begin.

BLADE GRIP

This grip is often used by cooks with larger hands, who find it difficult to comfortably fit four fingers under the knife handle. This grip requires a bit more strength in the wrists and fingers. Because the hand is moved slightly forward, this grip can also provide somewhat more control over the blade.

1. Let the knife rest in your open hand, with the index finger on the blade and your other three fingers perpendicular to the knife. Fold your fingers and tighten the grasp of your palm. The tip of the index finger should now be touching the bolster (the metal shank between the blade and the handle) and the index finger itself should rest flat against the blade.

2. Now place your thumb on the blade. The tip of the thumb should be on the opposite side of the blade from the second joint of the index finger.

3. Turn the knife so that it is now at a right angle to the cutting surface, and you are ready to begin cutting.

There are two ways to position the hand that is not holding the knife. Both are designed to prevent slippage, to control the size of the cut, and to protect the hand holding the item being cut. The one you use is simply a matter of which feels most comfortable and natural.

THE CLAW METHOD

In this method, the first joints of the fingers of the noncutting hand actually rest on the item being cut. The thumb and little finger should be parallel to each other and the three other fingers fairly close together. The blade should rest against the knuckle, which provides guidance but is in no danger of being cut.

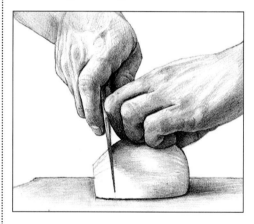

THE PARALLEL FINGER METHOD

In this method, the thumb and little finger are placed parallel to each other on the item being cut, the middle finger at the summit, and the other two fingers evenly spaced between them. The fingers remain bent so the blade can rest against the knuckle, providing guidance with no danger of being cut.

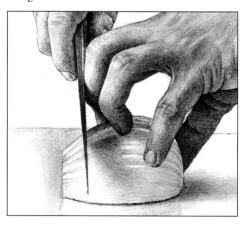

ILLUSTRATIONS BY ANATOLY

For best results with all of the cutting methods illustrated below, move the guiding hand and the knife instead of the item being cut.

USING THE HEEL END AS THE CUTTING EDGE

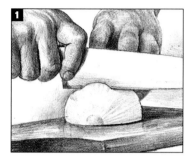

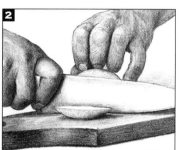

1. Position the knife with the tip pointing slightly upward. The cut begins with a downward motion that also moves the knife into a more horizontal position.

2. The cut ends as the blade reaches the cutting board. Note the area of the blade that is used and that horizontal as well as vertical movement is employed.

USING THE TIP OF THE KNIFE FOR CUTTING

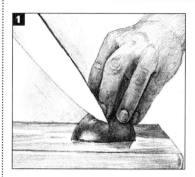

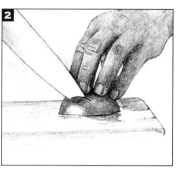

1. For objects with a skin that must be punctured, such as a tomato, it sometimes works best to use the tip of the knife to begin the cut.

2. Continue the cut by drawing the tip of the knife through the item being cut, maintaining the angle of the knife to the cutting board.

USING THE MAIN CUTTING EDGE

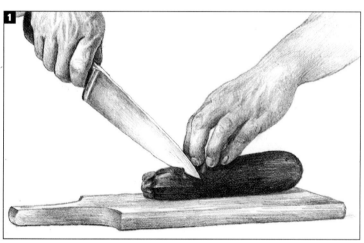

1. Hold the knife at about a 45-degree angle to the cutting board, touching the item being cut, which should be securely held with the other hand.

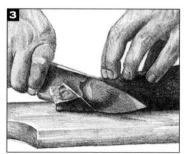

2. Cut the item by bringing the knife forward and downward with a smooth motion, simultaneously letting it become more horizontal. The cut continues in a smooth motion. The tip of the blade should remain in contact with the cutting board.

3. When the blade reaches the cutting board, it should be horizontal. To make the second cut using this technique, lift the knife to its position in step 1, keeping it constantly in contact with the cutting board. During the upward motion, move the guiding hand to determine the size of the next cut.

CHOPPING

1. This continuous, fast motion begins with the knife held high and the guiding hand held gently on top of the end of the blade. The guiding hand should provide just enough pressure to keep the blade in control and always in contact with the cutting board. Begin the chopping motion by lowering the knife, looking ahead to anticipate where you want to cut.

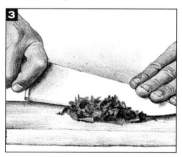

2. Continue the motion, bringing the curved edge of the blade into contact with the board.

3. The motion ends with the heel of the knife in contact with the board. Repeat this three-part motion rapidly, keeping the tip of the knife in contact with the board but moving the knife handle back and forth and redistributing the product on the cutting board, if necessary, until the food is as finely chopped as you would like. ■

Simple, Satisfying Beef Stew

Choose chuck, use a combination of broth and wine, and thicken at the beginning for a simple, but intensely flavored stew.

~ BY PAM ANDERSON WITH KAREN TACK ~

Browning the meat is a key to flavorful stew. The next step is to stir a bit of flour into the sautéing onions and garlic, the easiest way to thicken the stew.

Few dishes are as soul-satisfying as a hearty beef stew. What a gift to the cook that such a rich, hearty dish demands so little preparation and effort.

Our goal in developing a recipe for hearty beef stew was to keep that cooking process simple without compromising the stew's deep, complex flavor. We skipped over recipes that began with instructions for homemade beef stock, knowing that many home cooks barely have time to make stew, much less stock. At the other extreme, we ignored those that dumped meat, vegetables, and liquid into a pot to simmer for a couple of hours, understanding that the browning and caramelizing process was just too important to skip.

We focused on the issues that mattered. What cut or cuts of meat respond best to stewing? How much and what kind of liquid should you use? When and with what do you thicken the stew? And where should the stew be cooked: in the oven, on top of the stove, or does it matter?

Chuck Reigns

From our hamburger testing (*see* "A Better Burger," July/August 1995), we already knew that chuck is one of the most flavorful cuts of beef. Not surprisingly, chuck scored high in our stew tests as well (*see* "The Upper Cut," page 19). The intramuscular fat and connective tissue in chuck suit it well for the long, slow, moist cooking that is stewing. When cooked in liquid, the connective tissue melts down into gelatin, making

the meat juicy and tender. The fat helps, too, in two important ways. Fat carries the chemical compounds that our taste buds receive as beef flavor, and it also melts when cooked, lubricating the meat fibers by slipping between the cells to increase tenderness.

The Skinny on Thickeners

After determining the best cut of meat for stewing, we explored how and when to thicken the stew. We tried several thickening methods and found most methods acceptable, with the exception of quick-cooking tapioca, which produced a slimy and gelatinous stew. The thickener that works best for fruit pies (*see* "How to Thicken Fruit Pies," July/August 1995) delivered almost inedible beef stew.

Dredging beef cubes in flour is another round-about way of thickening stew. The floured beef is browned, then stewed. During the stewing process, some of the flour from the beef dissolves into the liquid, causing it to thicken. Although the stew we cooked this way thickened up nicely, the beef cubes had a "smothered steak" look: The flour coating had browned, not the meat. This coating often fell off during cooking to expose pale and therefore less flavorful meat.

We also tried two thickening methods at the end of cooking—a *beurre manié* (softened butter mixed with flour) and cornstarch mixed with water. Either method is acceptable, but the *beurre manié* lightened the stew's color, making it look more like pale gravy than rich stew juices. Also, the extra fat grams did not improve the stew's flavor enough to justify it. For those who prefer to thicken at the end of cooking, we found cornstarch dissolved in water did the job without compromising the stew's dark, rich color.

Pureeing the cooking vegetables is another thickening method. Once the stew is fully cooked, the meat is pulled from the pot. The juices and vegetables are pureed, creating a thick sauce. Some may like this thickening method, but we felt the vegetable flavor became too dominant. Hearty Beef Stew began to taste like Mixed Vegetable Stew with Beef Chunks.

Ultimately, we opted for thickening the stew with flour at the beginning—stirring it into the sautéing onions and garlic, right before adding

the liquid—not because stew thickened this way was any better but because it was easier. All the work is done at the beginning. Once the liquid starts to simmer, the cook's work is done.

The Liquid Test

Once we had figured out how and when to thicken, we moved on to stewing liquids. To determine which liquid or combination of liquids made the most flavorful stew, we made stew with the following:

—*all water*
—*water with a few shank bones thrown in for extra flavor*
—*all wine*
—*all low-sodium canned beef broth*
—*wine with various partners: low-sodium canned beef broth, low-sodium canned chicken broth, or water*

Neither of us preferred the stews made with only one liquid. Predictably, the all-wine stew was too strong while the all-water stew was thin and flat-tasting. The one made with water and bones was greasier; adding the bones didn't improve the flavor dramatically. The all-beef broth stews were acceptable but lacked that flavor edge that comes with wine. Of the stews that were made with part wine, the chicken broth-flavored stew had an edge over the one made with water. Neither of us, though, favored the one made with part beef broth.

During our research, we noticed the range of liquid used in different stew recipes. Some called for a minimum of liquid while others called for a large quantity. Quite logically, we confirmed that the more liquid the beef chunks must flavor, the less intensely flavored the stew. In order to preserve the pure intense beef flavor, we preferred a minimum of liquid. We found that about one cup of liquid per pound of meat gave us a sufficient amount to generously moisten a mound of mashed potatoes, polenta, or a pile of rice without drowning them.

We discovered as well that the body of the wine you use really makes a difference. Our first stews were made with a moderately priced but full-bodied shiraz. Without giving it much thought, we made our next group of stews with a young Beaujolais. We noticed, as we tasted the Beaujolais stews, that they weren't as rich and complex, and we began to question the wine/broth ratios we had decided on in our original testing. We finally realized that our first stews were made with a more full-bodied wine. It had, in fact, made a difference. For a richer stew, we suggest you select a moderately priced, but full-bodied wine (see "Wine for the Stew," page 20).

Cook in the Oven

At first we thought we should attempt to cook beef stew like pot roast or brisket, cooking the meat at a subsimmer and then pulling the stew as the meat passes from its juicy but tough stage into its dry but tender phase. A cooking colleague, however, convinced me that this goal was not only unimportant, but virtually impossible. While large chunks of meat like pot roast or brisket can be brought from a tough to a semitender, juicy state for a short time, the window of opportunity for smaller chunks of meat is incredibly small, requiring the cook to serve the stew *immediately* before the meat starts to dry out—a silly requirement since most people think stew tastes better the day after it has cooked.

We focused on low-temperature cooking methods since we already knew that high heat toughens and dries out meat. We cooked stews on the stovetop over low heat (with and without a flame-taming device) and in a 200-degree oven (any

temperature over 212 degrees would boil the meat, risking tougher, drier meat). The flame-taming device kept the meat from getting tender too soon and thus leaving the stew juices tasting as though the wine hadn't cooked off. Although either method is acceptable, we preferred the consistent, enveloping heat of the oven as opposed to the inconsistent heat of the burner. We found ourselves constantly adjusting the burner while the stews in the oven cooked evenly.

We did find that, regardless of whether you cook the stew on the stovetop or in the oven, the meat passes from the tough to tender stage fairly quickly. Often at the two-hour point, the tested meat would be chewy. Fifteen minutes later that same meat was tender. So though you can't achieve the same perfection with stew as with pot roast or brisket, we do think it important to stop the cooking as soon as the meat is tender.

HEARTY BEEF STEW
Serves 6 to 8
Make this stew in a large, heavy-bottomed soup kettle measuring at least ten inches in diameter. If

the kettle is any smaller, you may need to cook the meat in three batches rather than two.

- 3 pounds beef chuck, cut into 1½-inch cubes
- 1½ teaspoons salt
- 1 teaspoon ground black pepper
- 3 tablespoons vegetable oil
- 2 medium-large onions, chopped coarse (about 2 cups)
- 3 garlic cloves, minced
- 3 tablespoons flour
- 1 cup full-bodied red wine (see "Wine for the Stew," page 20)
- 2 cups chicken stock or low-sodium chicken-flavored broth
- 2 bay leaves
- 1 teaspoon dried thyme leaves
- 6 small boiling potatoes, peeled and halved
- 4 large carrots, peeled and sliced ¼ inch thick
- 1 cup frozen peas (6 ounces), thawed
- ¼ cup minced fresh parsley leaves

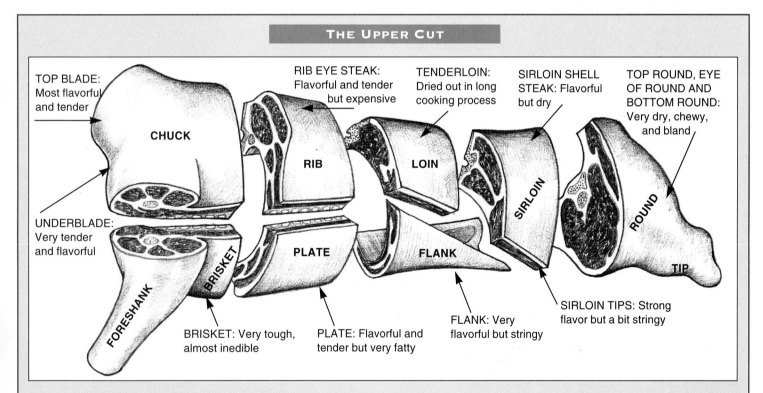

THE UPPER CUT

TOP BLADE: Most flavorful and tender

RIB EYE STEAK: Flavorful and tender but expensive

TENDERLOIN: Dried out in long cooking process

SIRLOIN SHELL STEAK: Flavorful but dry

TOP ROUND, EYE OF ROUND AND BOTTOM ROUND: Very dry, chewy, and bland

CHUCK

RIB

LOIN

SIRLOIN

ROUND

UNDERBLADE: Very tender and flavorful

FORESHANK

BRISKET

PLATE

FLANK

TIP

BRISKET: Very tough, almost inedible

PLATE: Flavorful and tender but very fatty

FLANK: Very flavorful but stringy

SIRLOIN TIPS: Strong flavor but a bit stringy

To compare texture and flavor, we sampled twelve different cuts of beef. We browned each, marked them for identification, and stewed them in the same pot according to our beef stew recipe.

The results were not surprising: Chuck proved the most flavorful, tender, and juicy. As detailed in the illustration above, after stewing, most other cuts were either too stringy, too chewy, too dry, or just plain bland. The exception was rib eye steak, which made

good stew meat, but is too expensive a cut to use for this purpose.

What does this mean to you at the market? Our advice is to buy a steak or roast from the chuck and cube it yourself instead of buying precut stewing beef.

The reason for this is simple: Prepackaged stewing beef is often made up of irregularly shaped end pieces from different cuts (all within the same primal cut) that cannot be sold retail as steaks or roasts because of their uneven

appearance. Because of the differences in their origin, precut stewing cubes in the same package may have inconsistent cooking, flavor, and tenderness qualities. If you cut your own cubes from a single piece of chuck, on the other hand, you are assured that it will all have the same cooking characteristics, as well as the flavor and richness of chuck.

The names given to different cuts of chuck vary, but the most commonly used names for retail

chuck cuts include boneless chuck-eye roasts, cross-rib roasts, blade steaks and roasts, shoulder steaks and roasts, and arm steaks and roasts. Both Jack Ubaldi, a butcher and author based in New York, and National Beef Council Test Kitchen Director Marlys Bielunski specifically mention chuck-eye roast as an excellent choice for stewing beef, though all our sources agree that any chuck cut would work well in a stew.—*Adam Ried*

1. Heat oven to 200 degrees. Place beef cubes in large bowl. Sprinkle with salt and pepper; toss to coat. Heat 2 tablespoons of the oil over medium-high heat in large nonreactive soup kettle; add beef to kettle in two separate batches. Brown meat on all sides, about 5 minutes per batch, adding remaining tablespoon of oil if needed. Remove meat and set aside. Add onions to now empty kettle; sauté until almost softened, 4 to 5 minutes. Reduce heat to medium and add garlic; continue to sauté about 30 seconds longer. Stir in flour; cook until lightly colored, 1 to 2 minutes. Add wine, scraping up any browned bits that may have stuck to kettle. Add stock, bay leaves, and thyme; bring to simmer. Add meat; return to simmer. Cover and place in oven; simmer about 1 hour.

2. Remove kettle from oven, add potatoes and carrots, cover, and return to oven. Simmer until meat is just tender, 1½ to 2 hours. Remove stew from oven. (Can be cooled, covered, and refrigerated up to 3 days.)

3. Add peas and allow to stand 5 minutes. Stir in parsley, adjust seasonings, and serve.

BEEF STEW WITH BACON, MUSHROOMS, AND PEARL ONIONS
Serves 6 to 8

Rather than the portions of liquid in Hearty Beef Stew, use equal portions of red wine and stock (one and one-half cups of each). Instead of the frozen pearl onions called for here, you can use an equal amount of fresh pearl onions that have been blanched, peeled, and steamed.

1. Follow recipe for Hearty Beef Stew, making the following changes: Before preparing beef, fry 4 ounces sliced bacon, cut into small dice, in bottom of kettle until brown and crisp. Drain bacon, reserving bits and drippings. Substitute drippings for oil when browning meat. Return bacon to kettle with stock, bay leaves, and thyme.

2. Omit potatoes, carrots, and peas. Heat 2 tablespoons of reserved drippings in large skillet until hot and add 1 pound white mushrooms, quartered; sauté over high heat until browned, 5 to 7 minutes. Remove from skillet, then add 1 cup (8 ounces) frozen pearl onions, cooked according to package directions. Sauté until lightly browned, 2 to 3 minutes. When meat is almost tender, 2 to 2½ hours, add mushrooms and pearl onions to stew. Cover and return to oven. Cook until meat and pearl onions are tender, 20 to 30 minutes longer. Stir in parsley, adjust seasonings, and serve.

BEEF STEW WITH TOMATOES, ORANGE ZEST, AND OLIVES
Serves 6 to 8

1. Follow recipe for Hearty Beef Stew, making the following changes: Substitute 1 cup chopped tomatoes with their juice for 1 cup of the stock. Add two strips orange zest when adding stock. Substitute equal portion herbes de Provence for the thyme.

2. Omit potatoes, carrots, and peas. Stir in 1 cup black olives such as Kalamata to fully cooked stew. Cover and let stand 5 minutes. Stir in parsley, adjust seasonings, and serve.

BEEF STEW WITH TOMATOES, CINNAMON, AND CLOVES
Serves 6 to 8

1. Follow recipe for Hearty Beef Stew, making the following changes: Stir in 1 tablespoon tomato paste after flour has colored. Substitute 1 cup tomatoes for 1 cup of the stock and add 1 teaspoon ground cinnamon and ⅛ teaspoon ground cloves along with stock, bay leaves, and thyme.

2. Omit potatoes, carrots, and peas. Heat 1 tablespoon oil in medium skillet; add 1 cup frozen pearl onions, cooked according to package directions, and sauté until lightly browned, 2 to 3 minutes. When meat is almost tender, 2 to 2½ hours, add pearl onions and ⅓ cup currants to stew. Cover and return to oven. Cook until meat and pearl onions are tender, 20 to 30 minutes longer. Stir in parsley, adjust seasonings, and serve. ∎

WINE FOR THE STEW

Although most home cooks realize that "cooking wine"—the dreadful, usually oxidized stuff sold in supermarkets—is not going to cut it when it comes to beef stew or any other dish that relies upon red wine for much of its flavor, I frequently run into people who overcompensate. It wasn't long ago, in fact, that I had to virtually snatch a bottle of good $20 burgundy from the hands of a friend who had read, in a recipe for coq au vin, that he should "use the best red wine you can afford." He could afford it, it was true, but the difference in flavor contribution between this wine and one costing a third as much would have been subtle at best, and more likely not at all discernible.

I have tried beef stews with many different wines over the years and have always felt that the best solution is to use a fruity, assertive, young, fairly cheap, sturdy specimen: Chianti, zinfandel (red, not pink, of course), some of the newer wines from southern France, or cabernets from California. What you're looking for, mostly, is fruit, some of the flavor of wood, and not too much in the way of tannins, which might make a dish bitter. You can get all of this from a lovely, mature—and costly—wine from Burgundy or Bordeaux, or from many of the far less expensive wines mentioned above.

In sum, my long-term experience and short-term experimenting leads me to this bit of advice: When cooking with wine, use the least expensive, decent wine you think you can get away with. Save the most expensive, best wine you can afford for drinking.

—*Mark Bittman*

THE VERY BEST BEEF STEW: THE VEGETABLES LAST

In order to determine when to add the vegetables, we made three different stews, adding carrots, celery, and onions to one stew at the beginning of cooking, and halfway through the cooking process to another stew. For our final stew, we cooked the onions (and garlic) with the meat but added steamed carrots and celery when the stew was fully cooked.

The results of these tests make perfect sense to us in retrospect, but we couldn't have predicted the outcome up front. The stew with vegetables added at the beginning ended up being thin and watery. The vegetables, which had given up their flavor to the stew, diluted the liquid, making the stew taste more like a beef-vegetable soup. The stew with vegetables added halfway through cooking was less watery, but the liquid from the vegetables still somewhat diluted the rich beef flavor we wanted, and the vegetables themselves had lost a good deal of their flavor and texture. The beef stew with the cooked vegetables added at the last minute, though, gave us what we wanted—a rich, uncompromised stew with fresh, bright, intensely flavored vegetables.

It is a bit more work (but only a bit) to steam vegetables separately from the stew, but many cooks do not consider a dish "real American beef stew" unless their vegetables are cooked in the same pot with the beef. Thus, the main recipe that we have provided adds the vegetables partway through cooking.

When you want the very best-tasting stew, though, follow the recipe for Hearty Beef Stew but omit the potatoes (I like my potatoes mashed and served as a base for the stew rather than included with the beef) and do not add the carrots and peas to the stew pot raw. Instead, just before serving, bring one inch of water to a boil in a steamer pot. Place the carrots in a steamer basket, lower them into the pot, and steam them until just tender, about six minutes. Then add the peas and steamed carrots, cover the kettle, and let the stew stand for approximately five minutes in order to blend all the flavors.

—*P.A.*

Cooking with Walnuts

To bring out walnuts' full flavor, don't blanch, but do toast in a skillet.

❧ BY DARRA GOLDSTEIN ❧

Walnuts are much more than flavor enhancers. In addition to accenting sweet snacks, they can also form the basis of savory dishes, from sandwich spreads to omelettes to rich, yet healthy sauces.

Some older cookbooks suggest blanching walnuts to remove the papery inner skin, or pellicle, which protects the nut from oxidation. This procedure was supposed to remove any bitterness from the nut, but I consider it unnecessary. I happen to like the assertive taste of the nut, which is diminished by blanching.

Other techniques for treating walnuts, however, enhance their flavor rather than lessen it. I have found a marked difference in taste when the nuts are lightly toasted before use. Most directions for toasting are generic and recommend baking any sort of nut for ten minutes in an oven at 350 degrees. But with walnuts, the best flavor is released when you toast the nuts briefly in a skillet, preferably a cast-iron one that heats quickly. The direct and vigorous contact with the hot surface lightly crisps the nuts and intensifies their flavor, making them taste richer than when oven-toasted.

To toast walnuts, place the nut halves in a dry cast-iron skillet, then turn the heat to medium and cook, stirring frequently, for four to five minutes, just until the nuts begin to sizzle and become fragrant. Be careful not to let them scorch. This process releases essential oils, which will subtly infuse any dish to which the nuts are added.

The other crucial technique for walnuts involves grinding. There are several tools with which this can be done: a mortar and pestle (the most ancient and time-consuming device), a chef's knife, a manual nut grinder, a blender, or a food processor.

When a thick paste is called for, as in many Middle Eastern recipes, the mortar and pestle is the instrument of choice. While the process of crushing the nut meats against stone is tedious, it is the continuous action of the pestle that releases the oil and intensifies the flavor. Also, there is really no other way to achieve the type of finely-textured paste called for in these dishes.

For regular ground nuts, the most reliable method is to use the kind of nut grinder that attaches to a table or countertop and has a grinding arm that is turned by hand. This method ensures perfectly ground, fluffy nuts.

Lacking this special equipment, it is acceptable to mince walnuts finely by hand. Use a large, heavy chef's knife against a wooden board and chop until the nuts are very fine. A quarter cup of walnuts will take about five minutes to process this way. As with a manual grinder, the nuts stay fluffy, but because a uniformly ground mass is hard to achieve by hand, the finished nuts should be pushed gently through a coarse sieve and large pieces minced a second time.

Grinding nuts in a blender is faster, though trickier, since the action of the blade tends to be uneven. For this reason, it is best to grind only a small quantity of nuts at a time and to keep scraping down the sides of the jar to release any nuts that have been thrown there. Walnuts ground in a blender are generally denser and oilier than those worked by hand.

Food processors definitely offer the easiest method of grinding. The danger is that the heat of the motor and the speed of the machine can quickly turn the nuts into an oily mass; if the cook is careful, however, food processor grinding can achieve very good results: fluffy texture along with the desired release of the walnut oil. The essential precaution is to use the pulse action and to check frequently to make sure that the nuts are ground only to the point at which you can still detect separate pieces. If you wish to use the nuts in sweet dishes, grind them together with any granulated sugar called for in the recipe so that they will be less likely to clump.

For convenience, most of us buy walnuts already shelled, in halves or in pieces. The nuts should appear firm and oily; shriveled or whitish nut meats indicate that much of the oil, and therefore the flavor, has been lost. It is better to buy the more expensive halves rather than the bits—the larger the pieces, the longer they will keep. Also, because of their high fat content, walnuts tend to absorb other flavors, so once opened, store them in an airtight container in the refrigerator or freezer, where they will keep for months.

TOASTED WALNUTS WITH CURRY SPICES
Makes 2 cups

These sweet, spicy nuts can be kept for three to four weeks in an airtight container.

- ¾ teaspoon curry powder
- ¾ teaspoon ground cumin
- ¼ teaspoon each: ground coriander, ground ginger, and cayenne pepper
- ⅛ teaspoon ground cinnamon
- 2 cups shelled walnuts, halved
- 1 tablespoon unsalted butter
- 3 tablespoons sugar
- ½ teaspoon salt
  Oil or cooking spray for cookie sheet

1. Mix spices in small bowl; set aside.
2. Place nut halves in dry cast-iron skillet over medium heat and cook, stirring frequently, 4 to 5 minutes, just until the nuts begin to sizzle and become fragrant. Add butter and stir until melted. Add spices and stir constantly until they are fragrant and begin to darken, about 1 minute.
3. Add sugar, 1 tablespoon water, and salt; continue cooking, stirring occasionally, until sauce thickens and walnuts are glazed, 5 to 6 minutes.
4. Turn nuts onto greased cookie sheet; arrange in single layer, using two forks to separate individual nuts. Let cool completely and store.

LINGUINE WITH WALNUT, GARLIC, AND HERB SAUCE
Serves 4 to 6

- 2 tablespoons unsalted butter
- 2 tablespoons olive oil
- 1¼ cups shelled walnuts, chopped fine
- 4 large garlic cloves, minced
- ½ cup grated Parmesan cheese, plus more for sprinkling on top
- ⅓ cup each: minced fresh basil and parsley leaves
- 3 tablespoons heavy cream
- ½ teaspoon salt, plus more for cooking water
- ½ teaspoon ground black pepper
- 1 pound dried linguine

1. Heat butter in large cast-iron skillet over medium heat until it begins to brown, 4 to 5 minutes. Add oil and walnuts; cook, stirring frequently until walnuts are fragrant and begin to brown, 3 to 4 minutes. Add garlic and cook until softened, about 1 minute longer. Remove skillet from heat; stir in cheese, basil, parsley, cream, salt, and pepper.
2. Meanwhile, cook linguine in large pot of boiling salted water until al dente. Drain, reserving ½ cup cooking water.
3. Toss reserved sauce and pasta together, adding just enough cooking water to moisten the dish. Serve with additional Parmesan cheese. ∎

Darra Goldstein's most recent cookbook is the award-winning *The Georgian Feast* (HarperCollins, 1993).

Solving the Mystery of the Chewy Chocolate Chip Cookie

After testing forty different variations, we discover how to make a thick, chewy gourmet shop cookie at home.

～ BY GAIL NAGELE-HOPKINS ～

Melting the butter before adding it and adding an extra egg yolk to the batter turned out to be the keys to a gourmet shop cookie.

The quest began simply enough: I wanted to duplicate, at home, the big, delicious, chewy chocolate chip cookies bought in the trendy specialty cookie shops. For me, first and foremost, this new genre of home-baked chocolate chip drop cookie had to look and taste like the ultimate, sinful cookie: thick (about one-half inch high), jumbo (three inches in diameter), and bursting with chocolate. It also had to have a mouthwatering, uneven surface texture with rounded edges, be slightly crispy but tender on the outside, and rich, buttery, soft, and chewy inside. In other words, it needed to be a "melt-in-your-mouth" kind of cookie. It also had to be quick and easy to make, not fussy or labor-intensive.

I tried innumerable published recipes claiming to produce a thick, chewy cookie. After many unsuccessful attempts, I wondered whether or not a conspiracy existed to prevent home cooks from making these cookies. The search was on.

Chipping Away at the Mystery

In order to establish a point of departure, I compared about twenty-five published recipes from various sources, analyzing and comparing such basic variables as ingredients, their quantities and relative proportions, oven temperature, yield, and baking time. With the basic common denominators clearly laid out, I began experimenting and testing. I consulted professional literature and food professionals, and bought and analyzed specialty shop cookies and the dough from which they were made.

In my earliest trials, I turned to well-known cookbooks for recipes that claimed to yield chewy chocolate chip cookies. I ended up with either crispy, feathery light cookies with flattened edges, or doughy, underbaked, pliable creations. Several recipes suggested that baking the cookies at a very low oven temperature (275 degrees) would produce chewy, dense cookies, so I dutifully cooked a batch that way. What it produced was an insufficiently browned, doughy-textured cookie that tasted underbaked. Other recipes suggested a shorter baking time, and still others suggested that refrigerating the dough would slow its spread and produce thick, chewy cookies. I tried them all, but none worked.

I began to suspect that the solution lay not in the cooking time or temperature, but in the dough itself. I needed to create a more dense dough that would spread less when baked, thus producing a thicker, and therefore chewier, cookie.

Early on in my quest for a dense dough, I tried increasing the proportion of flour to see if, with a slightly drier dough, the cookies would hold their shape better and flatten less. I also tried adding ground oatmeal, expecting that a chewy grain might add a chewy quality to the finished product. Both of these experiments caused the cookies to hold their shape better as they baked, but, unfortunately, in both cases the cookies became cakey, puffy, and dry, not chewy.

Still unsuccessful, I next tried adding molasses, which helps retain moisture (molasses is 24 percent water), and then corn syrup in the hope that these ingredients might lend a gluey, caramel quality to the dough. The impact of the corn syrup was unremarkable. The taste was nice with the molasses, and the cookie was slightly moister, but, as they baked, the cookies stubbornly continued to spread toward crispy flatness.

Thoughts of the dense, stiff, almost caramel-like texture of the dough I had bought from the specialty cookie shop began to amble through my head. I literally began pulling and pushing at this guaranteed chewy dough; the cookie shop dough and my dough were obviously at two opposing ends of a texture spectrum. The key to achieving a denser dough and possibly a denser cookie continued to elude me.

Changing Course in the Right Direction

About this same time, a professional baker commented that she had once mistakenly used a "blondie" recipe (a light-colored version of brownies, with chocolate chips in place of melted chocolate) to make chocolate chip cookies and that they were somewhat chewy. Other than differences in proportions of ingredients, the main difference between the "blondie" dough and the traditional chocolate chip cookie dough is in the treatment of the butter. When making blondies, the butter is melted; in traditional chocolate chip cookies, butter is creamed together with sugar into a light, airy state.

According to food scientist Shirley Corriher, when butter is melted, free water and fat are separated from each other. When this melted butter is combined with flour, the proteins in the flour grab the water and each other to immediately form elastic sheets of gluten. This creates a product with a chewy texture. At the same time, the sugars and fats are working to inhibit gluten formation, which prevents the cookies from becoming too tough.

Clearly, my next task was to create a chocolate chip cookie from a blondie recipe. I thought I was almost there when I realized this, but I was far from it. Although it was only tinkering, my final adjustments included seventy-two recipe variations! My first results yielded chewy, somewhat dense, well-formed chocolate chip somethings that were neither brownies nor cookies. The taste still needed lots of work, but the texture was definitely on the right track. The logical next step was to return to the

PHOTOGRAPHS BY ERIC ROTH

same ingredients and proportions of the traditional chocolate chip recipe, except with melted, not beaten, butter. In the initial trials, there was too much butter in the dough; it clearly had more fat than the flour could absorb. As a result, the dough was greasy, and when baked, the cookies flattened, were gummy, and practically slid off the cookie sheet. The addition of more flour in order to remedy this problem resulted in a dry, cakey cookie with little spread. When I then underbaked these cakelike cookies in order to get a chewy effect, they tasted gummy and undone.

Gradually, however, by eliminating the molasses and judiciously reducing the quantities of vanilla and flour (as well as substituting bleached for unbleached), I was able to achieve the appropriate proportion of wet to dry ingredients in order to maintain the desired dough consistency and degree of spread that I was looking for. I had achieved the chewy texture of my quest.

Pursuit of Tenderness

Though I now had good-tasting, chewy cookies, they were still somewhat tough, and became increasingly harder with each hour out of the oven. The problem to be addressed now was tenderness.

Since flour plays a major role in the structure of baked products, I decided to experiment with flour and flour substitutes. First, I wanted to determine how the differences in the protein content of the flours affected the texture of the dough and the cookies. We know that higher protein (hard) flour will result in more gluten development and yield a tougher product. Lower protein (soft) flour will yield a more tender, but crumbly product. After numerous tests, varying the types of flours, proportions of flour to butter, and sifting and not sifting, my faithful taste testers unanimously agreed that the best cookie—chewy on the inside, crispy/crunchy on the outside, but also tender—resulted from unsifted, bleached, all-purpose flour. In comparing different all-purpose flours, bleached and unbleached, I realized why. The protein content of the bleached, all-purpose flour, which was between 8 and 10 percent, provided precisely the right balance of gluten development for chewiness yet tenderness. In spite of this newest achievement, however, the problem of the texture hardening with time still persisted.

Perhaps, I thought, flour was not the culprit, and the solution to the persistent hardening problem was in the sugar. I moved on to examine and compare how different sugars affected the taste and texture of my cookie. I eventually found that the best taste and texture resulted from using two parts brown sugar to one part white sugar—the cookie was rich, flavorful, and had a great aroma and appearance.

But I still wasn't completely satisfied with the texture of the cookie I had produced. In particular, though I had tested countless batches, the problem of the cookies hardening when several hours old persisted. I baked on, searching for ever more tenderness, chewiness, and softness.

Sweet Success

Just when I began to believe it impossible to create chewy, tender/crispy, yet soft cookies, I thought about the egg! It was the only ingredient quantity I hadn't varied after initially concluding that one whole egg provided the necessary quantity of moisture to maintain the desired dough consistency. Since fat is a tenderizer in baked goods, I reasoned, and since the yolk of an egg is fat, an additional egg yolk should add enough fat to tenderize and soften, yet not too much additional liquid to change the proper balance of dry to liquid ingredients. I tested and retested for this factor, and there was no doubt: The problem of the cookie hardening after several hours was eliminated by the addition of a single egg yolk. With a slight reduction in the amount of flour combined with the additional egg yolk, I had finally achieved my goal! The cookie was crispy/tender on the outside, soft and chewy on the inside, and hours after emerging from the oven, it remained pliable and soft. The key to the mystery had been found.

While the ideal baking time for these cookies is fifteen to eighteen minutes, just to be sure, I recommend you set the timer for thirteen minutes and then evaluate the cookies every two minutes thereafter. The cookies are done when they are light golden brown in color and the edges are hard but the center still looks a little puffy and is still soft to the touch. It is also important to remember that the quantity of cookies on the cookie sheet and the number of cookie sheets in the oven will influence baking time; the more cookies in the oven, the longer they will take to bake. All ovens are different, so be vigilant and remove the cookies from the oven promptly when they are done. Even the method of cooling turns out to be an important step in maintaining the chewy texture of this cookie. To maintain their soft, chewy texture, leave the cookies on the cookie sheet until cooled.

THICK AND CHEWY CHOCOLATE CHIP COOKIES
Makes 1½ dozen 3-inch cookies
These truly chewy chocolate chip cookies are delicious served warm from the oven or cooled. To ensure a chewy texture, leave the cookies on the cookie sheet to cool. You can substitute white, milk chocolate, or peanut butter chips for the semi- or bittersweet chips called for in the recipe. In addition to chips, you can flavor the dough with one cup of nuts, raisins, or shredded coconut.

- 2⅛ cups (2 cups plus 2 tablespoons) unsifted bleached all-purpose flour
- ½ teaspoon salt
- ½ teaspoon baking soda
- 12 tablespoons unsalted butter (1½ sticks), melted and cooled until warm
- 1 cup brown sugar (light or dark)
- ½ cup granulated sugar
- 1 large egg plus 1 egg yolk
- 2 teaspoons vanilla extract
- 1–2 cups semi- or bittersweet chocolate chips/chunks

1. Heat oven to 325 degrees. Adjust oven racks to upper- and lower-middle positions. Mix flour, salt, and baking soda together in medium bowl; set aside.

2. Either by hand or with electric mixer, mix butter and sugars until thoroughly blended. Mix in egg, yolk, and vanilla. Add dry ingredients; mix until just combined. Stir in chips to taste.

3. Form scant ¼ cup dough into ball. Holding dough ball using fingertips of both hands, pull into two equal halves. Rotate halves ninety degrees and, with jagged surfaces exposed, join halves together at their base, again forming a single cookie, being careful not to smooth dough's uneven surface. Place formed dough onto one of two parchment paper-lined 20-by-14-inch lipless cookie sheets, about nine dough balls per sheet. Smaller cookie sheets can be used, but fewer cookies can be baked at one time and baking time may need to be adjusted. (Dough can be refrigerated up to 2 days or frozen up to 1 month—shaped or not. *See* "Freezing the Dough.")

4. Bake, reversing cookie sheets' positions halfway through baking, until cookies are light golden brown and outer edges start to harden yet centers are still soft and puffy, 15 to 18 minutes (start checking at 13 minutes). (Frozen dough requires an extra 1 to 2 minutes baking time.) Cool cookies on cookie sheets. Serve or store in airtight container. ∎

Gail Nagele-Hopkins is a Pennsylvania-based baker and freelance writer.

FREEZING THE DOUGH

One of the best things about the dough in this recipe is that the dough will keep in the refrigerator for a couple days and in the freezer for a month. Cookies can be baked when needed, one at a time, to instantly gratify an inveterate sweet tooth, or a tray at a time, when company comes unexpectedly. They can also be frozen the day they are baked. If the dough is to be frozen, you may want to preform individual pieces before freezing. Experimenting, I froze an entire mass of dough and was, in fact, able to cut off individual pieces to be baked. Because the dough was frozen and unworkable, however, I was unable to get precisely sized pieces. With an adjustment in baking time, the results were fine. For the standard scant one-quarter cup dough per chocolate chip cookie, baking time for the frozen dough was only two to three minutes longer. If you prefer, the frozen dough mass can be defrosted until it is workable, probably around one hour depending on the mass size, and then formed and baked.—*G.N.*

Rating Dijon Mustards

Dijon mustard originated in France, but a mass market American product takes third place in our blind tasting.

⮑ BY DOUGLAS BELLOW ⮑

Although mustard has always been a favorite condiment and flavoring in American cooking, most American mustards have been characterized by their blandness, particularly in comparison to their spicier cousins from France and England. In recent years, however, as Americans' palates have become more receptive and spicy flavors in general have gained favor, one type of mustard, Dijon, has gained tremendous popularity in the United States.

Dijon mustards differ from both American and English versions of the condiment. American mustards are generally distinguished by their color—a garish bright yellow created by the addition of turmeric—as well as their blandness. English mustards are spicier than their American counterparts but traditionally have been dry rather than wet. While Dijon mustards are similar to English mustards in spiciness and similar to American mustards in that they are wet, they differ from both in flavor and texture.

The singular nature of Dijon mustard comes from its strictly prescribed list of ingredients and from its method of manufacture, both of which have a long history.

Historically, the process of making Dijon mustard began by soaking mustard seeds in an acidic mixture composed of water, vinegar, and wine. The softened seeds were then ground in a device called a "mustard quern," which basically consisted of two stones turned by hand. The resulting mixture was strained to remove the hulls and then mixed with more vinegar to form a smooth, yellow paste. After the addition of spices and salt, the mustard was aged for a short time, and then packed into barrels.

In 1390, the French government passed an ordinance codifying part of this process. The ordinance stated that, for a mustard to bear the label "Dijon," it could contain only three ingredients—brown or black mustard seeds, vinegar, and salt (wine was used only in the initial soaking process)—and that it could not be aged for longer than twelve days between manufacture and sale. In the eighteenth century, verjuice, the juice from very sour, unripe grapes, was accepted as a replacement for vinegar. In 1937 a law was passed codifying the methods by which the various ingredients were to be mixed.

Vinegar, Aging, and Seeds

Today, Dijon mustards made in France are still subject to these regulations. Three aspects of the prescribed method—the required use of vinegar, the length of aging, and the type of mustard seeds used—continue to have a particularly strong effect on the final product.

The heat of mustard seeds is dormant until the seeds are mixed with a liquid, which releases the heat. In the manufacture of Dijon mustard, this chemical reaction is precipitated by the original soaking in vinegar and water. Vinegar, however, has a second effect: It cools the heat of the mustard even as it releases it. Therefore, when the strained, softened seeds are mixed with the second batch of vinegar, the longer the vinegar and mustard stand before bottling, the less heat there will be in the final product. It is for this reason that the regulations governing Dijon manufacture state that it must be bottled within twelve days of manufacture. In fact, most companies bottle their mustards after far less standing time in order to preserve the desired spiciness.

Dijon is also distinguished from other varieties of mustard by the type of seeds that are used. The mustard plant, which is of the same family as radishes and turnips, produces seeds that come in three basic varieties: white (also known as *Sinapis alba*), black (*Brassica nigra*), and brown (*Brassica juncea*). The color names refer only to the outside shells, or husks, of the seeds, as the insides of all three are a muddy yellow color. Recently, use of the black seed plant was abandoned almost entirely because of its resistance to mechanized harvest. These days, all commercially raised seeds referred to as black or brown are actually the *Brassica juncea,* or brown, seeds.

Generally, mustard seeds supply an uncomplicated sort of background heat and mustiness, which enhance other flavors. The difference in flavor between white and brown seeds is rather subtle, but there is a marked difference in the degree and type of heat they provide. White seeds supply their heat at the front of the mouth and tongue whereas brown seeds supply a more intense heat, which affects the back of the throat, nose, and eyes. Both English and American mustards are made with a combination of white and brown seeds while Dijon mustard is made with brown alone, which thus gives it that more intense, nasal type of heat.

Tasting the Mustards

We decided to limit our tastings to mustards that mostly contain only the regulation list of ingredients—mustard seeds, vinegar, spices, and salt—with the only allowable addition being white wine. We allowed white wine because many Dijon-style mustards manufactured outside of France do contain it, and we wanted to sample more than just French mustards. However, keeping the ingredients list even this pure did eliminate a great many of the Dijon mustards made outside of France, which are not subject to French regulation and therefore contain ingredients as widely divergent as sugar and horseradish.

Even using these criteria, we discovered dozens of mustards from which to choose. We eventually selected a cross section of the most popular and available American and imported brands, including mustards from very old, established French firms and new versions by American producers. Suggestions came from local food distributors, from The Mount Horeb Mustard Museum in Mount Horeb, Wisconsin, and straight off supermarket shelves.

Two tastings were held, the first for a small group of food experts and the second for a group of twenty nonprofessional food lovers. In both tastings the participants tasted the mustards raw and were asked to rate them according to seven criteria: aroma; color; silkiness of texture; flavor; balance of acidity, spiciness, saltiness, and sweetness; finish, which should pleasantly echo the original taste; and overall impression.

Both tastings produced remarkably similar results. Essentially what we found was that tasters in both groups were looking for a very spicy and very balanced, yet relatively simple mustard. Most tasters, feeling that Dijon mustards should be quite hot, tended not to like mustards whose heat faded too rapidly. At the same time, tasters were very sensitive to the dominance of a single flavor—particularly too much vinegar, not enough mustard flavor, or too much of what was called a "musty," "old," or "eggy" flavor. This "off" flavor is caused by aging in the bottle, since both light and the air in the head of the bottle cause mustard to age. Unfortunately, it is difficult to tell when a mustard has been manufactured, and the "use by" dates on all the mustards tasted were at least two years from the date of the tastings.

The three victors all shared the qualities of heat and balance, with tasters opting for what they felt were "simpler, more complementary" mustards over more complex but distracting mustards. The addition of wine or spices may have affected the flavors of the mustards but did not do so in a way that tasters could easily detect. Interestingly, the three victors did not share a common ancestry, but all did share spiciness, distinct mustard flavor, and smoothly blended taste components. ■

Douglas Bellow lives and cooks in Cambridge, Massachusetts.

Eleven mustards were tasted blind, just as they came from the bottle, in two separate tastings, and are listed in the order of preference based on the combined scores awarded by judges in the two tastings. The first tasting was held at The Blue Room restaurant in Cambridge, Massachusetts. Participants included four members of the *Cook's Illustrated* staff plus Steve Johnson, chef at Mercury Bar in Boston, and Peter Sagansky, a Massachusetts-based wine consultant.

The second tasting was held in Wellfleet, Massachusetts, and participants included twenty nonprofessional food enthusiasts. Unless otherwise noted, all mustards in the list contain only the traditional ingredients of Dijon mustard, plus a preservative for shelf life. All mustards are available at supermarkets or may be purchased by mail order from The Mount Horeb Mustard Museum in Mount Horeb, Wisconsin (*see* Sources and Resources, page 32, for details).

HIGHLY RECOMMENDED

Bornier Genuine Dijon Mustard (Europé en de Condiments, Couchey, France), $3.49 for 16 oz. One of the spiciest of the mustards, Bornier appealed to almost all of the tasters. Tasters found it to have "an appealing, vinegary nose," with a "full, smooth texture." Flavor was "decently balanced," "building to an intense bright heat," followed by a "pleasant, mustardy finish."

Maille Dijon Originale (Segma-Maille, Longvic-les-Dijon, France), $2.29 for 7.5 oz. Not quite as spicy as Bornier, Maille nevertheless scored very highly in our taste tests. Tasters enjoyed the "spicy nose" and "smooth" texture. The flavor of Maille was "well balanced" yet "active, with serial sensations in the mouth."

French's Dijon Mustard (Reckitt & Colman Inc., Wayne, New Jersey), $1.99 for 8 oz. Most tasters found French's to be "straightforward and a little hot." Like the other two winners, French's had a "spicy aroma," "nutty brown color," and "smooth texture." French's had a "hot finish, with a slightly salty aftertaste." Most tasters rated French's highly and felt that although it was "not terribly distinctive," it was nonetheless "very pleasant." In addition to the traditional ingredients, this mustard contains white wine, but no preservatives.

RECOMMENDED

Edmond Fallot Moutarde de Dijon (Edmond Fallot, Beaune, France), $3.75 for 7 oz. Tasters found Fallot to have a "good, fresh aroma" and a "bright, attractive color." Fallot also had a good "balance of heat and flavor," and a "pleasant, consistent aftertaste." Many tasters felt that Fallot tasted "real" and that it "nailed a style of mustard well," but that the "touch of flame" was not enough.

Grey Poupon Dijon Mustard (Nabisco Foods, East Hanover, New Jersey), $2.39 for 8 oz. Tasters found that this highly advertised and highly successful mustard had "little aroma" and "more watery texture" but still "survived as good basic mustard." Grey Poupon is a very vinegary mustard, and tasters felt that the "mustard flavor could be more aggressive." Despite this, its "good general quality" and (interestingly) its "familiarity" gained it a number of high votes. In addition to the traditional ingredients, this mustard contains white wine, but no preservatives.

Amora Traditional Dijon Mustard (Amora, Dijon, France), $3.25 for 7 oz. Amora is the best-selling mustard in France. Much like Grey Poupon, most tasters felt that Amora was "undistinguished" yet "pleasant and sort of toothsome," with a "silky-smooth texture." Amora rated a "clean mustard flavor" and a bit of "character" but was also deemed "a bit weak." Amora was chosen "mostly for its lack of faults than for its vibrant character."

NOT RECOMMENDED

Beaufor Moutarde de Dijon (Beaufor, Reims, France), $3.25 for 7 oz. Beaufor was judged to have a "musty, mustardy aroma" and "slightly grainy" texture. Most tasters found Beaufor to have "indistinct," or "unexciting," flavor, which "disappears in the mouth as if by magic." Many tasters felt Beaufor tasted "odd, as if old mustard seeds were used." Beaufor contained a flavor that tasters found distracting, making it seem "not bright."

Etoile de Dijon Dijon Mustard (ETS Fallot, Beaune, France), $4.25 for 13 oz. Etoile was noted for its "garish color" and "smooth, flat texture." Like Beaufor, Etoile had a flavor that most tasters found distinctly distracting and unappealing. Comments tended to point out a "dull, heavy" yet "slightly vinegary" flavor. Again, Etoile was criticized for tasting as if it "used old spices." Interestingly, Etoile contains no preservatives.

Le Cordon Bleu Extra Strong Dijon Mustard (Le Cordon Bleu, Paris, France), $4.25 for 7 oz. Le Cordon Bleu had a "strong vinegar aroma," with a "slightly grainy texture." Tasters found Le Cordon Bleu to have a "dull, indistinctive flavor," "not off like some of the others, but not strong." Some felt that it was "a bit too salty" and that it generally lacked the strong character Dijon mustard needs. This mustard contains no preservatives.

Old Monk Dijon Mustard (Old Monk, Nice, France), $3.25 for 7 oz. Old Monk had a "heavy, musty nose," "bright yellow color," and "thick, lumpy texture." Tasters felt that Old Monk was "not spicy or hot enough," "lacking zip or character." Tasters also noticed that same "odd flavor that makes it taste old or cheap." Old Monk contains no preservatives.

Roland Extra Strong Dijon Mustard (Made in France for American Roland Food Co., New York, New York), $2.75 for 8.5 oz. Roland had a "good mustardy aroma," which, unfortunately, led to a "salty, anemic flavor." Like some of the other mustards, Roland had a flavor that tasters felt was "old, without liveliness ... just sits there on the tongue." The overriding flavor seemed to be "salty, but generally mediocre."

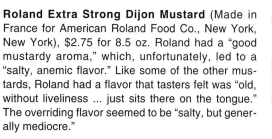

Braised Winter Vegetables

Braising enhances the deep flavors of winter's squashes and root vegetables.

∼ BY ANDY HUSBANDS AND KEN GOODMAN ∼

Braising is an ideal cooking method for foods that are fibrous and tough and need long cooking periods to break down tissue. Any vegetable can be braised, but the hearty, flavorful squashes and root vegetables of fall and winter are particularly well suited to the method.

We tried several versions of each recipe, and found that most vegetables could be simply braised on top of the stove. The onion and squash dishes, however, which are a little heartier, worked best in the oven with a little longer cooking time and a uniform heat, as opposed to heat from below.

PAN-BRAISED ROOT VEGETABLES WITH RED CABBAGE AND ROSEMARY
Serves 4 as a side dish

- 2 tablespoons olive oil
- 2 large garlic cloves, minced
- 1 medium shallot, minced
- 4 medium parsnips, peeled and cut into ½-inch pieces
- 2 medium carrots, peeled and cut into ½-inch pieces
- ¼ pound celery root, peeled and cut into 2-by-⅛-inch julienne strips
- ⅓ cup dry full-bodied red wine
- 1½ tablespoons minced fresh rosemary
- ½ tablespoon minced fresh sage leaves
- 1½ cups chicken stock or low-sodium broth
- ½ cup shredded red cabbage
  Salt and ground black pepper

1. Heat oil in medium skillet over medium-high heat. Add garlic and shallot; sauté until aromatic, about 1 minute. Increase heat to high; add parsnips, carrots, and celery root; sauté until vegetables start to brown, 4 to 5 minutes.

2. Add wine, rosemary, and sage; continue to cook to blend flavors, about 3 minutes longer. Lower heat to medium; add stock and cabbage. Cover and simmer until knife easily pierces vegetables, about 5 minutes. Season to taste with salt and pepper.

BRAISED ONIONS WITH RED WINE, THYME, AND PANCETTA
Serves 4 to 6 as a side dish

- 1 tablespoon olive oil
- 4 ounces pancetta, chopped fine (about ¼ cup)
- 1 medium garlic clove, minced
- 1 celery stalk, sliced thin, diagonally
- 1 small carrot, peeled and sliced thin
- 3 medium red onions, peeled and quartered, lengthwise
- 1 cup dry full-bodied red wine
- 1 tablespoon fresh thyme leaves
- ½ tablespoon chopped fresh sage leaves
- 1 bay leaf
- 1 cup chicken stock or low-sodium broth
  Salt and ground black pepper

1. Heat oven to 400 degrees. Heat oil in medium skillet over medium heat. Add pancetta; cook until crisp, about 4 minutes. Add garlic; sauté until fragrant, about 1 minute. Add celery and carrot; sauté to soften slightly, about 2 minutes. Increase heat to high. Add onions; sauté until spotty brown, being careful not to burn other ingredients, about 2 minutes. Add wine; cook to reduce slightly, about 30 seconds. Add herbs and stock; bring to simmer.

2. Cover skillet and braise vegetables in oven 10 minutes. Uncover skillet and continue to braise vegetables until onions are soft but not mushy, about 10 minutes longer. Season to taste with salt and pepper.

QUICK-BRAISED BOK CHOY, TURNIPS, AND WATERCRESS WITH GINGER AND SOY
Serves 6 as a side dish

- 1 tablespoon sesame oil
- 1 tablespoon vegetable oil
- 1 small garlic clove, minced
- 1 tablespoon minced fresh gingerroot
- ½ pound turnip roots, peeled, halved, and sliced thin
- 2 heads (about 12 ounces) bok choy, washed and cut crosswise into 1-inch pieces
- 1 bunch (4 ounces) watercress, rinsed
- ¼ cup chicken stock or low-sodium chicken broth
- 2 tablespoons soy sauce
- 2 tablespoons sake
  Ground black pepper
- 2 tablespoons toasted sesame seeds

1. Heat oils in large sauté pan over medium heat. Add garlic and ginger; sauté until aromatic and starting to brown, about 2 minutes. Increase heat to medium-high. Add turnips; sauté to soften slightly, about 3 minutes. Increase heat to high; add bok choy and watercress and sauté until wilted, about 1 minute.

2. Add stock, soy, and sake; cover and reduce heat to low. Simmer until turnips are just tender, about 3 minutes. Season to taste with pepper and garnish with sesame seeds.

BRAISED BUTTERNUT SQUASH WITH DRIED APRICOTS, RAISINS, AND MADRAS SPICES
Serves 6 as a side dish

- ¼ cup dark or golden raisins
- ¼ cup dried apricots, cut into ¼-inch strips
- ½ cup dry full-bodied red wine
- 3 tablespoons olive oil
- 1 tablespoon minced fresh gingerroot
- 1 medium garlic clove, minced
- 1 large Spanish onion, chopped coarse
- 1 red bell pepper, stemmed, seeded, and cut into ¼-inch dice
- 1 or more serrano or jalapeño peppers, stemmed, seeded, and minced
- 1½ pounds butternut squash or pumpkin, peeled, seeded, and cut into ½-inch chunks
- 1 teaspoon each: ground cinnamon, ground cumin, ground coriander, and whole mustard seed
- 2 teaspoons curry powder
- 2 cups chicken stock or low-sodium broth
  Salt and ground black pepper
- ½ cup minced fresh cilantro leaves

1. Heat oven to 400 degrees. Soak raisins and apricots in wine; set aside.

2. Heat oil in medium skillet over medium heat. Add ginger and garlic; sauté until fragrant but not brown, about 1 minute. Increase heat to medium-high; add onion, peppers (sweet and hot), and squash. Sauté until squash starts to brown, 3 to 5 minutes. Add dried fruit, wine, and spices; cook to blend flavors, about 1 minute. Add stock, bring to simmer.

3. Cover skillet and braise vegetables in oven until squash is tender but not mushy, 10 to 12 minutes. Season to taste with salt and pepper; garnish with cilantro. ∎

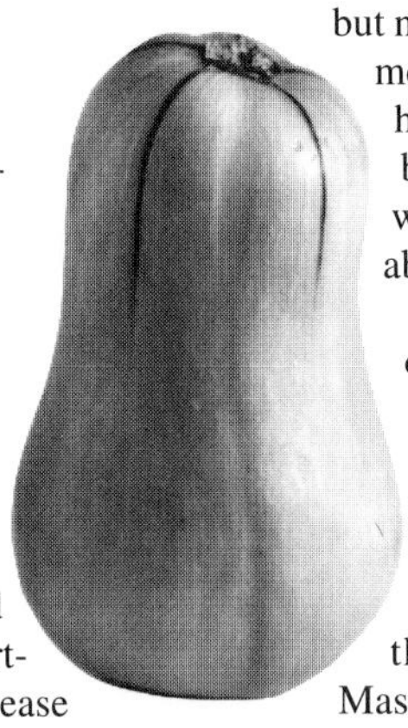

Andy Husbands and **Ken Goodman** are former and present chefs, respectively, at the East Coast Grill in Cambridge, Massachusetts.

PHOTOGRAPHS BY DAVE HENDERSON

The Best Coffee-Brewing Method

We test eight ways to make regular coffee and find that while the most complicated method rates high, the low-tech method is our top choice.

~ BY JACK BISHOP ~

While I usually make espresso for myself, in recent months I have had a string of house guests ask for regular coffee with milk. I certainly have collected enough equipment over the years (including an automatic drip machine, a plunger, a funky stovetop number, and a plastic drip cone with thermos) that I should be capable of handling these requests. But all this paraphernalia begs the question: Which setup makes the best coffee? Furthermore, which is the most reliable? Fastest? Easiest to use?

For this article, I purchased widely available equipment from top manufacturers. I included examples of all major brewing methods: a percolator, an expensive automatic drip machine with a thermos, a cheap automatic drip with a burner plate, a manual plastic drip cone that fits over a thermos, a manual plastic cone that fits over a glass carafe, a flip pot, a plunger pot, and a vacuum coffee maker.

With the machinery in hand, I ran a series of experiments to determine the best grind of coffee to use for each method, then proceeded to the actual testing. I designed my tests to rate each machine on the temperature, flavor, and body of the coffee it produced, as well as on ease of use.

As soon as the coffee finished brewing in each device, I took its temperature with an instant-read thermometer. I waited fifteen minutes and took the temperature again. I also tasted the coffee as soon as it was made, noting flavor, aroma, and body. But since these latter tests were subjective, I also arranged for six members of the *Cook's*

Illustrated editorial staff to participate in a blind tasting of the coffee made in each device.

The Losers

I quickly dismissed several methods based on the poor quality of the coffee or the hassle involved in getting the device to work. A flip pot (also called a drip pot, café filtre, napoletana, or machinetta) consists of two metal chambers separated by a filter holder. Grounds are placed in the filter area, water is added to the bottom pot, and the whole device is sealed

---

RATING COFFEE METHODS

Eight methods of brewing were tested and judged on the following criteria. These methods are listed in order of preference. Among the criteria listed below, flavor and body were the most important, followed by convenience.

Price: Average cost of devices in category. (*See* Sources and Resources, page 32, for specific brands that I used and can recommend.)

Best Grind: I tested several grinds for each machine and have listed the grind I found made the best coffee.

Time: Actual brewing time is listed first for six cups (thirty-six ounces of water to twelve tablespoons of ground coffee) or maximum amount device can accommodate. Second figure represents brewing time plus setup time (e.g., time to assemble device, time to boil water, if necessary).

Temperature: Figure is average for just-brewed coffee and coffee that has sat for fifteen minutes. Each measurement was taken twice.

= superior performance

= average performance

= poor performance

Flavor: All devices were tested with the same premium Costa Rican coffee, which was tasted blind by six members of the *Cook's Illustrated* editorial staff. We compared flavor, noting the methods that captured more nuances in the coffee. Coffee that tasted burned or bitter was downgraded. A full cup indicates superior quality. A half cup indicates average quality. An empty cup indicates poor quality.

Body: In judging body, the panel looked for sediment on the tongue and at the cup bottom. Coffee with too much sediment was downgraded as was watery or thin coffee. We were looking for a medium between these two extremes. (*See* "Flavor" listing, above, for description of icons.)

Convenience: Given the fact that most of us make coffee first thing in the morning, the setup and brewing should involve minimal fuss. A full cup indicates hassle-free brewing (can almost be done in your sleep). A half cup indicates the need for some concentration, and an empty cup indicates that brewing demands full attention.

METHOD	PRICE	BEST GRIND	TIME	TEMPERATURE	FLAVOR	BODY	CONVENIENCE
Manual drip into insulated thermos	$25 to $40 for thermos; $5 for plastic filter cone	Fine	6 mins/14 mins	180°/177°	superior	superior	superior
Manual drip into glass carafe	$15 to $20 for set with glass carafe and plastic filter cone	Fine	6 mins/14 mins	178°/148°	superior	superior	superior
Vacuum	$50 for basic stovetop model	Fine	5 mins/19 mins	200°/178°	superior	superior	poor
Automatic drip into insulated thermos	$75 to $150, depending on other features	Fine (for cone filter)	10 mins/12 mins	180°/178°	average	superior	superior
Percolator	$50 to $80	Coarse	7 mins/10 mins	194°/190°	average	superior	average
Plunger pot (or French press)	$20 to $50	Coarse	4 mins/12 mins	186°/171°	average	poor	average
Flip pot	$30 to $50	Fine	2 mins/20 mins	192°/175°	average	poor	poor
Automatic drip into glass carafe on burner	$20 to $70, depending on other features	Medium (for basket filter)	9 mins/11 mins	178°/166°	poor	poor	superior

and placed on a burner. When steam comes out through a tiny hole at the top of the chamber with the water, the pot is flipped over, allowing the boiling water to drip through the grounds into what was the top pot.

A flip pot can only brew one or two cups of coffee at a time (all other setups make five or ten cups), takes at least twenty minutes to work, seems excessively dangerous (you must wear a thick mitt to flip the burning hot metal pot), and makes gritty, slightly burnt coffee (no doubt due to the fact that excessively hot water is dripping through the grounds; *see* "The Science of Brewing," page 29).

A plunger pot, or French press, is easier to use. Grounds and nearly boiling water are mixed together in a glass container. When the water has extracted enough flavor from the beans (about four minutes), a plunger covered with a fine-mesh screen is pushed down through the mixture. The grounds end up at the bottom. Strained coffee stays above the filter, ready to be poured.

Unfortunately, both the blind tasting panel and I found that too much sediment passes through the mesh filter. I played around with the cheap plunger in my pantry as well as a brand new, top-of-the-line model and got the same results, even though I was using the coarsest setting on my grinder. I was surprised, however, to discover that another common complaint I have heard about plunger pots can be mitigated. Since there is no direct heat source involved, coffee made in a press tends to be cooler than coffee made by other methods. But I found that filling the glass pot with hot water from my tap (140 degrees) until just before brewing raised the initial temperature of the coffee from a too cool 162 degrees to a pleasantly hot 186 degrees. Of course, cooling off still occurs fairly rapidly in a plunger pot.

The percolator performed much as expected. This old-fashioned device forces boiling water up through a tube and then sprays it over grounds. Because the water passes so quickly over the grounds, the coffee is very weak at first. Therefore, the thin brew is recycled back down to the bottom of the percolator, pushed up through the tube when it comes to a boil, and sprayed again (and again) over the grounds.

The label on my new but retro-looking percolator promised "super hot," "super fast" coffee, and the percolator delivered. Only coffee made in a vacuum was hotter; the percolator coffee also had the highest temperature after fifteen minutes. As for brewing time, the percolator made six cups of coffee faster than any other method. But there was a downside. The coffee was only fair. Tasters consistently used the words "light" and "weak" to describe this thin, clear brew. This results from the fact that as the water is sprayed over the grounds repeatedly, it drains through quite rapidly each time and therefore does not spend much actual time in contact with the grounds.

Next I came to what is probably the most widespread type of coffee maker in the United States today, the automatic drip machine. These machines are certainly the easiest coffee makers to use. No parts to assemble, no water to boil and pour through grounds—just grind the coffee, pour cold water into the machine, and press a button. You can leave the kitchen to get the paper and come back to brewed coffee.

I knew from past experience that many drip coffee machines brew quite slowly, especially when making large quantities. Besides the time factor, slow brewing can negatively affect the quality of the coffee (*see* "The Science of Brewing," page 29). The experts I talked with cited a range of four to six minutes as the time it should take the water to drip through the grounds.

I tested a cheap automatic drip with a glass carafe that sits on a burner and a more expensive model that drips right into an insulated carafe. Both machines brewed two cups relatively quickly (four minutes for each) but took way too long (nine minutes and ten minutes, respectively) to brew six cups. As the experts had predicted, coffee brewed in four minutes tasted fine. But the six-cup batch was bitter in both machines. Making the grind coarser did not help since the slow brewing was due to the rate at which the machines dripped water into the filter.

The model with the burner had an added problem: Coffee from the two-cup batch that tasted decent right after brewing was horrible after "cooking" on the hot plate. The coffee that dripped into a thermos was better, es-

BEST BREWING METHOD

Manual Drip into Insulated Thermos: Simple, fast, and convenient, plus coffee stays hot for hours.

BEST BUY

Manual Drip into Glass Carafe: Same benefits as brewing into a thermos except coffee must be served immediately.

Vacuum: The most spectacular way to make coffee. Great results but not practical for everyday use.

Flip Pot (Napoletana): Very slow, only makes a cup or two, and must be handled with oven mitts.

Plunger: Easy to use but even the best models cannot filter out all the bitter sediment.

Percolator: The hottest, fastest coffee, but it tends to be weak and thin.

Automatic Drip into Glass Carafe on Burner: Coffee develops a cooked flavor in minutes.

Automatic Drip into Insulated Thermos: Better than dripping into a carafe on a burner, but coffee is only average.

PHOTOGRAPHS BY ERIC ROTH

pecially when made in batches of four cups or less. However, I don't think the average coffee quality and convenience of being able to brew almost in my sleep are worth the $100 this coffee maker cost me.

I was so disappointed with the two automatic drip machines I had selected for this article, I went out and purchased two more top models, both fairly expensive. One machine had the slow brewing problem I had already uncovered, although it was not quite as bad. The other machine, which promised brewed coffee in record time, actually delivered six cups in just four minutes. Obviously, slow brewing affects many but not all automatic drip coffee makers. In a future issue, we will test all leading models on the market.

The Winners

In my opinion, two brewing methods stand out as superior, at least in terms of quality. Coffee made in the vacuum has much to offer: properly hot temperature, a rich flavor that captures the nuances in expensive beans without any bitterness or harshness, and a full body without sediment. To my mind, this was the best-tasting coffee, although the panel I assembled ranked it second. The real problem here is convenience.

This showy method relies on a vacuum created between two glass bowls. When water in the lower bowl comes to a boil, it is drawn up through a funnel to the top bowl where the grounds have been placed. As long as heat is applied (the bottom bowl can rest on a burner or over a spirit lamp), the hot water and grounds remain in the top bowl. When the contraption is removed from the heat (about three minutes is long enough for water to extract flavor from the grounds), a vacuum develops in the lower pot and the water (now coffee) drops back through the funnel in a matter of seconds. A filter in the funnel keeps the grounds in the top bowl. The coffee is then served from the lower bowl.

Although it's not that hard to use a vacuum coffee maker, it does require concentration. In addition, the glass bowls are wobbly and liable to break eventually. As an intriguing finale to a special meal, this conversation piece makes sense—the coffee tastes great, and your guests will think you have discovered something truly exotic. However, as a way to make coffee at six in the morning every day, I'll pass.

Last but not least is my favorite method (and the top choice of the tasting panel), the manual drip. The convenience factor is second only to that of an automatic drip machine. Grind and measure the coffee into a filter, bring water to a boil, let it cool slightly, and then pour. Of course, since you must add the water in batches, you can't leave the kitchen during brewing. In addition, to ensure that the water runs evenly through the grounds, first moisten the grounds with a little of the water just removed from the boil, stir to make sure they are evenly damp, then add water to the filter basket.

The difference between the two manual drip setups that I tested became apparent when I took the temperature of the brew after fifteen minutes. While coffee that was brewed directly into an insulated carafe (prewarmed by rinsing it with very hot tap water) dropped only three degrees after fifteen minutes, coffee dripped into a prewarmed glass carafe that sat on the counter dropped thirty degrees during the same period. Putting the carafe on a burner solved this problem, but the coffee developed a burned flavor.

Given the fact that coffee brewed into a thermos stays hot for hours with no loss of flavor (the temperature dropped only eight degrees in three hours), this is my first choice. A thermos and plastic cone insert cost twice as much as a glass carafe and cone (I laid out $35 versus $16), but for convenience and quality, this is money well spent. ∎

THE SCIENCE OF BREWING

There are many variables involved in brewing coffee, including the ratio of beans to water, the temperature of the water, how finely the beans are ground, and the length of time that the grounds and water are in contact. Adjustments in the first category are fairly straightforward. Use more water, and the coffee will be weaker; use more beans, and it will be stronger. The other three factors are more complicated, and all affect the amount of flavor extracted from the beans.

"You can brew coffee with room temperature water," says Ted Lingle, executive director of the Specialty Coffee Association. "However, there are approximately eight hundred flavor compounds in coffee, with varying solubility temperatures, and those that taste the best are released by water between 195 degrees and 205 degrees."

Water temperature determines *which* flavor compounds end up in your cup, but brewing time determines *how much* of each of these compounds you imbibe—and more is not necessarily better. Lingle says that if all the flavor compounds were extracted from the beans, the result would be something undrinkable. Studies have shown that an extraction rate between 18 and 22 percent tastes best.

Luckily, the most flavorful and aromatic compounds in coffee are released first, according to Lingle. Unpleasant elements require greater brewing time to be extracted from the grounds. Hence, the obvious dangers of overlong brewing, called "overextraction" by experts.

There is no single ideal brewing time for all methods. "You must match the particle size to the design of your equipment," says Lingle. An espresso machine extracts flavor in seconds, so the coffee must be very finely ground. A drip coffee machine takes much longer, so the grounds should be coarser. In general, Lingle notes that brewing should be completed in less than six minutes, no matter the method, or you risk overextraction.

"Many electric drip machines don't turn out very good coffee because they have an extended brewing time," says Lingle. He cites small brew baskets as another factor for mediocre quality. "If there is not enough room for the grounds to swell and agitate, the particles become pressed together, the water passes through the grounds in channels, and you don't get full extraction."

Manual drip setups allow you to moisten and then stir the grounds, which ensures that water passes through them uniformly—just another reason why Lingle recommends this brewing method.

CHOOSING A FILTER

Buying paper filters has become somewhat confusing during recent years, but fortunately things now seem headed back toward more simplicity. Until about five years ago, most paper filters were bleached white with chlorine, which is not particularly earth-friendly. Hence, the advent of unbleached brown filters. Although better for the planet, unbleached filters were reported to add woody notes to coffee that passed through them. A third process (which now seems to be the choice of most companies) relies on oxygen to bleach filters white. This process is safer and removes any pulpy or woody notes.

I purchased three brands of oxygen-bleached filters, one brand of unbleached brown filters, and used some old chlorine-bleached filters from my pantry. Upon careful tasting, I was able to pick up some differences in coffee brewed in the brown filter and preferred the cleaner taste of coffee made in bleached filters. I could not detect any differences among the various bleached filters.

An alternative choice is a gold-plated, fine-mesh filter. The theory is that paper filters (whether bleached or not) absorb flavorful coffee oils during brewing. Permanent gold filters, which cost from $15 to $20, allow the coffee to pass through without removing (or adding) anything. When I compared coffee brewed through an oxygen-bleached filter with that brewed through a gold filter, I thought the cup made in the gold filter had more character and nuances. However, when I slipped a batch of gold-filtered coffee (made with the manual drip method) into the general tasting, it finished just behind the manual drip coffee brewed through a paper filter. Gold filters are in some respects easier to use, and you never run out. Whether or not you can taste the difference may depend on your taste buds and ability to perceive nuances in coffee.—*J.B.*

Ranking Inexpensive Bordeaux

In between the cheap no-name wines and the classified growths are some terrific values in Bordeaux.

⌖ BY MARK BITTMAN ⌖

Much as we might like it, the word "Bordeaux" is not a guarantee of quality. There are seven thousand châteaus in what is arguably the world's most important wine-growing region, and countless wines bottled with appellations such as "Bordeaux" or "Bordeaux Supérieur," which isn't superior at all.

Finding great red Bordeaux is easy: Just take your checkbook (or, if you don't have overdraft protection, your credit card) to the best wine store you know, and go to the classified growth section. Here you'll find a couple of dozen labels with well-known names, and few bottles selling for less than $50. We set out to find the best wines in that next section over there, the one with the vaguely familiar-sounding names, the ones that lifelong devotees consider lesser but eminently decent.

Like the great Bordeaux, these near-greats are made predominantly from cabernet sauvignon (which dominates in blends from the great Médoc and Graves areas) or merlot (which makes up the majority in wines from Pomerol and St. Emilion). All the châteaus in these areas usually blend the primary grape with lesser amounts of merlot, cabernet sauvignon, cabernet franc, petit verdoc, malbec, and/or assorted other minor grape varieties. And, like their more expensive cousins, a couple of generalizations can be made about these wines: Those made mostly from cabernet are slower to mature, rougher when young, somewhat more "austere"—displaying their fruit rather reluctantly—and, in the long run, more complex. Those relying on merlot are smoother, quicker to mature, more rewarding when young, and more often described as "lovely."

Even limiting our choices by price as we did—none of the wines cost more than $20—we had a tough time narrowing the field. There are around two hundred *cru classés* (classified growths) in Bordeaux, and some of these fell within our price range. In addition, there are many nonclassified growths—the 240 best of which, at least as recently as 1978, are officially titled *cru bourgeois*—that can be sensational. And, of course, there are châteaus that no one officially recognizes as great but have loyal followings because they consistently produce wines that are of good value.

After poring over what is currently available at good prices from good recent vintages (1991 was essentially a washout), we narrowed the list to fifteen wines. (It would have been quite easy to choose twenty-five, still staying under $20 and still keeping the quality level high, but our experience has shown that tasters' palates begin to fa-tigue after a dozen wines or so.) In the end, one of our wines was a classified growth (Lynch-Moussas) and several were *cru bourgeois,* but the majority were on no official lists. Some were just wines with good reputations; others were "second label" wines, meaning wines made by classified châteaus that don't quite measure up to the standards of the main label. These are often considered good value and can be quite widely sought after.

The results were sensational. Although we did have a clear winner, we had very few "losers." Almost all the wines were enjoyed by some and adored by one or two, and the tasters unanimously agreed that this tasting (the eighteenth in the *Cook's Illustrated* series) was among the best in displaying a group of solid, affordable wines. ∎

1990 CHÂTEAU MARTINET

VERY HIGHLY RECOMMENDED

1990 Château Martinet (St. Emilion Grand Cru), $15. *"Grand cru"* doesn't mean much in St. Emilion (there are sixty-three of them), but this was a pleasant surprise. Nearly every taster placed it near the top, and many raved about it: "This wine sings with fruit, and has weight, too." Quite young; will last for years.

HIGHLY RECOMMENDED

1988 Château Potensac (Médoc), $18. This wine had some loving it ("Brilliant, good now, with a great future"), and a few thinking it was "short on fruit."
1992 Franc-Mayne (St. Emilion Grand Cru), $19. Merlot-based wine that has been a hot item in recent years. Many found it "elegant," "well balanced," and "lovely." Several tasters thought it was "thin" or "little." Probably best for current drinking.
1990 Château Meyney (St. Estephe), $16. A *cru bourgeois* with a long-standing, solid reputation that did not disappoint. Although some found it "bland" or "simple," most thought it had "terrific flavor."
1990 Amiral de Beychevelle (St. Julien), $18. Second label of the much-loved fourth-growth Château Beychevelle. Three tasters loved this wine: "Delicious, wonderful structure, good fruit and tannin; a bit young." Some found it short on fruit.
1990 Lynch-Moussas (Pauillac), $19. A fifth-classified growth, this wine's quality varies, but this one is a good one: "Spicy," "lush," and "complex." One taster found it a "bit old," so you may not want to wait on it.
1990 Château de Rochemorin (Pessac-Léognan), $15. This is from a ten-year-old appellation within Graves. It will probably show much better in a couple of years, but most tasters still ranked it highly.
1990 Château Greysac (Médoc), $11. A well-known *cru bourgeois* that usually offers good value (note price), as it did here: "Rich, luscious, good balance, very tasty." "Would be great with cheese."

RECOMMENDED

1989 Château Plagnac (Médoc), $12. A solid *cru bourgeois* that showed quite nicely: "Full-flavored and fruity." Three tasters detected off-odors.
1992 Château Les Ormes de Pez (St. Estephe), $16. A *cru bourgeois* owned by the makers of Château Lynch-Bages, a sometimes great fifth growth. Solid, if not great: "Spicy and lush but light."
1992 Reserve de la Comtesse (Pauillac), $15. With vineyards abutting those of Château Latour, this wine can be great. Not in this vintage, though. One taster found it "intense." But more found it "flat."
1990 Château Fourcas-Hosten (Listrac-Médoc), $13. A *cru bourgeois* with a bit of a following, this wine disappointed some of its admirers here.
1992 Château de Clairefont (Margaux), $16. Second label of Prieure Lachine. "Attractive, round, sweet, but a little bit simple" sums it up nicely.

NOT RECOMMENDED

1992 Lady Langoa (St. Julien), $18. This can have very good years, but this was not one of them.
1990 Mouton Cadet (Bordeaux), $8. This commercial wine, produced by Baron Philippe de Rothschild, was out of its league here.

From the Earth to the Table
John Ash's Wine Country Cuisine
with Sid Goldstein
Dutton, $35

I've long been a fan of John Ash's food. His restaurant, John Ash & Co., was among the best in Sonoma County, California, and his food translates decently to the home kitchen. While there are exceptions, it's generally direct and simple, without a lot of exotic ingredients. Better still, there are helpful tips scattered throughout this book, the kinds of things I wish that more people who cooked for hours every day would share with the rest of us. Ash offers two unusual ways to peel garlic, for example: One is to soak the whole bulb in water overnight; the other is to dry-roast unpeeled cloves in a skillet for a few minutes. Both make peeling easier and give you whole, un-smashed cloves.

Another nice tip comes at the end of one of my favorite recipes from this book, Scallops with Sautéed Apples and Vanilla-Scented Sauce. Here, Ash sears large scallops, sautés apples in the same skillet, and tops them with a sauce of mushrooms, stock, shallots, butter, cream, and mustard, all scented with vanilla. There are many ingredients, it's true, but the whole thing takes only a half hour, and the result is beautiful, both in flavor and appearance. It's even nicer if you follow Ash's directions for oven-drying the apples, an easy process that requires a couple of hours but no extra work.

Other recipes I tried and enjoyed include Cold Tomatillo-Tequila Soup, a light, refreshing gazpacho (to which, in fact, the tequila added little); Veggie Burger, the best I've ever made; Baked Olives, which were quick and out of this world; and a simple Flourless Walnut Cake that has few ingredients but explosive flavor.

As you might expect, there are times Ash goes over the top. The Veggie Burger, for example, was an inordinate amount of work: I roasted eggplant, cooked potatoes, and sautéed carrots all before assembling it. And other recipes that could be simple require an extra step or two that make an easy recipe needlessly harder in the home kitchen. Ash's White Bean Salad, for example, is delicious, and I didn't even mind roasting garlic to make it—but do you really want to grill tomatoes, too? Not me. Fortunately, this is the exception. More often, Ash makes things simple, as "wine country cuisine" should be.

—*Mark Bittman*

Fear of Wine: An Introductory Guide to the Grape
Leslie Brenner and Lettie Teague
Bantam, $11.95

This book has a fresh, not-too-cute format, a basic approach that has no attitude at all (it's the least snobbish wine book I've ever seen), and enough current information so that even people who know about wine may be inclined to glance at it. Its premise—that most Americans fear, even dread, wine—may be a bit overstated (ignorance and fear, after all, are hardly equivalent, and most Americans just don't care). But its remedial approach is a simple, textbook course that falls short in only two areas; unfortunately, these are not insignificant.

The first shortcoming is that *Fear of Wine* presumes, as has almost every other wine book preceding it, that to enjoy wine you must first understand how it is made. This point of view is a trap: Americans don't understand how food is grown (or even cooked, in many instances), they have little idea how movies are put together, and few have more than a cursory understanding of the workings of the internal combustion engine. Yet they enjoy and even adore these things. Wine need not be different.

The other problem is that, although *Fear of Wine* does make some recommendations for wines to buy, they are neither specific enough nor plentiful enough. There is, for example, a list of Wines to Bring to a Dinner Party. It's a nice enough list (of "impressive" and "interesting" wines that "won't break the bank"), but it gives no specific recommendations. It's difficult to believe that the clearly knowledgeable authors have found that New Zealand Sauvignon Blanc or Châteauneuf-du-Pape are categories made up of wines so consistently worth the money that they deserve blanket recommendations.

Given all of this, I would not recommend *Fear of Wine* to people who *only* want to know what wine they should buy in a given circumstance. But if you are looking for a clearly stated, anti-snob wine course, then this offering is a good one. It's filled with simple truths that summarize in a few sentences what takes most wine books pages to say. For example: "In Germany, sweetness is the big deal. After *Auslese*, the longer the word the sweeter the wine." Not untrue, not even an oversimplification, and about all that most of us need to know.

—*Mark Bittman*

Everybody Eats Well in Belgium Cookbook
Ruth Van Waerebeek
Workman, $24.95

It's hard to imagine there's a western European cuisine that has yet to receive full airing in the pages of an American cookbook. But there is, and Ruth Van Waerebeek, a Belgium-born cooking teacher who has lived and taught in New York for many years, has done an excellent job of capturing the spirit of Belgian cuisine.

Many individual dishes seem familiar, with French-like quiches and tarts, German-style meat-and-potato dishes, and smoked and pickled fish preparations reminiscent of Northern European cooking. In some respects this is the author's point. Belgium has long been a crossroads in Europe, and the food reflects diverse influences.

So what exactly defines Belgian cuisine? The author provides this list of favorite foods: potatoes, mussels, meat (including charcuterie and game), beer, waffles, and chocolate. Needless to say, there are few diet recipes in this book, but there are definitely many delicious ones.

Superb Cognac-Scented Flemish Waffles are made with yeast, but, unlike similar recipes, this batter requires only one hour to rise. The waffles themselves are light and tender. Gratin of Belgian Endive is made by boiling whole heads until tender, wrapping each in a thin slice of ham, and then covering them with béchamel sauce (too much for my taste) and grated Swiss cheese. This side dish is incredibly rich, if not overly decadent.

Likewise, Chicken Braised in Belgian Beer is a rustic dish with plenty of heft. Chicken, mushrooms, carrots, and pearl onions braise in a mixture of beer and beef stock. The chicken is removed when tender, and the sauce is reduced and enriched with cream. A substantial Potato and Leek Pancake, scented with thyme and nicely browned in butter and olive oil, makes a good accompaniment to the chicken dish.

Even better was the dinner I started with Poached Leeks in a Shallot-Parsley Vinaigrette (thickened with egg yolks), followed by Belgian Steamed Mussels. Minced celery and shallots, along with thyme and parsley, gave the simple white wine broth a clean, vegetal flavor that contrasted nicely with the briny, sweet mussels.

Instructions are clear, no doubt a reflection of the author's teaching experience. Cooks interested in rustic, hearty home cooking with a European flavor will find this book a pleasure. ∎

—*Jack Bishop*

Most of the ingredients and materials necessary for the recipes in this issue are available at your local supermarket, gourmet store, or kitchen supply shop. The following are mail-order sources for particular items. Prices listed below were current at press time and do not include shipping or handling unless otherwise indicated. We suggest that you contact companies directly to confirm up-to-date prices and availability.

ROASTING RACKS

Give your chicken a little rise (above the bottom of the pan, that is) as it roasts by placing it on a V-shaped, nonstick roasting rack from the Williams-Sonoma catalog (800-541-2233). Roasting on a rack, as specified in our roast chicken article on page 9, allows air to circulate underneath the bird, which promotes even cooking and browning. Also, in the name of even cooking, a bird sitting steady in a rack can be rotated so that either wing, or the breast, faces up. The small Williams-Sonoma rack costs $12 and measures thirteen and one-half inches long (ample space for the three- to four-and-one-half-pound birds called for in the roast chicken article); the large model measures fifteen inches long and costs $18; and the extra large rack measures seventeen and one-half inches long and costs $22.

COFFEE EQUIPMENT

Part highly rated coffee-brewing method and part stovetop sideshow (*see* "The Best Coffee-Brewing Method," page 27), a vacuum coffee maker provides both excellent brew and after-dinner entertainment value. Though it is possible to spend up to $150 on such a device, we used the Bodum Santos Vacuum Coffee Maker, available through the Bodum catalog (800-23-BODUM) for $50, and found it performed admirably. Equally good results can be attained with less esoteric equipment, for which we turned to the Green Mountain Coffee Roasters catalog (800-223-6768). Our top-rated cup

was brewed using the venerable manual drip method into an insulated thermos by Nissan. The thermoses come in three sizes (sixty-ounce for $39.99, thirty-ounce for $29.99, and a slim sixteen-ounce unit also for $29.99) and all feature high-impact plastic containers with brushed stainless steel exteriors. You can brew directly into the thermoses using the Nissan Coffee Cone ($4.99) since it fits over the opening of each. Green Mountain also offers a choice of filters. We liked the Swiss Gold Filter (buy the #4 size for $16.99 to fit into the Nissan Coffee Cone) because it produces a clean-tasting brew, is reusable, and rinses clean. Glass carafes, which we recommend as the best buy (when paired with a cone) for manual drip coffee making, are widely available in house and kitchenware stores.

MUSTARD MECCA

If you love mustard, turn toward Mount Horeb, Wisconsin, the home of The Mount Horeb Mustard Museum (109 East Main Street, P.O. Box 468, Mt. Horeb, WI 53572; 800-438-6878). The Dijon mustards rated in the article on page 24 may be familiar, but you are sure to discover something new in the museum's ever-growing collection of 2,250 mustards from around the world. The mail-order catalog sells all of the Dijons we tasted (with the exceptions of French's and Grey Poupon, which are both widely available in supermarkets) as well as multitudinous hard-to-find prepared mustards, mustard-making ingredients and cookbooks, and mustard theme accessories. In addition, the museum staff publishes "The Proper Mustard," a biannual mustard newsletter that proclaims itself to be "yellow journalism at its best." A one-year subscription costs $5.

REAL MAPLE SYRUP

What do you think of first when someone mentions pancakes (besides our story on page 6)? How about when they mention Vermont? For many,

the answer in both cases is maple syrup. The King Arthur Flour Baker's Store (not the catalog) in Norwich, Vermont (802-649-3361), sells, and happily accepts phone orders for, three brands of syrup from small Vermont producers. Package sizes vary, so it is easy to order according to your needs. A thirty-two-ounce jug of Highland Sugarworks syrup costs $24.75; a five hundred-milliliter bottle (roughly sixteen fluid ounces) of Seldom Seen syrup sells for $12; and a twelve-ounce, log cabin–shaped, ceramic bottle of Wards Pond Farm syrup costs $17.25, all exclusive of shipping costs. All of these syrups result from authentic wood-fired evaporation processes and are Grade A Medium Amber, which is slightly more viscous, concentrated, and darker than Fancy grades, and often preferred by true Vermonters for baking as well as eating.

GRIDDLES

The breakfast cook's companion extraordinaire is a wide, flat griddle that easily handles all the standard breakfast dishes such as pancakes (*see* page 6). The Williams-Sonoma catalog (800-541-2233) sells two varieties. The $40 Reversible Grill Pan is an oversized (ten inches by twenty inches), anodized aluminum griddle that covers two gas or electric burners. The cooking surfaces are stick-resistant (as opposed to nonstick) and safe for metal utensils. One side has raised grates to impart the characteristic grill lines while cooking stovetop, and the other side is smooth. Both sides have edge channels to drain extra fat. If a two-burner griddle is too large or nonstick is a priority, you might try the Berndes Griddle and Grill Pan Set for $140. This pair of pans features cast-aluminum construction, thick aluminum disks on the bottom to conduct heat quickly and evenly, and wooden handles

that stay cool. The ridged pan measures nine and one-half inches square, and the smooth one measures eleven inches square.

PANCETTA

Generally used in small quantities to flavor savory dishes such as the Braised Onions with Red Wine, Thyme, and Pancetta on page 26, pancetta is a cured Italian bacon distinctive because it is left unsmoked. The meat is dressed with salt, pepper, and spices, cured briefly, and then either rolled or left flat, depending on the producer. Zingerman's Delicatessen (422 Detroit Street, Ann Arbor, MI 48104; 313-663-3400) sells pancetta by mail order for $13 per pound, prepared to your specifications (sliced, chunked, or left whole) and in any quantity. ■

UNITED STATES POSTAL SERVICE

Statement of Ownership, Management, and Circulation (Required by 39 U.S.C. 3685)

1. Publication Title	2. Publication No.	3. Filing Date
Cook's Illustrated	0 1 2 - 4 8 7	9/26/95

4. Issue Frequency	5. No. of Issues Published Annually	6. Annual Subscription Price
Bimonthly	6	$24.95

7. Complete Mailing Address of Known Office of Publication (Street, City, County, State and Zip+4) (Not Printer)
17 Station St., Brookline Village, MA 02147

8. Complete Mailing Address of Headquarters or General Business Office of Publisher (Not Printer)
Same as 7

9. Full Names and Complete Mailing Addresses of Publisher, Editor, and Managing Editor (Do Not Leave Blank)

Publisher (Name and Complete Mailing Address)
Christopher P. Kimball 17 Station St., Brookline Village, MA 02147

Editor (Name and Complete Mailing Address)
Christopher P. Kimball 17 Station St., Brookline Village, MA 02147

Managing Editor (Name and Complete Mailing Address)
Maura Lyons 17 Station St., Brookline Village, MA 02147

10. Owner (If owned by a corporation, its name and address must be stated and also immediately thereafter the names and addresses of stockholders owning or holding 1 percent or more of the total amount of stock. If not owned by a corporation, the names and addresses of the individual owners must be given. If owned by a partnership or other unincorporated firm, its name and address as well as that of each individual must be given. If the publication is published by a nonprofit organization, its name and address must be stated.) (Do Not Leave Blank.)

Full Name	Complete Mailing Address
Boston Common Press Limited Partnership	500 Boylston St. #1880 Boston, MA 02116
WDH, Inc.	500 Boylston St. #1880 Boston, MA 02116
Auchincloss, Wadsworth & Co.	500 Boylston St. #1880 Boston, MA 02116
Denny East-West Partnership	500 Boylston St. #1880 Boston, MA 02116
John D. Halpern	500 Boylston St. #1880 Boston, MA 02116
Christopher P. Kimball	500 Boylston St. #1880 Boston, MA 02116

13. Publication Name	14. Issue Date for Circulation Data Below
Cook's Illustrated	9/26/95

15. Extent and Nature of Circulation	Average No. Copies Each Issue During Preceding 12 Months	Actual No. Copies of Single Issues Published Nearest to Filing Date
a. Total No. Copies (Net Press Run)	244,835	257,003
b. Paid and/or Requested Circulation		
(1) Sales Through Dealers and Carriers, Street Vendors, and Counter Sales (Not Mailed)	31,312	31,598
(2) Paid or Requested Mail Subscriptions (Include Advertisers' Proof Copies/Exchange Copies)	173,357	186,577
c. Total Paid and/or Requested Circulation (Sum of 15b(1) and 15b(2))	204,669	218,175
d. Free Distribution by Mail (Samples, Complimentary, and Other Free)	2,920	2,963
e. Free Distribution Outside the Mail (Carriers or Other Means)	0	0
f. Total Free Distribution (Sum of 15d and 15e)	2,920	2,963
g. Total Distribution (Sum of 15c and 15f)	207,589	221,138
h. Copies Not Distributed (1) Office Use, Leftovers, Spoiled	175	175
(2) Return from News Agents	37,071	35,690
i. Total (Sum of 15g, 15h(1), and 15h(2))	244,835	257,003
Percent Paid and/or Requested Circulation (15c/15g x 100)	98.59%	98.66%

16. This Statement of Ownership will be printed in the Jan/Feb '96 issue of this publication. ☐ Check box if not required to publish.

17. Signature and Title of Editor, Publisher, Business Manager, or Owner	Date
[signature] VP	9-26-95

I certify that all information furnished on this form is true and complete. I understand that anyone who furnishes false or misleading information on this form or who omits material or information requested on the form may be subject to criminal sanctions (including fines and imprisonment) and/or civil sanctions (including multiple damages and civil penalties).

GRAVLAX page 13

HEARTY BEEF STEW page 19

THICK AND CHEWY CHOCOLATE
CHIP COOKIES page 23

TARTE TATIN page 15

BRAISED BUTTERNUT SQUASH WITH DRIED APRICOTS,
RAISINS, AND MADRAS SPICES page 26

LIGHT AND FLUFFY PANCAKES page 8

Braised Carrots with Sour Cream–Cilantro Sauce

Heat 3 tablespoons butter in medium skillet. Add 1 pound carro[ts] that have been peeled and cut into 2-by-¼-inch julienne strip[s]; cook over medium heat until carrots just begin to soften, abou[t] 5 minutes. Add ¼ cup chicken stock, 2 teaspoons coarsely choppe[d] fresh cilantro leaves, and 1 teaspoon honey, as well as salt an[d] ground black pepper to taste; cover and simmer until carrots a[re] tender, about 5 minutes longer. Transfer carrots to serving bow[l] with slotted spoon; cover and keep warm. Increase heat [to] high; cook until pan juices thicken slightly, about 1 minu[te] longer. Turn off heat and stir in ¼ cu[p] sour cream and 1 additional tea[-] spoon coarsely chopped fres[h] cilantro leaves. Pour sauc[e] over carrots and serv[e] immediately. *Serves*

COOK'S
ILLUSTRATED

Throw Out Your Wok!
Skillet Works Best for Home Stir-Frying

Classic Cream Pies
Creamy Filling, Crisp Crust, and Lush Topping

90-Minute Chicken Soup
Sauté Chicken Parts for a Rich, Homemade Soup

Testing Pepper Mills
New Design Wins; Traditional Models Score Well

SUPERMARKET BACON TASTING

·

HOW TO QUICK-COOK CARROTS

·

DECORATING WITH CHOCOLATE

RATING TUSCAN WINES

$4.00 U.S./$4.95 CANADA

TABLE
OF CONTENTS

"Papayas"

ILLUSTRATION BY
BRENT WATKINSON

Compote of Oranges,
adapted from
*The Vegetarian Table:
France* by
Georgeanne Brennan
(Chronicle, 1995)

ILLUSTRATION BY
CAROL FORTUNATO

COOK'S
ILLUSTRATED

Publisher and Editor	CHRISTOPHER KIMBALL
Consulting Editor	MARK BITTMAN
Senior Editor	JOHN WILLOUGHBY
Food Editor	PAM ANDERSON
Senior Writer	JACK BISHOP
Articles Editor	ANNE TUOMEY
Editorial Production Director	MAURA LYONS
Editorial Prod. Coordinator	KARIN L. KANEPS
Assistant Editor	ADAM RIED
Copy Editor	GARY PFITZER
Editorial Assistant	ELIZABETH CAMERON
Test Cook	MELISSA HAMILTON

Art Director	MEG BIRNBAUM
Food Stylist	MARIE PIRAINO
Special Projects Designer	DEBBIE WOLFE

Marketing Director	ADRIENNE KIMBALL
Circulation Director	ELAINE REPUCCI
Ass't Circulation Manager	JENNIFER L. KEENE
Circulation Coordinator	JONATHAN VENIER
Circulation Assistant	C. MARIA PANNOZZO
Production Director	JAMES MCCORMACK
Project Coordinator	SHEILA DATZ
Production Coordinator	PAMELA SLATTERY
Systems Administrator	MATTHEW FRIGO
Production Artist	KEVIN MOELLER

Vice President	JEFFREY FEINGOLD
Controller	LISA A. CARULLO
Accounting Assistant	MANDY SHITO
Office Manager	TONYA ESTEY
Special Projects	FERN BERMAN

Cook's Illustrated (ISSN 1068-2821) is published bimonthly by Boston Common Press Limited Partnership, 17 Station Street, P.O. Box 569, Brookline, MA 02147-0569. Copyright 1996 Boston Common Press Limited Partnership. Second-class postage paid at Boston, MA, and additional mailing offices, USPS #012487. For list rental information, please contact Direct Media, 200 Pemberwick Road, Greenwich, CT 06830; (203) 532-1000. Editorial office: 17 Station Street, P.O. Box 569, Brookline, MA 02147-0569; (617) 232-1000, FAX (617) 232-1572, E-mail: cooksill@aol.com. Editorial contributions should be sent or E-mailed to: Editor, Cook's Illustrated. We cannot assume responsibility for manuscripts submitted to us. Submissions will be returned only if accompanied by a large self-addressed stamped envelope. Subscription rates: $24.95 for one year; $45 for two years; $65 for three years. (Canada: add $3 per year; all other countries: add $12 per year.) Postmaster: Send all new orders, subscription inquiries, and change of address notices to Cook's Illustrated, P.O. Box 7444, Red Oak, IA 51591-0444. Single copies: $4 in U.S., $4.95 in Canada and other countries. Back issues available for $5 each. PRINTED IN THE U.S.A.

EDITORIAL

TOO BLESSED TO COMPLAIN

We receive more than fifty letters a week from readers. Many are predictable—questions about cooking or purchasing cookware—while others speak in a more personal voice. Georgie Johnson from La Conner, Washington, writes, "I love your continued belief in the simplicity of food, its inherent way of revealing us to ourselves and community at each meal, the act of faith called forth when one lives and breathes with the seasons." Kathy Bungard from Ione, Washington, has written to say that *Cook's Illustrated* has "given me wings" despite a chronic illness that leaves her with little energy and much pain. Wiley and Nancy McCall from Fort Pierce, Florida, look to *Cook's Illustrated* as an old friend and invite us down to Florida to share a meal: "Ya'll are welcome anytime."

CHRISTOPHER KIMBALL

But, I was most touched by a letter I just received from Sharlene Spina of Baldwinsville, New York, who won first place at the New York State Fair using our Hazelnut Butter Cookie Dough from the November/December 1993 issue. The letter is really about winning a different sort of prize. She writes, "Most important was the news of my winning to my grandmother whom, God bless her, we buried on this beautiful fall day today. If only you could have seen the smile on her face (when I told her at the nursing home); she was so happy. Although she never said it, I believe her thoughts were that the baton had been passed and the tradition of baking and Christmas cookies would go on for future generations. Thank you so much for what you may think of as just another research article completed—but, due to your staff, I was able to have yet another moment with my grandmother that I will always cherish."

A few months ago, our family attended a service at the Ebenezer Baptist Church in the South End of Boston, a short walk from our home. When I first stepped out of the brisk, mid-November wind into the warm, Gothic sanctuary, it reminded me of my first foray into a kitchen. It was all very foreign—the male ushers dressed in black suits, white gloves, and bow ties; women in starched white dresses; others in hats, some squat and black, some wild, soaring with architectural abandon—but it was welcoming and stirring. You haven't lived until you've heard two fired-up choirs get hold of "Have a Little Talk with Jesus" and pump it full of raw faith and harmony.

In his sermon, the Reverend Kirk Jones spoke about a stranger he had met the other day in front of the church. He had asked her how she was, and she replied, "I'm too blessed to complain." As I thought about her words, I realized that home cooks are also blessed with the power to give something special to others. Food and religion are intimately entwined for a reason. Both kitchens and churches are filled with common purpose, with the repetition of the familiar, which, through time and experience, transcends the commonplace. Making soup, baking biscuits, or even preparing oatmeal for the kids is not an act of faith but is a simple act of kindness, of service, of community.

When compared to the art of the gourmet cook, home cooking may seem a bit commonplace, even threadbare, but this is the essence of its appeal. Putting good food on the table every day is a service performed for others; making elaborate dishes for a dinner party is more for the glory of the cook. Whereas gourmet cooking is about the art of cooking somebody else's food, home cooking is about nourishing family and friends. As a minister once told me, "Preaching isn't about the preacher, it's about the congregation."

As the service continued, I held our sleeping ten-month-old son in my arms and watched the lazy sunlight come and go through the soft green and yellow stained glass windows, heard the strong, clear voices of witnesses testifying to their faith, noticed an impeccably dressed man with salt-and-pepper hair weeping softly in the pew ahead of me, and looked on as the red- and yellow-robed choir waved white paper fans donated by the nearby Davis Funeral Home. And then, my five-year-old daughter tugged on my sleeve and said, "Daddy, I think we're supposed to hold hands now." She was right—the congregation was holding hands, praying for the health of a sick member—and as I gripped her perfect, small fingers, I suddenly realized that both cooking and praying are best when done collectively. Baking cookies for a state fair can connect one generation to the next. A woman in pain can find strength through shared recipes. A congregation singing "We Gather Together" can refresh and bind the souls of strangers. We all experience these moments of lucid stillness when the turbulence of modern times washes clear, and we peek beneath the surface to see that we are, all of us together, too blessed to complain. ■

NOTES FROM READERS

POLENTA VERSUS CORNMEAL

What is the difference between polenta and cornmeal, except the price?

FREDDA HARDY
New York, NY

Polenta is simply the Italian name for cornmeal. As you note, cornmeal sold as polenta in gourmet stores is often expensive. What's more important than the name or price is the grind. We find that medium-grind cornmeal makes the best cooked polenta. Powdery cornmeal (the grind of most inexpensive supermarket cornmeal, including the best-selling brand, Quaker) is not suited for this purpose. When preparing polenta, look for cornmeal that has a texture similar to that of granulated sugar. To find this kind of cornmeal, try a health foods store, where it is generally much cheaper than the "polenta" sold in gourmet specialty shops. Also, note that instant polenta is something completely different: It consists of cornmeal that has been cooked and dried.

ICE IN YOUR GROUND BEEF

Your article on hamburgers (July/August 1995) was very interesting. I am surprised that the authors did not mention the oldest trick in the book that some retail meat markets used to do to "bulk" up their ground beef, namely adding ice cubes to the meat while grinding it. The consumer paid for the added water weight, thus increasing the butcher's profits. Butchers rationalized this practice by saying that the ice cubes helped "cool off" the meat grinder.

TOM RYAN
Elmwood Park, IL

JUDGING THE ACCURACY OF THERMOMETERS

Stephen Schmidt's tip to test a meat thermometer by placing it in boiling water (Quick Tips, May/June 1995) works well at sea level. However, I have another way to test a meat thermometer that works at any altitude. Just fill a glass up with ice cubes and water. After fifteen seconds the thermometer should read 32 degrees, the freezing point of water. Follow Mr. Schmidt's instructions for adjustment of the thermometer using pliers to twist the small nut beneath the thermometer.

CARRON HARRIS
Minneapolis, MN

ELECTRONIC SCALE BATTERIES

In your September/October 1995 issue, you recommend electronic kitchen scales over mechanical versions. While I do not take issue with that recommendation, you didn't discuss the type of batteries used in electronic scales.

Many years ago we were given an electronic scale that was, as you describe, compact, accurate, and easy to store. Its one major drawback was the expensive battery it required, which was especially hard to find in the rural area where we live. Consequently, when the battery ended its useful life, so did the scale. While there has been much progress in battery technology since then, and small, powerful, long-life batteries are common, the type, cost, and availability of batteries should be a consideration when choosing an electronic scale.

LEE GEHRKE
Drummond, WI

Good news awaits you the next time you try an electronic scale. As you point out, battery technology and availability has improved over the years, and so have electronic scales. The electronic scales we tested require batteries in very common sizes. For instance, the Terraillon Electronic Food Scale BE 225, which we rated as the best buy among the electronic models, is powered by four AA batteries, while the Cuisinart Precision Electronic Scale SA 110 is powered by four AAA batteries. Both AAs and AAAs are inexpensive and very widely available in hardware and drug stores as well as in rural general stores.

JUDGING MERLOTS

As a wine varietal, merlot is often overlooked and underappreciated, so we were pleased to see Mark Bittman's column about inexpensive merlots in the September/October 1995 issue. We were disappointed, though, with the taster's impressions of our nonvintage Vendange wine.

A merlot, whether ours or someone else's, that is described as "odd," "sour," "thin," or "vegetal" is obviously a wine that has oxidized due to poor shipping or storage. Any wine in this condition should be removed from a tasting as it is not a proper sample of a winery's final product. It would be akin to judging the quality of a magazine if it arrived with its cover torn or shredded by the mail.

Our Vendange merlot is generally considered to be a medium-bodied, well-balanced wine with

a pleasant berry hint and a combination of vanilla and toasty oak flavors.

JASON BREAW
Sebastiani Vineyards
Sonoma, CA

Mark Bittman responds: I don't believe that the Vendange merlot at our tasting was oxidized; indeed, two tasters liked it enough to rank it in their top seven. Furthermore, three other wines also wound up in the Not Recommended category. None of these wines were "bad" in the sense that a consumer could return them to their retailer or send them back in a restaurant; they were, in the opinion of the vast majority of tasters, not worth drinking.

In fact, the parallel to be drawn is not between these inferior wines and a magazine with a torn cover, but rather between them and a magazine with a lovely cover but articles that you are not really anxious to read. Neither one is worth the money, but it is up to the consumer to avoid them despite the best efforts of marketers. That is why we taste wines in groups and look for consensus, and that's why some wines end up in the Not Recommended category.

REGIONAL CORNBREAD PREFERENCES

Judy Monroe's description of Southern-type cornbread in the September/October 1995 article "The Best Northern Cornbread" moved one reader to the following response:

Judy, Judy, Judy. What so-called Southerner has been feeding you cornbread? Dry, crumbly, and flat!? And you said that Southerners prefer their cornbread this way? You got the white cornmeal right, and Southern cornbread might, in some instances, be somewhat flatter than Yankee cornbread, but "dry" and "crumbly"? Not when made by Southerners who know how!

I've had Northern cornbread many times, and it lacks only one thing—a frosting. It is bread after all, not cake. I'm a transplanted Southerner from Kentucky, and I was brought up on Southern cornbread. There must be at least two dozen ways Southerners worth their culinary salts prepare cornbread and ten times that many recipes. I use a heaping tablespoon full of bacon fat—the fresher the better—to subtly flavor my cornbread, and I bake it in a cast-iron skillet. Heat the fat in the skillet in the oven while you prepare the other ingredients, and definitely add the fat last. If you use bacon fat, cut out the sugar altogether, and don't mix the batter too much.

Cornbread without buttermilk, real buttermilk, is less than perfect. Of course, you cannot buy real buttermilk anymore. Supermarkets everywhere sell only cultured buttermilk, with 1½ percent butterfat. This ain't real buttermilk, but we have to make due with what we have. Stone-ground meal goes without saying.

Cornbread is still quite popular in the South, and made by a good cook with the best ingredients, it is the best cornBREAD in the world.

CURTIS BALLS
Long Island City, NY

The differences in the way people make their cornbread in different regions of the country is very clear to us—as is the passion with which these preferences are felt. In her article, Judy Monroe specifically focussed on Northern-style cornbread precisely because we understand that this is a different animal than its Southern cousin. While both styles have their respective champions and detractors, we believe that each of them can stand on its own merits. In a future issue, we will investigate Southern cornbread.

WHEN TO CARVE PRIME RIB

As soon as the November/December 1995 issue arrived, we tried Pam Anderson's and Karen Tack's method for prime rib. We will never make prime rib in any other way again.

But, when we brought the slices of meat to the table, they were not warm. We got to thinking that there are two traditional reasons to let meat sit for twenty minutes or so after it comes out of the oven. The first reason is to allow the heat in the meat to distribute evenly from the outside to the inside. The second reason is to allow the juices to retreat throughout the roast. The method of roasting long and low, however, ought to render both ancient requirements irrelevant. The meat cooks evenly during the whole process, as demonstrated by its negligible rise in temperature after leaving the oven. Similarly, since the roast loses so little weight during cooking, no juices are being extruded. Hence, there is no need to allow the juices to retreat to the interior of the roast.

We think you could probably slice this roast as soon as it reaches the desired temperature on the meat thermometer without any loss of juice or any significant change in the interior temperature. The benefit here is clear: a roast as hot going to the table as it was coming from the oven.

SARAH AND MARC COGAN
Ypsilanti, MI

Your reasoning is excellent. The low heat used in this method ensures that the heat is distributed evenly from the exterior to interior of the roast, and because of the even heat, the proteins give up less of their moisture. Thus, the need for a rest time to reabsorb the juices is eliminated. To test this, we roasted two prime ribs side by side and carved one immediately after it emerged from the oven, and the other after a twenty-minute rest. Both roasts were equally (very) juicy. If you do not need the twenty minutes of rest time to put the finishing touches on other dishes you are serving, go ahead and carve the roast right out of the oven, and enjoy fully hot slices of meat.

QUESTIONING COCOA

Am I correct in inferring from your September/October 1995 article "Dutched vs. Natural Cocoas" that I cannot substitute dutched cocoa for cocoa in recipes that require cocoa plus some leavening agent? My favorite cake recipe (from Hershey's) calls for, among other things, one-third cup cocoa, one and one-fourth teaspoons baking soda, and one-fourth teaspoon baking powder.

SKY COLE
Ridgefield, CT

Essentially, your assumption is correct. We should clarify, however, that the leaveners in question are the chemical leaveners—baking soda and powder, which react with acid ingredients to create the rising action—not egg foams and air.

The cocoa article points out that, historically, most of the cocoas on the American market have been natural, whereas their European counterparts have been Dutch-processed, meaning the natural acidity is neutralized by adding a small amount of alkaline solution. Unless otherwise specified, then, American recipes (such as your Hershey's cake recipe) suit the type and proportion of chemical leaveners that work with the natural, mildly acidic cocoa that dominates our market. In fact, the leavening action in this recipe depends on the chemical reaction between the baking soda, which is alkaline, and the natural cocoa, which is acidic. Our tests for this article, and others, show that natural cocoa tastes great—often better than Dutch-processed—in baked goods. And natural cocoa offers the additional advantage of costing less than Dutch-processed.

In short, your best bet is to stick with the type of cocoa specified in the recipe.

ON COCOA IN CAKE

When I recently reviewed Stephen Schmidt's articles on chocolate cake in the July/August 1994 issue and all-purpose birthday cake in the May/June 1995 issue, the following question occurred to me. Why does the master recipe for chocolate cake require all-purpose flour while "Cake Baking 101," a sidebar to the all-purpose birthday cake article, calls on the baker to use only cake flour? Is this in order to get a fine-grained texture, or something else?

MARI KEEFE
Austin, TX

You ask an excellent question about the different flours used in chocolate and white cakes. All-purpose flour has a higher protein content than cake flour (about 10 to 11 percent versus 7 to 8 percent), and it is the protein that gives cakes their structure by forming gluten. In chocolate cake batter, some of the flour is replaced with cocoa, which has no protein. All-purpose flour is used, then, to make up for that protein loss; it gives the cake sufficient structure. If cake flour were used instead, the batter would contain too little protein to give the cake structure enough to withstand splitting and hold up to the frosting process. The cake would generally be too tender for easy handling. In fact, such a delicate cake might even crumble as it is removed from the baking pan.

The batter for the white cakes described in "Cake Baking 101" contains the full amount of flour. Therefore, the batter will accommodate lower-protein cake flour and still provide enough gluten to give the cake good structure for handling, along with a tender crumb. If higher-protein, all-purpose flour were used, the batter would have too much protein, leading to a tough cake. ∎

ILLUSTRATION BY DAN KROVATIN

Quick Tips

GRINDING MEAT WITHOUT MESS

To keep meat juices from spattering during grinding, Philipina Vlismas of Brooklyn, New York, suggests the following tip.

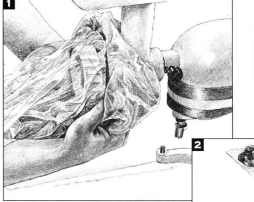

1. Secure a large plastic bag over the grinder mouth with a rubber band.

2. The meat grinds neatly into the bag with no mess—not even a bowl to clean up.

RINSING GRAINS

To rinse rice and other small grains without losing them down the drain, follow this suggestion from Pamela Lee of Pullman, Washington.

1. Pour the rice or other grain into a wide-mouth quart Mason jar, preferably with cup measures marked on the side. Replace the lid with a piece of screen, then secure it with the jar lid's ring.

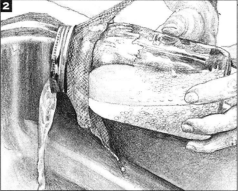

2. Run water through the screen into the jar; swish, shake, and drain. Repeat as many times as necessary.

MAKING YOGURT CHEESE

For a simple method of draining yogurt to make the cheese called labne, Laurel Cowan Knutson of Desert Hot Springs, California, makes the following suggestion.

1. Using an ice pick, poke several holes in the bottom of a 16-ounce plastic yogurt container, starting from the inside and pushing out.

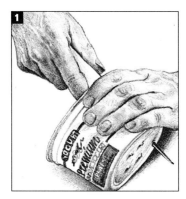

2. Fill the container with yogurt and snap on the lid, then slip it into a 32-ounce container.

LEVELING A CAKE LAYER

Rather than use a long-bladed knife to level a cake, Amy Hird of Benton, Wisconsin, suggests the following.

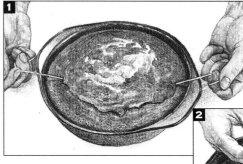

2. Pull the severed section from the top of the layer.

1. After the cake has cooled, return the cake layer to the pan. Run the appropriate length of fishing line or dental floss across the cake top, using the top edge of the pan as a guide.

ILLUSTRATIONS BY ALAN WITSCHONKE

MAKING PERFECT DIPPED BERRIES

Cara Morris of New York City has solved the problem of uneven-looking chocolate-dipped strawberries. Rather than laying them on waxed paper once they've been dipped, she suggests following this procedure.

1. Use a scissors to trim the edges from an empty egg carton.

2. Trim the tall center divider from the egg carton.

3. Place the strawberries, dipped side up, in the egg holes in the trimmed carton.

TO MAKE PERFECT TARTLETS

Fitting rounds of dough into muffin tins to make tartlets can be difficult. You must overlap a part of each dough circle in order to fit it into the tin, and this creates a portion that is thicker than the rest. Sally McQuail of Downington, Pennsylvania, has devised this method to solve the problem.

1. Roll the dough out to a thickness of ⅛ inch and cut it into rounds using a 2¾ inch cookie cutter. Then use the cookie cutter to cut a small crescent-shaped section out of each round.

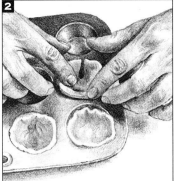

2. Place the notched crusts into the pan; they will conform well to the sides. To seal, simply press lightly on the seam.

KEEPING HERBS FRESH

David Eichorn of Kensington, California, uses the following method to preserve fresh herbs and greens, including parsley, cilantro, and watercress.

1. Cut off the stems of the herbs with a scissors or knife.

2. Place the entire bunch in a water glass half filled with water. Cover it with a plastic bag and refrigerate.

CUTTING BAR COOKIES

George Erdosh of Sacramento, California, has developed this method in order to prevent the jagged edges that often occur when cutting cooled cookie bars.

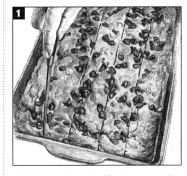

1. Use a sharp knife to score the bars as soon as the pan comes out of the oven.

2. Then cut the cooled bars along the scored lines.

A SIMPLE RECIPE CARD HOLDER

Follow this tip from Rita Durkheimer of Portland, Oregon, to keep recipe cards easily visible while you are cooking. Thread the recipe card on fork tines, then set the fork in a water glass.

Thanks to our readers for Quick Tips: The editors of *Cook's Illustrated* would like to thank all of the readers who have sent us their quick tips. We have enjoyed reading every one of them, and have learned a lot. Keep them coming. We will provide a one-year complimentary subscription for each quick tip that we print. Send a description of your special technique to *Cook's Illustrated,* P.O. Box 569, Brookline Village, MA 02147-0569. Please write "Attention: Quick Tips" on the envelope and include your name, address, and daytime phone number. You can also e-mail us at cooksill@aol.com. Unfortunately, we can only acknowledge receipt of tips that will be printed in the magazine. In case the same tip is received from two readers, the one postmarked first will be selected. Also, be sure to let us know what particular cooking problems you would like us to investigate in upcoming issues.

Crisp, Sweet Sea Scallops

For a crispy exterior and meltingly sweet interior, sauté uncoated, unprocessed scallops in butter—and don't move them around during cooking.

∽ BY STEPHANIE LYNESS ∽

Properly sautéed scallops have crisp, nicely browned tops and bottoms and meltingly tender interiors.

The idea was to find out how to sauté sea scallops so they taste the way I like them— the top caramelized to a concentrated, nutty-flavored, brown-and-tan crust, cracked across the surface as if it can hardly contain the creamy, sweet, barely cooked meat inside.

Scallops come in different sizes and species. For this article, I chose to deal with the larger, marshmallow-shaped sea scallops and not the smaller, cork-shaped bay scallops or the even smaller calicoes, which are cooked somewhat differently than sea scallops but are not as readily available (*see* "The Little Scallops," page 8).

The most common problem a cook runs into with scallops is how to get the scallop well caramelized (which greatly enhances its natural sweetness) before it has a chance to overcook, which makes the flesh rubbery and tough. I found that it's easy to have perfectly crusted, creamy scallops by cooking them in whole butter, moving them only to turn, and learning to gauge doneness by touch and eye.

Getting the Best Crust Possible

My first question was whether one type of fat would brown the scallops better than the others would. Since scallops cook quickly, I knew it would be important to choose the fat that browned

the most efficiently. So, I cooked seasoned sea scallops in a heated, stainless steel frying pan over medium-high heat in whole butter and in olive and canola oils as well as in a combination of oil and butter. I also tried sautéing the scallops in canola oil until the crust was formed and then finishing with butter at the very end, the idea being that the oil might allow me to brown on a higher heat, while the butter would add flavor at the end. I decided to experiment with clarified butter only if all the other options were unsatisfying; my experience is that very few home cooks, including myself, have the time or patience for clarifying butter.

To preserve the ethereal, creamy texture of the flesh, I cooked the scallops to medium-rare, which means that the scallop is hot all the way through but the center still retains some translucence. As a scallop cooks, the flabby flesh firms and you can see an opaqueness that starts at the bottom of the scallop, where it sits in the pan, and slowly creeps up towards the center. The scallop is medium-rare when the sides have firmed up and all but about the middle third of the scallop has turned opaque.

Intuitively, I was pretty sure that butter was going to be the ticket here, and I was right. The scallops browned well in all the fats and combinations thereof, and I even liked the taste the olive oil delivered. The butter, however, succeeded in combining and reducing with the scallop juices as in deglazing, seeming almost to infuse the scallop with the thick, even, richly colored crust I was looking for. The nutty taste of the butter complemented the sweetness of the scallop without compromising its delicate flavor. I did find that a com-

bination of two-thirds butter and one-third canola oil browns as well as butter and can be heated to a higher temperature, with less risk of burning the fat. But, since I'm big on simplicity, I decided just to monitor the heat and cook with butter— which is appropriate unless there's a good reason not to (for example, a dish in which scallops are served with an olive oil-based sauce, such as Ed Brown's Cilantro Pesto, or perhaps in an Asian preparation).

Having settled on butter, I briefly considered the idea of a coating. I knew that I didn't want to use any kind of heavy breading, because I was getting a great crust already with the butter, and from a purely taste point of view, the less you do to a scallop the better. I thought a light coating of flour on both ends might encourage browning even more, however, so I tested a plain, seasoned scallop sautéed in butter against one with both ends lightly dipped in flour and then sautéed. Not only did the floured scallop brown significantly less well than the other, missing the shiny, rich crust I'd grown accustomed to, but it also tasted less sweet because it tasted of flour.

Type and Heat of Pan

I had been told by a friend that an excellent way to sauté scallops in very little fat is to toss them in a tiny amount of olive oil and then sauté them in a heated, nonstick pan. By coating the scallops rather than the pan with the oil, the oil stays in contact with the scallop rather than beading up on other parts of the pan. (Impassioned by the low-fat option after days of sautéing in butter, I also tried sautéing in a dry pan and, somewhat to my relief, was utterly disappointed.) Although this coating technique didn't yield nearly the crust provided by butter, it browned credibly with far less fat than I had been using. I also found that this technique browned the scallops even better in a traditional pan, although it is hard on the pan, which got brown spots on it that were tough to clean. So, while this is a good low-fat option, I prefer more butter better.

Having now entered the world of nonstick, I tried

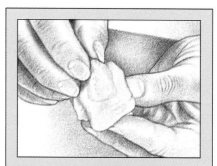

The small, rough-textured, crescent-shaped muscle that attaches the scallop to the shell is often not removed during processing. You can readily remove any muscles that are still attached. If you do not, they will toughen slightly during cooking.

my butter method in both traditional and nonstick pans. The scallops browned just about the same (unlike oil, butter doesn't bead up in a non-stick pan), although it was more difficult to monitor the heat in my black-bottomed nonstick pan because I couldn't see how quickly the butter was browning.

While I was testing, I wanted to come up with a timing system to determine, by holding my hand over the bottom of the pan, when the pan was just the right temperature to sauté. This timing is particularly important when using butter since butter burns quickly if the pan preheats too long. Unfortunately, I found that my two pans reflect heat so differently that while, after two minutes, it was uncomfortably hot to hold a hand about two inches over one, the other felt barely hot. So I cheat: I heat the pan one minute, until a drop of water spits aggressively, then add the butter and heat it until I can smell and see it just begin to turn nutty brown.

In the midst of all this, I spoke to a few restaurant chefs in the New York area to make sure I wasn't overlooking anything. Rick Moonen, the chef at Oceana, a seafood restaurant in Manhattan, swept me off my feet with his enthusiasm for scallops and gave me a unique technique for sautéing his extravagantly large scallops (three or four make a meal for most people): He brushes only the top of each seasoned scallop with softened butter and then sautés them in a nonstick pan. The idea here is that he gets the butter on the scallop, where it belongs, rather than melting it in the pan. When I heard the reasoning behind his technique—he says he's always made grilled cheese sandwiches this way—I knew I had to check it out.

I used the largest scallops I could find (they're called U-10's in the industry, which means they're so large that it takes less than ten to make up a pound) and "brushed" the top of each with one-half teaspoon of butter, using the fork with which I had just mashed the cold butter to soften it. I tested the scallops in both nonstick and traditional pans. The scallops browned beautifully (my traditional pan worked better), and the technique offered the added advantage of using only two teaspoons of butter to sauté four huge scallops (I would normally have used about one tablespoon). When I tested this technique against my melted-butter technique, however, I found that the scallops browned and tasted pretty much the same with both. So, while I may use this technique to sauté very large scallops because it works and it's fun, in the end it's quite difficult for the average cook to get hold of such large scallops and I can't recommend it over the melted butter technique for standard-sized scallops.

When sautéing scallops, make sure not to overcrowd the skillet or they will not brown properly. Use tongs to turn the scallops in the sauté pan.

Searing and Sizing the Scallops

Despite the origin of the word "sauté," which means "to jump" in French, it's critical to the formation of a good crust that, once the scallop hits the pan, you not move it at all until you're ready to turn it; you're really searing the scallops as you do meat. I found that the optimal method for cooking was to carefully place the scallops in the pan one at a time, with one flat end down for maximum contact until a crust formed. Then I turned them, again one at a time, and cooked them through. Although a spatula works for this in a pinch, tongs are far superior.

Scallops obviously cook differently depending on size. If you end up with a jumble of sizes, you can either remove the scallops from the pan, in order of size, as they finish cooking, or you can cut the large ones down to size. Katherine Alford, who teaches cooking in New York, recommends cutting the scallops vertically rather than into horizontal disks (the thin, horizontal disks overcook before they brown). I tried her idea, cooking the scallops cut side down first, and got much better results than with the traditional cut.

Sea scallops are available year-round throughout the country. They require very little, if any, preparation because they are almost always shucked at sea. The guts and roe, or milt, are jettisoned along with the shells, because these organs are much more perishable than the scallop proper that we know of from supermarkets and fish counters—the dense, ivory- to pink- or tan-colored, disk-shaped muscle that vigorously propels the live scallop in its shell through the water. You may notice a small, rough-textured, crescent-shaped muscle attached to one side of some scallops when you get them home. This muscle holds the live scallop to its shell and may or may not be pulled off during shucking. It toughens during cooking, however, so you'll need to remove it. You'll spot it easily because of the slight difference in texture and color. It peels off effortlessly.

"PROCESSED" SCALLOPS

When asked how they sauté scallops, the chefs I spoke to aggressively prefaced their responses with the admonition not to use "processed" scallops, that is, scallops that are "dipped" for a short time in a phosphate-and-water mixture that may also contain citric and sorbic acids. According to these experts, the processing ruins the flavor of the shellfish and inhibits browning by causing the scallop to throw off liquid when it hits the hot pan. Distributors and retailers who I questioned at the Fulton Fish Market in Manhattan told me that scallops are dipped primarily to preserve their shelf life. According to a distributor in the market who carries both fresh and processed scallops, the processed product lasts at least four days longer than the fresh. By federal law, processed scallops must be identified on a wholesale level (the cans scallops are packed in show the name of the chemical dip), but there is no regulation at the retail level, so the uninformed consumer is unprotected.

Once the difference was pointed out to me, I had no trouble telling the difference between the fresh and the processed scallops. While the processed scallops are bright white, I've never seen a fresh (called "dry" in the industry) scallop that comes even close to that color; they vary from ivory to pinkish beige to tan or orangish, and are sometimes even slightly grayish, depending on where they're dredged. Another visual clue is that, whether open to the air on the fish counter or wrapped in individual shrink-wrapped packages, processed scallops are usually swimming in milky liquid; just as the scallop readily absorbs the dip, so it gives it up over time. This is only a clue, however, since you may also see dry scallops sitting in their natural juices as well.

The most reliable tests are touch and smell. Dry scallops are sticky and flabby while the processed shellfish are slippery and swollen. Dry scallops smell distinctly of the sea; the processed ones may have no smell or give off a faint whiff of perfume.

I did some kitchen tests comparing processed with dry scallops to determine the truth about how they cook and taste. I weighed out four ounces each of dry and processed sea scallops, sautéed them in oil, weighed them again, and then did a taste comparison. Each cost $11.99 a pound; I bought the dry scallops at a retail fish market and the processed at a supermarket next door.

Although neither type of scallop threw off more water than the other, the dry scallops browned much better than the processed, and the crust on the processed didn't crack the way it does on a dry scallop. The cooked weight was the same for both. The big difference was in the taste: While the dry scallop was sweet and meaty, the processed scallop was bitter and unappetizing. The processed scallop also had a somewhat different texture than the dry, but I confess that, spoiled by excellent-quality dry scallops, I wasn't motivated to eat enough of the processed to figure it out. Since something like 90 percent of the scallops on the market are processed, and consumers aren't complaining much, I must assume that my experience with processed scallops was unusually bad. I'm confident, however, that most people would taste the difference between a dry and a processed scallop.—S.L.

MASTER RECIPE FOR
SEARED SCALLOPS
Serves 4

This recipe was developed for a standard sea scallop, about the size of a short, squat marshmallow. If using smaller scallops, turn off the heat as soon as you turn them; they will finish cooking from the residual heat, fifteen to thirty seconds longer. For very large scallops, turn the heat to low once they have browned and continue cooking for one minute. Turn the scallops, raise the heat to medium, and cook them at least two minutes on the second side.

 1½ pounds sea scallops, about 30 to a pound, small muscles removed (*see illustration, page 6*)
   Salt and ground black pepper
 1½ tablespoons butter (or olive oil, *see note above*)

Sprinkle scallops on both sides with salt and pepper. Heat large (11-inch) sauté pan over medium-high heat until hot, about 1 minute. Add half the butter; swirl to coat bottom. Continue to heat pan until butter begins to turn golden brown. Add half the scallops, one at a time, flat side down; cook, adjusting heat as necessary to prevent fat from burning, until scallops are well browned, 1½ to 2 minutes. Using tongs, turn scallops, one at a time; cook until medium-rare (sides firmed up and all but middle third of scallop opaque), 30 seconds to 1½ minutes longer, depending on size. Repeat cooking process using remaining half of butter and scallops. Serve immediately.

WATERCRESS SALAD WITH SEARED
SCALLOPS AND ORANGE
VINAIGRETTE
Serves 4 as first course, 2 as main course

 2 teaspoons zest and 2 tablespoons juice from 1 small orange
 1 teaspoon red wine vinegar
 ⅛ teaspoon salt
   Ground black pepper
 ¼ cup plus 1 teaspoon olive oil
 4 cups lightly packed watercress, washed, trimmed, and dried
 ½ recipe Simple Seared Scallops
 1 small shallot, minced
 1 teaspoon minced fresh thyme leaves

1. Whisk zest and juice, vinegar, salt, and pinch of pepper in small bowl. Slowly whisk in ¼ cup of the oil; set aside. Put watercress in medium bowl; set aside.

2. Follow recipe for Simple Seared Scallops, wiping fat from skillet once scallops have cooked. Return skillet to burner; reduce heat to low. Add remaining 1 teaspoon oil, shallot, and thyme; cook, stirring with wooden spoon, until shallot softens slightly, 1 to 2 minutes. Remove pan from heat; let cool about 1 minute. Pour in vinaigrette, scraping pan bottom with wooden spoon to loosen caramelized bits.

3. Spoon about two-thirds of vinaigrette over watercress. Toss and divide among plates. Arrange portion of scallops on top of each watercress bed, spoon remaining vinaigrette over scallops, and serve immediately.

RICK MOONEN'S ANGEL HAIR PASTA
WITH SEARED SCALLOPS
Serves 4 to 6

The only tricky part of this recipe is ensuring that the pasta and sauce are done at the same time. Start the pasta after adding the ginger and shallots to the sauté pan and you'll be fine.

 1 recipe Simple Seared Scallops
 1 medium shallot, minced

 1½ ounces (2-inch-long piece) fresh gingerroot, peeled, sliced thin, and julienned
 1 pound angel hair pasta
 ⅔ cup dry white wine
 2 tablespoons white wine vinegar
 1 cup heavy cream
 ½ teaspoon salt
 ⅛ teaspoon ground black pepper
 ¼ cup snipped fresh chives, or ½ cup chopped scallion greens
 2 plum tomatoes, peeled, seeded, and diced (optional)

1. Bring water to boil in large pot; heat oven to 200 degrees for keeping scallops warm.

2. Follow recipe for Simple Seared Scallops, transferring scallops to heatproof plate and then to warm oven with door ajar.

3. Return skillet to burner; reduce heat to low. Add shallot and ginger; cook until shallot softens slightly, 1 to 2 minutes. (Add pasta to pot of boiling water.) Increase heat to high; add wine and vinegar and boil, scraping pan bottom with wooden spoon to loosen caramelized bits, until liquid reduces to a glaze, 4 to 5 minutes. Add cream, salt, and pepper; bring to boil. Reduce heat; simmer until cream reduces very slightly, about 1 minute longer. Stir in chives or scallions, and tomatoes if desired. Drain pasta; pour into large bowl. Add sauce; toss to coat.

4. Divide pasta among individual serving plates, arranging a portion of scallops around or on top of each. Serve immediately.

ED BROWN'S
SEARED SCALLOPS WITH
CILANTRO PESTO
Serves 4

If made ahead, the pesto separates slightly but the flavor doesn't suffer. If grilling or broiling scallops, Brown recommends brushing this pesto directly onto the scallops before cooking.

 1 cup packed cilantro leaves
 1 tablespoon pine nuts
 1 garlic clove, chopped coarse
 ½ teaspoon grated zest from 1 small lemon
 ¼ teaspoon salt
 ⅛ teaspoon ground black pepper
 ¼ cup olive oil
 1 recipe Simple Seared Scallops (using olive oil)

1. Pulse cilantro, pine nuts, garlic, zest, salt, and pepper in bowl of food processor until minced. With motor running, gradually add oil. Process until smooth; set aside.

2. Follow recipe for Simple Seared Scallops, dividing scallops among four plates. Drizzle portion of pesto over each plate of scallops. Serve immediately. ■

Stephanie Lyness is the author of the forthcoming *Cooking with Steam*, to be published by William Morrow this spring.

THE LITTLE SCALLOPS

In addition to the sea scallops that we tested for this article, you will probably also run into two other smaller types of scallops, known as bays and calicoes.

Small, cork-shaped bay scallops are harvested in a small area from Cape Cod south to Long Island. Bay scallops are seasonal—available from fall until mid-winter—and very expensive, up to $15 a pound in Manhattan.

Calico scallops are a smaller species harvested around Florida and the Carolinas and farmed worldwide. They are on the opposite end of the expense spectrum from bays, and can be found for as little as three dollars a pound in supermarkets. Unlike other scallops that are shucked by hand, calicoes are shucked by machine-steaming them open. (Hand-shucking is too time-consuming for such small scallops.) This steaming partially cooks them and gives them an opaque look, meaning that they're easy to overcook in the skillet.

I tested both the bay scallops and calicoes to taste the difference. The bays won easily on the basis of taste. I found, over a season of eating them, that the flavor of both varies noticeably—they range from unbelievably sweet to merely delicious. The calicoes were much better than I had imagined, though, given their reputation. Much less sweet, their flavor can't compare to the bays, but if carefully watched so they don't overcook, the texture can be every bit as good.

I also compared bay scallops cooked and cleaned of their muscles with other scallops having the muscle still attached. Trained to be picky about these sorts of things, I was surprised to find that I was hard-pressed to choose. Although the muscle was noticeably chewier than the body of the scallop, it wasn't as objectionably tough as on a sea scallop. And because the scallop surface caramelizes to such a thick, almost sticky, candylike texture, the muscle gets hidden in the crust. Did I notice? Absolutely. Did I care? Nope.—S.L.

Quick Seafood Pasta Sauces

With minimal work clams, tuna, mussels, and shrimp can be turned into quick sauces for pasta.

~ BY JACK BISHOP ~

Pasta and seafood have a natural affinity; just read the menu at any Italian restaurant. Since seafood requires only the briefest cooking, these sauces, each of which makes enough for one pound of pasta, can be prepared in less than thirty minutes.

Although there are an infinite number of pasta and seafood combinations, they all have one thing in common: They should be served without cheese. Many Italian restaurants in this country bring grated cheese to the table, but I agree with waiters in Rome, Venice, and Genoa who routinely deny such "sacrilegious" requests.

TOMATO SAUCE WITH TUNA AND GREEN OLIVES
Enough for 1 pound of pasta

This pantry sauce relies on canned tomatoes, green olives, and Italian-style canned tuna packed in olive oil. Serve it with farfalle, fusilli, or other shapes that will trap small bits of the sauce.

- 3 tablespoons olive oil
- 2 medium garlic cloves, minced
- 1 can whole tomatoes (28 ounces), chopped coarse, with liquid reserved
- 1 can tuna (6 ounces) packed in olive oil, drained and flaked
- 12 large or 18 medium green olives, pitted and chopped (about ⅔ cup)
- 2 tablespoons minced fresh parsley leaves
- Salt and ground black pepper

1. Heat oil over medium heat in large saucepan. Add garlic; sauté until golden, about 1 minute. Add chopped tomatoes and ¾ cup tomato liquid; simmer until tomatoes soften and sauce thickens somewhat, about 15 minutes.

2. Add tuna and olives; simmer to blend flavors, about 5 minutes longer. Stir in parsley and season to taste with salt and pepper. Toss sauce with cooked pasta and serve immediately.

BASIL SAUCE WITH SAUTÉED SHRIMP
Enough for 1 pound of pasta

This simple but delicious sauce is really nothing more than sautéed shrimp tossed with pesto minus the cheese. Serve it with linguine or other long, thin pasta. Reserve one-half cup of the pasta cooking liquid and drizzle it in as needed when tossing the pasta with the sauce.

- ¾ cup packed fresh basil leaves
- 1 small garlic clove, peeled
- 1 tablespoon pine nuts
- 6 tablespoons extra-virgin olive oil
- Salt and ground black pepper
- 1 pound small shrimp, peeled and deveined (if desired)

1. Process basil, garlic, and pine nuts in workbowl of food processor, scraping down sides as needed, until minced. With motor running, slowly pour 4 tablespoons of the oil through feed tube, processing sauce until smooth. Scrape sauce into serving bowl large enough to hold cooked pasta. Stir in ½ teaspoon salt and ¼ teaspoon pepper.

2. Heat remaining 2 tablespoons oil in large skillet. Add shrimp; sauté over medium-high heat until pink, 3 to 4 minutes. Season to taste with salt and pepper. Transfer shrimp to bowl with pesto; toss well with cooked pasta and reserved cooking liquid (*see* note above). Serve immediately.

CLAM SAUCE WITH TOMATOES AND GARLIC
Enough for 1 pound of pasta

If you can, make this sauce with tiny Manila clams, which are particularly tender and sweet. As a second choice, buy small littlenecks. If only large clams are available, chop them into bite-size pieces. Serve with linguine or spaghetti.

- 3 pounds Manila or littleneck clams, thoroughly scrubbed
- ¼ cup dry white wine
- 1 bay leaf
- 3 tablespoons olive oil
- 3 medium garlic cloves, minced
- 2 cups canned whole tomatoes, chopped coarse, with liquid reserved
- 1 tablespoon minced fresh oregano leaves or 1 teaspoon dried
- Salt and ground black pepper

1. Bring clams, wine, and bay leaf to boil in large soup kettle over high heat, then lower heat to steam clams until most have opened, about 5 minutes. Remove clams and set aside, discarding clamshells, bay leaf, and any clams that have not opened. Strain liquid through paper towel-lined sieve and reserve. Wipe out soup kettle with another paper towel.

2. Meanwhile, heat oil over medium heat in the now empty soup kettle. Add garlic; sauté until golden, about 1 minute. Add tomatoes and their liquid; simmer to thicken, about 5 minutes. Add strained clam broth and oregano. Simmer until sauce thickens slightly and flavors blend, 5 to 7 minutes. Season to taste with salt and pepper. Return clams to kettle; heat to warm through. Toss sauce with cooked pasta and serve immediately.

STEAMED MUSSEL SAUCE WITH LEMON AND WHITE WINE
Enough for 1 pound of pasta

This sauce is fairly soupy, so serve it with bread. Use linguine or spaghetti and feel free to substitute littleneck clams for the mussels.

- 3 dozen black mussels, rinsed thoroughly, weedy beards removed
- ½ cup dry white wine
- ¼ cup olive oil
- 2 medium garlic cloves, minced
- ½ teaspoon hot red pepper flakes
- 1 teaspoon grated zest and 2 tablespoons juice from 1 medium lemon
- 2 tablespoons minced fresh parsley leaves
- Salt

1. Bring mussels and wine to boil in large soup kettle over medium-high heat. Lower heat to steam mussels until most have opened, 4 to 5 minutes. Discard any that have not opened. Remove mussels from shells if desired; set aside. Strain liquid through paper towel-lined sieve and reserve. Wipe out soup kettle with another paper towel.

2. Heat oil over medium heat in now empty soup kettle. Add garlic and pepper flakes; sauté over medium heat until garlic is golden, about 1 minute. Add strained mussel broth, zest, and juice; simmer to blend flavors, 3 to 4 minutes. Return mussels to kettle; heat to warm through. Stir in parsley and add salt to taste. Toss sauce with cooked pasta and serve immediately. ■

Frittatas Made Easy

For a firm yet tender frittata, start cooking it on the stovetop and finish it in a moderately heated oven.

～ BY DIANA SHAW ～

Frittatas can be filled with virtually anything, and are equally delicious hot, cold, or at room temperature.

My interest in cooking nearly ended with an omelette. I was nine years old and saw Julia Child make one on TV. It was the most daunting demonstration I'd ever seen. Despite her confidence and dexterity, it appeared inordinately—impossibly—difficult. Fortunately, for those who love the idea of omelettes but can't handle the execution, there are frittatas, an Italian version of the dish consisting of eggs and a filling, but requiring no fancy pan work.

To make an omelette, you must place a filling on top of partially set eggs, wait a second for the eggs to set further, then turn the contents out onto a serving plate in one graceful swoop. For a frittata, you simply prepare the filling in a pan, pour the eggs on top, and cook until the eggs are set. The difference in preparation yields different results: While an omelette is soft, delicate, and slightly runny, a frittata is tender, but firm. An omelette encases its filling while a frittata incorporates it evenly throughout. Aside from simplicity, frittatas have another advantage: They're delicious hot, cold, or at room temperature—so you don't have to sweat the timing as you do with most omelettes, which must be served warm.

Since few cookbooks agree on a method for making frittatas, I tested a number of techniques to determine which would consistently yield a frittata that was moist but not runny, firm but not tough, and light but substantial. The filling would

need to meld with the eggs, not overwhelm them. To get the results I desired, I had to find the optimal ratio of eggs to cooking fat to pan size, as well as the best proportion of filling to eggs. But I also had to avoid getting too fussy or precise; the whole point is to make a dish that takes little thought and even less technique. In fact, in Italian, the expression "to make a frittata" (*fare una frittata*) means to make a mess.

To discover the best proportion of eggs to pan size to filling to cooking fat, I began with the recipes in my Italian cookbooks, most of which called for six eggs and roughly two tablespoons of oil for a frittata for four. None of the recipes specified pan size, but having eaten very thin frittatas in Italy, I guessed the pan was at least twelve inches.

Two tablespoons of oil proved to be too much in the first version I tested; the frittata tasted of the oil when the oil should mainly have just facilitated the cooking, lending only a faint flavor to the dish. Also, the frittata was very thin, almost crêpelike, which I liked but which didn't seem substantial enough for a lunch or supper dish. To retest, I cut the oil in half, to one tablespoon, and used a ten-inch skillet. This turned out to be the right proportion for firm, flavorful frittatas when the filling had few ingredients. However, when the filling had more substantial ingredients, such as mushrooms, potatoes, or asparagus, I found that it was better to return to the original two tablespoons of oil.

To determine the ideal amount of filling, I decided to judge it by sight, adding only enough to cover the bottom of the pan. I didn't want to risk having the filling overwhelm the eggs, and it just seemed sensible that a layer spread across the pan would be adequate for flavor and substance. This approach turned out to be correct, amounting to about two-thirds cup filling for a ten-inch skillet.

To keep the preparation as simple as possible, I began each test by sautéing the ingredients for the filling in the same nonstick pan in which I would cook the frittata. Then I beat the eggs lightly and poured them over the filling, stirring them with a fork to distribute the white and yolk

evenly, then proceeded with the following cooking methods, getting the results described:

Stovetop only. Judging from the old cookbooks I have from Italy, this is the original method. Once I'd poured the eggs into the pan, I cooked them over medium-low heat until all but the top was set. To set the top, I flipped the frittata with a large spatula, a move that called for more dexterity than I possess, and that involved the risk of tearing. The next time, I covered the pan with a heat-resistant plate. This action caused the underside to overcook and turn tough.

Oven only. Once I'd poured the eggs into the pan, I placed the pan in the center of a 375-degree oven for thirty minutes. The frittata cooked evenly and looked impressive, puffing up a bit and turning golden brown. But it was on the dry side. Hoping to keep it moist, I tinkered with the following: oven temperature (lowering it to 350 degrees), placement of the pan (putting it on a lower rung), and timing (baking it for twenty to twenty-five minutes). Cooked at the lower temperature, the frittata was still dry. Cooked at the lower temperature in the lower part of the oven, it set unevenly, with parts still runny while others were dry. Cooking it for a shorter period of time left part of it uncooked.

Starting on the stovetop and finishing under the broiler. I cooked the frittata on the stove until all but the top was set. Then I placed the pan under a preheated broiler three inches from the heat for about forty seconds.

Provided you work swiftly to keep from overcooking, this method ties for the best, making a slightly crispy outer layer, but leaving the inside creamy and moist. The only reason I don't rate this method absolute tops is because the care you have to take not to burn the top while broiling adds an element of stress to what's meant to be an entirely casual process.

Starting on the stovetop and finishing in the oven. I found this method best overall. Instead of going under the broiler as above, the nearly set frittata is placed in the upper third of a 350-degree oven for two to four minutes. While the top won't turn crispy as it would under the broiler, it sets evenly. Moreover, there's more leeway before the frittata burns or dries out.

I also found during these tests that nonstick skillets with ovenproof handles are best for frittatas. Conventional skillets require so much oil to prevent sticking that frittatas cooked in them are likely to be greasy. Eggs often cook more evenly in a nonstick pan because they won't cling to the surface in various places.

Trying to Reduce Fat and Cholesterol

Having discovered the best cooking method and the best type of pan, I tried a couple of options designed to reduce fat and cholesterol without sacrificing texture and flavor.

First I tried dry-cooking the frittata. I stirred together the filling and the eggs, adding a little buttermilk to compensate (I hoped) for some of the moisture I'd lose by eliminating the cooking fat. I then poured the ingredients into a preheated, nonstick skillet and cooked them over medium-low heat, finishing in a 350-degree oven. Unfortunately, the results were tough, rubbery, and relatively bland.

Next I tried eliminating several yolks from the total number of eggs used. I tried a number of combinations: one egg white plus one whole egg; two whites to one whole; two whole to two whites, and so on. But it seems that nature created eggs in the ideal proportions for frittatas. Made with a preponderance of whites, frittatas are gelatinous in texture and the filling flavor takes over.

So the lesson is, when making frittatas, use a bit of fat in the pan and stick to whole eggs. The results will be worth it.

FRITTATA WITH CHEESE AND FRESH HERBS
Serves 4

1 tablespoon olive oil or unsalted butter
½ small onion, 1 medium scallion, or 1 medium shallot, chopped fine
2 tablespoons minced fresh herb leaves, such as parsley, basil, dill, tarragon, or mint
2 tablespoons to ⅓ cup grated cheese of your choice (½ to 1 ounce)
¼ teaspoon each salt and ground black pepper
6 large eggs, lightly beaten

1. Adjust oven rack to upper-middle position and heat oven to 350 degrees.
2. Heat oil or butter in 10-inch nonstick, oven-proof skillet over medium heat. Swirl skillet to distribute evenly over bottom and sides. Add onions and sauté until softened, 3 to 4 minutes. Stir in herbs.
3. Meanwhile, stir cheese, salt, and pepper into eggs.
4. Pour mixture into skillet; stir lightly with fork until eggs start to set (*see* illustration 1). Once bottom is firm, use thin, nonmetallic spatula to lift frittata edge closest to you. Tilt skillet slightly toward you so that uncooked egg runs underneath (illustration 2). Return skillet to level position and swirl gently to evenly distribute egg. Continue cooking about 40 seconds, then lift edge again, repeating process in illustration 2 until egg on top is no longer runny.
5. Transfer skillet to oven; bake until frittata top is set and dry to touch, 2 to 4 minutes, making sure to remove frittata as soon as top is just set.
6. Run spatula around skillet edge to loosen frittata; invert onto serving plate. Serve warm, at room temperature, or chilled.

ASPARAGUS FRITTATA WITH MINT AND PARMESAN
Serves 4

2 tablespoons olive oil or unsalted butter
1 shallot, minced
1 tablespoon minced fresh mint leaves
2 tablespoons minced fresh parsley leaves
⅓ pound trimmed asparagus, blanched
5 tablespoons grated Parmesan cheese
¼ teaspoon each salt and ground black pepper
6 large eggs, lightly beaten

1. Adjust oven rack to upper-middle position and heat oven to 350 degrees.
2. Heat oil or butter in 10-inch nonstick skillet over medium heat. Swirl skillet to distribute evenly over bottom and sides. Add shallot; sauté until softened, 3 to 4 minutes. Add mint, parsley, and asparagus; toss to coat with oil. Spread in single layer.
3. Meanwhile, stir 3 tablespoons of the cheese, salt, and pepper into eggs.
4. Complete frittata following steps 4, 5, and 6 in Frittata with Cheese and Fresh Herbs, sprinkling remaining 2 tablespoons cheese over frittata before baking.

FETA CHEESE FRITTATA WITH OLIVES AND SUN-DRIED TOMATOES
Serves 4

1 tablespoon olive or sun-dried tomato oil
1 small garlic clove, peeled and flattened
1 tablespoon minced fresh basil leaves or 1 teaspoon crumbled dried leaves
1 tablespoon minced fresh oregano leaves or 1 teaspoon crumbled dried leaves
¼ cup sun-dried tomatoes, packed in oil, chopped coarse
¼ cup cured olives, pitted and minced
⅓ cup crumbled feta cheese
¼ teaspoon ground black pepper
6 large eggs, lightly beaten

1. Adjust oven rack to upper-middle position and heat oven to 350 degrees.
2. Heat oil and garlic in 10-inch nonstick skillet over medium heat. Remove garlic from skillet as it begins to color. Swirl skillet to distribute oil evenly over bottom and sides. Add herbs, tomatoes, and olives; stir to coat with oil. Spread in single layer.
3. Meanwhile, stir cheese and pepper into eggs.
4. Complete frittata following steps 4, 5, and 6 in Frittata with Cheese and Fresh Herbs.

FRITTATA WITH LEEK AND POTATOES
Serves 4

2 tablespoons olive oil or unsalted butter
1 large leek, white part only, rinsed and sliced thin
2 medium red potatoes (8 ounces), boiled and cut into medium dice
2 tablespoons minced fresh parsley leaves
⅓ cup shredded Emmenthaler cheese
¼ teaspoon each salt and ground black pepper
6 large eggs, lightly beaten

1. Adjust oven rack to upper-middle position and heat oven to 350 degrees.
2. Heat oil or butter in 10-inch nonstick skillet over medium heat. Swirl skillet to distribute evenly over bottom and sides. Add leek; sauté until softened, 5 to 6 minutes. Add potatoes and parsley; toss to coat with oil.
3. Meanwhile, stir cheese, salt, and pepper into eggs.
4. Complete frittata following steps 4, 5, and 6 in Frittata with Cheese and Fresh Herbs. ∎

Diana Shaw is the author of several cookbooks, her most recent being *Almost Vegetarian* (Clarkson Potter, 1995).

SETTING EGGS FOR A FRITTATA

1. Pour the egg mixture into the nonstick skillet and stir lightly with a fork until it starts to set.

2. Once the bottom of the eggs is firm, use a thin, nonmetallic spatula to push the frittata back so the uncooked egg runs underneath.

ILLUSTRATIONS BY WENDY WRAY

Food Processor Sausage

Sausage expert Bruce Aidells shares his secrets for making high-quality sausage without fancy equipment.

≈ BY JACK BISHOP ≈

Making sausage at home doesn't have to be tedious or require a huge investment in equipment. While a meat grinder, sausage stuffer, and other specialized equipment are necessary for making sausage in large quantities, you can make small quantities without these expensive items. In fact, Italian and Polish grandmothers have been doing it this way for centuries.

Bruce Aidells, owner of Aidells Sausage Company in San Francisco, coauthor with Denis Kelly of *Hot Links and Country Flavors* (Knopf, 1990) and *Flying Sausages* (Chronicle, 1995), and arguably the country's leading expert on the subject, says a food processor (a modern convenience that's a lot faster than knife chopping) can do the grinding and a pastry bag can be used to fill casings if you want to form links. If filling links seems like too much work, you can season the ground meat and then form it into patties or just divide it into small bulk packets and freeze it for later use.

Bruce Aidells started his San Francisco sausage company as a lark, supplying local chefs. Today his sausages are sold nationwide.

Great Taste, Less Fat
In addition to equipment issues, many home cooks are concerned about the fat content in sausage. Aidells says the commercial Italian sausage in supermarkets, made with pork, typically has about 30 percent fat. His chicken links have just 15 percent fat.

The most important key to successful sausage making, according to Aidells, is moisture. "I think juiciness in sausage is an admirable, if not necessary characteristic," he notes. When making chicken sausage, juiciness is a result of the cut (breast meat is way too dry, so Aidells only uses the thigh) and the grinding. "Coarse-textured sausage has a better mouth feel since larger pieces of meat are more likely to hold their moisture, and moisture translates into juiciness," he adds. For this reason, special care must be taken when grinding meat for all sausage, and especially for lower-fat chicken sausage.

Aidells bones the thighs himself and separates the skin from the meat. The meat is chopped into rough one-inch chunks and frozen for fifteen minutes, as is the skin. He then pulses the meat in a food processor in small batches until it is roughly ground. The particles should be about three-eighths of an inch in size. The skin is pulsed separately and should be fairly smooth, although small particles can still remain.

Another key to good texture, then, is cold temperatures. Freezing the meat keeps it cold during grinding and firms up the texture so that the food processor blade can cut it more evenly. Excessive mixing of the ground meat and seasonings can warm up the mixture and cause safety as well as quality concerns. "The meat must be kept cold at all times," warns Aidells. "You can't start a batch and then not finish it." Once the meat warms up, bacteria can multiply, and the ability of the meat to hold moisture decreases. After the food processing, Aidells mixes the meat, fat, and seasonings by hand and makes sure that some particle definition remains. It's essential to work quickly.

Cooking the Right Way
You can use homemade chicken sausage in pasta sauces, soups, rice dishes, stuffings, or whatever you like. As for links, Aidells has a few cooking tips that will ensure maximum juiciness. "I'm totally against pricking, especially during grilling. Chicken sausage has so little fat and moisture that you want to keep it all in." Before grilling, Aidells slides his links into a pot of boiling water, removes the pot from the heat, and covers it for about ten minutes. He then finishes these partially cooked links on a grill, preferably with the cover on to keep the flames down. When cooking on top of the stove, add a little water to prevent the links from sticking, but keep the water to a minimum.

CHICKEN SAUSAGE WITH APPLES AND SAGE
Makes seven or eight ½-pound packages or twenty 5-inch links

You can serve this all-American country breakfast sausage with eggs or pancakes. However, it's just as appropriate as a flavoring for bean or rice dishes or as part of a poultry stuffing.

- 1 cup apple cider
- 4½ pounds chicken thighs with bones and skin
- 3 ounces dried apples, chopped fine
- 2 teaspoons kosher or 1 teaspoon table salt
- 2 teaspoons each ground black pepper and dried sage
- ⅛ teaspoon each ground cinnamon and ground nutmeg
- ¼ teaspoon ground ginger

1. Boil down cider in nonreactive saucepan almost to syrup, 2 to 3 tablespoons. Let cool and set aside.

2. Bone and grind chicken, grinding skin separately (*see* illustrations 1 through 6).

3. Combine cider, chicken, skin, and remaining ingredients in large bowl. Blend thoroughly but gently with hands. (Don't overmix, or the fat will melt. There should be some particle definition when done.) Fry a small patty until done. Taste and adjust seasonings.

4. Divide sausage into ½-pound portions, wrap tightly in plastic or aluminum foil, and refrigerate or freeze for later use. Or, stuff sausage into casings that have been thoroughly flushed with cold running water or soaked for ½ hour; make smaller links if desired (illustrations 7 through 11). Sausage can be refrigerated 2 days or frozen several months.

CHICKEN SAUSAGE WITH MEDITERRANEAN FLAVORS
Makes seven or eight ½-pound packages or twenty 5-inch links

This aromatic sausage is not overly spicy but has plenty of flavor. It is particularly good with lentils, greens, seafood soups, or pasta dishes.

- 2 tablespoons olive oil
- 2 medium onions, sliced
- 4½ pounds chicken thighs with bones and skin
- 1 tablespoon tomato paste
- 4 large garlic cloves, minced
- 2 tablespoons paprika
- 2 teaspoons fennel seed, ground coarse

2 teaspoons kosher or 1 teaspoon
  table salt
2 teaspoons each ground cumin, ground
  coriander, and ground black pepper
1 teaspoon ground turmeric
1 teaspoon sugar
½ teaspoon each ground allspice and
  cayenne pepper
2 teaspoons minced zest and
  1 tablespoon juice from 1 large
  lemon
¼ cup minced fresh parsley leaves

2 tablespoons minced fresh mint leaves
  or 2 teaspoons dried

1. Heat oil in medium skillet over medium heat. Add onions; sauté until soft but not colored, about 7 minutes. Transfer to food processor fitted with the steel blade; pulse until onions are ground coarse. Set aside.

2. Bone and grind chicken, grinding skin separately (*see* illustrations 1 through 6).

3. Combine onions, chicken, skin, and remaining ingredients in large bowl. Blend thoroughly

but gently with hands. (Don't overmix, or the fat will melt. There should be some particle definition when done.) Fry a small patty until done. Taste and adjust seasonings.

4. Divide sausage into ½-pound portions, wrap tightly in plastic or aluminum foil, and refrigerate or freeze for later use. Or, stuff sausage into casings that have been thoroughly flushed with cold running water or soaked for ½ hour; make smaller links if desired (illustrations 7 through 11). Sausage can be refrigerated 2 days or frozen several months. ∎

STEPS FOR MAKING CHICKEN SAUSAGE

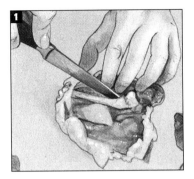

1. Remove the skin from the chicken thighs and set it aside. Cut along the bone with a small, sharp knife to expose it.

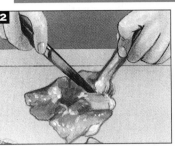

2. After loosening the meat from one end, lift the bone up so that it is perpendicular to the thigh and continue to cut the meat away from the bone. (The boned meat should weigh about 3½ pounds.)

3. Dice the meat into 1-inch pieces.

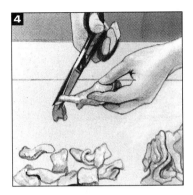

4. Snip the skin into 1-inch pieces. Freeze the skin and meat for 15 minutes.

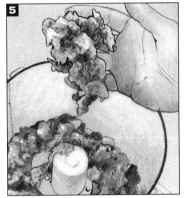

5. Process the meat in 1-pound batches into ⅜-inch pieces. Do not overprocess the meat into a slurry.

6. Process the skin into ⅛-inch pieces. (The fat should be fairly smooth.) Pick through and discard any large pieces.

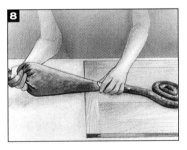

7. Place the sausage mixture in a large pastry bag. Pull about 2½ feet of well-rinsed casing completely over the end of the bag, leaving 3 inches dangling. Knot the dangling end closed.

8. Squeeze the pastry bag to push the meat into all but the last 3 or 4 inches of the casing. While doing this, use your fingers to make sure that the unfilled casing stays on the bag. Twist the open end of the casing closed.

9. Beginning at the knotted end, pinch the casing between your thumb and forefinger at 5 inches (or desired link length). Move down 5 inches more (a total of 10 inches from the knotted end) and pinch again with the thumb and forefinger of the other hand to form a second link. Repeat the pinching along the length of the casing.

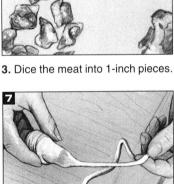

10. In the pinched areas, tie a knot at each of the two sausage ends with extra casing.

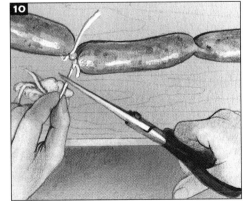

11. Use a clean hat pin or open safety pin to pierce the links and get rid of any air bubbles. Cut through the middle of each pinched casing, leaving a knot with each link.

Quick Homemade Chicken Soup

A broth developed from an Edna Lewis recipe makes full-flavored chicken noodle soup possible in less than ninety minutes.

⁓ BY PAM ANDERSON WITH KAREN TACK ⁓

We've always made good vegetable soup—but unfortunately, it was often the product of a failed chicken soup. We would start off by adding a standard homemade chicken broth to sautéed celery, carrots, and onions. To the simmering broth and vegetables we would add some diced chicken and rice or noodles. The resulting chicken soup was so weak and characterless that we invariably added a can of tomatoes, a few potatoes, a turnip or two, and a package of green peas or mixed vegetables. It took all that to make the soup finally taste satisfying. Thus chicken soup became vegetable soup.

And, when making broth, it always bothered us to strain out and throw away all that celery, carrot, and onion, only to turn around and chop more of the same for the soup. Maybe we wouldn't have minded if the soup had tasted rich and hearty. But it didn't. No matter whose stock or broth recipe we tried, the resulting soup was unsatisfying.

The problem, obviously, was the broth. So when we set out to make a really good chicken soup, we knew we needed to begin with the broth. Since we also knew that standard chicken stocks or broths weren't flavorful enough for the robust chicken soup we wanted, we focused on more offbeat methods to see if somehow we couldn't develop an easy-to-make broth that tasted so good, you'd long to be sick.

When we set out to test a dish, it's not unusual for us to try it thirty or forty times before we're satisfied with the results. Chicken soup was different. After making only four broths, we knew we had a winner.

A Few Good Broths

We started with a Chinese recipe that we found in Bruce Cost's *Asian Ingredients* (Morrow, 1988). This rich, clear broth is made by blanching a whole chicken (blanching keeps it from releasing foam during cooking). The blanched chicken is then partially covered with water and placed in a heatproof bowl over a pan of simmering water for four hours. Cooked this way, the chicken never simmered, and the resulting broth was remarkably clear, refined, and full-flavored. This very special broth was perfect for floating dumplings or blanched vegetables, but too fine a base for a hearty main-course soup. We also noted that our four-pound chicken was good for nothing but the compost heap after being cooked so long. Only special occasions warrant this kind of sacrifice.

A number of recipes promoted roasting chicken bones with the celery, carrot, and onion for a rich, full-flavored stock. We gave it a try, roasting three pounds of chicken backs, necks, and bones for twenty minutes in a 400-degree oven. We added one small carrot, one medium onion, and a small piece of celery to the pan and roasted forty minutes longer before adding water and simmering for an hour. The resulting stock was dark in color and had a nice, roasted-chicken and caramelized-onion flavor, but it still wasn't the full-flavored stock we were looking for.

James Beard believed gizzards make especially good stock. Following his directions, we made a stock of two and one-fourth pounds of chicken backs and wings and three-fourths of a pound of gizzards. The resulting stock was acceptable, but all the stocks made to this point turned out to be weak cousins compared to the one we were about to experience.

Liquid Gold

The winning broth recipe came from Edna Lewis's *In Pursuit of Flavor* (Knopf, 1988) and was different from any we'd ever seen. The method was so fast and simple that we were a bit skeptical at first. From our experience, offbeat methods are fun to try but rarely yield spectacular results. Her broth proved the exception.

Rather than simmering chicken bones, aromatic vegetables, and herbs for hours, Lewis's recipe called for sautéing a chicken, hacked into small pieces, with an onion until the chicken lost its raw color. The pot was then covered and the chicken and onion cooked over low heat until they released their rich, flavorful juices, fifteen to twenty minutes. Only at that point was water added, and the broth was simmered for

MAKING CHICKEN STOCK AND BROTH

The terms chicken broth and stock appear to have become synonymous. Most recipes you see these days call for chicken stock or low-sodium canned chicken broth. Although the broths and stocks share common ingredients—chicken, onions, carrots, celery, and a bouquet garni (thyme, bay leaf, parsley)—the similarities end there.

Broth is made with a whole chicken or chicken parts and simmered until the chicken is done. The chicken is pulled from the pot and used in soup or salad. Stock, on the other hand, is made from the bird's bones, which are simmered until they're completely spent, having given every ounce of their flavor to the liquid.

You can easily use the Master Recipe for Hearty Chicken Noodle Soup (see page 15) to make a quick, full-flavored chicken broth for another use. To do so, simply set aside the chicken breast, then follow the recipe through the end of step 1, ignoring references to the breast. At the end of step 1, strain and discard the solids, and the broth is ready to use. You will have a scant two quarts of rich broth.

The recipe can also be adapted to make chicken stock. To do so, simply follow the instructions above for making broth, but substitute four pounds of chicken backs for the three pounds of whole legs.

The problem with this, however, is that chicken backs are difficult to come by these days.

The chicken parts sold in most supermarkets, as well as boneless cuts such as breasts and thighs, are separated and boned by suppliers and packagers long before they arrive at the market's refrigerated meat cases. We surveyed eight retail supermarkets in the Boston area, and found that only one sells chicken backs and necks on a regular basis. The meat manager at a second market expressed a willingness to special-order backs for us—but only in frozen, forty-pound blocks. The meat manager at a third, decidedly upscale market said that they occasionally bone out chicken breasts themselves for ready-to-cook specialty preparations, and that he would sell the resultant bones to us. However, he made it clear that this would be an extra benefit from an occasional undertaking. Virtually all of the other retail poultry sellers we contacted said that they could not get chicken backs or bones, even in relatively small quantities.

just twenty minutes longer.

We knew we were onto something as we smelled the chicken and onions sautéing, and the finished broth confirmed what our noses had detected. The broth tasted pleasantly sautéed, not boiled. We had some refining to do, though. For once, we had made too strong a broth; this one had almost demi-glacé intensity. And like Cost's recipe, this broth required a whole chicken's life, its meat worthless after cooking.

For our final broth, we followed Lewis's technique but substituted chicken backs and wing tips for the whole chicken and increased the water from three cups to two quarts. The broth was obviously less intense, but just the right strength to make a base for some of the best chicken soup we've ever tasted. We made the stock twice more—once without the onion and once with onion, celery, and carrot. The onion added a flavor dimension we liked; the extra vegetables neither added nor detracted from the final soup, so we left them out.

Where to Get the Goods

So how do you come up with useless chicken parts for this stock? The Buffalo chicken wing fad has made wings more expensive than legs and thighs. Some cooks freeze chicken bones as they get them, but unless you're careful about wrapping and marking freezer packages, you may find yourself with an unidentifiable, unusable bag of freezer-burned bones in six months. We came up with three alternatives.

For those who can buy chicken backs, this is clearly an inexpensive way to make stock for soup. Our local grocery store usually sells them for almost nothing, but in many locations they may be difficult to get (see "Making Chicken Stock and Broth," page 14).

But there are other ways to get chicken bones for stock. Rather than freeze chicken bones as we acquire them, we often cook them right away. For example, we rarely roast a whole chicken; we usually remove the backbone and butterfly it. Opening the chicken up this way allows the chicken to cook quicker and more evenly than one roasted whole (see "The Secrets of Butterflied Chicken," September/October 1994). So from most chickens, we end up with a back, a neck, wing tips, and giblets. Once we've removed the chicken's back, we add it to the pot of giblets and make a quick quart of stock while we're cooking the chicken. You can make a small pot of soup from this amount. Or you can freeze it—stock is much easier to freeze than bones.

We also found that relatively inexpensive whole legs make incredibly full-flavored broths for soup. In a side-by-side comparison of stock made from backs and broth made from whole legs, we found the whole leg broth was actually more full-flavored than the all-bone stock. For the less frugal, broth made from legs and thighs is, in fact, superior; just don't try to salvage the meat. After five minutes of sautéing, twenty minutes of sweating, and another twenty minutes of simmering, the meat is void of flavor.

Our third method was actually our favorite for

those who want to make a pot of soup. Like Lewis's method, it requires a whole chicken. But rather than using the whole chicken for the broth, we removed the breast and reserved it for the final soup. The rest of the bird—the legs, back, wings, and giblets—are tossed into the stock pot. We particularly liked the tidiness of this method: one chicken yields one pot of soup.

Hack It Up

Cutting the chicken into small pieces is actually the most difficult part of making this soup. A meat cleaver, a heavy-duty chef's knife, or a pair of heavy-duty kitchen shears makes the task fairly simple. Cutting up the chicken for broth doesn't require precision. The point is to get the pieces small enough to release their flavorful juices in a short period of time.

To cut up a whole chicken, start by removing the whole legs and wings from the body; set them aside. Separate the back from the breast, then split the breast and set the halves aside. Hack the back crosswise into three or four pieces, then halve each of these pieces. Cut the wing at each joint to yield three pieces. Leave the wing tip whole, then halve each of the remaining joints. Because of the larger bones, the legs and thighs are most difficult to cut. Start by splitting the leg and thigh at the joint, then hack each to yield three to four pieces.

MASTER RECIPE FOR HEARTY CHICKEN NOODLE SOUP
Makes about 3 quarts, serving 6 to 8

- 1 tablespoon vegetable oil
- 1 whole chicken (about 4 pounds), breast removed, split, and reserved; remaining chicken cut into 2-inch pieces
- 2 medium onions, cut into medium dice
- 2 quarts boiling water
     Salt
- 2 bay leaves
- 1 large carrot, peeled and sliced ¼-inch thick
- 1 celery stalk, sliced ¼-inch thick
- ½ teaspoon dried thyme leaves
- 2 cups (3 ounces) hearty, wide egg noodles
- ¼ cup minced fresh parsley leaves
     Ground black pepper

1. Heat oil in large soup kettle. When oil shimmers and starts to smoke, add chicken breast halves; sauté until brown on both sides, about 5 minutes. Remove and set aside. Add half of chopped onions to kettle; sauté until colored and softened slightly, 2 to 3 minutes. Transfer to medium bowl; set aside. Add half of chicken pieces; sauté until no longer pink, 4 to 5 minutes. Transfer to bowl with onions. Sauté remaining chicken pieces. Return onions and chicken pieces (excluding breasts) to kettle. Reduce heat to low, cover, and simmer until chicken releases its juices, about 20 minutes. Increase heat to high; add boiling water along with both breast halves, 2 teaspoons salt, and bay leaves. Return to sim-

mer, then cover and barely simmer until chicken breasts are cooked and broth is rich and flavorful, about 20 minutes.

2. Remove chicken breasts from kettle; set aside. When cool enough to handle, remove skin from breasts, then remove meat from bones and shred into bite-size pieces; discard skin and bone. Strain broth; discard bones. Skim fat from broth, reserving 2 tablespoons. (Broth and meat can be covered and refrigerated up to 2 days.)

3. Return soup kettle to medium-high heat. Add reserved chicken fat. Add remaining onions, along with carrot and celery; sauté until softened, about 5 minutes. Add thyme, along with broth and chicken; simmer until vegetables are tender and flavors meld, 10 to 15 minutes. Add noodles and cook until just tender, about 5 minutes. Adjust seasonings, stir in parsley, and serve.

HEARTY CHICKEN SOUP WITH ORZO AND SPRING VEGETABLES
Serves 6 to 8

Follow steps 1 and 2 of Master Recipe for Hearty Chicken Noodle Soup. In step 3, substitute 1 medium leek, rinsed thoroughly, quartered lengthwise, then sliced thin crosswise, for one onion. Substitute ½ cup orzo for egg noodles. Along with orzo, add ¼ pound trimmed asparagus, cut into 1-inch lengths, and ¼ cup fresh or frozen peas. Substitute 2 tablespoons minced fresh tarragon leaves for parsley.

HEARTY CHICKEN SOUP WITH SHELLS, TOMATOES, AND ZUCCHINI
Serves 6 to 8

Follow steps 1 and 2 of Master Recipe for Hearty Chicken Noodle Soup. In step 3, add 1 medium zucchini, cut into medium dice, to sautéing onions, carrots, and celery. Increase sauté time from 5 to 7 minutes. Add ½ cup chopped tomatoes (fresh or canned) along with broth to kettle. Substitute 1 cup small shells or macaroni for egg noodles and simmer until noodles are cooked. Substitute an equal portion of fresh basil for parsley. Serve with grated Parmesan, if you like.

HEARTY CHICKEN SOUP WITH LEEKS, WILD RICE, AND MUSHROOMS
Serves 6 to 8

Follow steps 1 and 2 of Master Recipe for Hearty Chicken Noodle Soup. While broth is simmering, cook ½ cup wild rice, following package instructions. Use 1 cup hot chicken broth to rehydrate ½ ounce dried wild mushrooms, about 30 minutes. In step 3, substitute 1 leek, rinsed thoroughly, quartered lengthwise, then sliced thin crosswise, for one onion and omit celery. When leek and carrot have softened (about 5 minutes), add ¼ pound sliced mushrooms (domestic or wild); continue to sauté until mushrooms are softened, about 5 minutes longer. Drain and chop dried wild mushrooms; reserve soaking broth. Pour soaking broth through strainer lined with coffee filter to remove grit. Add this liquid and dried mushrooms, along with chicken broth, to kettle. Simmer according to Master Recipe, stirring in cooked rice during last 5 minutes of cooking. ∎

Simple Chocolate Decorations

Chocolate decorations give cakes and other desserts an especially professional and attractive appearance. It often seems, however, that these decorations are too difficult for most home cooks to master. No longer. Chocolate expert Alice Medrich, author of *Cocolat: Extraordinary Chocolate Desserts* (Warner Books, 1990) and *Chocolate and the Art of Low-Fat Desserts* (Warner Books, 1994), has devised these simple methods of creating chocolate decorations. ■

FINE CHOCOLATE SHAVINGS

It takes less than three-quarters of an ounce of chocolate to coat the side of an eight- or nine-inch cake, and a fraction of that to decorate just the bottom edge of a cake. Shavings may be used on both refrigerated and room-temperature desserts.

1. Hold a sharp paring knife against the flat side of a bar of chocolate at a 45-degree angle and scrape toward you, anchoring the bar with your other hand.

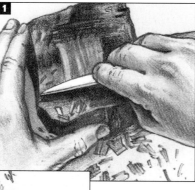

2. Transfer the shavings to a plate by sliding a metal frosting spatula (or pancake turner) under them. Do not pick them up with your hands, as they will melt almost instantly.

3. To apply, hold the dessert over the plate of chocolate shavings. Using the spatula, lift the shavings and gently touch them to the moist or sticky side of the dessert, letting the rest fall back onto the plate. Continue until you achieve the desired effect.

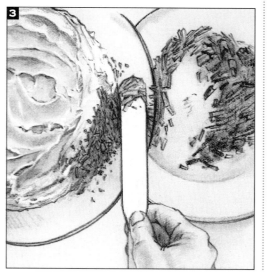

THICK CHOCOLATE SHAVINGS

Milk chocolate and white chocolate are softer than dark, so they yield larger shavings with less warming.

1. Warm a bar of chocolate in one of these ways: letting it sit in a warm kitchen; rubbing it with the heel of your hand; setting it briefly under a desk lamp; or sweeping it with a hairdryer (shown here), taking care not to melt the chocolate.

2. Hold a knife blade at a 45-degree angle to the chocolate and scrape toward you, anchoring the bar with your other hand. This action yields thick, sturdy shavings.

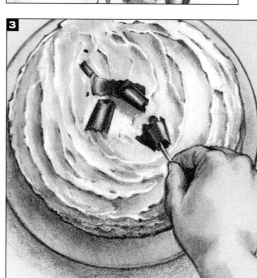

3. Pick up the shavings with a toothpick and transfer them to the dessert.

ILLUSTRATIONS BY JUDY LOVE

CHOCOLATE SHARDS

Ultrathin pieces mean a little goes a long way. But these tiny pieces will melt at room temperature, so use them only on desserts that will be served immediately or kept refrigerated until serving time.

Before you begin, microwave chopped chocolate on medium (50 percent) power or melt it in a water bath or double boiler, stirring frequently until it is completely melted and smooth.

1. Using a spatula, spread the melted chocolate on a sheet of waxed paper.

2. Cover the chocolate with another sheet of waxed paper; spread it with a rolling pin until very thin. Refrigerate it for at least 1 hour or until needed.

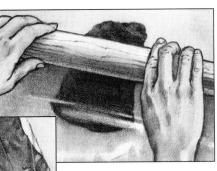

3. Remove the chocolate from the refrigerator and peel away the top sheet of waxed paper. Slide a thin spatula under the chocolate and break it into irregular pieces.

CHOCOLATE SPLINTERS

This technique yields long, narrow shapes with a little curve to them instead of flat shards. Use as an alternative to chopped or shaved chocolate.

1. Melt chopped chocolate, as you would for shards. Tear off several square sheets of plastic wrap. Use a small spatula to spread a 2½-inch-wide band of melted chocolate, slightly thicker than paper thin, down the center of a sheet of plastic wrap. It is not necessary to spread very neatly or to the exact width.

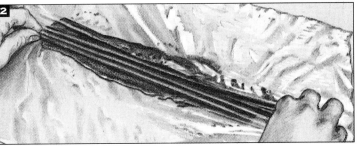

2. Use the fingers of both hands to pinch and gather the plastic on both sides of the chocolate into tiny pleats so the chocolate-coated plastic becomes pleated as well. The chocolate pleats can touch one another. Continue to spread and pleat more sheets as desired, then refrigerate them for at least 1 hour.

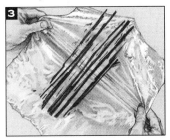

3. Remove and pull the pleated plastic flat. Splinters will pop up and off the plastic. If they stick or melt, refrigerate the remaining plastic sheets longer, or freeze them to speed up the process.

CHOCOLATE CURLS

To simplify the challenging and time-consuming traditional method of making chocolate cigarettes or curls, Medrich has created a chocolate mixture that is simple to make and easy to work with. To make the mixture, place six ounces of finely chopped semisweet or bittersweet chocolate (not chocolate chips) and one tablespoon of vegetable shortening in a small heatproof bowl. Set the bowl in a pan of barely simmering water and stir constantly until the mixture is melted and smooth.

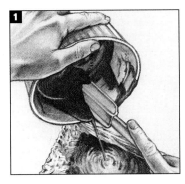

1. Line a 5¾-inch by 3½-inch loaf pan with plastic wrap. Scrape the chocolate mixture into the pan and chill it for at least 2 hours, or until it is firm.

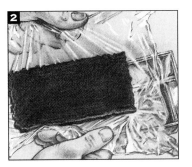

2. Remove the chocolate from the refrigerator and lift the plastic to remove the chocolate from the pan. Let it stand at room temperature for 10 to 15 minutes to soften the chocolate slightly.

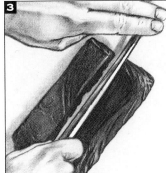

3. Cut the chocolate lengthwise to form two long bars no wider than the length of the cutting blade of a vegetable peeler.

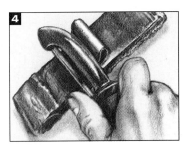

4. Scrape the chocolate firmly with the peeler to make curls and cigarette shapes. If the curls splinter or crack, the chocolate is too cold; wait a few more minutes and try again. If the chocolate becomes too soft, put it back in the refrigerator to harden. Handle the curls with a toothpick to avoid fingerprints.

Note: Wrapped tightly or placed in an airtight container, curls and unused chocolate can be stored indefinitely in the refrigerator or freezer.

Throw Out Your Wok!

The most important rule for stir-frying at home is this: Don't use a wok. Woks aren't designed for a flat stovetop and provide less heat than a large skillet.

∼ BY CHRISTOPHER KIMBALL ∼

The summer before college I spent three months in a Land Rover driving from London to Nairobi, over ten thousand miles of potholes and the famous English rock-hard suspension (the joke was that if you ran over a penny with a Land Rover, you could feel whether it was tails up or down). The most memorable part of the trip was the drive through the Sahara Desert, especially the six-hundred-mile trek to Agadez, which was devoid of human life except for a small military outpost that consisted of one small building and half a dozen very hot, unhappy soldiers. On the second day out, we stopped for lunch and a siesta—we never drove during midday—in a canyon where the thermometer registered just over 120 degrees. I thought that New York City in July was hot, but this was transcendent heat, heat that could make an American teenager immobile and speechless for hours.

The difference between an ordinary hot day and that canyon in Niger is the difference between home wok cooking and the real thing. To stir-fry properly you need plenty of shimmering, intense heat; enough to caramelize sugars, deepen flavors, and evaporate unnecessary juices. The problem is that a wok married to a home stovetop is a lousy partnership, one that provides, at best, moderate heat.

Why Are Woks Shaped Like Woks?

Woks are conical because in China they traditionally sat on cylindrical pits containing the fire. Food was cut into small pieces to shorten cooking time, thus conserving fuel. Only one cooking utensil was required for many different methods including sautéing (stir-frying), steaming, boiling, and deep frying.

Unfortunately, what is practical in China makes no sense in America. Simply put, woks don't work for American home cooks. A wok was not designed for stovetop cooking, where the heat comes only from the bottom; the bottom of the wok gets very hot, and the sides get only very warm. A horizontal heat source requires a horizontal pan. Therefore, if you want to stir-fry at home, consign your wok to the basement and use a large skillet or Dutch oven, twelve to fourteen inches in diameter.

The other dirty little secret of stir-frying at home is that, even with a skillet, you don't have enough heat to quickly sear and cook either large amounts or large pieces of food. This completely changes the home cook's approach. You simply don't have enough horsepower to stir-fry as they

do in China or in restaurant kitchens in the United States. (In restaurants, woks fit into a special gas-fired burner unit that provides a tremendous amount of heat from all sides—I've seen a wok go from room temperature to being hot enough to vaporize cooking oil in under thirty seconds.)

This leaves the home cook with two options. You can blanch (cook briefly in boiling water until barely tender) the denser vegetables, such as carrots, snow peas, asparagus, green beans, broccoli, and cauliflower, ahead of time so that they require almost no cooking in the wok. I tested this method and found that while it did work, it was cumbersome. I think a stir-fry should be an easy, last-minute cooking method. For that reason, I simply chop the vegetables into smaller pieces so they will cook quickly. This is the approach I follow in the Master Recipe for Stir-Fry on page 20.

You also need to cook relatively small amounts of food at one time—too much volume will draw down the heat of the pan, and you will end up with stewed meat and vegetables. In addition, to cook each vegetable to its proper degree of doneness, I suggest that you add vegetables in batches (see illustrations 3 through 5, page 19). Onions, carrots, and cauliflower require a good deal of cooking and should be added first. Fresh herbs, scallions, tomato wedges, and tender greens should be added at the end of cooking. All other vegetables are added in between.

Meat, fish, and tofu should also be cut into bite-size pieces for quick cooking. To make cutting beef or chicken easier, freeze it for an hour or two. The slightly frozen texture is perfect for slicing, cubing, or dicing. If the meat is already frozen, transfer it from the freezer to the refrigerator in the morning; by evening the not-quite-thawed texture should be perfect (the exact timing depends on the size of the cut).

Testing the Theories

To test my own and other theories about stir-frying, I visited Mindy Schreil in her home in Marin County, just north of San Francisco. Mindy was first hired as a line cook at China Moon (a well-known eatery near Union Square in San Francisco, the brainchild of Barbara Tropp) and graduated to sous-chef a few years later. She and I set out to cook three different stir-fries: one with beef, one with sea bass, and one with cubes of firm tofu. We started off with a few basic premises. We used a fourteen-inch nonstick skillet instead of a wok (a twelve-inch skillet will also work well), divided the vegetables into two or three batches depending on the particular recipes

(see "Batching Vegetables for Stir-Fry," page 20, for specific sizes), and cut the vegetables into very small pieces without any precooking.

We tested the beef stir-fry first. The meat took just under one minute to cook—you should cook meat only about three-quarters done and then remove it from the pan, since carryover cooking will finish it up. However, the pan was not properly preheated and the beef did not sear properly. When the heat is high enough, it will sear the meat deeply, a process that adds a tremendous flavor to the rest of the stir-fry ingredients as you cook. Despite this failure we forged on, adding the onions and carrots plus about a teaspoon of oil. These cooked for about four minutes. Then we added the rest of the vegetables—broccoli and peppers—plus another teaspoon of oil. After three more minutes we cleared out a space in the center of the pan and added the garlic and ginger. We sprinkled a little more oil on top and then mashed the garlic and ginger mixture down into the pan using a metal spatula. After just ten seconds we took the pan off the stove, reduced the heat to medium, waited about thirty seconds, and then replaced the pan on the burner. The timing is important here—you want to cook the garlic and ginger, but you want to avoid burning them. The garlic is then stirred into the vegetables, and the meat is added back to the pan along with the sauce. Everything is cooked another thirty seconds, and the dish is finished.

The resulting stir-fry was good but lacking in flavor. The pan was simply not hot enough. Hence we came across the first and most important rule of stir-frying: The pan must be hot, real hot. The food should sizzle, steam, and smoke. I suggest heating the pan for about four minutes over high heat. To find out whether the pan is hot enough, place your outstretched hand about one inch above the pan's surface. If you can hold it there no more than three seconds because of the heat, the pan is ready for stir-frying. At this point you should add the oil, then wait to add the meat and/or vegetables until the oil starts to shimmer and smoke. As Mindy pointed out, stir-frying is a delicate balance between cooking and burning—you really have to live on the edge to develop the right textures and flavors.

With the stir-fry of sea bass, we made sure the pan got good and hot—the oil was just starting to smoke before we added the cubes of fish. These cooked in about twenty seconds. We then let the pan come back up to temperature and added a bit more oil along with the onion and cauliflower. They sizzled when they hit the pan, and the pan

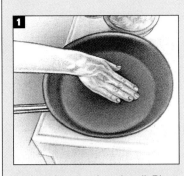

1. Heat the pan, then the oil. Place your hand two inches above the surface of the pan; when you can keep it there only two seconds, the oil is ready.

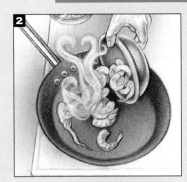

2. Add the meat, seafood, or tofu and cook until about three-quarters done, then remove from the pan.

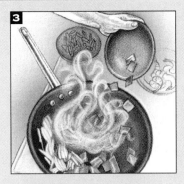

3. After the pan comes back to heat, add additional oil and the longer-cooking vegetables and stir-fry.

4. Add additional oil and the remaining vegetables (in two batches if necessary), stir together, and stir-fry.

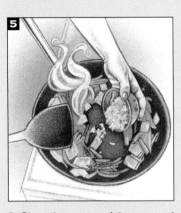

5. Clear the center of the pan and add the garlic, ginger, and scallions. Drizzle with oil, cook for 10 seconds, remove from heat, and stir into the vegetables.

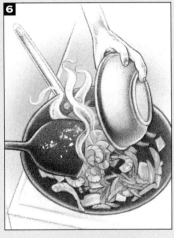

6. Return the pan to heat and add the cooked meat, seafood, or tofu.

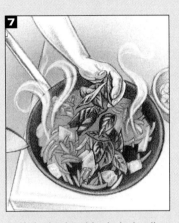

7. If desired, add whole basil or mint leaves, without the stems and stir-fry for 20 seconds or untill leaves wilt.

8. Stir in the sauce and stir-fry to coat all ingredients, then serve at once with rice.

---

smoked and spattered, just as it should. A cook once told me that when you can barely see the food through the smoke and steam, you know the wok is hot enough. We finished up the recipe, using the same method as in the beef stir-fry, and the results were much better. The dish had twice the flavor, thanks to the right amount of heat; the tiny cauliflower florets were browned, for example, which imparted a nutty flavor. Finally, we tried the tofu stir-fry, which was also very good. Keep in mind that tofu needs about two tablespoons of oil to start, otherwise it will stick to the pan. It also requires about two minutes of initial cooking, about twice as long as meat.

Other Conclusions

Through this testing, I came to a few other interesting conclusions. First, most American home cooks use too much meat or seafood. A good stir-fry should be heavy on the vegetables and light on the meat. This is both more authentic—meat is a luxury and is used sparingly in China—and, to my mind, preferable. The vegetables should be at least double the meat or seafood by weight.

Another interesting conclusion is that there is absolutely no reason to use cornstarch or other thickeners. This makes a gloppy sauce, one that is close to my childhood memories of bad suburban Chinese restaurants. Why thicken? The stir-fry is much brighter and cleaner in taste with a purer, thinner sauce. The cornstarch simply gunks it up, muddying the texture and flavor.

Finally, be wary of sugar. A stir-fry should not be sweet. We are used to overly sweet Chinese restaurant food, but this is neither desirable nor authentic. Would you add a tablespoon of sugar to a bowl of fresh, steamed peas? Then why add it to a vegetable stir-fry? A small amount of sweetness can enhance flavor, but I have used a minimal amount in the sauces that follow.

I also confirmed or learned several other valuable lessons:

• Proper vegetable preparation is crucial. Nothing should be bigger than a quarter.

• Because tofu, eggplant, and mushrooms tend to soak up oil, you'll have to use about twice as much oil as normal when using large quantities of these ingredients. Fish has a tendency to stick to the pan, so I suggest adding an extra two teaspoons of oil at the outset of cooking.

• I call for equal amounts of garlic and ginger. However, beef can stand more garlic and fish can stand more ginger. If you like, increase one ingredient by one-half teaspoon and lower the other by the same amount.

• If you prefer a spicy stir-fry, add about one-half teaspoon of hot red pepper flakes or minced hot peppers at the end of cooking and sauté for thirty seconds.

• A great last-minute addition to a stir-fry is a small handful of fresh basil or mint leaves. Just add them whole, without the stems, and stir-fry for twenty seconds or until the leaves are wilted.

• Many home cooks feel compelled to confine themselves to "Chinese" ingredients—broccoli, water chestnuts, sugar snap peas, scallions, etc. There is no reason why you cannot stir-fry virtually any vegetable found in an American supermarket. Tomato wedges, added at the last thirty seconds, are great with beef. Spinach leaves are wonderful added whole (stemmed first) and then cooked until wilted. Peas, fennel, cabbage, butternut squash, and chard are just a few other items that can be successfully stir-fried.

• You can use cooked, leftover meats such as chicken. Just add it to the end of the stir-fry. You can also use ground meats such as beef or pork, cooking them as you would the cubed meat.

• Always let the pan come back up to temperature between batches. This may take up to two minutes, depending on your stovetop and pan.

• I found that aromatics (garlic, chives, ginger)

BATCHING VEGETABLES FOR STIR-FRY

In order to get the maximum heat out of your pan, it is best to divide your vegetables into two or even three batches, depending on the required cooking time. This is not a rigid system—these vegetables are simply listed in the approximate order in which they should be added to the pan.

FIRST BATCH	SECOND BATCH	THIRD BATCH	FOURTH BATCH
Carrots	Asparagus	Cabbage	Fresh Herbs
Cauliflower	Green beans	Celery	(basil, mint)
Onions	Broccoli	Chard	Scallions
Peppers	Butternut Squash	Fennel	Tender Greens
		Mushrooms	Tomatoes
		Peas	
		Sugar Snaps	
		Summer Squash	
		Zucchini	

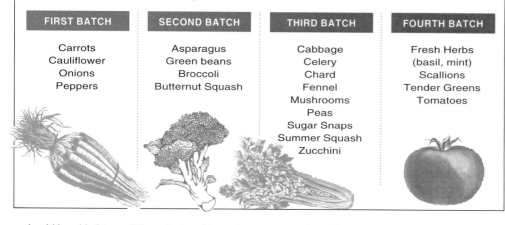

should be added toward the end of cooking rather than at the beginning. Otherwise, these delicate ingredients will burn, ruining your dish. However, onions are always added first so that they have a chance to develop flavor.

Finally, I have tested many different combinations of foods and offer the following suggestions. Beef—flank steak is a good choice—has an affinity with asparagus, mushrooms, chard, and broccoli. Chicken does well with celery and summer squash. Fish—use a firm fish such as swordfish, tuna, sea bass, salmon, or halibut—is great with greens, fennel, celery, peas, and corn and also works nicely with a curry sauce.

MASTER RECIPE FOR STIR-FRY
Serves 4
The secret to good stir-frying is lots of heat, so preheating the pan is crucial. During cooking, there should be lots of smoke, lots of steam, and lots of sizzle. Otherwise, you are braising the food and it will not develop the proper texture or flavor. To give you as much surface area as possible, you should use a large (twelve- to fourteen-inch) nonstick skillet. This recipe can be halved to serve two (if you halve the recipe, the cooking times will decrease) but it cannot be increased, as a home stovetop has insufficient heat to cook greater quantities of vegetables.

Meat , Seafood, or Tofu
  ¾ pound meat, seafood, or tofu cut into small, even-sized pieces and drained
  1 tablespoon soy sauce or tamari
  1 tablespoon dry sherry

Vegetables
  1½ pounds vegetables, cut into small pieces (none bigger than a quarter) and divided into two or three batches (*see* chart above)
  2 tablespoons chopped scallions, white part only
  1 tablespoon minced garlic

  1 tablespoon minced fresh gingerroot
Sauce
  1 recipe flavoring sauce (*see* below)
  2–4 tablespoons canola or peanut oil

1. Toss meat, seafood, or tofu with soy sauce and sherry in medium bowl; set aside. Prepare flavoring sauce. Divide vegetables into two or three batches, following guidelines in chart above.

2. Heat 12- or 14-inch nonstick skillet over high heat, 4 minutes (pan should be so hot, you can hold your outstretched hand 1 inch above its surface for no more than 3 seconds); add 1 tablespoon oil (add 2 tablespoons for tofu or fish) and rotate pan so that bottom is evenly coated. Let oil heat until it just starts to shimmer and smoke. Check heat with hand (*see* illustration 1, page 19). Drain meat, seafood, or tofu, then add to pan and stir-fry until seared and about three-quarters cooked (about 20 seconds for fish, 60 seconds for meat, 2 minutes for tofu, 2½ to 3 minutes for chicken). Spoon cooked meat or seafood into serving dish. Cover and keep warm (illustration 2).

3. Let pan come back up to temperature, 1 or 2 minutes. When hot, drizzle in 2 teaspoons of oil, and when oil just starts to smoke, add vegetables from first category. Stir-fry until vegetables are just tender-crisp, about 2 minutes (illustration 3). Leaving first batch in pan, repeat with remaining vegetables, cooking each set of vegetables until tender-crisp, or for fourth category, wilted (illustrations 4 and 5). Add about a teaspoon of oil for each new batch (amount of oil will depend on skillet you are using—nonstick pans require about a teaspoon; other pans may require 2 teaspoons). Clear center of pan and add garlic, ginger, and scallions. Drizzle with ½ teaspoon of oil. Mash into pan with back of a spatula. Cook for 10 seconds. Remove pan from heat and stir garlic/ginger mixture into vegetables for 20 seconds (illustration 6).

4. Return pan to heat and add cooked meat, seafood, or tofu (illustration 7). Stir in sauce and

stir-fry to coat all ingredients, about 1 minute. Serve immediately with rice (illustration 8).

FLAVORING SAUCES
Each of the following recipes makes enough sauce for one Master Recipe for Stir-Fry.

GINGER SAUCE

  3 tablespoons light soy sauce
  ½ teaspoon sugar
  1 tablespoon dry sherry
  ¼ cup minced fresh gingerroot
  2 scallions, minced
  2 tablespoons chicken stock

Combine all ingredients in small bowl and set aside.

ORANGE SAUCE

  2 teaspoons minced zest and ¼ cup juice from 1 large orange
  ½ teaspoon sugar
  2 tablespoons chicken stock
  1 tablespoon light soy sauce
     Pinch salt

Combine all ingredients in small bowl and set aside.

LEMON SAUCE

  2 teaspoons minced zest and 3 tablespoons juice from 1 large lemon
  1 teaspoon sugar
  2 tablespoons chicken stock
  1 tablespoon light soy sauce
     Pinch salt

Combine all ingredients in small bowl and set aside.

CURRY SAUCE

  3 tablespoons light soy sauce
  ½ teaspoon sugar
  1 tablespoon dry sherry
  2 teaspoons curry powder
  2 scallions, minced
  2 tablespoons chicken stock

Combine all ingredients in small bowl and set aside.

HOT-AND-SOUR SAUCE

  2 tablespoons cider vinegar
  2 teaspoons minced hot chiles
  2 teaspoons sugar
  2 tablespoons chicken stock
  1 tablespoon light soy sauce
     Pinch salt

Combine all ingredients in small bowl and set aside. ■

Magnificent Madeleines

We find the best-tasting recipe for these classic French cake-cookies —and discover how to keep them from sticking to the pan.

～ BY SHARON KEBSCHULL BARRETT ～

B akers tend to argue over the authenticity of their madeleines, each one thinking that theirs is the exact re-creation of the cookie that famously stirred Proust's imagination. What everyone does agree on is that madeleines are small, feather-light, spongy cakes, which are eaten like cookies. They are baked in a special pan with scallop shell indentations (*see* Sources and Resources, page 32) and typically have a hump on the back.

Shortly after I began my search for the perfect madeleine, I gave up on history in favor of taste, texture, and simplicity. What I wanted was a cake-cookie that tasted lightly buttery and eggy, with a hint of vanilla; it also had to barely weigh down my tongue, and it had to be as simple as possible to prepare.

Making Molds Work

The first step in making madeleines is to prepare for the last and most difficult step: getting the cookies out of the pan. I tried coating the forms with plain melted butter, melted butter dusted with flour, and a combination of softened butter and clarified butter, but none of these methods proved absolutely reliable. I then mixed a little melted butter with a dash of flour, and since using that method, not one madeleine has stuck to the pan. It is particularly helpful to coat not only the inside of the molds, but the rims as well.

Releasing the cookies immediately after removing them from the oven also proved crucial. To avoid imprinting lines on your cookies from wire cooling racks, turn the cookies out onto a tea towel, tapping the mold gently on the counter to release them, if needed.

I tested both aluminum and tinned steel molds. Both worked, but the slightly heavier steel produced cookies that fell out exceptionally easily, leaving almost no residue behind. I avoided nonstick molds because of their tendency to overdarken baked goods.

Creating a Cookie to Remember

With the sticking problem solved, I turned to the actual recipe. I made my tests by changing each element in a basic recipe I liked. It called for one-quarter cup of butter, melted; two eggs; one-quarter cup of granulated sugar; one-half teaspoon of vanilla; and one-half cup of all-purpose flour.

First, I experimented with the butter, trying creamed butter rather than melted. But I found it didn't fold in well and bubbled out of the cakes during baking, resulting in a heavy, dense texture. Increasing the butter to one-third of a cup only

changed the crumb slightly, and didn't improve on the original. And the resulting browned butter cookie looked hideous.

Changing the amount of egg did improve the original, however. By substituting two yolks for one of the whole eggs, I had the perfect amount of batter for twelve madeleines and a cookie that rose higher and had a fuller, more eggy flavor. The separated eggs, with the whites whipped stiff, rose higher, but they were no longer delicate. Beating the eggs with both the sugar and flour, rather than folding the flour in, created a very loose batter and a cookie that looked great, but had all the delicacy of rubber.

The biggest surprise came with the flour. For a light texture, I thought using cake flour alone would be the obvious choice. To my surprise, the best cookie, with a light, tight crumb, came from a combination of cake and all-purpose flours.

With that, I was close to my perfect recipe. A few more tests showed that one and one-half teaspoons of vanilla was a tasty but not overwhelming amount. A test with one-quarter teaspoon of baking powder—for those who long for a hump on their cookies—produced an open crumb that doesn't seem worth the hump. (If you're hooked on the hump, I found that refrigerating the batter in the molds for one hour before baking will produce a slight hump.) I still thought the cookies were missing an edge in their flavor, though, and started experimenting with salt. One-half teaspoon in the cookies tasted truly disgusting, and even one-eighth teaspoon was too much. My final recipe calls for a pinch of salt, and I mean it: not a grain more.

While the perfect madeleine proved perfectly pleasant, I was beginning, after nineteen dozen, to long for a flavor variation. So I created some citrus and nut cookies, a chocolate madeleine, and, my favorite, a rosemary version. A day after baking, the madeleines become pleasantly dry without going stale and easily withstand a dunking in tea or coffee. Tightly wrapped, they freeze fantastically well and thaw quickly.

MADELEINES
Makes 12

To coat the molds, mix two teaspoons of melted butter with one teaspoon of all-purpose flour. Brush the molds and rims thoroughly, but not thickly, with this mixture.

 ¼ cup all-purpose flour
 ¼ cup cake flour

  Pinch of coarse salt
 2 egg yolks, plus 1 whole egg
 ¼ cup sugar
 1½ teaspoons vanilla
 4 tablespoons unsalted butter, melted

1. Adjust oven rack to low center position; heat oven to 375 degrees. Sift flours and salt together in small bowl; set aside.

2. Beat yolks with whole egg in bowl of electric mixer until light yellow and fluffy, about 5 minutes on high speed if using hand mixer, about 3 minutes if using heavy-duty mixer. Add sugar and vanilla and beat until a ribbon drops from beaters, about 5 minutes with hand mixer, 3 minutes with heavy-duty mixer. Gently fold in flour mixture, then melted butter.

3. Spoon batter into molds. (Batter should come just flush with mold rim.) Bake until tops are golden and cakes spring back when pressed lightly, about 10 minutes. Turn madeleines onto dry tea towel; cool to room temperature. (Can be stored in airtight container up to 3 days or frozen up to 1 month.)

LEMON OR ORANGE MADELEINES
Follow recipe for Madeleines, beating in 2 teaspoons grated lemon or orange zest with sugar and vanilla.

ROSEMARY MADELEINES
Follow recipe for Madeleines, mixing 1 teaspoon very finely minced fresh rosemary leaves into flour mixture and reducing vanilla from 1½ to 1 teaspoon.

CHOCOLATE MADELEINES
Follow recipe for Madeleines, reducing both all-purpose and cake flours from ¼ cup to 2 tablespoons each. Sift ¼ cup Dutch-processed cocoa with flours and salt, adding 1½ teaspoons instant espresso powder if desired.

ALMOND MADELEINES
Follow recipe for Madeleines, reducing both all-purpose flour and cake flour from ¼ cup to 3 tablespoons each. To flour mixture, stir in ¼ cup very finely ground almonds. Reduce vanilla from 1½ teaspoons to 1 teaspoon and add ¼ teaspoon almond extract. ∎

Sharon Kebschull Barrett is a food writer and baker living in Chapel Hill, North Carolina.

Classic Cream Pies

We investigate each crucial component of these luscious pies—custard filling, prebaked crust, flavoring, and whipped cream topping.

～ BY PAM ANDERSON WITH KAREN TACK ～

Leftover cream pies can be refrigerated and eaten the next day, but they are best eaten the day they are made.

Chocolate, banana, coconut, and butterscotch—everyone has a favorite flavor, but virtually no one can resist the lure of cream pie. Our mission in developing a great cream pie was to explore its four parts—the custard filling, the prebaked crust, the specific flavoring ingredients, and the whipped cream—making sure each was the best it could be.

The filling required the greatest effort since not even great chocolate or a crisp crust can save a pie made with filling that's too stiff, soupy, gummy, or flat. Just what cooking method and thickener would guarantee a substantial, yet velvety filling? What combination of ingredients would deliver a custard filling unobtrusive enough to complement its rich counterparts, yet lush and irresistible on its own?

Developing a filling with great body and flavor was key, but preventing that filling from dampening the crust was just as important. Unlike pumpkin or pecan pie, in which filling and crust bake together, cream pie unites a fully cooked crust with a moist, fluid filling. Was a soggy pie shell inevitable? Some recipes that we consulted said to pour hot filling into the cooked pie shell. Wouldn't steam from the hot filling dampen the crust, we questioned? Others suggested cooling the filling to warm while others required a complete chill, uniting filling with crust shortly before serving. We set out to find which of these recommendations really worked best.

Filling First

After looking at a range of recipes for cream pie filling, we developed a basic vanilla filling consisting of milk, egg yolks, sugar, cornstarch, butter, vanilla flavoring, and a small amount of salt. The first issue we had to decide was the method we would use to prepare the filling. In this department, we had two choices. Some cooks heat the sugar, cornstarch, and milk to a simmer, gradually add enough of this mixture to the yolks to stabilize them, then add the stabilized yolks to the simmering milk. Our other choice was to dump everything (except flavorings and butter) into a saucepan and cook, stirring fairly constantly, until the thickened mixture began to bubble.

We opted for the latter, simpler cooking method, since we had learned from food scientist Shirley Corriher that starch prevents eggs from curdling. According to Corriher, heat causes starch to swell so that it prevents egg protein molecules from coagulating. She cited pastry cream and crème anglaise to prove her point. The formulas are virtually identical, except that pastry cream contains starch (usually flour or cornstarch). Crème anglaise curdles easily; pastry cream does not. So, by cooking the starch and the eggs together from the very start, our filling avoided the curdling problem.

Some of the filling recipes we found were lean, with skim milk and whole eggs; others were extravagant, with heavy cream and yolks. To find out just how rich the filling needed to be, we started by testing the range of milks, making the basic filling with skim milk, 2 percent, whole milk, half-and-half, evaporated milk, and cream.

Since skim milk is more translucent than the other milk choices, the yolks colored the filling a vivid yellow. Rich color, however, did not mean full flavor. The skim milk filling tasted thin and lacked that creamy mouth feel you need from pudding. On the other hand, we liked the fillings made from 2 percent and whole milk, 2 percent offering just enough fat to enrich without masking other flavors, and whole milk offering a slightly fuller flavor.

The fillings enriched with half-and-half and cream proved that richer is not always better. Though pleasant enough, these fillings were too much of a good thing, especially when teamed with a butter-rich crust, a generous mound of whipped cream, and flavoring ingredients such as coconut, bananas, and chocolate.

Evaporated milk, the dark horse in this little series of tests, showed promise. Although we found the filling made with straight evaporated milk too assertive, its rich caramel flavor had potential. We eventually settled on one-half cup of evaporated milk for every two cups of regular milk, which provided a filling with a richer color and a rounder, subtly caramelized flavor than that made with all milk (*see* "What Is Evaporated Milk?" page 24).

Deciding on the number of eggs or yolks we should use in our filling was a fairly simple exercise. The fillings made with whole eggs were grainy and characterless, lacking the smooth, velvety texture and richness of the all-yolk fillings. But an excessive number of yolks turned our pie filling into a pastry cream more appropriate for a tart. We settled on five yolks.

Next we turned to thickeners. We wanted a cream pie filling that was soft and creamy, yet stiff enough to give us a clean cut. Flour yielded a gummy filling and no clean cut. Although a gelatin-thickened pie certainly cut clean, its stiff, rubbery texture did not fulfill our soft-and-creamy requirement. Quick-cooking tapioca contributed its distinctive but unpleasant fish-eye texture while tapioca flour produced a filling with the texture of stewed okra. A combination of flour and cornstarch made a filling that was too soft to cut properly. So, we finally returned to cornstarch for thickness, relying on the egg yolks for softness and creaminess.

At this point our pie filling had the right texture, richness, and creaminess, but it was still totally dependent on extra ingredients like coconut and bananas to make it taste great. Switching from vanilla flavoring to vanilla bean and adding a touch of brandy nudged a mediocre-tasting filling into the realm of greatness.

Strong, Yet Fragile Bonds

To determine how the crust would respond to fillings of various temperatures, we made three pies. The first pie shell contained hot filling straight from the saucepan. The second pie shell held filling that had cooled for thirty minutes. These two pies were refrigerated for three hours. Chilled filling was spooned into the final crust and refrigerated for an hour.

To our surprise, neither the hot nor the warm fillings dampened their shells. However, we preferred using the warm filling for different reasons.

Since the hot filling was more liquid when poured into the crust, it settled in a very compact way. The warm filling, having had a chance to set a bit, mounded when poured into the shell. When cut, the squatter, denser filling from the hot-filled pie tended to fall apart. The warm-filled pie sliced neater, its mounded filling standing peaked and tall.

The chilled filling—the one you might think would work best—turned soupy and moistened our once-crisp crust. We subsequently learned from Shirley Corriher that you can't disturb the filling once the starch bonds have completely set. If you break the starch bonds, you destroy the filling's structure. Those who have tried stirring liqueur into a chilled pastry cream may be familiar with similar results. When we stirred the cold filling to put it into the crust, we broke the starch bonds so that the filling went from stiff to runny. We learned a major lesson. You can cool the filling to warm, but once it has set, don't stir it.

We also found that coating the pastry lightly with graham cracker crumbs when rolling it out helped it to retain its light, crisp texture when the filling was added.

The Topping

With the filling refined and a crisp, flaky crust preserved, we moved on to the whipped cream topping. Since we had seen so many tips for keeping whipped cream stable, we thought the cream might have trouble holding up on the pie for several hours without some help.

After whipping cream with gelatin, corn syrup, confectioner's sugar, and granulated sugar, we discovered that the whipped cream actually required no special tricks to hold up on the pie overnight. That time length was certainly long enough for us. Why try to make the cream last longer than the pie? Given a choice between pasteurized and ultrapasteurized cream, though, cooks should choose the former. Although it has a shorter shelf life, it tastes noticeably fresher (less cooked) than ultrapasteurized, which is heated to a higher temperature during processing. Also, if you do whip the cream just before serving the pie, you might prefer quicker-dissolving confectioner's sugar over granulated. But after it was fully whipped, we could tell no difference between creams whipped with different sugars.

GRAHAM CRACKER–COATED PIE SHELL
Makes one 9-inch pie shell

1¼ cups all-purpose flour
½ teaspoon salt
1 tablespoon sugar
6 tablespoons chilled unsalted butter, cut into ¼-inch pieces
4 tablespoons chilled all-vegetable shortening
3–4 tablespoons ice water
½ cup graham cracker crumbs

1. Mix flour, salt, and sugar in food processor fitted with the steel blade. Scatter butter pieces over mixture, tossing to coat butter with a little of the flour. Cut butter into flour with five one-second pulses. Add shortening; continue cutting in until flour is pale yellow and resembles coarse cornmeal, with butter bits no larger than a small pea, about four more one-second pulses. Turn mixture into medium bowl.

2. Sprinkle 3 tablespoons of the water over mixture. Using rubber spatula, fold water into flour mixture, then repeatedly press down on dough mixture with broad side of spatula until dough sticks together, adding up to 1 tablespoon more water if dough will not come together. Shape dough into ball with hands, then flatten into 4-inch wide disk. Dust lightly with flour, wrap in plastic, and refrigerate 30 minutes before rolling.

3. Generously sprinkle 18-inch work area with 2 tablespoons graham cracker crumbs. Remove dough from wrapping and place in center of work area. Scatter a few more crumbs over disk top. Roll dough from center to edges to make 9-inch disk, rotating a quarter turn after each stroke and sprinkling additional crumbs underneath and on top, as necessary, to heavily coat dough. Flip dough and continue to roll, without rotating, into 13-inch disk just under ⅛-inch thick.

4. Fold dough in quarters, then place dough point in center of 9-inch Pyrex pie pan. Unfold dough to cover pan completely, with excess dough draped over pan lip. Trim and flute crust (*see* illustrations 1 through 4, below).

5. Refrigerate dough until firm, about 30 minutes. Prick shell at ½-inch intervals to keep dough

CRUSTS FOR CREAM PIES

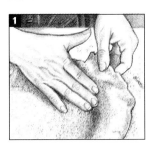

1. Lift the edge of the pie dough with one hand and press at the pan bottom with the other hand; repeat around the circumference of the pan.

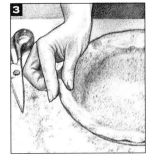

2. Use kitchen scissors to trim the dough to ½ inch of the lip all around.

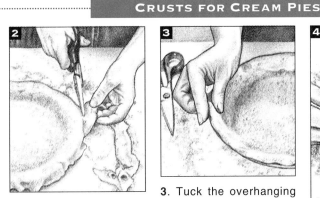

3. Tuck the overhanging dough back under itself so the folded edge is flush with the pan lip; press to seal.

4. Flute the edges all around.

5. Prick the shell at ½-inch intervals to keep the dough from ballooning.

ILLUSTRATIONS BY WENDY WRAY

from ballooning during baking (illustration 5). Press a doubled 12-inch square of aluminum foil inside pie shell. Prick foil to prevent further ballooning. Refrigerate to let dough relax, at least 30 minutes longer.

6. Adjust oven rack to lowest position and heat oven to 400 degrees. Bake, checking occasionally for ballooning, until crust is firmly set, about 15 minutes. Reduce oven temperature to 350 degrees, remove foil, and continue to bake until crust is crisp and golden brown in color, about 10 to 15 minutes longer. Transfer to wire rack and cool completely.

VANILLA CREAM PIE
Serves 8

½ cup plus 2 tablespoons granulated sugar
¼ cup cornstarch
⅛ teaspoon salt
5 large egg yolks, lightly beaten
2 cups 2 percent or whole milk
½ cup evaporated milk
½ vanilla bean, about 3 inches long, split lengthwise
2 tablespoons butter
1–2 teaspoons brandy
1 Graham Cracker–Coated Pie Shell (*see* recipe, page 23), baked and cooled completely
1 cup heavy whipping cream
2 tablespoons confectioner's sugar
½ teaspoon vanilla extract

1. Whisk sugar, cornstarch, and salt in medium saucepan. Add yolks, then immediately but gradually whisk in milk and evaporated milk. Drop in vanilla bean.

Cook over medium heat, stirring frequently at first, then constantly as mixture starts to thicken and begins to simmer, 8 to 10 minutes. Once mixture simmers, continue to cook, stirring constantly, for 1 minute longer. Remove pan from heat; whisk in butter and brandy. Remove vanilla bean, scrape out seeds, and whisk them back into filling.

2. Pour filling into shallow pan (another pie pan works well). Put plastic wrap directly over filling surface to prevent skin from forming; cool until warm, about 30 minutes. Pour warm filling into pie shell and, once again, place sheet of plastic wrap directly over filling surface. Refrigerate pie until completely chilled, at least 3 hours.

3. Whip cream to soft peaks. Add confectioner's sugar and vanilla; continue to whip to barely stiff peaks. Spread over filling and refrigerate until ready to serve.

CHOCOLATE CREAM PIE
Follow recipe for Vanilla Cream Pie, adding 2 tablespoons unsweetened cocoa to cornstarch

mixture and stirring in 4 ounces good-quality semisweet or bittersweet chocolate with butter. Substitute 1 teaspoon vanilla extract for vanilla bean.

COCONUT CREAM PIE
Adjust oven rack to lower-middle position and heat oven to 300 degrees. Scatter

1¼ cups sweetened flake coconut in 9-inch square pan. Bake, stirring occasionally, until evenly golden brown, 20 to 25 minutes. Cool to room temperature. Follow recipe for

Vanilla Cream Pie, stirring 1 cup of the coconut into filling once butter has melted. Continue with recipe, sprinkling remaining toasted coconut over whipped cream topping.

BANANA CREAM PIE
The safest and best place for the banana slices is sandwiched between two layers of filling. If sliced over the pie shell, the bananas tend to moisten the crust; if sliced over the filling top or mashed and folded into the filling, they turn brown faster.

Follow recipe for Vanilla Cream Pie, spooning half the warm filling into baked and cooled pie shell. Peel 2 medium bananas and slice them over filling. Top with remaining filling. Continue with recipe.

BUTTERSCOTCH CREAM PIE
Whisking the milk slowly into the brown sugar mixture keeps the sugar from lumping. Don't worry if the sugar does lump—it will dissolve as the milk heats—but make sure not to add the egg-cornstarch mixture until the sugar completely dissolves.

¼ cup cornstarch
¼ teaspoon salt
½ cup evaporated milk
5 large egg yolks
6 tablespoons unsalted butter
1 cup light brown sugar
2 cups whole milk
1½ teaspoons vanilla extract
1 Graham Cracker–Coated Pie Shell (*see* recipe, page 23), baked and cooled completely
1 cup heavy whipping cream
2 tablespoons confectioner's sugar

1. Dissolve cornstarch and salt in evaporated milk; whisk in egg yolks and set aside.

2. Meanwhile, heat butter and brown sugar in medium saucepan over medium heat until candy thermometer registers 220 degrees, about 5 minutes. Gradually whisk in whole milk. Once sugar dissolves, gradually whisk in cornstarch mixture. Continue cooking until mixture comes to boil; cook 1 minute longer. Turn off heat, then stir in vanilla. Pour filling into shallow pan (another pie pan works well). Put plastic wrap directly over filling surface to prevent skin from forming; cool until warm, 20 to 30 minutes. Pour filling into pie shell and, once again, place sheet of plastic wrap over filling surface. Refrigerate until completely chilled, at least 3 hours.

3. Whip cream to soft peaks. Add sugar and vanilla; continue to whip to barely stiff peaks. Spread over filling and refrigerate until ready to serve. ∎

WHAT IS EVAPORATED MILK?

As an ingredient, evaporated milk offers cooks a subtle, sweet flavor that can deepen the overall taste of many dishes. The process that yields evaporated milk has four parts.

First, pasteurized milk is "forewarmed," a process of heating the milk to about 200 degrees, then cooling it to between 36 and 39 degrees. This procedure both softens the milk proteins and increases the stability of the concentrated product during the sterilization process to come.

Next, the milk is evaporated under a vacuum, reducing its water content by 60 percent. In step three, the milk is homogenized by forcing it through a tiny nozzle at very high pressure onto a hard surface, breaking

the fat globules down to about one-quarter of their original size and dispersing them evenly throughout.

In the fourth step, heat sterilization, the evaporated milk takes on its telltale trait—a soft flavorful note of caramel. The milk is poured into cans, sealed, and heated to almost 240 degrees, destroying any dangerous bacteria and stabilizing the product for an extended shelf life. The high temperature reached during this process, coupled with the greater than usual concentration of lactose (milk sugar), causes the sugar to undergo some browning, which imparts the delicate caramel sweetness.

Unopened cans of evaporated milk can be stored at a cool room temperature—for nine months for the skimmed product and twelve months for the whole—but must be refrigerated and consumed within five to seven days once opened.   —Adam Ried

How to Quick-Cook Carrots

Braising, followed by sautéing in the same pan, produces carrots that are sweet, bright orange, and tender-crisp.

∽ BY PHILLIS M. CAREY ∽

Crisp, raw carrots are universal favorites, but when carrots are cooked, people often turn away. We find them used more often to provide an accent with their brilliant color, rather than for their distinctive taste. Admittedly, carrots can be mushy and earthy-tasting if overcooked, but when treated correctly, they are wonderful with a hint of sweetness and a crisp-tender texture.

To find the best and simplest way to prepare carrots, I chose to investigate boiling, steaming, microwaving, and braising. I limited my testing to peeled carrots, sliced one-quarter inch thick on the diagonal. I was looking for a crisp-tender, slightly sweet, bright orange cooked carrot that was simple to prepare.

I began my testing with boiling and steaming, the two most common cooking techniques for carrots. After three minutes of cooking with both methods, I started testing for tenderness. The carrots were firm in texture but underdone. After four minutes, they had softened a bit and were pleasant-tasting, yet still not done. At five minutes, they were crisp-tender and still a bright orange color. Unfortunately, the sweetness I was searching for was not there—and further cooking only produced mushy, unappealing carrots.

Perhaps the microwave would be the answer. Microwaved vegetables cook in very little water, and I thought this might help retain the carrots' natural sweetness. I added one-half cup of water to the sliced carrots, cooked them covered on high, and first checked them after three minutes. They were definitely not done and didn't begin to soften until after five minutes. At six minutes, they were crisp-tender and bright in color, and after seven minutes, tender with a buttery carrot flavor. Surprisingly, this activity took longer than steaming or boiling and produced carrots that were tasty but not terribly sweet.

Braising was next. For my first trial, I brought one-half cup of water to a boil in a two-quart saucepan. This only took about two minutes. I then added the carrots, along with a bit of salt, and cooked them tightly covered. Again, I started testing after three minutes, at which point the carrots were still rather crunchy. At five minutes the carrots were still a bit firm, but at six minutes they were ready to eat. However, they seemed to have cooked a bit unevenly. I retested using one cup of water and found that the carrots cooked evenly in five minutes. Still, the carroty-sweet taste was missing.

At this point, I took a step back to rethink the project. The best carrots I had ever tasted were sautéed in butter. Sautéed carrots are delicious, but they take a long time to cook and require too much attention to keep the butter and carrots from overly browning. I then thought of combining two techniques by using the French method of cooking vegetables, which is to blanch them in boiling water and then sauté in butter. Would that produce the best results?

Back to the kitchen. I knew that I didn't want to spend the time boiling too much water, so braising seemed the best answer. I also had another thought: To help the natural carrot sweetness along, why not add a small amount of sugar to the water along with the salt? I had found that salting the water during cooking eliminated the need to season further after cooking, so adding sugar might also increase the flavor of the carrots.

I started the test, and felt I was finally beginning to reach the desired result. One cup of water took about three minutes to boil. I added the carrots, along with the salt and sugar, and cooked them for only three to four minutes, then drained and sautéed them. Cooked this way, the carrots were sweet, crisp-tender, and bright orange with a slight buttery flavor.

But part of my original goal was to find a truly simple method. Did this technique, with two pots and two separate preparations, really qualify? Or could I simplify the process by combining these two cooking techniques into one?

Back into the kitchen one last time. Instead of using a saucepan to cook the carrots, I chose a ten-inch skillet with a lid. The water, butter, sugar, and salt were all stirred into the carrots. I spread the carrots out over the bottom of the pan to encourage more even cooking, and began to try different quantities of water. After several attempts, I found that two tablespoons was the correct amount. I cooked the carrots in the water, covered, for three minutes, then cooked them uncovered for an additional minute to evaporate the remaining water. This left the carrots coated in butter and ready to sauté. I then sautéed the carrots for one to two minutes to finish cooking them and to pick up the buttery flavor. Seasoned with a bit of pepper and a sprinkle of fresh parsley leaves, the carrots were ready for the table—and with only one pan to clean.

QUICK-COOKED CARROTS WITH BUTTER AND PARSLEY
Serves 3 to 4

1 pound carrots, peeled, ends trimmed, and sliced on the diagonal ¼-inch thick
2 tablespoons unsalted butter
1 teaspoon sugar
½ teaspoon salt
  Ground black pepper
1 tablespoon minced fresh parsley leaves

In 10-inch skillet, bring carrots, 2 tablespoons water, butter, sugar, and salt to boil over medium-high heat. Cover and cook 3 minutes. Uncover skillet; continue to cook over medium-high heat until remaining water evaporates, about 1 minute. Sauté carrots until tender, 1 to 2 minutes longer. Season to taste with pepper, sprinkle with fresh parsley leaves, and serve.

QUICK-COOKED CARROTS WITH ORANGE AND PISTACHIOS
Follow recipe for Quick-Cooked Carrots with Butter and Parsley, substituting ¼ cup fresh orange juice and 1 teaspoon orange zest for the water and increasing sugar from 1 teaspoon to 1 tablespoon. Once liquid has evaporated, add ¼ cup toasted pistachio nuts and continue with recipe.

QUICK-COOKED CARROTS WITH MUSTARD–BROWN SUGAR GLAZE
Follow recipe for Quick-Cooked Carrots with Butter and Parsley, omitting sugar. Once liquid has evaporated, stir in 2 packed tablespoons dark or light brown sugar and 1½ tablespoons Dijon-style mustard. Continue cooking until carrots are tender and glazed, about 2 minutes longer. Substitute 2 tablespoons snipped fresh chives for the parsley.

QUICK-COOKED CARROTS WITH VINEGAR AND THYME
Follow recipe for Quick-Cooked Carrots with Butter and Parsley. Once liquid has evaporated, add 2 tablespoons red wine vinegar and ¼ teaspoon dried thyme leaves. Cook until carrots are tender and glazed, about 2 minutes longer. Stir in parsley. ■

Phillis M. Carey is a cooking instructor and writer based in San Diego, California.

Oscar Mayer Wins Bacon Tasting

The highest-rated supermarket bacons were those with a good balance of pork, sweet, and salty flavors.

≈ BY DOUGLAS BELLOW ≈

In a world that is increasingly conscientious about health, bacon stands as a throwback to less cautious times. So, on those occasions when you do go whole hog (you'll pardon the expression), you should make sure you are getting your money's worth.

To find out what that might be, we decided to taste a range of bacons generally available in supermarkets. For the tasting, we assembled a group of twelve bacon brands: nine nationally available supermarket brands, a preservative-free natural brand, and two mail-order brands. Our choice of supermarket brands was based on what is most commonly available to consumers. As for the three nonsupermarket brands, we chose representatives nearly at random, with recommendations from experts in both gourmet and natural foods.

We also assembled a brave, and somewhat hedonistic, set of tasters willing to sit down and rate all twelve different brands. Tasters were asked to rate the bacon according to preferences based on flavors, balance of fat to lean, and overall qualities of the meat.

Our tasting showed that both the flavor of the meat itself and the flavors provided by the curing process were crucial factors in judging a bacon. With regard to the meat, the extreme ends of content—too much fat or too much lean—both caused tasters to mark down certain bacons. With those bacons that had relatively equal fat-to-meat ratios, the texture, thickness of the cut, and appearance all aided the bacon's scores.

As concerns the meat itself, the quality of the pork flavor was judged strongly. It is important to note here that although all bacons look similar at first glance on the shelf, there are actually quite pronounced differences between manufacturers. For one thing, different manufacturers may use different parts of the pork belly for making their bacon (see "Where Does Bacon Come From?" above). In addition, bacon is a natural product, not

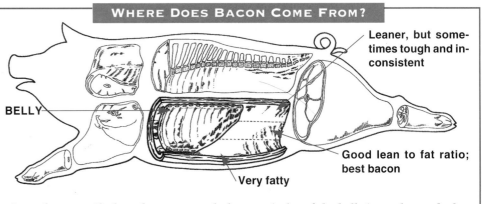

WHERE DOES BACON COME FROM?

Leaner, but sometimes tough and inconsistent

BELLY

Good lean to fat ratio; best bacon

Very fatty

Once the spareribs have been removed, the remainder of the belly is used to make bacon. However, some sections of the belly are better for making bacon than others.

a recipe like sausage or bologna. Since not all pigs grow the same, quality and taste will even vary to some degree from package to package from the same manufacturer.

In terms of the flavors provided by curing, tasters were looking for a strong balance of salt and sugar in their bacon. The top finishers all had a good dose of sweetness to their taste whereas those finishing lower in the standings tended to taste salty only, with little sugar or pork flavors. Along with the balance of fat to lean, this balance of flavors was the single most important determining factor in the preferences of the tasters.

Although all of the bacons make claims of "smokiness" or of being "hardwood smoked," none of our samples was deemed a truly smoky-flavored product. The essence of smoke in the palate was a very favorable addition, but, for the most part, the smoky flavor in bacon is a subtle backdrop to the salt, pork, and sweetness rather than a formal presence. This is due in part to the quick smoking times employed by modern manufacturers as well as the reliance on preservatives

rather than cooking to preserve the meat. Most manufacturers smoke their bacon for not much longer than six to eight hours. In historic processes, smoking occurred over a much longer time period, which allowed the smoke particles to mix with the bacon's juices, marinating it as it cooked.

Interestingly, the one bacon in our testing that is smoked for a relatively long time—about twenty hours—was judged so vastly superior to the other bacons, with such a different taste, that most tasters put it in its own special category. This was Ham I Am's Ozark Trails Bacon, one of our mail-order "ringers," which is flavored with brown sugar and pepper after the long smoking. It was included in our test to highlight the flavors in normal bacon and show what a more creative approach to bacon can produce. For the sake of our results, we keep it separate because it is a very different product than the supermarket variety.

However, the other mail-order brand—Edwards Country Style Hickory Smoked Bacon—did not place well, demonstrating that spending more money does not necessarily ensure a superior product.

It is interesting to note that none of the manufacturers who we contacted wanted to talk about the processes they use in making their bacon, considering that to be "proprietary information." However, when asked about our results, one industry representative did comment that our tasters seemed to have chosen according to a very Northeastern palate, as our victors tended to be somewhat less fatty and slightly less sweet than those brands preferred in the South. ∎

Douglas Bellow lives and cooks in Cambridge, Massachusetts.

HOW MUCH FAT IS LOST?

Tasting so much bacon made us curious about the actual amount of fat each package would render when cooked. To find out, we cooked a whole package of each bacon, weighing each both before and after to see how much fat was rendered. Of course, some weight was lost in the form of steam during cooking, but we still felt the test provided a good rough idea of how much fat is lost during cooking.

Our observations were consistent, if a little scary. With the exception of Ozark Trails (which lost 58 percent of its initial weight), all of the bacon tested fell within an 8 percent window, losing between 69 and 77 percent of its initial weight. There seemed to be little correlation between how much fat each bacon lost during cooking and its standing in the tasting, but one thing is sure: Cooking any bacon will produce plenty of fat, if you care to use it for later cooking.

—Adam Ried

ILLUSTRATION BY JUDY LOVE/PHOTOGRAPHS BY DAVE HENDERSON

Twelve bacons were baked until just crispy and then tasted blind at The Blue Room restaurant in Cambridge, Massachusetts. Bacons are listed in order of preference based on the scores awarded by our judges.

In addition to the author and two members of the *Cook's Illustrated* editorial staff, tasters included John Dewar of John Dewar & Sons, a specialty butcher and wholesaler in Boston; Ihsan Gurdal of Formaggio Kitchen in Cambridge; Andy Husbands, chef of East Coast Grill, also in Cambridge; Lydia Shire, executive chef/owner of Biba and Pignoli in Boston; Susan Regis, chef of Biba and Pignoli; Peter Sagansky, wine consultant and president of Wineworks, Inc. in Groton, Massachusetts; and Bob Sargeant, chef/owner of Flora in Arlington, Massachusetts.

HIGHLY RECOMMENDED

Oscar Mayer Bacon (Oscar Mayer Foods Corp., Madison, Wisconsin), $3.49 for sixteen ounces. Cured with water, salt, sugar, sodium phosphates, sodium erythorbate (made from sugar), and sodium nitrite, then smoked. Oscar Mayer is a relatively thick and irregular cut of bacon with "tender texture" and good "balance of fat and lean." Tasters liked the "nice pork flavor and the hint of smoke" along with the "balance of sweet and salt."

John Morrell Hardwood Smoked Bacon (John Morrell & Co., Cincinnati, Ohio), $2.49 for sixteen ounces. Cured with water, salt, sugar, sodium phosphate, sodium erythorbate, and sodium nitrite, then smoked. Our close second-place finisher, Morrell is also "slightly thicker than most other bacon and shows better presentation," with a "rustic sort of look"; some felt it even looked "hand-cut." Morrell had "good overall flavors, with a sweet aroma," "sweet mapley taste," and "strong pork flavor."

RECOMMENDED

Hillshire Farm Country Smoked Brand Bacon (Hillshire Farm, Cincinnati, Ohio), $2.99 for sixteen ounces. Cured with water, salt, sugar, sodium phosphate, sodium ascorbate (vitamin C), and sodium nitrite, then smoked. Hillshire Farm has the highest fat-to-meat ratio of the high finishers but also has a "nice thick slice to it." It demonstrated a "good overall taste" with a "salty beginning followed by sweetness for balance." Hillshire Farm is one of the smokier of the contestants.

Colonial Genuine Hickory Smoked Special Cut Bacon (Colonial Quality Meats, Boston, Massachusetts), $2.59 for sixteen ounces. Cured with water, salt, sugar, sodium phosphate, sodium erythorbate, and sodium nitrite, then smoked. Like the other top finishers, Colonial is a "thick-sliced cut, more like a ham than a bacon, with an irregular, but appealing shape." "A little lean" for most, Colonial had "strong pork flavor, and an otherwise straightforward taste."

Plumrose Old Fashioned Hardwood Smoked Premium Bacon (Plumrose USA, Inc., East Brunswick, New Jersey), $2.49 for sixteen ounces. Cured with water, salt, sodium phosphate, brown sugar, sodium erythorbate, and sodium nitrite, then smoked. Plumrose is a "fatty and plump" bacon that also looks "hand-cut." It has an "almost perfect ratio of meat to fat" and was dubbed "very salty with a good hog underneath." Plumrose was admired mainly for its "nice texture" along with a "balance of sweetness even to its strong salt taste."

NOT RECOMMENDED

Jones Dairy Farm Hickory Smoked Sliced Bacon (Fort Atkinson, Wisconsin), $2.99 for sixteen ounces. Cured with water, salt, sugar, sodium phosphate, sodium ascorbate, and sodium nitrite, then smoked. Jones Dairy Farm is a "very thin, straight bacon, with even strips of dark brown meat and yellowy fat." Jones had a "decent balance of flavors" with "no overwhelmingly bad tastes," but was generally deemed too "weak and thin to compete" with the other strong finishers.

Smithfield by Luter Hickory Smoked Bacon (Smithfield Packing Co., Inc., Smithfield, Virginia), $2.59 for sixteen ounces. Cured with water, salt, sodium phosphate, sodium erythorbate, and sodium nitrite, then smoked. No sugar is added. As one might guess, then, Smithfield was judged "too salty" with "little sweetness or texture." Although appearing to have a "good fat-to-lean ratio," its flavor was thought to be "imitation-tasting" and "kind of dead."

Armour Premium Bacon (Armour Foods Co., Downers Grove, Illinois), $2.99 for sixteen ounces. Cured with water, salt, sugar, sodium phosphate, sodium erythorbate, and sodium nitrite, then smoked. Armour is "very generic-looking bacon with even ribbons of meat and fat." Many tasters found the texture of Armour to be distracting, calling it "too rubbery" or "plasticky." Critics felt that it was "flat and uninteresting" or "high in fat with no smoke and sugar." One ventured, "No smoke, no salt, no sugar, no flavor, no way!"

Hormel Black Label Center Cut Bacon (Hormel Foods Corp., Austin, Minnesota), $2.59 for sixteen ounces. Cured with water, salt, sugar, dextrose, sodium erythorbate, and sodium nitrite, then smoked. Although Hormel enjoys some fairly high respect inside the bacon industry, our panel was generally unimpressed. "Very high in fat," with "distracting yellow and red colors," Hormel proved "thin and uninspirational." The only outstanding flavor to Hormel was the high salt content, but with "little sweetness and no smoke to speak of."

Edwards Country Style Hickory Smoked Virginia Bacon (S. Wallace Edwards and Sons, Inc., Surry, Virginia), $14.95 for a three-pound package. Cured with water, salt, sugar, and sodium nitrite. You can purchase this bacon in slab form by mail (call 800-222-4267) or buy it sliced from specialty butcher shops. It was the only one of our bacons that comes in a slab, and was also the highest priced of all of them. Interestingly, it was also ranked as the second lowest. Described as "lacking color and texture" largely due to the extremely high fat content, and most felt it had only a "thin, salty flavor."

The Pork Schop of Vermont Maple Sugar Cured Bacon (The Pork Schop of Vermont, Inc., Hinesburg, Vermont), $3.99 for twelve ounces. Contains pork cured with water, sea salt, and maple sugar, then smoked. This is the only one of our bacons that does not contain sodium nitrite or sulfites. It was also the most distinct-looking—other than Ham I Am—of all of the competitors. Pork Schop is "very meaty" bacon, which "seems uncured." ("There is no cure for this bacon," said one.) Most found its "gray color" and its "plasticky texture" disturbing. Pork Schop is not salty at all, with most of its flavors characterized as "sweet and porky."

Traditional Designs Score Well in Pepper Mill Testing

Traditional pepper mills take three out of four top places in a packed field that includes one-handed mills and electric mills with lights.

∼ BY JACK BISHOP ∼

Although most cooks use their pepper mills at least once a day, few of us give any thought to which mill is really the best. Even cooks who insist on owning the newest gadgets tend to stick with the same old pepper mill year after year. I know, because I have been using the same mill for as long as I can remember. I just assumed all mills are created equal. After testing twenty-six mills from eleven companies, I now know that my old mill is decent but far from the best.

The Tests

The criteria for judging a pepper mill are fairly straightforward. First and foremost, can you load up the mill without spilling peppercorns all over the kitchen? To be fair, I used a small funnel and found that most mills could be filled without too much hassle. A few mills, however, had openings so small that lost peppercorns were unavoidable.

A wide range of grinds (something most mills could not produce) is also very important. It's true that medium-grind pepper is fine for most uses, but why not own a mill capable of a much greater range? Really coarse pepper is essential for steak *au poivre,* for example, while delicate sauces require extremely fine pepper.

Most but not all models I tested have a knob either on top of the mill or under the grinding mechanism that can adjust the grind. (A few mills could not be adjusted and consequently fared poorly in the testing.) In conventional mills, the knob, called a finial, is attached to a long shaft that runs through the area where the peppercorns are stored. The shaft in turn is attached to the grinding mechanism, which actually has two parts. The top portion is moved by the shaft and, hence, the finial. The bottom portion is stationary. The greater the distance between the top and bottom parts of the grinder, the coarser the ground pepper will be.

The last general factor I used to judge the mills is what I call "overall design," a category that includes ease of use. There are two traditional designs. The most common is a bulbous top that you turn to grind the pepper. Another less common but still traditional design requires you to turn a crank to move the grinding mechanism. About half of the mills tested are based on one of these two designs.

But pepper mill manufacturers

RATING PEPPER MILLS

Legend: ● = Good Performance ◐ = Fair Performance ○ = Poor Performance

Twenty-six pepper mills from eleven different companies were tested for this article and evaluated on the following criteria. If mills from the same company were quite similar, I included only my favorite. If mills from the same company were dissimilar, I included the various mills in the chart. Mills are listed in order of preference.

Price: Suggested retail prices are listed. *See* Sources and Resources, page 32, for mail-order outlets for top mills.
Capacity: Mills capable of holding a half-cup or more peppercorns are preferred for kitchen use. If the mill will be used at the table, then capacity is not as important.
Speed: Time it takes to grind a half-teaspoon. Extremely slow mills are downgraded. Note that very fast mills may be better in the kitchen (when grinding larger amounts) than at the table.
Ease of Filling: All mills were filled using a small funnel. Mills with an opening too small for the funnel are downgraded.
Range of Grinds: Along with overall design, this test was the most important. Few mills can produce both a really fine and a really coarse grind. Those that can do both earn top marks.
Overall Design: Mills that are especially easy to operate, comfortable, and easy to clean are preferred here. Mills that are overly complicated or awkward to use are downgraded.

NAME	PRICE	CAPACITY	SPEED	EASE OF FILLING	RANGE OF GRINDS	OVERALL DESIGN
Unicorn Magnum Plus Restaurant Use Peppermill	$45	1⅓ cups	10 sec	●	●	●
Chef Specialties 10" Natural Maple Pepper Mill 10250	$25	½ cup	20 sec	●	●	●
Mr. Dudley Willow 9173 Peppermill	$24	⅜ cup	20 sec	●	●	●
Olde Thompson Manor Pepper Mill & Salt Shaker Set 3564-36	$28	¼ cup	15 sec	●	●	●
Peppermate Pepper Mill 623	$50	⅔ cup	9 sec	●	◐	●
Unicorn Peppergun	$23	½ cup	17 sec	●	●	○
Peugeot Auberge P808-1	$46	⅓ cup	8 sec	◐	◐	●

NAME	PRICE	CAPACITY	SPEED	EASE OF FILLING	RANGE OF GRINDS	OVERALL DESIGN
Perfex "Office" Moulin à Poivre	$46	¼ cup	15 sec	○	●	●
Atlas Pepper Mill 103	$52	9⁄16 cup	13 sec	●	●	●
William Bounds Ultimate Cooking Mill 09000	$25	¼ cup	12 sec	●	●	●
Banton Pepper Mill	$42	⅛ cup	11 sec	●	●	●
Mr. Dudley Saturn 6003 Illuminated Peppermill	$20	⅜ cup	25 sec	●	○	●
Pyramill Salt and Pepper Grinder APM-2	$20	⅜ cup	60 sec	●	○	○
Chef'n Salt 'n Pepper Machine ASPM-88CBK	$19	⅛ cup	15 sec	○	○	●

are constantly trying to reinvent the wheel. Innovative designs rely on a host of newfangled mechanisms—everything from a battery-powered button (with spotlight) to side crank-keys and double ears. I found some of these innovative mills to be comfortable in my hands, but others were awkward to use.

In addition to these general factors, I also considered two specific measurements: capacity and speed. I soon realized that larger, faster mills were not necessarily better for all tasks. If you plan on using the mill to grind pepper for recipes, then speed and capacity are important. You don't want to spend several minutes grinding a tablespoon of pepper for a spice rub, for example. Likewise, a mill with only a one-quarter cup capacity will need to be refilled quite often if you use a fair amount of pepper in the kitchen.

However, if the mill will be used at the table, then speed and capacity are not so important. Since many people buy separate mills for the table and kitchen, I decided to judge each mill on its own merits. As long as it met the other criteria listed above, I didn't downgrade a mill obviously meant for the table just because it was small or fairly slow.

The Results

A few personal preferences became clear almost immediately. I was not wild about the crank-turned mills such as the Perfex and Atlas. I found the cranks cumbersome, especially when I was trying to grind a large amount of pepper. It's easier to turn the large, bulbous top on a standard mill.

As for innovative design, some models were duds. In fact, the two models at the bottom of the rankings (both distributed by a company called Progressive International) were so bad, I would have returned them immediately under normal circumstances. Other newfangled designs, however, had a point. The Peppermate relies on a large turning crank-key on the side of the mill to move the grinding mechanism. This model also comes with a cup that catches the pepper and makes measuring especially easy. If the range of grinds were a tad better, this model might have finished at the top of the ratings.

The Peppergun, another nontraditional mill, also finished high in the rankings. Although the range of grinds here is quite good, I was less

enthralled with the one-hand operation. The two "ears" must be squeezed together to operate the grinder. With some practice this awkward motion can be mastered, but it never really felt natural. There are occasions when grinding pepper with one hand might come in handy, but I'm not sure it's worth the hassle the rest of the time.

When I tallied the results, I was surprised to see three traditional wooden mills near the top of the list. Besides delivering good results, these mills were comfortable and easy to use. Mills from Chef Specialties, Mr. Dudley, and Olde Thompson were not terribly sexy but worked well. Since the Chef Specialty mill had a slightly better range of grinds, larger capacity, and low price, it's a strong second choice as well as a best buy. This mill can be used on the table or in the kitchen.

The overall winner is a take-off on these classic mills with some important differences. The Magnum is made of black acrylic (not wood) and has a slim, comfortable feel. The mill, however, works on the same general premise: the top portion is turned to grind pepper. The Magnum has a number of distinguishing features that make it my first choice for kitchen use, including a super-large capacity and blinding speed. The large hole on the side of the mill is an easy way to load up the peppercorns. For serious pepper users, this is the best choice.

So why did some mills outperform the others? Although most mills were decent, the top mills had a much wider range of grinds. Not surprisingly, experts I talked with pointed to the grinding mechanism. With one exception, all of the grinding mechanisms are stainless steel. (The William Bounds Ultimate has a ceramic grinder.)

The quality of the stainless steel, the built-in tolerances (a tight fit between the top and bottom portions of the mechanism is required to yield very fine pepper), the sharpness of the teeth on the grinder, and the size of the mechanism (larger grinders can crush more pepper at once) are all factors that affect the performance of the mill. Unfortunately, a casual inspection of a grinding mechanism reveals little information even to the savvy shopper. However, the grinder in the bottom of the top-rated Magnum does have a very large circumference. ∎

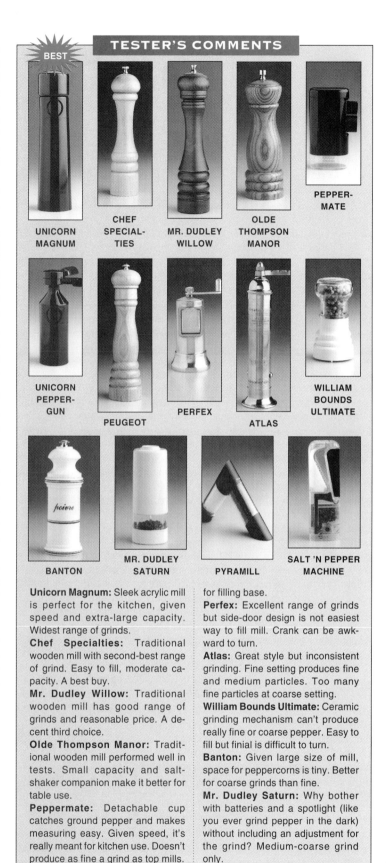

TESTER'S COMMENTS

BEST

UNICORN MAGNUM

CHEF SPECIAL-TIES

MR. DUDLEY WILLOW

OLDE THOMPSON MANOR

PEPPER-MATE

UNICORN PEPPER-GUN

PEUGEOT

PERFEX

ATLAS

WILLIAM BOUNDS ULTIMATE

BANTON

MR. DUDLEY SATURN

PYRAMILL

SALT 'N PEPPER MACHINE

Unicorn Magnum: Sleek acrylic mill is perfect for the kitchen, given speed and extra-large capacity. Widest range of grinds.

Chef Specialties: Traditional wooden mill with second-best range of grind. Easy to fill, moderate capacity. A best buy.

Mr. Dudley Willow: Traditional wooden mill has good range of grinds and reasonable price. A decent third choice.

Olde Thompson Manor: Traditional wooden mill performed well in tests. Small capacity and salt-shaker companion make it better for table use.

Peppermate: Detachable cup catches ground pepper and makes measuring easy. Given speed, it's really meant for kitchen use. Doesn't produce as fine a grind as top mills.

Unicorn Peppergun: Nice range of grinds, but two-eared mill can be hard to operate, although it can be mastered. Do you really need to grind pepper with one hand?

Peugeot: Somewhat expensive traditional mill should have slightly more capacity and wider opening for filling base.

Perfex: Excellent range of grinds but side-door design is not easiest way to fill mill. Crank can be awkward to turn.

Atlas: Great style but inconsistent grinding. Fine setting produces fine and medium particles. Too many fine particles at coarse setting.

William Bounds Ultimate: Ceramic grinding mechanism can't produce really fine or coarse pepper. Easy to fill but finial is difficult to turn.

Banton: Given large size of mill, space for peppercorns is tiny. Better for coarse grinds than fine.

Mr. Dudley Saturn: Why bother with batteries and a spotlight (like you ever grind pepper in the dark) without including an adjustment for the grind? Medium-coarse grind only.

Pyramill: High-concept but low-quality. "Adjustable" grind only produces fine pepper. Very awkward to use.

Salt 'n Pepper Machine: Squeeze handle is easy to use but slices, rather than grinds, the peppercorns to yield a very coarse grind.

Rating Tuscan Wines

There is good Tuscan wine beyond Chianti, and it's becoming more appealing every year. Our tasting turns up an inexpensive beauty.

∾ BY MARK BITTMAN ∾

For many of us, Tuscan wine *is* Chianti (for some, *Italian* wine is Chianti). And, although Chianti is rarely great—I've had a total of perhaps two that swept me off my feet—it is generally solid wine, great to drink by itself, good enough to have almost any time you have food that calls for a red. Like Tuscan food, it is eminently approachable.

But there is Tuscan wine beyond Chianti, and it should not be ignored. Although Chianti has been around forever—arguably, it is the earliest named wine still in existence—so have a number of other wines made in Tuscany. Traditionally, these carried elegant place names like Brunello (or Rosso) di Montalcino or Vino Nobile di Montepulciano, wines with long, solid reputations. Now, Tuscan wines are just as likely to carry the names of vineyards, grapes, or the winemaker's grandmother as anything else.

The Tuscan revolution began a decade or so ago, when Piero Antinori and other winemakers realized that their warm, lush hills were just as good as Napa Valley, or almost any place on earth, for growing not only sangiovese, the classic red wine grape of Tuscany, but cabernet sauvignon (which has been grown in Tuscany since the eighteenth century) and other "foreign" grapes. Antinori used cabernet to replace the 10 percent white wine grape content that was not only traditional in Chianti but mandated by law, and he aged the resulting wine in new, small barrels of French oak rather than the traditional huge *barriques*.

When he was finished, he could not call the wine Chianti, but that did not bother him a bit. He named it Tignanello, after one of the oldest vineyards in Tuscany, and began a new era of winemaking in the region. The result has been the introduction of a number of brilliant new non-Chiantis in recent years (and now even the mandated percentages of grapes in Chianti are changing), and a new round of accolades for the region, which has seen a resurgence.

With Chianti prices escalating, these new Tuscan wines seem even more appealing. Furthermore, the 100 percent sangiovese wines, or wines that blend sangiovese (the dominant grape of Chianti) with cabernet and/or other grapes, are often a better value than Chianti, whose name alone probably costs consumers a dollar or two a bottle.

Tignanello, along with a few other new and traditional Tuscan wines, are on the pricey side (some are outrageous, costing $50 or more for wine that is very good but rarely exquisite). But many of the new wines, including the wine that won our tasting in convincing fashion (a $9 Rosso di Montalcino from Banfi) and Antinori's own $7.50 Santa Cristina (which contains some merlot) are inexpensive by any standards. And, for the most part, the wines are good: Sangiovese is a strong, full-bodied grape capable of producing delicious, well-structured wine. (The Californians realize this and have more than trebled plantings of sangiovese in recent years.)

In our tasting we found no fewer than ten wines generally regarded as good. Some of the wines are on the expensive side, but there was little correlation that we could establish between price and quality. Two or three wines (including our "ringer," the $35 Brunello from Il Poggione) will definitely improve with time, but most of these are enjoyable wines for everyday drinking right now—just like Chianti. ∎

BOOK

REVIEWS

Roasting, A Simple Art
Barbara Kafka
William Morrow, $25

In her latest book, well-known food writer and culinary expert Barbara Kafka aims very high; she seeks nothing less than to reinvent roasting for the home cook. Her premise is that high-heat roasting is both simple and universal in application. Almost every recipe starts off with "Heat oven to 500 degrees," a remarkable notion given the fact that the author is roasting everything from chicken to beef to fruit to vegetables to a five-pound hunk of swordfish. This loyalty to a high-heat technique seems particularly dangerous to me since I start out with a bias, based on months of testing, towards low-heat roasting for many meats and poultry. To avoid prejudice, I asked some of the *Cook's Illustrated* editorial staff to assist in the recipe testing.

I personally made the most interesting and, as it turned out, the most disastrous, recipe in the book: As-Good-As-Meat Roasted Swordfish. The premise of the recipe is intriguing: Roast a garlic-studded five-and-one-quarter-pound piece of swordfish as you would a rack of lamb, then slice and serve it at the table. Kafka used the Canadian theory of fish cookery—ten minutes per inch of thickness—to arrive at the overly precise cooking time of thirty-seven and one-half minutes. When I pulled my gorgeous, $68 piece of fish out of the oven after just this amount of time, the outer layer had been pulverized into mush by the high heat and the inside was raw and unappealing.

Perfect Beef Stew, however, was excellent. Both the meat and the vegetables are roasted in the oven and then combined with the liquids and seasonings on top of the stove. This method eliminated the need for browning the cubes of beef (a tedious process), and the roasted vegetables were a winner. I did have two minor complaints, however. The recommended saucepan size was too small, and I would have roasted the carrots longer, though I must admit that the other staff member who tried this recipe thought the carrots were just fine.

Other recipes were a mixed bag. For starters, Roast Chicken with Crispy Potatoes calls for a five- to six-pound chicken. This size is hard to find unless you purchase a pumped-up Perdue chicken, which is not worth eating in the first place. Also, roasting a chicken at 500 degrees breast side up seemed to me to be a recipe for disaster. Sure enough, the white meat was over-

cooked by the time the dark meat was up to speed.

The Roasted Broccoli with Lemon-Garlic Bath was very tasty, but, when pressed into service as a pasta sauce (Roasted Broccoli Spaghettini), it failed amidst a spider's web of stringy cheese. The prime rib was overcooked even though I followed the directions to the letter, but the potatoes that went along for the ride were sensational. I also agree with our food editor Pam Anderson that prime rib is best cooked at 200, not 500, degrees (*see* "Perfect Prime Rib," November/December 1995). There is certainly room for differences of opinion here, but the point is that Kafka's method does not work as well as many others.

Of the nonmeat dishes, the Melting Potatoes were delicious but the Roasted Pears with Asian Glaze were fussy. You make a sauce, peel, core, baste—and end up with pears that aren't as good as simply cutting them in half, sprinkling on five-spice powder, and throwing them in the oven for twenty-five minutes at 375 degrees.

I also found it puzzling that many of the recipes were extremely specific, especially in reference to pan sizes and cooking times, yet were inaccurate. Sometimes recipes are vague on purpose, and that is fine—not every oven or piece of food is the same. But if you specify a specific pan size that turns out to be too small or a precise cooking time that is much too long, what's the point?

In addition, heating an oven to 500 degrees is not always the most practical cooking method; pan-searing scallops, for example, is faster and easier on top of the stove. And, if you have a smoke alarm, you'd better unplug it before roasting the fattier foods.

But the overall problem with Kafka's approach is that high-heat roasting simply doesn't work for everything. Although I agree that high-heat roasting can produce a wonderful exterior, lower oven temperatures promote more even cooking, a critical step for most thick pieces of meat or poultry. When we tested the Roast Leg of Lamb with Herb Rub, for example, the meat around the bone was still raw at the point at which the outer layers were properly cooked. A combination of high- and low-heat roasting often gives you the best of both worlds: a caramelized exterior and even cooking. In my experience, roasting is anything but a simple art.

All in all, cooking from this book is like driving a Maserati. It's stylish (Kafka is a good writer) and it's interesting (some of the recipes were revelatory), but the mechanics are flawed.
—*Christopher Kimball*

Roasting
Kathy Gunst
Macmillan, $16

If Barbara Kafka is a pedagogue, bending foods to her will, Kathy Gunst is a New Age mentor, allowing individual foods the freedom to roast at a variety of temperatures. Roast chicken, for example, is started at 475 degrees for fifteen minutes and is then reduced to 325; a rib roast is begun at 450 degrees and then finished at 350; and a basic eye of round is simply roasted at a constant 400 degrees. While Kafka roasts her swordfish at 500 degrees, Gunst cooks her fish steaks at 350 degrees, less ingenious but vastly preferable in terms of the final results.

Members of the *Cook's Illustrated* editorial staff tried a dozen recipes from this book. All were very good, if a bit pedestrian. The prime rib, for instance, was cooked perfectly, and Roasted Fennel Parmigiana was a model of delicious simplicity—fennel slices, olive oil, salt, pepper, and a dusting of Parmesan near the end of cooking. The Roast Chicken with Lemon and Herbs resulted in well-cooked, juicy white and dark meat, although the skin was not quite as crispy as Kafka's high-heat roaster.

In addition, Gunst instructs her readers to rely on internal temperatures as a measure of doneness, which, as all home cooks know, is the only practical method given variable ovens and foods.

While the recipes in this book worked well, we did find the seasonings on the bland side. Top Round with Sweet Potatoes and Shallots cooked up perfectly but needed some more dynamic flavors. Provençal-Flavored Eye of Round Roast was fine, but unaccountably the recipe did not call for any salt. Roasted Squash with Parsnips and Apple Cider was very good (the parsnips were outstanding, absorbing wine and cider as they cooked) but could have used more maple syrup and thyme. And Roasted Pork with Rum and Vidalia Onions sounded better than it tasted—the onions were on the crunchy side, the roast was unsalted, and the pork was overcooked at 155 degrees. (Although the USDA will tell you otherwise, pork should be cooked only to 145 degrees if you want it moist and tender.)

But these are quibbles with a book that is a lesson in good home cooking, neither pedantic nor revelatory. These are solid, well-tested recipes, and although this book may not break new culinary ground, its lessons are well learned. ∎
—*Christopher Kimball*

SOURCES
AND RESOURCES

Most of the ingredients and materials necessary for the recipes in this issue are available at your local supermarket, gourmet store, or kitchen supply shop. The following are mail-order sources for particular items. Prices listed below were current at press time and do not include shipping or handling unless otherwise indicated. We suggest that you contact companies directly to confirm up-to-date prices and availability.

PEPPER MILLS
In the testing article on page 28, we ground out ratings of twenty-six pepper mills from eleven different companies. The top-rated Unicorn Magnum Plus Restaurant Use Peppermill is available by calling the manufacturer, Tom David, Inc., directly at 800-634-8881. The ten-inch mill comes only in black, shatterproof ABS plastic and costs $45, postage paid. Our second- and third-rated mills, the Chef Specialties 10" Natural Maple Pepper Mill (Model 10250) and the Mr. Dudley Willow 9173 Peppermill, come from larger manufacturers that make hundreds of different models distributed by retailers around the country. Customer service representatives at each company can help track down these specific mills by directing you to the nearest retailer. Call Chef Specialties at 800-440-2433 and Mr. Dudley at 619-439-3000. Prices will vary slightly among retailers, but expect to pay roughly $25 for each mill.

THE FILL OF THE MILL
Whole black peppercorns are available in just about every supermarket, but how about white, green, pink, and Szechuan? Those who want to vary their pepper can find each of these types, as well as two kinds of black pepper and several blends, through the mail-order catalog of Spices Etc... (P.O. Box 5266, Charlottesville, VA 22905; 800-827-6373). Nine ounces of Malabar black peppercorns, the most popular of the four mass-produced black pepper varieties, costs $3.70. We prefer tellicherry peppercorns ($5.25 for nine ounces) because they are larger, more mature, and more flavorful than Malabar. White peppercorns ($5.75 for ten ounces), which are really black peppercorns without their dark outer skin, are often called for in light-colored soups and sauces. Green peppercorns ($12.50 for six ounces), have a milder flavor because they are harvested before they are fully ripe. Pink peppercorns ($21 for ten ounces) are not actually pepper but are considered so because of the size and sweet, fresh flavor of the berries. Like pink pepper, Szechuan peppercorns ($7.50 for nine ounces), which are a common ingredient in many Asian and Russian recipes, are reddish brown berries the same size as peppercorns, but not truly pepper.

MADELEINE PANS
The distinctive, elongated scallop shape of madeleines, which sets them apart from all other tea cakes and cookies, comes from baking them in specially formed madeleine pans, also called madeleine tins or plaques. Although these pans can be manufactured from a variety of metals, we found in our investigation of madeleines (see page 21) that the best pans are made from tinned steel. The King Arthur Flour Baker's Catalog (800-827-6836) sells two types of tinned steel madeleine pans. The traditional French Madeleine Pan measures 15½ by 7 inches, has twelve 2-by-3-inch cups, and costs $13.75. The Shell Madeleine Pan produces cookies in a rounder, seashell shape. It measures 13 by 7 inches overall, has eight 2½-inch cups, and costs $10.75.

SPECIALTY TEAS
Marcel Proust, in *Remembrance of Things Past*, unwittingly catapulted the madeleine to fame and cemented its reputation as the unparalleled partner for tea. To find the perfect partner for the madeleines you'll make using our recipes on page 21, consult the Upton Tea Quarterly, which is the newsletter and mail-order catalog of Upton Tea Imports (231 South Street, Hopkinton, MA 01748; 800-234-8327). The company sells all manner of tea paraphernalia, including English and German Chatsford teapots and mugs; cozies; strainers and infusers; and canisters. The real focus, however, is on tea. Single-estate and specialty teas from India, Sri Lanka, Nepal, China, Taiwan, Japan, and Africa are all available. The catalog is organized by country, and further by regional types of tea and districts within the country, where applicable. For instance, because teas from different regions of India have their own particular characteristics, you can choose among teas from the Darjeeling, Sikkim, Assam, and Nilgiri districts. The Chinese teas for sale include Congou, China Green, Scented, White, and Oolong & Souchong. Distinctive tea blends and flavored teas are also available.

FAT-SKIMMING LADLE
The healthfulness and consistency of broths and soups—including our Hearty Chicken Soup recipes on page 15—benefit greatly from skimming away excess fat. If you have ever chased a puddle of liquid fat around the surface of a stock or broth, though, you know how elusive it can be. To banish a maximum of fat with a minimum of effort, try the Fat-Off Ladle, available in the Williams-Sonoma catalog (800-541-2233) for $15. This Swiss-made stainless steel ladle is specially designed with edge slots around one side of the three-and-three-quarter-inch diameter bowl. When you lower the ladle into broth, the fat flows through the slots and collects in the bowl. When it fills up, remove it from the pot and pour off the fat from the side without the slots.

"DRY" SEA SCALLOPS
Sea scallops, the mollusks discussed in our story on page 6, are harvested all year in North Atlantic waters. In our recipes, we prefer unprocessed, or "dry," sea scallops (which have not been dipped in a liquid solution to extend shelf life) because they do not leak liquid while sautéing. If you are unsure whether the scallops available to you locally have been processed, you can order dry sea scallops from Jake's Fish Market (2425 Broadway, New York, NY 10024; 212-580-5253). The size of these untreated scallops varies according to what is on the market, but they are available year-round for $12.99 per pound, plus the cost of packing and overnight shipping.

SAUSAGE CASINGS
If you want to make links from the chicken sausage recipes from Bruce Aidells' Master Class on page 12, you will need to purchase sausage casings. Often, you can order casings from your local butcher, but they are also available by mail from The Sausage Maker (26 Military Road, Buffalo, NY 14207; 716-876-5521). Natural casings, made from the intestines of sheep, hogs, and beef, come in a variety of sizes suitable for everything from narrow frankfurters to whole bolognas. Aidells recommends using one-inch to one-and-one-quarter-inch hog casings, which are sold in bundles called "hanks." Each hank costs $23.95 and will accommodate approximately ninety to one hundred pounds of meat, which will last a home sausage maker for many batches. The hanks are packed in dry salt and, when left in the packing salt and refrigerated, will keep for about a year. Another option, recommended by the people at The Sausage Maker, is to buy collagen casings derived from cattle hides. One package of collagen casings containing three coils is called a caddy, which sells for $14.95 each in both the one-inch and one-and-one-quarter-inch diameters. A caddy of one-inch casings will accommodate roughly thirty pounds of meat whereas a caddy of the one-and-one-quarter-inch size will hold between forty and forty-three pounds. Collagen casings will keep for six months in the refrigerator. ∎

BEEF STIR-FRY
page 20

HEARTY CHICKEN NOODLE SOUP
page 15

CHOCOLATE CREAM PIE
page 24

**WATERCRESS SALAD WITH SEARED
SCALLOPS AND ORANGE VINAIGRETTE**
page 8

PASTA WITH STEAMED MUSSELS
page 9

QUICK-COOKED CARROTS WITH BUTTER AND PARSLEY
page 25

Orange Compote with Star Anise

Remove zest from 3 of 4 oranges with vegetable peeler. Bring 1 cu[p]
water, ½ cup sugar, 4 star anise, and all but two strips of the ze[st]
to boil in medium saucepan. Reduce heat and simmer until flavo[rs]
blend and a thin syrup has formed, about 20 minutes. Meanwhil[e]
peel remaining orange and remove outer white pith from all fo[ur]
oranges, without separating oranges into segments. Slice orang[es]
a scant ½-inch thick or section them; remove seeds. Arrange [in]
medium shallow bowl. Remove and discard zest from hot syru[p]
stir in 2 tablespoons crème de cassis, then immediately pour ov[er]
oranges. Cool oranges to room temperature, then refrigerate u[n]
til ready to serve. Cut remaining two strips zest into
fine julienne strips. Garnish oranges with zest
when ready to serve.
Serves 4.

COOK'S
ILLUSTRATED

No-Knead American Bread

Homemade Bread in Just Two Hours

Steak Taste Test

Supermarket Beats Omaha

Best Chiffon Cake

Richer, Moister, More Tender

Rating Standing Mixers

Inexpensive Models No Bargain

HOMEMADE FROZEN YOGURT

CHICKEN POT PIE REINVENTED

PERFECT LONG-GRAIN RICE

RATING INEXPENSIVE RED WINES

$4.00 U.S./$4.95 CANADA

"Strawberries"
See page 15 for a frozen yogurt recipe that uses fresh stawberries.

ILLUSTRATION BY
BRENT WATKINSON

"Espresso Granita"
adapted from
The Stars Dessert Book
by Emily Luchetti
(HarperPerennial, 1991)

ILLUSTRATION BY
CAROL FORTUNATO

COOK'S
ILLUSTRATED

Publisher and Editor CHRISTOPHER KIMBALL

Executive Editor MARK ZANGER

Senior Editor JOHN WILLOUGHBY

Food Editor PAM ANDERSON

Senior Writer JACK BISHOP

Consulting Editors MARK BITTMAN
STEPHANIE LYNESS

Assistant Editor ADAM RIED

Editorial Assistant ELIZABETH CAMERON

Test Cook MELISSA HAMILTON

Art Director MEG BIRNBAUM

Food Stylist MARIE PIRAINO

Special Projects Designer DEBBIE WOLFE

Managing Editor KEITH POWERS

Editorial Prod. Coordinator KARIN L. KANEPS

Copy Editor GARY PFITZER

Marketing Director ADRIENNE KIMBALL

Circulation Director ELAINE REPUCCI

Ass't Circulation Manager JENNIFER L. KEENE

Circulation Coordinator JONATHAN VENIER

Circulation Assistant C. MARIA PANNOZZO

Production Director JAMES McCORMACK

Project Coordinator SHEILA DATZ

Production Coordinator PAMELA SLATTERY

Systems Administrator MATTHEW FRIGO

Production Artist KEVIN MOELLER

Vice President JEFFREY FEINGOLD

Controller LISA A. CARULLO

Accounting Assistant MANDY SHITO

Office Manager TONYA ESTEY

Special Projects FERN BERMAN

EDITORIAL

A GOOD DAY FOR MUG-BREAD

There is a story in *Old Squire's Farm* in which C. A. Stephens tells of his grandmother's mug-bread, so named because it was started in a lavender- and gold-banded, white porcelain mug. (This bread is an old Yankee recipe and was also called milk-yeast bread, patent bread, milk-emptyings bread, and salt-rising bread. A recipe for the latter can be found in *Beard on Bread*.) In the evening his grandmother would mix "two tablespoons of cornmeal, ten of boiled milk, and half a teaspoonful of salt in that mug, and set it on the low mantel shelf behind the kitchen stove funnel, where it would keep uniformly warm overnight." At breakfast time, his grandmother would peer into the mug to see if the little "eyes" had begun to open in the mixture. If everything worked out as planned, water and flour were stirred in and the mixture was put back on the shelf to rise until lunchtime. It was baked into "cartwheels"—foot-wide, yellow-brown loafs just an inch thick—and served with fresh Jersey butter and all the canned berries a boy could eat. But some mornings, the jug would disappear suddenly, and a strong sulfurous smell would linger in the kitchen. In that case, the wrong microbe had "obtained possession of the mug." One never knew how it was going to turn out. It was this element of chance, the not-knowing that made that mug-bread taste so fine.

CHRISTOPHER KIMBALL

Even today, with standardized yeasts and flour, some breads rise faster than others, some rise higher, and some bake up lighter. The fifty loaves of bread we baked for the article on page 9 of this issue proved that, although one can develop a standardized recipe that works admirably, no two loaves are exactly the same. Somehow, cooking, like everything else in life, is not an exact science. It is a bit of adventure and should be approached with a big helping of wild enthusiasm and risk taking. As Harriet Van Horne once said, "Cooking is like love. It should be entered into with abandon or not at all."

Growing up on a Vermont farm, I found that the unknown was a constant neighbor, sharpening the appetite for a host of activities from hunting to fishing, from hitching up a new team to boiling off maple sap to make sugar. The sap might run well or it might not, the fish might be biting or not, a six-point buck might walk right past your tree stand or not, and that new team might hitch up well together or it might not, turning your wagon over in a ditch or running your seeder into a pile of rocks. Like the New England weather, one just never did know what was in store. Our family used to hike up to the top of our mountain near the small abandoned barn on the ridge to pick blackberries. Some years we would get a bucketful and other years, even when the weather was good, we'd get no more than a quart of hard, small berries. It was a chance we were used to taking. But when the berries were fat and plentiful, the sky was bluer, the air scented more sweetly with fern and pine, as if all of the good memories of the lean years were collapsed into that one enchanted summer.

These days, our small Vermont town has a "coming of age" ritual, which also has unexpected outcomes. There is a cave at the mouth of the Green River up in Beartown, its entrance hidden by a patch of stinging nettles. Dads take their sons and daughters through the cave when they think they're ready to negotiate the long, dark passage. Last summer it was time for Whitney, my seven-year-old daughter, to make her first visit. She is a bit shy and never the first to rush into the unknown. I was apprehensive about the trip.

With some friends, we packed a bunch of local kids into the flatbed of a large Chevy pickup. The truck was left at the end of the road, and we walked up through an abandoned camp, then to the mouth of the cave, where each child was given a candle. I went first, with five kids in line behind me, Whitney in the middle of the pack. The cave starts out narrow—about five feet high—and the stream that runs through it was deep and searingly cold. In the weak half-light of the candles, we scrambled back to a large, circular room, where we climbed up a funnel to the next level. The cave narrowed considerably at this point, and I made my way to the end, a small opening where the water bubbled up from a deep spring. I looked back and saw my daughter's mud-streaked face in the flickering glow. She looked confident, more mature than usual, and gave me a quick, intimate smile that said "I did it." I was proud, of course, but also filled with the wild joy of the unexpected. It was the journey together that provided the yeast that day, struggling through the dark cave, not knowing if she would make it all the way to the end. Next year it would be her younger sister's turn, but that could wait. On that hot August day, the mug-bread had turned out just fine. ∎

NOTES

FROM READERS

CHOCOLATE CHIP COOKIE CONUNDRUM

I would like to try the chocolate chip cookie recipe in the February 1996 issue, but the "turn 90 degrees and put back together" technique for forming the cookies has me somewhat at a loss. Do I put the two sides so it looks like a figure eight, do I turn and flip so it looks like an hourglass, or do I just turn one half to the right and one half to the left so it ends up looking the same?

CERI ESCODI
Washington, D.C.

You are one of several readers who let us know that they were having a tough time understanding how to form these cookies. We hope that the illustration below, and these instructions, will clarify matters. Essentially, you form a ball from a scant quarter cup of the dough (*see* part 1, below) and pull the ball apart into equal halves (part 2). Each half will have a jagged surface where it was ripped from the other. Rotate each half *up* so the jagged surface faces the ceiling (part 3). Now, jam the halves back into one ball so that the top surface remains jagged (part 4). The nooks and crannies you have created will give the finished cookies an attractive and somewhat rough, uneven appearance.

FORMING CHOCOLATE CHIP COOKIES

COLD-BREWING COFFEE

Your article entitled "The Best Coffee-Brewing Method" in the February 1996 issue has, in my opinion, one glaring omission—the cold-brewing method. This method produces what anyone who has ever tasted it agrees is the smoothest cup of coffee to be had. Cold brewing involves soaking the coffee grinds for up to twelve hours in cold water and then filtering through a dense fiber filter. What remains is a coffee concentrate free of the acids and oils that wreak havoc on delicate stomachs, but with no loss of flavor (or caffeine). The concentrate is added to hot water in a 3:1 ratio for "instant" coffee that rivals any heat-brewed coffee.

MAJEL R. STEIN
Richmond, VA

As you note, cold brewing produces a concentrated coffee—almost an extract, in fact—which, when mixed with hot water, results in a mild, low-acid cup. This may be a major advantage for those with delicate stomachs easily upset by the more common, heat-brewed coffee. As Ted Lingle of the Specialty Coffee Association notes, however, the most desirable of the roughly eight hundred flavor compounds in coffee are released by water between 195 and 205 degrees. Water that is at room temperature or colder misses some of the lighter aromatic flavors, along with many of the acids and oils in the coffee. If your stomach can stand it, acidity, along with body, aroma, and flavor, is one of the traits that give good coffee its character.

The relative absence of acidity in the finished product and the clear inconvenience of a brew period of ten to twenty-four hours are the reasons we chose not to include cold brewing in our round of tests.

DRIP-BREWING COFFEE

I agree with you on the top-rated manual drip method for brewing coffee; it's the one I use—but with one modification. To resolve the problem of water channeling right through the dry grounds, I first mix the grounds

directly with the hot water to ensure complete contact, allow better control of the extraction time, and improve filtering speed.

Usually, I make one-quart batches by microwaving the water in a one-quart measure. When the water boils, I remove it from the microwave and stir it briefly (this cools the water slightly, as the microwave tends to superheat it) before adding the coffee. If you add the coffee without the stirring, the mixture suddenly boils over and you end up with quite a mess. Near the desired extraction time, pour the mixture into the filter. Pouring the liquid off the settled grounds avoids clogging the filter and speeds extraction.

BILL STRENK
Caledonia, NY

Your method sounded really good to us, so we tested it several times. Our results, however, were just the opposite of yours: a slightly slower filtering speed. As you describe, we heated one quart of water in the microwave, mixed in the coffee grounds, and allowed a four-minute extraction time. Although a portion of the grounds was still suspended in the water at the end of the four minutes, most had settled to the bottom of the container, as you noted. Then we poured the mixture through a manual drip setup. The coffee took two minutes to drip through the filter and fill an eleven-ounce mug, and we noticed that the grounds had collected at the bottom of the filter, slowing the drip speed slightly. When we followed our usual procedure of simply placing coffee grounds in the filter and pouring water through, the same eleven-ounce mug filled thirty seconds faster, in one and one-half minutes, and the grounds were distributed evenly over the sides of the filter. In both cases, the coffee was excellent.

RETRO-BREWING COFFEE

I was interested to read that coffee brewed in a vacuum pot was preferred. Vacuum pots were quite common in the 1950s. The pot was manufactured by the Silex Company and was always referred to as a "Silex." The pots were fragile, however, and required frequent replacement. And as Mr. Bishop found, it takes a deft touch to handle the pot well.

The Chemex pot came along shortly after and became the pot of choice among fussy coffee brewers. It was a more elegant design, with a wooden collar, and was marketed as a more upscale item. The Chemex marked the beginning of

ILLUSTRATION BY ALAN WITSCHONKE

the use of paper filters. The Melitta pot, with a re- placeable plastic cone for the filter, was a more practical pot for everyday use and gradually re- placed the Chemex.

TONI MATSU
Marblehead, MA

The Chemex pot is still around. International Housewares Corporation, the Massachusetts- based manufacturer of the Chemex, sells the pot in three sizes: a six-cup for about $24; an eight- cup for about $28; and a ten-cup for about $32. Call 413-274-3396 for ordering and shipping in- formation.

FOAMING PASTA WATER

R *ecently, I cooked some lasagna noodles in a large pot of boiling water, removing them when they were done. Rather than waste the wa- ter, I added the ziti that I wanted to cook next. As soon as the first ziti hit the water, it was compa- rable to a mini-explosion. The water foamed and bubbled over violently. Why did this happen?*

MARILYN MAGGI
Surfside Beach, SC

Dr. Susan Brewer, associate professor of food chemistry at the University of Illinois; a repre- sentative from the National Pasta Association; and an associated cereal chemist all agree that your mini-explosion occurred because of the starch in the pasta. The cooking lasagna noodles release starch molecules into the water that, like protein molecules, concentrate at the surface to form a skin that traps the steam beneath, causing pressure to build.

At the same time, as the water continues to heat, some of its molecules transform from their liquid state to their gaseous state. That is, they turn to steam. The gaseous molecules, which move much faster than their liquid counterparts and require about three hundred times as much space, cause a rapid expansion in volume.

In addition to forming a surface skin, the starch molecules also coat the vaporized steam bubbles, giving them the extra strength that allows them to accumulate into foam. When you broke the starch skin by adding the second batch of pasta, the pres- sure beneath forced the trapped foam bubbles and steam skyward. They escaped so abruptly, in fact, that the force was explosion-like, as you wit- nessed.

Although there is a downside to this method, you could try adding a teaspoon of oil to the wa- ter to reduce the foam. Because molecules are at- tracted to like molecules, the oil will prevent the starch molecules from bonding into a continuous skin at the water's surface. Thus, steam will be able to escape better as the water molecules va- porize, keeping foam buildup to a minimum. The downside to this method is that the oil will film the pasta, making it difficult for the sauce to ad- here. Alternatively, cooling the water slightly by simply blowing on it or stirring it with a spoon be- fore adding the second batch of pasta will reduce (though not eliminate) the foaming.

PECAN PIE AND ITS KIN

R *egarding Stephen Schmidt's article on pecan pie and its references to chess pie in the December 1995 issue, I always thought that real chess pie contained both white vinegar and corn- meal, in small amounts. Though I don't know what these two ingredients are supposed to do, I know I have made pies that way before and had success.*

ELLEN WILSON
Pittsburgh, PA

During the course of his research on pecan and chess pies, author Stephen Schmidt did run across recipes calling for minute quantities of both corn- meal and vinegar. He posits that the cornmeal, like the flour and cornstarch with which he ex- perimented in the kitchen, is added to stabilize and thicken the pie filling. Our pecan pie recipes eliminate the need for stabilizers because the pies are baked at a temperature sufficiently low to avoid the danger of curdling the eggs in the fill- ing. We found that any flour or cornmeal added to the filling tasted slightly raw and felt grainy in our mouths, again because the pies are cooked at a low oven temperature. Vinegar may be present in some recipes to help cut the overwhelming sweet- ness by providing a taste counterpoint of tang, much like our Buttermilk Pecan Pie with Raisins.

ELECTRIC FRYERS NEEDN'T DISAPPOINT

I *purchased a DeLonghi Roto-Fryer based on a recommendation in the charter issue of* Cook's Illustrated *and I've experienced problems with food sticking to the fryer basket.*

It seems that any recipe, such as sesame chicken, that calls for an egg—as opposed to a bread—coating sticks mercilessly to the basket. I have tried immersing the basket in hot oil before adding the food, as well as using Pam cooking spray on the basket. Neither helps. Are these recipes better suited to wok cooking, where you ease the food down the side of the pan and let it fry on its own rather than in a basket?

BILL LUISI
Clinton, MA

After receiving your letter, we pulled out our elec- tric fryer and tried a few experiments. To no one's surprise, our egg white–dipped chicken pieces stuck to the fryer basket just as you described. Egg whites are essentially liquid protein, which expands quickly upon contact with intense heat. If the egg coating on the pieces of chicken is too thick, the excess egg will expand around the wires in the mesh of the fryer basket, causing the food to cling.

To get around this sticking problem, we adapted the following method for sesame chicken from Nina Simonds' *China Express* (Morrow, 1993). After marinating one and one-half pounds of boneless, skinless chicken breasts in an Asian- style marinade, we added one egg white to the mixture at the end of the marinating time. We turned the breasts to coat them evenly with the egg white and then dredged them in a mixture of one cup sesame seeds and one-half cup corn starch. After dredging, we removed the chicken to a wire rack to dry for thirty minutes, and then fried it in the deep fryer with absolutely no stick- ing. The cornstarch makes the sesame seeds ad- here evenly to the surface of the chicken pieces, ensuring that no egg white is exposed to touch— and thus stick to—the wire mesh fryer basket. ■

WHAT IS IT?

I *n going through some boxes left by my mother, who died recently, I came across this item. The bottom outer shell and the top are shinier than the inset with the holes, which fits snugly into the bottom. It was in a box with other kitchen items, so I am certain it is a cooking tool of some kind. Can you tell me what it is and how to use it?*

JEAN EISENHART
Sandgate, VT

Do you remember the warm rolls your mother used to serve at dinner? Chances are they ar- rived at the table in your mystery device, which is a Top of the Stove Bun Warmer. Popular throughout the 1930s, '40s, and '50s, the warmer was used by adding a table- spoon or two of water to the

bottom of the pan, putting the rolls in the in- sert and the insert in the pan, covering it with the top, and heating it on the stove burner un- til the water turned to steam. The limited num- ber of holes, and their placement on the side of the insert, prevented the rolls from becoming soggy due to too much contact with steam. Although no longer common, bun warmers are still made and can be special-ordered for about $25 through La Cuisine Kitchenware (323 Cameron Street, Alexandria, VA 22314; 800-521-1176).

Quick Tips

PEELING A FEW TOMATOES

When peeling large quantities of tomatoes, you'll find nothing's faster than a quick dip in boiling water. But for only a few tomatoes, David Smith of Pittsford, New York, finds it quicker and simpler to use the gas flame of a stove burner. (We find this technique works over a hot electric burner as well.)

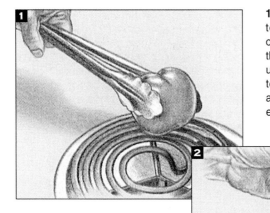

1. Use kitchen tongs to hold the tomato over the burner. Hold the tomato in position until the skin just blisters, then rotate it so another area of skin is exposed to the flame.

2. After rotating the tomato all around, the blistered skin will slip right off.

SLICING HARD WINTER SQUASH

Acorn and other winter squashes can be very difficult to slice. Because they tend to slip, it is hard to begin cutting. Rebecca Shelton of Champaign, Illinois, has found a way to avoid this problem.

1. Place the squash, stem side down, in the drain hole of your sink. This secures the squash and keeps it from rolling around.

2. Cut nearly all the way through, then snap the remaining connective fibers apart.

CHOCOLATE-COATING BAR COOKIES

Terri Dates of Smithville, Texas, passes along this tip from her grandmother for an easy way to give bar cookies a chocolate topping without having to use a double boiler or microwave to melt the chocolate.

1. When the cookies come out of the oven, lay chocolate bars directly on top of the pan contents.

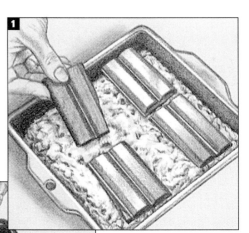

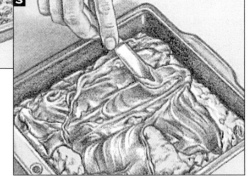

2. Once the chocolate bars have melted, use a table knife to spread the chocolate.

3. Continue spreading until the chocolate makes a thin, even layer over the entire top of the cookies.

MINCING GINGER

Ginger can be minced quickly and easily by using a standard garlic press.

ILLUSTRATIONS BY ALAN WITSCHONKE

ATTRACTIVE VEGETABLE SALADS

Lisa Keys of Middlebury, Connecticut, suggests using a citrus zester to grate vegetables like carrots, cucumbers, and jicama. The long, thin strands that result are ideal for salads and relishes.

MAKING PITA TRIANGLES

For years, Suzanne Burzyk of Wellesley, Massachusetts, had difficulty cutting large quantities of pita with a chef's knife or cleaver. She has since discovered that heavy-duty kitchen shears are quicker and easier for this task.

RETRIEVING BAKED POTATOES

Repeatedly reaching into a hot oven to remove baked potatoes can be a chore—and can lead to burns. Mr. and Mrs. John Victory of Brooklyn Park, Minnesota, make the task easier by baking their potatoes in a muffin tin so they can all be removed at once. They also suggest using this method for baked apples and baked stuffed peppers.

PREPARING GUACAMOLE QUICKLY

Ann L. Harvey, who works at the Four Seasons Resort in Irving, Texas, is a guacamole fan who has found a simple trick to make its preparation easier. To prepare the avocado, simply cut it in half, remove the pit, then press each half through a wire rack set over a bowl. There are no messy cutting boards to clean up, and the job is much quicker.

ASSEMBLING SPRING ROLLS QUICKLY

For restaurant-style speed when making spring and egg rolls, John Pease of Snowmass Village, Colorado, suggests this setup.

1. Ten at a time, arrange wrappers in a vertical line so that only ½ inch of each wrapper is exposed. Now you can easily brush egg wash along the top edges of all ten.

2. Place several tablespoons of the filling mixture just below the center line of the first wrapper, then fold the bottom portion of the wrapper over the filling.

3. Holding the wrapper over the filling with one hand, fold in one side of the wrapper with the other hand.

4. Holding the wrapper with the opposite hand, fold in the opposite side.

5. Roll the wrapper up completely, then set aside, seam side down. Moving up the line, repeat the process with each wrapper.

NOTE: In the January/February issue, we neglected to credit Martha Demetriou of Eden Prairie, Minnesota, with the Quick Tip "Making Spaetzle." Thanks again, and sorry for the slipup.

Thanks to our readers for Quick Tips: The editors of *Cook's Illustrated* would like to thank all of the readers who have sent us their quick tips. We have enjoyed reading every one of them, and have learned a lot. Keep them coming. We will provide a one-year complimentary subscription for each quick tip that we print. Send a description of your special technique to *Cook's Illustrated,* P.O. Box 569, Brookline Village, MA 02147-0569. Please write "Attention: Quick Tips" on the envelope and include your name, address, and daytime phone number. Unfortunately, we can only acknowledge receipt of tips that will be printed in the magazine. In case the same tip is received from two readers, the one postmarked first will be selected. Also, be sure to let us know what particular cooking problems you would like us to investigate in upcoming issues.

Secrets of Chiffon Cake

For a moist, tender cake that still has enough structure, decrease the flour, add an egg yolk, and beat only *some* of the egg whites.

～ BY STEPHEN SCHMIDT ～

Huge, high, and light as a feather, the chiffon cake was one of the most popular desserts of the 1950s, and is still excellent today.

Like the Hollywood stars of the 1920s who were the first to taste Harry Baker's secret-recipe cakes, I was delighted by the uniquely light yet full richness and deep flavor of this American invention, which came to be known as the chiffon cake. To perfect this twentieth century classic, I decided to go back to Betty Crocker's version, as first put before the public by General Mills in 1948 (*see* "A Classic Cake Restored," page 8). If the original seemed in need of fixing, I would then proceed to consult the countless variations, tinkerings, and revisions that have accumulated over the years.

With the exception of the chocolate variation, all of Betty Crocker's original chiffon cakes call for two and one-quarter cups sifted cake flour, which translated to about one and two-thirds cups measured by dip-and-sweep, one and one-half cups sugar, one tablespoon baking powder, one teaspoon salt, one-half cup oil, five egg yolks, three-quarters cup water or other liquid, one cup egg whites (seven to eight large), and one-half teaspoon cream of tartar.

I made a plain, an orange, and a walnut chiffon cake according to the original formula and found that I had three complaints. The cakes were a bit dry—cottony and fluffy rather than moist and foamy, the way I thought chiffon cakes should be—and they seemed to lack flavor, punch, pizzazz. In addition, the cakes rose a bit too high for the pan, a consequence of the downsizing of tube

pans, from eighteen to sixteen cups, that took place around 1970.

Since fat increases perceived moistness and also transmits flavor, I thought that adding more oil might help, but it did not. An orange chiffon cake made with an additional one-quarter cup of oil (up from one-half cup) turned out not only dry and flavorless but also greasy and heavy, an outcome that was as unexpected as it was disappointing.

Most of the cookbook authors whom I consulted wisely stuck with Betty's one-half cup of oil. The changes they had made usually involved the eggs. Predictably, many contemporary recipes called for reducing or eliminating the egg yolks, the idea being to produce a low-cholesterol or cholesterol-free cake. I could not fathom the health advantages of cutting back the yolks from six to two or three, so I didn't bother trying the recipes. (Assuming that the cake serves twelve, the savings per person is only one-quarter to one-third yolk, around a teaspoon.)

However, the idea of using *only* egg whites greatly intrigued me because I thought that the result might be a sort of angel chiffon cake, easier than true angel food cake to make and, I dared hope, perhaps even more delectable. But eleven flops later, I reluctantly concluded that egg white chiffon cakes, no matter how they are made, are tough, wet, bouncy, low-rising disasters. Beware such recipes.

Writers more interested in taste than in health tended to increase the egg content of their chiffon cakes, particularly the whites. These recipes proved successful, but the cakes, even though they were lighter and richer than Betty Crocker's original, still struck me as dry. I instinctively felt that adding more liquid would be a poor idea, but at this point I felt I had no choice but to try. Unfortunately, experimentation proved my instincts right. Increasing the water from three-quarters cup to one cup made the texture gummy and heavy—and the cake still managed to taste dry! There was now only one ingredient left to play with, the

flour, and the thought of touching this one terrified me. Since the problem was dryness, the flour obviously had to be decreased, but I knew from my experience with other sponge-type cakes that decreasing the flour could have very messy consequences. I might end up with a rubbery sponge (*à la* my egg white chiffon experiments) or, worse, with a demonic soufflé that heaved plops of batter onto the floor of my oven.

Whenever a sponge-type cake decides to collapse or explode, the culprit is the same: a lack of structure. Since eggs as well as flour provide structure, I reasoned that I could compensate for a decrease in flour by adding an extra egg yolk. I made an orange chiffon cake using the Betty Crocker formula but decreasing the flour by one-third cup (dip-and-sweep) and increasing the yolks from five to six. The effect was magical. Instead of being fluffy, cottony, and crumbly, the cake was wonderfully moist and so tremblingly tender that slices flopped over at the middle if cut too thin. And the moistness transmitted all of the taste that had been lacking in my first experiments.

The cake, however, was not quite perfect. Evidently the structure was borderline, and so the cake rose very high, spilling over onto the lip of the pan. This made it difficult to cut the cake free from the pan without tearing the top crust. Furthermore, because its top was humped, the cake did not sit flat when turned upside down onto a serving plate. I figured that removing an egg white would help to shrink the cake, but I feared that it might also undercut the structure to the point where the cake wouldn't rise at all. Nonetheless, I gave the idea a try. The resulting cake was lovely coming out of the oven, risen just to the top of the pan and perfectly flat—but its perfection was illusory. I hung the cake upside down to cool and started to clean up the kitchen when I heard a soft plop: My cake had fallen out of the pan.

Once I had taken a few nibbles of the mess, my fears were confirmed. The cake was pasty and overly moist. There was simply not enough structure to hold it together. It had to have that egg white. But perhaps, I thought, using an extra egg *yolk*

PHOTOGRAPHS BY DAVE HENDERSON

in place of that white would save the structure but prevent the excess puffiness. Unfortunately, when I tried this formula, my test cake bulged almost as much as the one I had made with five yolks and eight whites, though it didn't fall out of the pan, which meant that it had sufficient structure.

At this point a chiffon cake recipe that I had seen in Carole Walter's *Great Cakes* (Ballantine, 1991) came to mind. Rather than whipping all of the egg whites, Walter mixed some of them, unbeaten, into the dry ingredients along with the yolks, water, and oil. Thus she incorporated less air into the batter, which should, I reasoned, make for a smaller cake. I tried Walter's technique using seven eggs, two of them added whole to the batter and five of them separated with the whites beaten. Eureka! At last I had the perfect chiffon cake: moist, tender, flavorful, and just the right size for my pan.

Stiff Egg Whites

In the original recipes for chiffon cake published by General Mills, the directions for beating the egg whites read, "WHIP until whites form *very stiff* peaks. They should be much stiffer than for angel food or meringue. DO NOT UNDERBEAT."

These instructions, with their anxiety-inducing capitalized words and italics, are well taken. If the whites are not very stiff, the cake will not rise properly, and the bottom will be heavy, dense, wet, and custardlike. Better to overbeat than underbeat. After all, if you overbeat the egg whites and they end up dry and "blocky," you can simply smudge and smear the recalcitrant blobs with the flat side of the spatula to break up the clumps.

MASTER RECIPE FOR CHIFFON CAKE
Serves 12

If the egg whites to be whipped are not at room temperature, set them in a pan placed in hot tap water and stir them until they are tepid.

1½	cups sugar
1⅓	cups *plain* cake flour (measured by dip-and-sweep)
2	teaspoons baking powder
½	teaspoon salt
7	large room-temperature eggs, 2 left whole, 5 separated
½	cup vegetable oil
1	tablespoon vanilla extract
½	teaspoon almond extract
½	teaspoon cream of tartar

1. Adjust rack to lower-middle position and heat oven to 325 degrees. Whisk sugar, flour, baking powder, and salt together in large bowl (at least 4-quart size). Whisk in two whole eggs, five egg yolks (reserve whites), ¾ cup water, oil, and extracts until batter is just smooth.

2. Pour reserved egg whites into large bowl; beat at medium speed with electric mixer until foamy, about 1 minute. Add cream of tartar, increase speed to medium-high, then beat whites until *very thick and stiff,* just short of dry, 9 to 10 minutes with hand-held mixer and 5 to 7 minutes in KitchenAid or other standing mixer. With large rubber spatula, fold whites into batter, smearing in any blobs of white that resist blending with flat side of spatula.

3. Pour batter into large tube pan (9-inch diameter, 16-cup capacity). Rap pan against countertop five times to rupture any large air pockets. If using two-piece pan, grasp on both sides with your hands while firmly pressing down on the tube with thumbs to keep batter from seeping underneath pan during this rapping process (*see* illustration 1). Wipe off any batter that may have dripped or splashed onto inside walls of pan with paper towel (illustration 2).

4. Bake cake until wire cake tester inserted in center comes out clean, 55 to 65 minutes. Immediately turn cake upside down to cool. If pan does not have prongs around rim for elevating cake, invert pan over bottle or funnel, inserted through tube (illustration 3). Let cake hang until completely cold, about 2 hours.

MAKING A CHIFFON CAKE

1. Grasping the pan on both sides while firmly pressing down on the tube with your thumbs, rap the pan against the counter five times to rupture any large air pockets.

2. If batter has dripped or splashed onto the inside walls of the pan, wipe it off with a dry paper towel.

3. After baking, invert the pan over a bottle or funnel, inserted through the tube. Let the cake hang until it is completely cold, about 2 hours.

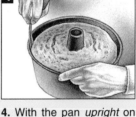

4. With the pan *upright* on the counter, insert a frosting spatula or thin knife between the cake and the wall of the pan. Always pressing *against the pan,* run the spatula or knife around the circumference of the cake.

5. To loosen the cake from the tube, scrape around the tube with a wire cake tester.

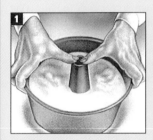

6. If glazing the cake, use a fork or a paring knife to gently scrape all the crust off the cake.

7. If using a two-piece pan, loosen the bottom of the cake from the pan bottom with the spatula or knife.

8. Carefully invert the cake onto a plate. To keep the serving plate from becoming smudged with glaze, slip small pieces of waxed paper beneath the edge of the cake all along the bottom.

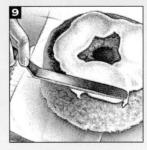

9. Pour the glaze onto the top of the cake. A little at a time, spread the glaze over the top of the cake, letting the excess dribble down the sides.

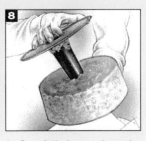

10. If you like, spread the dribbles, before they have a chance to harden, to make a thin, smooth coat.

ILLUSTRATIONS BY HARRY DAVIS

5. To unmold, turn pan upright. Run frosting spatula or thin knife around pan's circumference between cake and pan wall, always pressing *against the pan* (illustration 4). Use cake tester to loosen cake from tube (illustration 5). For one-piece pan, bang it on counter several times, then invert over serving plate. For two-piece pan, grasp tube and lift cake out of pan. If glazing the cake, use a fork or a paring knife to gently scrape all the crust off the cake (illustration 6). Loosen cake from pan bottom with spatula or knife (illustration 7), then invert cake onto plate (illustration 8). (Can be wrapped in plastic and stored at room temperature 2 days or refrigerated 4 days.)

BANANA-NUT CHIFFON CAKE

Follow Master Recipe for Chiffon Cake, decreasing baking powder from 2 teaspoons to 1¼ teaspoons and adding ¼ teaspoon baking soda. Decrease water from ¾ to ⅔ cup and vanilla from 1 tablespoon to 1 teaspoon; omit almond extract. Fold in 1 cup very finely mashed bananas (about 2 large or 3 medium) and ½ cup very finely ground toasted walnuts or pecans to batter before folding in whites. Increase baking time to 60 to 70 minutes.

CHOCOLATE MARBLE CHIFFON CAKE

Combine ¼ cup unsweetened cocoa (any type) and 2 tablespoons firmly packed dark brown sugar in small bowl. Stir in 3 tablespoons boiling water, mixing until smooth. Follow Master Recipe for Chiffon Cake, equally dividing batter into two separate bowls. Mix scant ½ cup of one batter portion into cocoa mixture, then partially fold this mixture back into the batter from which it came. *Sieve or sift* 3 tablespoons cake flour over the now-chocolate batter and continue to fold until just mixed. Pour half the white, then half the chocolate, batter into pan; repeat. *Do not rap pan against countertop.*

DATE-SPICE CHIFFON CAKE

Follow Master Recipe for Chiffon Cake, substituting 1½ cups firmly packed dark brown sugar for white sugar and adding ¾ cup chopped or snipped dates, 2 teaspoons ground cinnamon, ½ teaspoon ground nutmeg, and ¼ teaspoon ground cloves to dry ingredients. Rather than mixing, process dry ingredients in work bowl of food processor fitted with metal chopping blade until dates are reduced to ⅛-inch bits and any lumps of brown sugar are pulverized. Continue with Master Recipe, omitting almond extract.

LEMON OR LEMON-COCONUT CHIFFON CAKE

Follow Master Recipe for Chiffon Cake, substituting ½ teaspoon baking soda for baking powder, decreasing water from ¾ to ⅔ cup and vanilla from 1 tablespoon to 1 teaspoon, and omitting almond extract. Along with vanilla, add grated zests of 2 large lemons and 2 tablespoons strained lemon juice. (For Lemon-Coconut Chiffon Cake, proceed as above, adding ⅔ to 1 cup lightly packed sweetened flaked coconut,

chopped a bit with chef's knife, to batter before folding in whites.)

MOCHA-NUT CHIFFON CAKE

Follow Master Recipe for Chiffon Cake, substituting ¾ cup brewed espresso-strength coffee for the water and omitting almond extract. Add ½ cup finely chopped toasted walnuts and 1 ounce grated unsweetened baking chocolate to batter before folding in whites.

ORANGE OR CRANBERRY-ORANGE CHIFFON CAKE

Follow Master Recipe for Chiffon Cake, substituting 2 tablespoons grated orange zest and ¾ cup strained orange juice for the water, decreasing vanilla from 1 tablespoon to 1 teaspoon, and omitting almond extract. (For Cranberry-Orange Chiffon Cake, proceed as above, adding 1 cup cranberries, chopped to ⅛-inch flecks in food processor, and ½ cup finely chopped toasted walnuts to batter before folding in whites.)

RED VELVET CHIFFON CAKE

A perfect kid's cake—frost it with a fluffy white icing and sprinkle it with coconut.

Follow Master Recipe for Chiffon Cake, adding 1 tablespoon cocoa with dry ingredients, decreasing water from ¾ to ⅔ cup, and adding 2 tablespoons liquid red food coloring with extracts.

OPTIONAL GLAZE FOR CHIFFON CAKE
Enough for 1 cake

Since lumps in the confectioners' sugar don't dissolve completely in the liquid, they really show up once the cake is glazed. Unless you are certain that your sugar is lump-free, better to sift it. Before you glaze the cake, the crumbs must be scraped. With a fork or paring knife, gently scrape all the crust off the cake (*see* illustration 6). To keep the serving plate from becoming smudged with glaze, slip small pieces of waxed paper beneath the cake edge all along the bottom. If making the milk variation, stir in one-half teaspoon of lemon juice to cut the intense sweetness.

    4   tablespoons unsalted butter, melted
  4–5   tablespoons orange juice, lemon juice,
          milk, or coffee (for date-spice
          or mocha-nut variations)
    2   cups sifted confectioners' sugar

Beat butter, 4 tablespoons of the liquid, and sugar in medium bowl until smooth. Let glaze stand 1 minute, then try spreading a little on cake. If cake threatens to tear, thin glaze with up to 1 tablespoon more liquid. A little at a time, spread glaze over cake top, letting excess dribble down sides (illustration 9). Let cake stand until glaze dries, about 30 minutes. If you like, spread dribbles to make a thin, smooth coat (illustration 10). ■

Stephen Schmidt is a regular contributor to *Cook's Illustrated* and the author of the forthcoming *Dessert America* (Scribners, 1996).

PHOTOGRAPH COURTESY OF GENERAL MILLS ARCHIVES

No-Knead Sandwich Bread

Now you can make full-flavored American bread in just two hours and without any hand kneading.

∼ BY CHRISTOPHER KIMBALL WITH EVA KATZ ∼

American loaf breads are quite different from their European cousins, primarily because they contain fat in the form of milk and melted butter. This produces a more tender crumb and a softer loaf particularly well suited for sandwiches, for which less assertive bread works best (notwithstanding the current ill-conceived trend of using thick slabs of focaccia with dainty fixings). As we discovered during the testing process, this is not just an exercise in convenience either. American loaf bread is every bit as inspiring as those toothier imports—there is nothing like a fresh-from-the-oven loaf cut into slabs and slathered with butter and honey.

These days, many home cooks might choose to use a bread machine to make this type of bread. In our experience, this method produces a crust that is mediocre at best and an interior of unpredictable quality that is, all too often, cakelike. As for purchasing this type of bread at the store, it's actually not that easy. Most gourmet shops don't carry a basic sandwich bread; when they do, it's a whole lot more expensive than making your own, and you can't purchase the many variations listed below, such as anadama or buttermilk bread. Of course, many people who might enjoy making terrific sandwich bread at home don't even try it because they think it takes most of a day. So we set out to develop a good, solid recipe that could be done in two hours, start to finish, including baking time.

No Hand Kneading Required

For many home cooks, the other great impediment to making bread at home is the notion of kneading bread by hand. To find out if this was essential, we used a standard American loaf bread recipe and tested hand-kneaded bread against bread kneaded by machine—both in a standing mixer and a food processor—to find out if hand kneading makes better bread. The results were eye-opening. The hand-kneaded loaf *was not as good as the two loaves kneaded by machine!* It was denser, did not rise as well, and the flavor was lacking the pleasant yeastiness found in the other loaves. After some additional testing and discussion, we hit on a reasonable explanation: When kneading by hand, most home cooks cannot resist the temptation of adding too much additional flour, because bread dough is notoriously sticky. In a machine, however, you add no additional flour, and the resulting bread has the correct proportion of liquid to flour.

Now that we knew that machine-kneaded

bread was actually preferable to the hand method, we set out to refine the techniques. We wanted to include separate recipes for a standing mixer and a food processor, given that most home kitchens have one or the other, but not both.

Starting with the standing mixer, we tested the dough hook versus the paddle attachment. (Some recipes use the paddle for part or all of the kneading process.) The hook turned out to be vastly preferable, as dough quickly got caught in the paddle, requiring frequent starting and stopping to free it. We also found that a medium-speed setting (number 4 on the KitchenAid mixer) is better than a slow setting. Although the hook appears to move at an alarming rate, the resulting centrifugal force throws the dough off the hook, resulting in a more thorough kneading. At slower speeds, the dough has a tendency to cling to the hook like a child on a tire swing.

Next we turned to the food processor. This method, to our surprise, was very successful, although the dough did require about four minutes of hand kneading at the finish. (A food processor does not knead as thoroughly as a standing mixer.) Using a metal blade, we pulsed the dry ingredients to combine them. Then, with the machine running, we added the liquid ingredients through the feed tube and processed the dough until it formed into a rough ball. After a rest of two minutes, we processed the dough a second time for about thirty seconds and then removed it to a lightly floured counter for hand kneading. We did test this recipe without any hand kneading but found the resulting bread inferior—coarser in texture, with less rise.

We also noted that the action of the food processor was quite different from that of the standing mixer. A relatively dry dough had worked well in the mixer because it was less likely to stick to the dough hook. However, in the food processor a slightly wetter dough seemed preferable, as the metal blade stretched and pulled it better than a dry dough, which ended up simply being cut into pieces. Therefore, to improve the performance of the food processor, we added two tablespoons of water to the dough.

In addition, we found that the difference in action between food processor and mixer called for

When making bread for use as a sandwich loaf, a tender crumb and a softer crust are virtues.

different types of flour. The reason for this has to do with the difference in protein content of the two types of flour. Bread flour, which has a low protein content, requires a thorough, slow kneading process to properly develop the gluten. This type of kneading action does occur in a mixer, so bread flour worked well there. In the rapid food processor kneading, however, all-purpose flour with its high protein content worked better.

Oven Temperatures and Baking Times

With our dough and kneading methods set, we turned to oven temperatures and baking times. When we baked our bread at 350-, 375-, and 400-degree oven temperatures, the two higher temperatures overcooked the crust by the time the inside of the loaf was done. Again, unlike most European breads, because this American loaf contains milk, butter, and honey, it is prone to quick browning.

To decide the proper baking time, you have to figure out how to gauge when your bread is done. Most cookbooks tell you to tap the bottom of a loaf of bread to see if it is done. This is, at best, an inexact method. It is much better to use an instant-read thermometer, which we inserted halfway into the loaf in the middle of the bottom. After testing bread taken from the oven at 190,

We tried four different shaping methods for this bread and found that the simplest methods were best. This confirmed our opinion that bread dough should be handled gently between rises, with no kneading and a minimum of handling. Other shaping methods, which required more working of the dough, resulted in a squatter, denser loaf. Here is our favorite method:

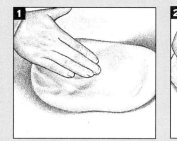

1. Gently press the dough into a rectangle, one inch thick and no wider than the length of the loaf pan.

2. Roll the dough firmly into a cylinder, pressing with your fingers to make sure the dough sticks to itself.

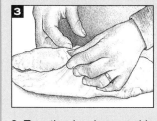

3. Turn the dough seam side up and pinch it closed.

4. Place dough in the pan and press it gently so it touches all four sides of the pan.

5. Place loaf pan in the oven, then immediately pour heated water into the empty loaf pan and close the oven door.

195, and 200 degrees internal temperature, the 195-degree reading was clearly the winner. The lower temperature produced dense bread, and the higher temperature produced dry and overcooked bread. (Note that different types of bread should be baked to different internal temperatures. The recipe for Rustic Country Bread in the January/February 1995 issue, for example, requires an internal temperature of 210 degrees because the dough is extremely wet. I have also made very dry doughs that were completely cooked at 165 degrees.) It should be noted that the length of time the bread is in the oven has a tremendous effect on texture and quality, and the judicious use of an instant-read thermometer is therefore critical.

When our food editor, Pam Anderson, set out to test our final recipes one last time, however, she added a simple enhancement. Instead of removing the loaf from the pan and inserting the thermometer into the bottom, she pushed the thermometer into one end of the loaf, angling it down toward the middle. We tested this ourselves and found the technique to produce the same reading without having to remove the bread from the pan.

Good Bread in Two Hours?

As stated above, one of the objectives in developing this recipe was to produce bread as quickly as possible. My first thought was to use rapid-rise yeast even though I was certain that it would produce inferior bread—another example of technology run amok.

However, not only did the rapid-rise yeast greatly reduce rising times, but, in a blind tasting, the *bread actually tasted better!* (see "Best Yeast for American Sandwich Bread?" page 11). To further speed this process, we preheated the oven to 200 degrees for ten minutes, turned it off, then used it as our proofing box, allowing the dough to rise in a very warm, draft-free environment. Next we tried heating the milk and water to jump-start the yeast. When the liquids were too hot, well over 130 degrees, we had some failures because the yeast was killed by the excess heat. We did find, however, that when we warmed the liquids to about 110 degrees, the rising times were reduced by five to ten minutes. These three changes brought the first rise down to forty minutes and the second rise to a mere twenty. Now we could make homemade bread in two hours, including kneading, both risings, and the baking time, which for us was no more than forty minutes.

At the end of two months of testing, we had produced a terrific loaf of bread in just two hours, start to finish. Using rapid-rise yeast, we kneaded the dough in a standing mixer for ten minutes (and then by hand for a mere fifteen seconds). We then proofed it in a warmed oven for forty to fifty minutes, at which point we gently shaped it and placed it in a loaf pan.

The second rise took twenty to thirty minutes, after which we baked the dough at a moderate 350 degrees for about forty minutes or until the internal temperature reached 195 degrees. And to make the payoff even bigger, we worked out

six variations on the master recipe, from anadama to whole wheat.

MASTER RECIPE FOR AMERICAN LOAF BREAD
Makes one 9-inch loaf

This recipe uses a standing electric mixer, but a food processor variation follows. You can hand-knead the dough, but we found it's easy to add too much flour during this stage, resulting in a somewhat tougher loaf. If you don't have bread flour, you can use all-purpose flour.

3½ cups bread flour, plus extra for work surface
2 teaspoons salt
1 cup warm milk (110 degrees)
⅓ cup warm water (110 degrees)
2 tablespoons butter, melted
3 tablespoons honey
1 package rapid-rise yeast

1. Adjust oven rack to low position and heat oven to 200 degrees. Once oven temperature reaches 200 degrees, maintain heat 10 minutes, then turn off oven heat.

2. Mix flour and salt in bowl of standing mixer fitted with dough hook. Mix milk, water, butter, honey, and yeast in 1-quart Pyrex liquid measuring cup. Turn machine to low and slowly add liquid. When dough comes together, increase speed to medium (setting number 4 on a KitchenAid mixer) and mix until dough is smooth and satiny, stopping machine two or three times to scrape dough from hook if necessary, about 10 minutes. Turn dough onto lightly floured work surface; knead to form smooth, round ball, about 15 seconds.

3. Place dough in *very lightly* oiled bowl, rubbing dough around bowl to lightly coat. Cover bowl with plastic wrap; place in warm oven until dough doubles in size, 40 to 50 minutes.

4. Form dough into loaf as shown in illustrations 1 through 4, at left, placing dough in greased 9-by-5-by-3-inch loaf pan.

5. Cover with plastic wrap; set aside in warm spot until dough almost doubles in size, 20 to 30 minutes. Heat oven to 350 degrees, placing empty loaf pan on bottom rack. Bring 2 cups water to boil.

6. Remove plastic wrap from loaf pan. Place pan in oven, immediately pouring heated water into empty loaf pan (illustration 5); close oven door. Bake until instant-read thermometer inserted at angle from short end just above pan rim into center of loaf reads 195 degrees, about 40 to 50 minutes. Remove bread from pan, transfer to a wire rack, and cool to room temperature. Slice and serve.

FOOD PROCESSOR METHOD

American Loaf Bread made in the food processor was slightly better made with all-purpose flour, but regardless of the flour you use, add an extra two tablespoons of water to the dry ingredients. The food processor blade kneads the softer dough more effectively. During the hand-kneading

ILLUSTRATIONS BY WENDY WRAY

phase, you may need to add a little flour to make a workable dough. To ensure a tender bread, however, add as little as possible.

Follow Master Recipe for American Loaf Bread, substituting equal amount of all-purpose flour for the bread flour and increasing the warm water by 2 tablespoons. Mix flour and salt in bowl of food processor fitted with steel blade. Add liquid ingredients; process until rough ball forms. Let dough rest 2 minutes. Process 35 seconds. Turn dough onto lightly floured work surface and knead by hand until dough is smooth and satiny, 4 to 5 minutes. Continue with master recipe.

SLOW-RISE LOAF BREAD
If you do not have rapid-rise yeast on hand,
try this slow-rise variation.

Follow Master Recipe for American Loaf Bread, substituting an equal amount of dry active yeast for the rapid-rise yeast. Let dough rise at room temperature, instead of in the warm oven, until almost doubled (about 2 hours for first rise and 45 to 60 minutes for second rise).

BUTTERMILK LOAF BREAD
Follow Master Recipe for American Loaf Bread, bringing the water to boil rather than 110 degrees. Substitute cold buttermilk for the warm milk, adding it to the hot water. (The mixing of hot water and cold buttermilk should equal the right temperature—about 110 degrees—for adding the yeast.) Increase the first rise to 50 to 60 minutes.

WHOLE WHEAT LOAF BREAD
Follow Master Recipe for American Loaf Bread, substituting 1⅓ cups whole wheat flour for 1⅓ cups of the bread flour. Increase first rise to 50 to 60 minutes and second rise to 40 minutes.

OATMEAL LOAF BREAD
Bring ¾ cup water to boil in small saucepan. Add ¾ cup rolled oats; cook to soften slightly, about 90 seconds. Follow Master Recipe for American Loaf Bread, decreasing flour from 3½ to 2¾ cups, adding the cooked oatmeal to flour, and omitting the warm water from wet ingredients.

To turn this loaf into Oatmeal-Raisin Bread, simply knead three-quarters cup of raisins, tossed with one tablespoon of flour, into the dough after it comes out of the food processor or mixer.

CORNMEAL LOAF BREAD
Bring ½ cup water to boil in small saucepan. Slowly whisk in ¼ cup cornmeal. Cook, stirring constantly, until mixture thickens, about 1 minute. Follow Master Recipe for American Loaf Bread, decreasing flour from 3½ to 3¼ cups, decreasing milk from 1 cup to ¾ cup, and adding the cornmeal mixture to flour (before incorporating liquids).

ANADAMA LOAF BREAD
Follow recipe for Cornmeal Loaf Bread, substituting molasses for the honey. ∎

PHOTOGRAPHS BY DAVE HENDERSON

BEST YEAST FOR AMERICAN SANDWICH BREAD?

The staff of *Cook's Illustrated* taste-tested our final American bread loaf with eight different yeasts, including Fleischmann's Rapid Rise Yeast, Fleischmann's Active Dry Yeast, Fleischmann's Cake Yeast, Red Star Quick-Rise, King Arthur Regular Instant Yeast, King Arthur Special Instant Yeast, Fleischmann's Instant Yeast, and Red Star Instant Yeast. (We should note, by the way, that many of these yeasts are recommended for breads quite different from the all-purpose American loaf tested in this article, and, therefore, the results might be quite different with another recipe.)

The surprising winner of our mini-tasting was Fleischmann's Instant Yeast, with Fleischmann's Cake Yeast and Fleischmann's Rapid Rise Yeast close seconds. The instant yeast is a mail-order yeast (*see Sources and Resources*, page 32) not always available in supermarkets ("instant" yeast is not the same as "rapid-rise," which is more commonly available), and cake yeast can also be somewhat difficult to locate. For these reasons, we recommend the Fleischmann's Rapid Rise as an excellent, all-purpose yeast.

The most startling result from this taste test, however, was that while Fleischmann's Rapid Rise came out near the top, the regular Fleischmann's Active Yeast placed dead last. It should be noted that the rising methods were also different— we placed the doughs made with rapid-rise yeast in a warmed oven for just forty minutes, whereas breads made with the regular active yeast took about two hours when left to rise on top of the stove. The faster rise, in fact, yielded more flavor and produced a noticeably sweeter bread. One theory is that a rapid rise provides less time for the creation of the acidic by-products of fermentation, hence a sweeter loaf. It is also true that rapid-rise yeast has a superior enzyme structure, which converts starches to sugar faster than regular-rise varieties.

But even with all this, it still seems logical that a longer, gentler rise would allow the dough more time to produce complex flavors. This may be true for a European-style loaf, but an American bread contains both fat (milk and butter) and sugar (honey) so that the complexity of flavors, which would be evident in a plainer loaf, is easily missed here. Even more to the point, though, is the fact that rapid rise is not necessarily an inferior product. Yeast is a plant, not a bacteria, and different varieties have quite different qualities, just as do different varieties of, say, roses. Rapid-rise yeast was genetically engineered to reproduce the best characteristics of yeasts from around the world. Although genetic engineering often results in loss of flavor, our blind taste tests confirmed that, in this case, it produced an excellent product.

As for why the yeast works faster, two primary reasons exist. Besides the more rapid enzyme activity described above, rapid-rise yeast also has an open, porous structure, which means that it absorbs liquid instantly. When these yeasts were first introduced, consumers had difficulty with them because, following habit rather than the manufacturer's directions, they proofed the yeast rather than mixing it directly into the flour. Due to its efficiency, the yeast rapidly ran out of food (starch) and died during the proofing process.

To correct this problem, scientists went back and added more starch to the mix, providing enough food for the yeast to survive proofing. Today, however, most yeast does not have to be proofed. Proofing used to serve two functions. First, it was an indicator of the health of the yeast. Today, yeast is both refrigerated and marked with an expiration date for freshness. (Note that these expiration dates should be taken seriously. I tried baking a loaf with yeast that was one month past expiration, and the rising times were double those experienced with fresh yeast. The resulting loaf was denser with a smaller rise.) Second, although most yeast consists of dead cells encapsulating live cells, and the dead cells do need to dissolve first in order for the live cells to start working, this hydration process occurs quickly when yeast and water are mixed together; it will also occur in short order in the dough mixture during kneading. For this article, therefore, I have opted not to proof the yeast, but I do mix it directly into the warm liquid to speed up rising time. However, feel free to mix yeast in with the flour for any bread recipe if a few extra minutes of rising time is not an issue.

Although proofing is not necessary, keep in mind that the temperature of the water or milk is crucial. Dry yeast will die either in ice water or in liquids at 130 degrees or higher (some yeasts can live up to 170 degrees). When testing the recipes below, we found that hot milk often killed off the yeast and therefore suggest using warm milk (about 110 degrees).—*C.K.*

One-Pot Chicken Pot Pie

Make full-flavored, fresh-tasting chicken pot pie without spending all afternoon.

∽ BY PAM ANDERSON WITH KAREN TACK ∽

Poached chicken, sautéed vegetables, milk, and a dash of sherry combine to make the best one-pot pie.

Most everyone loves a good chicken pot pie, though few seem to have the time or energy to make one. Not surprising. Like a lot of satisfying dishes, traditional pot pie takes time. Before the pie even makes it to the oven, the cook must poach a chicken; take the meat off the bone and cut it up; strain the broth; prepare and blanch vegetables; make a sauce; and mix and roll out biscuit or pie dough.

Given the pie's multistepped, time-consuming nature, our goal was to make the pot pie the best it could be as quickly as possible. Pot pie, after all, is supper food.

From the many recipes we reviewed, it was obvious we weren't the first to try to simplify this dish. Canned vegetables, soups, biscuits, and other processed convenience foods made for short ingredient lists and recipe instructions, but obviously compromised flavor. Because we were looking to beat the clock, though, we were open to shortcuts. Ingredients like boneless, skinless chicken breasts, frozen puff pastry, and frozen green peas were welcome possibilities.

Besides the time concern, my own recent experiences with making pot pie made me also realize two other difficulties. First, the vegetables tend to overcook. A filling that is chock full of bright, fresh vegetables going into the oven looks completely different after forty minutes of high-heat baking under a blanket of dough. Carrots become mushy and pumpkin colored, while peas and fresh herbs fade from fresh spring to drab green. We wanted to preserve the vegetables' color as long as it didn't require any unnatural acts to do so.

I had also made a number of pot pies I thought were too juicy. Before baking, the filling was thick and creamy. When cut into after baking, however, the pie looked like chicken soup en croute. Although we wanted the pie moist and saucy, we also wanted it thick enough to eat with a fork.

Poach It in Broth

We began by determining the best way to cook the chicken. In addition to making pies with roast chicken and poached chicken, we steamed and roasted whole chickens, and braised chicken parts.

Steaming the chicken was time-consuming, requiring about one hour, and the steaming liquid wasn't a strong enough broth for the pot pie sauce. Roast chicken also required an hour in the oven, and by the time we took off the skin and mixed the meat in with the sauce and vegetables, the roasted flavor was lost. We had similar results with braised chicken: It lost its delicious flavor once the browned skin was removed, and the sauce made from the braising liquid tasted too pronounced, distracting us from the meat, vegetables, and crust.

Next we tried poaching, the most traditional cooking method. Of the two poaching liquids we tried, we preferred the chicken poached in wine and broth to the one poached in broth alone. The wine infused the meat and made for a richer, more full-flavored sauce. To our disappointment, however, the acidity of the wine-broth sauce caused the green peas and fresh herbs to lose their bright green color in the oven. Vegetables baked in the broth-only sauce kept their bright color, though the bland sauce needed perking up—a problem we'd have to deal with later. Now we were ready to test this method against quicker-cooking boneless, skinless chicken breasts.

Boneless Breasts, the Best

Because boneless, skinless breasts cook so quickly, sautéing was another possible cooking method. Before comparing poached parts to breasts, we tried cooking the breasts three different ways. We cut raw breast meat into bite-sized pieces and sautéed them; we sautéed whole breasts, shredding the breast meat once cool enough to handle; and we poached whole breasts in canned broth, also shredding the meat.

Once again, poaching was our favorite method. The resulting tender, irregularly shaped chicken pieces mixed well with the vegetables and, much like textured pasta, caused the sauce to cling. The sautéed chicken pieces, however, floated independently in the sauce, their surfaces too smooth to attract sauce. For simplicity's sake, we had hoped to like the sautéed whole breasts. Unfortunately, sautéing caused the outer layer of meat to turn crusty, a texture we did not like in the pie.

Our only concern with the poached boneless, skinless breasts was the quality of the broth. Though both the parts and the breasts were poached in canned broth, we thought the long-simmered poaching liquid of the parts would be significantly better. But in our comparison of the pies, we found no difference in quality, and we were able to shave one-half hour off the cooking time (ten minutes to cook the breasts compared with forty minutes to cook the parts). For those who like either dark or a mix of dark and white meat in the pie, boneless, skinless chicken thighs can be used as well.

No Overcooked Vegetables

A good pot pie with fresh vegetables, warm pastry, and full-flavored sauce tastes satisfying. One with overcooked vegetables tastes stodgy and old fashioned. So we made pies with raw vegetables, sautéed vegetables, and parboiled vegetables.

After comparing the pies, we found that the vegetables sautéed before baking held their color and flavor best, the parboiled ones less so. The raw vegetables were not fully cooked at the end of baking time and gave off too much liquid, watering down the flavor and thickness of the sauce.

Of course, the other means of keeping the vegetables fresh is removing the pie from the oven as quickly as possible. To keep the pie from becoming overly rich and complicated, we had ruled out a double crust. The vegetables became our third reason for keeping the pie single-crusted. To get a bottom crust fully cooked, the pie would have to cook for at least forty-five minutes, at which point the peas and carrots would be lifeless.

Milk, What a Surprise

Our final task was to develop a sauce that was flavorful, creamy, and of the proper consistency.

PHOTOGRAPH BY DAVE HENDERSON

Chicken pot pie sauce is traditionally based on a roux (a mixture of butter and flour sautéed together briefly), which is thinned with chicken broth and often enriched with cream.

Because of the dish's inherent richness, we wanted to see how little cream we could get away with using. We tried three different pot pie fillings, with one-quarter cup of cream, one-quarter cup of half-and-half, and one cup of milk, respectively. Going into the oven all the fillings seemed to have the right consistency and creaminess; when they came out, however, it was a different story. Vegetable and meat juices diluted the consistency and creaminess of the cream and half-and-half sauces. To achieve a creamy-looking sauce, we would have needed to increase the cream dramatically. Fortunately, we didn't have to try it, because we actually liked the milk-enriched sauce. The larger quantity of milk kept the sauce creamy in both color and flavor.

To keep the sauce from becoming too liquid, we simply added more flour. A sauce that looks a little thick before baking will become the perfect consistency after taking on the chicken and vegetable juices that release during baking.

We had worked out the right consistency, but because we had been forced to abandon the wine for the vegetables' sake, the sauce tasted a little bland. Lemon juice, a flavor heightener we had seen in a number of recipes, had the same dulling effect on the vegetables as the wine. I shared this cooking dilemma with *Cook's Illustrated* contributor Stephen Schmidt, who suggested we stir a couple tablespoons of dry sherry into the sauce. Because sherry is more intensely flavored and less acidic than wine, he thought we'd get the flavor boost we wanted without affecting the vegetables. He was right. The sherry gave us the flavor we were looking for without harming the peas and carrots.

This magazine has already featured great recipes for pie pastry and biscuits, so we did not explore this aspect of pot pie in depth. We teamed each of these already published toppings with our newly developed filling and found them extremely compatible. We had achieved our pot pie goals—the method is simple and the pie is good.

SIMPLE CHICKEN POT PIE
Serves 6 to 8
You can make the filling ahead of time, but remember to heat it on top of the stove before topping it. Mushrooms can be sautéed along with the celery and carrots, and blanched pearl onions can stand in for the onion.

- 1 recipe pastry topping
- 1½ pounds boneless, skinless chicken breasts and/or thighs
- 2 cups homemade chicken broth or 1 can (15 ounces) low-sodium chicken broth with water added to equal 2 cups
- 1½ tablespoons vegetable oil
- 1 medium-large onion, chopped fine
- 3 medium carrots, peeled and cut crosswise ¼-inch thick

- 2 small celery ribs, cut crosswise ¼-inch thick
  Salt and ground pepper
- 4 tablespoons butter
- ½ cup flour
- 1½ cups milk
- ½ teaspoon dried thyme leaves
- 3 tablespoons dry sherry
- ¾ cup frozen green peas, thawed
- 3 tablespoons minced fresh parsley leaves

1. Make pastry topping and refrigerate until ready to use.
2. Adjust oven rack to low-center position; heat oven to 400 degrees. Put chicken and broth in small Dutch oven or soup kettle over medium heat. Cover, bring to simmer; simmer until chicken is just done, 8 to 10 minutes. Transfer meat to large bowl, reserving broth in measuring cup.
3. Increase heat to medium-high; heat oil in now-empty pan. Add onions, carrots, and celery; sauté until just tender, about 5 minutes. Season to taste with salt and pepper. While vegetables are sautéing, shred meat into bite-sized pieces. Transfer cooked vegetables to bowl with chicken; set aside.
4. Heat butter over medium heat in again-empty skillet. When foaming subsides, add flour; cook about 1 minute. Whisk in chicken broth, milk, any accumulated chicken juices, and thyme. Bring to simmer, then continue to simmer until sauce fully thickens, about 1 minute. Season to taste with salt and pepper; stir in sherry.
5. Pour sauce over chicken mixture; stir to combine. Stir in peas and parsley. Adjust seasonings. (Can be covered and refrigerated overnight; reheat before topping with pastry.) Pour mixture into 13-by-9-inch pan or any shallow baking dish of similar size. Top with desired pastry dough; bake until pastry is golden brown and filling is bubbly, 30 minutes for large pies and 20 to 25 minutes for smaller pies. Serve hot.

RICH, FLAKY PIE DOUGH
Enough to cover one 13-by-9-inch (or the equivalent) pan or six 12-ounce ovenproof baking dishes
This pastry dough was developed by the publisher, Christopher Kimball, and was featured in the September/October 1994 issue. Refer to the article if you need more detailed instructions.

If you like a bottom crust in your pot pie, you can duplicate that soft crust texture by tucking overhanging dough down into the pan side rather than fluting it.

- 1½ cups all-purpose flour
- ½ teaspoon salt
- 8 tablespoons (¼ pound) unsalted chilled butter, cut into ¼-inch pieces
- 4 tablespoons chilled all-vegetable shortening

1. Mix flour and salt in workbowl of food processor fitted with the steel blade. Scatter butter pieces over flour mixture, tossing to coat butter with a little of the flour. Cut butter into flour with five one-second pulses. Add shortening; continue cutting in until flour is pale yellow and resembles coarse cornmeal, keeping some butter bits the size of small peas, about four more one-second pulses. Turn mixture into medium bowl.
2. Sprinkle 3 tablespoons ice-cold water over the mixture. Using rubber spatula, fold water into flour mixture. Then press down on dough mixture with broad side of spatula until dough sticks together, adding up to 1 tablespoon more cold water if dough will not come together. Shape dough into ball, then flatten into 4-inch-wide disk. Wrap in plastic and refrigerate 30 minutes while preparing pie filling.
3. Roll dough on floured surface to approximate 15-by-11-inch rectangle, about ⅛-inch thick. If making individual pies, roll dough ⅛-inch thick and cut 6 dough rounds about 1 inch larger than pan circumference. Lay dough over pot pie filling, trimming dough to ½ inch of pan lip. Tuck overhanging dough back under itself so folded edge is flush with lip. Flute edges all around. Or don't trim dough and simply tuck overhanging dough down into pan side. Cut at least four 1-inch vent holes in large pot pie or one 1-inch vent hole in smaller pies. Proceed with Simple Chicken Pot Pie recipe.

FLUFFY BUTTERMILK BISCUITS
Enough to cover one 13-by-9-inch (or the equivalent) pan or six 12-ounce ovenproof baking dishes
For more information about biscuit making, refer to Stephen Schmidt's "The Art of Biscuit-Making" in the May/June 1993 issue.

- 1 cup all-purpose flour
- 1 cup plain cake flour
- 2 teaspoons baking powder
- ¼ teaspoon baking soda
- 1 teaspoon sugar
- ½ teaspoon salt
- 8 tablespoons (¼ pound) chilled unsalted butter, quartered lengthwise and cut crosswise into ¼-inch pieces
- ¾ cup cold buttermilk, plus 1 to 2 tablespoons extra, if needed

1. Pulse first six ingredients in workbowl of food processor fitted with the steel blade. Add butter pieces; pulse until mixture resembles coarse meal with a few slightly larger butter lumps.
2. Transfer mixture to medium bowl; add buttermilk; stir with fork until dough gathers into moist clumps. Transfer dough to floured work surface and form into rough ball, then roll dough ½-inch thick. Using 2½- to 3-inch pastry cutter, stamp out 8 rounds of dough. If making individual pies, cut dough slightly smaller than circumference of each dish. (Dough rounds can be refrigerated on lightly floured baking sheet covered with plastic wrap up to 2 hours.)
3. Arrange dough rounds over warm filling and proceed with Simple Chicken Pot Pie recipe. ∎

Homemade Frozen Yogurt

Gelatin creates a smooth, creamy texture, while plain low-fat yogurt and real fruit, vanilla, coffee, or cocoa provide great taste.

∾ BY JACK BISHOP ∾

Talk about bad deals. You pay a king's ransom for a small scoop of commercial frozen yogurt, and frankly it never tastes all that good. Of course, the idea of eating something creamy and cold that is low in fat holds plenty of appeal. But the reality is always a disappointment. When my local yogurt shop changed its flavor names to "Not Just Plain Old Vanilla" (which, in fact, was still regular vanilla) and "Razzleberry" (boy, did I feel stupid asking the yogurt clerk if this was raspberry!), I figured it was time to try making my own frozen yogurt at home.

A faddish health food turned into a mainstream American treat, frozen yogurt is a commercial product that, unlike ice cream or sorbet, has no real history in either home kitchens or restaurants. My initial research did turn up a number of fairly recent recipes, but I started out pretty much on my own with only a few models.

To begin, I listed the things I like about commercial frozen yogurt. The list was pretty short: creamy texture and low fat content. What didn't I like? Plenty. Most commercial frozen yogurt has an unpleasant artificial flavor. I wanted vanilla frozen yogurt that tastes like vanilla beans, not an aroma factory. Likewise, strawberry frozen yogurt should taste like fruit, not bubble gum. In addition to the lack of true, strong flavors, most shop-style yogurt bears no resemblance to regular yogurt. While I don't want to eat something harsh or overly acidic, a little yogurt kick would be nice. Otherwise, why not eat sherbet or some other form of low-fat ice cream?

Flavor First

Although I had come across a few recipes for homemade frozen yogurt that started with flavored yogurt, I was confident that plain yogurt was the way to go. After a few tests, it was clear that strawberry frozen yogurt made with plain yogurt and ripe berries was better than the version made with strawberry yogurt. The same held true for other flavors.

These early tests also pointed the way to an important discovery. Freezing plain yogurt and fruit did not make the best frozen dessert. The yogurt flavor was very strong, and more important, the sugar did not dissolve properly. I needed to add some milk not only to tame the yogurt flavor but to have a liquid in which I could dissolve the sugar over low heat. Adding milk to the base also gave me an easy way to add vanilla bean flavor.

Getting the Texture Right

Soon I was turning out yogurt that tasted very good but whose texture remained a problem. My frozen yogurt was too icy. The smoothness of commercial products—achieved with emulsifiers and gums—was proving elusive.

From experience I knew that water causes iciness in frozen desserts. Obviously, I needed to eliminate some of the water from my base. The first place I looked was the milk. I had been using whole milk in my tests. I considered using half-and-half or heavy cream but resisted due to fat content. Draining the yogurt to remove some of its liquid seemed a better option.

I scooped two cups of plain yogurt into a fine-mesh strainer set over a glass measuring cup. I put the whole contraption in the refrigerator and waited. After about two hours, one-half cup of liquid had drained down into the measuring cup. I experimented with shorter and longer draining periods but eventually realized I had hit the mark the first time out. Draining yogurt less than two hours did not remove enough liquid, while longer periods yielded only a bit more whey and tended to give the yogurt a cheesy flavor.

Although draining the yogurt really cut down on the iciness, I wondered if more improvements could be made. Gelatin is often used to give low-fat desserts a creamy, smooth texture. In some sense it acts like eggs, and because egg yolks are responsible for the smooth texture in premium ice creams, I figured it was worth a try.

When I added an envelope of unflavored gelatin to my working base, though, I did not like the results. The base gelled while chilling in the refrigerator and the frozen yogurt had an unpleasant, gummy quality. However, I had eliminated the problem of icy texture (this frozen yogurt was quite smooth), and by cutting back on the amount

To make frozen yogurt with smooth texture, set the yogurt in a strainer and drain for a couple of hours. This removes enough water to keep the yogurt from becoming icy in the freezer.

of gelatin, I was able to eliminate the rubbery quality in the finished product. Although the base still gels as it chills, the gelatinous texture disappears during freezing. (*See* "How Does Gelatin Work," page 15, for more information on this popular thickener.)

Subtle Tweaking

I was happy with my results at this point but wondered if the fat content of the plain yogurt and/or milk really mattered. When I tried using nonfat yogurt, the texture really suffered. Some fat is required to create a pleasant mouth-feel. I also tried some organic full-fat yogurt. It made frozen yogurt with a richer flavor and texture. The difference was perceptible but not tremendous. Given the fact that this kind of boutique yogurt can be hard to find and does have a higher fat content, I decided to stick with low-fat yogurt in my recipes. However, feel free to use full-fat yogurt.

When I tried using low-fat and nonfat milk, the results were as I expected. Low-fat milk made decent frozen yogurt, but it was definitely icier than batches made with whole milk. The savings in fat grams was not worth the compromise. Frozen yogurt made with skim milk was unacceptable in my opinion.

I own both an electric and manual ice cream machine. As has been my experience with other frozen desserts, frozen yogurt benefits from the extra air that constant electric churning provides. (*See* Sources and Resources on page 32 for a recommendation.)

A few thoughts on serving. Right out of the ice cream machine, my frozen yogurt is soft and supple, much like frozen yogurt dispensed in shops. However, at this point it is fairly warm (the temperature is in the mid-20s), so it needs to be chilled in the freezer for several hours. As the temperature drops, the frozen yogurt becomes firmer, akin to the frozen yogurt you buy in supermarket freezer cases. If your freezer works properly (i.e, it gets down to 0 degrees), you will want to soften frozen yogurt (to around 10 or 12 degrees) on the counter before scooping.

Finally, unlike commercial products, which are usually filled with stabilizers and/or preservatives, homemade frozen yogurt has a short shelf life. Temperature fluctuations in home freezers promote iciness in all homemade frozen desserts, with melting and freezing taking their toll fairly quickly. After two days frozen yogurt becomes icy, so it is best eaten the day it is made, or perhaps the following day.

VANILLA FROZEN YOGURT
Makes 1 generous quart

2 cups low-fat plain yogurt
2 teaspoons unflavored gelatin
1 ¾ cups whole milk
1 cup minus 2 tablespoons sugar
1 5-inch piece vanilla bean, slit
   lengthwise

1. Spoon yogurt into fine-mesh strainer set over glass measuring cup. Place measuring cup in refrigerator; let drain until yogurt releases ½ cup liquid, 1 to 2 hours.

2. Sprinkle gelatin over ¼ cup of the milk in a small bowl; let stand, stirring frequently, until gelatin swells, about 10 minutes.

3. Meanwhile, heat remaining 1½ cups milk, sugar, and vanilla bean in small saucepan, stirring occasionally to dissolve sugar. Remove pan from heat.

4. Add swelled gelatin to hot milk-sugar mixture, stirring until completely dissolved. Scrape seeds from softened vanilla bean into mixture, whisking seeds to evenly distribute; discard bean. Cool to room temperature, then mix with drained yogurt.

5. Refrigerate yogurt mixture until it cools to at least 40 degrees. Pour chilled gelatinous mixture into canister of ice cream machine; churn until frozen. (Can be served as soft frozen yogurt at this point, or can be stored in a sealed plastic container for 2 days before it becomes icy.)

CHOCOLATE FROZEN YOGURT
Makes 1 generous quart
Cocoa powder delivers a strong chocolate punch without adding an excessive amount of fat or calories. I prefer Dutch-processed cocoa in this recipe. It has a mellower flavor and is not as harsh as natural cocoa.

Follow recipe for Vanilla Frozen Yogurt, increasing sugar to 1 cup and whisking 6 tablespoons unsweetened cocoa, along with sugar, into milk. Omit vanilla bean but stir in 1 teaspoon vanilla extract after the milk mixture cools to room temperature.

COFFEE FROZEN YOGURT
Makes 1 generous quart
If you prefer to use fresh-brewed coffee, steep three tablespoons of coarse-ground coffee in the hot milk until strongly flavored, about 20 minutes. Strain and discard the coffee grounds. Reheat the mixture before mixing in the gelatin.

Follow recipe for Vanilla Frozen Yogurt, increasing sugar to 1 cup and whisking 6 to 7 teaspoons instant espresso powder into hot sugar-milk mixture. Omit vanilla bean but stir in 1 teaspoon vanilla extract after mixture cools to room temperature.

STRAWBERRY FROZEN YOGURT
Makes 1 generous quart
Really ripe, sweet fruit will make a tremendous difference in this recipe. The liquid in the strawberries means that this frozen yogurt will become icy fairly quickly, so rather than storing it, you are better off eating it the day it is made.

2 cups low-fat plain yogurt
1 pint fresh strawberries, hulled
   and sliced
¾ cup sugar
1 teaspoon vanilla extract
1 cup whole milk
2 teaspoons unflavored gelatin

1. Follow step 1 in recipe for Vanilla Frozen Yogurt.

2. Meanwhile, mix berries, ¼ cup of the sugar, and vanilla in medium bowl. Crush fruit lightly with potato masher; macerate at room temperature for 1 hour.

3. Pour ¼ cup of the milk into small bowl. Sprinkle gelatin over milk; let stand, stirring frequently, until gelatin swells, about 10 minutes.

4. Meanwhile, heat remaining ¾ cup milk and ½ cup sugar in small saucepan, stirring occasionally to dissolve sugar. Remove from heat.

5. Add swelled gelatin into hot milk-sugar mixture, stirring until completely dissolved. Cool to room temperature, then mix, along with crushed strawberries, with drained yogurt.

6. Follow step 5 in recipe for Vanilla Frozen Yogurt. (Can be kept frozen for 1 day before becoming icy.)

RASPBERRY FROZEN YOGURT
Makes 1 generous quart
Raspberries can be handled much like strawberries. However, the fruit mixture needs to be strained to remove the seeds.

Follow recipe for Strawberry Frozen Yogurt, substituting 4 cups fresh raspberries or 1 bag (20 ounces) frozen and thawed raspberries for the strawberries. After macerating 1 hour, strain fruit through fine-mesh strainer to remove seeds, then proceed with the recipe. ■

HOW DOES GELATIN WORK?

If only all those Jell-O-eating kids knew how gelatin was made, I doubt that it would remain among their favorites. The woman on the phone at the consumer hot line for Knox Unflavored Gelatin tells me that gelatin is derived from the skin and connective tissue of cows and pigs. This protein-rich material is boiled, filtered, dried, and mechanically ground into a fine powder that can be used to thicken mousses, cheesecakes, parfaits, and various liquids.

But gelatin has a number of distinctly nonculinary uses. As a protein, gelatin can be used to correct brittle nails. It also can be used to set your hair, starch rayon and lace fabrics, or preserve decorative fruit displays. Why is gelatin so versatile? Because it has a tremendous ability to tie up water. When the individual water molecules are bonded to gelatin, they can't bond with each other to form large, perceptible ice crystals.

As with my recipes, most culinary uses for gelatin rely on a two-step process—soaking and then dissolving. Gelatin is usually soaked in some cool or cold liquid so it can swell and expand. It is then dissolved in hot liquid. This dual process results from the fact that when unsoaked gelatin is added directly to hot liquid, the outside edges of each granule expand instantly and form a gel coating, preventing the inside from becoming hydrated. The center of each gelatin particle then remains hard and undissolved. In contrast, soaking in cold or cool liquid allows the particles to expand slowly so that they can tie up the maximum amount of liquid.

Once the gelatin has expanded, it should be dissolved in hot but not boiling liquid. Boiling breaks down gelatin and causes it to lose some effectiveness.

Quick and Easy Antipasti

~

Italian antipasti consists of a group of small dishes set out before the meal—or, as the name implies, before the pasta course. The recipes illustrated below were developed by Michelle Scicolone, author of *The Antipasto Table* (Morrow, 1991). Use them alone or together as appetizers, cocktail snacks, or to make a light meal with salad and pasta.

PROSCIUTTO AND GOAT CHEESE ROULADES

Serves 8

1

1. Mix 8 ounces of mild fresh goat cheese, 2 tablespoons of minced fresh parsley leaves, and 1 small minced garlic clove in a small bowl until well blended. Cut 12 strips of prosciutto in half, forming 24 strips, each about 3 inches by 1½ inches. (You'll need about 4 ounces of prosciutto in all.)

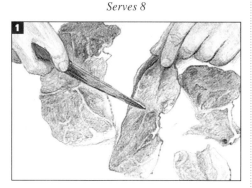

2

2. Place about 2 teaspoons of the cheese mixture on each prosciutto strip.

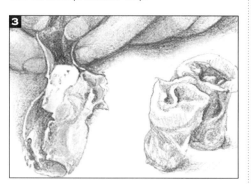

3

3. Fold the sides of each strip over the cheese mixture, then fold one end over, forming a roll. Arrange the rolls on a plate and sprinkle them with 1 tablespoon of olive oil, 1 tablespoon of fresh lemon juice, and ground black pepper to taste. Serve them at room temperature.

PARMESAN WITH DATES

Serves 8

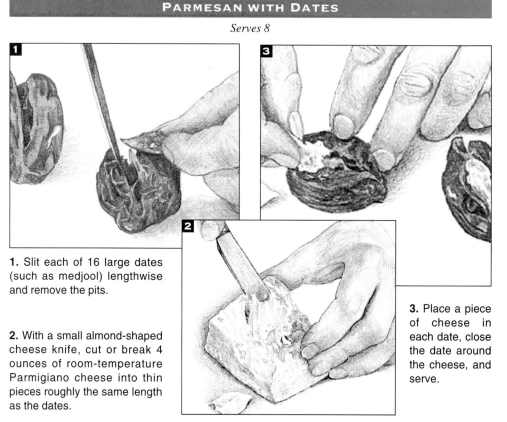

1

1. Slit each of 16 large dates (such as medjool) lengthwise and remove the pits.

2. With a small almond-shaped cheese knife, cut or break 4 ounces of room-temperature Parmigiano cheese into thin pieces roughly the same length as the dates.

3

3. Place a piece of cheese in each date, close the date around the cheese, and serve.

MARINATED ZUCCHINI WITH PARMESAN

Serves 8

1

1. Using a mandolin, V-slicer, or food processor, slice 1 pound of well-rinsed zucchini into very thin slices.

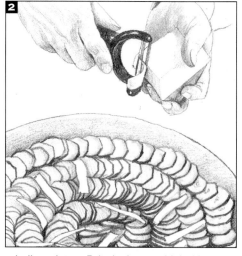

2

2. Arrange the slices, overlapping them slightly, on a shallow platter. Drizzle the zucchini with ½ cup of olive oil, 3 tablespoons of fresh lemon juice, and salt and pepper to taste. With a vegetable peeler or a small, sharp paring knife, shave 4 ounces of Parmigiano-Reggiano cheese over the zucchini. Serve.

ILLUSTRATIONS BY ANATOLY

CRISPY CHEESE WAFERS

Makes about 2½ dozen

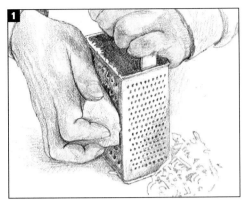

1. Grate 1 pound of Parmigiano-Reggiano or Montasio cheese on the largest holes of a box grater.

2. Heat 1 teaspoon of butter in a medium skillet over medium-low heat, coat the pan bottom with butter, and pour out the excess. Sprinkle a 3-inch area of the pan with a pinch of cornmeal. Spread 2 tablespoons of the grated cheese in the 3-inch circle. (Do not make the layer of cheese too thick or the wafer will be chewy instead of crispy.)

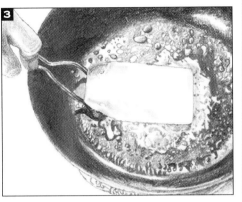

3. Cook the cheese, flattening it with a spatula if necessary, until melted and golden on one side, about 2 minutes.

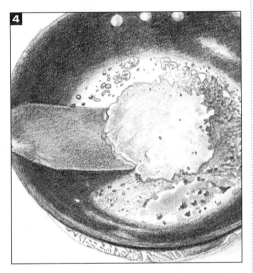

4. Carefully flip the wafer over and cook until it is golden and set, about 1 minute more. Do not let the wafer brown or it will become bitter. Transfer the wafer to a paper towel to drain. Wipe out any crumbs from the pan and repeat with the remaining cornmeal and cheese.

GRILLED MOZZARELLA AND SUN-DRIED TOMATO SKEWERS

Serves 8

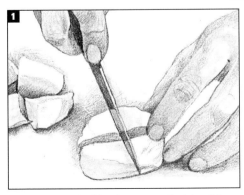

1. Cut 1 pound of fresh mozzarella into sixteen 1-inch cubes. (*Ciliegine,* that is, small, 1-ounce fresh mozzarella balls, can be used in place of the cut cheese.)

2. On each of 8 short bamboo or wooden skewers, alternately thread marinated sun-dried tomatoes, mozzarella, and basil leaves. Brush the cheese with some tomato oil, then grill or broil the skewers until the cheese just begins to melt, turning once. Serve immediately.

ARTICHOKE CROSTINI

Makes 8 crostini

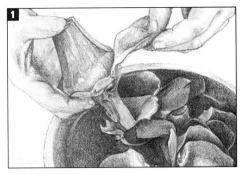

1. Remove the leaves from 4 steamed and cooled artichokes. Reserve the leaves for another use.

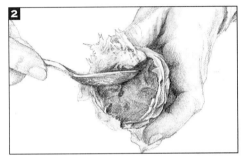

2. Scrape the fuzzy choke away from the artichoke heart.

3. Mash the artichoke hearts and stems with a fork. Stir in 1 to 2 teaspoons of lemon juice, 2 tablespoons of olive oil, and salt and pepper to taste. (Can be covered and kept at room temperature up to 3 hours.)

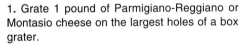

4. Grill or broil 8 slices of 3-by-2-by-½-inch Italian or French bread on both sides. Rub one side with a peeled garlic clove.

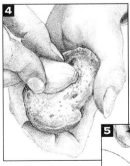

5. Spread the artichoke mixture on the toast. Serve immediately.

Cooking with Fennel

To discover fennel's virtues, slice it thin and cook it slowly.

∾ BY JACK BISHOP ∾

Although fennel is almost always available in supermarkets these days, most Americans have little idea what to do with this anise-flavored vegetable. Maybe it's the funny Italian name, *finocchio*, or its odd appearance. A white, squat bulb narrows into several light green stems, which are topped with feathery, dark green fronds.

Raw fennel is crisp and has a fairly strong anise flavor. Cooking softens the fennel and causes this licorice flavor to fade. No matter how it is cooked, fennel will be slightly sweet. Although each portion—the bulb, stems, and fronds—has different culinary uses, for most recipes only the white bulb is used. The stems can be reserved for making stock while the fronds can be minced and used as a garnish for dishes made with the bulb. In this article, I focus on the bulb, the most commonly used portion in Italian cooking.

At the outset, my goals were twofold: I wanted to figure out how to prepare fennel for cooking and find out which cooking methods would deliver the best results. I soon realized that these two questions are intertwined. The tricks with cooking fennel are to cook it evenly and to use methods that accentuate its subtle anise sweetness. To do that, you must combine the proper cooking method with the proper way of cutting the vegetable.

Slicing the Bulb

The first step in slicing fennel is to remove the long green stems and fronds. A heavy chef's knife can be used to cut through the bottom of the stems where they meet the white bulb (*see* illustration 1, page 19).

Most fennel, especially larger bulbs, has an outer layer of dried or blemished flesh. Of course, when at the market, you should try to pick firm bulbs with a bright white color and as little blemishing as possible. But even on the freshest fennel, the outer layer should be removed, much as you might peel away the outer layer on a large onion.

I find it best to start out by trimming a thin slice from the bottom of the bulb (illustration 2). Invariably, this flesh is discolored and needs to be removed. This cut usually loosens the outer layer on the bulb sufficiently so that it can be peeled away with your fingers. If the outer layer will not yield to your fingers, make a shallow vertical cut through this layer and then slide your fingers into the cut to pry off this first layer of the bulb.

Now that the tough portions of the bulb have been removed, there are several options for slicing. Fan-shaped wedges are good for grilling

Although it looks a little like frizzy celery, fennel has a sweet licorice flavor that softens and mellows when the vegetable is cooked.

(these large pieces won't fall through the grates) or for braising. To form these wedges, simply cut the bulb vertically so that each slice includes a portion of the base, which will serve to hold the various layers together (illustration 3).

Most cooking methods other than grilling or braising rely on smaller pieces. In this case, I find it useful to cut the bulb in half through the base. Each half contains a small portion of the core at its base. Use a small, sharp knife to remove this pyramid-shaped piece (illustration 4). This small refinement helps promote even cooking because the core can remain tough long after the rest of the bulb has softened.

The next step is to lay each fennel half on a work surface with the flat side down, then cut each half crosswise to yield three or four thick slices (illustration 5). These slices can then be cut lengthwise to yield long strips that are about one-half-inch thick (illustration 6). I find this size perfect for sautéing and roasting. Larger slices take too long to soften with either method, and the exterior can burn before the interior is fully cooked.

In contrast, this is not such a problem when braising, because the liquid prevents too much browning. That's why fennel for braising can be left in larger pieces. If you want to dice fennel for use in salads or risotto, simply cut slices horizontally.

Slow-Cook for Best Texture and Taste

Unlike most vegetables, raw fennel has a long history of use in salads or antipasti. Italians often put out strips of fennel along with a bowl of fine olive oil and salt as a quick antipasto. The fennel is simply dipped in the oil, sprinkled with salt, and enjoyed with cocktails. Raw fennel can also be cut into thin strips or diced and used in salads. Add a handful of diced fennel to a leafy salad or use thin strips of fennel in a citrus salad.

When it comes to cooking, fennel generally responds best to dry-heat methods. Sautéing and roasting cause the natural sugars in the fennel to caramelize, thereby enhancing its flavor. The exception to the "dry heat is best" rule is braising. This method involves wet heat, with the fennel absorbing flavors from the cooking liquid (usually stock or wine) and, therefore, delivering very good results, as well.

The common thread in all my testing was to achieve uniform tenderness throughout the fennel pieces. It's easy enough to cook fennel until mushy, but I prefer that it offer some resistance. However, fennel that is soft on the exterior and crunchy on the inside is not to my taste either. Fairly slow cooking turned out to be the key. Sautéing over medium heat for a considerable period (about fifteen minutes), braising for thirty minutes, and roasting for thirty-five minutes all worked beautifully. Attempts to hurry fennel along by using faster methods such as boiling and microwaving did not succeed; the fennel became mushy with both methods, and boiling also washed out much of its flavor. Steaming not only was time consuming and turned the fennel a bit mushy, but because it did not brown the fennel, it did little to elicit or enhance its sweet flavor.

The following recipes illustrate several basic cooking techniques for fennel. Once you have mastered them, feel free to change the seasonings.

BRAISED FENNEL WITH WHITE WINE AND PARMESAN
Serves 4

In this recipe, the fennel cooks slowly in butter and white wine until tender, then receives a dusting of cheese just before serving. This rich side dish works well with beef or veal.

3 tablespoons butter
2 medium or 3 small fennel bulbs
  (about 2¼ pounds), stems,
  fronds, and base trimmed,
  bulb cut vertically into ½-inch
  thick slices (*see* illustrations
  1 through 3, below)
  Salt and ground black pepper
⅓ cup dry white wine
¼ cup grated Parmesan cheese

1. Heat butter over medium heat in sauté pan large enough to hold fennel in almost single layer. Add fennel and sprinkle with salt and pepper to taste. Add wine and cover pan. Simmer over medium heat 15 minutes. Turn slices and continue to simmer, covered, until fennel is quite tender, has absorbed most of pan liquid, and starts to turn golden, about 10 minutes longer. Turn fennel again and continue cooking until fennel starts to color on other side, about 4 minutes longer.

2. Sprinkle fennel with cheese. Transfer to platter or individual plates and serve immediately.

SAUTÉED FENNEL WITH GARLIC AND PARSLEY
Serves 4

Sautéing causes the anise flavor of fennel to fade but concentrates the natural sugars in the vegetable. This side dish particularly complements seafood or poultry.

2 medium fennel bulbs (about 2
  pounds), stems, fronds, and base
  trimmed (*see* illustrations 1
  and 2), 1 tablespoon minced
  fronds reserved
3 tablespoons olive oil
4 medium garlic cloves, minced
  Salt and ground black pepper
2 tablespoons minced fresh parsley
  leaves

1. Halve and core fennel (illustration 4). With cut side down and knife parallel to work surface, slice each fennel half crosswise to yield ½-inch slices (illustration 5). Then, with knife perpendicular to work surface, cut each fennel half lengthwise into long thin strips (illustration 6).

2. Heat oil in large skillet. Add garlic; sauté over medium heat until lightly colored, about 1 minute. Add fennel strips; toss to coat with oil. Cook, stirring often, until fennel has softened considerably but still offers some resistance, about 15 minutes.

3. Season generously with salt and pepper to taste. Stir in minced fronds and parsley. Serve immediately.

ROASTED FENNEL WITH RED ONIONS AND CARROTS
Serves 4

Drizzle a tablespoon of balsamic vinegar over the vegetables during the last minutes of roasting to highlight their sweetness. Serve this fennel as a side dish with chicken or veal.

1 large or two small fennel bulbs
  (about 1½ pounds), stems,
  fronds, and base trimmed
  (*see* illustrations 1 and 2)
1 medium red onion, peeled and cut
  lengthwise into 8 wedges
2 medium carrots, peeled, halved
  lengthwise, and cut into 2-inch
  lengths
2 tablespoons olive oil
  Salt
1 tablespoon balsamic vinegar

1. Heat oven to 425 degrees. Halve and core fennel (illustration 4). With cut side down and knife parallel to work surface, slice each fennel half crosswise to yield ½-inch slices (illustration 5). Then, with knife perpendicular to work surface, cut each fennel half lengthwise to yield long thin strips (illustration 6).

2. Toss fennel, onion, and carrots in large roasting pan with oil. Season generously with salt. Roast 30 minutes, turning vegetables once after 20 minutes.

3. Drizzle vinegar over vegetables and toss gently. Continue roasting until vegetables are richly colored and tender, about 5 minutes longer. Adjust seasonings. Serve hot or warm.

FENNEL-ORANGE SALAD WITH BLACK OLIVES AND MINT
Serves 4

This salad is popular in southern Italy, where fennel grows wild. Use small black olives in brine, such as Niçoise or Gaeta olives.

2 large seedless oranges, zest and pith
  removed, fruit sections and
  juice saved
1 medium fennel bulb (about 1¼
  pounds), stems, fronds, and
  base trimmed (*see* illustrations
  1 and 2)
⅓ cup small black olives
12 fresh mint leaves, cut crosswise into
  thin strips
  Salt and ground black pepper
2 tablespoons extra-virgin olive oil

1. Place orange sections and juice in large bowl.

2. Halve and core fennel (illustration 4). With cut side down and knife parallel to work surface, slice each fennel half crosswise to yield ¼-inch slices. Then, with knife perpendicular to work surface, cut each fennel half lengthwise to yield long ¼-inch-thin strips.

3. Add fennel, olives, and mint to oranges. Season with salt and pepper to taste. Drizzle with oil and toss gently. Serve immediately. ∎

PREPARING FENNEL FOR COOKING

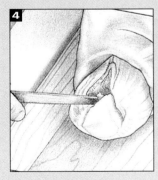

1. Trim and reserve stems and fronds from fennel.

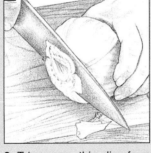

2. Trim a very thin slice from base and remove any tough or blemished outer layers from bulb.

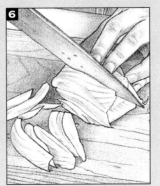

3. Slice bulb vertically through base into ½-inch-thick pieces that resemble fans. Or see step 4.

4. Cut bulb in half through base. Use small, sharp knife to remove pyramid-shaped core.

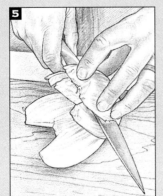

5. Cut cored fennel, crosswise, to yield 3 or 4 slices.

6. Cut these slices, lengthwise, to yield long strips about ½-inch thick.

How to Roast a Bell Pepper

After flaming, broiling, and baking dozens of bell peppers of every color, we find cutting and oven-broiling the peppers yields superior results.

∾ BY STEPHANA BOTTOM ∾

Roasting bell peppers has become a very popular process for very good reasons. When roasted, sweet, crunchy raw red bell peppers assume a whole new layer of complex, smoky flavor.

My own pepper-roasting experience began, appropriately enough, as a baptism by fire. On my first day of restaurant employment, I was given two crates of beautiful, crisp red bell peppers to transform into perfect one-inch triangles of roasted peppers. I duly carried out the chef's orders to roast the peppers over a gas burner, steam them in a bag for ten minutes, then peel and rinse them. Needless to say, after the first crate the peppers no longer seemed so beautiful, nor the method sufficiently swift.

But I did not give up on roasting peppers. Instead I decided to look for the best possible way to accomplish the task. In testing the many different methods of roasting peppers, I sought the most efficient way to achieve a tender but not mushy flesh, smoky flavor, and skin that would peel off easily.

Despite my restaurant experience, I was still in the gas burner camp, sure that charring the pepper over the open flame was the most satisfying and quickest method. It pays to keep an open mind, though, because it turned out that I was completely wrong. After flaming, broiling, baking, and steaming dozens of peppers, I found that oven broiling is clearly superior. It's neater, faster, and the peppers are delicious. End of debate!

It took me a while to get to that end, though. First I had to try every pepper-roasting method I had ever heard or read about. Along the way, I discovered a point that applies to any method you might choose: You must take care not to overroast the peppers. When the skin of the pepper just puffs up and turns black, you have reached the point at which flavor is maximized and the texture of the pepper flesh is soft but not mushy. After this point, continued exposure to heat will result in darkened flesh that is thinner, flabbier-textured, and slightly bitter.

Testing All Techniques
The first method I tested was my previous favorite, the stovetop gas burner. The one benefit of this method is that whole peppers retain the liquid that would be released during roasting. The disadvantages, however, are many. The peppers require constant tending and must be turned with tongs after each exposed area of flesh has charred. The clever tong manipulation doesn't end there, as both ends of the pepper need to be charred to promote even peeling. Also, only two peppers can be roasted at a time, unless you want to try to double this number by using two burners. That, however, requires two pairs of tongs and deft eye-hand coordination and invites both arm-scorching and over-roasting. Forget about using a long-handled fork instead of tongs, since, after three to four minutes of roasting, the softened pepper will fall off the fork.

The second approach I tested was oven-roasting peppers at high heat, 550 degrees. Whether the peppers are kept whole or split open and flattened, this method takes longer, usually from twelve to fifteen minutes, which in turn creates overcooked, soggy flesh. Lower oven temperatures, favored by so many chefs and writers, also yield overcooked peppers and require even longer cooking times, up to one hour at 325 degrees.

A third option, broiling whole peppers, also has problems. The broiler element in most ovens is approximately three inches away from the upper rack, which means that whole peppers usually touch the element. A lower rack level takes too long and cooks the flesh too much.

The answer, then, is to cut the peppers. This method yields less juice (some does collect in the bowl as the pepper steams) but that's an easy tradeoff for me given the many benefits of this method. Primary among these is the fact that the peppers consistently achieve a meaty-textured, richly flavored flesh. In addition, peppers that have been cut open and roasted under the broiler are easier to peel than peppers roasted by any other method. The skin blackens and swells up like a balloon and, after steaming and sometimes even without steaming, it lifts off in whole sections. Open flame roasting, no matter how long peppers are steamed, results in small patches of skin peeling off at a time. It is messy, your fingers get covered with charred bits, and you yearn to throw the whole pepper away.

Incidentally, peppers should not be rubbed with oil before they are roasted. The skins will char and blister faster without the oil coating. It does help to use foil in the pan. With no foil, sticky, dark spots form on the pan where the juices dripped and evaporated during roasting. When using foil, I found it made no difference which side was turned up, shiny or matte.

To Steam or Not to Steam
Unless you have asbestos fingers, roasted peppers need time to cool before handling, and steaming during this time does help make the charred skin a bit easier to peel off. The ideal steaming time is fifteen minutes—any less and the peppers are still too hot to work with comfortably. Any more time (I tested lengths of time up to one hour) provided no discernible advantage, and I did not find it helpful to refrigerate the bowl while the peppers steamed. The best method is to use a heat-resistant bowl (glass, ceramic, or metal) with a piece of plastic wrap secured over the top. The wrap holds in the heat, creating more intense steam, and one piece of wrap is all you need for dozens of peppers.

Rinsing and Storing
The broiler method makes it possible to peel the pepper without having to rinse it. If you are still tempted to rinse, notice the rich oils that accumu-

---

NOT COLOR BLIND

I had long wondered whether color makes a difference when it comes to roasting bell peppers. After roasting every color pepper I could find, I can now say that the answer is an unequivocal yes.

Red peppers give the best and most even results. Yellow peppers are generally more delicate, their flesh thinner and more prone to overcooking, which gives it a brownish hue. Since they are also more expensive than the red, I would only roast them if the yellow color was important to the dish I was preparing. Orange peppers are equally delicate and need subtle timing. With both yellow and orange varieties, watch for the skin to just char and lift up, making sure the edges are slightly blistered, then remove them from the broiler immediately. Purple peppers are a waste of money to roast, as they lose their expensive shade when cooked, turning a muddy green. Green peppers, which are simply unripened red peppers, are not yet sweet and gain nothing by being roasted.

PHOTOGRAPH BY DAVE HENDERSON

late on your fingers as you work. It seems silly to rinse away those oils, rather than saving them for your meal.

How the peppers are treated after they are peeled will determine how long they keep. Unadorned and wrapped in plastic wrap, peppers will keep their full, meaty texture only about two days in the refrigerator. Drizzled with a generous amount of olive oil and kept in an air-tight container, peppers will keep about one week without losing texture or flavor. Completely covered with olive oil, peppers will last in the fridge three to four weeks. All of the recipes that follow may be made with freshly roasted peppers or peppers made ahead and stored in oil.

ROASTED RED BELL PEPPERS
Makes 4 roasted peppers
Cooking times vary, depending on the broiler, so watch the peppers carefully as they roast. You will need to increase the cooking time slightly if your peppers are just out of the refrigerator instead of room temperature. Yellow and orange peppers roast faster than red ones, so decrease their cooking time by 2 to 4 minutes.

> 4 red bell peppers (6 to 9 ounces each), prepared following illustrations 1 through 5

1. Adjust oven rack to top position. Turn broiler on. With oven door closed, let oven heat for 5 minutes. Oven rack should be 2½ to 3½ inches from heating element. If not, set a jelly-roll pan, turned upside down, on oven rack to elevate pan (*see* illustration 6). Place prepared room-temperature peppers on a foil-lined 17-by-11-inch baking sheet and flatten peppers with palm of your hand. Broil peppers, with oven door closed, until spotty brown, about 5 minutes. Reverse pan in oven; roast until skin is charred and puffed but the flesh is still firm, 3 to 5 minutes longer.

2. Remove pan from oven; let peppers sit until cool enough to handle; peel and discard skin from each piece (illustration 7). For those who prefer, peppers can be transferred to a large heat-resistant bowl, covered with plastic wrap, and steamed for 15 minutes before peeling skin.

SWEET AND SPICY ROASTED RED PEPPER DIP
Makes about 2 cups
Adapted from Chris Schlesinger and John Willoughby's *Big Flavors of the Hot Sun* (Morrow, 1994), this sweet and spicy Middle Eastern–style dip should be served with grilled or toasted pita. An equal portion of pomegranate molasses, available at Middle Eastern or Indian markets, can be substituted for the molasses in this recipe.

> 6 tablespoons olive oil
> 1 small onion, roughly chopped
> 1 small garlic clove, peeled and minced
> 1 tablespoon ground cumin
> ½ minced jalapeño or other hot red or green fresh chile

STEPS TO PERFECT ROASTED PEPPERS

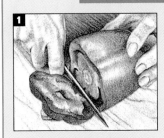

1. Slice ¼ inch from the top and bottom of the pepper.

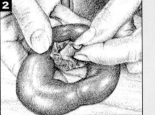

2. Gently remove the stem from the top lobe.

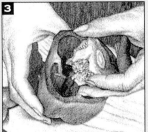

3. Pull core out of the pepper.

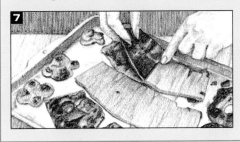

4. Slit down one side of the pepper, then lay it flat, skin side down, in one long strip. Use a sharp knife to slide along the inside of the pepper removing all ribs and seeds.

5. Arrange the strips of peppers and the top and bottom lobes on a baking sheet, skin-side up. Flatten the strips with the palm of your hand.

6. Adjust oven rack to its top position. If the rack is more than 3½ inches from the heating element, set a jelly-roll pan, bottom up, on the rack under the baking sheet.

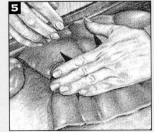

7. Roast until the skin of the peppers is charred and puffed up like a balloon but the flesh is still firm. You may steam the peppers at this point or not, as you wish. Start peeling where the skin has charred and bubbled the most. The skin will come off in large strips.

> ¾ recipe Roasted Red Bell Peppers
> ¼ cup coarsely chopped fresh parsley leaves
> 2 tablespoons molasses
> 2 tablespoons juice from 1 lime
> Salt and ground black pepper

1. Heat oil in a medium skillet over medium-high heat. Add onion; sauté until softened, about 5 minutes. Add garlic, cumin, and chile; sauté until garlic softens, about 1 minute longer.

2. Transfer mixture to a food processor fitted with steel blade. Add peppers, parsley, molasses, and juice; process until very smooth. Season to taste with salt and pepper. Transfer to a bowl and serve with toasted pita. (Can be covered and refrigerated up to 1 week.)

ROASTED RED PEPPER SALAD WITH RED ONIONS AND CUCUMBERS
Serves 4 to 6
In this simple salad, the cucumbers are salted to remove some of the water, which gives them a crisp texture that contrasts nicely with the tender roasted peppers.

> 1 large (1-pound) seedless cucumber, halved lengthwise and cut into ¼-inch-thick half circles
> Salt
> 2 tablespoons balsamic vinegar
> Ground black pepper
> 4 tablespoons olive oil
> 1 small red onion, halved and sliced thin
> 1 recipe Roasted Red Bell Peppers, cut into bite-sized pieces
> 2 tablespoons minced fresh mint leaves

1. Toss cucumber slices with ½ teaspoon salt in a colander; drain until at least ¼ cup juice is given up, about 45 minutes.

2. Meanwhile, whisk vinegar with salt and pepper to taste in medium bowl. Slowly whisk in oil to make a vinaigrette. Add onions; let stand while cucumbers are draining, about 30 minutes. When ready to serve, add cucumbers, which have been patted dry, peppers, and mint; toss to combine. Adjust seasoning. Serve. ∎

Stephana Bottom, a food writer, editor, and cook, is developing recipes for a book on food and health.

The Best Way to Cook Long-Grain White Rice

For the best rice, use less water, a quick sauté, and a "resting period."

BY KATHERINE ALFORD

Few foods are as satisfying as perfectly cooked rice. But this elemental food can be temperamental—it can resist the cook and be a pot of true grit or dissolve to an unpleasant, gummy mess. Advertisements stress perfect rice, but package instructions are unreliable when you want a tasty bowl of fluffy rice with separate grains. I wanted to find an easy method for making really great long-grain white rice.

Of the many types of rice, long-grain white rice is preferred for dishes such as pilafs and salads, in which individual grains and a fluffy, almost flaky, texture are important. There were four varieties of long-grain rice at my local market, ranging in price from a popular converted brand (Uncle Ben's) at $5.50 for a five-pound bag down to $1.50 for the same quantity of the market's generic long-grain white rice. I also tested the widely distributed Carolina Rice and Goya's Canilla brand.

Hoping for clues, I queried cooks who had mastered the grain, and found an alarming pattern: Their secret was almost always an electric rice cooker. But what if you don't have a rice cooker?

I started my tests by following the package directions. The technique was a variation on a simmer-covered method, with one cup rice for two to two-and-one-half cups water. Some packers suggested salt, some didn't, and there were recipes with and without butter. All the recipes were disappointing, the results mostly insipid, with mushy, frayed grains. There was gritty rice, there was fatty rice, but there was no rice I liked.

Next I tried a method popular with both French and Indian cooks, boiling the rice in a generous quantity of salted water as if cooking pasta. Cooked this way, all types of rice came to the table evenly done, with separate kernels, but waterlogged and bland.

Then I experimented with baking the rice in casseroles, with one and three-quarters to two and one-half parts water to one part of rice, some with butter, salted and unsalted. Boiling water was poured over the rice, then the vessels were sealed with foil and baked for twenty-five to thirty minutes. The rice made with less water and salt was better. However, that was somewhat beside the point because baked rice, while slightly creamy, did not have the well-defined grains I wanted.

I next tried a routine advocated by Asian cooks, a combination of uncovered boiling and covered steaming. For this technique the quantity of water is gauged by the length of a finger joint over the rice, or one-half to three-quarters inch. First the water is boiled until it evaporates to the level of the grains, then the heat is turned down to low, the pot is covered, and cooking continues over low heat for ten to sixteen minutes. The four varieties took unevenly to this method, some better than others, but the rice was always sticky—easier to handle with chopsticks but still not the distinct grains I wanted.

I wondered if a microwave oven could resolve these problems, but I found no advantage to cooking rice in the microwave; it was awkward, no speedier, and produced starchy rice.

Pilaf vs. Steeped
The perfect method still eluded me, but I had discerned a pattern: Less water and an even, gentle heat worked better. So I tried a pilaf method because pilaf recipes generally use less water and produce distinct grains of rice. First I sautéed the rice in two teaspoons of butter or oil, with water varying from one to two cups. After the water came to a boil, I covered the pan and let the rice simmer for fifteen minutes, then removed it from the heat and let it rest a bit prior to serving. With this method, the rice cooked up in separate grains, and sautéing the rice added a rich dimension of flavor.

No matter the variety, I preferred rice made with one cup rice to one and one-half cups water. It was light and tender but not mushy, with individual grains. The kernels should be sautéed and stirred until some become milky white. For stronger, nutty flavors, the raw rice can be fried to a toasted golden brown.

Fine-tuning the method produced different nuances in the grain. It was like choosing a white paint. White is white—until you've compared twenty paint chips and realized the contrast between eggshell, Navajo, and ecru. For example, I had several pans with lids that did not fit very well, so I laid a folded kitchen towel over these pans before I put the lid on, creating a snug seal. There was a marked improvement, even with matched lids, because condensed water droplets no longer plopped onto the rice. (When using this method, take care to fold the towel back over the lid to avoid setting it ablaze.)

In repeated tests I found the rice was less starchy when the pan was swirled to incorporate all the ingredients instead of stirred with a fork. But, surprisingly, adding rice to boiling water made stickier rice than when the rice was added to cold water and the mixture heated to a boil. I also rinsed rice before cooking to see if it contributed to a fluffier, drier grain. It did not.

I was curious to try the same formula (one cup rice, one and one-half cups water, one-half teaspoon salt) without sautéing the rice. Fluffed with a fork, rice cooked in this manner was almost as fluffy as the pilaf-method rice, with a mild flavor that brings out the subtly floral, "ricey" aromatics. At a small sacrifice of texture, this is the ideal rice for many chicken stews and fish dishes.

Finally, I played with timing, cooking the rice for as little as ten minutes to as much as twenty-five. There was some flexibility with the cooking time, as long as the rice was allowed to rest, covered, after cooking. The most consistent timing was fifteen to eighteen minutes from when the pot was sealed to the time the rice was done, with a fifteen-minute rest on the turned-off burner. (Don't pull the cover off the pot to peek.) Before serving, fluff the rice easily with a fork.

MASTER RECIPE FOR FLUFFY WHITE RICE
Serves 4
This recipe is designed for one cup of raw rice in a tight-lidded pot. As you cook more rice, you should reduce the proportion of water. With two cups of rice, you can get these results with two and one-half to two and three-quarters cups of water. But it is very hard to get a reliable result with less than a cup of rice, so do not halve this recipe.

2 teaspoons unsalted butter or oil (vegetable or olive)
1 cup long-grain white rice (not converted)
1½ cups water
½ teaspoon salt

1. Heat oil in medium saucepan over medium heat. Add rice; cook, stirring constantly, for 1 to 3 minutes, depending on desired amount of nutty flavor. Add water and salt; bring to boil, swirling pot to blend ingredients.

2. Reduce heat to low, cover with tight lid lined with a towel, and cook until liquid is absorbed, about 15 minutes.

3. Turn off heat; let rice stand on burner, still covered, to finish cooking, about 15 minutes longer. Fluff with fork and serve. ■

Katherine Alford is a cooking teacher and food writer living in New York.

How to Grill a Steak

A month's worth of testing shows that the solution involves lots of charcoal, an open grill, and a fire built with two levels of heat.

❧ BY STEPHANIE LYNESS ❧

In order to get a good sear on the outside of your steaks, and also to cook them through, you need to use a two-level fire.

I love a good steak. And during the summer I'm in love with the *idea* of grilling steaks because there's very little prep or cleanup, and grilling gives me an excuse to stay outdoors and cook over a real fire. The reality, unfortunately, has often been something different.

Some nights I've ended up with a small bonfire fueled by steak fat, and my expensive steaks have come off the grill charred and tasting of resinous smoke. Then maybe the next time I've let the coals burn down so the fire's not so hot, but the steak ends up with those pale, wimpy grill marks and the flavor just isn't there. In those cases I have tried leaving it on the grill long enough to develop flavor, but it just overcooks.

My favorite cuts, porterhouse and T-bone, are especially tricky. Both of these consist of two muscles with a T-shaped bone in between. When I grill them so that the strip section is perfectly cooked, the lean tenderloin is inevitably overcooked, dry, and flavorless.

So, last summer I went to battle; I vowed to figure out how to use the grill. I wanted to end up with the quality of steak that I love: the meat seared evenly on both sides so that the juices are concentrated into a powerfully flavored, dark

brown, brittle coating of crust; the juicy inside cooked a little past rare; and the outside strip of rich, soft fat crisped and browned slightly on the edges.

Cuts and Grills

Since I knew I couldn't cover all cuts of steaks in one article, I thought it would be best to concentrate on a few popular cuts. So I narrowed my testing to strip sirloin steaks, on and off the bone, and porterhouse and T-bone steaks. I figured these steaks were bound to cook pretty much the same because they were all cut from the loin. I was particularly interested in porterhouse and T-bone steaks because their two muscles pose such a specific problem for the cook. In the course of my testing, I also found that my master grilling technique works just as well for other popular cuts.

Having chosen the steaks, I needed to select my grill. The question I faced was whether gas and charcoal grills give comparable results, or if the best steak needs to be grilled over one or the other. To determine this, I compared three brands of gas and two types of charcoal grills. While two of the gas grills marked the steaks effectively, neither gave the steak the all-over seared crust that both charcoal grills delivered (when I used enough charcoal). I also preferred working with charcoal to gas because I had subtler control of the heat. So for this article, I decided to stick to charcoal grilling.

Two Heats Are Better Than One

Early on in my testing, I determined that I needed a very hot fire to get the crust I wanted without overcooking the steak. I could get that kind of heat by building the charcoal up to within two or two and one-half inches of the grilling grate. But with this arrangement, I ran into problems with the fat dripping down onto the charcoal and flaming. I had already decided that a thick steak—about one and one-half inches thick, to be specific—was optimal because, at that thickness, I got a tasty contrast between the charcoal flavoring on the outside of the steak and the beefy flavor on the inside. But I couldn't cook a thick steak over consistently high heat without burning it.

BUILDING A TWO-LEVEL FIRE

1. Use enough briquettes to make a pile on one half of the grill that rises to within 2 to 2½ inches of the grilling grate. This will amount to about 10 pounds of standard briquettes for a 22½-inch kettle grill, or a little over 5 pounds for an 18½-inch kettle.

2. Light the briquettes using one or two chimney starters, an electric firestarter, or a couple of firestarter cubes. Let the charcoal burn until it's completely covered with a thin coating of gray ash, about 30 minutes. Use a fire shovel to scrape some of the coals off the mound to make a single, sparse layer of coals on the other half.

3. The end result should consist of a large pile of lit coals on one side of the grill and a single layer of lit coals on the other side.

ILLUSTRATIONS BY NEMAD JAKESEVIC.

For all cuts of steak, look for meat that has a bright, lively color. Beef normally ranges in color from pink to red, but dark meat probably indicates an older, tougher animal. The external fat as well as the fat that runs through the meat (called intramuscular fat) should be as white as possible. As a general rule, the more intramuscular fat (marbling), the more flavorful and juicy the steak will be. But the marbling should be smooth and fine, running all through the meat, rather than showing up in clumps; smooth marbling melts into the meat during cooking, while knots remain as clumps of fat pockets. Stay away from packaged steaks that show a lot of red juice (known as "purge"). The purge may indicate a bad job of freezing; your steak will be dry and cottony.

You can grill all the cuts shown here following the master grilling technique on page 25. Steaks sport different names depending on locale. I've used industry names that I feel best describe where the steaks lie on the loin; in parentheses you'll find some other common names.

Rib eye (rib, Delmonico): Very tender and smooth-textured; distinctive, robust, beefy taste; very rich, with pockets of fat; moderately expensive.

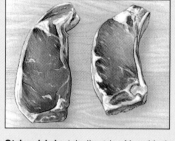

Strip sirloin (shell, strip, New York strip, top loin): Medium chewy with noticeable grain; very good flavor (what I expect from a steak); more fat than hip sirloin but much less than rib; slightly more expensive than rib.

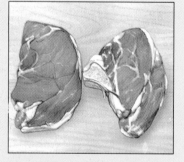

Hip sirloin (sirloin, London broil, boneless butt, boneless hip): Quite chewy; very flavorful; often less fat than strip though not always; less expensive; in supermarkets usually sold without tenderloin.

T-bone: Combines an oblong piece of strip sirloin with a round of tenderloin—tenderloin measures less than one and one-quarter inches in diameter; grain of sirloin piece is finer and, so, more desirable than that of porterhouse because it's closer to the rib.

Tenderloin (filet, filet mignon): So tender it's soft; mild-flavored; very lean; very expensive.

Porterhouse: Like T-bone, combines tenderloin and sirloin, but the tenderloin section is larger; grain of sirloin piece is rougher than that of T-bone because it is closer to the hip.

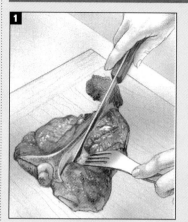
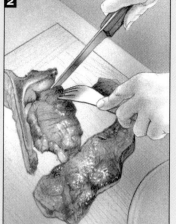

1. Slice close to the bone to remove the strip section.

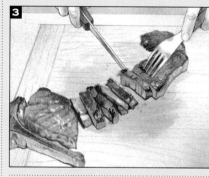

2. Turn the steak around and cut the filet section off the bone.

3. Slice each of the resulting pieces crosswise about ⅓ inch thick and serve immediately.

If the steaks begin flaming, pull them immediately to the cooler part of the grill. The charring caused by flaming masks the flavor of the meat. A squirt bottle aimed at the charcoal will also douse the flame.

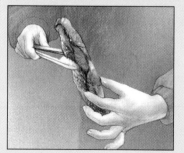

By texture: Pick the steak up and check its texture to that of your hand: Feel between thumb and forefinger to approximate the soft, squishy feel of rare, or make a fist and do the same to give the springy feel of medium, or touch the tip of your nose for well done.

By temperature: Use an instant-read thermometer, sticking it through the edge of the steak into the eye, so that most of the shaft is embedded in the steak. Pull the steak off the grill when it registers 120 degrees for rare; 130 degrees for medium rare; 135 to 140 degrees for medium.

ILLUSTRATIONS BY NEMAD JAKESEVIC

After considerable experimentation, I found the answer to this dilemma: I had to build a fire with two levels of heat (see "Building a Two-Level Fire," page 23). Once I realized that I needed a fire with a lot of coals on one side and much fewer coals on the other, I could sear the steak properly at the beginning of cooking, then pull it onto the cooler half to finish cooking at a lower temperature. I could also use the dual heat levels to cook thin steaks properly as well as thick ones, and the system also ensured against bonfires—if a steak flared up, I simply moved it off the high heat. An added bonus was the pleasure of working with the fire rather than against it. I had the sense of playing with a live entity, much as when playing a musical instrument.

I found I could be sure I had the right levels of heat on both sides of the fire by holding my hand about five inches over the cooking grate: When the hot side of the grill was hot enough for searing, I could only hold my hand over the grill for about two seconds. For the cooler side of the grill, I could count four to five seconds.

My two-level fire also solved the porterhouse/T-bone problem. I found that if I grilled the steak with the tenderloin toward the cooler side of the fire, it cooked more slowly and reached proper doneness at the same time as the strip. I could even engineer it so the tenderloin came off the grill rare while the strip was cooked to medium-rare.

But one question kept bugging me. The literature that came with the kettle grill I was using recommended grilling covered. Most cooking professionals I spoke to, however, were not in favor of covered grilling. So I ran a test comparing the taste of steak grilled covered to that grilled uncovered. I found that, depending on the type of charcoal used, steak cooked with the lid on picked up a mild to unpleasant, smoky, resinous flavor. Grilling steak uncovered, on the other hand, allowed me to avoid that resinous taste, as well as to control any flare-ups by moving the steak off the hotter side of the grill.

More Kitchen Tests

Common cooking wisdom suggests that bringing meat to room temperature before grilling will cause it to cook more evenly and that letting it rest for five to ten minutes after taking it off the grill will both preserve the juices and provide a more even color. I tested the first of these theories by simultaneously grilling two similar steaks, one straight from the refrigerator and a second that stood at room temperature for one hour. I noticed no difference in the cooked steaks except that the room temperature steak cooked a couple of minutes faster than the other. This result suggests that it might even be an advantage to cook meat straight from the refrigerator if you want it medium-rare; the heat will be slower to reach the center of a cold steak, and it won't overcook as quickly as room-temperature meat.

On the resting front, I found that while it was certainly true that five minutes of resting gave the meat an even, pink color, it did nothing to keep the juices in. The resting steak lost the same vol-

ume of juices while it rested as the other did when I cut into it. The color is important visually, however, so I suggest that you do let the meat rest.

I tried lightly oiling steaks before grilling to see if they browned better that way, as well as brushing with butter halfway through grilling to see if the flavor improved. Although the oiled steaks browned a tiny bit better, the difference wasn't significant enough to merit the added ingredient. As for the butter, I couldn't taste any difference.

I also tried grilling steaks that I had frozen at home for one week and for six weeks, respectively, against fresh meat. I couldn't tell the difference between the fresh steaks and those that had been frozen for one week and then thawed. The steak frozen for six weeks, though, was noticeably less juicy than the fresh.

On the advice of Ed Seh at Pacific-Seh, a purveyor of prime meats in Manhattan, I next tried grilling a steak that had been frozen one week without thawing it first. (The traditional advice is to thaw steaks as slowly as possible, in the refrigerator.) I grilled over two levels of heat, just as I would for a fresh steak, and found that, although the frozen steak took a little more than half again as long as the fresh steak to cook, there wasn't a discernible difference between the two when they came off the grill.

MASTER RECIPE FOR GRILLED STRIP SIRLOIN STEAK
Serves 4

Strip sirloins, on or off the bone, are my first choice for individual steaks. A one-and-one-quarter- to one-and-one-half-inch-thick steak gives you a solid meat flavor as well as a little taste of the grill; cut any thicker and the steak becomes too thick for one person. If your guests are more likely to eat only an eight-ounce steak, grill two one-pounders, slice them, and serve each person a half steak.

> 4 strip sirloin steaks with or without
> bone, 1¼- to 1½- inch thick
> (12 to 16 ounces each), patted dry
> Salt and ground black pepper

1. Following illustrations 1 through 3, page 23, build a two-level fire. Set grill rack in place, cover grill with lid, and let rack heat up, about 5 minutes.

2. Meanwhile, sprinkle both sides of each steak with salt and pepper to taste.

3. Position steaks over higher-level (hotter) fire. Grill, uncovered, until well browned on one side, 2 to 3 minutes. Turn each steak over with tongs; grill until well browned on second side, 2 to 3 minutes longer. (If steaks start to flame, pull them to lower, cooler, level or extinguish flames with a squirt bottle.)

4. Once steaks are well browned on both sides, slide each one to lower level; continue cooking to desired doneness, 5 to 6 more minutes for rare (120 degrees), 6 to 7 minutes for medium-rare on the rare side (125 degrees), 7 to 8 more minutes for medium-rare on the medium side (130 degrees), or 8 to 9 more minutes for medium (135 to 140 degrees). Let steaks rest 5 minutes, then serve immediately.

GRILLED PORTERHOUSE OR T-BONE STEAK
Serves 4

Like many professional cooks, I prefer the robust taste and tooth of other steaks to filet mignon, cut from the tenderloin. On a porterhouse steak, however, the buttery, delicate tenderloin suddenly makes sense. How can you argue with a steak that gives you two different tastes and textures in one cut, plus the bone?

Since a porterhouse is so large, it's best to have the butcher cut it thick (one and one-half inches) and have it serve two people. Sliced, as in the recipe below, it makes a more elegant meal than a single strip steak, until four people start to fight over the two bones.

> · 2 porterhouse or T-bone steaks, each
> 1½ inches thick (about 3½
> pounds total)
> Salt and ground black pepper

Follow Master Recipe for Grilled Strip Sirloin Steak, positioning steaks on the grill so the tenderloin pieces are over the lower-level (cooler) fire. Grill exactly as in Master Recipe, browning steaks over the higher (hotter) level, then sliding the steaks to the cooler level to finish cooking. Cooking times remain the same. Once steaks have rested 5 minutes, cut the strip and filet pieces off bones and slice them each crosswise about ⅓ inch thick (see "Cutting Two-Part Steaks," page 24) Serve immediately. ∎

Tasting Mail-Order Steaks

A $24-per-pound mail-order steak comes in first, but to our surprise, an inexpensive supermarket steak holds its own.

∾ BY STEPHANIE LYNESS ∾

Our panel rated mail-order Prime Access as the top steak, but some mail-order steaks did not fare as well as a supermarket choice.

As experienced local butchers become a wistful memory in most of the United States, most cooks buy whatever steak the supermarket has to offer for everyday meals, and call a pricey mail-order house when they want something really special.

A survey of several mail-order houses across the country shows that you can pay up to almost $30 per pound, plus shipping, for that really special steak. In my supermarket, the same cut costs just more than $10 per pound. Does a fabulously expensive, dry-aged, prime grade, mail-order steak really taste better than what the supermarket has to offer? Our panel found that two mail-order houses really do deliver, but that for everyday eating, you might as well save your money and take your chances at the supermarket.

The Grading Game

Mail-order houses and top butchers charge a lot of money for their steaks based on the alleged quality. So what makes for a quality steak? Experts in the industry told me in one word: prime, which is the top grade in the USDA (United States Department of Agriculture) grading program.

The USDA grades beef on the basis of "the expected flavor, tenderness, and juiciness" of the meat—the higher the grade, the tastier the steak. (Note that this USDA grading service is *voluntary* and paid for by the processor as opposed to the *mandatory* USDA health inspection program.)

Grading inspectors look at a number of factors to make their decision, but in terms of taste, the most important of these is the degree of marbling, which means the *intra*muscular, rather than *external,* fat. Theoretically, fat that is well distributed within the eye of the meat gives the beef more flavor and keeps it tender and juicy even as it loses moisture during cooking. Fat also mitigates the steely, metallic taste of the iron-rich muscle. Therefore, the more marbling in the meat, the more desirable it is and, consequently, the higher the grade and the price.

At the retail level we're familiar with the top three grades, which are, in descending order, prime, choice, and select. Prime beef is the most heavily marbled and so commands top dollar. Only 2 to 3 percent of graded beef is stamped prime, so it's tough for many Americans to get it. According to Marlys Bielunski, test kitchen director at the National Live Stock and Meat Board, prime beef is available only in "pockets throughout the United States" and, of course, through mail order.

Choice meat has somewhat less marbling than prime; most of the beef graded in the United States is choice. Select has still less marbling. Although an occasional supermarket sells prime beef, most sell choice, select, or ungraded cuts.

While Stanley Lobel, part owner of M. Lobel & Sons, Inc., a butcher in Manhattan, says, without equivocation, that a prime steak is always a better eating experience than a lesser grade, wholesale purveyors and chefs with whom I spoke disagreed. First of all, they say, grading is done by human beings, so it is to a certain extent subjective. Further, grading is a visual determination based on *expected* results; given the variation from one animal to another, the process is hardly an exact science. To further muddy things, in the industry the grades are broken down into subgrades such as top, middle, and low end. So it stands to reason that low-end prime meat could be very similar to high-grade choice, yet cost more.

In this tasting, I wanted to find out whether tasters actually preferred prime steak over choice or select and whether they could even tell the difference between prime and top choice. Four of the steaks tested (Allen Brothers, Balducci's, M. Lobel & Sons, and Prime Access) were prime. Coleman was choice or select (the company does not specify which one), and the others (Allen Brothers, Certified Angus Beef, Omaha Steaks

International, Pfaelzer, and Supermarket Choice) fell into the choice grade.

Besides the grade, the other buzzword among purveyors of expensive steaks is "dry aging." Generally, beef can be aged by the wet method, which involves letting it age after it has been vacuum-packed, or by dry aging, a much more expensive process in which the beef is allowed to hang and dry by air. Purveyors of dry-aged steaks insist that one simply can't compare the two methods: Wet aging makes a soft, mushy steak while dry aging yields firm meat. Dry aging also concentrates and develops the flavor of the meat.

I thus wondered whether tasters could tell the difference between dry-aged and wet-aged steak and which method they'd prefer. Three of the steaks (Prime Access, Balducci's, and Lobel's) were dry-aged for twenty-one days, thirty-two days, and six weeks, respectively. The remaining entries were wet-aged.

The Results

Panelists tasted for the flavor and texture of the meat. The two top-ranking steaks—both of which were prime grade and dry-aged—received praise for their buttery, tender textures and rich, round, complex flavors, typical characteristics of prime grade, dry-aged meat. Dissenters found the flavor too gamy, presumably because they were unaccustomed to the flavor of dry aging. The third dry-aged prime steak, from M. Lobel & Sons, rated surprisingly badly, possibly because Lobel ages its sirloins longer than the competition, giving it a stronger flavor and denser texture.

The wet-aged steaks, by and large, had a pleasant mix of chew and tenderness, and tasters liked them well enough for their mild, clean, beefy flavors. Reactions such as "a tad one-dimensional" and "plain" may indicate the flavor compromise of wet aging as well as the smaller amount of marbling in the wet-aged choice steaks.

The Supermarket Choice steak, though, was a big surprise, ranking above some well-respected mail-order houses and Certified Angus Beef. One of the tasters, Hugh Ross at Wotiz, suggests two reasons for this result: First, Ross's hands-on experience is that, because the choice grade indicates a range of quality, one out of five boxes of choice beef will be of exceptional quality. So when you buy choice in your supermarket, you have about a one in five chance of getting a really terrific steak. Secondly, he surmises, the Supermarket Choice steak being tested was thinner than most of the other steaks; in a bite of the steak, therefore, the appealing taste of the broiled

PHOTOGRAPH BY DAVE HENDERSON

outside crust is proportionately larger and has greater potential to influence the taste of the beef itself. This may also be a case of panelists liking the taste they find most familiar.

Tasters disliked the lean, organic Coleman steak mostly as a result of its strong metallic taste. This flavor is probably due to the low degree of marbling in the meat; marbling softens the metallic taste of the minerals in the muscle.

It seems that the best advice is to eat steak like you often drink wine: Occasionally it's worth it to spend the money with the top mail-order houses to buy a tender, buttery-textured, delicious, dry-aged steak. But for weeknight dinners, a wet-aged, supermarket steak of choice grade will generally deliver acceptable, albeit unexceptional, flavor and texture (and sometimes much better than that) at about one-third the price. ∎

RATING THE STEAKS

Our panel blind-tasted seven mail-order and three supermarket steaks, including three national brands, at 9 Jones Restaurant and Bar in Manhattan. The steaks appear below in order of preference based on numerical scores given each steak by the tasters. All steaks were strip sirloins without the bone; the bone-in Balducci's steak was boned by the chef before cooking. All were one and one-quarter to one and one-half inches thick, with the exception of the Supermarket Choice and Certified Angus steaks, which were three-quarters of an inch to one inch thick. With the exception of the Prime Access steak, which was shipped fresh, all mail-order steaks were shipped frozen and then thawed in a refrigerator before the tasting.

Tasters included the author; Katherine Alford, food writer and cooking teacher; Marcy Bassoff, 9 Jones Restaurant and Bar chef; Jack Bishop, *Cook's Illustrated* senior writer; Sal Caciccia, buyer for Balducci's meat department; Hugh Ross, part-owner of Wotiz, a New Jersey meat purveyor; Michele Scicollone, cookbook author; Cathy Schwartzman, food lover; and Diana Sturgis, director of the test kitchen at *Food & Wine*.

HIGHLY RECOMMENDED STEAKS

These steaks received positive comments from almost every taster.

Prime Access (White Plains, NY; 800-314-2875), $24.99 per pound plus shipping ($99.95 for four 16-ounce, boneless steaks). Tasters were almost overwhelmingly positive about these three-week, dry-aged prime steaks, the only steaks shipped fresh. The steak "glistened" and had a "wonderful smell" with a "complex flavor that bursts in the mouth." Another panelist detected "buttery notes." Tasters called the steak "very tender" with a good balance of "chew and tenderness" as well as a "buttery" texture. One taster compared the texture favorably to sushi while one of the few dissenters found it "cottony."

Balducci's (Greenwich Village, NY; 800-225-3822), $16.25 per pound plus shipping ($65 for four 16-ounce, bone-in steaks). Tasters gave these thirty-two-day, dry-aged prime steaks high marks for their "round," "complex and changing" flavor, which was "strong but not overwhelming" and which "lingers and grows." Several tasters loved its "buttery" texture, which was "tender without being soft"; one suggested the steak could be cut "with a butter knife." A few tasters objected to the aged flavor; one found it to be "too strong" and "gamy."

ACCEPTABLE STEAKS

Reviews of these steaks were mixed.

Allen Brothers Sterling Silver Certified (Chicago, IL; 800-957-0111), $22.72 per pound plus shipping ($119 for six 14-ounce, boneless steaks). This choice steak is aged three to four weeks; specifications for USDA-certified Sterling Silver brand require that it be culled from the top two-thirds of the choice grade or higher. This steak came in with two first-place votes and rated over the Allen Brothers prime entry, below. Leaky vacuum-packing didn't seem to harm this steak too much. Tasters liked the "clean steak" flavor, which had a "nice beefiness," if "a tad one-dimensional." Tasters' experience with the texture ranged from "sawdust" to "soft but dry" to "very tender with just a hint of chew."

Supermarket Choice, $10.39 per pound at a local Manhattan supermarket for a boneless steak. This wet-aged steak pulled in two first places, a lot of fairly positive comments, and only one overwhelmingly negative review. Both industry tasters rated it very high. One taster appreciated its "rich flavor" while another termed it "mild" and two others rated it "unhappy looking" with "no flavor," and as tasting "better than it looks but cheesy." Almost all comments on the texture were positive, from "tender, almost delicate" to "chewy but tender" and "very good."

Omaha Steaks International (Omaha, NE; 800-228-9872), $21 per pound plus shipping ($63 for four 12-ounce, boneless steaks). Probably the best known mail-order steak house due to its aggressive marketing,

Omaha did not mention grading in the written sales material I saw, but I was told by telephone that their beef was choice and wet-aged at least twenty-one days. All but one taster rated this steak as middle-of-the-road: The flavor was "mild," "sort of bland," "not very complex," "plain," and "beefy but not rich." The texture was rated "chewy" with "nice bite," but many found it somewhat "dry."

Certified Angus Beef (Wooster, OH; 216-345-2333); $11.49 per pound for boneless at a local Manhattan supermarket. This popular USDA-certified national brand has an excellent reputation in the industry. The meat comes from the top two-thirds of the choice grade or better and is wet-aged. Tasters split on this one, rating the flavor from "good" and "beefy but not overwhelming" to "thin," "disappointing," and "lacks depth." Comments on the texture ranged from "good" and "soft" to "tough" and "dry."

Allen Brothers (Chicago, IL; 800-957-0111), $27.25 per pound plus shipping ($109 for four 16-ounce, boneless steaks). This wet-aged prime steak (also with damaged packaging) rated far below the same company's choice offering. Tasters gave it satisfactory reviews on flavor, commenting that it had a "nice beefy" and "typically beef" flavor, with "some sweetness," but almost everyone gave it a thumbs-down on texture, calling it "wet paper," "dryish," "sawdust," and "mushy."

STEAKS NOT RECOMMENDED

Most tasters commented negatively on these steaks.

Coleman Natural Meats (Denver, CO; 800-442-8666), $13.29 per pound at a local Manhattan supermarket for boneless. Coleman has gone after the health-conscious consumer. Its wet-aged beef, which is "certified natural and organic" and lean, ranges from choice to select, with no prime. Most tasters didn't like the flavor, finding it to be "metallic," "grassy," or unpleasantly "strong"; one industry taster found the meat tasteless. The texture was generally rated "chewy" but "good."

M. Lobel & Sons, Inc. (New York, NY; 212-737-1372/3/4), $21 per pound for boneless. Lobel provides prime meat; strip sirloins are dry-aged six weeks. This very well reputed butcher (and a favorite of mine) rated surprisingly poorly. Although several tasters thought that the steak "smelled great," they were almost overwhelmingly negative about the taste and texture. Many were put off by the flavor created by the aging. Two tasters found the texture "rubbery," and some called it "chewy," although one dissenter found it "tender without being mushy."

Pfaelzer Brothers (Burr Ridge, IL; 800-621-0226), $24.98 per pound plus shipping ($74.95 for four 12-ounce, boneless steaks). This choice steak got no points at all from tasters, who called the flavor "harsh," "old, not aged," "bitter," and "almost chemical." The texture was rated both "gristly," and "mushy."

Rating Free-Standing Mixers

High-end machines perform well; inexpensive models are no bargain.

∽ BY RONNIE FEIN ∽

Years ago, free-standing mixers were a kitchen staple. Grandma probably had a "mixmaster," which is a generic term for a free-standing mixer, though it is actually a brand name for units manufactured by Sunbeam. For a while, these large machines went out of favor as new food processors and more powerful hand mixers, which were better suited for many of the tasks of standing mixers, became available. If all you want to do is whip egg whites or cream, or if you only make cakes from a mix, you don't really need a heavy-duty standing mixer.

However, for those who do like to bake from scratch, a standing mixer is an invaluable kitchen tool. Provided it's a good one, a standing mixer allows the maximum flexibility for baking traditional and authentic breads and cookies, because it reduces the rather tiresome task of mixing or kneading dough to a matter of turning a switch. Models with

the most options, such as a whisk, beater, and dough hook, will open up the most possibilities for baking.

Perhaps the best use for standing mixers is for mixing and kneading bread dough. They knead perfectly in about one-third the time of hand kneading, and with far more control and satisfaction than bread machines. Hand-held mixers are supposed to be able to knead bread dough but in fact lack the stability and power to do a good job. Some large food processors can knead bread dough, but often make a bread that bakes up tough.

Unfortunately, not all brands of standing mixers are helpful kitchen allies. In the process of testing seven of the top-selling standing mixers, I found that some models are simply too difficult and frustrating to work with to make them worthwhile purchases. Outdated engineering and poorly designed beaters and bowls made it a challenge, rather than a

pleasure, to prepare baked goods in several of the models I used.

On the other hand, three of the seven models were outstanding, and making cakes, cookies, and bread with them was enjoyable and gratifying. The Rival Select KM210B was exceptional, performing every task flawlessly. The two KitchenAid models I tested, the K5SS and the K45SS, were outstanding as well, although the Rival's dough hook is better designed and kneaded bread dough quicker. These three models are also the most expensive of the group. Are they worth it? Plainly and simply, yes. Each is designed for endurance, so it makes sense to spend the money up front, since you will derive years of use and pleasure from these models.

Design Differences

In selecting the appliances to test, I chose models that had good name-brand recognition and reputation, in-

cluding models from KitchenAid, Rival, Krups, Hamilton Beach, and Sunbeam. Each model came equipped with at least one bowl plus one or two beaters and a dough hook or hooks. The KitchenAid models also came with a whisk, as did the Rival, which had a splashguard and spatula as well.

Unlike some kitchen appliances, in which the design of all brands is basically the same, standing mixers have distinct design differences that are the key to differing performance.

Both the Rival Select and the two KitchenAid mixers operate by "planetary action," in which a wide, flat beater moves around a stationary bowl. This proved the most effective way of blending ingredients, since the beater reaches the sides as well as the center of the bowl and gathers particles quickly. As a result, there is little need to stop the machine and scrape the sides of the bowl.

In the more old-fashioned Sun-

FREE-STANDING MIXER PERFORMANCE CHART

The free-standing mixers were evaluated based on the following tests and are listed in order of preference. Prices are suggested retail. For information on purchasing the top models, see Sources and Resources, page 32. Tests performed on each mixer included the following:

Whipped Cream: Bowls and beaters were refrigerated for fifteen minutes. One cup of cream was whipped on low speed for twenty seconds, then the speed was increased gradually to the top speed. Whipped cream was observed for smoothness and volume, measured in cups.

Egg Whites: Five egg whites were beaten on low speed for twenty seconds, then the speed was increased gradually to the top speed. Whites were observed for fluffiness and volume, measured in cups.

Cake Batter: Mixers were required to blend butter with sugar, then incorporate dry and liquid ingredients alternately. Mixers were rated on the ability to do the task without sending flour or milk flying out of the bowl, and for efficient beating of ingredients into a smooth, uniform batter.

Cookie Dough: Mixers were required to blend

butter with sugar, then incorporate eggs, flour, oatmeal, and raisins. Mixers were rated on stability during performance, ability to incorporate dry ingredients without them flying out of the bowl, and on efficiency in creating a uniform dough.

Bread Dough: Mixers were required to blend and knead ingredients for egg-yeast bread. Models were rated for stability during performance and for efficient gathering and kneading of ingredients into a smooth, elastic dough.

= above average performance

= average performance

= poor performance

MIXER	PRICE	SPEEDS	WHITES	CREAM	COOKIE	CAKE	BREAD
Rival Select KM210B	$349	variable	above avg	above avg	above avg	above avg	above avg
KitchenAid K5SS	$415	10	above avg	above avg	above avg	above avg	above avg
KitchenAid K45SS	$300	10	above avg	above avg	above avg	above avg	above avg
Krups Power Mix Pro 610	$100	3 plus pulse/turbo	above avg	average	above avg	above avg	above avg
Hamilton Beach 60600	$130	12	above avg	above avg	above avg	above avg	poor
Sunbeam 2360	$100	12	above avg	above avg	above avg	above avg	poor
Sunbeam 2359	$160	12	above avg	above avg	average	average	poor

beam and Hamilton Beach units, though, the beaters are stationary while the bowl moves. That means you have to turn the unit off several times and scrape the sides with a spatula to move the mixture to the middle of the bowl.

The Krups model has an unusual design that combines features of the other units: The bowl spins around and the beaters also move from the sides to the center of the bowl.

Putting Them Through the Paces
I put each of the seven models through five tests: whipping cream, beating egg whites, mixing cake batter, mixing stiff oatmeal-raisin cookie dough, and mixing and kneading bread dough.

With the exception of the Krups Power Mix Pro 610, all the models made lovely, velvety whipped cream within two minutes. The Krups took several minutes longer and the whipped cream wasn't as fluffy. All models did a good job with egg whites too, with the Rival Select, both KitchenAid models, and Krups giving the greatest volume in the shortest amount of time.

But the dividing line was drawn when I tested each machine's prowess in blending cake, cookie, and bread ingredients. Basically, each machine's performance depended on its mixing method.

Preparing cake batter in the Sunbeam models and the Hamilton Beach unit, with their stationary beaters, was annoying because they took twice as long as the Rival and the two KitchenAid models. In addition, the beaters in these old-fashioned models have center posts, which caused ingredients to repeatedly get clogged in the beaters. This added even more time, since I had to stop several times to scrape the batter off the beaters. Also, the Sunbeam bowls didn't always spin as they were supposed to, which made the process even more frustrating. To make the necessary adjustments for the bowls to spin correctly, I had to fidget with the beater head, which was messy and time consuming.

The Krups fared better than the Sunbeam and Hamilton Beach models. The in-and-out movement of the beaters reduced scraping time considerably, though not as much as in the models with planetary action. The Krups beaters are also well designed, without center posts to cause clogging. However, the best performers by far in blending ingredi-

ents, were the Rival and KitchenAid models, with their planetary action.

Another critical point of comparison among the mixers was stability. The Rival and KitchenAid models are heavy and barely vibrate even when put to the test of mixing stiff cookie and bread dough. The Hamilton Beach and the Krups models, although lighter, are also stable, with well-designed heads that balance the base. These models only wobbled slightly during heavy mixing and kneading. The Sunbeam models, however, were dangerously unstable. They bounced up and down considerably, and sometimes the plate holding the bowl popped up from its base. I had to hold the head down to make sure the machines didn't fall over. Moreover, both units crept along the counter so quickly that they would have fallen off had I not held onto them. A standing mixer you have to hold with one or two hands is not a labor-saving device. And what if the phone rings?

The Rival and the KitchenAids were the best at kneading bread dough, performing the task quickly, smoothly, and efficiently without the motors having the slightest strain, and with no spilling of flour. All three models had the weight, stability, and power needed to make smooth, elastic, tender dough.

Safety is paramount when you're cooking and baking, so, in addition to the stability factor, I also considered safety features of each model. In the Rival and KitchenAid K5SS units, the bowl locks onto the machine; there is no chance it will fly off or wobble up and down. The Krups, Hamilton Beach, Rival, KitchenAid K45SS and the two Sunbeam machines all have tilt-back beater heads that lock into place when the head is down. However, only the Hamilton Beach and Rival heads lock when the head is up, which gives them better stability than the others.

I also considered the mixing speeds when comparing the standing mixers. Having a slow speed is important for adding flour or cream, or blending butter and sugar together without ingredients flying out of the bowl. All but the Krups proved worthy in this respect. Fortunately, the Krups model's mixing method and its modern beaters made up for this lack. ∎

Ronnie Fein is the author of *The Complete Idiot's Guide to Cooking Basics* (Alpha Books, 1995).

Rival Select KM210B: A top choice, with efficient performance and solid construction.

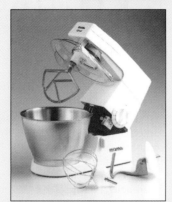

KichenAid K5SS: Outstanding performer, widest variety of attachments.

KitchenAid K45SS: Smaller bowl capacity, fewer attachments than the K5SS, but a fine machine and very popular.

Krups Power Mix Pro 610: A lightweight machine that does a decent job on dough but lacks real power.

Hamilton Beach 60600: Fair job on bread dough and whipped cream, not much else.

Sunbeam MixMaster 2360: Poor performance and dangerous lack of stability make this a poor choice.

Sunbeam MixMaster 2359: All the drawbacks of the 2360 plus hard-to-clean chrome body, and a higher price.

PHOTOGRAPHS BY DAVE HENDERSON

Cheap, Drinkable Red Wines

Yes, you can find a decent red wine in a supermarket or convenience store.

∾ BY MARK BITTMAN ∾

Finding good value in a red wine, even one that costs just a few dollars, is not difficult when you're in a good wine store. Most committed shop owners can recommend their current $6 favorite, or you can go in and ask for a wine you've been told about or read about.

But what happens when you're in a supermarket, a convenience store, or an old-fashioned liquor store and need a bottle, like, now? Chances are you'll be confronted by a few stale wines that no one wanted (and neither do you) and a handful of well-known, mass-produced reds—wines of which literally hundreds of thousands of cases are made each year. Are you destined to buy something virtually undrinkable on such occasions? Or will you simply opt out of the battle and settle for beer instead?

Neither extreme is necessary. Although some cheap red wine is absolutely vile, there are good buys in the mass market category—reasonably well-made wines that pack neither power nor complexity but can still make a contribution to a good meal. From a group of fifteen wines, limited to $8 a bottle (why spend more?), our tasting panel found three we liked very much and six we could live with; the remaining six went from not too terrible to downright awful.

Although the type of grape didn't seem to matter (inexpensive grapes don't have a lot of varietal character anyway), country of origin did: Most of the best wines came from California and France. One might explain this by saying that shipping costs add little to the expense of California wines, and the French simply have a lot of decent grapes—as long as you allow that our second-place finisher, a wine from Australia, is the exception that proves the rule.

In any country, making good, inexpensive red wine is a real challenge. To produce and sell the necessary quantities profitably requires mega-tons of grapes, usually far more than a winery can grow or even purchase from favored growers, which leads to buying grapes on the open market. There's nothing wrong with this. But no matter how careful and conscientious the winery is, each year the wine is affected not only by the vintage but also by the fact that the grapes may have originated hundreds of miles away from the previous year's batch. Remember, too, that a bottle labeled "Merlot" may contain up to 25 percent (more in some countries) nonmerlot grapes. In one vintage, those blended grapes may have been decent quality cabernet sauvignon; in the next, they may be under-ripe gamay. Even if the merlot grapes are top-notch and the winemaking process remains identical, you are looking at two completely different wines.

Thus, this year's results are unlikely to be of much use to you a year from now. For that reason, we held our tasting as close to publication as possible to make sure that the wines we're writing about are ones you're likely to find in the store. Since none of these are designed to be sold for more than a year or so, it's not likely that you'll see these vintages much past the end of this summer, when the next batch makes its appearance. ∎

BLIND TASTING RESULTS

As usual, the wines in our tasting were judged by a panel made up of both wine professionals and amateur wine lovers. In the judging, seven points were awarded for each first-place vote; six for second; five for third; and so on. The wines were all purchased in the Northeast; prices will vary somewhat throughout the country. Within each category, wines are listed based on the number of points scored.

In general, Highly Recommended wines received few or no negative comments; Recommended wines had predominantly positive comments; and Not Recommended wines had few or no positive comments.

HIGHLY RECOMMENDED

1994 Fetzer Eagle Peak Merlot (California), $8. Placed in the top five by all tasters but one. While some found it "bland" or "simple," others saw "surprisingly good tannin and balance," with "very nice fruit."

1992 Lindeman's Bin 50 Shiraz (Southeastern Australia), $7. Nearly everyone liked this wine, too, although it was "stronger," and some felt it could use a little more age.

1993 Glen Ellen Proprietor's Reserve Merlot (California), $6. From the best-known maker of inexpensive varietal wines, a pleasant surprise: "Light and fruity," "has weight," and "finishes as pleasantly as it starts."

RECOMMENDED

1992 Beautour Cabernet Sauvignon (Napa Valley), $8. This wine's top fan called it "a Cabernet of some weight." Others who liked it also found it "somewhat short," and detractors thought it either "too sweet" or "vegetal."

1994 Georges Duboeuf Beaujolais-Villages, $8. "A young wine of good quality," said one booster. Others thought it "most quaffable" even if it did have a nose "like Kool-Aid."

1990 Mouton Cadet (Bordeaux), $8. The classic inexpensive red wine from France did fairly well: "Definitely French," wrote one taster, "and not at all bad." But some found it "weak-willed" and "not in good shape."

1993 La Vieille Ferme (Côtes du Ventoux), $6. "A bit sweet, but well-balanced and fresh," according to one panel member. But "sour," "hot,"

and "burnt" were other comments.

1993 Woodbridge (Mondavi) Barrel Aged Cabernet Sauvignon (California), $7. "Fairly sweet cab," with "some fruit and nice finish," said some. "Vegetal," said others.

N.V. Ernest and Julio Gallo Hearty Burgundy (North Coast, California), $4.50. No one loved this wine, but almost no one hated it either.

NOT RECOMMENDED

1993 Los Vascos Cabernet Sauvignon (Colchagua, Chile), $7. This did have one fan, who found it "drinkable at least." But most thought it "unbalanced," "vegetal," and "poor."

1994 Concha y Toro Cabernet Sauvignon/Merlot (Rapel Valley, Chile), $4.50. Again, one taster thought this "drinkable," and another "not bad." More found it "unpleasant."

1993 Napa Ridge Pinot Noir (North Coast, California), $7. A good example of the wide quality swings of inexpensive wines. Two years ago, this wine did well in one of our tastings, now tasters found it "like gasoline."

1990 Montecillo Viña Cumbrero (Rioja, Spain), $6.50. Many tasters found "some" fruit here, but most also found it "bitter" and "unappealing," with "fuel-oil" aromas.

1994 Antinori Santa Cristina Sangiovese Toscano (Tuscany), $7.50. "Drinkable but sweet" was the best said about this. Generally: "Insipid."

N.V. Corvo Duca di Salaparuta (Sicily), $8. Singularly distasteful. Voted "among the worst wines I've every tasted" by three-fourths of the panel members.

Chez Panisse Vegetables
Alice Waters
HarperCollins, $30

Alice Waters is a product of Berkeley, a cultural biosphere that has no more in common with the average American lifestyle than Henry Miller's Paris. In this food lover's arcadia, Waters has often pursued arcane culinary visions, pampered by just-picked, hard-to-find ingredients that are devoutly prepared and sold at stiff prices at her world-famous eatery, Chez Panisse. Her first book, *The Chez Panisse Menu Cookbook* (Random House, 1982), reflected this devotion to culinary elitism, with recipes like Sautéed Duck Livers with Celery Root, which called for twelve very *fresh* duck livers, two tablespoons of duck fat, one cup of duck stock, and one teaspoon of minced black truffle.

But times have changed and so has Waters. Her charm and her reputation are both based on a religious devotion to the relationship between farmer and cook. By focusing on fresh ingredients, simply prepared, she cast a powerful spell over the American food revolution of the 1980s. While many chefs were busy squirting goat cheese designs on pools of red pepper puree, Waters was, to her credit, lavishing time and attention on the grower and the baker. With the publication of *Vegetables*, a topic that is well suited to both her culinary philosophy and kitchen skills, we were eager to determine whether Waters had finally come full circle, merging the realities of home cooking with her unquestioned genius with fresh ingredients.

The first question we ask about any cookbook is "How's the food?" After the *Cook's* editors tested eleven recipes from *Vegetables,* we'd have to answer that question, with a few caveats, "Pretty darn good." Let's start with the winners. Cauliflower with Ginger and Cilantro, White Bean and Wilted Greens Soup, Caramelized Fennel, Spicy Baked Onions, Spinach Roman Style, Roasted Wild Mushroom Salad, Wild Mushroom Pasta Gratin, and Chard, Spinach and Escarole Pasta were all excellent. When Waters is firing on all cylinders, her food is both simple and full-flavored. In the cauliflower recipe, for example, the ginger kicks up the taste of dull cauliflower, yet the recipe takes just minutes to make and uses only five ingredients (not including salt and pepper). Her genius shines through the clever simplicity of her approach. The marriage of sherry and balsamic vinegars, for exam-

ple, overcomes the deficiencies of both ingredients and produces an unexpected and delightful result. What more could a home cook ask for?

Well, one might expect a modicum of instruction as to how to make a dish. Waters' instructions are often vague and assume more than a passing knowledge of the culinary arts in that the reader, for example, needs to know how to deglaze, make a julienne, and correctly guess about pan sizes, ingredient amounts (how much is a "small piece of prosciutto"?), and on some occasions, even cooking times. In her defense, specificity is not always required when preparing vegetables, but providing a higher level of guidance and comfort would certainly broaden her audience.

A few recipes had problems. When I made the batter for the Batter Fried Beets, it was as thick as bread dough. The recipe then instructed me, after letting the batter rest, to fold in beaten egg whites, a futile proposition. The batter needed more liquid. The Celery Root, Potato, and Olive Oil Gratin was bland, the potatoes were mealy, and the pan size, not indicated in the recipe, was crucial to success. The Spicy Broccoli Sauté was on the dry side and desperately needed the accompaniments suggested in the headnote; as a stand-alone main course, it was lackluster. Finally, some of our editors had a quibble with the Shallot Flan. It tasted great and the recipe worked just fine, but it seemed better suited as a restaurant side dish than as a home recipe.

But when Waters is good, she's very, very good. If you can skip recipes calling for purple artichokes, white asparagus, black cabbage, and wild fennel (such ingredients, thankfully, are in the minority in this cookbook), and manage with spare recipe instructions, you will be amply rewarded.

Waters' saving grace is her devotion to simplicity of preparation, allowing the deep, natural flavors of fresh-picked vegetables to shine through. For that alone, we owe her our undying gratitude. Most chef cookbooks are elaborately staged magic shows, impossible to replicate at home without years of experience and fancy props. Ms. Waters stands there on a bare stage and, with modest sleight of hand, works wonders with a few garden vegetables. For the most part, her sorcery is transparent—we can go home after the show and, indeed, pull a rabbit out of the hat. If a few of the props are hard to find and a bit of practice is necessary, so be it. To our surprise and her credit, her illusions are based in reality.

—*Chris Kimball*

Home Food
Debbie Shore and Catherine Townsend
Clarkson Potter, $25

I'm not usually attracted to cookbooks by restaurant chefs. The stylish food chefs create for their restaurant rarely translates to the home kitchen. And it shouldn't. Generally, home cooks respond to need; chefs satisfy want.

But sometimes the roles reverse. Chefs have to cook at home, and home cooks have to entertain. *Home Food* bridges the two worlds, offering forty-four home-entertaining menus designed by chefs, most of which are extraordinary and appealing. With few exceptions, *Home Food* lives up to its name, offering home food with flair. As if that were not enough, profits from book sales benefit SOS, a nonprofit hunger-relief organization.

—*Pam Anderson*

With the Grain
Raymond Sokolov
Alfred A. Knopf, $25

If you like to think about your food as you cook and eat, whole grains can help you think about nature, or about life in earlier times, or about distant cultures. Ray Sokolov has become our most popular food historian, and brings both considerable knowledge and a light touch to this book of two hundred recipes for twelve different grains.

He is also enough of a food lover to make sure that his recipes are delicious, not just healthful, historic, or authentic. Some of the best recipes in this book are simple substitutions. There is a typical recipe for grape leaves stuffed with rice, for instance, but also a really good, easy, interesting one for grape leaves stuffed with pearl barley, mushrooms, and garlic. Technical directions are kept simple, with the risk that it may take a couple of tries to get them just right. But for cooks who are comfortable with fine-tuning a recipe, this cookbook goes beyond the usual recipes and conveys a real excitement about grains.

—*Mark Zanger*

Congratulations: *Three cookbooks by staff members will be published this spring:* Pasta e Verdura *(HarperCollins, $25) by Jack Bishop,* Cooking with Steam *(William Morrow, $19.95) by Stephanie Lyness, and* Lettuce in Your Kitchen *(William Morrow, $25.00) by John Willoughby and coauthor Chris Schlesinger.* ∎

SOURCES
AND RESOURCES

Most of the ingredients and materials necessary for the recipes in this issue are available at your local supermarket, gourmet store, or kitchen supply shop. The following are mail-order sources for particular items. Prices listed below were current at press time and do not include shipping or handling unless otherwise indicated. We suggest that you contact companies directly to confirm up-to-date prices and availability.

STANDING MIXERS

By virtue of their power, weight, and excellent overall performance, two KitchenAids—the Heavy Duty series, 325-watt Model K5SS, and the Classic series, 250-watt Model K45SS—and the Rival Select Model KM210B led the pack in our standing mixer testing (page 28). The Krups Powermix Pro Model 610, though less solidly built and less powerful (at 240 watts) than the others, deserves consideration because it performed adequately and costs significantly less. Because of the willingness of the company to special-order particular products at a customer's request, you can obtain each of these mixers by mail order through A Cook's Wares (211 37th Street, Beaver Falls, PA 15010; 412-846-9490) even though they do not all appear in the catalog. The KitchenAid K5SS sells for $319, the K45SS for $239; the Rival for $269; and the Krups for $69.90. Call for details about capacities, features, colors, and shipping.

ELECTRIC ICE CREAM MACHINE

Working on recipes for the frozen yogurt story on page 14, as well as for "Secrets of Creamy Fruit Sorbets" in the July/August 1995 issue, revealed an important fact about homemade frozen desserts: The more air you beat into the base mixture, the better the texture of the finished product. And when it comes to incorporating air, you can't beat the constant churning of an electric ice cream machine. Our favorite electric machine is still the Simac II Gelataio Magnum that

won our rating in July/August 1993, but at $500, it is something of a budget breaker. An excellent and reasonably priced alternative is the newer Krups La Glacière, featuring a coolant-filled canister, which must be frozen overnight, and an electric motor for easy churning. The La Glacière is available for $60 through the Williams-Sonoma catalog (800-541-2233).

BREAD PANS

In making loaf after loaf of bread for the "No-Knead Sandwich Bread" article on page 9, we found that our heavy, commercial-grade loaf pans consistently turned out the best crusts. Typically sold in restaurant or bakery supply stores, such top-quality, extra-heavy loaf pans can also be purchased through the King Arthur Flour Baker's Catalogue (800-827-6836). Made by Ecko-Glaco, these pans are formed from a strong steel-aluminum base; to release loaves easily, the interior surfaces are coated with nonstick silicone. The cost is $10.50 for one pan, or $19.95 for two.

INSTANT YEAST

Fleischmann's Instant Yeast, the winner among the eight yeasts we tested for the "No-Knead Sandwich Bread" piece, is a new product developed by Fleischmann's, which also makes the familiar red-and-yellow packets of active dry yeast. Fleischmann's Instant is especially strong and fast-acting, so much so, in fact, that you can mix it directly with the other dry ingredients without first proofing it. Vacuum-packed, one-pound packages of Fleischmann's Instant Yeast are available through the King Arthur Flour Baker's Catalogue (800-827-6836) for $5.25 each.

TUBE PANS

For baking the chiffon cakes from the story on page 6, a tube pan allows the batter to heat from the center as well as from the outside edges, so the cake sets quickly and without loss of volume. The King Arthur Flour

Baker's Catalogue (800-827-6836) sells a 16-gauge aluminum tube pan (which they call the Classic Angel Food Pan) that measures nine and five-eighths inches in diameter for $24.50.

FRESH MOZZARELLA

Mass-produced mozzarella cheese is available at every market in the nation, but the Mozzarella Company (2944 Elm Street, Dallas, TX 75226; 214-741-4071 or 800-798-2954) sells mozzarella of a completely different nature: It is made from fresh milk, by hand, every day. The Mozzarella Company's namesake cheese, ideal for use in the antipasti illustrated on pages 16 and 17, comes in impressive variety, including buffalo milk for $16 per pound; goat's and cow's milk combination for $10 per pound; smoked (over pecan shells) for $8.25 per pound; and rolled with savory fillings for $10 per pound. Straightforward cow's milk mozzarella comes, salted and not, in one-half-pound balls for $8 per pound, and in one-and-one-half-ounce, bite-sized balls (roughly ten in a pound) for $10 per pound.

MEDJOOL DATES

Medjool dates are arguably the largest, plumpest variety of the fruit on the market. Excellent for use in either the antipasto recipe on page 16 or the Date-Spice Chiffon Cake recipe on page 8, medjools are primarily grown in Israel, though California also produces a small crop. Adriana's Caravan (409 Vanderbilt Street, Brooklyn, NY 11218; 800-316-0820 or 718-436-8565), a New York mail-order house that bills itself as "the ultimate international food source," sells medjools for $5.95 per pound with a one-pound minimum order. There are roughly fifty dates in a pound.

FIRE FIXIN'S

Because it is free from the additives and chemicals used in briquettes, lump hardwood charcoal burns hotter and cleaner and imparts no undesir-

able flavors or odors to the grilled foods. The People's Woods Company (75 Mill Street, Cumberland, RI 02864; 800-729-5800) sells 8 kg (17.6-pound) lots of kiln-fired, sugar maple lump hardwood charcoal for $8.90 each, or $7.90 each if you buy two or more. Also available are thirty-six-count packages of hardwood lighters, which are firestarters made from sawdust bound with paraffin, for $2.50, and chimney starters in regular and large sizes, for $10.95 and $15.95, respectively.

EMILE HENRY OVENWARE

Used for everyday cooking in France for more than one hundred years, Emile Henry high-fired ceramic bakeware is a favorite around here. Produced by hand in Burgundy, the entire line is safe for the oven, microwave, and dishwasher. The pieces come in a wide range of useful shapes and sizes, but what clinches it for us are the terrific colors, which include vibrant cobalt blue, bright red, saffron yellow, forest green, and pure white, all with white interiors. The Wooden Spoon Catalog (P.O. Box 931, Clinton, CT 06413; 800-431-2207) carries an impressive collection. Try the fifteen-by-eight-inch lasagne pan ($49) for a full recipe of our chicken pot pie (see page 12), or the five-and-one-half-inch-diameter all-purpose bowls ($34 for a set of four) for individual pies.

OZARK TRAILS BACON

Because the focus of our "Oscar Mayer Wins Bacon Tasting" article in the March/April issue was supermarket bacon, no information was given on the availability of Ozark Trails brand bacon, a specialty product included in the test as a clear ringer. But since Ozark Trails was a favorite among the tasters, many readers have asked for ordering information. The bacon in question is available by mail order from the distributor, Ham I Am! (1303 Columbia Drive #201, Richardson, TX 75081; 800-742-6426) for $4.45 per one-and-one-half-pound package. ∎

ROASTED RED PEPPER SALAD WITH
RED ONIONS & CUCUMBERS page 21 &
FENNEL-ORANGE SALAD WITH BLACK
OLIVES & MINT page 19

SIMPLE CHICKEN POT PIE
page 13

LEMON CHIFFON CAKE
page 8

STRAWBERRY FROZEN YOGURT
page 15

ASSORTED ANTIPASTI
page 16

GRILLED STRIP SIRLOIN STEAK
page 25

ESPRESSO GRANITA

(YOU DON'T NEED AN ESPRESSO
MACHINE TO MAKE THIS DESSERT;
YOU CAN SIMPLY MAKE ESPRESSO-
STRENGTH COFFEE IN A DRIP
MACHINE. THIS GRANITA CAN ALSO
BE MADE WITH DECAFFEINATED
ESPRESSO.)

In large bowl, dissolve 1½ cups sugar in 4 cups espresso. Cool to room temperature, then pour coffee mixture into loaf pan and freeze, scraping mixture with fork tines every half hour or so until mixture is light-textured and icy, 6 to 8 hours. Whip ¾ cup heavy whipping cream to soft peaks with 1 tablespoon sugar, ¼ teaspoon vanilla extract, and 2 teaspoons brandy. Serve each portion of granita with dollop of whipped cream.
Serves 6

NUMBER TWENTY-ONE

AUGUST 1996

COOK'S
ILLUSTRATED

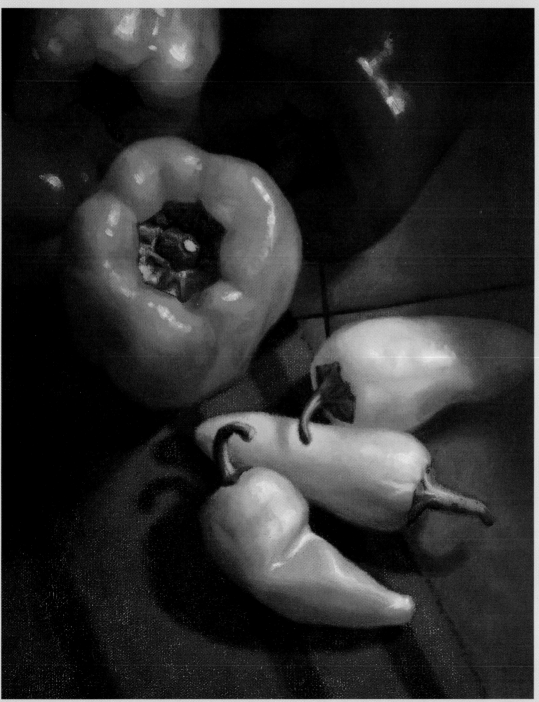

Fruit Cobblers
Combine 10 Fruits with
4 Different Toppings

Salad Dressing 101
More Oil, Less Vinegar

Dannon Wins
Yogurt Tasting
Lowfat Supermarket
Yogurts Score Well

Rating & Using
Pressure Cookers
Are They Really Faster?
Which One Should I Buy?

GRILLING CHICKEN
LEGS AND THIGHS

CHOCOLATE MOUSSE

BEST KITCHEN GADGETS

GRILLING VEGETABLES

FULL-FLAVORED PESTO

$4.00 U.S./$4.95 CANADA

TABLE
OF CONTENTS

"Peppers"
ILLUSTRATION BY
BRENT WATKINSON

"Poached Plum and Raspberry Compote in Sweet Wine Syrup"
adapted from
Classic Home Desserts
by Richard Sax
(Chapters, 1994)

ILLUSTRATION BY
CAROL FORTUNATO

COOK'S
ILLUSTRATED

Publisher and Editor CHRISTOPHER KIMBALL

Executive Editor MARK ZANGER

Senior Editor JOHN WILLOUGHBY

Food Editor PAM ANDERSON

Senior Writer JACK BISHOP

Consulting Editors MARK BITTMAN
STEPHANIE LYNESS

Assistant Editor ADAM RIED

Editorial Assistant ELIZABETH CAMERON

Test Cook MELISSA HAMILTON

....

Art Director ANNE MURDOCK

Food Stylist MARIE PIRAINO

Special Projects Designer AMY KLEE

....

Managing Editor KEITH POWERS

Editorial Prod. Coordinator KARIN L. KANEPS

Copy Editor GARY PFITZER

....

Marketing Director ADRIENNE KIMBALL

Circulation Director CAROLYN ADAMS

Circulation Coordinator JONATHAN VENIER

Production Director JAMES MCCORMACK

Project Coordinator SHEILA DATZ

Advertising Prod. Manager PAMELA SLATTERY

Systems Administrator MATTHEW FRIGO

Production Artist KEVIN MOELLER

....

Vice President JEFFREY FEINGOLD

Controller LISA A. CARULLO

Accounting Assistant MANDY SHITO

Office Manager TONYA ESTEY

Special Projects FERN BERMAN

Cook's Illustrated (ISSN 1068-2821) is published bimonthly by Boston Common Press Limited Partnership, 17 Station Street, P.O. Box 569, Brookline, MA 02147-0569. Copyright 1996 Boston Common Press Limited Partnership. Second class/periodical postage paid at Boston, MA, and additional mailing offices, USPS #012487. For list rental information, please contact List Services Corporation, 6 Trowbridge Drive, P.O. Box 516, Bethel, CT 06801; (203) 743-2600, FAX (203) 743-0589. Editorial office: 17 Station Street, P.O. Box 569, Brookline, MA 02147-0569; (617) 232-1000, FAX (617) 232-1572. Editorial contributions should be sent to: Editor, *Cook's Illustrated*. We cannot assume responsibility for manuscripts submitted to us. Submissions will be returned only if accompanied by a large self-addressed stamped envelope. Subscription rates: $24.95 for one year; $45 for two years; $65 for three years. (Canada: add $3 per year; all other countries: add $12 per year.) Postmaster: Send all new orders, subscription inquiries, and change of address notices to *Cook's Illustrated*, P.O. Box 7444, Red Oak, IA 51591-0444. Single copies: $4 in U.S., $4.95 in Canada and other countries. Back issues available for $5 each. PRINTED IN THE U.S.A.

EDITORIAL

COOKING LESSONS

CHRISTOPHER KIMBALL

Our white Vermont farmhouse sits in an old cornfield at the top of a narrow valley, which runs from the Green Mountains due west toward New York State. Most of our weather blows in from the west, and in the summer I sit with the kids on the narrow front porch watching great walls of rain sweep down Walnut Mountain or towering shrouds of mist that change color and shape as they slowly drift up our dirt road. But when the weather comes from the east, we know it will be a hard blow. Last March, we endured such a storm, a mini-tornado that ripped through our valley like a freight train, plucking out old maples and scattering the roofs of sheds and barns over the sodden, dormant fields.

After church the Sunday after the storm, I picked up my chain saw and went over to a neighbor's to help cut up three large sugar maples that were leaning precariously toward his house. When I arrived, I started up my sixteen-inch Stihl and got started on the first tree, which by this point had been felled by the local woodsman, Harley, a born Vermonter.

I started cutting down through the tree, and as the saw got toward the bottom, the trunk started to close in and bind my saw. After a few minutes, I noticed that Harley was standing right next to me with his own chain saw fired up. He started cutting through the massive maple from the bottom up, and as he neared the top of the log, the cut would widen, leaving plenty of room for the chain. After a couple of cuts, he went away. I then realized that he had just given me a silent lesson in chainsawing. He had quietly watched me do it the wrong way, and in the great tradition of old-time Vermonters, Harley had stepped in and taught me a lesson without a word spoken between us.

Most of what I have learned about cooking has come not from experts telling me what to do but from watching others. In the early 1960s, I learned how to knead bread by watching Marie Briggs, our town baker, work the rich, nut-brown dough back and forth over a plastic red-checked tablecloth, her shockingly pale arms full of hidden muscle and sinew. On those rainy summer afternoons when I was helping out in the kitchen, not the hayfields, she treated me like an equal, expecting me to learn by watching. She quietly demonstrated how to stir up the fire in the woodstove that baked the bread, to cut out doughnuts, and to roll out sugar cookies, but thirty years later, I can't remember one word of explicit instruction. All those engaged in hard work were treated equally and accorded a large measure of respect. My terrible fear of disappointing Marie was her great strength as a teacher.

Since that day in March, I have spent many hours thinking about other teachers. I have shared the immense benefits of a hard day's work with Charles Bentley, a local farmer; I have witnessed from Julia Child the invigorating pleasures of giving assistance to others; I have seen the vivid joy of faith in the eyes of ushers at our church; I have been energized by the great intellectual curiosity of my mother; I have been softened and humbled by the total love and acceptance of our children; I have learned to savor the idiosyncrasies of daily life from my father, who was a keen observer of the human condition. Good teachers share themselves with others, leaving behind a bit of their energy and enthusiasm even as we begin to grow and move apart. What remains is the sharing, not so much the instruction itself.

Perhaps that is why I find cooking not to be a solitary task. Preparing food is most enjoyable when we realize that each of us is both a teacher and a student in the kitchen. Cooking is about studying other people, watching their actions, not their words, and it is also about assuming the role of teacher, treating others with respect, the same way Marie taught a know-nothing eight-year-old many years ago in that small yellow farmhouse. Few of us today know what to watch for in life. But in a time when everything is explicit, what is left unsaid takes on greater meaning.

The lesson I most remember was taught to me by my wife, Adrienne, just after our first child was born. It was a tough labor, lasting well into a Sunday morning in June, which, by coincidence, was also my birthday. As the nurses handed Adrienne our daughter, freshly weighed, cleaned, and swaddled, she took her for just a second and then gave her, arms outstretched, to me. She was too tired to say much, but she wanted me to be the first one to hold her tightly and gaze into her eyes. It was not a casual gesture; it taught me much about selflessness and caring for others, and every year on my birthday, I remember a small child held out for me by her mother, a precious gift from my greatest teacher. ∎

THICKENING FRUIT PIES

I've always had mixed results using flour as a pie thickener, but never had the initiative to sort out the other thickeners and their characteristics. So it was terrific to read about tapioca in the July/August 1995 issue.

As all of my pie recipes now use flour as a thickener, how do I convert the amount of flour in each recipe to the appropriate amount of tapioca needed?

SKY COLE
Ridgefield, CT

We suggest using the amount of fruit in the recipe, rather than the amount of flour, to determine how much instant tapioca to use. There are two reasons for this. First, recipes are not always consistent; they call for all sorts of different amounts of flour per cup of fruit. If the amount of flour is off to begin with, chances are that any amount of tapioca based on that flour will also be off. Second, all fruit is not created equal in terms of inherent thickening ability or quality. For instance, local berries at the height of their season are juicier, and might require more thickening, than their out-of-season, imported counterparts. Personal tastes also come to bear in thickening fruit pies. Some people like a truly set, gelatinous filling whereas others prefer juicier versions.

To our tastes, a good fruit pie filling is firm, with a little bit of juice. The recipes in "How To Thicken Fruit Pies" in our July/August 1995 issue call for three to four tablespoons of instant tapioca for six cups of juicy fruit, which works out to a generous, rounded one and one-half teaspoons per cup of fruit. If your fruit is a little less juicy, use a scant one and one-half teaspoons per cup. These amounts are a good starting point from which you can adjust the thickening to your tastes.

CHASING THE CHEW

With reference to your January/February 1996 article about chewy chocolate chip cookies, I have an answer to share. Years ago, I arrived early at a friend's house and she was baking chocolate chip cookies. When the stove timer went off, she removed the cookie sheet from the oven, banged it flat on the counter once or twice, and returned the sheet to the oven. When I asked why she did this, she told me it was because her husband liked chewy chocolate chip cookies.

Laugh if you will, but I have done it for more than thirty years. Try it—it works!

VIRGINIA FAST
Chagrin Falls, OH

Your suggestion prompted us to go to the kitchen to do some testing. We tried your method using both our chocolate chip cookie recipe from the January/February 1996 issue of *Cook's Illustrated* and the Toll House cookie recipe from the back of the chocolate chips bag. Rapping the cookie sheet with the partially baked cookies against the counter made a more noticeable difference in the height and chewiness of the Toll House cookies than it did with our recipe for a couple of reasons.

The first reason is the amount of chemical leavening in the dough. Leavening in the cookies occurs because the baking soda produces carbon dioxide gas in the dough as it bakes. The cookies rise as the gas tries to force its way out. Banging the cookie sheet against the counter causes the gas to escape suddenly from the cookies, which collapses their structure before it is set. Thus, the cookies sink in the middle. The result is fairly flat, compact, chewy cookies. Our recipe uses one-half teaspoon less baking soda than does the Toll House recipe, so less gas is created during baking. Because the structure of our cookies gets less of a rise to begin with, it falls less when disturbed. The Toll House cookie recipe includes more baking soda, so a greater quantity of carbon dioxide gas develops as the cookies bake, forcing a higher rise. The higher the rise, the more the cookies deflate when the gas escapes suddenly. The Toll House cookies that were rapped against the counter fell almost one-quarter of an inch, from three-eighths of an inch to just under one-quarter of an inch in height.

A second factor is the quantity of dough used to make the cookies before baking. One aim of our recipe is to create cookies that are, if you will, full-figured. In our technique, each cookie is made from about one-quarter cup of dough, or four tablespoons. Thus, the cookies start out taller and plumper than Toll House cookies, which begin with one generous tablespoon of dough, dropped on the baking sheet in the traditional manner. The extra height and mass of our unbaked cookies helps ensure that they will be thick and rounded when baked, about three-quarters of an inch high. Our cookies fell only one-eighth of an inch, from three-quarters of an inch to five-eighths of an inch when they were rapped on the counter during the baking process.

PRESERVING THE CHEW

My chocolate chip cookies sometimes get hard and difficult to bite. To solve this problem, I put a slice of bread into the storage container along with the cookies. The bread gets stale, but the cookies stay soft and chewy. If there is a large quantity of cookies, I tear the bread into two or three pieces, which I distribute evenly among the cookies. This tip also works well with cookies that have already gotten tough. If you can figure out how this works, I'd love to know.

JANICE NAGUIT
San Rafael, CA

Guided by our food science consultant Shirley Corriher, we did figure out why the cookies stay moist and the bread goes stale. The answer can be summed up in one word, hygroscopicity, which is the quality of attracting moisture. Sugar is, by nature, highly hygroscopic.

Compared to bread, chocolate chip cookies (any cookies, really) are much higher in sugar and fat and lower in water. Cookies' low moisture content, coupled with their high proportion of sugar and the sugar's hygroscopicity, means that cookies will grab moisture wherever they can get it. In this case, you are providing extra moisture from the bread. Dr. Brian Strouts, Biscuit Products Research Director at the American Institute of Baking in Manhattan, Kansas, noted the moisture differential between bread and cookies more specifically. According to the FDA's standard of identity, commercial white bread is allowed a maximum moisture content of 38 percent. Homemade cookies, on the other hand, have a moisture content of 10 to 12 percent. When the bread and cookies are placed together in the canister, the moisture in the bread raises the relative humidity inside the canister. The sugar in the cookie dough attracts the excess humidity provided by the bread in an attempt to equalize the moisture levels of the two products.

CLABBERED MILK

I have been searching for someone who knows about something my grandmother made from whole milk or cream (I am not sure which one, since I was very young and don't remember such details). She would set a bowl of milk or cream to stand for a few days (again, I do not recall whether it was refrigerated), and it would solidify into what she called "clabbered milk," which she used in baking and sometimes as a topping for desserts. Do you know how to safely make this type of milk product?

LEVENIA KELEMAN
Cupertino, CA

Traditionally associated with the South, clabbered milk or "clabber," as it is also called, is a soured, thickened milk product that results from the activity of naturally occurring acid-producing bacteria in raw milk. The sour taste comes from the lactic acid produced by the bacteria, which in turn causes the caseins, or milk-solid proteins, to aggregate, or curdle. Essentially, this is a fermentation process that happens at room temperature, thus your grandmother probably left her milk out while it cured and then refrigerated it to stop fermentation once it had reached her desired texture and piquancy.

The homogenized, pasteurized milk that is available widely in supermarkets has been heated and held briefly at the elevated temperature to destroy any enzymes and bacteria that could cause disease as well as the fermentation process necessary to make clabbered milk.

You can sour and slightly curdle room-temperature pasteurized milk by adding an acid ingredient such as lemon juice or white vinegar in a ratio of one tablespoon per cup of milk. The resulting product would be acceptable used in baking as a buttermilk substitute, but the texture is not smooth and thick. You would certainly not want to use it as a dessert topping.

To make clabbered milk from pasteurized milk, you must reintroduce the live cultures that the pasteurization process eliminated. *Cook's Illustrated* Food Editor Pam Anderson, who was born and raised in the South, where her parents regularly made clabber, suggests adding one-half cup of buttermilk (a cultured milk product) to three and one-half cups of warmed whole milk, and allowing the mixture to ferment at room temperature until it thickens and sours, at least overnight. This process could take up to thirty-six hours. The clabbered milk that results is thicker and richer than buttermilk. The flavor is noticeably tangy, but less tart than buttermilk.

BAKEWELL CREAM

*F*or years, I have used Bakewell Cream when I make biscuits (they come out high, fluffy, and light), and now I can no longer obtain it. The contents of Bakewell Cream are acid sodium pyrophosphate and redried starch. What can I use in its place?

CHERYL ANN HARTMAN
Estero, FL

We have good news and better news. The good news is that you can substitute cream of tartar for Bakewell Cream. Both substances are acidic compounds that will interact with baking soda, a base, to make a double-acting baking powder. Cream of tartar is a natural precipitate of the tartaric acid present in grape juice, and it collects in crystalline form inside the wooden casks in which wine is aged. Because cream of tartar was in short supply during the wartime 1940s, Bangor,

Maine, chemist Byron Smith developed Bakewell Cream as an alternative acid to combine with baking soda for use as a leavening agent.

The better news is that the Apple Ledge Company, makers of Bakewell Cream, is alive and well in East Holden, Maine. Apple Ledge manufactures both Bakewell Cream and a Bakewell Cream premade biscuit mix, both of which are distributed primarily in New England and by mail order through the company. The cost of an eight-ounce can of Bakewell Cream is $2; $1.75 for a sixteen-ounce box of the biscuit mix. Shipping is extra in both cases. To order, call Apple Ledge at 207-989-5576.

HOW TO CHECK A PROPANE TANK

*T*he time for outdoor grilling is upon us again, and with it a season's worth of wondering how much propane is left in the tank. Here is an easy, accurate way to check.
  1) Boil one cup of water.
  2) Pour the boiling water down the side of your propane tank.
  3) Feel the metal with your hand. Where it has been warmed by the water, it is empty. Where there is still propane inside, it will be cool to the touch.
  No more guesswork about whether it is time to refill.

CINDI PETERSON
Stationed in Japan

We tried your boiling water method of checking a propane tank and it worked well. Arch Corriher,

an electrical engineer by profession and husband of our food science consultant, explained how your trick works. Where the propane has been depleted, there is nothing against the metal of the tank. This means that the boiling water has to heat a single layer—the metal only—which it can do quickly. Where propane remains in the tank, the boiling water must heat a double layer—the metal and the liquid next to it. This the water cannot do, so the metal remains cool.

ERRATA

In the article entitled "No-Knead Sandwich Bread" in the May/June 1996 issue, an error during editing resulted in the inadvertent reversal of the protein contents of bread flour and all-purpose flour. In the original version of the story, as well as in all testing, the authors correctly noted the relative protein contents of the two flours, so all testing results remain valid. We apologize for any confusion that this may have caused our readers.

The article entitled "Roasting Chicken 14 Ways" in the January/February 1996 issue included a discussion of the testing of a vertical roaster, accompanied by a picture of a vertical roaster. The vertical roaster shown in the article, a Spanek Roaster, was not the roaster tested in the article. *Cook's Illustrated* apologizes for any inconvenience that this may have caused.

Since learning of the inadvertent use of a picture of the Spanek Roaster, *Cook's Illustrated* has begun further testing of vertical and V-rack roasting, the results of which will be reported in a future issue. ∎

WHAT IS IT?

I recently found this object and would like to know what it is and how it is used. It consists of a pair of heavy terra-cotta plates with concentric grooves in the interior, joined with a lightweight metal frame with plastic handles. The plates are eleven inches in diameter and about three-quarters of an inch deep. The device is made in Italy, and the outside of the plates are stamped "La Cotta." What is it?

ROWLAND AERTKER
Hancock, NH

We consulted Italian chef and author (most recently of *La Vera Cucina*, Simon and Schuster, 1996) Carlo Middione, along with several importers and retailers of Italian

cookware including La Cuisine Kitchenware in Alexandria, Virginia, and VillaWare Manufacturing in Cleveland, Ohio. Everyone agreed that your La Cotta, which translates loosely to "cooked" in Italian, is a type of grilling device used to approximate a Tuscan technique of grilling pigeons or small chickens under a brick or a specially designed terra-cotta weight called a *mattone*. In a dish called *pollo al mattone*, seasoned, marinated chicken parts (or halves, if the chicken is small) are weighted on the grill under a mattone or a brick. As we found in the "Secrets of Butterflied Chicken" in the September/October 1994 issue of *Cook's Illustrated*, weighting the birds during cooking promotes more even browning and reduces the cooking time by a few minutes.

You can achieve a similar effect using the La Cotta. The marinated chicken gets flattened and compressed between the two terra-cotta plates (which are ridged inside to mark the meat) when the La Cotta is closed. Taking care not to burn the plastic handles of the La Cotta, you can place it directly on the hot coals in the grill to cook the contents.

Quick Tips

KEEPING HERBS FRESH

Dan Drislane of Farmington Hills, Michigan, has found a way to keep parsley and other herbs fresh for weeks.

1. Wash and dry the herbs, trim the stem ends, and place the herbs in a tall, airtight container with a tight-fitting lid, such as a plastic powdered-drink container. Add water up to the top of the stems, but don't cover the leaves.

2. Seal the container tightly and refrigerate it. The combination of water and relatively little air keeps the herbs fresh for much longer than other storage methods.

KEEPING STRAWBERRIES FRESH

Care Morgenstern of Los Angeles, California, keeps strawberries fresh for up to ten days by refrigerating them (unwashed) in an airtight container between layers of paper toweling.

BLANCHING GARLIC

Blanching garlic reduces its bite and mellows its flavor a bit (*see* "Pesto at Its Best," page 29, for details). Mrs. L. R. Ledbetter of Orange Park, Florida, discovered an easy way to blanch garlic cloves.

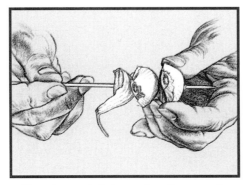

1. Thread unpeeled cloves of garlic onto a long wooden, bamboo, or metal skewer.

2. Dip the skewer into boiling water for about 45 seconds or until the garlic is slightly softened.

FREEZING STOCK

Karen Prater of Eugene, Oregon, has found an easy way to freeze and store stock without taking up very much room in your freezer.

1. Line a mug with a zipper-lock bag. (This way, the bag will stay open, freeing both hands for pouring.)

2. Fill the bag with stock and seal it.

3. Place the bag flat in a large, shallow pan, then stack ensuing bags on top of one another and freeze them. Once the stock is solidly frozen, the bags can be removed from the pan.

ILLUSTRATIONS BY ALAN WITSCHONKE

POURING FROM A FOOD PROCESSOR

Ms. Prater also recommends the following tip to prevent the food processor blade from falling out of the bowl when pouring.

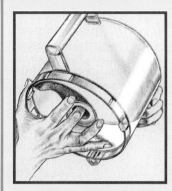

1. Simply hold the workbowl in one hand and push your finger into the bowl shaft and the hollow of the blade.

2. When the bowl is turned upside down, the blade stays in place.

QUICK-CHOPPING HARD-BOILED EGGS

Bridget Tracy of Campbell, California, and Pegg Makolondra of Sturgeon Bay, Wisconsin, both find a pastry blender to be the perfect tool for quickly and easily chopping large quantities of boiled eggs. It is quicker than a knife, and it chops more coarsely than a food processor.

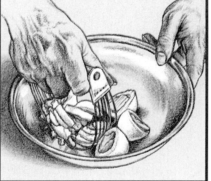

ROLLING AND TRANSFERRING PIE DOUGH

Mayumi Akiyoshi of Chicago has found a foolproof way to roll out and transfer dough to a pan.

1. Place the flattened disk of dough inside a large plastic bag.

2. Roll out the dough, inside the bag, just as you usually would.

3. Once the dough is rolled, cut open the sides of the bag.

4. Slide the rolled-out dough off the bag and onto the pie plate.

5. Finally, just peel the bag off the top of the crust.

SLICING A TOMATO

Unless you have a very sharp knife, slicing a tomato through the skin can be somewhat difficult, because the skin resists the knife surface and the tomato can get a bit crushed. Helen Rowell of Lake Havasu City, Arizona, finds this method helpful.

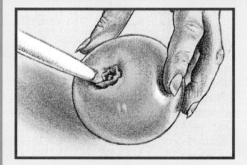

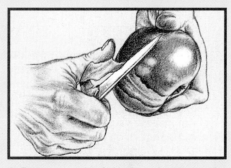

1. Slice off the stem end of the tomato.

2. Remove a strip of skin from the stem to the blossom end.

3. Slice the tomato along the skinned strip so that the knife does not have to cut through skin before it can enter the tomato.

Thanks to our readers for Quick Tips: The editors of *Cook's Illustrated* would like to thank all of the readers who have sent us their quick tips. We have enjoyed reading every one of them, and have learned a lot. Keep them coming. We will provide a one-year complimentary subscription for each quick tip that we print. Send a description of your special technique to *Cook's Illustrated,* P.O. Box 569, Brookline Village, MA 02147-0569. Please write "Attention: Quick Tips" on the envelope and include your name, address, and daytime phone number. Unfortunately, we can only acknowledge receipt of tips that will be printed in the magazine. In case the same tip is received from two readers, the one postmarked first will be selected. Also, be sure to let us know what particular cooking problems you would like us to investigate in upcoming issues.

The Ultimate Chocolate Mousse

The proper ratio among ingredients gives a smooth, creamy texture and a deep but balanced chocolate flavor.

∾ BY MARIE PIRAINO ∾

Chocolate mousse is one of America's best-known desserts, a standby of cooks who want to create something with the allure of French baking but without the difficulty of, say, a Gâteau St. Honoré. However, exactly what defines a chocolate mousse turned out to be something of a mystery.

When I went to my cookbooks, I found that all the recipes for this dessert started with chocolate and eggs, but that's where the similarity ended. Most of the recipes added some other elements, most frequently (but not always) butter, sugar, and cream. In addition, all sorts of different flavorings could be present, apparently at the whim of the individual cook.

So I started by setting some standards of my own. I wanted a creamy mousse and a deep chocolate flavor, but I didn't want either of these aspects to dominate. Chocolate flavor is essential, yes, but when I crave a solid-chocolate experience, I'd rather have real fudge, a truffle, or a flourless chocolate cake instead of one of the sticky, heavy chocolate mousses I found in some cookbooks. This position, therefore, helped me eliminate one whole folder's worth of obviously leaden recipes. At the other extreme, diet chocolate mousse is a contradiction in terms. When I want more air than flavoring, there are meringues and sponge cakes.

As a starting point, I turned to the most basic definition of chocolate mousse that I could find. Surprisingly, it was in a book by the late British cookbook author, Elizabeth David. In her *French Provincial Cooking* (Harper & Row, 1962), she refers to the "old and reliable formula for chocolate mousse—four yolks beaten into four ounces of bitter chocolate, and the four whipped whites folded in." I decided to stick with the four eggs,

then test mousses using varying amounts and proportions of the other possible ingredients, including not only the chocolate that David's bare-bones recipe specified, but also the butter, cream, sugar, and flavorings that other cookbooks recommended.

Getting the Proportions Right

Because chocolate mousse derives almost all of its flavor from the starring ingredient, I first wanted to see how much chocolate in proportion to eggs would give me a flavor I liked. Although I knew I would probably have to fine-tune this proportion and add more chocolate later on, a tentative amount would give me a consistent basis for testing various texture-affecting ingredients such as cream, butter, gelatin, whipped cream, and liquid flavorings. And because chocolate contains sugar, as well as saturated fat in the form of cocoa butter, the amount of chocolate affects the texture of the final mousse as well.

I started with Elizabeth David's four ounces of chocolate to four eggs. While I liked it, I found that it didn't have enough chocolate flavor for my taste. Six ounces of chocolate provided a much

After trying dozens of recipes for this classic dessert, we settled on one that includes both butter and whipped cream, but not too much chocolate.

richer chocolate flavor. So in the spirit of experimentation, I upped the chocolate again, adding eight ounces to my next mousse. At that level, however, the chocolate was too much the predominant flavor, giving the mousse an underlying edge of bitterness that seemed inappropriate. I settled on six ounces.

Because most of the French recipes I had found in my cookbook research used butter to some degree, I next tried adding unsalted butter to the mixture. I discovered that it did make the mousse denser and gave it a rich mouth feel. With one ounce of butter, the four-egg mousse was airy and light, but two ounces of butter gave it more creaminess and density without obliterating the lightness. When I moved up to four and six ounces of butter, the mousses took on a solid, trufflelike consistency and were so rich they could only be eaten in very small amounts, so I stuck with the two ounces.

Balancing Flavor with Whipped Cream

Cooks have often used whipped cream as a garnish for chocolate mousse. Many newer recipes add heavy cream to the mousse itself, so I tried

---

PHOTOGRAPH BY DAVE HENDERSON

some variations with whipped cream (and no butter) to determine the effect. Whipped cream, like the butter, made the mousse a little denser in texture and it also softened the flavor, taking some of the deep chocolate hit out of the finished dish. Although chocolate maniacs may stop reading right here, I wanted a more balanced flavor, and thus found this effect useful and desirable. One cup of heavy cream, whipped and folded in, smoothed out the flavor without much diluting the chocolate impression.

As a check on my own personal leanings, I held a number of informal tastings at this point in my mousse odyssey. (In the process, I also confirmed the enduring popularity of this classic dessert—it's no problem to find willing tasting participants when the subject in question is a chocolate mousse.) In these tastings, almost everyone picked the mousse that I had made with one-half cup of whipped cream, so I went with the prevailing opinion.

Having tested butter and cream separately, I decided to try the ultimate creamy mousse, one with both butter and cream. To do this, I made eighteen different mousses for another informal tasting. The version with two ounces of butter and a half cup of whipped cream was the clear winner.

Because chocolates vary so much in sugar content, and because sugar is also a structural element in mousse, the recipes I encountered varied widely in the type and quantity of sugar specified. While your choice of chocolate will determine exactly how much sugar you need, I got a nicely balanced flavor using two tablespoons of sugar with most bittersweet and semisweet chocolates (three tablespoons actually made the chocolate flavor weaker, and didn't seem any sweeter). Professional dessert chefs stock superfine sugar to ensure that it dissolves completely, but I had no difficulties in several tests with ordinary granulated sugar or with confectioners' sugar.

I next tested adding various flavoring liquids, including strong coffee and a variety of liquors and liqueurs. Not surprisingly, all such additions made the final product less firm. More than two tablespoons of such liquid (in addition to the teaspoon of vanilla extract) started to make the mousse slightly soupy, and more than two tablespoons of any alcohol-based liquid overwhelmed the flavor as well. If you prefer a stronger alcohol kick, I recommend you try whipping some additional liquer into a whipped cream topping.

Final Fiddling
After almost three dozen tests, I was beginning to feel more confident, but one test did make me worry that I would have to return to square one. About half the recipes I researched called for whisking the egg yolks one by one into the chocolate mixture, and this was the technique I had been using to standardize my other ingredients. I had set aside another, more time-consuming approach to the egg yolks, in which they are beaten with some sugar until lightened in texture and color, then added to the chocolate. When I got around to trying a recipe that followed this procedure with the yolks, the volume of the mousse increased by

as much as one-fourth, and the texture was much lighter and more airy.

However, in a side-by-side test, I found that I preferred the flavor of mousse made with unbeaten yolks. As with recipes emphasizing egg whites and those made with extra whipped cream, more air in the mousse meant less flavor per mouthful. So this time, the easier technique was also the winner.

Once I had the master recipe proportions, I went back and fiddled with the amounts of chocolate and sugar. Beyond a certain point, of course, it becomes a matter of personal taste. Having chosen six ounces of chocolate over four ounces and even played with eight ounces, the question remained: What about seven ounces? The difference was subtle, and some chocoholics will prefer the seven-ounce variation, but in a blind tasting with four *Cook's Illustrated* editors, all four preferred the six-ounce recipe. The extra chocolate added a sticky, gelatinous texture that just didn't prove to be the ideal chocolate mousse; it also overpowered the other flavors, making the mousse taste duller and flatter.

By the end of all this experimentation, I had found my ultimate recipe and found myself sitting comfortably in my kitchen, eating a large bowl of chocolate mousse.

CHOCOLATE MOUSSE
Serves 6 to 8
For an extra creamy chocolate mousse, fold in one cup of heavy cream that's been whipped instead of the one-half cup called for here. Make this mousse at least two hours before you wish to serve it to let the flavors develop, but serve it within twenty-four hours because flavor and texture will begin to deteriorate.

6 ounces bittersweet or semisweet chocolate, chopped coarse

4 tablespoons unsalted butter
  Pinch salt
1 teaspoon vanilla extract
2 tablespoons strong coffee or 4 teaspoons brandy, orange-flavored liqueur, or light rum
4 large eggs, separated
2 tablespoons sugar
½ cup heavy cream, plus extra for garnish

1. Melt chocolate any of the following three ways: in medium bowl set over large saucepan of barely simmering water; in uncovered Pyrex measuring cup microwaved at 50 percent heat for 3 minutes, stirring once at 2 minute mark; or in ovenproof bowl set in 350-degree oven for 15 minutes. Whisk butter into melted chocolate, 1 tablespoon at a time; stir in salt, vanilla, and coffee or liquor until completely incorporated. Whisk in yolks, one at a time, making sure that each is fully incorporated before adding the next; set chocolate mixture aside.

2. Stir egg whites in clean mixing bowl set over saucepan of hot water until slightly warm, 1 to 2 minutes; remove bowl from saucepan. Beat with electric mixer set at medium speed until soft peaks form. Raise mixer speed to high and slowly add sugar; beat to soft peaks. Whisk a quarter of the beaten whites into chocolate mixture to lighten it, then gently fold in remaining whites.

3. Whip cream to soft peaks; gently fold into mousse. Spoon portion of mousse into six to eight individual serving dishes or goblets. Cover and refrigerate to blend flavors, at least 2 hours. (Can be covered and refrigerated up to 24 hours.) Serve with additional whipped cream. ■

Marie Piraino is a Boston-based food stylist and recipe developer.

Great Grilled Vegetables

To avoid precooking, slice them right and use the correct cooking temperature.

∼ BY JACK BISHOP ∼

Grilling vegetables should be easy. You've made a fire to grill a couple of steaks, some swordfish, or maybe a few pieces of chicken. There are some vegetables in the fridge, and you want to turn them into a side dish without having to heat up your kitchen. Sounds simple, but a number of issues immediately arise. Do you have to precook the vegetables? How thick should each vegetable be sliced? What's the best temperature for grilling them? Are hickory chips or marinades worth the effort?

For this story, I decided at the outset that I wanted to develop guidelines for grilling as many vegetables as possible without precooking them. Blanching, baking, or microwaving is not hard, but it does add an extra step and time to what should be a simple process. In addition, blanching and baking heat up the kitchen.

What Kind of Grill? What Kind of Heat?

My first experiments revolved around the type of grill and the intensity of the fire. While steaks taste best when grilled over a superhot charcoal fire (*see* "How to Grill a Steak," May/June 1996), I was pretty sure that the grill setup wouldn't make all that much difference when it came to vegetables. After some tests, I learned I was right, with a few caveats.

Vegetables don't respond well to blazing fires—incineration is a real possibility. I found that most vegetables are best cooked over a medium-hot fire. In some cases, even lower heat is needed to cook through vegetables with a low moisture content, like potatoes.

What does a "medium-hot" fire mean? To gauge the temperature, hold your hand about five inches above the fire. If you can keep your hand there for four seconds, the fire is medium-hot. For medium-low, you should be able to keep your hand above the fire six seconds.

Because even a fairly wimpy gas grill has enough BTUs to reach this heat level, the type of grill used to cook vegetables is not very important. I did find that leaving the cover off can make a difference. Unless the grill cover is scrupulously clean (and it never is), delicate vegetables can pick up some resinous flavors if cooked in a covered grill. It is also imperative that the grate be scraped clean. Tiny bits of charred-on food can cause flare-ups and give mild-tasting vegetables an off flavor.

Flavor and Equipment

I played around with wood chips (both hickory and mesquite) and found no perceptible change in flavor. Vegetables do not cook long enough to pick up any wood flavor. A better way to add flavor is to brush vegetables with a flavored oil just before grilling. (Marinating is not advised because the acids will make vegetables soggy.) Make sure the oil is a good-quality olive oil. (I tried other oils and found vegetables brushed with canola, corn, or other bland oils to be similarly boring.) Try adding fresh herbs, garlic, and/or grated citrus zest to the oil, or purchase one that is already flavored. Seasoning with salt and pepper both before and after grilling is another way to maximize flavor.

A lot of equipment exists out there for grilling, much of it designed for vegetables. I tried grilling vegetables in a hinged metal basket and felt that this tool was not very practical. One part of the grill is always hotter or colder than another and invariably some vegetables are ready to be turned before others. Large vegetables (everything from asparagus spears to sliced zucchini) are best cooked right on the grill grate.

You can skewer smaller items (like cherry tomatoes and white mushrooms) to prevent them from falling onto the coals, but my favorite tool for handling small items is a vegetable grid. I used a tightly woven grid with handles that can be set down right onto the grate. A piece of fine mesh, like that used in a window screen, also works well.

And the small items are easy enough to turn with a pair of metal tongs (I've always found flipping skewers to be a tricky business). A grid is also good for grilling onion rings that otherwise might fall through grate openings.

The chart on page 9 lists my favorite vegetables for grilling without precooking, along with preparation information (slicing, trimming, and so forth), cooking methods (use of a grid, temperature, and how often to turn), and grilling times.

Grilled vegetables are good not only hot, but also at room temperature. So if there isn't room on the grill for both the vegetables and main course, do the vegetables first.

GRILLED ITALIAN VEGETABLES WITH THYME AND GARLIC
Serves 6

These vegetables are fine warm or at room temperature, so grill them before the main course. Drizzle the grilled vegetables with balsamic vinegar if you like.

½ cup olive oil
3 medium garlic cloves, minced
1 tablespoon minced fresh thyme leaves, plus several sprigs for garnish
Salt and ground black pepper
2 large red onions, prepared according to chart instructions
3 medium zucchini, prepared according to chart instructions
3 small eggplant, prepared according to chart instructions
1 large red bell pepper, prepared according to chart instructions

1. Light grill fire. Combine oil, garlic, thyme, and salt and pepper to taste in small bowl. Place vegetables on platter; brush both sides with flavored oil.

2. Place vegetable grid over medium-hot fire and heat several minutes. Place sliced onions on

grid. Arrange as many vegetables as possible on open parts of grill. (Grill remaining vegetables in batches as openings are available.)

3. Grill uncovered, turning onions frequently but other vegetables just once, until everything is marked with dark stripes, 5 to 6 minutes for onions and 8 to10 minutes for zucchini, eggplant, and pepper.

4. As each vegetable looks done, transfer to large platter. Garnish platter with thyme sprigs and adjust seasonings. Serve hot, warm, or at room temperature. (Vegetables can be covered and kept at room temperature for several hours.)

GRILLED PORTOBELLO MUSHROOMS, RED PEPPER, AND GARLIC CROUTONS
Serves 4

This grilled bread salad can be served as a side dish or even better as a first course for an outdoor grilled meal. Because the grilled croutons will become soggy fairly quickly, do not add them until the last minute if you want to prepare this dish in advance.

5 tablespoons olive oil
2 medium garlic cloves, minced
1 teaspoon grated zest and 1 tablespoon juice from medium lemon
Salt and ground black pepper
2 large portobello mushrooms, prepared according to chart instructions
1 large red bell pepper, prepared according to chart instructions
4 1-inch-thick slices Italian bread
3 tablespoons minced fresh parsley leaves

1. Light grill fire. Combine 4 tablespoons of the oil, garlic, lemon zest, and salt and pepper to taste in small bowl. Place mushrooms, red pepper, and bread slices on large platter; brush both sides of vegetables and bread with flavored oil.

2. Place vegetables and bread over medium-hot fire, making sure that gill-like undersides of mushrooms are facing up. Grill uncovered, turning pepper and bread once but leaving mushrooms in place, until vegetables and bread are streaked with dark grill marks, about 2 minutes for bread and 8 to 10 minutes for mushrooms and pepper.

3. Transfer grilled vegetables and bread to cutting board. Halve mushrooms, then cut into ½-inch-wide strips. Cut pepper into ¼-inch-wide strips, and bread into 1-inch croutons.

4. Toss vegetables in large serving bowl with remaining 1 tablespoon oil, lemon juice, and parsley. Adjust seasonings. (Vegetables can be covered and kept at room temperature for 1 hour.) Stir in croutons and serve immediately. ∎

GRILLING VEGETABLES AT A GLANCE

Use this chart as a guide to grilling the following vegetables. Lightly toss the vegetables or brush them on both sides with olive oil, preferably extra-virgin, before grilling. Unless otherwise specified, vegetables should be cooked over a medium-hot fire.

VEGETABLE	PREPARATION	COOKING METHOD/TIME
Asparagus	Snap off tough ends.	Grill over medium-low fire, turning several times, until tender and streaked with light grill marks, 6 to 8 minutes.
Corn	Remove husk and silk.	Grill, turning often, until kernels start to char, about 8 to 10 minutes.
Eggplant	Remove ends. Cut large eggplant crosswise into ½-inch-thick rounds. Slice small eggplant lengthwise into ½-inch-thick strips; remove peel from outer slices so that they match the others.	Grill, turning once, until flesh is darkly colored, 8 to 10 minutes.
Endive	Cut in half lengthwise through stem end.	Grill, flat side down, until streaked with dark grill marks, 6 to 8 minutes.
Fennel	Remove stalks and fronds. Slice vertically through base into ½-inch-thick pieces.	Grill, turning once, until streaked with dark grill marks and quite soft, 10 to 15 minutes.
Mushrooms, white and cremini	Clean with a damp towel and trim thin slice from stems.	Grill on a vegetable grid, turning several times, until golden brown, 6 to 7 minutes.
Mushrooms, portobello	Clean with a damp towel and remove stems.	Grill, with gill-like underside facing up, until cap is streaked with grill marks, 8 to 10 minutes.
Onions	Peel and cut into ½-inch-thick slices.	Grill, turning occasionally, until lightly charred, about 5 to 6 minutes.
Peppers	Core, seed, and cut into large wedges.	Grill, turning once, until streaked with dark grill marks, 9 to 10 minutes.
Potatoes, new	Choose very small potatoes (no larger than a whole walnut) and cut them in half.	Grill on vegetable grid over medium-low fire, turning several times, until richly colored and tender throughout, 25 to 30 minutes.
Squash, butternut	Cut in half lengthwise and scoop out seeds and string pulp. Remove thin slices from either end. Cut crosswise into ¼-inch-thick half circles.	Grill, turning once, until streaked with dark grill marks, 8 to 10 minutes.
Tomatoes, cherry	Remove stems.	Grill on vegetable grid, turning several times, until streaked with dark grill marks, about 3 minutes.
Tomatoes, plum	Cut in half lengthwise and seed.	Grill, turning once, until streaked with dark grill marks, about 8 minutes.
Zucchini (& summer squash)	Remove ends. Slice lengthwise into ½-inch-thick strips. Remove peel from outer slices so that they match the others.	Grill, turning once, until streaked with dark grill marks, 8 to10 minutes.

The Truth About Pressure Cookers

Many great dishes can be sped up for weekday suppers—but not every one.

~ BY LISË STERN ~

When microwave ovens were first introduced, they were touted as time-savers for every kind of cooking. But they ended up not saving any time at all on most actual cooking. Now, with the new wave of interest in pressure cookers, the question arises: Will they prove any more helpful for real cooking than the microwave? Can pressure cookers produce food as good-tasting as traditional methods, and rapidly enough so that weeknight suppers can be as satisfying as weekend dinners?

The mechanism by which the pressure cooker cuts cooking times is simple. In order to steam, boil, simmer, or braise foods without pressure, you increase the heat to the boiling point of water, 212 degrees. Just fifteen pounds of added air pressure in a pressure cooker, however, raises that boiling point to between 245 and 250 degrees. And at this higher temperature, cooking times become one-third to one-half of what they would be at 212 degrees. What is not so straightforward is the potential impact of pressurized cooking upon the quality of food. This is because higher temperatures can affect flavor and texture in unpredictable ways.

For this article I tested a variety of dishes that you can cook by moist-heat methods and that usually take forty-five minutes or more: soups, stocks, stews, pot roasts, artichokes, custards, Indian pudding, brown rice, beans, potatoes, and risotto. I tested for quality and time savings against traditional methods, often as they were detailed in master recipes from *Cook's Illustrated*. While a pressure cooker enthusiast

can refine many recipes to succeed in a familiar cooker, I wanted recipes that would allow readers trying out pressure cooking for the first time to produce outstanding results right from the start, in any pressure cooker. With this in mind, I tested the recipes in a wide variety of cookers.

My successes came mostly with foods that tolerate some overcooking, such as stews and pot roasts. These dishes all turned out well. And the time savings were significant except for those recipes that involved a lot of preparation or a lengthy sauté step.

Some foods are too sensitive to high heat for first-time success. A recipe for potato salad, for example, turned into a recipe for mashed potatoes unless I used red Bliss potatoes. And custards overcook so easily that my master recipe for quick custards remains a work in progress. And there were the clear failures, such as traditional New England Indian pudding, which takes longer in a pressure cooker than in an oven.

Certain dishes passed the quickness test, but not the quality test. Thus, the time saved on brown rice was significant, but in a side-by-side test, the rice was not as good as the one-step oven-baked brown rice I usually make.

The recipe that really sold me on pressure cookers, though, was risotto. Like a lot of people, I had made risotto once to prove to myself that I could. I followed the classic instructions to stir constantly for a half hour or more while adding small amounts of stock. While I loved the dish, I knew it would never fit into a home life in which children demand attention and the telephone rings.

Then a pressure cooker recipe in Lorna Sass's *Recipes from an Ecological Kitchen* (Morrow, 1992) prompted me to try risotto again. The result was amazing: creamy, flavorful, perfectly cooked risotto, ready from scratch in less than fifteen minutes, with no stirring. Because risotto can easily overcook to mush, though, I now keep pressure-cooking time down to four to five minutes and finish the dish conventionally, with the lid off, and a little stirring at the end.

I also wanted to see what the pressure cooker would do with tougher legumes such as chickpeas—especially given that canned chickpeas have such a tinny taste. (Many other canned beans are too soft for salads and soups, and are oversalted as well.) I was further motivated to use the cooker to reduce cooking time, since chickpeas can take an hour or two to soften in boiling water. After overcooking a few batches (and enjoying the resulting hummus), I found that chickpeas take five to seven minutes under pressure, yielding the "fresh bean" flavor I want for stews and salads, as well as for hummus.

For artichokes I started with the forty-to-fifty-minute master recipe from "Steam, Don't Boil, Artichokes" in the May/June 1994 issue. I tried pressure-steaming the artichokes in one inch of water, as recommended for traditional steaming, but they ended up waterlogged. Using a thin layer of water under a rack turned out better. When I steamed them stem side down, the bottom also got a little soggy. The best method for the pressure cooker proved to be steaming stem side up for only fifteen minutes.

To test pot roasts for this article, I began with the master recipe from "Pot Roast Perfected" in the January/February 1994 issue, then made adaptations for the pressure cooker. In all kinds of pressure cookers, at high and low pressure, and with quick or natural steam releases, the pot roasts were juicy and tender.

In summary, risotto will sell you on the pressure cooker, and soups, pot roasts, and beans will keep it on the stove. From there you may find yourself perfecting custards, root vegetables, and every two-hour stew you know.

"REAL" COOKING WITH A PRESSURE COOKER

Some cooks do not want to just seal the lid and forget about it. Some of us want the time savings of pressure cooking but also the satisfaction of finishing the dish to our own standards of texture and seasoning.

For those cooks, Lorna Sass, the author of *Cooking Under Pressure* (Morrow, 1989) recommends a technique of pressure cooking to about 80 percent doneness. As she says, "A complexity of flavor is achieved quickly in the pressure cooker, but it also mutes flavor. The muting and the mingling are a companion thing. If you want a burst of flavor, add it at the end—a burst of fresh herbs, toasted mustard seeds, whatever." The final few minutes represents the ideal time to thicken stews, given the fact

that thick sauces burn in a 250-degree pressure cooker more quickly than we expect from our experience with 212-degree stovetop cooking. The last minutes are also good for adding quick-cooking ingredients like tender vegetables or seafood.

If you undershoot the goal, you can always lock the lid back on and repressurize quickly, because the food is already at a simmer. The cooking time under pressure is the same no matter how many episodes are used; just add about four minutes for each natural release. Stovetop quick releases add almost no cooking time. Cold water quick releases are a little slower, which adds cooking time, but are also a little less traumatic to the food.

PRESSURE COOKER RISOTTO

Serves 6

Proper timing is essential with pressure cooker risotto. If you cook it too long, you end up with a sticky, glutinous pot of mush. Better to undercook the rice and simmer it on the stovetop for a few minutes. During this final cooking, you can stir in wild mushrooms, fresh spinach, or slices of thin asparagus, almost any cheese, diced tomato or ham, chopped olives, scallops or small shrimp, or fresh herbs.

  2   tablespoons butter
  1   tablespoon olive oil
  1   small onion, chopped fine
  1 ½ cups arborio rice
  ½   cup dry white wine
  3 ½–4 cups chicken broth, homemade
      or low-sodium canned
  ¼   cup grated Parmesan cheese,
      plus extra for sprinkling on top
      Salt and ground black pepper

1. Heat butter and oil over medium-high heat in 6-quart pressure cooker. Add onion; sauté until softened, about 2 minutes. Stir in rice to coat with oil. Add wine; simmer until almost absorbed. Increase heat to high; add 3 ¼ cups broth. Cover cooker, securing lid, and bring to high pressure. Reduce heat to maintain high pressure; cook 4 minutes. Quick-release pressure.

2. When pressure has dropped, carefully remove lid away from you. Return slightly soupy risotto to medium heat. Continue to stir, adding additional broth if necessary, until rice is swelled, yet firm at its center, and liquid has thickened, 2 to 3 minutes longer. Stir in cheese and salt and pepper to taste. Serve immediately.

PRESSURE-STEAMED ARTICHOKES
Serves 4
Artichokes are particularly flavorful when steamed under pressure, and they're fully cooked in just fifteen minutes. Chicken stock or wine can be substituted for the water. Serve the artichokes warm with lemon butter or cold with a vinaigrette.

  4   medium or 3 medium-large artichokes,
      stems and tops trimmed (individual
      leaves trimmed with scissors,
      if desired)

1. Bring 1 ½ cups water to boil over high heat in 6-quart pressure cooker fitted with steamer rack. Carefully place artichokes, stem side up, in cooker. Cover, securing lid; bring to high pressure. Reduce heat to maintain high pressure and cook 15 minutes. Quick-release pressure.

2. When pressure has dropped, carefully remove lid away from you. Test artichokes for doneness; leaves should remove easily and a toothpick inserted into base should go in easily.

PRESSURE-COOKED POT ROAST
Serves 6 to 8
The pressure cooker is extremely forgiving for tougher cuts of meat such as pot roast. It yields a good, juicy roast. Although slices will look grey and overcooked, they aren't. I prefer a juicy gravy like the one in this recipe, but you may also thicken it. Once you've removed the vegetables from the cooker, skim one tablespoon of fat off

the surface of the juices and mix it with two tablespoons of flour. Whisk this mixture back into the juices, one teaspoon at a time, until it can coat the back of a spoon. Simmer the gravy for two minutes.

  1   medium bay leaf
  ½   teaspoon dried thyme
  2   whole cloves
  ¾   teaspoon black peppercorns
  ¾   teaspoon salt
  2   large garlic cloves, cut into a total of
      16 thin slices
  1   boneless chuck roast (about 3 pounds),
      tied
  2   tablespoons flavorless oil such as
      canola
  1   medium onion, chopped fine
  1   small carrot, cut into small dice
  1   small celery stalk, cut into small dice
  1   cup chicken or vegetable stock
  1   cup red wine
  3   medium potatoes, peeled and cut into
      eighths
  4   medium carrots, peeled and cut into 2-
      inch chunks

1. Grind bay leaf, thyme, cloves, and peppercorns to fine powder in spice grinder or small food processor. Add salt; pulse to mix. Transfer to small bowl, add garlic slivers, then toss to coat with spice mixture. Poke sixteen, ½-inch-deep slits in meat with paring knife; stuff each with garlic sliver. Rub remaining spice mixture over meat.

2. Heat oil in 6-quart pressure cooker over medium-high heat. Put roast in pot and brown thoroughly on all sides, maintaining heat so fat sizzles briskly but does not smoke, about 15 minutes. Transfer roast to plate. Add onion, small carrot, and celery to heated fat; sauté to soften slightly, 2 to 3 minutes. Stir in stock and wine; increase heat to high. Lower trivet into pot; set browned roast on trivet. Cover cooker, securing lid; bring to high

pressure. Reduce heat to maintain high pressure and cook 1 hour. Quick-release pressure.

3. When pressure has dropped, carefully remove lid away from you. Test meat; it should be fork-tender. Remove meat and wrap in tin foil; set aside.

4. Remove trivet from cooker and reserve vegetables that were cooked with meat. Add potatoes and medium carrots. Once again cover cooker, securing lid; bring to high pressure. Reduce heat to maintain high pressure and cook 4 minutes. Quick-release pressure. When pressure has dropped, carefully remove lid away from you. Transfer vegetables to large platter; cover with foil.

5. With handheld immersion blender, puree juices left in cooker, or puree them in food processor or blender.

6. Cut pot roast into thin slices. Arrange on platter and surround with vegetables. Ladle a few spoonfuls of gravy over meat. Pass remaining gravy in separate gravy boat.

PRESSURE-COOKED NORTH AFRICAN LAMB STEW
Serves 4
Any stew—beef, pork, or lamb—can be adapted to the pressure cooker. This lamb tagine simply exemplifies the basic technique. Lamb shoulder is better for stewing but is often expensive and hard to find. You can substitute meat from the leg, but the stewed meat will be drier.

  1   tablespoon flavorless oil
  2   pounds boneless lamb shoulder or leg
      of lamb, cut into 1-inch cubes
  1   large onion, chopped coarse
  2   large garlic cloves, minced
  1   cup dried apricots, halved
  ⅓   cup raisins
  ½   cup blanched whole almonds
  1   tablespoon minced fresh gingerroot
  ½   teaspoon ground cinnamon
      Salt and ground black pepper
  ¾   cup water
  ¼   cup juice from 1 large orange
  ⅓   cup packed mint leaves,
      plus extra for garnish

1. Heat oil in 6-quart pressure cooker over medium-high heat. Add lamb cubes in batches to avoid overcrowding; brown on all sides, about 5 minutes per batch. Transfer browned lamb to plate with slotted spoon. Add onion and garlic to heated fat; sauté to soften slightly, 2 to 3 minutes. Return lamb to pot and stir in remaining ingredients, including ¾ cup water and salt and pepper to taste. Cover cooker, securing lid; bring to high pressure. Reduce heat to maintain high pressure and cook 15 minutes. Let pressure release naturally, 10 to 15 minutes.

2. When pressure has dropped, carefully remove lid away from you. Test meat; it should be fork-tender. If not, replace lid and cook under high pressure 5 minutes longer, then quick-release pressure. ∎

Lisë Stern is a freelance writer and publisher of *The Cookbook Review.*

Make Perfect French Fries at Home

Bathe the raw potatoes in ice water, spike the oil with bacon grease if you like, always fry twice—and use a brown grocery bag for draining.

~ BY FRED THOMAS ~

I have loved french fries since I was a toddler. I have tasted truly great french fries in the usual places—steakhouses, drive-in restaurants, and fish joints—but never at a home dining room table. So years ago, I tried replicating the great fries. To my dismay, I found that drive-in fare was far superior to my own efforts.

But I didn't give up. My goal was to find a recipe and method for the home cook that would rival restaurant fries. For me, the ideal french fry is long and crisp, with right-angle sides, a nice crunch on the outside, and an earthy potato taste. Its bass flavor note should be rustic, like a mushroom, and its high note should hint of the oil in which it was created. It should definitely not droop, and its coloring should be two-tone, blond with hints of brown.

After testing every component of french fries, I finally found a

Idaho potatoes yield long, elegant fries, the classic shape. All-purpose baking potatoes are equal from a taste standpoint, but their rounder shape produces shorter fries.

method that yields fries better than any restaurant's. You will not find this recipe in cookbooks; it is a hybrid. Unlike many other such recipes, you won't need restaurant cooking gear. The most exotic equipment you'll need for this recipe is a clip-on-the-pot candy thermometer and a large Dutch oven or other five-quart (or larger) heavy pot.

Obviously, a good french fry requires the right potato. The immediate question was whether this meant a waxy or a starchy variety. I tested two of

the most popular waxy potatoes, the Yukon Gold and the red La Soda potato (similar to a red Bliss). Neither was even close to ideal, both being too watery. During the frying, water evaporated inside the potato, leaving hollows that would fill with oil, so the finished fries were greasy.

Next I tested the starchy potato most readily available nationwide, the russet Burbank baking potato, often called the "Idaho." This potato turned out to be ideal, frying up with all the qualities that I require in a fry.

Because these are starchy potatoes, it is important to rinse the starch off the surface after you cut the potato into fries. To do this, simply put the cut fries into a bowl, place the bowl in the sink and run water into it, swirling with your fingers until the water runs clear. This might seem like an unimportant step, but it makes a real difference. When I skipped the starch rinse, the fries weren't quite right, and the oil clouded.

At this point, you take the second crucial step: Fill the bowl with clear water, add ice, and refrigerate the potatoes for at least thirty minutes. That way, when the potatoes first enter the hot oil, they are nearly frozen, which allows a slow, thorough cooking of the inner potato pulp. When I tried making fries without this chilling, the outsides started to brown well before the insides were fully cooked.

If you like, you can leave the cut potatoes in the refrigerated ice water for up to three days.

I also found that I preferred peeling the potatoes. A skins-on fry keeps the potato from forming those little, airy blisters that, to me, signal a really great fry. Peeling the potato also allows home cooks to see—and remove, if they want to—any imperfections and greenish coloring.

Finding the Right Oil

Next question: What is the right oil for making perfect french fries?

To find out, I experimented with five common oils: lard, vegetable shortening, canola oil, corn oil, and peanut oil. For my taste, and that of various friends conscripted into taste tests, lard—with all its saturated fat—made the best-tasting fry. But how could I propose cooking with a known

health enemy? To keep in step with the times, I put the other oils through the paces to determine if there was an adequate substitute for the lard.

Vegetable-shortening fries rivaled the lard fries, providing an exquisite flavor balance between oil and potato. But common wisdom is that vegetable shortening is not that much healthier than lard. So I moved on to canola oil, the much-ballyhooed oil of the '90s, now used in a blend with safflower oil by McDonald's, which produces four million pounds of finished fries a day. But I was unhappy with the results: bland, almost watery fries, with no mouth feel.

My next try, corn oil, was the most forgiving oil in the test kitchen. It rebounded well to temperature fluctuations and held up very well, and the fries tasted marvelous. I felt I was getting pretty close to finding an oil that really worked.

A potato fried in peanut oil is light, and the flavor is rich but not dense. The earthy flavor of the potato is there, as with corn oil, but is not overbearing. I was very close, and yet there was still something missing. The high flavor note, which is supplied by the animal fat in lard, was lacking.

I started by adding a few tablespoons of sausage drippings to the various oils, an experiment not worth replicating. The greasy taste of sausage came through with remarkable clarity and left the oil dirty, ugly, and useless. I then tried a dollop of strained bacon grease, about two generous tablespoons per quart of oil. The meaty flavor came through, but without its nasty baggage.

So bacon grease seemed the fat of choice. To be certain of this, I added bacon grease to each of the oils, with these results: vegetable shortening, no discernible difference; canola oil, extra body, but still short on flavor; corn oil, more body, more flavor, nearly perfect; peanut oil, flavor, bite, body, bass notes, high notes galore. At last, an uncompromised equal to lard.

A Study in Temperatures—Less Is More

So now it was time to get down to the frying, which actually means double-frying. First, one par-fries the potatoes at a relatively low temperature to release the inner beauty of the potato: pulpy, mealy, potato-y. Then the potatoes are quick-fried at a higher temperature and served.

The garden variety cookbook recipe calls for par-frying at 350 degrees and doing the final frying at 375 to 400 degrees. But I found these temperatures to be far too aggressive. I prefer an initial frying at 325 degrees, with the final frying at 350 degrees. To arrive at this conclusion, I tried a

1. Peel the potatoes and slice them lengthwise into planks about ¼-inch thick. Stack the planks on top of each other and slice them at ¼-inch intervals.

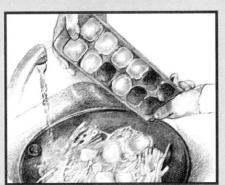

2. Rinse the cut potatoes well, then place them in a bowl of ice and water and refrigerate for at least 30 minutes.

3. Drain and dry the potatoes, then fry, stirring with a Chinese skimmer or large-hole slotted spoon, until potatoes are limp and blond.

4. After the first frying, remove the potatoes from the hot oil, then place on a brown paper bag to drain. Repeat the process for the second frying.

variety of temperature combinations in first and second fryings. Lower temperatures allowed for perfect monitoring, but with higher temperatures the fries could get away from the cook. Most of all, I was really pleased with the final results at the lower temperatures.

For the sake of convenience, I also attempted a single, longer frying. But like many cooks before me, I found that with standard french fries (as opposed to the much thinner shoestring fries), I could not both sear the outside and properly cook the inside with a single visit to the hot fat. When I left them in long enough to sear the outside, I wound up with wooden, overcooked fries.

Be sure to pat the fries dry very well with a tea towel before dropping them into the preheated oil, or the oil will spatter. And drop in a handful all at once; this quick handful breaks the surface tension of the oil, reducing the possibility of boiling over. As the fries cook, stir them occasionally to separate them, because they tend to cluster in hot spots in the oil.

The Paper Bag

When the fries are cooked, they need to drain and rest for at least ten minutes—or as long as two hours, another advantage to the twice-frying method, because the initial frying can be done well ahead of serving time.

But here is yet another decision to be made: What is the best draining medium?.

I've tried paper towels but have found that rather than wick the oil, they merely return it to the cooked potatoes. I also drained fries on newspaper, the delivery conveyance of fish-and-chips. Because newspaper is fibrous, it did wick the oil. However, the fries were left gray from the newsprint. I thus haven't found anything better than, or even close to, brown paper bags. Restaurants toss the fries on a drain table under an infrared lamp, but because the home cook doesn't have such a luxury, I tried substituting a stainless steel rack over paper towels. The oil stayed on the rack and congealed on the french fries. So my advice is to use a grocery bag.

Like gnocchi, when fries are done, they are done and must be removed rapidly from the oil. I have lost countless servings of fries to overcooking. I use a Chinese skimmer—a brass wire sieve with holes big enough to poke your finger through, commonly used in wok cooking—to gather the fries in a hurry, leaving the oil in the pot. A slotted spoon will also work but tends to transfer too much of the cooking oil.

Toss the fries with a little salt and pepper as they are glistening with oil. During the second frying, many of the fries will have become puffy, the hallmark of one of the great culinary ideals, *pommes soufflées.* But don't bother your guests with such trivia. Rather, spend your time plating the fries and rushing them to the table. You can guarantee that they'll be eaten up just as fast as you can get them there.

CLASSIC FRENCH FRIES
Serves 4

For those who like it, flavoring the oil with a few tablespoons of bacon grease adds a subtle, meaty flavor to the fries. Their texture, however, is not affected if the bacon grease is omitted. Once you've peeled the potatoes, you can use a mandolin or V-slicer, rather than cut them by hand. To prepare steak fries, cut the potatoes one-third-inch to one-half-inch thick, and increase the cooking time to ten to twelve minutes during the initial frying and just a few seconds longer in the final fry.

> 4 large russet Burbank (Idaho) potatoes, peeled and cut into ¼-inch-by-¼-inch-thick lengths (*see* illustration 1, left). Reserve nonuniform pieces for another use.)
> 2 quarts peanut oil
> 4 tablespoons strained bacon grease (optional)
> Salt and pepper

1. Rinse cut fries in large bowl under cold running water until water turns from milky colored to clear. Cover with at least 1 inch of water, then cover with ice (illustration 2). Refrigerate at least 30 minutes. (Can be refrigerated up to 3 days ahead.)

2. In 5-quart pot or Dutch oven fitted with clip-on-the-pot candy thermometer, or in larger electric fryer, heat oil over medium-low heat to 325 degrees. As oil heats, add bacon grease. Oil will bubble up when you add fries, so be sure you have at least 3 inches of room at top of cooking pot.

3. Pour off ice and water, quickly wrap potatoes in a clean tea towel, and thoroughly pat dry. Increase heat to medium-high and add fries, a handful at a time, to hot oil. Fry, stirring with Chinese skimmer or large-hole slotted spoon, until potatoes are limp and soft and start to turn from white to blond, 6 to 8 minutes (illustration 3). (Oil temperature will drop 50 to 60 degrees during this frying.) Use skimmer or slotted spoon to transfer fries to brown paper bag to drain (illustration 4); let rest at least 10 minutes (can stand at room temperature up to 2 hours or be wrapped in paper towels, sealed in zipper-lock bag, and frozen up to 1 month).

4. When ready to serve fries, reheat oil to 350 degrees. Using paper bag as a funnel, pour potatoes into hot oil. Discard bag and set up second paper bag. Fry potatoes, stirring fairly constantly, until golden brown and puffed, about 1 minute. Transfer to paper bag and drain again. Season to taste with salt and pepper, or other seasoned salt. Serve immediately. ■

Florida-based freelance writer **Fred Thomas** is working on a restaurant cookbook, *The A.J.'s Catfish Cookbook.*

Salad Dressing 101

A high ratio of oil to vinegar softens the harshness of supermarket vinegars and creates a foolproof emulsion in just seconds.

∽ BY MARK ZANGER ∽

Food writers do get invited to dinner parties, but sometimes we have to perform. Over the last few years I have often been asked to "make the salad dressing," in the same serious tones in which, twenty years ago, I was offered the honor of carving the roast. Apparently, salad dressing is now a bigger household anxiety than slicing.

And we are right to be anxious. There is a lot of bad salad dressing on the supermarket shelves. To make it at home, we grab a cookbook off the shelf, but the instructions look tricky—do we really have to mash garlic with a fork and then beat in vinegar and a thin stream of olive oil? Or worse, we are told just to mix oil, vinegar, salt, and pepper "to taste." Whose taste? How can we tell?

For my testing of salad dressings, I wanted to emphasize the flavor of olive oil, enhanced but not upstaged by the other ingredients. I particularly wanted to avoid nose-burning excesses of vinegar or garlic.

For my oil, I picked Colavita Extra Virgin, overall winner of the comparative tasting in the charter issue of *Cook's Illustrated* (*see* "Taste-Testing Olive Oils") and still both delicious and widely available. Vinegar was obviously a crucial variable; because vinegars vary widely in acidic strength, I began testing with Heinz Gourmet Fine Wine Vinegar, winner of our blind tasting conducted for the September/October 1993 issue (*see* "Rating Red Wine Vinegars").

Because so much of the cookbook confusion involved the word "emulsion," I wanted to find out if I actually needed one of those. Do we have to make an emulsified salad dressing—known as vinaigrette—at all? Maybe, I thought, it would be just as good to simply toss the lettuce leaves in unmixed oil, vinegar, salt, and pepper.

The resulting experiment was so striking in its results that I recommend readers repeat it. Using a packaged mixture of salad greens (for uniformity and blandness), I made two salads, each dressed with one-quarter teaspoon of salt, a couple fine grinds of pepper, a tablespoon of vinegar, and three tablespoons of olive oil. But for one salad, I made a vinaigrette by mixing the ingredients for twenty seconds with a small whip until the mixture was translucent and had no visible bubbles. For the second salad, I simply tossed the greens first in the olive oil, then in a mixture of the other three ingredients.

The difference was clear to everyone who tasted the two salads. The salad dressed with the ingredients in sequence had much more of the bite of the vinegar; the vinaigrette dressing produced a smoother impression, with an initially stronger flavor of the oil. The reason for this is that in the oil-then-vinegar salad, the oil and vinegar don't mix, so both race up the tongue—and the less viscous vinegar wins. In the emulsion, the oil medium hits the tongue first while the vinegar is held back in tiny dispersed droplets. I tried adding more oil to the tossed salad, but the vinegar remained prominent.

The correct ratio of oil to vinegar in vinaigrettes is much discussed. In my own tastings using the Heinz Gourmet Fine Wine Vinegar, preferences among my tasters varied from 2.5:1 to 4.5:1. I concluded that the oil and vinegar I was using as standards make a delicious vinaigrette for most tastes at 4:1. At that ratio, neither ingredient predominates, and you get a smooth, fine-tasting mixture that is neither harsh nor greasy.

To compensate for the varying strengths of vinegars, you can simply vary the oil ratio. Most supermarket vinegars are standardized at 5 percent acidity, but sherry, champagne, and balsamic vinegars are often 7 percent acid, with rice vinegars at 4 percent or a little less. I love lemon and lime juices with olive oil, but they, too, vary in strength. Because lime, especially, can interact with air and olive oil to create bitter flavors, I use only fresh-squeezed juices and stay at around the 4:1 ratio. Another approach is to reduce the acidity of strong vinegars with water or with wine (which approximates the flavor of homemade vinegar).

Most recently published recipes involve adding emulsifiers, most often mustard, to vinaigrettes in order to help them stay emulsified over time. This addition may be necessary for a cold buffet table at a grand hotel, but irrelevant for home cooks. My hand-whipped or fork-stirred vinaigrettes begin to break up in five to ten minutes. That is plenty of time to serve and eat a salad at home, so I add only small amounts of mustard and other flavorings for their flavors

If you do add flavorings, it turns out to make a difference whether they are first added to the oil or to the vinegar! As chef Louis Szamarthy wrote in *The Chef's Secret Cookbook* (Galahad Books, 1971), "Many people commit a great error when making vinaigrette by dissolving the salt, sugar, and spices in the vinegar and then adding the oil. It is much better to mix the spices in the oil....You will taste the difference." I thought this advice was preposterous, but when I tried it, I could taste the difference when certain additions were present, notably mustard and garlic. Apparently, flavor components can be dissolved in the vinegar and thus get hidden inside the oil of the emulsion; alternatively, fine particles suspended in the oil can be sent more quickly to the tongue.

MIXED GREEN SALAD WITH CLASSIC FRENCH DRESSING
Serves 4

Salt and pepper are mixed first with the vinegar for subtlety, while the garlic is rubbed into the bowl for aroma without bitter flavor.

- ½ medium garlic clove, peeled
- 4 teaspoons red wine vinegar
- ½ teaspoon salt
- ¼ teaspoon ground black pepper
- 5 tablespoons extra-virgin olive oil
- 2 quarts mild salad greens, such as romaine, Boston, Bibb, or other leaf lettuces

Rub bottom and sides of large salad bowl (at least 4-quart) with garlic clove. In the rubbed bowl, mix vinegar, salt, and pepper. Add oil, then whisk or mix with fork until smooth, about 30 seconds. Add greens, and toss to coat. Serve immediately.

VINAIGRETTE WITH MEDITERRANEAN FLAVORS
Makes about ½ cup

This vinaigrette draws on Mediterranean flavors—lime, thyme, capers, and garlic—that enhance the fruity, piney flavors of good olive oil. Serve it with grilled or roasted chicken.

- 1 tablespoon drained capers, minced
- 1 teaspoon minced fresh thyme leaves
- 1 tablespoon minced fresh Italian flat parsley leaves
- 1 medium garlic clove, minced fine
- ½ teaspoon salt
- ¼ teaspoon ground black pepper
- 5 tablespoons extra-virgin olive oil
- 4 teaspoons juice from one-half of a medium lime

Mix first seven ingredients with fork in small bowl. When ready to serve, whisk in juice. ∎

Simple Scallop Ceviche

For quick, clean-tasting ceviche, lightly "cook" thin-sliced scallops for thirty minutes in lemon, lime, or a combination of citrus juices.

∽ BY STEPHANIE LYNESS ∽

Ceviche (also known as seviche or cebiche) —a dish of very fresh seafood marinated or "cooked" in acid and served as a first or main course salad—is mostly a restaurant dish in this country, rarely served at home. But this is a shame, because this technique offers the home cook a great alternative to cooking during the dog days of summer, when stovetop cooking is out and mosquitoes have claimed airspace around the grill.

My early research showed ceviche to be as varied in method, timing, and ingredients as it is geographically far-ranging. So for the purposes of this short piece, I defined ceviche by the technique of actually "cooking" seafood in citrus juices. This approach eliminated recipes using precooked seafood as well as impromptu recipes that simply drizzled the fish with acid. Armed with this definition, I proceeded to perform a range of kitchen experiments, comparing different citrus juices, seafoods, and marinating times to come up with ceviche that proves quick to make, tastes fresh and clean, and produces a happy balance of tart and sweet.

After experimenting with a variety of fish, I settled on sea scallops for the master recipe. I not only liked their sweet taste and silky texture, but the fact that they're available across the country and that, for those concerned about eating raw or lightly cooked seafood, there's little chance of parasites in cleaned scallops. I was surprised to find that, with the exception of tuna, my experiments with a variety of finfish proved disappointing; unless sliced very thinly and marinated very briefly, the fish quickly took on too fishy a taste, at least to my taste buds. (That said, if you can get very fresh fish, the soy-ginger scallop ceviche is delicious made with tuna.)

To ensure speedy cooking, I cut the scallops into very thin rounds. I then marinated them in the refrigerator over a twenty-four-hour period in lime, lemon, orange, and grapefruit juices, tasting every fifteen minutes for the first two hours and then every several hours.

Thirty minutes of soaking in lemon or lime juice turned out to be ideal. The tart taste of the acid was strong enough by that time to accentuate the sweetness of the scallop; in addition, the outside of the scallop was opaque and firm while the inside was contrastingly tender and silken. Longer marinating developed an unpleasantly fishy flavor and brought out a dry, almost tannic quality in the lime and lemon juices.

The scallops marinated in orange juice and grapefruit juice tasted bland in comparison; the juices weren't acidic enough to highlight the sweet scallop taste, and they cooked the scallops much more slowly. However, I did find that these less acidic juices worked well when combined equally with lemon or lime juice. In a final test, I determined that the seafood marinated more evenly in a liberal amount of acid (one cup of lime juice to one pound of scallops) than with the scallops barely covered (one-third cup of juice per pound).

BASIC CEVICHE
Serves 4

Add one or several of the following ingredients to flavor this ceviche while marinating: one jalapeño pepper or one-half of a bell pepper, peeled, seeded, and diced fine; one tablespoon of chopped cilantro, parsley, scallion (green and white parts), or red or white onion; one peeled, seeded, and diced tomato; one clove of minced garlic; or one teaspoon of chopped fresh oregano. Serve the well-chilled ceviche on a bed of tender lettuces.

- 1 pound sea scallops, small, crescent-shaped muscles removed, scallops sliced crosswise into ⅛-inch-thick rounds
- 1 cup strained citrus juice (at least ½ cup from lime or lemon)
  Salt and ground black pepper

Place scallop rounds in glass or porcelain bowl and pour juice over them. Refrigerate 30 minutes. Season with salt and pepper to taste.

SCALLOP CEVICHE WITH SWEET PEPPER CONFETTI
Serves 4

Adapted from a recipe developed by Jonathan Waxman for Jams Restaurant in Manhattan, this ceviche can be served with avocado slices and tortilla chips.

Follow recipe for Basic Ceviche, using juice of 2 limes, 2 oranges, and 1 lemon to make up the 1 cup of citrus juice. To marinating scallops add 1/2 fine-diced small red and yellow bell pepper, 1 fine-diced jalapeño pepper, 2 tablespoons fine-diced red onion, and 1 tablespoon minced fresh cilantro or parsley leaves.

SOY-GINGER SCALLOP CEVICHE
Serves 4

Follow recipe for Basic Ceviche, cooking scallops in 1 cup fresh lime juice. Drain and toss with 2 tablespoons flavorless oil, 1 tablespoon thinly-sliced scallion (white and green parts), 1 tablespoon minced fresh cilantro, 1½ teaspoons minced fresh ginger, 1½ teaspoons soy sauce, and 1 teaspoon rice wine vinegar. Serve on a bed of cucumber rounds or strips. ∎

BUT IS IT SAFE?

Many people worry about eating ceviche because the seafood is not fully cooked. On the safety front, according to the National Institute of Medicine's report on *Seafood Safety* (February 1991), the major risk of acute food-borne illness is associated with the consumption of raw shellfish *other* than scallops. Parasites are not an issue with scallops. Bacteria, however, will certainly be present in ceviche as with any raw protein. (A thirty-minute acid bath will kill some but not all bacteria.) According to Ruth Welch at the FDA Seafood Hotline, the severity of symptoms from food-borne illness is in large part dependent on the health of the consumer. Take the same precautions with ceviche as with raw fish: Buy from a reputable source that stores the seafood on ice, eat it as quickly as possible upon arriving home, and if you do need to store it briefly, do so in your refrigerator on ice. Those at high risk—the very young or the frail and elderly, as well as pregnant women, those with liver disease, and those who are immuno-compromised—should not eat ceviche or any other raw protein.

And remember: The reported number of people made ill from eating shellfish over the ten-year period between 1978 and 1987 is still *fewer* than the number of those made ill from eating beef, turkey, chicken, or pork over the same period.

Useful Kitchen Gadgets

~

Whether you are shopping in a department store, gourmet shop, supermarket, or by catalog, kitchen gadgets abound. To the discerning and knife-handy among us, ninety percent of these gadgets are worth neither the price nor the kitchen storage space. But there are exceptions. After testing dozens of different gadgets, we found that those illustrated below *really work*. Each one of these unusual tools makes it easier and quicker to perform the task for which it is designed. These gadgets are especially helpful for preparing large quantities of ingredients—pitting piles of olives for tapenade, for example, or hulling dozens of strawberries for jams, tarts, and other desserts.

DOUBLE BOILER STAND

If you don't have a double boiler, this little circular stand fills in nicely. Simply place it in a large pot, fill the pot with water to just below the top of the stand, and place a smaller pot on top of the stand.

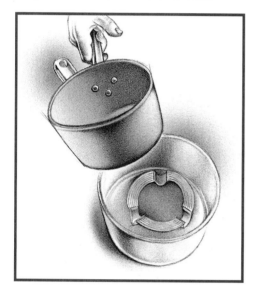

NUTMEG GRATER

You can use a regular grater to grate fresh nutmeg, but you are likely to end up with skinned knuckles. With this gadget, a knuckle-sparing carriage glides up and down the grater board, against which the spring-loaded carriage cap pushes the whole nutmeg. The unused portion of the nutmeg can be kept in the handle storage compartment.

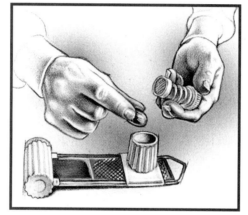

1. Place the whole nutmeg in the carriage and screw on the spring-loaded cap.

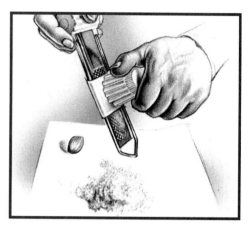

2. Glide the carriage back and forth against the grater board. When finished, place the unused portion of the nutmeg into the storage compartment located in the handle of the grater.

OLIVE PITTER

Cleaner and infinitely quicker than removing the pits of olives with a knife, the spring-loaded pitter offers the additional advantage of leaving the olive intact.

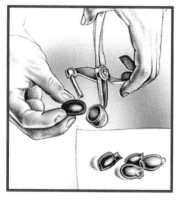

1. Holding the pitter open with one hand, load the small cupped ring with an olive stem side up.

2. Squeeze the handles shut. This action pokes a 1-inch rod through the center of the fruit, punching the pit out of the bottom end without appreciable loss of juice.

GARLIC PEELER

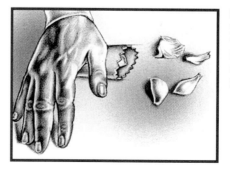

This gadget, made of smooth-finish rubber and shaped like a cannoli, causes papery garlic skins to stick to the inside. The whole cloves emerge, perfectly peeled, without bruising or mashing.

1. Place garlic clove inside the peeler.

2. Roll briskly with the heel of your hand, with some downward pressure, on a hard surface until you can hear the skin crackle, indicating that it is released from the clove.

ILLUSTRATIONS BY HARRY DAVIS

MAGI-CAKE STRIPS

By providing a buffer between the sides of a cake pan and the oven heat, these little strips prevent cakes from overcooking near the outside edges.

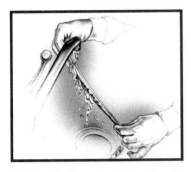

1. Saturate the cake strip with cold water and run your fingers along it to squeeze out excess water.

2. With the aluminized side facing out, wrap the strip around the outside of the batter-filled pan.

3. Secure the strip with the provided pin. Two strips can be used together for larger or oblong pans. Bake as directed, but be aware that baking times may increase slightly.

4. Because all areas of the cake—top, bottom, and sides—cook at an equal pace, the end result is a level cake (on right) that does not shrink, crack along the top, or have a tough crust along the outside edges.

HEARTWATCH GOURMET FAT SKIMMER

Of the three styles of skimmers tested, we preferred this one because of its trigger action. With this gadget, you can defatten still hot broth without having to refrigerate it in order to skim off the solidified fat at the surface.

1. Holding the skimmer level, lower the ladle slowly into the stockpot until the liquid and surface fat run through the canals along the top rim of the ladle.

2. Lift the ladle and wait for a moment while all the fat collects at the surface, trapping the broth at the bottom of the ladle. Pull the trigger, releasing the broth back into the pot. Toss out the fat that has collected in the ladle and repeat as necessary.

MULTI CORER

This tool resembles a small melon baller, with the addition of sharp teeth around the rim. It effectively removes cores from tomatoes, and hulls and stems from strawberries, without damaging the fragile flesh of the fruit in either case. To use the corer, simply scoop out the core of the fruit using a circular motion.

WOODEN OVEN RACK ADJUSTER

When checking the contents of a hot oven, a carelessly placed pot holder or an oven mitt worn thin can result in burns. The oven rack adjuster keeps hands clear of the hot rack. A magnet is attached so the adjuster can be kept right on the oven.

1. Use the notch carved into the base of the adjuster to pull out the hot oven rack. To push the rack back in, use the notch at the end.

FOOD MILL

Also called a mechanical sieve, this kitchen tool has lost favor as food processors have gained popularity. However, this hand-powered tool has a definite advantage: It separates pulp from skin, seeds, and cores as it purees, an important attribute when making applesauce, tomato sauce, and so forth.

1. The mill consists of a hopper with a perforated disk in the bottom, topped by a flat, curving blade attached to a crank. To use, simply place food in the hopper and turn the crank.

2. The cranking action causes the blade to rotate over the disk, forcing the food through the holes; while cranking, grip the handle for stability. Food mills come with three disks of varying fineness.

Mix-and-Match Fruit Cobblers

Four cobbler toppings and a fruit chart give cooks freedom of choice based on fruit, time, and ingredients on hand.

∼ BY PAM ANDERSON WITH KAREN TACK ∼

Baked and topped fruit desserts like crisps, cobblers, and crumbles have been my standard casual company dessert for years. Served with whipped or ice cream, they taste as good as most fruit pies and are much quicker to assemble.

The difference among these simple desserts is the topping—cobblers usually have a pastry or biscuit topping, while crisps and crumbles have crumb toppings. To further differentiate, crisps are topped with a mixture of butter, sugar, flour, and nuts, while crumbles have the same topping, with oatmeal taking the place of the nuts.

I had been eyeing this group of desserts for a while, thinking that I'd like to bring them all together by developing one formula based on the fruit, topping ingredients, and time I had on hand. As it was, my topping recipes were scattered, and I was never quite sure in which cases the fruit should be sweetened or thickened.

Because I make these desserts so often during the summer, I wanted a recipe that fit in a simple eight-inch pan (or doubled for the equally common nine-by-thirteen-inch size). Even ill-supplied vacation houses usually have one of the two, and if not, there are always disposables in both sizes at the grocery.

Lastly, to honor the humble, friendly roots of these desserts, I wanted to make sure they remained easy to make and simply flavored.

Mission Impossible
After only a few hours in the kitchen, we realized these goals were too ambitious. Cobblers, we determined, ought to be juicy, while crisps and crumbles are necessarily dry. There were just too many variables to play the mix-and-match game we initially thought possible.

So we narrowed the focus to cobblers, still a' big topic because they vary widely depending on decade and region. We found recipes for the usual pastry- and biscuit-topped fruit, but we also saw custardy clafouti-style desserts, fruits baked in sweet pancake batters, and double-crusted juicy fruit pies, all confidently called cobbler. Among the many, we isolated four cobbler styles for our mix-and-match format: toppings of butter cookie dough, biscuit (shortcake), and pastry as well as a batter-based topping.

Before refining the toppings, we first wanted to understand the dynamics of the fruit. Because cobblers are so casual, would *x* amount of fruit, regardless of variety, bake up

more or less the same under the crust? Did the fruit need to be thickened, sweetened, flavored? If so, how much?

Fruit First
First we needed to check the juice and sugar level of each baked fruit. So we tested both fresh and frozen fruits—apples (Winesaps, Granny Smiths, McIntoshes, and Empires), peaches, nectarines, plums, dark sweet and sour cherries, strawberries, blueberries, pears, blackberries, rhubarb, and raspberries. We baked a small portion of each, lightly sweetened, until fully cooked.

Most of the fruits, when baked with sugar, produced a nice quantity of slightly thickened juices. Two fruits, however, responded very differently. Cobblers made with apples, at one extreme, were so dry we ultimately added water to make them juicy enough. At the other end, cobblers made

with sour cherries were too watery, and ultimately demanded more thickener than the other fruits.

Having figured out the juiciness quotient, we moved on to sweetenings. Stated simply, baked fruit needs sugar. On its own, most fruit is too tart for this type of dessert, and sweet cobbler toppings and ice cream accentuate its tartness, rather than mellowing it. It turns out that sugar also helps with the thickening, turning the fruit juices into a very light syrup. After a number of tests with each fruit, we came up with the sugar amounts listed on the chart. Since fruit sweetness varies, we recommend you start by adding the lower of the suggested amounts, then taste and increase as needed. Also, be mindful that cooked fruit tends to be a bit tarter than its fresh version, so add a bit more sugar than you think you need.

Even though sugar helped thicken the juice, it wasn't quite enough. All fruits benefit from a little thickener, which helps in two ways. It gives the juice body and sheen, which translates into good mouth feel. It also tones down the intensely sweet-tart flavor of the baked fruit.

Which starch to use? For a natural, thin, silky syrup, we preferred cornstarch, arrowroot, or potato starch. Used in small quantity, we found it difficult to tell much difference among the three. Though they all worked equally well at unobtrusively thickening the juices, we recommend cornstarch because it is the most widely available. Unlike fruit pie, for which a good clean cut is important, cobblers are meant to be on the moist and messy side. Thus, instant tapioca, while great for thickening pie fruit (*see* "How to Thicken Fruit Pies," July/August 1995) gave the cobbler fruit too jellylike a texture. Flour turned the juices cloudy.

Because we knew that minced apple is often used to thicken fruit jams, we tried this thickening method with cobblers as well. The method showed promise, but it was more complicated and less effective than starch in taming the flavor intensity of the baked fruit.

One final observation about thickener: The riper the fruit, the lower the pectin level, so if baking prime specimens, you may want to add a tad more starch.

Top Dressing
While exploring fruits, we also test-piloted various cobbler toppings. Christopher Kimball's excellent pastry (featured many times in this magazine),

sprinkled generously with sugar and baked over any of the suggested fruits, makes a delicious cobbler. We got good advice from another *Cook's Illustrated* contributor, Stephen Schmidt, who suggested tucking the dough into the pan side rather than fluting the edges. The fruit juices keep the side crust tender while the dry oven heat crisps up the top. This tucking method gave us both soft and crisp textures without making a double crust.

After testing a number of biscuit toppings, we opted for a rich, sweet shortcake dough to help anchor the assertive fruit. Given a choice between drop or cutout biscuits and a rolled sheet, we voted for the latter. We preferred the even distribution of crust. Like the pastry, you can also tuck this shortcake dough into the pan side to create dual textures.

Since tasting a blueberry cobbler featured in an article titled "Boarding House Cuisine" in *Cook's* magazine six years ago (May 1990), I've never met a cobbler I liked better. Similar to butter cookie dough, this third cobbler topping bakes up soft and rich at the center and delicately crisp on top. After testing this topping with many of the fruits on the chart, we endorse them all.

Finding a batter-based cobbler was more difficult. Fruit baked in rich yellow cake batter was technically a buckle, and the dessert looked and tasted too much like cake. Fruit baked in a lean, sweet pancakelike batter looked like coarse quick bread. Both batters absorbed the fruit's excess juice, looking more like cake than cobbler. Stiffer batters, dropped by the tablespoonful onto the

fruit, baked into mediocre cobblers that just couldn't compete with our other winners. The batter cobblers, in general, were uniformly soft, lacking the crisp contrast of topping and fruit.

I casually mentioned my defeat to *Cook's Illustrated* consulting science expert, Shirley Corriher, who knew just where to find the perfect batter-based cobbler. Nathalie Dupree, in *New Southern Cooking* (Knopf, 1986), shares a recipe for just such a Peach Cobbler. To make it, butter is melted in the cobbler pan in the preheating oven. Once the butter melts, a mixture of flour, baking powder, salt, sugar, and milk are poured over it, then fruit and juices are poured over the batter. Since the butter is not actually mixed into the batter, it surfaces to form a thin, crisp top.

It's all here—a fruit chart and four cobbler toppings—enough combinations to keep you baking right through the summer and into the fall.

MASTER RECIPE FOR FRUIT COBBLER
Enough for one 8-inch square or one 9-inch round pan

Clearly, these fruits can be mixed. If sugar quantities for the selected fruits are different, simply average the two amounts. Any of the toppings listed below can be used with any of the fruits. If you're short on time, the Butter Cookie Dough Topping and the Batter Fruit Cobber can be put together very quickly. These recipes can easily be doubled and baked in a thirteen-by-nine-inch pan.

Serve any of the cobblers that follow with ice cream or lightly whipped cream.

1. Prepare pastry, shortcake or cookie-dough topping for fruit. (Refrigerate shortcake or pastry topping.) Batter Fruit Cobbler that follows is self-contained.

2. Adjust oven rack to lower-middle position and heat oven to 375 degrees. Mix cornstarch, sugar to taste, and optional dry spices in medium bowl. Add prepared fruit and optional liquid flavorings; toss to coat.

3. Place fruit in 8-inch square or 9-inch round baking pan. Cover with selected topping, and bake on cookie sheet until golden brown, 45 to 55 minutes.

BUTTER COOKIE DOUGH TOPPING
This recipe was featured in an article titled "Boarding House Cuisine," which ran in the May 1990 issue of *Cook's* magazine. All of us who tasted the cobbler thought it was one of the best we had ever tasted. Six years and a lot of cobblers later, I still feel this topping makes one of the best cobblers you'll probably ever eat. Because the cookie dough is quite sweet, use the smaller amount of sugar suggested in the fruit chart.

½ cup all-purpose flour
¼ teaspoon baking powder
    Pinch salt

FRUIT	QUANTITY	PREPARATION	CORNSTARCH	SUGAR QUANTITY	FLAVORINGS
Blueberries	2 pints fresh (or 24 ounces frozen)	Rinse and pick over	2 teaspoons	½ to ⅔ cup	½ teaspoon ground cinnamon, 1 teaspoon vanilla extract
Blackberries	2 pints fresh (or 24 ounces frozen)	Rinse	1 tablespoon	⅓ to ½ cup	1 teaspoon vanilla extract
Strawberries or strawberry/ rhubarb	2 pints fresh (or 24 ounces frozen) or 10 ounces each of rhubarb and strawberries	Stem and rinse, leave whole with small or medium berries, but halve if large; cut rhubarb into ⅓-inch chunks	1 tablespoon	⅓ to ½ cup	1 teaspoon vanilla extract
Raspberries	2 pints fresh (or 24 ounces frozen)	Rinse	1 tablespoon	½ to ⅔ cup	1 teaspoon vanilla extract
Sour cherries	1 ¾ pounds fresh (or 24 ounces frozen)	Stem and pit	1 ½ tablespoons	⅔ to ¾ cup	½ teaspoon almond extract, 1 tablespoon kirsch
Italian plums	1 ¾ pounds	Pit and quarter	2 teaspoons	½ to ⅔ cup	½ teaspoon ground cinnamon, 1 teaspoon vanilla extract
Apples	1 ¾ pounds tart, firm	Peel, quarter, core, and slice thick	2 teaspoons dissolved in ¼ cup water	⅓ to ½ cup	½ teaspoon ground cinnamon, 1 teaspoon vanilla extract, 1 tablespoon brandy
Pears	1 ¾ pounds	Peel, quarter, core, and slice thick	2 teaspoons	⅓ to ½ cup	¼ teaspoon powdered ginger or nutmeg, 1 teaspoon vanilla extract
Apricots	1 ¾ pounds	Pit and halve	2 teaspoons	½ to ⅔ cup	1 teaspoon vanilla extract, ½ teaspoon almond extract
Peaches/ nectarines	1 ¾ pounds	Peel, pit, and slice thick	2 teaspoons	⅓ to ½ cup	Pinch cloves, 1 teaspoon vanilla extract, 1 tablespoon brandy

8 tablespoons unsalted butter, softened
½ cup sugar
½ large egg or 1 yolk
¼ teaspoon vanilla extract

1. Mix flour, baking powder, and salt in small bowl; set aside.

2. Beat butter and sugar until well blended. Beat in egg and vanilla. Add flour mixture; stir until just combined.

3. Drop dough onto prepared fruit by heaping tablespoons. Bake, following instructions in master recipe.

RICH SHORTCAKE TOPPING

Because the biscuit easily absorbs juices, this shortcake topping is particularly nice with berries. If you want to top the cobbler with individual biscuits, increase the recipe by half and roll it to three-quarters inch thick, brushing the dough rounds with milk and sprinkling them with sugar.

1 cup all-purpose flour
1 ½ teaspoons baking powder
¼ teaspoon salt
4 tablespoons cold unsalted butter, cut into ¼-inch pieces
2 tablespoons cold vegetable shortening
7 tablespoons milk
1 tablespoon sugar

1. Mix flour, baking powder, and salt in food processor fitted with steel blade. Scatter butter pieces over mixture, tossing to coat butter with a little of the flour. Cut butter into flour with five 1-second pulses. Add shortening; continue cutting in until flour is pale yellow and resembles coarse cornmeal, with butter bits no larger than a small pea, about four more 1-second pulses. Turn mixture into medium bowl.

2. Pour 6 tablespoons milk into flour mixture. Toss with fork until mixture forms large clumps. Turn mixture onto work surface; lightly knead until mixture just comes together. Place dough on sheet of plastic wrap and press into either square or round disk, depending on pan shape. Refrigerate while preparing fruit. (Can be refrigerated up to 2 hours before baking.)

3. On a lightly floured work surface, roll dough to 10-inch square or circle. Lay dough over prepared fruit; tuck excess dough in between pan side and fruit. Brush dough with remaining tablespoon of milk; sprinkle on sugar. Cut four two-inch air vents in dough top and follow baking instructions in master recipe.

FLAKY PASTRY TOPPING

You can effortlessly achieve a soft and crisp-textured crust by tucking the pastry between the fruit and pan wall. The fruit juices keep the side crust tender while the dry oven heat crisps up the top. To turn your cobbler into a pandowdy, follow Master Recipe for Fruit Cobbler, topping it with Flaky Pastry Topping. Once the crust has fully set, but not browned (about thirty minutes into baking), remove the dessert from the oven, scoring the crust lengthwise and crosswise to form two-inch squares. Using a large spoon or metal spatula, press the partially baked crust down into the fruit. Continue to bake until the crust is set and golden.

1 cup all-purpose flour
¼ teaspoon salt
1 tablespoon sugar, plus 1 additional tablespoon for sprinkling over dough top
6 tablespoons chilled unsalted butter, cut into ¼-inch pieces
2 tablespoons chilled all-vegetable shortening

2–3 tablespoons ice water
1 tablespoon milk (or water)

1. Mix flour, salt, and sugar in food processor fitted with steel blade. Scatter butter pieces over flour mixture, tossing to coat butter with a little of the flour. Cut butter into flour with five 1-second pulses. Add shortening; continue cutting in until flour is pale yellow and resembles coarse cornmeal, with butter bits no larger than a small pea, about four more 1-second pulses. Turn mixture into medium bowl.

2. Sprinkle 2 tablespoons ice water over flour mixture. Using rubber spatula, fold water into mixture. Then press down on mixture with broad side of spatula until dough sticks together, adding up to 1 tablespoon more water if dough will not come together. Place dough on sheet of plastic wrap and press into either square or round disk, depending on pan shape. Refrigerate while preparing fruit. (Can be refrigerated up to 2 days before baking.)

3. On a lightly floured work surface, roll dough to 10-inch square or circle. Lay dough over prepared fruit; tuck excess dough in pan between pan side and fruit. Brush dough top lightly with milk or water and sprinkle with additional sugar. Cut four 2-inch air vents in dough top and bake following instructions in master recipe.

BATTER FRUIT COBBLER
Serves 4 to 6

After testing a number of batter-based cobblers, we found this recipe, adapted from *New Southern Cooking* (Knopf, 1986), to be one of the best in its category. Many of the batter cobblers reminded us too much of cake, quick bread, or custard. Unlike the others, this one had a real cobbler feel to it.

6 tablespoons unsalted butter
¼ cup all-purpose flour
¼ cup plus 1 tablespoon sugar
1 teaspoon baking powder
¼ teaspoon salt
¼ cup milk
2 cups sliced fruit or berries (not sweetened or thickened)

1. Adjust oven rack to lower-middle position and heat oven to 350 degrees. Put butter in 8-inch square or 9-inch round pan; set in oven to melt.

2. Whisk flour, ¼ cup sugar, baking powder, and salt in small bowl. Add milk; whisk until just incorporated into dry ingredients. When butter has melted, remove pan from oven. Pour batter into pan, without stirring it into butter, then arrange fruit over batter. Sprinkle with remaining tablespoon sugar. Bake until batter browns, about 40 to 50 minutes. ∎

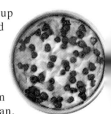

Easy Summer Salsas

These highly flavored "little dishes" add intense flavor with minimal effort.

∽ BY JOHN WILLOUGHBY AND CHRIS SCHLESINGER ∽

To most Americans, the word "salsa" conjures up the spicy, hot concoction of tomatoes, onions, chile peppers, and garlic that is known as *salsa mexicana.* While this is the most well known version of salsa, it is far from the only one. One thing that almost all salsas have in common, though, is that they contain many bold, intense flavors. When making these little dishes, the only trick is to make sure that you balance these flavors so that they stimulate your taste buds in rapid succession, rather than allowing one flavor or ingredient to dominate. Use these flavorful mixtures as dips, side dishes, or accompaniments to dress up simple meat or fish.

CLASSIC RED TABLE SALSA
Makes about 5 cups
If you cannot find chipotle peppers (dried, smoked jalapeños), you can substitute any minced, fresh chile pepper of your choice.

- 3 large, very ripe tomatoes (about 2 pounds), diced small
- ½ cup tomato juice
- 1 small chipotle pepper, minced (about 2 tablespoons)
- 1 medium red onion, diced small
- 1 medium garlic clove, minced
- ½ cup chopped fresh cilantro leaves
- ½ cup juice from 4 medium limes
- Salt

Mix all ingredients, including salt to taste, in medium bowl. Cover and refrigerate to blend flavors, at least 1 hour or up to 5 days.

AVOCADO-CORN SALSA
Makes about 5 cups
This salsa goes great with any grilled seafood.

- 3 ears of corn, husked
- 3 ripe but firm avocados, peeled, pitted, and diced large
- 1 medium red onion, diced small
- 1 red bell pepper, cored, seeded, and diced small
- ⅓ cup olive oil
- ¼ cup red wine vinegar
- 3 medium garlic cloves, minced
- 4 dashes hot red pepper sauce, or to taste
- 1 tablespoon ground cumin
- 1 teaspoon chili powder
- ¼ cup chopped fresh oregano leaves

- ½ cup juice from 4 medium limes
- Salt and ground black pepper

1. Bring large pot of water to boil; add corn and boil until just cooked, 3 to 5 minutes. Drain and immediately cool ears of corn under cold, running water, then cut kernels from each cob.
2. Mix corn with remaining ingredients, including salt and pepper to taste, in medium bowl. Cover and refrigerate to blend flavors, at least 1 hour or up to 3 days.

SIMPLE PEACH SALSA
Makes about 3 cups
If you don't have peaches, substitute any yellow-orange fruit, including mangoes, pineapples, or papaya.

- 2 ripe but not mushy peaches, pitted and chopped coarse
- 1 small red bell pepper, cored, seeded, and sliced thin
- 1 small red onion, sliced into long, thin slices
- ¼ cup chopped fresh parsley leaves
- 1 medium clove garlic, minced
- ¼ cup pineapple juice
- 6 tablespoons juice from 3 medium limes
- 1 jalapeño or other medium hot chile pepper, minced
- Salt and ground black pepper

Mix all ingredients, including salt and pepper to taste, in medium bowl. Cover and refrigerate to blend flavors, at least 1 hour or up to 4 days.

BLACK BEAN–MANGO SALSA
Makes about 5 cups
This Caribbean-inspired mixture is great with grilled fish, but it is also very tasty just by itself—use it as a spicy, summer salad course, or scoop it up with chips as a snack or appetizer.

- 1 cup cooked black beans
- 2 mangoes, peeled, seeded, and diced small
- ½ medium red bell pepper, cored, seeded, and diced small
- ½ medium green bell pepper, cored, seeded, and diced small
- ½ medium red onion, diced small

- ¾ cup pineapple juice
- ½ cup juice from 4 medium limes
- ½ cup chopped fresh cilantro leaves
- 2 tablespoons ground cumin
- 1 small jalapeño or chile pepper of your choice, seeded and minced
- Salt and ground black pepper

Mix all ingredients, including salt and pepper to taste, in medium bowl. Cover and refrigerate to blend flavors, at least 1 hour or up to 4 days.

GRILLED JALAPEÑO SALSA
Makes about 3 cups
In addition to serving this salsa with tortilla chips, you might try mixing it in with pasta—about a tablespoon or so per serving. You'll still get a good dose of heat.

- 2 tablespoons vegetable oil
- 1 medium garlic clove, minced
- 6 plum tomatoes, halved
- Salt and ground black pepper
- 10 large jalapeño chile peppers, stems removed
- ¼ cup juice from 2 medium limes
- ¼ cup chopped fresh cilantro leaves
- ¼ cup olive oil

1. Mix 1 tablespoon of vegetable oil and garlic together in small bowl; rub tomato halves with this mixture, then sprinkle with salt and pepper to taste. Place over medium-hot fire and grill, turning once, until they begin to color, 6 to 8 minutes. Remove from grill, cool to room temperature, dice, and transfer to medium bowl; set aside.
2. Rub peppers with remaining tablespoon of vegetable oil and grill over same medium-hot fire until slightly colored, 2 to 3 minutes. Remove from fire and cool to room temperature; seed, mince, and add to tomatoes.
3. Mix remaining ingredients with tomatoes and peppers. Cover and refrigerate to blend flavors, at least 1 hour or up to 4 days.

John Willoughby and **Chris Schlesinger** are the coauthors of four cookbooks, including *Salsas, Sambals, Chutneys, and Chowchows* (Morrow, 1993), from which several of the recipes above were adapted. ■

Grilling Chicken Legs and Thighs

The secrets to grilling dark meat are a quick brine and a two-level fire.

∼ BY JOHN WILLOUGHBY AND CHRIS SCHLESINGER ∼

Grilling is about as straightforward a cooking method as there is: You build the fire, you put the food over the fire, and you cook it until it's done. But that doesn't mean that there is no technique involved. In fact, the pleasing simplicity of grilling is nicely balanced by the fact that, when using what is essentially a quick, high-heat cooking method, the griller has to mesh the desire for a good, strong surface sear—the part that gives food that ineffable grilled flavor—with the need to cook the food all the way through before the outside gets incinerated.

So we set out to find the best method for cooking chicken pieces on the grill. Like everybody else who lights the grilling fire, we were looking for a juicy, tender, evenly cooked interior, a nicely seared exterior, and robust grilled flavor. Over the years we'd heard all the tales and backyard improvisations and figured we'd check them all out to see if any of them held particular promise for the griller. While you can get great results with just about any approach to grilling, some methods are more likely than others to give you what you're looking for.

Combo Cooking Methods

We soon realized that in order to test every possibility, we would have to eliminate breasts and stick to the dark meat portions of the chicken. That was no problem, because these pieces have a higher fat content, which not only gives them more inherent flavor but also makes them better for grilling. We cooked the whole leg with thigh attached and also cooked thighs by themselves, which turned out to affect the cooking time (thighs alone took about two to four minutes less).

We divided the tests into three sets. The first set involved partial cooking off the grill; the second involved particular ways of moving the chicken around on the grill surface, as well as using the grill cover for part of the cooking time; and the third involved various ways of treating the chicken before it cooked, both to add flavor and to improve texture.

We had thought that some of the methods of partially cooking the chicken off the grill would work pretty well, but we were wrong.

Poaching the chicken before grilling resulted in dry chicken with a cottony texture. Microwaving prior to grilling was even worse: The chicken ended up not only dry but rubbery, and the skin failed to crisp despite its postmicrowave time on the grill.

Our next approach was to sear the thighs and legs on the grill first, then finish the cooking off the grill. Using the microwave to finish cooking after a two-minute sear on the grill wasn't bad and would be acceptable for those times when you're in a hurry to get food on the table. Unlike the chicken that was microwaved before grilling, these pieces had crispy skin, and the meat was evenly cooked throughout. But this chicken, too, was slightly less juicy than those that were cooked only on the grill.

Our final attempt at combined cooking methods came even closer to the goal. Again we seared the thighs and legs on the grill but this time finished cooking them in a 350-degree oven. The meat was evenly cooked and remained juicy, with none of the toughness experienced with other methods; the skin, which had crisped up nicely during its time on the grill, remained quite crisp after its sojourn in the oven.

The differences between this method and our final favorite were differences of degree: The meat was just slightly less tender, the skin a bit less crispy. More importantly, this oven method used two different appliances and required you to do part of the cooking outside on the grill and the rest in the kitchen. Not only was this needlessly cumbersome, it was also less fun, given that part of the appeal of grilling is standing around the fire sipping your favorite beverage and passing the time of day as you cook. So we consigned this method to the reject pile along with the other, less successful combination cooking techniques.

Moving Around the Grill

We next moved on to test methods that involved cooking on the grill alone. Each method involved

Coating chicken with a spice rub or paste prior to grilling forms a flavorful crust on the outside of the chicken.

some variation on the two-level fire, that is, a fire with one area that is hotter than the other. The idea in every case was to get the sear from the hotter fire and cook the chicken evenly all the way through over the cooler fire.

The first of these methods seemed particularly contrary, but a friend had insisted that it worked, so we had to give it a test run. In this method, the chicken was to be cooked on a low fire first, then finished up on a hot fire. Like microwaving, however, this backwards approach resulted in dry meat—a lame result for a method that saved no time or energy.

Next we tried the method recommended by the manufacturers of many covered grills and sworn to by legions of backyard cooks across the country: searing chicken over a hot fire, then moving it to a medium fire, putting the cover on, and cooking until done. We found that with this method the chicken indeed cooked through without burning on the outside, stayed relatively moist, and cooked a couple of minutes faster than with other grill-only methods. There was just one problem: It didn't taste that great. Every time we tried it, the chicken had a faint but definitely noticeable "off" taste, which we can best describe as resembling the odor of stale smoke. We later found that, with larger or tougher cuts of meat that stay on the grill longer—in other words, when "smoke-roasting"—the flavor of the smoke from the coals overpowers this off taste. But with foods that are not going to be on the grill long, putting the cover on seems to cause the food to absorb the taste of the inside of the cover.

Next we tried the method that intuitively seemed most likely to succeed: searing the chicken over a medium-hot fire and then moving it to a medium-low fire to finish cooking. This approach did prove the winner. While the chicken took a couple of minutes longer to cook this way than with covered cooking, it ended up just as we liked it, the interior evenly cooked, moist, and tender, and the skin dark and crisp.

Adding Flavor—and a Surprise

It was now time to consider ways of adding flavor to the chicken. In this area, options included marinating, spice rubs and pastes, and brining.

Marinating the chicken was disappointing. Even several hours in a classic oil-and-acid marinade added only a small amount of flavor to the finished chicken, and oil dripping off the marinated chicken caused constant flare-ups during the initial searing period.

Rubbing the chicken with a spice rub or paste prior to grilling proved far more satisfactory. Because the rubs and pastes are composed almost entirely of spices, they have enough flavor intensity to stand up to the smoky grilled flavor and as a result come through much more clearly.

As a final test, we tried brining the chicken before grilling it. Admittedly, we didn't approach this test with a lot of enthusiasm—it seemed like too much bother for what should be a simple cooking process. This just goes to show how preconceptions can be faulty, though, because it turned out to be an excellent idea.

We tried brining for various amounts of time and found that, by using a brine with a high concentration of salt and sugar, we could achieve the result we wanted in only about one and one-half hours. The brine penetrated the chicken, seasoning it and slightly firming up its texture before grilling. On a molecular level, what actually happened was that the salt caused the strands of protein in the chicken meat to unwind, get tangled up with each other, and trap water in the resulting matrix. When the chicken was grilled, this matrix formed a sort of barrier that kept water from leaking out of the bird. As a result, the finished chicken was juicier and more tender.

The sugar in the brine had one very good effect and one minor negative aspect. The traces of sugar left on the exterior of the chicken, while not enough to affect the taste in itself, did cause the chicken to brown more quickly and thoroughly. Since browning adds rich, deep flavor to any food, this was a decided advantage. However, the browning also took place more quickly than with nonbrined chicken, so on our first try we managed to burn the skin of some pieces. Thus, when grilling brined chicken, be sure to watch it very carefully during the initial browning period.

If you don't have time to brine your chicken, you can still get excellent results with the two-level fire method and by adding deep flavor with a spice rub or paste. If you choose not to brine, sprinkle the chicken with salt and freshly cracked pepper before heading to the grill.

MAHOGANY GRILLED CHICKEN THIGHS OR LEGS
Serves 4

Brining improves the chicken's flavor, but if you're short on time, you can skip step number 1 and simply flavor the chicken with one of the spice rubs or pastes below. Because no two live fires are exactly the same, the cooking time remains an estimate. To check the fire temperature for this recipe, hold your hand about five inches above the grill grid. If you can hold it there for two to three seconds, you have a medium-hot fire; if for four to five seconds, you have a medium-low fire. To check for doneness, cut into one piece at the thickest point; it should show no redness.

¾ cup sugar
¾ cup kosher salt
8 chicken thighs or 4 whole legs
Ground black pepper

1. In gallon-size zipper-lock plastic bag, dissolve sugar and salt in 1 quart water. Add chicken, pressing out as much air as possible; seal and refrigerate until fully seasoned, about 1 ½ hours.

2. Light 5 quarts charcoal (one chimney starter heaped full) and allow to burn until flames have died down and all charcoal is covered with a layer of fine gray ash. Build two-level fire by stacking half of the hot coals on one side of grill to within 3 inches or so of grill rack for medium-hot fire. Arrange remaining coals in single layer on other side of grill for medium-low fire. Return grill rack to position; cover grill and let rack heat 5 minutes.

3. Meanwhile, remove chicken from brine, dry thoroughly with paper towels, and season with pepper (or one of the spice rubs or pastes below).

4. Cook chicken, uncovered, over medium-hot fire, extinguishing any flames with squirt bottle, until seared, about 1 to 2 minutes on each side. Move chicken to medium-low fire; continue to grill uncovered, turning occasionally, until chicken is dark and fully cooked, 12 to 16 minutes for thighs, 16 to 20 minutes for whole legs. Transfer to serving platter. Serve warm or at room temperature. ■

John Willoughby and **Chris Schlesinger** are co-authors of *The Thrill of the Grill* (Morrow, 1990).

RUBS AND PASTES

Each of the following rubs and pastes can be used to flavor the grilled chicken, brined or not. If the chicken has not been brined, make sure to salt and pepper it before grilling. Each rub or paste makes about enough for one recipe (above).

SWEET-AND-SOUR CURRY SPICE RUB
Makes about 3/4 cup
In small bowl, mix 1 tablespoon each of ground cumin, curry powder, crushed coriander seeds, paprika, and brown sugar; 2 medium garlic cloves, minced; ¼ cup red wine vinegar; ¼ cup distilled white vinegar; and ¼ cup peanut oil. Grill chicken following instructions in Mahogany Grilled Chicken. When chicken is almost fully cooked, brush some mixture on both sides of each piece. Continue to grill chicken, brushing with remaining rub, until fully cooked.

CHILI SPICE PASTE WITH CITRUS AND CILANTRO
Makes about ⅓ cup
In food processor or blender, puree 1 teaspoon each of ground cumin, chili powder, paprika, and ground coriander; 2 tablespoons fresh cilantro leaves; 1 small garlic clove; 1 tablespoon each of orange juice, pineapple juice, lime juice, and olive oil; and 2 dashes Tabasco sauce. Rub paste generously under chicken skin. Grill, following instructions in Mahogany Grilled Chicken.

ASIAN SPICE PASTE
Makes about ½ cup
In food processor or blender, puree 2 tablespoons fresh cilantro leaves, 1 tablespoon minced fresh chile pepper of your choice, 2 medium garlic cloves, 1 tablespoon coarse-chopped gingerroot; 2 tablespoons soy sauce; and 2 tablespoons peanut oil. Rub paste generously under chicken skin. Grill, following instructions in Mahogany Grilled Chicken.

MEDITERRANEAN SPICE PASTE
Makes about ½ cup
In food processor or blender, puree 4 medium garlic cloves, 2 tablespoons finely grated lemon zest, ¼ cup fresh parsley leaves, ¼ cup olive oil, and 1 tablespoon each of fresh thyme, rosemary, and sage leaves. Rub paste generously under chicken skin. Grill, following instructions in Mahogany Grilled Chicken.

Dannon Lowfat Wins Yogurt Tasting

Two surprises surfaced in this tasting: Plain supermarket yogurts outpolled health foods store brands, and our panel actually preferred low-fat versions.

～ BY JACK BISHOP ～

Plain yogurt may not be the world's sexiest food, but there is plenty of mystique surrounding this refrigerator staple. Maybe it's due to that ad campaign featuring centenarian Georgians (the Soviet variety) who ate yogurt by the cupful every day. For whatever reason, the health food crowd certainly latched on to yogurt, with its active cultures promising all kinds of benefits to the body, and slowly but surely brought this food into the mainstream. Once consumed mainly by hippies and ethnic Americans hailing from Eastern Europe or the Middle East, yogurt is now a favorite with kids, dieters, cooks (who use it in everything from dips to dressings), and bakers (who know that yogurt can add moistness to muffins and cakes).

Because I always have plain yogurt in the fridge, the question naturally arose, does it matter what kind? I designed this tasting to address three factors that would answer that question.

First, I wanted to know whether the inclusion of certain bacteria (the "active cultures" in yogurt) would cause particular yogurts to rate higher than others. Second, I wanted to find out whether the fat content would make a difference in yogurt taste and/or texture. The leading yogurt companies, Dannon and Colombo, make low-fat and nonfat versions, but several smaller companies start with whole milk. Could experts tell the difference, and would they care?

The final question, and one I always have before starting a tasting article, has to do with overall quality. Is yogurt a case in which the leading supermarket brands are just fine, or are specialty brands worth searching out?

The Bacteria Bug

Yogurt was no doubt first made by chance when milk was accidentally fermented by wild bacteria. Today, the process is more controlled. Milk (either whole, low-fat, or skim) is pasteurized and usually homogenized. (Some companies leave whole milk unhomogenized to retain a separate cream layer in their yogurt.) Active bacteria cultures are then added to the milk.

This milk with active cultures is then poured directly into the cups, which are incubated for several hours in a warm environment. The bacteria turns the milk sugars (called lactose) into lactic acid, causing the proteins in the milk to coagulate and thicken. Lactic acid also gives yogurt its characteristic tang. Next, the yogurt is cooled and then refrigerated. If re-pasteurized (something that is rarely done today), the bacteria will be killed. All the yogurts we tested contain live and active cultures.

Exactly which cultures, however, proved to be unimportant at least as far as taste goes (see "No Cultural Differences," below). We therefore moved quickly on to the issues of fat content, texture, and flavor.

Less Fat Is Better

We tasted a total of thirteen commercial brands plus one homemade yogurt. Three commercial brands, plus the homemade yogurt, were made with whole milk. When you open a container of whole milk yogurt, you notice an immediate difference. These yogurts are topped with a thick, yellow layer of cream.

I had assumed that these rich products would do well in the tasting. After all, they contain 9 or 10 grams of fat per cup as compared to 2 to 5 grams in a cup of low-fat yogurt and 0 fat grams in nonfat yogurt. Well, I was wrong. While the organic whole milk yogurt from Stonyfield Farm took fifth place (this brand is available in many supermarkets as well as most health foods stores), the other whole milk yogurts finished eighth and tenth. The homemade yogurt did not fare any better, ending up tied for eighth place.

That's not to say that all low-fat and nonfat products scored well. Two nonfat and one low-fat brand finished at the bottom of the rankings. But the first four finishers were either low-fat or nonfat. Tasters said they felt overwhelmed by yogurts made with whole milk. They seemed overly rich. Lower-fat yogurts, as long as they were well made, suited our panel just fine. As one taster remarked when the results were announced, "I guess our palates really have been trained to like less fat."

The Right Balance

Our panel found taste and texture considerations even more important than fat. Yogurts that demonstrated a combination of desirable qualities rose to the top of the pack. In terms of consistency, yogurts on either end of the spectrum did not score well. Tasters reacted negatively to extremely stiff or gelatinous yogurts as well as to those that were too thin or soupy.

NO CULTURAL DIFFERENCES

By law, *Lactobacillus bulgaricus* and *Streptococcus thermophilus* must be among the active cultures added to all yogurts made in the United States. All the yogurts we tested also contained a third bacteria, *Lactobacillus acidophilus*. This bacteria has been linked with a number of good traits, including a reduction in the lactose that makes dairy products hard for some people to digest. A fourth bacteria, *Bifidus*, is added to most natural foods store yogurts. Like *Lactobacillus acidophilus*, *Bifidus* has been associated with a number of health benefits. With the exception of Dannon, Colombo, and Erivan, *Bifidus* cultures were also a part of all the yogurts tested.

Despite some manufacturers' claims, however, our panel could not detect any relationship between particular bacteria and specific flavor characteristics. Because most of the health claims are anecdotal, most shoppers will want to rely on other issues, such as fat content, texture, and flavor, when choosing a specific brand.

Topping even thickness in the yogurt desirability sweepstakes, though, was smoothness. Although a few tasters did not mind lumps, most of the panel downgraded yogurts that were not perfectly smooth. Even worse were a few smooth yogurts with a grainy or chalky quality. Better a few lumps than grittiness.

Flavor proved to be a less complicated issue for our tasters, and there was greater agreement. Tasters liked some acidity but downgraded a few brands that were bitter or overly tart. A happy medium between bland and tart carried the day. A nice milk flavor was valued as well.

Stick with the Supermarket

The tasting results make it clear that a special trip to the health foods store to pick up yogurt is not necessary. Low-fat yogurts from Dannon and Colombo took first and third place. Alta Dena nonfat yogurt, which is available in some supermarkets (mainly on the West Coast) and health foods stores across the country, was a strong second. Horizon nonfat yogurt, another smaller brand found in health foods stores, finished fourth.

A few final thoughts about natural food yogurts. Unlike so many items, they are priced about the same as their supermarket counterparts, and all but one are actually cheaper than Dannon. Also, if you are interested in buying an organic product, the Horizon and Stonyfield products are worth seeking out. ∎

RATING PLAIN YOGURT

Thirteen commercial yogurts were tasted blind at Byblos, a Lebanese restaurant in New York, and are listed in order of preference based on scores awarded by our judges. The yogurts were mixed just prior to the tasting to incorporate any separated liquid or cream at the top of the containers. The yogurts were sampled with plastic spoons, since metal affects flavor perceptions in acidic foods. Manufacturing locations are listed in each entry as well as prices paid in supermarkets or health foods stores in New York. Unless otherwise noted, the prices pertain to thirty-two-ounce containers.

In addition to the author, the panel included three *Cook's Illustrated* editors (Pam Anderson, Mark Bittman, and Stephanie Lyness); Geraldine Ackert, dairy buyer for Dean & DeLuca; Dalia Carmel, Middle Eastern food expert; food writer Cara De Silva; Sabeh Kachouh, owner of Byblos restaurant; and Julie Sahni, cookbook author and Indian food expert.

RECOMMENDED YOGURTS

These yogurts elicited positive or mixed comments from tasters.

 Colombo Lowfat Plain Yogurt (Minneapolis), $2.49. The "lumpy," "almost curdled" texture of this yogurt was a turnoff for some tasters, but most liked the "mild, milky" flavor, which reminded several panelists of cottage cheese. Several tasters wrote that this entry reminded them of "real" or "authentic" yogurt.

 Horizon Organic Plain Nonfat Yogurt (Boulder, Colorado), $1.99 for twenty-four-ounce container. The texture of this yogurt was deemed "very creamy" and "very smooth," if not "the smoothest." Panelists found the flavor to be "mild but nice" and "not very acidic." As one taster summed up, "could use a little more edge, but quite enjoyable."

 Stonyfield Farm Organic Plain Yogurt (Londonderry, New Hampshire), $2.69. "Very thin," "lumpy" texture divided the panel as did "yellowish" color and "fatty" mouth feel. This whole milk yogurt comes with a cream layer on top, which is responsible for the unusual hue and texture. "Cheesy," "strong dairy flavor" was deemed "distinctive" by most tasters although a few naysayers were put off by the "intense sourness."

 Colombo Fat-Free Plain Yogurt (Minneapolis), $2.49. Tasters all noticed the thick texture. Some liked the "nice mouth feel," but others felt that it was "unnaturally stiff." Panelists picked up on a "decent acid kick" while some thought that this yogurt was "inoffensive but not great."

 Stonyfield Farm Organic Lowfat Plain Yogurt (Londonderry, New Hampshire), $2.89. As with the whole milk product, this Stonyfield yogurt was deemed "quite thin" and "a tad lumpy." However, most tasters liked the flavor, which was described as "sweet but not bland," "close to sour cream," and "strong dairy with cheesy bite." Note that this product has half the fat of other low-fat yogurts.

Brown Cow Farm Plain Yogurt (Newfield, New York), $2.79. The texture of this whole milk yogurt was judged to be "thin" and "almost runny."

As for flavor, some tasters thought there was "too much fat" and that this yogurt "was like eating dessert." The yogurt had a "nutty" or "smoky, aged in wood" quality that some liked and others deemed "horrible." Interesting, but how much of this could you eat?

 Stonyfield Farm Nonfat Plain Yogurt (Londonderry, New Hampshire), $2.69. "Thin, lumpy, chalky" texture was a real drawback for most tasters although the flavor was deemed good to acceptable, with comments like "delicate," "slightly tangy," and "OK but not exceptional."

 Erivan Acidophilus Yogurt (Oreland, Pennsylvania), $1.80 for sixteen-ounce container. This whole milk yogurt had a "thin, lumpy" texture that sparked little controversy. The flavor was another matter. A few panelists liked the "sour," "acidic," "complex" nature of this yogurt that "tasted like lemons," but others were overwhelmed by the "god-awful sourness." As one taster summed up, "a very mature yogurt."

YOGURTS NOT RECOMMENDED

These yogurts earned negative comments from most tasters.

 Dannon Fat Free Plain Nonfat Yogurt (Minster, Ohio), $3.09. "Thick," "puddinglike" texture was deemed unacceptable by most tasters. Several loud complaints about "grittiness" and an "unpleasant gelatinous quality." Panelists were underwhelmed by the "dull" flavor, which was described as "inoffensive," "generic," and "bland."

 Brown Cow Farm Plain Nonfat Yogurt (Newfield, New York), $2.79. "Thick," "almost like Jell-O" texture was a turnoff for most tasters, but "bland and boring" flavor was deemed a more serious flaw. Panelists wanted more punch from this "nothing special" yogurt.

 Brown Cow Farm Plain Lowfat Yogurt (Newfield, New York), $2.79. This "thin, smooth" yogurt, as one taster noted, "pours like crème anglaise." As another wrote, "it's so watery you could drink it." Panelists thought this "porridge-like" yogurt tasted "watered down," "wimpy," and "flat."

Spring-Valve Pressure Cookers Top Testing

Their new design makes these cookers more precise cooking utensils than the classic jiggle-top models; bottom construction and steam-release features are also important.

BY LISË STERN

Although pressure cookers have been marketed for home cooking in the United States since before World War II, the recent arrival of second-generation spring-valve designs from European makers has revived enthusiasm for this timesaving kitchen tool.

To see how much better the new pressure cookers are, I tested fourteen cookers, produced by nine manufacturers from the United States, France, Spain, Italy, and Switzerland. The result: The new, spring-valve designs are so much easier to use and so much more precise that they could take over a majority of stovetop cooking chores in many homes. Older designs and cruder cookers can still make many timesaving dishes, but the hassles add up—and become obvious with comparative testing.

How Pressure Cookers Work

At sea level, air pressure is 14.7 pounds per square inch (psi), and water boils at 212 degrees Fahrenheit. When you heat water in a sealed container, the steam from the boiling water collects and the pressure begins to rise. The temperature at which the water boils likewise rises.

Pressure cookers take advantage of this phenomenon by forming a sealed environment (the seal is made when a rubber gasket is locked between the lid and the base) in which the temperature of boiling water can be raised. For the average cooker, high pressure is fifteen pounds psi higher than normal, and the boiling point is 250 degrees. Because food cooks at a hotter temperature, it cooks significantly faster—usually in a third the time of conventional methods.

There are basically three designs for pressure cookers. The first generation of home pressure cookers used a weight balanced loosely on top of a pipe vent to maintain pressure, and this is still the dominant design in the United States. As pressure inside the cooker builds, steam pushes up the weight, and the pressure regulator begins to move. When the pot is fully pressurized, the weight begins to jiggle and emit bursts of steam—hence cookers of this design are known as "jiggle tops." Each machine has its own characteristic sound, but it's always hard to know exactly when it is fully pressurized, when it is over-pressurized, and when it has dropped below pressure. This design also typically requires

more adjustments to keep a steady pressure over low heat.

The spring-valve design, introduced by Kuhn Rikon in Switzerland in 1949 but only available in the United States since 1990, uses a precision spring inside the valve to set pressure, which is indicated by a pin or rod. As the pressure builds, the rod rises. Marks on the rod indicate the pressure that is being reached. Little steam is released, and these cookers are much quieter than those with weight valves. They also need less cooking liquid and fewer heat adjustments.

There is also a third design, a new version of the weight-valve model, with what I think of as a disguised jiggle top; one manufacturer describes it as a "developed" jiggle top. These new machines are quieter than the metal shaking on metal of the earlier jiggle tops, but the sign that they are working is still aural: They hiss and release steam.

The Tests

Whatever the design, the key issue for successful pressure cooking is knowing exactly when the pot has reached full pressure so you can time the dish successfully. You then lower the flame to maintain pressure for the appropriate cooking time, ideally without too many adjustments along the way. Another aid to precise timing is a quick release at the end of cooking.

To test how well—and how conveniently—the various cookers performed their task, I devised a series of both formal and informal tests using all fourteen cookers. Informally, when I developed the recipes for the accompanying article on page 10, I tried each of them in several different cookers to see how they handled real recipes. Formally, I conducted four tests: browning flour; timing a run (going from no pressure to full pressure, then releasing the pressure) with a quart of tap water; cooking a custard; and cooking split peas.

First, I simply sprinkled an even layer of flour over the bottom of each pan and heated it over high heat with the lid off to determine how evenly each cooker heated food. Hot and cold spots might lead to burning or would make for less flavor in recipes with a sauté or browning step. Most of the stainless steel cookers with aluminum sandwich bases heated the flour evenly. The all-aluminum cookers—the Mirro, WearEver, and Presto Super Six—each had oddly shaped bot-

toms and heated the flour unevenly, as did the all-stainless Presto Stainless.

The next test was what I dubbed the "water test." I brought a quart of tap water to high pressure, reduced the heat to maintain high pressure for five minutes, then let the pressure release naturally, that is, without using cold water or a pressure release valve. I timed how long each cooker took to reach high pressure and how long it took for all the pressure to be released naturally.

The times ranged significantly, from six to almost ten minutes to come up to high pressure, and from around eight to fourteen minutes to release it. The Monix weight-valve model, which reaches only a pressure of six pounds, was an exception to the averages, coming up to its low pressure quite quickly and releasing it in only a bit more than five minutes. But a low pressure–only cooker is relatively slow and relatively useless. The T-Fal Clipso, which has an excellent quick-release feature, had an unusually slow natural release, about twenty-five minutes in our tests, which obviates any time advantage to pressure cooking with the many recipes that recommend a natural release, such as most bean and grain recipes.

As part of my water test, I measured to see how much water had evaporated during this process. Ideally, a pressure cooker should be perfectly sealed; the less steam released during cooking, the less fluid you need at the beginning of a given recipe, and the more the flavors become concentrated in stews and risottos. The spring-valve cookers released little steam while cooking, but some of the jiggle-top cookers, including the Monix Vitralia Press, and the T-Fal Safe 2, lost as much as one-quarter cup of liquid at this point. But surprisingly, one of the jiggle tops, the Presto Stainless, also got a top rating for retaining water.

I also timed how long it took each cooker to go back to high pressure and then did two quick releases. Quick releases, which are vital to recipes for foods like vegetables that can easily overcook, can be achieved by two methods. The old fashioned cold-water release means carrying a pot full of food to the kitchen sink, and spraying it with cold water to condense the steam. The valve on newer models that allows you to diffuse the steam pressure right on the stovetop is a tremendous feature—but not if it sprays scalding steam and has to be held down with a wooden spoon, as was the case with the Lagostina.

The final amount of water lost after all these water tests ranged from three-quarters cup to one and one-half cups. The highest ratings for overall reliability went to cookers that had lost less water throughout the tests.

I next tested cooking two items that can be a little tricky in pressure cookers, custard and split peas. None of the fourteen pots had any problem cooking the peas, but the way they cooked them and how long it took varied considerably. Some turned the peas to soup-perfect puree in as little as eight minutes.

Ultimately, I was also able to make a successful custard in every cooker, but all required minor adjustments, with none performing this task significantly more easily than others.

The Results

Once I had worked with the spring-valve models, the jiggle tops could not really compete. While some of the developed jiggle-top cookers are well made and have some attractive features, I actually found them more frustrating to use than the older jiggle tops because they are even harder to "read" for pressure. Although no one should throw away an old jiggle top—several are fine and produce pleasing results—the spring-valve models are much easier to work with. For many cooks, a spring-valve cooker will become an everyday appliance, while a jiggle-top model will only come off the shelf for special situations.

With that said, however, do not draw the conclusion that all spring-valve cookers are created equal. The Magefesa and the Kuhn Rikon are significantly superior for their ease of use and excellent design. During testing, both went to the top of the class for their easy and accurate pressure control at all three stages—low, high, and quick release. In cooking, I preferred the Kuhn Rikon's long handle, but it lost points for a quick release button you have to hold down for a long time. The Magefesa has a simple switch you flip once. The Kuhn Rikon also has a pressure-valve screw that can come loose, keeping it from attaining pressure at all. The Fagor Multirapid and the Monix Vitralia Press spring-valve model are still preferable to the jiggle tops, but the Fagor lid is the most difficult to open, and the Monix Vitralia Press's pressure valve is very confusing to read. ∎

RATING PRESSURE COOKERS

Four spring-valve, three "developed" weight-valve, and seven "jiggle-top" pressure cookers were evaluated based on the following characteristics. The cookers are organized according to valve type, then listed in order of preference within those categories. Among the criteria listed below, ease of use was the most important, followed by overall reliability.

Price: Suggested retail prices are listed. See Sources and Resources, page 32, for information on purchasing the top models.

Ease of Use: Of utmost importance in this category, it needed to be simple to determine when the desired pressure had been reached. High marks also went to cookers with lids that open and shut without difficulty.

Overall Reliability: Reliability was also evaluated on how well the cooker performed in further water tests and when cooking split peas, custard, and some of the recipes found on pages 10 and 11.

very good performance

average performance

poor performance

Quick-Release Option: Highest ratings went to pots with quick release buttons that felt safe and dispersed the steam well.

Flour Test: Two tablespoons of flour were sprinkled over the bottom of the cooker. The pot was then heated, lid off, over high heat until the flour began to brown. Cookers that produced even browning were rated highest.

Water Test: One quart of cool water was brought to high pressure and maintained at high pressure for five minutes. The pressure was then allowed to come down naturally and the water measured. Those that lost one tablespoon of water or less rated highest; losing two tablespoons rated average, and losing three or more rated lowest.

Manuals: Highest ratings went to cookers with clear instructions that included well-written recipes (sometimes in the form of an extra booklet). An asterisk (*) next to the rating in this column indicates that the company has particularly helpful toll-free customer service.

	MANUFACTURER	MODEL	PRICE	PRESSURE SETTINGS	EASE OF USE	OVERALL RELIABILITY	QUICK REALEASE	FLOUR TEST	WATER TEST	MANUALS
SPRING VALVE	MAGEFESA	Super Rápida	$99	8/10/12/16 lb.	very good	very good	very good	very good	very good	average*
	KUHN RIKON	Duromatic	$164	8/15 lb.	very good	average	average	very good	very good	very good*
	FAGOR	Multirapid	$110	11/14/18 lb.	average	average	average	very good	average	average*
	MONIX	Vitralia Press	$99.99	7/9/12 lb.	average	average	very good	poor	poor	average
DEVELOPED WEIGHT VALVE	SITRAM	Prima	$140	8.5/17 lb.	average	average	N/A	very good	very good	average
	FAGOR	Rapid Express	$90	11/16 lb.	average	average	N/A	very good	average	average*
	T-FAL	Clipso	$149	8/13 lb.	average	average	very good	very good	average	average
WEIGHT VALVE	NATIONAL-PRESTO	Presto Stainless	$69.99	15 lb.	poor	poor	N/A	poor	very good	very good
	NATIONAL-PRESTO	Presto Super Six	$50.99	15 lb.	poor	poor	N/A	poor	poor	very good
	T-FAL	Safe 2	$89	13 lb.	average	average	N/A	average	poor	poor
	MIRRO	6 Qt.	$49.99	5/10/15 lb.	average	poor	NA	poor	poor	poor
	WEAREVER	6 Qt.	$49.99	5/10/15 lb.	average	poor	NA	poor	poor	poor
	LAGOSTINA	Amica	$120	15 lb.	poor	poor	poor	poor	poor	poor
	MONIX	Monix	$79.99	6 lb.	poor	poor	N/A	average	poor	poor

SPRING VALVE

HIGHLY RECOMMENDED   **NOT RECOMMENDED**

Magefesa Super Rápida: Easiest cooker to use, with a quick-release valve that switches on or off. Documentation is weak, but customer service is very good. Best cooker and best buy.

Kuhn Rikon Duromatic: A close second in performance and the best documentation by far.

Fagor Multirapid: Allows you to preset pressure, an excellent feature. But the most difficult to open and loses a lot of water.

Monix Vitralia Press: Confusing pressure switch, loose handle that leaks steam, recipes only in Spanish.

DEVELOPED WEIGHT VALVE

Sitram Prima: Solid feel and function, but some problems coming up to pressure. Asymmetrical rubber gasket is a pain.

Fagor Rapid Express: Quiet, but loses steam during cooking. Hard to open and close.

T-Fal Clipso: The lid, which is easy to put on, is also very heavy and sometimes awkward to use.

TRADITIONAL WEIGHT VALVE

Presto Stainless: Easiest jiggle top to use, but uneven heating with the all-stainless base. Very good manual and recipes.

Presto Super Six aluminum: Actually an eight-quart cooker; the company found people like the larger size but are intimidated by the idea.

T-Fal Safe 2: Nonstick, but food sticking to pressure cookers is not a big problem.

Mirro: Heats unevenly, loses a lot of water during cooking, and both looks and feels cheap.

WearEver: Made by Mirro; same overall qualities and looks even cheaper.

Lagostina Amica: Awkward lid fell into the food more than once.

Monix: Awkward to use and much slower than the other cookers, as its one level of pressure is only six pounds. Difficult lid, too.

PHOTOGRAPHS BY DAVE HENDERSON

Pesto at Its Best

To balance the flavors, bruise the basil and blanch the garlic.

≈ BY ADAM RIED ≈

Most Italians agree that making pesto, the pounded basil sauce from Liguria, is instinctual cooking. The ingredients—basil, garlic, nuts, olive oil, and cheese—can be adjusted endlessly for individual tastes.

In my experience with pesto, the bright herbal fragrance of basil always hinted at more flavor than it ever really delivered. Also, though I love garlic, the raw article can have a sharp, acrid taste that bites through other flavors in a dish, as it does the basil in pesto. So my goals were there before me: If I could heighten the basil and subdue the garlic, I thought, I'd have a sauce with well-rounded flavors, each major element balancing the next. Special treatment of the nuts had not even entered my mind—yet.

I started my tests by using a mortar and pestle to make pesto. The advantage of this method was that it produced a silky paste with an unusually full basil flavor. The disadvantage was that it required plenty of time and effort; I pounded away for fifteen minutes to get the right texture. The blender and the food processor are more practical, contemporary tools for the job, and of the two, I preferred the food processor because it made a sauce with a much finer, more consistent texture. In the blender, the ingredients tended to bunch up beneath the blade, which prevented them from being chopped and mixed uniformly. Also, to keep the solids moving in the blender I had to add more oil than I care for in pesto. And last, I found it difficult to remove the finished sauce from the blender.

Now, back to the advantage of the mortar and pestle: the basil flavor. Because the basil was broken down totally, it released its full range of herbal and anise flavor notes in a way that the chopping action of the food processor alone did not accomplish. Attempting to approximate that flavor in the processor, I tried the separate tests of chopping, tearing, and bruising the leaves (packed into a zipper-lock bag) with a meat pounder before processing. Bruising them worked well, making for a mellow, full-tasting pesto.

Garlic is a star player in pesto, but often I think the star shines a little too brightly. Wondering how to cut the raw garlic edge, I tried roasting it, sautéing it, and even infusing its flavor into olive oil, but none of these methods were ideal. Blanching the whole garlic cloves in boiling water, an approach suggested by George Germon, chef-owner of Al Forno restaurant in Providence, Rhode Island, turned out to be the best solution for several reasons:

It's quick (you can use the pasta water before boiling the pasta), it loosens the papery skin for easy peeling, and it eliminates the raw garlic sting. Also, I found it worthwhile to mince the garlic before adding it to the food processor. Otherwise, the pieces never become fine enough in the finished sauce.

With the basil boosted and the garlic toned down, I began to experiment with the nuts. Most of the seventy recipes I studied called for either pine nuts or walnuts, with almonds making an occasional appearance as well. I was surprised, though, that none of the recipes mentioned toasting the nuts, a common technique that accentuates flavor by releasing the nuts' essential oils. So I went for it, and in every case my tasters favored the pestos made with the toasted nuts.

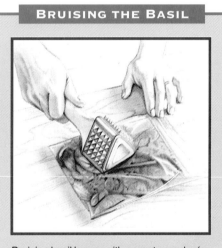

BRUISING THE BASIL

Bruising basil leaves with a meat pounder (or rolling pin) is a quick but effective substitute for hand-pounding with a mortar and pestle.

Each type of nut has its own characteristics in pesto. Almonds are relatively sweet, which works beautifully with the basil, but they are also hard, so they give the pesto a coarse, granular texture. Walnuts break down a little more, but they still remain distinctively meaty in flavor and texture. All but one of the tasters agreed that pine nuts were best. They become very creamy when processed, yielding pesto with a smooth, luxurious texture.

The cheese is equally important. Cheeses should be grated on the fine side of a box grater so they become powdery enough to blend smoothly with the other ingredients. All of my tasters agreed that a

mixture of both Parmesan and sharper pecorino Romano tasted better than either did alone.

Without exception, the Italian chefs who advised me about pesto stressed the same point: It must be thinned with some pasta cooking water before being tossed with the pasta. Thinning the pesto with two or three tablespoons of the pasta water allows good distribution throughout the pasta, softens the flavors, and highlights the creaminess of the cheese and nuts.

PESTO
Makes ¾ cup

Basil usually darkens in homemade pesto, but you can boost the green color a little by adding the optional parsley. For sharper flavor, substitute one tablespoon finely grated pecorino Romano cheese for one tablespoon of the Parmesan. This recipe, thinned with two or three tablespoons of pasta cooking water, is sufficient to dress a pound of pasta.

- ¼ cup pine nuts, toasted (or substitute almonds or walnuts)
- 3 medium garlic cloves, threaded on a skewer
- 2 cups packed fresh basil leaves, rinsed thoroughly
- 2 tablespoons fresh flat Italian parsley leaves (optional)
- 7 tablespoons extra-virgin olive oil
  Pinch salt
- ¼ cup finely grated Parmesan cheese

1. Toast nuts in small heavy skillet over medium heat, stirring frequently, until just golden and fragrant, 4 to 5 minutes.

2. Meanwhile, bring small saucepan of water to boil. Lower skewered garlic into water; boil until garlic is partially blanched, about 45 seconds. Immediately run cold water over garlic to stop the cooking. Remove from skewer; peel and mince.

3. Place basil and parsley in heavy-duty, quart-size, zipper-lock bag; pound with flat side of meat pounder until all leaves are bruised.

4. Place all ingredients except cheese(s) in bowl of food processor fitted with steel blade; process until smooth, stopping as necessary to scrape down bowl with flexible spatula.

5. Transfer mixture to small bowl, stir in cheese(s), adjust salt, and serve. (Can be covered with a sheet of plastic wrap placed directly over the surface or filmed with oil and refrigerated up to 5 days.) ■

A Sampling of German Rieslings

German wines are unfamiliar to most of us, but they can be great, with or without food. Our panel picks a few winners.

～ BY MARK BITTMAN ～

Germany is the world's most important producer of fruity white wines, and arguably the country producing more great wines than any other save France. Although many of these wines are well suited to American palates and American foods—the best have a beautiful balance of acid and fruit that makes them wonderful partners to spicy foods—most of us remain ignorant of them.

There are reasons for this: One is that there are around 2,500 individual vineyards in Germany, many of which are divided among different growers; this situation makes learning about German wines as challenging as learning about the wines of Burgundy. These German producers often make several wines from the same vineyard, and there is little blending. The best grapes are used to make one wine, those not so great go into another, and so on. As a result, there are well-known producers whose total production for a given wine is limited to several hundred bottles.

Another reason is that the German language is generally less familiar to us than French; understanding long, compound German nouns is made even more difficult by the changing but still common practice of printing labels with Gothic type, whose letters are sometimes nearly impossible to make out.

Most important, however, is the wine itself. The best German wines are made from the riesling grape, the world's best white wine grape after chardonnay. Riesling is fruity, elegant, and, handled with luck and skill, enormously complex. But it is undeniably different, and few Americans have been exposed to it. Furthermore, because Germany is the northernmost of the world's great wine-growing districts (it is actually on a parallel with Labrador), the grapes do not ripen as readily or completely as they do elsewhere. Thus, the wines are delicate and often subtle—some might say weak. At their best, they are a perfect balance of fruit and acid that is unmatched elsewhere. Short of that, these wines can be flabbily fruity or even sour.

As a result of their unusual character, German wines have developed a reputation as being non-food wines. And, indeed, they are wonderfully refreshing on a sunny afternoon; given their scant alcohol levels—often well under 10 percent, compared to 12 percent and more for most other wines—they could be considered ideal. But they are also fitting partners for some of the foods considered challenging to pair with wines, especially the highly seasoned foods of Asia and South America, as well as certain delicate dishes—pasta with light sauces, dishes made with eggs, lightly seasoned fish. (Almost all of these wines were sampled with Chinese food in a nonjudgmental atmosphere following our tasting; verbal reviews were enthusiastic.)

I have become increasingly fond of German wines in recent years, and wanted to assemble a tasting that would provide not only encouragement but guidance to readers of *Cook's Illustrated.* Naturally, this called for a number of judgment calls on my part, because there are literally dozens of categories of German rieslings. If I made the tasting too narrow, the recommendations would be too specific, but if I left it broad, the choices would be overwhelming.

In choosing to taste high-quality, reasonably priced Kabinett wines from more than one region, I believe I found a decent middle ground. Kabinetts are the lightest, least expensive, and most accessible of the highest-quality German wines, and those produced in the greatest quantity. Still, there are not millions of bottles of any of these; in fact, only four hundred cases of our winning wine will be sold in the United States this year, not a great amount by any standards. But eleven out of fourteen of the wines in our tasting were enjoyed enough by our tasters to end up in the Highly Recommended or Recommended categories, and given that many choices you should be able to find some in the best-stocked wine store in your area. ∎

BLIND TASTING RESULTS

As usual, the wines in our tasting were judged by a panel made up of both wine professionals and amateur wine lovers; in this case it should be noted that even our professionals are not highly experienced judges of German wines. In the judging, seven points were awarded for each first-place vote; six for second; five for third; and so on. Prices are national suggested retail and will vary. In general, Highly Recommended wines received few or no negative comments; Recommended wines had predominantly positive comments; and Not Recommended wines had few or no positive comments.

All of these wines are from the 1994 vintage.

HIGHLY RECOMMENDED

Joh. Jos. Prüm Estate (Mosel), $16. Not a single-estate wine, but a "solid, almost flawless" wine from a top producer; all tasters put it in their top six. A great starting place.

Dr. Loosen Erdener Treppchen (Mosel), $16. An "enticing, peachy" aroma gives way to a "beautifully balanced" wine.

Gunderloch "Jean Baptiste" (Rheinhessen), $14. "Pretty, balanced, and elegant."

Robert Eymael Mönchhof Ürziger Würzgarten (Mosel), $14. "Graceful," "intense" wine.

Dr. Heinz Wagner Nachf Ockfener Bockstein (Saar), $14. "Well-balanced riesling, start to finish."

RECOMMENDED

Joh. Haart Piesporter Goldtröpfchen (Mosel), $14. "Floral and rich."

Dr. F. Weins-Prüm Graacher Himmelreich (Mosel), $14. "Intense nose," "decent weight."

J. Wegeler Erben Oestricher Lenchen (Rheingau), $12. "Almost dry," "wonderfully balanced."

von Hovel Oberemmeler Hütte (Saar), $13. "A little flabby" but "mouthwatering."

Karthäuserhof Estate (Ruwer), $16. "Light" but "very well balanced."

J. Wegeler Erben Bernkasteler Graben (Mosel), $13. "A little acidic" but "nice intensity."

NOT RECOMMENDED

Baron zu Knyphausen Erbacher (Rheingau), $14.

R. Müller Piesporter Goldtröpfchen (Mosel), $12.50.

Schloss Vollrads Riesling (Rheingau), $16.50.

Fish and Shellfish
James Peterson
William Morrow, $40

Any work of art (and I include cookbooks in this category) must be judged by how well it accomplishes what it sets out to do. *Ace Ventura, Pet Detective,* a modest movie by any standards, fulfilled its rather limited goals by simply making the audience laugh, whereas *Godfather III* fell short of delivering on the towering vision of the original. Yet, while giving the former a good review and the latter mixed grades, one needs to be reminded that one aimed low and the other high.

In the same vein, James Peterson's *Fish and Shellfish* has taken the high road, promising to deliver "a monumental cookbook that will take its rightful place as the first and last word on seafood preparation and cooking." On its own terms, this tome falls considerably short, but it does deliver some fine performances along the way.

Peterson was trained in Paris and has also spent time in the Far East, which may account for the heavy French, Southeast Asian, and Indian influences that together result in an eclectic rather than an encyclopedic collection. The chapter on steaming, for instance, has one basic recipe, followed by Assorted Steamed Fish and Shellfish in Thai Spice-Scented Broth, Chinese Steamed Sea Bass with Scallions, Ginger, and Black Beans, and Vietnamese-Style Whole Steamed Striped Bass. These recipes redefine the notion of "hard-to-find ingredients" by calling for preserved black beans, Thai fish sauce, unsweetened coconut milk, lemongrass, and kaffir lime leaves. And this is in a basic technique chapter! Nor was this an exception. When looking through the mussel section, I noted that there were few approachable recipes for home cooks, since every one calls for some nonstandard ingredient such as fish stock, sorrel, or green curry paste.

Some of the recipes we tested were sublime. The Panfried Croaker Fillets with Porcini Dust and Chive Sauce, while it may not be a typical Tuesday night recipe, was excellent and took just forty-five minutes to make. The Linguine with Lobster Basil Sauce, the Italian-Style Steamed Mussels with Garlic and Tomatoes, the Braised Red Drum Fillets with Tomato Sauce, and the Indian-Style Baked Pompano with Yogurt and Spices all received high marks as well. The Venetian-Style Marinated Cooked Pompano Fillets were perhaps overly complex, but good.

On the other hand, some of the recipes were problematic at best. I made the Fillets of Sole Bercy, the first ingredient of which is "three pounds whole sole, fluke, or flounder, filleted, head and bones reserved." Maybe whole sole or flounder is readily available in Paris (as Peterson points out in his introduction), but stateside it's pretty tough to find. So most of us will be left with the option of purchasing fillets, which, of course, will be a complete mystery given that we aren't told how much to buy. And because I didn't have the heads and tails, I couldn't make the fish stock, which left me with white wine as a mediocre substitute; with the added lemon juice, the resulting sauce was too acidic. Furthermore, the basic preparation method calls for finishing the cooking in a 400-degree oven, allowing ten minutes per inch of thickness. I am no fish expert, but a flatfish fillet ain't thick (try an eighth of an inch or so), which means that the fish is cooked as soon as the oven door closes. Why oven-braise a flatfish fillet that is pretty much cooked already on top of the stove?

We also made the Roast Monkfish with Sage and Whole Garlic Cloves, which was a bit gluey due to a combination of heavy cream and the flour used for dredging, and the Sautéed Crab Cakes, which were too watery and used enough cayenne pepper to overwhelm the delicate lump crabmeat.

Fish and Shellfish does have its shining moments. The step-by-step photographs are comprehensive, there is plenty of information about fish and shellfish to make this a good reference book for the food hobbyist or professional food writer, and the recipes are interesting and occasionally excellent. Like some movie directors, however, Peterson views the world through an arcane lens that often leads him far afield from an audience becoming increasingly restless in the darkened theater. Flashes of brilliance are dimmed by a fundamental neglect of the tastes and lifestyles of his relatively "downscale" American audience, reminiscent of badly dubbed French art-house classics. You know that this guy is a serious director, but you have the uncomfortable feeling that you aren't supposed to make out the words.

—*Christopher Kimball*

BRIEFLY NOTED
Savoring Herbs and Spices
Julie Sahni
William Morrow, $25

While it is hardly the first herb-and-spice cookbook to be published, this may be the only one many home cooks ever need. Most of the recipes are quick and easy, and they are chosen to illustrate how to use both common and uncommon herbs and spices while avoiding overseasoning.

In dishes such as an East African–inspired Fish Fillet Braised in Vanilla Sauce, Sahni uses subdetectable amounts of seasonings to enhance foods. When she does use a powerful dose of spice, as in her Tomato-Cumin Rice or Lemon Saffron Sauce, she does so to bring out an unusual aspect of the flavor. The piney quality of cumin comes out particularly well in the rice, and by adding a little sugar to the yogurt-based saffron sauce, the author brings up the flowery aroma of saffron while muting its bitter taste.

In short, Sahni takes simple techniques and dishes from Asia, Europe, and Latin America without vulgarizing them, nor does there seem to be anything forced or exotic on her table. The only minor flaw in this book is an overemphasis on herb-and-spice mixtures, apparently in coordination with an effort to market Sahni's signature blends.

—*Mark Zanger*

Nicole Routhier's Fruit Cookbook
Nicole Routhier
Workman, $15.95

Dietitians revere fruit for its vitamins, minerals, and fiber; foodies love it for its flavors, scents, and colors. From either perspective, eating more fruit is a good idea.

In Nicole Routhier's new book, she provides a multitude of interesting recipes that will spur you to do just that. An accomplished food writer and chef with both imagination and common sense, Routhier weds all types of fruit with everyday ingredients and cooking techniques from many cultures. The writing is a bit flowery for my taste, but her impressive breadth of recipes is clearly geared for home cooking. Each one of the dozen dishes I tried was simple to prepare and delicious, and several, the Roasted Pork Chops in Grape Sauce and Watercress Soup with Asian Pears among them, were downright inspirational. With appealing flavor combinations like these, Routhier uses her fine palate to elevate fruit far beyond its usual role as dessert or side dish. That should please the nutritionists and gastronomes alike. ■

—*Adam Ried*

SOURCES
AND RESOURCES

Most of the ingredients and materials necessary for the recipes in this issue are available at your local supermarket, gourmet store, or kitchen supply shop. The following are mail-order sources for particular items. Prices listed below were current at press time and do not include shipping or handling unless otherwise indicated. We suggest that you contact companies directly to confirm up-to-date prices and availability.

PRESSURE COOKERS
After testing fifteen pressure cookers for the article on page 28, we consistently preferred the models with the quiet, reliable performance of the new spring-valve type, as opposed to the traditional jiggling weight valves. Among the cookers equipped with spring valves, two proved clearly superior to the rest of the pack. Our first choice was the Magefesa Rapid II Pressure Cooker (also known by its Spanish name, Super Rapida, as it is manufactured in Spain). Made of heavy-gauge 18/10 stainless steel and featuring a particularly well designed quick-release button for easy depressurization, the Rapid II is available by mail order only, through Magefesa USA (P.O. Box 328, Prospect Heights, IL, 60070; 800-923-8700). The cooker comes in four-, six-, and eight-liter sizes, all of which sell for the same price of $99. Our second winner was the Swiss-made Kuhn-Rikon Duromatic, which is available in two-, four-, five-, and seven-liter sizes through the Gold Mine Natural Food Company catalog (3419 Hancock Street, San Diego, CA 92110; 800-475-3663). We tested the seven-liter size, which sells for $159.95. The five-liter cooker sells for $149.95 and the four-liter model for $139.95, as does the two-liter pressure frying pan.

KITCHEN GADGETS
We experimented with a formidable array of gadgets to arrive at the few illustrated on pages 16 and 17. Though our collection was amassed from a number of different stores and catalogs, one impressively stocked shop called Kitchen Arts (161 Newbury Street, Boston, MA 02116; 617-266-8701), near our Boston-area offices, can provide one-stop shopping, in person or by mail order, for all the gadgets. The wooden oven rack adjuster, complete with magnet so it can be kept at the ready on the oven door, sells for $4.95; the E-Z-Rol garlic peeler costs $7.95; the Italian-made hand-operated olive pitter costs $6.25; the nutmeg grater by Zyliss costs $14.50; the Heartwatch Gourmet Fat Skimmer costs $10.95; the Multi Corer for use on tomatoes and strawberries costs $3.25; the Magi-Cake strips cost $5.95; the double boiler stand costs $3.95; and the manually operated Mouli food mill costs $24.95. Kitchen Arts accepts phone orders from any U.S. or Canadian location, though there is a $5 handling fee, above the normal shipping costs, to ship to Canada.

CHINESE SKIMMER
Since it was designed to retrieve deep-fried foods from hot oil in a wok, it is no surprise that we found a brass wire–mesh Chinese skimmer to be the perfect implement for scooping the french fries out of their hot cooking oil in our story on page 12. Available for $5 from A Cook's Wares catalog (211 37th Street, Beaver Falls, PA 15010; 412-846-9490), the skimmer is fitted with an eleven-inch bamboo handle that will not conduct heat, so it stays comfortable to hold. The long handle also keeps your hand far away from the hot oil, which drains efficiently from the five-inch open-mesh bowl.

CANDY/JELLY/DEEP-FRY THERMOMETER
Frying in oil that is at the proper heat is crucial to making french fries (from the story on page 12) the best they can be. In all deep-fat frying, food added to oil that is too cool will absorb the oil rather than form a crisp outer seal that prevents the fat from permeating the food. The only tool suitable for monitoring such high oil temperatures in a cooking pot—325 degrees for the par-fry and 350 degrees for the second fry, in the case of our french fries—is a candy/jelly/deep-fry thermometer. As the name indicates, the same thermometer can also be used to measure the temperature of sugar syrup for candy and jelly making. A Cook's Wares catalog (412-846-9490) sells such thermometers, which register temperatures as high as 400 degrees and feature stainless steel bodies, insulated handles, adjustable pot clips, and both Fahrenheit and Celsius scales, for $13.60.

GRILLING RACK
From asparagus to zucchini, a standard grill grate accommodates most of the vegetables in the "Great Grilled Vegetables" article on page 8. Onion rings, though, proved a little tricky because they tended to fall through the grate openings into the coals. An excellent solution for grilling onion rings and smaller vegetables like mushrooms and cherry tomatoes is to arrange them on a metal rack with a tightly spaced grid and put the rack on the grill grate. For $39.95, The Wooden Spoon catalog (P.O. Box 931, Clinton, CT 06413; 800-431-2207) sells a cast-iron grilling rack, measuring roughly eleven inches by seventeen inches, that can be placed directly on the grate. The rack has handles so it is easy to lift, and the metal bars are spaced closely to keep the vegetables and other small foods, such as shrimp, in place. Remember that cast iron retains heat especially well, so use oven mitts when you lift the rack off the grill.

BAMBOO SKEWERS
Slender Asian bamboo skewers have a number of uses in cooking. You can keep small vegetables from falling through grill grates into the fire by threading them, kebab style, onto a skewer. These skewers also work well for holding garlic cloves to be blanched (see Quick Tips, page 4). In addition, the skewers—especially the long ones—make fine cake testers because you can reach the cake without removing it from the oven (which reduces the chances of the cake deflating) and crumbs stick readily to the bamboo, whereas they usually slip right off metal cake testers. The Oriental Pantry (423 Great Road, Acton, MA 01720; 800-828-0368) carries bamboo skewers in three lengths. Sold in packages of one hundred, the six-inch skewers cost $1.19 per package, eight-inch skewers cost $1.39, and ten-inch skewers cost $1.59.

HOT PEPPERS
The heat provided by chile peppers is a crucial flavor component in almost all salsas. Several of the salsa recipes on page 21 feature chipotle peppers, which are dried, smoked jalapeños. Chipotles are available either in dried form or packed in adobo sauce (a mixture of garlic, herbs, and vinegar) in cans. For salsa, we prefer the canned version. Among an impressive array of authentic international ingredients, the CMC Company (P.O. Box 322, Avalon, NJ 08202; 800-CMC-2780) carries Mexican brand Herdez chipotles en adobo in seven-ounce cans for $3.50. Besides the chipotles, CMC also sells canned serranos for $2 per seven-ounce can, jalapeños for $4.25 per eleven-ounce can, and habañeros for $6 per twelve-ounce can.

GERMAN WINE INFORMATION
Whether you are searching for some of the wines recommended in our article "A Sampling of German Rieslings" on page 30 or just want to pick up your education about German wines where we left off by obtaining some detailed consumer information, the German Wine Information Bureau (79 Madison Avenue, New York, NY 10016; 212-213-7028) can help. The bureau can provide not only volumes of written material about German wines, but also a list of major retailers and importers who can help you track down sources in your area for specific wines. ∎

**GRILLED ITALIAN VEGETABLES
WITH THYME AND GARLIC**
page 8

RECIPE INDEX

CLASSIC FRENCH FRIES
page 13

CHOCOLATE MOUSSE
page 7

MAHOGANY GRILLED CHICKEN page 23
WITH AVOCADO-CORN SALSA page 21

PEACH-CHERRY COBBLER
page 19

SCALLOP CEVICHE WITH SWEET PEPPER CONFETTI
page 15

Poached Plum and Raspberry Compote in Sweet Wine Syrup

Bring 1 cup sweet dessert wine, ¼ cup water, ⅓ cup sugar, ½ split vanilla bean, 4 thin slices peeled fresh gingerroot, ½ cinnamon stick, and two 2-inch strips lemon zest to simmer in large saucepan. Simmer to dissolve sugar and reduce poaching liquid slightly, about 3 minutes. Add 1 pound purple or red plums, quartered; cover and continue to simmer, turning plums once or twice, until tender, about 5 minutes longer. Remove from heat and carefully stir in ½ pint fresh raspberries; let stand to allow flavors to blend, about 20 minutes longer. Remove vanilla bean, zest, and cinnamon stick. Spoon warm or cool compote into bowls or goblets. Top with lightly sweetened yogurt or sour cream or vanilla ice cream.

Serves 4

NUMBER TWENTY-TWO

OCTOBER 1996

COOK'S
ILLUSTRATED

How to Roast a Cheap Cut of Beef
Low Oven Temperature Wins Taste Test

Mastering the Chocolate Soufflé
For Intense Flavor, Use No Milk

Rediscovering Meat Loaf
Use Beef, Pork, Veal, and Filler

Rating Kitchen Timers
Forget Dial Timers; Electronic Models Win Big

EXTRA-VIRGIN OLIVE OIL TASTING

STOVETOP RICE PUDDING

AUTHENTIC BAKED BEANS

RATING RED JUG WINES

PIE CRUST TESTING

$4.00 U.S./$4.95 CANADA

Table of Contents

SEPTEMBER/OCTOBER 1996   NUMBER TWENTY-TWO

"Mixed Potatoes"

See page 2 for information about Yukon Gold potatoes.
ILLUSTRATION BY
BRENT WATKINSON

"Arugula Salad with Grilled Figs and Roasted Pepper Vinaigrette," adapted from *Lettuce in Your Kitchen* (Morrow, 1996) by Chris Schlesinger and John Willoughby

ILLUSTRATION BY
VINCENT McINDOE

COOK'S
ILLUSTRATED

Publisher and Editor	CHRISTOPHER KIMBALL
Executive Editor	MARK ZANGER
Senior Editor	JOHN WILLOUGHBY
Food Editor	PAM ANDERSON
Senior Writer	JACK BISHOP
Consulting Editors	MARK BITTMAN STEPHANIE LYNESS
Assistant Editor	ADAM RIED
Editorial Assistant	ELIZABETH CAMERON
Test Cooks	MELISSA HAMILTON EVA KATZ

Art Director	ANNE MURDOCK
Food Stylist	MARIE PIRAINO
Special Projects Designer	AMY KLEE

Managing Editor	KEITH POWERS
Editorial Prod. Manager	SHEILA DATZ
Copy Editor	GARY PFITZER

Marketing Director	ADRIENNE KIMBALL
Circulation Director	CAROLYN ADAMS
Fulfillment Manager	JAMIE AYER
Circulation Coordinator	JONATHAN VENIER
Production Director	JAMES MCCORMACK
Advertising Prod. Manager	PAMELA SLATTERY
Systems Administrator	MICAH BENSON
Production Artist	KEVIN MOELLER

Vice President	JEFFREY FEINGOLD
Controller	LISA A. CARULLO
Accounting Assistant	MANDY SHITO
Office Manager	TONYA ESTEY
Special Projects	FERN BERMAN

Cook's Illustrated (ISSN 1068-2821) is published bimonthly by Boston Common Press Limited Partnership, 17 Station Street, P.O. Box 569, Brookline, MA 02147-0569. Copyright 1996 Boston Common Press Limited Partnership. Periodical postage paid at Boston, MA, and additional mailing offices, USPS #012487. For list rental information, please contact List Services Corporation, 6 Trowbridge Drive, P.O. Box 516, Bethel, CT 06801; (203) 743-2600, FAX (203) 743-0589. Editorial office: 17 Station Street, P.O. Box 569, Brookline, MA 02147-0569; (617) 232-1000, FAX (617) 232-1572. Editorial contributions should be sent to: Editor, Cook's Illustrated. We cannot assume responsibility for manuscripts submitted to us. Submissions will be returned only if accompanied by a large self-addressed stamped envelope. Subscription rates: $24.95 for one year; $45 for two years; $65 for three years. (Canada: add $3 per year; all other countries: add $12 per year.) Postmaster: Send all new orders, subscription inquiries, and change of address notices to Cook's Illustrated, P.O. Box 7444, Red Oak, IA 51591-0444. Single copies: $4 in U.S., $4.95 in Canada and other countries. Back issues available for $5 each. PRINTED IN THE U.S.A.

EDITORIAL

JUST ONE MOMENT

CHRISTOPHER KIMBALL

I recently received a call from a Vermont neighbor, Jean, who said, "The fourth squirrel is in the freezer. See you Saturday night." For months, I had seen her hunkered down by the chicken coop at the side of the road with a .22 rifle loosely held across her lap. When queried about her objective, she admitted to a keen interest in squirrel hunting, but after she had bagged three fat specimens, the local population had been sufficiently decimated for it to take three months to bag the fourth and final quarry. As I soon found out, all of this small game hunting was in preparation for making the classic American dish, Brunswick stew, comprised of fresh lima beans, corn, tomatoes, onions, toasted bread crumbs, and, of course, squirrel.

Besides bagging the required number of squirrels (one per person), Jean had to skin them. She found directions in the *Joy of Cooking*, which instructed her to cut through the tailbone, make cuts in the back, turn the squirrel over, and while stepping on the base of the tail, pull on the hind legs until the skin came free. All of this took some time. Being thrifty and keenly devoted to living off the land, however, this was perfectly natural for Jean.

When Saturday night arrived, my wife Adrienne and I walked down our driveway past our lower field, where we often pick wildflowers. We headed across the dirt road past a few grazing sheep and then up the hilly path to Jean's home, a white clapboard farmhouse perched on top of a steep embankment.

Inside, the house was still, with the simplicity of a true Vermont home. The dining room has a wide-plank wooden floor painted gray and partially covered with a braided rug made by Jean's mother Dorothy. There are no curtains; the windows open onto a vast field of alfalfa framed by mountains. The table was simply set with a small glass dish of bread-and-butter pickles, ironstone china, an antique caster, and two beeswax candles. Just before dinner was served, there was a brief moment of silence. It captured the essence of one Vermont cook, a blueprint for frugality and plain living defined by the food, the room, the view—as if all the details of her daily life had been perfectly arranged in one posed snapshot.

The stew, incidentally, was excellent; squirrel is mild and lean, reminiscent of dark turkey meat. After a second helping, a simple salad of spinach and wild leek, and a thick slice of coconut cake, it occurred to me that few of us are blessed with such a moment, when everything we stand for as individuals comes together in a confluence of place and time. It is no wonder that great cooks are consistent in outlook and deeply devoted to their culinary views. Whether it is simple country cooking or the finest white tablecloth fare, the best of us have our moment, an instant in time when a picture of our lives emerges clearly, fully developed for all to see.

As in the kitchen, when all the small details and all the decisions we make when preparing food finally add up to a whole meal, I sometimes wonder if the same isn't true about a life well lived. If we are true to ourselves, the moment finally comes when we emerge clearly from the consuming back-and-forth of just getting by.

Once in a great while, these moments also happen to nations. Many of us remember the train carrying the Kennedy family to Washington, D.C., after the assassination of the president. We were all touched by the thousands of mourners who stood quietly by the side of the tracks. Their devout stillness, their waiting in the cold to bear witness to his life and a shared hope for our country, was such a moment, in some ways as moving as the indelible image of John and Caroline at their father's funeral.

But most of all I remember such a moment from Harper Lee's book *To Kill a Mockingbird*, when Atticus Finch, whose client was a hardworking black man accused of raping a local white girl, had just heard the guilty verdict given by an all-white jury. At that moment, the spectators in the balcony rose in silence to honor a man who had risked everything—including the lives of his children—to defend a neighbor who could find no other champion. As Atticus walked down the center aisle of the courtroom toward home, Reverend Sykes took hold of Atticus's daughter Scout and whispered, "Miss Jean Louise, stand up. Your father's passin'."

As a grown woman, Scout recalled that moment as the instant when her father's life came into focus, when all the difficult day-to-day decisions added up to a man who transcended the tired old town of Maycomb one hot summer. As cooks, as parents, as friends, it is comforting to remember that the details matter, that it all can add up to something after all. The thought of a neighbor taking your child in hand and saying "Stand up, your father's passin' " may be more than we can hope for, but it is no more than we should expect of ourselves. ■

Notes from Readers

YUKON GOLD POTATOES

I have seen references in Cook's Illustrated *to Yukon Gold potatoes. I live in New Orleans and have only seen them here once. Is there a season for Yukon Golds? Can I order some to be shipped to my home?*

ANNE GRACE
New Orleans, LA

Yukon Gold potatoes have flesh and skin that range in color from light tan to deep yellow and eyes with a distinctive pink hue. The National Potato Promotion Board currently classifies Yukon Golds as a specialty, or novelty, potato because they are still relatively new to the U.S. market. Originally from Scandanavia, Yukon Golds have become popular here only over the past five years. At this point, they are grown in smaller quantity than varieties more established in the U.S. market, such as Russets, Long Whites, Round Whites, and Round Reds. The harvesting season for most mature potatoes, including Yukon Golds, is the fall, and in this country they are grown primarily in Maine, Michigan, Minnesota, Colorado, northern California, Oregon, and Washington.

Generally, potatoes are classified according to their texture, which is determined by starch content. On the high end of the starch spectrum are the Russet varieties, which have a floury or mealy texture that suits them for baking. On the low end of the starch spectrum are waxy potatoes, including the Round Red varieties, which are great for boiling or in potato salads. Yukon Golds fall between the two, with a medium starch content and texture that makes them especially good for mashing.

From September through May, you can mail-order organically grown Yukon Golds, not to mention many other potato varieties, from New Penny Farm (P.O. Box 448, Presque Isle, ME 04769; 800-827-7551). New Penny mails potatoes in five-pound bags for $19.50 plus $2 for shipping, ten-pound bags for $24.50 plus $3 for shipping, and twenty-pound bags for $34.50 plus $5 for shipping. The shipping rates apply to addresses west of the Mississippi and change slightly with the seasons. There is no extra shipping cost for addresses east of the Mississippi.

BLISTERING PEPPER SKINS QUICKLY

In your May/June 1996 article "How to Roast a Bell Pepper," you neglected to try what I have found to be the very best way to roast a pepper: with a propane blowtorch.

I purchased a small, handheld, propane blowtorch to brown the sugar topping on my Crème Brûlée, à la Julia. This torch is absolutely perfect for charring the pepper skin as well. I skewer the pepper on a chef fork, and I can char the pepper in about two minutes. An additional advantage is that I can char the crevices without excessively burning the adjacent flesh.

ROBERT N. SCHWARTZ
Williamsville, NY

We have run tests using a blowtorch to char the skin on a pepper. As you point out, speed is the merit of the blowtorch method, but there are also disadvantages. Chief among them is flavor. The intense heat of the torch will blister the skin on the pepper before the flesh beneath can cook enough to caramelize the sugars to provide the sweet, fully roasted flavor we're after. The flesh of torch-roasted peppers was a little too crunchy for our tastes in addition to the flavor being underdeveloped. The second problem is control. Because the heat is so intense, you have to keep the torch moving rapidly and constantly over the pepper to char the skin and cook the flesh evenly. We found it much too easy to undercook some portions of the pepper while overcooking others if, for instance, we inadvertently slowed down while changing the pepper's position. In several cases, the flame burnt a hole right through the flesh before we knew it. Convenience is the last issue. Although we agree that a blowtorch is great for crème brûlée, we realize that most of our readers do not own one, which is why we recommend the oven method.

COOKWARE REACTIVITY

In various past articles your magazine has cautioned readers on the use of reactive pans in the deglazing and cooking process. Could you expand on this subject to include types of reactive pans and how they might react with food in terms of taste, color, and texture?

STU HOFFMAN
Camarillo, CA

In a discussion of pots and pans, "reactivity" refers to the potential chemical interaction between foods and the metals of the pans they are cooked in. Among the most reactive metals are aluminum, iron, and copper. When a recipe specifies a nonreactive pan for cooking or deglazing, the message is to steer clear of these materials.

According to University of Illinois Associate Professor of Food Chemistry Dr. Susan Brewer,

the foods most likely to react with these metals are highly acidic ones such as rhubarb, tomatoes, wine, vinegar, or lemon juice. Aluminum also reacts with highly alkaline foods such as corn, dried beans, and egg whites, as well as hard water. Though the texture of foods that contain these ingredients is unlikely to be affected by reactions with the metal, both taste and color can change.

With aluminum, this occurs because the high acid or alkali concentrations in these foods penetrate the naturally-occurring thin oxide layer on the surface of the metal. Minute traces of metal molecules then loosen and leech into the food. These molecules can impart a metallic, "off" flavor to the food. The metal molecules also exchange electrons and ions with the color pigments in many foods, especially vegetables, causing the foods to discolor. While this discoloration may not be appealing visually, it does not make the food dangerous to consume. These same reactions also leave the aluminum vulnerable to discoloration and corrosion. To prevent this, some aluminum cookware is anodized. Anodization is an electrochemical process that changes the molecular structure of the aluminum, making it denser, harder, and less porous. The decrease in porousness essentially seals the surface of the aluminum, rendering it not only less reactive, but also stick- and scratch-resistant.

Similar reactions can take place when acidic and alkaline foods are cooked in iron pans. Iron has a particularly distinctive, unpleasant taste, and so can change the taste of foods even more rapidly and noticeably than aluminum. Iron also causes foods that are high in unsaturated fat to oxidize faster than they would otherwise, so that the flavor of any leftover fatty foods cooked in iron will deteriorate markedly within twelve to twenty-four hours.

Copper is the most sensitive of all the reactive metals. It will react not only with substances in food, but also with those in the air. Both oxygen and sulfur can affect copper's oxide layer, forming a green coating that can be harmful to humans when ingested, since we can only excrete copper in limited amounts. For this reason, the interiors of copper pots and pans are covered with a very thin layer of another metal, often tin. The tin is nonreactive, but it is also soft and fragile. Tin linings must never be scrubbed forcefully or heated excessively, and even when treated with care they will wear down after a few years of use. This creates problems, since food should never, ever come into contact with unlined copper. An added disadvantage is the expense of tin-lined copper cookware.

Stainless steel, on the other hand, is nonreactive and safe to use with all types of food. Unfortunately, stainless steel is also a poor heat conductor, so pans made from it are often quite thin, which can lead to hot spots and uneven heating of the food. Our favorite choice for nonreactive pots and pans are those that are made from a combination of metals, with a stainless steel cooking surface bonded to an aluminum core for excellent heat conduction. Though somewhat less durable, enameled cast iron is also a fine nonreactive choice.

USING A FOOD PROCESSOR TO KNEAD DOUGH

Thank you for the article on American bread (May/June 1996). With all the fuss about crusty European loaves, this excellent bread is too often ignored. With regard to your food processor method, I would point out that most processors come with plastic blades specifically designed for kneading dough. The blade is shorter than the metal blade and lets the dough swing about more readily. If you use the steel blade and attempt to make a double recipe you could, as I have, end up with the blade jammed on the stem. The plastic blade does knead the dough and does not jam.

TERENCE JANERICCO
Boston, MA

Many food processors, including our KitchenAid, come with a stubby plastic blade that is about one-half inch shorter than the metal blade, designed specifically for mixing and kneading yeast doughs. According to Dan Sheehan, Food Processors Product Manager at KitchenAid, the quantity of flour in the recipe should determine which blade you use. KitchenAid recommends that you use the metal blade for recipes with two cups of flour or less, either the metal or the plastic blade for mixing two to three cups of flour, and the plastic blade for recipes with more than three cups of flour.

The reasoning behind this recommendation is fairly straightforward. In the smaller recipes, the longer metal blade will do a better job of moving the dough around in the bowl because it reaches under the entire dough mass. With larger batches of dough, however, there is a risk that the sharp metal blade will rip the gluten strands created by the flour as the dough is kneaded. Using the plastic blade minimizes this risk because it is meant to mix rather than to cut, and thus its edges are not sharpened.

We tested both the plastic and metal blades by making full recipes (three and one-half cups of flour) of the American Loaf Bread (May/June 1996) and the Basic Bread (from the charter issue of *Cook's Illustrated*) and our results were surprising. Overall, we found the difference in the performance of the two blades to be fairly subtle, and much less apparent in the basic bread than in its moister, fattier cousin, the American bread made with milk, butter, and honey. The plastic blade incorporated the liquid

and dry ingredients into dough in thirty seconds, which was twenty seconds faster than the metal blade, and it also moved the dough around in the work bowl a bit more efficiently. This dough had the familiar qualities of being firm and smooth, but when it was baked, the resulting bread had a slightly gummier texture than did its metal blade–mixed counterpart. The dough mixed with the metal blade was wetter and more like batter but surprisingly, we slightly preferred both the texture and flavor of this baked loaf to the other.

We also examined how each blade affected dough temperature. The action of the food processor motor, as well as the friction between the blade and the dough, can cause the blades to heat up slightly. Since metal retains heat better than plastic, we thought perhaps that yeast, which begins to lose viability at around 125 degrees, might be adversely affected in the dough processed with the metal blade. Not so. Because of the brief processing time of less than a minute, we found that the metal blade heats the dough only fifteen degrees more than the plastic blade. The temperature of the dough processed with the metal blade was 112 degrees, where as the dough processed with the plastic blade was 97 degrees. In neither case was the dough temperature high enough to kill yeast cells or inhibit rise.

ON HAND KNEADING

I've made almost all the bread eaten by this household for more than twenty years, so I was very interested in the article on no-knead American bread in the May/June 1996 issue. You may be right about the superior taste and texture of machine-kneaded bread, but I want to put in a word for the therapeutic value of hand kneading. When I make a batch of bread, I bring with me the accumulated irritations and vexations of the entire week. "Take that!" I mutter, dumping the dough onto the board, thinking about that nitwit administrator who refuses to see the forest through the trees. "You jerk!" as I ram my hands into the imagined face of a brain-dead colleague

who doubled the length of that meeting yesterday. As I turn and press the warm, smooth mass under my hands, all those negative feelings are being transmuted into something good; by the time I'm done, I'm almost always at peace with my world again. It's good exercise, too—for hands, arms, shoulders, back and so on. I'll take all that for a slight decrease in quality.*

DAVID EVETT
Cleveland Heights, OH

STEADYING YOUR WORK SURFACE

I have an idea for anyone who has a favorite board (wooden, plastic, or glass) upon which they knead bread dough, and which they constantly have to steady to prevent it from sliding. Simply scatter a handful of rubber bands, of any size or shape, on the counter and lay the board down on them. Bang it, jar it, hit it (kneading is such a tension release) as much as you like; it won't move.

LISA GRANT
Providence, RI

Your idea is a great one, and not just for kneading. We use this method to steady the board when we do a lot of chopping. If you do not have rubber bands handy, a dampened kitchen or paper towel underneath the board will stabilize it as well.

ERRATA

In the article entitled "Mix-and-Match Fruit Cobblers" in the July/August 1996 issue, the quantities of several ingredients in the Batter Fruit Cobbler recipe were printed incorrectly. The actual amounts should be: ¾ cup of flour, ¾ cup plus one tablespoon of sugar, and ¾ cup of milk. Accordingly, step two of the directions should instruct to whisk the flour, baking powder and salt with ¾ cup of sugar. We apologize for any confusion, or failed batter fruit cobblers, this mix-up may have caused. ∎

WHAT IS IT?

I bought this gadget at an antique market but use it only for a dinner table guessing game. I tried to trace it through the patent office, but the number had been rubbed off partially from use. The word "England," however, is still readable. Can you identify it for me?

CLAIRE ACKERMAN
Chevy Chase, MD

You've got an olive pick, designed specifically for reaching to the bottom of long, nar-

row jars to retrieve the last olives. With your index and middle finger on either side of the shaft, use your thumb to depress the plunger (like a syringe). This will open the pincers, allowing you to grab the olives. Also called automatic forks, the sturdy metal type that you have is difficult to come by these days. More often you will find plastic versions of this device, manufactured in the Far East, that use four thin, retractable wires as the pincers. Kitchen Arts (161 Newbury Street, Boston, MA 02116; 617-266-8701) sells a plastic Olive and Pickle Grabber for $1.95.

Quick Tips

STORING BACON

Now that many people eat bacon less often—or in smaller amounts—it can be difficult to use up a pound of bacon, once opened, before it goes rancid. To solve this dilemma, Janice Gross of Scottsdale, Arizona, rolls the bacon up in tight cylinders, with two to four slices of bacon in each. She then places them in a zipper-lock freezer bag and freezes them, easily pulling out the desired number of slices as needed.

CLEANING PUMPKINS AND WINTER SQUASHES

Daniel Katzen of Aptos, California, finds it difficult to remove the seeds and stringy fibers of pumpkins and winter squashes. A spoon can't easily sever the stringy mass, and a knife tends to poke the flesh. He has found that a hook-shaped French butter curler does a good job of scooping out the seeds as well as severing the fibers.

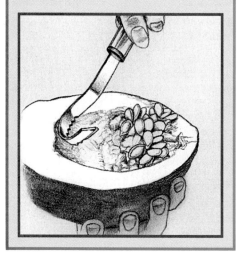

AVOIDING TONG CHAOS

Dottie Lewis of Sherman Oaks, California, has found that when she puts her spring-action tongs in the drawer where she keeps her other cooking tools, they often prevent it from opening and cause general chaos. She prevents this problem by storing the tongs in a heavy-duty cardboard tube from plastic wrap.

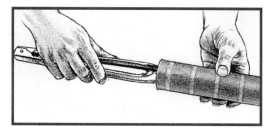

KEEPING FOOD PROCESSOR LIDS CLEAN

Food processors are real time-savers in the kitchen, but cleaning them can be quite annoying. Carol Banta of Cedar Grove, New Jersey, has come up with this method of keeping the food processor lid clean.

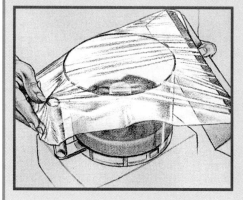

1. Before processing, cover the workbowl with plastic wrap or a thin plastic bag.

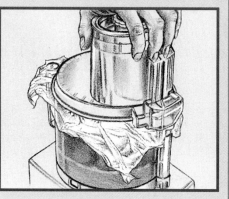

2. Fit the workbowl lid directly over the plastic. After processing, discard the splattered plastic.

KEEPING PANCAKES WARM

In our article entitled "Perfect Pancakes" in the January/February issue, we suggested keeping finished pancakes warm by folding them in a towel and placing them in a warm oven. To avoid firing up the oven, Marina Maroulis of Quebec, Canada, suggests keeping pancakes warm by covering them with an inverted colander.

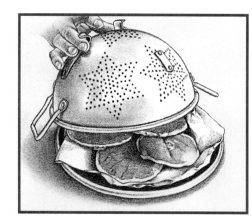

PEELING ONIONS

Terence Janericco of Boston, Massachusetts, finds that it is much easier to peel an onion in this fashion:

1. Halve the onion lengthwise.

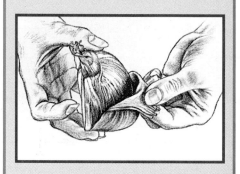

2. It is easy to get hold of the skin along the cut edge and peel it off each half.

ILLUSTRATIONS BY ALAN WITSCHONKE

FILLING PASTRY BAGS

Filling a pastry bag can be frustrating because you have to hold the bag open while simultaneously pouring or spooning in the food to be piped. Rosemary Leicht of Bethel, Ohio, has found a way to make the process easier.

1. Fit the pastry bag with the proper tip, then make a cuff at the top of the pastry bag. Then, set it in a Pilsner beer glass, folding the cuff of the bag over the top of the glass.

2. The glass is tall enough so you can fill the pastry bag most of the way. Now, with the bag supported by the weight of its own contents and still propped up by the beer glass, roll up the cuff and finish with any more filling that you need to add.

PEELING GINGER

Cook's Illustrated consulting editor Stephanie Lyness has found an easy and efficient way to peel ginger. She uses the bowl of a teaspoon to scrape off the knotty ginger skin.

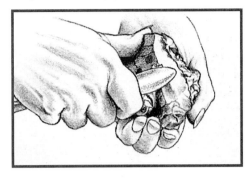

MEASURING LIQUID INGREDIENTS

Often several liquid ingredients need to be added to a recipe at the same time. Rather than measure each such ingredient separately, Susan Kato of Montebello, California, saves steps by using a single measuring cup and measuring each ingredient on top of the other.

DRYING GRATED POTATOES

When using grated potatoes for dishes like roesti or potato pancakes, you need to dry the grated potatoes before using them. To avoid the mess of wringing the potatoes dry in a dishcloth, Charles Robertson and Denise Rochat of Northampton, Massachusetts, have discovered the following technique:

1. Grate the potatoes to the desired thickness.

2. Place the grated potatoes in a salad spinner and spin them dry.

PEELING GARLIC

As an inexpensive stand-in for the cannoli-style garlic peeler we showed in our July/August issue (*see* "Useful Kitchen Gadgets"), Mary Hooten of Richmond, Virginia, uses an old-fashioned rubber jar opener.

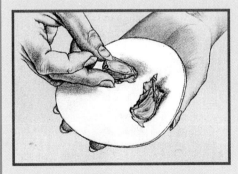

1. Place the garlic cloves in the center of the jar opener.

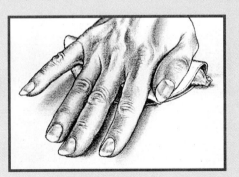

2. Roll the cloves around inside the soft, thin material.

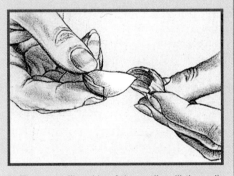

3. The paperlike skin of the garlic will then slip right off.

Thanks to our readers for Quick Tips: The editors of *Cook's Illustrated* would like to thank all of the readers who have sent us their quick tips. We have enjoyed reading every one of them, and have learned a lot. Keep them coming. We will provide a one-year complimentary subscription for each quick tip that we print. Send a description of your special technique to *Cook's Illustrated*, P.O. Box 569, Brookline Village, MA 02147-0569. Please write "Attention: Quick Tips" on the envelope and include your name, address, and daytime phone number. Unfortunately, we can only acknowledge receipt of tips that will be printed in the magazine. In case the same tip is received from two readers, the one postmarked first will be selected. Also, be sure to let us know what particular cooking problems you would like us to investigate in upcoming issues.

Macaroons Six Ways

We perfect almond macaroons and five flavorful variations.

~ BY STEPHEN SCHMIDT ~

These days, the only macaroons that you will find at most bakeries and supermarkets are made with coconut. Because almond macaroons (which, incidentally, are the original macaroon) are virtually unobtainable yet also very nice, I knew from the outset that they should be the focus of this article.

My standard recipe for almond macaroons is very traditional. To make the cookies, you simply grind almonds and sugar in a food processor, add egg whites and a little almond extract, and process until the mixture binds into a stiff but cohesive dough. Next you drop or pipe the paste onto a parchment-lined sheet and bake, and you should get perfect macaroons: moist and soft on the inside, crunchy-chewy on the outside—little nuggets of marzipan in a toasty crust.

I was very fond of this recipe but figured there was always a possibility for improvement. So I decided to try technique variations both old and new.

Seventeenth-century English and American bakers made macaroons with a third less sugar than we use today, and because contemporary taste seems to be running toward less sweet desserts, I decided to test out the old proportions. The resulting macaroons were surprisingly different from the usual modern kind, not only less sweet but also harder, drier, and crunchier, with a solid, heavy feel in the hand. Actually, I liked these cookies, but they were not macaroons as I know them.

I then tried a recipe based on commercial almond paste rather than almonds. I won't again. The cookies were gummy and lifeless, lacking both crunch and nuttiness. Another group of recipes that I will henceforth avoid are those that call for beating the egg whites and sugar into a meringue and then folding in ground almonds. These recipes promise soft and puffy macaroons but what I got, in three different tests, were sprawling, crumbly-crusted blobs with sticky goo in the center. To my mind, these cookies were kisses, not macaroons, and even as kisses I didn't like them the least bit.

I returned to my old standby recipe with renewed confidence, sure that there were no unknown tricks or variations that could give me a better macaroon. There was, however, an area where I had never had much luck over the years: the variations on almond macaroons. Because these variations had always sounded very good to me but never worked out very well, I was itching to try them again.

Sorting Out Flavor Variations

I began with a variation that simply adds another flavor to the almond, in this case, chocolate. My first few batches proved disappointingly pale and bland. Eventually, though, I realized that by simply adding a lot more cocoa, I could produce cookies with the black sheen and deep fudginess that I was after.

Next I moved on to the nut-flavored variations, substituting for the almonds first peanuts, then hazelnuts, then pistachios.

The peanut and hazelnut versions never did work out, but pistachio macaroons were a success. Even though making these cookies entails the skinning of nuts, they are so delicious—and so pretty, with their vivid green hue—that the task seems to me worthwhile. But I suggest making little macaroon "buttons" which require only a generous cupful of nuts. These make a lovely after-dinner nibble.

I also found that delicate new flavors could be added to my almond macaroons by simply rolling them sequentially in egg white and pine nuts or by making a drier almond paste, adding two tablespoons of grated lemon zest, and processing slightly longer.

As a final variation, I took on the coconut upstart that has become so popular. The instructions given in most nineteenth-century cookbooks for coconut macaroons suggest simply substituting coconut for almonds, and they couldn't possibly all be wrong. Or could they? I had tried this method innumerable times, and each time I ended up with coconut pancakes. I was quite sure that the problem was not the coconut: I had tried fresh, "sweetened, flaked," and desiccated. So what point was I missing?

One day, while grinding almonds in the food processor for another macaroon experiment, a thought occurred to me. I had always used shredded or grated coconut. But perhaps coconut, like almonds, needed to be ground for macaroons. Testing proved my hunch correct. When I ground the coconut, I got beautifully shaped, delicious macaroons. These old-fashioned coconut macaroons are lighter, softer, and generally more delicate than the usual modern kind, and they are also less sweet. I suspect that, like me, many people will actually prefer them.

ALMOND MACAROONS
Makes about 2 dozen 2-inch cookies
Macaroons must be baked on parchment paper. They will stick to an ungreased sheet and spread on a greased one. You need a slightly less stiff dough if piping the macaroons, so add water, as needed, to make a pipeable paste.

3 cups (12 ounces) blanched slivered almonds (measure without packing or shaking the cup)
1½ cups sugar
⅓ cup plus 1 tablespoon (3 large) egg whites
1 teaspoon almond extract

1. Set racks in upper-middle and lower-middle levels of oven and heat oven to 325 degrees. Line two large cookie sheets with parchment paper.

2. Turn almonds into food processor fitted with the metal chopping blade; process 1 minute. Add sugar; process 15 seconds longer. Add whites and extract; process until the paste wads around blade. Scrape sides and corners of workbowl with spatula; process until stiff but cohesive, malleable paste (similar in consistency to marzipan or pasta dough) forms, about 5 seconds longer. If mixture is crumbly or dry, turn machine back on and add water by drops through feeder tube until proper consistency is reached.

3. Allowing scant 2 tablespoons of paste for each macaroon, form a dozen cookies upon each paper-lined sheet, spacing the cookies 1½ inches apart. You can drop the paste from a spoon (*see illustration 1, left*) or for a neater look, roll it into 1-inch balls between your palms (illustration 2). (Rinse and dry your hands if they become too sticky.) To make fancy macaroons, pipe the paste using a large pastry bag fitted with a ¾-inch open star tip (illustrations 3 and 4).

4. Bake macaroons, switching cookie sheet positions midway through baking, until golden brown, 20 to 25 minutes. If overbaked, macaroons will dry out rather quickly when stored. Leave macaroons on papers until completely cooled or else they may tear. (Can be stored in an airtight container for at least 4 days or frozen up to 1 month.)

DELICATE COCONUT MACAROONS
Follow recipe for Almond Macaroons, substituting 14 ounces lightly packed sweetened flaked coconut for almonds and reducing almond extract to ½ teaspoon. After adding egg white and extract, process 1 full minute. The paste will now resemble slushy snow.

FUDGE-ALMOND MACAROONS
Follow recipe for Almond Macaroons, decreasing almonds to 1½ cups (6 ounces) and adding 1 cup Dutch-process cocoa and ¼ teaspoon salt along with the sugar. The macaroons are done when they have cracked lightly across top.

For Almond, Delicate Coconut, Fudge-Almond, and Lemon-Almond Macaroons

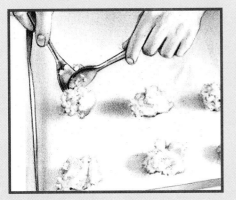

1. For a simple-shaped macaroon, drop a scant 2 tablespoons of paste for each macaroon onto a paper-lined sheet, spacing the cookies 1 ½ inches apart.

2. For a neater look, roll the dough into 1-inch balls between your palms.

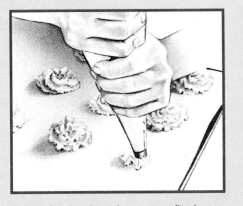

3. For a fancier-shaped macaroon, fit a heavy-duty pastry bag with a ³/₄-inch (No. 9) open star tip. Hold the pastry bag ½ inch above the baking sheet in a perpendicular position. Pipe.

4. When the base of the cookie is a little less than 2 inches across, raise the pastry bag slightly, still piping. When the macaroon is formed, twist the pastry bag slightly to disengage the tip from the cookie.

For Pine Nut–Crusted Almond Macaroons

5. Dip each ball into beaten egg white, then roll the balls in pine nuts, lightly pressing with your fingertips to adhere the nuts.

6. Transfer the nut-covered balls to the baking sheet and flatten them slightly with your fingers, making inch-wide buttons.

PINE NUT–CRUSTED ALMOND MACAROONS

Follow recipe for Almond Macaroons, rolling paste into balls between your palms. Dip each ball into beaten egg white, then roll in pine nuts, lightly pressing with fingertips (illustration 5). You will need 2 to 3 egg whites and 2½ to 3 cups (8 to 10 ounces) pine nuts altogether. Transfer cookies to baking sheet and flatten slightly with fingers, making inch-wide buttons (illustration 6).

LEMON-ALMOND MACAROONS

Follow recipe for Almond Macaroons, making the paste without water. Add 2 tablespoons grated lemon zest (2 large lemons) and process 10 seconds longer.

PISTACHIO MACAROON BUTTONS

Makes about 4 dozen cookies

The skinning of pistachios is a nuisance, but there is no point in bothering with this recipe unless it is done. Make sure to get pistachios that are raw or only lightly toasted. The flavor of these macaroons becomes more intense the day after baking.

- 1¼ cups (about 6 ounces) shelled pistachios
- ½ cup sugar
- 1 teaspoon grated zest from a small lemon
  Pinch salt
- 2 tablespoons (1 large) egg white

1. Boil pistachios hard in several quarts of water until skins begin to loosen, about 3 minutes. Drain nuts, then plunge into bowl of cold water; let stand in water until ready to peel. Remove skins, tossing skinned nuts onto paper towel–lined tray.

2. Thoroughly dry skinned pistachios on baking sheet set in center position in 200-degree oven, 45 minutes to 1 hour. Remove from oven before nuts begin to give off roasted aroma or take on any color. Increase heat to 325 degrees. Line cookie sheet with parchment paper.

3. Set aside forty-eight pistachios. Turn remainder into bowl of food processor, fitted with the metal chopping blade, and grind fine. Add sugar, zest, and salt and process 1 minute longer. Add egg white; process until dough wads into moist clumps.

4. Roll dough into 1-teaspoon balls and arrange 1 inch apart on baking sheet. Make dimple in center of each ball with moistened fingertip; press reserved pistachio into each little crater. Bake cookies until they look dry and have just begun to color, 10 to 12 minutes. Set baking sheet on rack; let macaroons cool completely before peeling them off parchment paper. (Can be stored in airtight container about 5 days.) ∎

Stephen Schmidt is a cooking teacher and the author of the forthcoming *Dessert America*.

Bruschetta: Italian Garlic Bread

The original version is toasted (not baked) and flavored with olive oil and raw garlic. Serve these crisp slices as is or with a variety of toppings.

～ BY JACK BISHOP ～

Authentic Italian garlic bread, called bruschetta, is never squishy or soft. Crisp toasted slices of country bread are rubbed with raw garlic, brushed with extra-virgin olive oil (never butter), and then slathered with various ingredients. Toppings can be as simple as salt and pepper or fresh herbs. Ripe tomatoes, grilled mushrooms, or sautéed onions make more substantial toppings.

Do not use narrow Italian bread for bruschetta. Crusty country loaves that will yield larger slices are preferable. Oblong loaves that measure about five inches across are best, but round loaves will work. As for thickness, about one inch provides enough heft to support weighty toppings and gives a good chew.

Toasting the bread, which can be done over a grill fire or under the broiler, creates little jagged edges that will pull off tiny bits of garlic when the raw clove is rubbed over the bread. For more garlic flavor, rub vigorously.

Oil can be drizzled over the garlicky toast or brushed on for more even coverage. One large piece of toast is enough for a single appetizer serving. Two or three slices will make a good lunch when accompanied by a salad.

BRUSCHETTA WITH TOMATOES AND BASIL
Makes 8 large slices

This is the classic bruschetta, although you can substitute other herbs. Decrease the quantity of stronger herbs, such as thyme or oregano.

- 4 medium ripe tomatoes (about 1 ⅔ pounds), cored and cut into ½-inch dice
- ⅓ cup shredded fresh basil leaves
  Salt and ground black pepper
- 1 12-by-5-inch loaf country bread, sliced crosswise into 1-inch-thick pieces, ends removed
- 1 large garlic clove, peeled
- 3 tablespoons extra-virgin olive oil

1. Heat broiler or light grill fire.
2. Mix tomatoes, basil, and salt and pepper to taste in medium bowl. Set aside.

3. Broil or grill bread until golden brown on both sides. Place toast slices on large platter, rub garlic over tops, then brush with oil.
4. Use slotted spoon to divide tomato mixture among toast slices. Serve immediately.

BRUSCHETTA WITH FRESH HERBS
Makes 8 large slices

- 5 tablespoons extra-virgin olive oil
- 1 ½ tablespoons minced fresh parsley
- 1 tablespoon minced fresh oregano or thyme leaves
- 1 tablespoon minced fresh sage leaves
  Salt and ground black pepper
- 1 12-by-5-inch loaf country bread, sliced crosswise into 1-inch-thick pieces, ends removed
- 1 large garlic clove, peeled

1. Heat broiler or light grill fire.
2. Mix oil, herbs, and salt and pepper to taste in small bowl. Set aside.
3. Broil or grill bread until golden brown on both sides. Place toast slices on large platter, rub garlic over tops, brush with herb oil, and serve immediately.

BRUSCHETTA WITH RED ONIONS, HERBS, AND PARMESAN
Makes 8 large slices

- 6 tablespoons extra-virgin olive oil
- 4 medium red onions (about 1 ½ pounds), halved lengthwise and sliced thin
- 4 teaspoons sugar
- 1½ tablespoons minced fresh mint leaves
- 2 tablespoons balsamic vinegar
  Salt and ground black pepper
- 1 12-by-5-inch loaf country bread, sliced crosswise into 1-inch-thick pieces, ends reserved
- 1 large garlic clove, peeled
- 3 tablespoons grated Parmesan cheese

1. Heat 3 ½ tablespoons of the oil in large skillet set over medium-high heat. Add onions and sugar; sauté, stirring often, until softened, 7 to 8 minutes. Reduce heat to medium-low. Continue to cook, stirring often, until onions are sweet and tender, 7 to 8 minutes longer. Stir in mint and vinegar and season to taste with salt and pepper. Set onion mixture aside. (Can be covered and refrigerated up to 1 week.)
2. Heat broiler. Place bread on large baking sheet; broil bread until golden brown on both sides.
3. Remove baking sheet from oven. Rub garlic over toast tops. Brush remaining 2 ½ tablespoons oil over bread. Divide onion mixture among slices, then sprinkle with cheese.
4. Broil until cheese just melts. Transfer bruschetta to large platter and serve immediately.

BRUSCHETTA WITH GRILLED PORTOBELLO MUSHROOMS
Makes 8 large slices

The mushrooms are grilled with the gill-like undersides facing up to prevent loss of juices. For serving, the mushrooms are flipped onto the bread so their juices seep down into the toast.

- 4 large portobello mushrooms (about 1⅓ pounds), stemmed
- 6 tablespoons extra-virgin olive oil
- 1 tablespoon minced fresh rosemary leaves
  Salt and ground black pepper
- 1 12-by-5-inch loaf country bread, sliced crosswise into 1-inch-thick pieces, ends removed
- 1 large garlic clove, peeled

1. Light grill. Place mushroom caps on large baking sheet. Mix 3½ tablespoons of the oil, rosemary, and salt and pepper to taste in small bowl. Brush oil mixture over both sides of mushrooms.
2. Grill mushrooms, gill side up over medium-hot fire, until caps are cooked through and grill-marked, 8 to 10 minutes.
3. Meanwhile, grill bread until golden brown on both sides. Place toast slices on large platter. Rub garlic over tops, then brush with remaining 2½ tablespoons oil.
4. Halve grilled mushrooms; place one half, gill side down, over each slice of toast. Serve immediately. ∎

PHOTOGRAPHS BY DAVE HENDERSON

How to Cook Cabbage

A quick braise-sauté creates cabbage that is tender-crisp and flavorful.

∾ BY JESSIKA BELLA MURA ∾

Cooked properly, cabbage is pliant and mildly sweet. It has an image problem because it turns mushy and smells bad when it is overcooked. I set out to find the best way to cook this surprisingly fickle vegetable, reasoning that quick cooking would minimize the unpleasant side effects.

Focusing on green cabbage, I chose to shred it for the quickest cooking and also to provide the greatest surface area for flavoring. I began with the fastest possible method, blanching. Plunging cabbage into boiling water for exactly one minute produced the desired crisp-tender texture and pleasant, mild flavor, but this technique also left the cabbage waterlogged.

To reduce the water involved, I considered microwaving. I sprinkled shredded cabbage with water and cooked it on high in a covered dish. After one minute, the cabbage was already limp, and by two minutes it was quite rubbery.

Steaming turned out to be a better solution to the problem of water uptake, but cooking times varied too much: four to six minutes with an electric steamer appliance; two to four minutes on the stovetop in a basket insert; less time for tender specimens, more time for fibrous heads. With steaming there is a thin line between delicious cabbage and the wan, flavorless, mealy kind.

I was not optimistic about the remaining options. I had heard that cabbage sautés terribly, and I went on to find truth in the rumor. Sautéed cabbage scorched before it could soften. In addition, cooking fat remained resolutely on the surface and contributed nothing to flavor other than an oily taste.

Testing the Braise-Sauté

Yet I was perplexed by the many cabbage recipes that refer to sautéing. Perhaps these cookbook authors, I reasoned, actually had a quick braise-sauté in mind. While braising usually refers to cooking slowly in a covered pan using a small quantity of fat or water-based liquid, I would describe a braise-sauté as a quicker process that employs the fat and the water-based liquid in combination. I hoped this gentle method would preserve texture while encouraging the development of more complex flavor.

I tried braising in cream, a strategy consistent with the notion of braise-sautéing because cream is basically an emulsion of butterfat and milk. Seven minutes later, I had found my ideal. For the first time, I could taste a subtle mix of flavors, complemented by a slight residual crunch. The cream also provided the perfect vehicle for both sweet and savory flavor variations. The only

problem is the inherent decadence of cream in an everyday cooking method.

But the quick braise-sauté also worked with every combination of four water-based liquids (white wine, chicken broth, apple juice, or tomato juice) and three common fats (butter, bacon fat, or vegetable oil). In each case the cabbage cooked in liquid alone tasted characterless while adding fat lent significant extra depth to the cabbage flavor and also improved its texture.

The quantity of fat required is less than a teaspoon per serving. You can obviously use more, but there is a lower limit, as I learned when I tried using dairy products that were lower in fat than cream. Light cream worked almost as well as heavy cream, but it started to scorch toward the end of cooking. Half-and-half and milk showed a greater affinity for the bottom of the pan than for the cabbage, and the cabbage cooked with them was porous with an insipid taste. Buttermilk and sour cream were wildly unsuccessful.

Contrary to the common advice to buy a tight, heavy head of cabbage, I had better success with smaller, looser heads that were covered with thin outer leaves.

To get the right texture and flavor, cabbage should be braise-sautéed in a combination of fat and liquid.

BRAISED CABBAGE WITH PARSLEY AND THYME
Serves 3

This dish is delicate and simple. For additional richness, increase the butter.

- 1 tablespoon butter
- 1 tablespoon chicken broth, canned or homemade
- 1 pound green cabbage (½ medium head), cut into ¼-inch shreds (about 4 cups)
- ¼ teaspoon crushed thyme
- 1 tablespoon minced fresh parsley leaves
  Salt and ground pepper, preferably white

Heat butter in large skillet over medium heat. Add broth, then cabbage and thyme. Bring to simmer; cover and continue to simmer, stirring occasion-

ally, until cabbage is wilted but still bright green, 7 to 9 minutes. Sprinkle with parsley and season to taste with salt and pepper.

CREAM-BRAISED CABBAGE WITH LEMON AND SHALLOTS
Serves 3 to 4

The French have been cooking cabbage in cream for ages. This is a variation on *chou croquant*, which means "crunchy cabbage."

- ¼ cup heavy cream
- 1 teaspoon juice from small lemon
- 1 small shallot, minced
- 1 pound green cabbage (½ medium head), cut into ¼-inch shreds (about 4 cups)
  Salt and ground black pepper

Heat cream, juice, and shallot in large skillet over medium heat. Add cabbage; toss to coat. Cover and simmer, stirring occasionally, until cabbage is wilted but still bright green, 7 to 9 minutes. Season to taste with salt and pepper. ■

Jessika Bella Mura is a freelance writer living in Malden, Massachusetts.

How to Roast a Cheap Cut of Beef

Contrary to accepted kitchen wisdom, the final internal temperature of the roast is only one factor in determining texture, taste, or juiciness. Choosing the proper cut and oven temperature are just as important.

BY CHRISTOPHER KIMBALL WITH EVA KATZ

Every August, my small town in Vermont holds an annual "ox roast," a covered dish supper that attracts everyone from mountain men to weekenders. The predinner entertainment is cloggers, who dance on plywood set up on two-by-fours. After dinner, the group assembles again to square-dance at the abandoned tennis court (lit by half a dozen table lamps duct-taped to the top of the posts so that we can see), where we "shuck the oyster" and "dig the clam."

The "ox" at that picnic is really a good-size heifer. The two steamship rounds (the back legs from the knee to the hip) are strapped to a homemade rotisserie, which is kept in working order by Russell Bain, our ninety-four-year-old expert metalworker. The fire is started the night before, attended by a half dozen locals stretched out on lawn chairs, drinking coffee, eating spice donuts, and trading gossip. The following morning at six o'clock, the meat is attached to the rotisserie using a length of sheep fencing and a few springs from an old metal bed. My job is to carve the rounds of beef. Over the years one thing has been consistent: Although the rest of the food is quite good, the meat is tough and dry.

I began to wonder what made this meat so tough. Was it just the animal? Was it the internal temperature of the meat? Was it the cooking method? With two dozen roasts and plenty of theories, we set out to find some answers.

The Secrets of Slow Roasting
First, we wanted to try the classic method of roasting beef. We cooked five separate bottom round roasts, each at a different oven temperature, ranging from 300 to 500 degrees. The results were disappointing, but we learned two things. First, the lowest oven temperature was best. The meat that was roasted at 500 degrees became dry, with most of the outer layers of the meat overcooked. The roast cooked at 300 degrees, however, was tenderer and juicier and had better internal flavor. Second, and most important, we found that the internal temperature of the meat does not necessarily determine the juiciness or texture of the roast. A roast cooked at 300 degrees until it reaches an internal temperature of 120 degrees is definitely tenderer and juicier than meat cooked to the same internal temperature in a 500-degree oven. In other words, it's not just where you are going but how you get there.

Why is this true? To fully understand what was happening inside the meat, we photographed four different roasts prepared at different temperatures—250, 350, 400, and 500 degrees. All were cooked to the same internal temperature—130 degrees—and allowed to sit for an additional ten minutes after they were removed from the oven. The roasts were then cut in half and photographed. When we compared the photographs, the answer was immediately apparent. The 500-degree roast was almost entirely overcooked. That is, the center was still red, but 70 percent of the remainder was gray and unappealing. By comparison, the roast cooked at 250 degrees was light red throughout, with only 10 percent of the outer layer gray and overcooked. The roasts cooked at the in-between oven temperatures varied between these two extremes. It's simply a matter of physics. Lower oven temperatures allow sufficient time for the even conduction of heat to the center of the roast from the outer layers. At higher oven temperatures, the outside and inside of the roast have a much larger temperature differential.

Testing Lower Oven Temperatures
Now that we knew that lower oven temperatures were best, we prepared five different bottom round roasts (we selected this cut because it is the worst of the cheap cuts in terms of texture and flavor) at oven temperatures ranging from 175 to 350 degrees. Once again, we encountered the same remarkable discovery as with the first round of tests. Although all the roasts were cooked to the same internal temperature, they were quite different in texture and juiciness. We found that 250 degrees was the ideal oven temperature, turning out a tender, juicy, and flavorful roast when cooked to an internal temperature of 130 degrees (*see* "Roasts Cooked at Constant Temperatures," below, for details). We repeated these tests using chuck roasts—with the same results.

In doing these tests, however, we found a problem with roasting at low temperatures: There is little flavor development on the exterior of the meat. To remedy this situation, we compared three new oven methods with the winner thus far, a constant 250 degrees.

In the first test, we roasted the meat at 350 degrees until it reached an internal temperature of 110 degrees, removed it from the oven for half an hour, then returned it to the oven and roasted it until it reached an internal temperature of 130

ROASTS COOKED AT CONSTANT TEMPERATURES

Bottom round roasts were browned on top of the stove in a Dutch oven and then transferred to a heated oven and roasted uncovered at five different oven temperatures until the internal temperature reached 130 degrees. Each roast weighed two pounds. These tests were repeated with chuck roasts with the same results.

OVEN TEMPERATURE	COOKING TIME	COMMENTS
175 degrees	2 hours, 10 minutes	Less flavorful than the other roasts. Slightly chewy; pale exterior. The next day, however, the interior had changed from deep red to a pale, pinkish gray. Very evenly cooked, however.
200 degrees	1 hour, 25 minutes	Juicy, tender, and evenly cooked. Better exterior color than the 175-degree roast.
250 degrees	1 hour	Wonderful flavor; very evenly cooked, tender, and juicy. A winner.
300 degrees	45 minutes	A bit tougher than the lower-temperature roasts. Good outside but uneven cooking inside. Outer crust layers were overcooked.
350 degrees	40 minutes	Exterior well browned. Very uneven cooking, although very good flavor.

Expensive cuts of beef, such as the tenderloin, can be roasted at very high heat with excellent results. Cheaper cuts, however, are best when roasted at low oven temperatures. I had heard various recommendations for cheap cuts and wondered which among them was actually the very best for slow roasting.

There is no lack of choices here. A side of beef has five sections, referred to in the trade as "primal" cuts. The more inexpensive boneless beef roasts come from one of three of these primal cuts: the chuck, the sirloin, or the round. The chuck is the area from the neck to the fifth rib of the side of beef; the round is the hind leg of the animal from the knee to the hip; and the sirloin is the section between the loin and round, in the hip area (*see* illustration, right). Generally speaking, the chuck is fattier and tenderer than any cut from the round, which

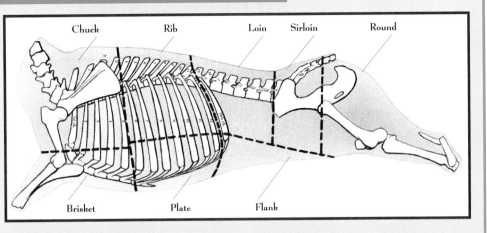

is lean and relatively tough. The sirloin falls in between the two.

We roasted ten different cuts: five from the chuck, two from the sirloin, and three from the

round. Although I tend to prefer juicier, fattier meat, the top round and the top sirloin were actually quite good. In general, however, the chuck provides more flavor and better texture than the round. —*C.K.*

CUTS FROM THE CHUCK

Blade Roast: This was clearly the best roast in the taste test—flavorful, juicy, and tender. However, it does contain connective tissues, which are unattractive, but not unpleasant to eat. The term "blade" refers to the shoulder blade, which is part of the chuck. A "blade roast" refers to the "top blade" muscle, which is similar to the muscle on your back over your shoulder blade.

Chuck-Eye Roast: This is a boneless rib roast that is cut from the center of the first five ribs (the term "eye" always refers to a center-cut piece of meat). The meat has good marbling throughout, which adds both flavor and moisture. This chuck is an extremely tender, juicy, and fatty piece of meat. It would have won first place in our tasting but was marked down for excessive fat content.

Chuck Fillet or Chuck Tender Roast: Made from the "mock tender" muscle located next to the top blade muscle, this cut is tougher, stringier, and less flavorful than chuck-eye. However, many super-markets mislabel this cut as chuck-eye. If the roast appears cone-shaped, it is probably the mock tender muscle and therefore an inferior chuck cut.

Shoulder Roast: Formerly referred to as an "arm roast" because it is the muscle at the top of the arm by the shoulder. It is chewy, the texture is grainy, and not the most flavorful chuck cut.

Under Blade Roast: This is the muscle underneath the shoulder blade. It is quite similar to a blade roast, with lots of connective tissue and lots of flavor.

CUTS FROM THE SIRLOIN

There are three important cuts for roasts from the sirloin: the top sirloin and the top and bottom rump roast, which are very similar.

CUTS FROM THE ROUND

Roasts from the round tend to be lean and relatively tough compared to chuck roasts. Generally speaking, they should be sliced very thin for serving. (We did not test the sirloin tip muscle, which is roughly equal to the top round in terms of flavor and texture.)

Top Round: Not quite as good as the top sirloin but had good flavor, texture, and juiciness.

Eye of the Round: Less juicy and flavorful than the roasts above.

Bottom Round: The least tender of all the cuts. Mediocre flavor as well.

Top Sirloin: Relatively juicy, flavorful, and tender. Good coloration on both the outside (dark brown) and inside (bright red). The clear winner among roasts from the sirloin or round.

Bottom Rump Roast: Juicy and with good flavor but not as tender as either the top sirloin or the top round roast. You can also purchase a top rump roast, which is slightly superior in flavor and texture.

degrees. (This technique worked well when roasting a loin of pork; *see* "Perfect Pork Roast," May/June 1995.) The results were terrible; the meat was very unevenly cooked, and a large portion was overcooked.

Next we tried roasting at 400 degrees for fifteen minutes, then reducing the heat to 200 degrees until the roast reached an internal temperature of 130 degrees. This method was not bad, resulting in a juicy roast with good texture and flavor inside. But the outer layers of meat were still overcooked.

Finally we tried roasting at 250 degrees until the meat reached an internal temperature of 110 degrees, then increasing the oven heat to 500 degrees and cooking another fifteen minutes or so until the roast reached 130 degrees internal temperature. This technique provided the best of both worlds—terrific flavor development on the exterior and an even, juicy, tender roast on the interior. The contrast of texture and taste between the inside and the outside was wonderful. (*See* "Roasts Cooked at Changing Oven Temperatures," page 21, for details.)

Finally we had found the best method. But we still wanted to go back and make sure that we were cooking the meat to the proper internal temperature. So we cooked five more bottom round roasts to different internal temperatures, starting at 120 degrees and ending at 160 degrees. We found that 130 degrees still delivered the most flavor, the best texture, and the most juice. At 120 degrees, the roast lacked flavor; at 140 degrees, it

was a bit chewy; and at 150 degrees internal temperature, it was dry, overcooked, and tough.

Chuck Wins Out

When we repeated these tests with chuck roasts, we did find some difference from the bottom round roasts. While the chuck was also best when cooked to 130 degrees, this fattier cut was acceptable cooked to somewhat higher internal temperatures because the fat kept it more flavorful and moist than a roast from the round. However, it could not go too much higher: The connective tissues, a common ingredient in a chuck roast, became tough and offensive at internal temperatures over 145 degrees. The lesson is that if you prefer your meat on the medium side or if you are concerned with the safety of eating meat that is rare or medium-rare, a roast from the chuck is a better choice than any cut from the round (*see* "The Best Cut for a Cheap Roast," page 19).

In fact, the chuck is on all counts the best cheap cut for slow roasting. In our tests, we found that, generally speaking, the chuck is more tender and flavorful than cuts from the lean and relatively tough round. The sirloin is a mixed bag; the bottom rump roast is not as good as the better round roasts, but the top sirloin and top rump roasts are indeed better than roasts from the round.

Why, then, is it so much easier to find a roast from the round than a chuck roast? Well, having spent some time with a local Boston butcher, we discovered that it is basically for the convenience of the butcher. Given the relatively complex con-

struction of the chuck, preparing a chuck roast is time-consuming. Butchers have to "seam out" the muscles (remove them intact, discarding bone and connective tissues) to create boneless roasts. But (and this is what most butchers do) they can more easily cut a cross section through the chuck to create steaks such as an arm or blade steak, or they can simply sell the chuck as stew or ground meat.

The round, on the other hand, has only one bone and relatively little connective tissue, so the meat is readily sliced off into roast-size cuts. The four muscles of the round—the top round, the bottom round, the sirloin tip, and the eye round—each correspond to the name of a roast. (In human terms, the sirloin tip is the front of the thigh, the top round is the inside, the bottom round is the outside, and the eye round is the back of the thigh. The top and bottom round were so named because butchers traditionally placed the round on a work surface with the inside of the thigh facing up; hence that portion of the thigh was the "top.") Also contributing to the relative abundance of round roasts in the supermarket is the fact that Americans claim a preference for leaner meats, and the round has much less fat than the chuck.

Other Factors: Covered Cooking, Resting Time, and Aging

Now that we had determined the best oven temperature, internal temperature, and type of roast, we decided to investigate some slightly less crucial elements involved in roasting beef, including whether to roast the meat in a covered container, how long to let it rest after cooking, and whether aging the beef would make a real difference.

Some cooks suggest cooking meat in a covered container. The theory is that in a relatively closed environment, moisture from the meat will be less likely to turn to steam and exit the meat. This idea is reminiscent of high school physics lessons: In a large, hot oven, the meat will lose a great deal of moisture in order to create equilibrium while in a smaller environment less water is likely to be released.

When we tested a covered roast, however, we found a slight loss in flavor caused by the fact that the outer crust did not brown sufficiently. Because we did not experience any significant improvement in juiciness or the texture of the interior of the roast when roasting covered, it seemed like a poor idea. These results confirmed our basic understanding of meat cookery, which is that the final temperature of the meat fibers and the quality of the cut, not the moisture content of the surrounding environment, are the determining factors in juiciness and texture.

We then wanted to determine the optimum amount of time a roast should sit after coming out of the oven. We let a roast sit for half an hour, testing it every five minutes until reaching the thirty-minute point. Twenty minutes—the amount of time suggested by most cooks—turned out, in fact, to be the proper waiting period. At that point, the roast was succulent, tender, and juicy, with more flavor than it had in previous tastings. Additional sitting time did not prove helpful to

THE SCIENCE OF ROASTING

Natural proteins, such as those found in beef, consist of many separate, coiled molecules. Bonds across the coils hold the protein together in a single unit. When the proteins are heated, however, some of these bonds break, causing the protein molecules to pop loose and unwind (this process is called denaturing). Almost immediately, these unwound proteins bump into each other and bond together. This process is the essence of cooking proteins. It is perhaps easiest to witness when you fry an egg and the white, which is translucent when raw, becomes opaque as it cooks. This change occurs because, while there is plenty of room for light to pass between the natural, bound protein molecules in the raw state, when these proteins become denatured in the heated state, they coagulate (join together) to create a dense, opaque structure.

The relevance of this process to the cooking of meat is that during cooking, these proteins also shrink. The way in which they shrink depends on how hot they are. Under 120 degrees, muscle proteins contract in diameter; over 120 degrees, these proteins start to shrink in length, expelling juices. Because more water is lost when the proteins shrink in length rather than diameter, meat tends to dry

out rapidly as it is heated above 120 degrees. The process is much like the wringing of a wet towel. The meat proteins get shorter and tighter, expelling more and more water. And because meat is 75 percent water, there is a dramatic change in texture and juiciness during the cooking process from raw all the way to well done. A roast can lose 30 percent to 40 percent of its weight by the time it reaches an internal temperature of 170 degrees, the point at which the meat is inedible and no additional liquid will be lost. (Cut into a piece of well-done meat, for example, and you'll notice that it will exude no juices.)

The good news, however, is that during cooking the connective tissues (collagen) in the meat start to turn soft and jellylike and act as a lubricant. So as the meat cooks, it is getting both tenderer and tougher at the same time. The trick is to find the point at which the tissue softening is maximized and the juice loss is minimized. The maximum benefit in terms of texture occurs when fatty beef, for example, is cooked to a final temperature of 130 to 140 degrees, the temperature at which the connective tissues start to gelatinize but relatively little juice has been squeezed from the meat.

the texture or flavor.

Next we tested the effect that a moderate amount of aging would have on the meat. Meat is aged to develop the flavor and improve the texture. This process depends upon certain enzymes whose function, while the animal is alive, is to digest proteins. After the animal is slaughtered, the cells that contain these enzymes start to break down, releasing the enzymes into the meat where they attack the cell proteins and break them down into amino acids, which have more flavor. In addition, the enzymes also start to break down the muscles, so the tissue becomes softer. This process can take from one to several weeks. (To age meat for more than a week, however, it must be done under carefully controlled conditions—it should not be done at home.)

To test aging meat at home, we placed a large eye round roast in the refrigerator, uncovered, on a rack above a pan. Each day we sliced off a piece, browned it for five minutes in two tablespoons of olive oil, and then roasted it in a 200-degree oven until the meat reached an internal temperature of 130 degrees. We found that the process does indeed have a tremendous effect on texture and flavor. In order to achieve this effect for the size of roast we were testing, though, the meat needed to sit for four days. After one day, the meat was flavorful and very juicy, but somewhat chewy. On the second day, it was slightly less chewy than the previous day, with the same amount of flavor. After three days, the meat was more tender, had better flavor, and was still juicy. On the fourth day, we hit the jackpot: The meat was still very juicy, extremely tender, and had a terrific, melt-in-your-mouth flavor. This was a winner. Aging the roast for more days did not seem to improve taste, texture, or juiciness.

So four days proved the optimum. Aging the meat for one or two days in the refrigerator, as most cookbooks advise you to do, is insufficient to develop flavor and texture fully. Although it obviously takes advance planning to age your meat for four days, this simple technique dramatically improves the flavor and texture of an inexpensive roast of beef.

SLOW-ROASTED BEEF WITH RED WINE PAN JUICES
Serves 6 to 8

If you have time, refrigerate the roast on a wire rack set over a paper towel–covered plate for four days. This aging process delivers a tender, more flavorful roast. Make sure, however, that before roasting you trim off the parts of the roast that have dehydrated and turned leathery. Tying the roast makes it compact and evenly shaped. Leftovers from a roasted cut of round, by the way, make excellent roast beef sandwiches.

1 boneless beef roast, 3 to 4 pounds (*see* "The Best Cut for a Cheap Roast," page 11), aged if possible (*see* note, above) and tied crosswise with twine every inch, then tied

---

To demonstrate the fundamental theory proposed by this article—that oven temperature is as important as the final internal temperature of the meat—we purchased two flank steaks and cut the first one into four 1-inch-wide pieces. One raw piece was removed and reserved, and the remaining pieces were then roasted at 250 degrees. We removed the strips from the oven at different internal temperatures starting at 120 degrees and increasing to 180 degrees. We then placed the cooked strips on a cutting board and compared them (left column in illustration, below). It was quite clear that the strip cooked to 180 degrees (top strip in left column) had shrunk (signifying a loss of juiciness and tenderness; *see* "The Science of Roasting," page 12) about 30 percent as compared to the raw strip. However, the strip cooked to 120 degrees had very modest shrinkage, about 10 percent. We repeated this test with the second flank steak (right column in illustration) but used a higher oven temperature, 375 degrees. The results were remarkable. Even the piece cooked to 120 degrees had shrunk a good 25 percent as compared to the raw piece. So lower oven temperatures will indeed cause meat to shrink less, even when it is cooked to the same internal temperature.—*C.K.*

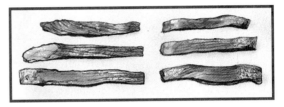

250 Degrees Versus 375 Degrees: When roasted at 250 degrees (left column), flank steak shrinks less than at 375 degrees (right column). However, regardless of oven temperature, meat shrinks more when roasted to an internal temperature of 180 degrees (top row) versus 120 degrees (bottom row–the middle row was roasted to 150 degrees).

---

lengthwise once or twice
Salt and ground black pepper
2 tablespoons olive oil
⅓ cup full-flavored red wine
1 cup low-sodium chicken or beef broth

1. Heat oven to 250 degrees. Sprinkle roast with salt and pepper as desired. Heat oil over medium-high heat in Dutch oven or large, heavy, ovenproof pot. Add roast; sear until brown, about 4 minutes each side.

2. Transfer pot to oven and cook, uncovered, until meat thermometer inserted into thickest part of roast registers 110 degrees, 45 minutes to 1 hour. Increase oven temperature to 500 degrees and cook until internal temperature reaches 130 degrees, about 15 minutes longer. (Cooking times will vary depending on size and shape of roast.) Remove roast from pot; let stand 20 minutes before carving.

3. Meanwhile, set pot over medium-high heat; spoon all but 1 tablespoon fat from pot. Add wine, stirring pan bottom with wooden spoon to loosen brown bits; simmer until wine reduces to glaze—about 2 minutes. Add broth; simmer until sauce reduces and thickens slightly, 1 to 2 minutes longer. (For pan juices with a little extra body, juices can be thickened at this point with 1 teaspoon cornstarch dissolved in 1 tablespoon water.) Cut roast into thin slices, adding meat juices to pan juices. Serve immediately with juices passed separately. ∎

ROASTS COOKED AT CHANGING OVEN TEMPERATURES

Bottom round roasts were browned on top of the stove in a Dutch oven and then transferred to a heated oven and roasted uncovered at changing oven temperatures until the internal temperature reached 130 degrees. Each roast weighed two pounds.

OVEN TEMPERATURE	COMMENTS
Constant 250 degrees	Evenly cooked, tender, and juicy. Exterior still lacking in flavor, however.
350 degrees until internal temperature reaches 110 degrees; remove from oven for 30 minutes; return to oven and cook until done.	Absolutely the worst method of all. Very uneven cooking. A large portion of roast overcooked by the time the internal temperature reached 130 degrees.
400 degrees for 15 minutes; reduce oven to 200 degrees until done.	Good texture and flavor inside and juicy. Outer layers of meat overcooked, however.
250 degrees until temperature reaches 110 degrees; increase oven to 500 degrees until done.	Excellent flavor, juicy, and tender. Wonderful contrast of texture and taste from outside to inside. A winner.

Boston Baked Beans

The best baked beans are meltingly soft but individually defined, with a rich sauce and true bean flavor.

∿ BY MARK ZANGER ∿

Boston baked beans have been known since the 1840s as slow-baked beans flavored with salt pork and molasses. The molasses, a by-product of Boston's sugar-refining industry, is the distinctly "Boston" part of the dish. Around one hundred years ago, the standard recipes became much sweeter and spicier as this farm village staple developed into a side dish and a popular canned convenience food.

I love Boston baked beans, but I don't love the oversweetened, mushy, chalky-tasting beans that come in cans. I wanted to develop a master recipe with old-fashioned flavor, and also to test several contending methods of cooking dried beans that have emerged in the last few years (*see* "Stop the Music?" page 15). As I made some of the traditional recipes for family and *Cook's Illustrated* staff, we agreed to try for beans that were meltingly soft inside, but with individually defined skins, in a rich sauce.

I was interested in saving time if it didn't compromise quality, but I quickly realized that there was no advantage for most readers in cutting the cooking time down from "overnight" to four or six hours. Even though baked beans are easily assembled and cook unattended in a slow oven, today's working families simply have no four- or six-hour brackets of at-home time, including weekends. I made my first fifteen pots of beans on weekends, then realized I could use an eight- to ten-hour recipe overnight or from breakfast to suppertime while I was at work. I made several attempts at a one-hour recipe using Goya canned small white beans, which have a reasonable texture, but even after a full hour of baking, the dishes tasted like I had just mixed up a sauce, poured it over the beans, and reheated. It takes time to bring together the flavors.

Keeping the structure of the individual beans looked to be a matter of soaking and cooking times, and I tried almost a dozen pots of beans with various methods and results before remembering the idea of using an acidic recipe. Many cookbooks say to never use acid ingredients with beans because the acid will prevent the beans from softening. In fact, some older recipes for baked beans from the days before preventive dentistry include baking soda (or its ancestor, saleratus) to soften the beans more completely.

Two scientific principles are involved here, both affecting only the bean skins. The structural carbohydrates of bean skins include intercellular glue called pectic substances. In bean cooking these pectic substances gradually change into water-soluble pectins, which dissolve, softening the bean skins. Acidity, from lemon juice or vinegar, inhibits the transformation of the pectic substances.

Because I was willing to bake the beans for eight hours, and because I wanted some residual structure, it was the acidity in vinegar, rather than the softening effect of baking soda, that proved helpful for this recipe. Acidity is used this way in certain European bean recipes that deliberately add vinegar, lemon juice, or tomato sauce to maintain the structure of lentils and black beans in slow-cooked stews.

I found that a little vinegar also added some tang and reinforced the sweetness, much as the acidity in wine increases the "fruit." As little as a teaspoon of vinegar preserved the structure of the beans, but a tablespoon added more flavor while two tablespoons proved too tangy.

Once I had the vinegar to solidify the bean skins, I had to work to get back to the creamy sauce. After a failed experiment using different sizes of beans, hoping that some would actually cook to mush and thus function as a sauce, I moved on to Plan B, which was to puree some of the beans before serving the dish. Following an old recipe that recommended removing the lid of the bean pot an hour before serving in order to brown the pork, I took that opportunity to scoop out and puree a half cup of beans. This tack was surprisingly unhelpful. But when, after fully cooking the beans, I again tried removing and pureeing some, the extra hour of cooking had made all the difference—now the fully cooked beans pureed into a rich sauce.

Much is made of the classic Boston or "Mesopotamian" round bean pot. In my tests of one-pound bean recipes, the efficient shape and narrow mouth of this casserole saved about one-half cup of water and rendered more fat and juices out of the meat than my other pots. Like an expensive brandy snifter, this classic pot is an enhancement but not a necessity.

I also own a Crock-Pot slow cooker and had high hopes for it as a more secure alternative to the unattended oven. But my Crock-Pot offers only two heat settings. With a full load of beans, the "low" setting never cooked the beans, and the "high" setting boiled them too vigorously.

In fact, a 200-degree oven (calibrated with a separate oven thermometer) is the least fussy tool to get the steady, slow cooking—just under a simmer—that produces the best-looking and -tasting beans, ones that never run dry or burn. The subsimmer cooks all kinds of beans, soaked or unsoaked, in the seven- to nine-hour period.

Testing the Individual Ingredients

The original beans for Boston beans were the dried white seeds of native American green beans. These beans are now sold in three sizes: small white beans (the smallest), navy (pea) beans, and Great Northern beans (the largest). Maine yellow eye beans, which are used in that state, are large and cook up relatively soft and floury. I found that all four made good baked beans and that mixtures of sizes were fun to eat.

Baked beans have not always been sickly sweet; this version lets real bean flavor come through.

PHOTOGRAPH BY DAVE HENDERSON

In the nineteenth century, salt pork was comparatively cheaper and leaner than it is today, and people ate the fat with relish. The meatiest pieces of salt pork I could pick out were very good, and the pork rind added some body to the sauce. But several nineteenth-century New England cookbooks mention corned beef as an alternative to salt pork, and I discovered that I actually preferred supermarket point-cut corned beef brisket to today's salt pork. (Flat-cut brisket and corned beef round were simply too lean; pork fatback had very little lean meat.) In my tests, corned beef added more juiciness and meat flavor to the pot of beans, and the cooked meat was easier to remove from the fat.

The earliest baked beans in Boston were not sweetened, and when cooks did eventually add a spoonful of molasses to them in the mid-nineteenth century, they still only had a hint of sweetness. When beans as sweet as our master recipe became popular at the turn of the century, there were family arguments about how sweet the baked beans should be, with some older relatives holding out against molasses.

With this in mind, I thought sweetening would make it difficult to pick a master recipe, but over a series of tastings, a clear preference emerged for moderately sweetened baked beans. When I slipped canned baked beans (which are much sweeter) into the tastings, they were always rejected as "too sweet." Some people still prefer barely sweetened beans. If this issue represents a division in your family, you can satisfy all parties with one bean pot, using less sweeteners. You can then add more sweetening to individual portions just before serving the baked beans because the sugars mostly stay in the sauce. None of my tasters could tell whether molasses had been cooked into the recipe all along or added just before the end of cooking.

This trick won't work for salt, which does work its way into the beans most pleasantly. Salting beans at the end just makes a salty sauce. The oldest recipes do not mention added salt, which is further evidence that they were using very meaty salt pork (meat holds more dissolved salt than fat). The adage that salt toughens the beans and slows down the cooking has been challenged by Russ Parsons of the *Los Angeles Times* (February 24, 1994). Our tests on various white beans agree with his tests of pinto and navy beans, and I went so far as to try soaking the beans in a heavy brine before cooking. Those beans cooked up quickly and well, but they were too salty.

At about the time that beans got sweeter, pepper gave way to mustard powder in printed recipes. Having tasted all the permutations, I believe that pepper is more complementary to beans, mustard to molasses. Thus the mustard came in as the beans got sweeter. Mustard powder is also a good emulsifier to help thicken the sauce.

Because my aim was to get a meaty flavor back into Boston baked beans, I'm not providing a vegetarian recipe here. In a pinch, however, one can use this master recipe, substituting two ounces of butter or canola oil and an onion stuck with one small clove for the salt pork.

It has long been known that beans are an especially musical fruit. Modern science has traced the problem to three complex sugars, or oligosaccharides, which make up 7 to 8 percent of the dry weight of beans. Unfortunately, most people cannot break down the oligosaccharides. They pass through to the colon where intestinal bacteria can ferment them, but with gassy results that vary from person to person.

Eating beans every day seems to diminish the effect, and in Mexico, where people eat beans daily, bean recipes usually start from dried beans and use none of the soaking or boiling routines developed in less bean-dependent cuisine.

New England Yankees liked to eat Boston baked beans once or twice a week and discovered that the beans were easier to digest if they were soaked overnight, with the soaking water discarded afterward, then heated in fresh water almost to boiling and held, as Fannie Farmer's 1896 *Boston Cooking-School Cook Book* stated, "until skins will burst—which is best determined by taking a few beans on the tip of a spoon and blowing on them, when skins will burst if sufficiently cooked." This somewhat confusing requirement, which measures the cracking of the bean skins when rapidly cooled by the breath, might have involved anywhere from half an hour (with ten minutes of simmering) to an hour for the oligosaccharides to dissolve in the water, which was again discarded.

Recent research by AkPharma Inc. (which produces Beano) indicates that soaking in cold water, even for twenty-four hours, removes less than 4 percent of the oligosaccharides.

But another study suggests that simmering removes up to 60 percent of these sugars.

However, the best method for no-gas beans was developed by the California Dry Bean Advisory Board in 1982. For each pound of beans, add ten or more cups of boiling water, boil for two to three minutes, cover the beans, and set them aside overnight. From 75 to 90 percent of the indigestible sugars dissolve into the soaking water overnight. Even a "quick soak" of as little as an hour after boiling will completely rehydrate the beans and remove a large fraction of the oligosaccharides.

The reason boiling is essential is that cold water soaking simply starts the process of germination. The living bean seed retains the stored sugars for future growth. Boiling "kills" the beans, so cell membranes break down and release the water-soluble oligosaccharides.

People who are especially sensitive to intestinal gas, including this author, find that it helps to supplement any bean recipe with a product such as Beano, which contains alpha-galactosidase, an enzyme that breaks up oligosaccharides for easier digestion. The enzyme is produced from *Aspergillus niger*, a safe mold organism. The only known side effects are allergic reactions among a few people with mold allergies, and the effects of the extra sugars on diabetics and galactosemics.

It must be added that most intestinal gas derives from swallowed air and dietary fiber, so no treatment of oligosaccharides will produce a completely gas-free pot of beans. To reduce swallowed air, chew thoroughly and don't eat hurriedly, no matter how good the beans are.
—M.Z. with John Ryan

Yankee families made double recipes of baked beans and reheated the leftovers with fish cakes or hot dogs, thinned them into a soup, or spread them cold on sandwiches (from my experience, I suggest rye or pumpernickel bread). As a final advantage, they also freeze well.

BOSTON BAKED BEANS
*Serves 4 to 6 as a main dish,
or 8 to 10 as a side dish*

This recipe yields a moderately sweet, meaty-flavored pot of beans. You can add familiar flavorings like onion or bacon or change the sweeteners without affecting the texture of the beans. Like many stews and soups, these beans improve in flavor the day after cooking.

    1   pound any size white beans (or a
        mixture), washed and picked clean
        of any debris or discolored beans
    1   pound fatty corned beef such as point-
        cut corned beef brisket or ½ pound
        meaty salt pork
    ¼   cup molasses
    3   tablespoons sugar or 6 tablespoons
        maple syrup
    1   tablespoon vinegar
    1¼ teaspoons salt
    1   teaspoon ground mustard

1. Bring 10 cups hot water and beans to boil in large pot; continue to boil 2 minutes. Remove from heat, cover, and soak until rehydrated, at least 1 hour and up to 8 hours to improve digestibility.

2. Heat oven to 225 degrees. Place meat in bottom of bean pot or other lidded ovenproof casserole. Drain and rinse beans; add them and remaining ingredients to pot. Cover with boiling water (about 2¾ cups for a bean pot or 3 to 3¼ cups for a wider-mouthed casserole).

3. Reduce oven temperature to 200 degrees; place pot or covered casserole in oven; cook until beans are tender, 7 to 9 hours. Skim rendered fat if you like. For creamier sauce, mash with a fork or puree ¾ cup of the cooked beans, stirring them back into pot. Serve or cool to room temperature and refrigerate. (Can be covered and refrigerated up to 1 week.) ■

Easy Decorative Pie Edgings

～

While few of us have the time to make fancy decorative pie edgings like leaves or other relatively complicated shapes, there are many simpler edgings that take only a minute or two and require no special tools. By following any of the instructions illustrated below, you can make your pies more visually appealing. In order to make these edgings, you need a relatively sturdy pie pastry that will hold its shape rather than shrink during baking, such as the Firm Crust Variation on page 24.

BOLD CROSSHATCH

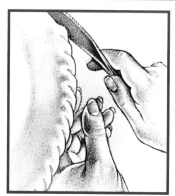 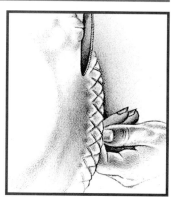

1. Use the blunt side of a table knife blade to make diagonal indentations about ¹/₂ inch apart around the pastry rim.

2. Now use the knife to make diagonal indentations around the rim in the opposite direction.

SCALLOPED EDGE

Holding a teaspoon (cutlery, not measuring) so the handle is positioned over the pie, use the bowl of the spoon to make a scalloped design around the pastry rim. Remove bits of excess dough around the indentations so that the scallop design is pronounced.

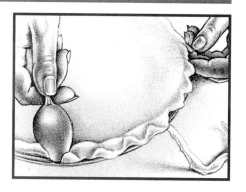

TRIPLE SCALLOPED EDGE

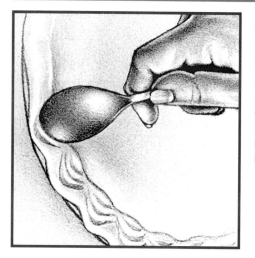

Holding a teaspoon so that the handle is positioned over the pie, use the bowl to make a triple scallop indentation, pulling the dough gently toward the center of the pie with each imprint. Repeat this process around the pastry rim.

ROUNDED POINTS

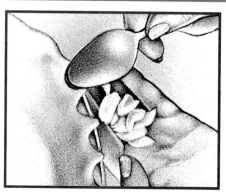

Holding a teaspoon so that the handle is positioned away from the pie, use the tip of the bowl to remove a semicircle of dough; continue this process, removing little semicircles of dough from around the pastry rim.

SHEAVES OF WHEAT

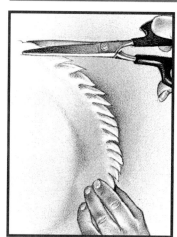

1. Using a clean pair of scissors, cut the dough on the diagonal at about ¹/₂-inch intervals around the pastry rim.

2. Turn one point of dough in toward the pie shell and the next point of dough away from the pie shell.

CHECKERBOARD

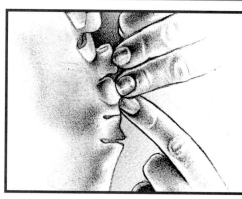

For a checkerboard edging, use a sharp knife to cut through the dough around the pastry rim at ¹/₂-inch intervals, then fold every other piece of dough toward the pie.

ROPE EDGES

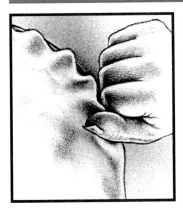

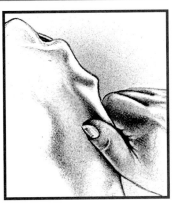

For a small rope edge, make a fist, then hold your thumb and index finger at a slight diagonal and pinch the dough; repeat at $\frac{1}{2}$-inch intervals around the pastry rim.

For a larger rope edge, hold the thumb and index finger at a more dramatic diagonal and pinch the dough; repeat every inch or so around the pastry rim.

FLUTED EDGES

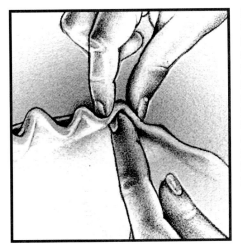

For a small fluted edge, hold your thumb and index finger about $\frac{1}{2}$ inch apart, press them against the outside edge of the pastry rim, then use the index finger or knuckle of your other hand to press the dough through the opening thus created. Repeat this process at $\frac{1}{2}$-inch intervals around the pastry rim.

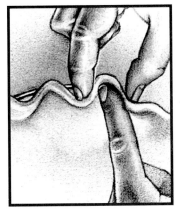

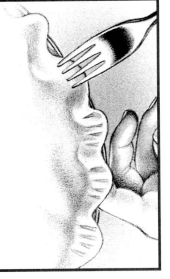

For a larger fluted edge, hold your thumb and index finger about 1 inch apart, press them against the outside edge of the pastry rim, then use the index finger or knuckle of your other hand to press the dough through the opening thus created. Repeat this process every inch around the pastry rim.

For a decorative flute, follow the instructions in the illustration at left, then use the tines of a fork to mark each flute.

CRIMPED EDGE

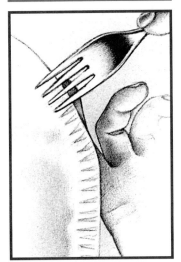

For a simple crimped edge, use the tines of a fork to mark the dough around the pastry rim.

HORIZONTAL CROSSHATCH

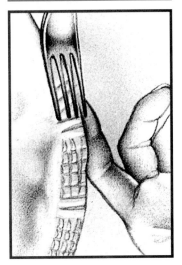

For a horizontal crosshatch effect, follow the instructions for a crimped edge, then mark the dough in the opposite direction.

FINE CROSSHATCH

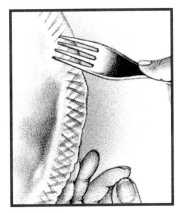

For a fine crosshatch effect, hold the fork on a slight angle and use the tines to mark the dough around the pastry rim, then repeat the process holding the fork at a slight angle in the opposite direction.

HERRINGBONE

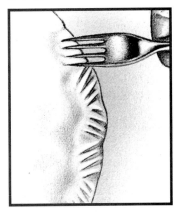

For a herringbone effect, hold the fork at a slight diagonal and use the tines to mark the dough. Holding the fork at a slight diagonal in the opposite direction, mark the dough next to the original mark. Repeat this process around the pastry rim.

SHARP POINTS

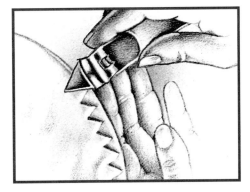

For a sharply pointed effect, use a can opener to cut out points around the pastry rim, pushing down with enough pressure to clearly cut the pastry before pulling out each section.

Mastering the Chocolate Soufflé

The secret to a bold, intense chocolate soufflé is a high proportion of chocolate and using beaten egg yolks instead of a classic béchamel or pastry cream.

∾ BY CHRISTOPHER KIMBALL WITH EVA KATZ ∾

What is the perfect soufflé? For my taste, it is a soufflé that has a crusty exterior packed with flavor, a dramatic rise above the rim, an airy but substantial outer layer, and a rich, loose center that is not completely set. A great soufflé must also convey a true mouthful of flavor, bursting with the bright, clear taste of the main ingredient. In a chocolate soufflé, the chocolate high notes should be clear and strong. A balancing act between egg whites, chocolate, yolks, and butter is the essence of a great chocolate soufflé.

A primary consideration when trying to create such a soufflé is what to use as the "base," the mixture that gives substance and flavor to the soufflé in contrast to the airiness and "lift" provided by the whipped egg whites. The base can be a béchamel (a classic French sauce made with equal amounts of butter and flour, whisked with milk over heat), pastry cream (egg yolks beaten with sugar and then heated with milk), or a bouillie (flour cooked with milk or water until thickened). After trying several versions of each of these options, we found that we consistently preferred the béchamel base. It provided the soufflé with good chocolate flavor and a puffed yet substantial texture. By contrast, the versions made with pastry cream and bouillie were too dense and puddinglike for our tasters' palates.

The Problem with Milk

After a week of refining a recipe using a béchamel base, we sent it off to our test kitchen for a final check. But when Food Editor Pam Anderson made the recipe, she noted that the chocolate was muted by the milk used in the béchamel, and decided to see if she could unmask the chocolate's full flavor. She had recently learned from Stephen Schmidt, a frequent contributor to *Cook's Illustrated*, about an interesting discovery he had made while preparing a chocolate truffle cake during a cooking class. He forgot to add the flour and came up with a dessert that was soufflélike in texture but with a more intense chocolate flavor than most soufflés.

Starting with this idea, Anderson removed the flour from our recipe, separated the eggs (whipping the whites separately), more than doubled the amount of chocolate, used six whole eggs, and reduced the amount of butter. This approach resulted in a base of egg yolks beaten with sugar until thick. This gave the soufflé plenty of volume but eliminated the milk, the ingredient that was holding back the chocolate. The result was fantastic—the most intense chocolate dessert I had ever tasted.

Our chocolate soufflé now had the intense flavor I had been looking for, but we still weren't completely happy with the texture because the outer layer was a bit cakey. After several more experiments, though, we discovered that adding two egg whites resolved the problem, giving the soufflé more lift and a better texture.

Investigating Other Variables

We now moved on to check other variables including oven tempera-

ture, a water bath, and the dish in which the soufflé was baked.

For most recipes a twenty-five-degree variance in oven temperature is not crucial, so we were surprised to find that it dramatically changed our soufflé. Our initial oven temperature was 375 degrees, but to be sure this temperature was optimum, we tested both 350 and 400 degrees as well. The higher oven temperature resulted in an overcooked exterior and an undercooked interior while the lower temperature did not brown the exterior enough to provide as much flavor and also produced a texture that was too even, given that we were looking for a loose center at the point at which the exterior was nicely

Despite what most cookbooks tell you, a soufflé will hold its shape if returned to the oven after you peek inside to check for doneness.

BEATING EGG WHITES

Beating egg whites to the proper consistency is considered both crucial to a good soufflé and extremely demanding in terms of split-second timing. To test this notion, we made three soufflés and used the so-called "raw egg method" to determine how much they had been beaten.

For the first soufflé, we beat the whites lightly so that they did not quite hold peaks, and a raw egg in the shell placed on top of them quickly fell to the bottom of the bowl. For the second test, we beat the whites to soft peaks, and the egg sunk just a bit, with the top 25 percent or so still showing. The last soufflé was made with whites that were beaten to firm (but still glossy) peaks—the raw egg was completely supported by the whites.

The results were completely unexpected. The underbeaten whites did rise more than those beaten to firm peaks, but because the initial volume was substantially less, the firm whites resulted in a higher soufflé. When the first soufflé was poured into the dish, the top of the mixture was one and one-half inches below the rim. After baking, the soufflé had risen two inches, ending up one-half inch above the rim. The third soufflé, however, started out at just a quarter inch below the rim and then rose to one and one-quarter inches above the rim after baking. In addition, the firm whites provided a slightly lighter, more ethereal texture. The other two soufflés were slightly wet and soggy. But perhaps the most interesting finding was that no matter how much you beat the egg whites, you still end up with a perfectly good soufflé! —*C.K.*

PHOTOGRAPH BY DAVE HENDERSON

1. Starting at the top of the bowl, use the spatula edge to cut through the middle of the mixture.

2. Turn the edge of the spatula toward you so it moves up the side of the bowl.

3. Continue this motion, going full circle, until the spatula is back at the center again.

4. Follow this procedure four more times, turning the bowl a quarter turn each time. Finally, use the spatula to scrape around the entire circumference of the bowl.

cooked. We decided to stick with 375 degrees.

A water bath was a truly awful idea. When we tested it, the outer crust of the soufflé turned out wet, with a gelatinlike appearance, and the soufflé did not rise well.

One factor we found to be of surprising importance was the baking dish. We tried using a standard casserole dish for one of the tests, and the soufflé rose right out of the dish onto the floor of the oven! The problem was that the dish did not have perfectly straight sides as a soufflé dish does. So it pays to make sure that you are using a real soufflé dish.

We also tested the theory that a chilled soufflé dish improves the rise, and discovered that it did cause chocolate soufflés to rise higher, but made little difference with nonchocolate soufflés.

During the course of all this testing, we also found that there are three ways to know when a chocolate soufflé is done: when you can smell the chocolate, when it stops rising, and when only the very center of the top jiggles when gently shaken. Of course, these are all imprecise methods. If you are not sure if your soufflé is done, simply take two large spoons, pull open the top of the soufflé, and peek inside. If the center is still soupy, simply put the dish back in the oven! Much to our surprise, this in no way harmed the soufflé.

The Make-Ahead Soufflé
For years, I had heard rumors about chefs who had devised secret recipes for chocolate soufflés that are prepared ahead of time, then refrigerated or frozen, and baked at the last minute. I wanted to develop just such a recipe to take the last-minute worry out of soufflés for busy cooks.

For the first test, we tried simply refrigerating and freezing the soufflé batter in individual ramekins. (We had discovered through earlier testing that individual soufflés hold up much better in the refrigerator or freezer than a full recipe held in a soufflé dish.) When we baked them, the refrigerated soufflés were a disaster (they hardly rose at all and were very wet inside), but the frozen versions worked fairly well. However, they were cakelike, without the loose center we were seeking.

For the second test, we heated the sugar used in the recipe with two tablespoons of water just

to the boiling stage and added it to the yolks while beating. Although this produced more volume, the final soufflé was only slightly better than in the first test. Finally, we also added two tablespoons of confectioners' sugar to the whites. This version was a great success, producing a soufflé that was light and airy with an excellent rise and a nice wet center. The actual texture of the whites changed as they were beaten, becoming stable enough so they held up better during freezing. We did find that these soufflés ended up with a domed top, but by increasing the oven temperature to 400 degrees, this problem was solved. I had my make-ahead soufflé at last.

CHOCOLATE SOUFFLÉ
Serves 6 to 8
Rather than one large soufflé, you can make individual ones. To do so, completely fill eight 8-ounce ramekins with the chocolate mixture, making sure to clean each rim with a wet paper towel and reduce baking time to sixteen to eighteen minutes. For a mocha-flavored soufflé, add one tablespoon of instant coffee powder dissolved in one tablespoon of hot water when adding the vanilla to the chocolate mixture. If you are microwave oriented, melt the chocolate at 50 percent power for three minutes, stirring in the butter after two minutes.

5	tablespoons unsalted butter (1 tablespoon softened, remaining 4 tablespoons cut into ½-inch chunks)
1	tablespoon plus ⅓ cup sugar
8	ounces bittersweet or semisweet chocolate, chopped coarse
⅛	teaspoon salt
½	teaspoon vanilla extract
1	tablespoon Grand Marnier
6	large egg yolks
8	large egg whites
¼	teaspoon cream of tartar

1. Adjust oven rack to lower middle position and heat oven to 375 degrees. Butter inside of 2-quart soufflé dish with the 1 tablespoon softened

butter, then coat inside of dish evenly with the 1 tablespoon sugar; refrigerate until ready to use.

2. Melt chocolate and remaining butter in medium bowl set over pan of simmering water. Turn off heat, stir in salt, vanilla, and liqueur; set aside.

3. In medium bowl, beat yolks and remaining sugar with electric mixer set on medium speed until thick and pale yellow, about 3 minutes. Fold into chocolate mixture. Clean beaters.

4. In medium bowl, beat whites with electric mixer set on medium speed until foamy. Add cream of tartar and continue to beat on high speed to stiff, moist peaks. (Mixture should just hold the weight of a raw egg in the shell when the egg is placed on top.)

5. Vigorously stir one-quarter of whipped whites into chocolate mixture. Following illustrations 1 through 4, above, gently fold remaining whites into mixture until just incorporated. Spoon mixture into prepared dish; bake until exterior is set but interior is still a bit loose and creamy, about 25 minutes. (Soufflé is done when fragrant and fully risen. Use two large spoons to pull open the top and peek inside. If not yet done, place back in oven.) Serve immediately.

MAKE-AHEAD CHOCOLATE SOUFFLÉ
This technique only works for the individual chocolate soufflés, which can be made and frozen up to two days before baking.

Follow instructions for Chocolate Soufflé, coating eight 1-cup ramekins with butter and sugar. Rather than beating sugar with yolks, bring sugar and 2 tablespoons water to boil in small saucepan, then simmer until sugar dissolves. With mixer running, slowly add this sugar syrup to egg yolks; beat until mixture triples in volume, about 3 minutes. Beat egg whites until frothy; add cream of tartar and beat to soft peaks; add 2 tablespoons confectioners' sugar; continue beating to stiff peaks. Fill each ramekin almost to rim, wiping excess filling from rim with wet paper towel. Cover and freeze until firm, at least 3 hours. Increase oven temperature to 400 degrees; bake until fully risen, 16 to 18 minutes. Do not overbake. ■

Homemade Oven-Dried Tomatoes

Surprisingly, the best technique does not use the lowest oven temperature, but it does call for seeding the tomatoes.

～ BY DEDE WILSON ～

As the wave of Italian cooking has swept over America, sun-dried tomatoes have become a staple in many kitchens. However, most cooks don't stock them in the pantry as consistently as other staples. This is largely due to their cost, which can range from expensive to exorbitant.

Although the original version of these flavorful, partially desiccated tomatoes was truly dried in the sun, these days most commercially dried tomatoes are prepared in dehydrators. These devices remove moisture from the fruit through a combination of long exposure at very low heat and a fan that circulates the warm air and helps remove moisture that has been released into the air. I wanted to assess whether tomatoes could alternatively be dried in a home oven, eliminating the need for the home cook to either buy the dried tomatoes at the store or purchase an expensive dehydrator.

One Method, Two Types

While I was at it, I hoped to be able to make not only a shelf-stable, extra-dry tomato but also a plumper, moister version. Although this partially dried tomato would have to be refrigerated, it would have different uses. It could serve, for instance, as a simple condiment or a flavorful addition to a sandwich. I also hoped that these two very different "dried" tomatoes could be made simply by varying oven time.

Of course, when I began to research the subject, I found that proper preparation of the tomatoes for drying was a matter of some debate. Various authors had success with peeled and unpeeled, cored and uncored, seeded and unseeded, and sliced and halved tomatoes. Some sources even suggested stuffing with herbs and drizzling with olive oil. One of the only factors that everyone agreed on was that plum tomatoes are the best choice for drying, as they offer more meat and less moisture than other varieties. With that as my starting point, I began testing various drying methods.

Searching for Technique

The lowest temperature on the majority of home ovens, whether gas or electric, is 150 degrees. I initially assumed that I would be best off proceeding at this temperature because it was the closest I could come to the even lower temperatures of dehydrators, which usually range from 125 to 135 degrees. I also began with the easiest preparation procedures, just in case they worked. I simply halved the tomatoes lengthwise, placed them cut side down on racks set upon baking sheets, and dried them in a 150-degree oven with the door closed.

Unfortunately, this approach did not work. The combination of the very low oven temperature and the amount of moisture held within the tomatoes via the seeds and core prevented the vegetables from giving off their moisture easily or evenly. As a result, it took up to twelve hours or more for the various sized pieces to become leathery.

I tried propping the door open for increased ventilation, cutting the tomatoes in slices, coring them, cutting across as opposed to lengthwise, in all manner of combinations. In most cases, the tomatoes dried fairly well up to a point but were then left with a wet pocket in the middle that just never seemed to dry out. I tried placing a bowl of water in the oven to increase air moisture, thinking, as one source suggested, that this might allow the tomatoes to dry more evenly. It did not seem to make a difference. Because some of my sources suggested peeling the tomatoes, I tried and got my first good results; the tomatoes finally dried much more evenly after being peeled and seeded. But because peeling the tomatoes adds a step with which many cooks would not want to bother, I kept searching.

Some helpful tips did surface as I played with preparation methods. Slicing the tomatoes in half lengthwise before coring them proved useful, as did scooping out all the seeds and gelatinous matter with a teaspoon.

Then I tried piercing the skin all over with the tip of a sharp paring knife. I proceeded to dry the tomatoes at 150 degrees, turning them over at least once during their oven time. This step also yielded good results, but there were still some overly moist pockets of flesh.

A Temperature Surprise

Finally I found two recipes that suggested using a higher oven temperature. Although at first

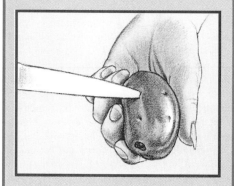

this seemed the wrong direction in which to go, I decided it was worth a try; maybe I would finally be able to get rid of those moisture pockets. I also decided, at the suggestion of Cook's Illustrated food editor Pam Anderson, to try placing the wire rack with the tomatoes on it directly on the oven rack, then putting a tray lined with aluminum on a rack below to catch any juices. This method, we agreed, might allow for maximum air flow, a nod toward the type of drying environment found in a dehydrator.

I halved, cored, and seeded the tomatoes and pricked the skins for good measure (*see* illustrations 1 through 3, page 20). I then placed them cut side down on the rack and baked them in a 200-degree oven, without flipping, for between four and eight hours. This turned out to be the method I had been searching for: The tomatoes were quite consistently dry, with nice texture, whether I took them out early for a plumper version or let them go for the longer stretch. Their color was bright and the flavor intense in both instances.

I tried this same technique at an oven temperature of 250 degrees, but at this level of heat, the tomatoes definitely "cooked" as opposed to dried out, so I went back to the combination that worked: plum tomatoes, halved lengthwise, cored, well seeded, skins pierced, and a 200-degree oven. With the four-hour time, you could accomplish your drying in the afternoon or evening while puttering around the house. The eight-hour version could be accomplished while getting a good night's rest.

OVEN-DRIED TOMATOES
Makes about 1¼ ounces dried tomatoes, depending on the degree to which the tomatoes are dried
Because these tomatoes need at least several hours in the oven, dry as many as possible at one time. Depending on your oven size, you can multiply the recipe, keeping in mind that drying times may increase.

2 pounds plum tomatoes (as uniform in size as possible), halved lengthwise, cored, thoroughly seeded, and skin pricked 6 to 8 times with the point of a sharp knife (*see* illustrations 1 through 3, page 20)

1. Adjust oven racks to middle and low positions; heat oven to 200 degrees. Line large tray or cookie sheet with aluminum foil.
2. Place tomatoes, cut side down, on large wire rack. Set wire rack on middle oven rack and foil-lined tray on lower rack. Dry, oven door closed, until desired texture is attained, 3 to 4 hours for plump tomatoes, 5 to 6 hours for leathery-textured ones, and 7 to 8 hours for completely dehydrated ones. When dry and cool, place in airtight containers. (Completely dried tomatoes can be stored at room temperature up to 1 year, leathery- textured ones can be refrigerated up to 6

months, and plump ones for 1 to 2 weeks.) If any off flavors or smells develop in the leathery or completely dried versions during storage, it may be due to mold or other bacteria; throw away the entire batch.

MUFFULETTA
Serves 6
This New Orleans–style sandwich takes advantage of the plumper version of our oven-dried tomatoes.

1 cup pitted brine-cured green olives, chopped coarse
1 cup pitted brine-cured black olives, chopped coarse
½ cup olive oil
¼ cup chopped fresh flat-leaf parsley leaves
1 medium roasted red bell pepper, peeled, seeded, and diced fine
2 tablespoons juice from a small lemon
1 teaspoon dried oregano
1 large (approximately 9-inch-diameter) round Italian or French loaf, halved crosswise, most of crumb removed
2 cups torn mixed lettuces
½ recipe Oven-Dried Tomatoes, dried to plump stage
¼ pound thin-sliced mortadella (or other soft salami)
¼ pound thin-sliced provolone or fresh mozzarella
¼ pound thin-sliced soppressata (or other hard salami)

1. Mix olives, oil, parsley, bell pepper, lemon juice, and oregano in small nonreactive bowl. Cover and refrigerate overnight.
2. When ready to assemble sandwich, drain olive mixture, reserving marinade. Generously brush all inside surfaces of bread with marinade. Fill bread bottom with half the olive mixture. Add layers as follows: half each of the lettuce and Oven-Dried Tomatoes, all of the mortadella, all of the provolone, all of the soppressata, and remaining tomatoes and greens. Pile rest of olive mixture on top. Cover with bread top; wrap with plastic wrap.
3. Set sandwich on large plate; top with small plate weighted with cans. Refrigerate at least 30 minutes. (Can be covered and refrigerated up to 6 hours.) Remove plates and plastic; cut into six wedges and serve.

OVEN-DRIED TOMATO SAUCE WITH PANCETTA AND HOT PEPPER
Makes about 3 cups
Oven-dried tomatoes add flavor depth to this pasta sauce. Substitute fatty prosciutto or even bacon for the pancetta if you like. Serve this sauce over bucatini or rotelle, passing Parmesan cheese separately. This highly concentrated sauce is enough to flavor one and one-half pounds of pasta.

1 recipe Oven-Dried Tomatoes, dried to leathery-textured stage
2 tablespoons unsalted butter
2 tablespoons vegetable or olive oil
¼ teaspoon hot red pepper flakes
2 medium onions, chopped medium
8 ounces thin-sliced pancetta
1 can (28 ounces) plum tomatoes, drained and chopped
Salt and ground black pepper
¼ cup minced fresh parsley leaves

1. Place dried tomatoes in small heatproof bowl. Cover with boiling water; let stand until plump, about 15 minutes. Drain, reserving tomato water. Chop coarse and set aside.
2. Meanwhile, heat butter, oil, and red pepper flakes in large sauté pan over medium heat. Add onions; sauté until softened, 7 to 9 minutes. Add pancetta; sauté until just crisp, 6 to 8 minutes longer. Add dried and canned tomatoes; bring to simmer. Reduce heat to low; cover and simmer to blend flavors, about 15 minutes. Season to taste with salt and pepper and stir in parsley. If sauce is too thick, thin it with a little of the reserved tomato water if you like.

PEPPERED OVEN-DRIED TOMATO RELISH
Makes about 4 cups
This relish, adapted from one that is served by Chris Schlesinger at the East Coast Grill in Cambridge, Massachusetts, is great with grilled meat of any kind or with strongly flavored fish such as bluefish.

3 tablespoons vegetable oil
¼ cup freshly cracked black pepper
2 tablespoons kosher salt
1 tablespoon minced garlic
2 pounds plum tomatoes (as uniform in size as possible), prepared as for Oven-Dried Tomatoes (left)
1 red onion, peeled and diced small
¼ cup roughly chopped fresh basil leaves
¼ cup large capers
¼ cup extra-virgin olive oil
¼ cup balsamic vinegar
Salt and ground black pepper

1. In a small bowl, combine olive oil, cracked black pepper, kosher salt, and minced garlic and mix well.
2. Rub mixture onto cut surfaces of tomato halves, then follow recipe for Oven-Dried Tomatoes, drying tomatoes until plump and slightly moist.
3. When tomatoes cool to room temperature, chop coarsely and place in large bowl. Add diced onion, chopped basil, capers, olive oil, vinegar, and season to taste. ∎

Dede Wilson is a freelance author living in western Massachusetts. She is currently writing a book on wedding cakes.

Memorable Meat Loaf

Use the right mix of meat, choose from three possible fillers, and bake the loaf free-form or in a perforated pan to keep it from stewing. The rest is up to the cook.

~ BY PAM ANDERSON WITH KAREN TACK ~

Our favorite loaf is wrapped in bacon, topped with a brown sugar–ketchup glaze, and baked free-form.

Not all meat loaves resemble Mama's. In fact, some ingredient lists look like the work of a proud child or defiant adolescent. Canned pineapple, cranberry sauce, raisins, prepared taco mix, and even goat cheese have all found their way into published recipes. Rather than feud over flavorings, though, we decided to focus on the meatier issues.

To begin with, we narrowed our testing to red-meat meat loaves. Poultry and vegetarian loaves presented different issues, so we decided to save those topics for another time. Even after narrowing our focus, we had plenty of questions to answer: What meat or mix of meats delivers good mouth feel and flavor? Which fillers offer unobtrusive texture? Should the loaf be cooked free-form or in a standard loaf pan, or are the new perforated pans designed for meat loaves worth the money? Should the loaf be topped with bacon, ketchup, both, or neither? Is it better to sauté the onions and garlic before adding them to the meat mix, or are they just as good raw and grated?

Many questions, but with meat loaf we knew there would be no absolute right or wrong an-swers. While there are rigid standards of excellence for some dishes, meat loaf just isn't one of them. There's too much personal preference about its flavor and texture. Our goal, then, was not to develop the ultimate meat loaf but to narrow the options so that cooks would know not so much what to do as what not to do. We developed a pretty outstanding meat loaf, but if you prefer your own recipe, you can still pick and choose what you like from the results of the tests that follow.

Mixed Meat Trio

In order to determine which ground meat or meat mix makes the best loaf, we used a very basic meat loaf recipe and made miniature loaves with the following meat proportions: equal parts beef chuck and pork; equal parts veal and pork; equal parts beef chuck, pork, and veal; two parts beef chuck to one part ground pork and one part ground veal; three-quarters beef chuck and one-quarter ground bacon; equal parts beef chuck and ham; all ground beef chuck; and all ground veal.

We found out that meat markets haven't been selling meat loaf mix (a mix of beef, pork, and veal, usually equal proportions of each) all these years for nothing. As we thought, the best meat loaves were made from the combinations of these three meats. Straight ground veal was tender but overly mild and mushy while the all-beef loaf was coarse-textured, liver-flavored, and tough. Though interesting, neither the beef/ham or the beef/bacon loaves looked or tasted like classic meat loaf. Both were firm, dense, and more ter-rinelike. Also, as bacon lovers, we preferred the bacon's smoky flavor and crispy texture sur-rounding, not in, the loaf.

Although both of the beef/pork/veal mixtures were good, we preferred the mix with the higher proportion of ground chuck. This amount gave the loaf a distinct but not overly strong beef fla-vor. The extra beef percentage also kept the loaf firm, making it easier to cut. Mild-tasting pork added another flavor dimension while the small quantity of veal kept it tender. For those who choose not to special-order this mix or mix it themselves at home, we recommend the standard meat loaf mix of equal parts beef, pork, and veal.

Fad Fillers Fail

After comparing meat loaves made with and with-out fillers or binders, we realized that starch in a meat loaf offers more than economy. Loaves made without filler were coarse-textured, dense, and too hamburger-like. Those with binders, on the other hand, had that distinct meat loaf texture.

But which binder to use? Practically every hot and cold cereal box offers a meat loaf recipe us-ing that particular cereal. We made several meat loaves, each with a different filler. Though there was no clear-cut winner in the category, we nar-rowed the number from eleven down to three.

Of the less-than-impressive fillers, rice left an obvious imprint, flecking the meat white and of-fering a taste and texture completely independent of the meat. Quick-cooking tapioca sucked every ounce of juice from the meat, leaving the loaf dry and very gelatinous.

Neither of our cereal-bound loaves scored well either. Grapenuts freckled its loaf and offered a wheaty aftertaste. The Corn Flakes loaf tasted funny too. Like the rice binding, grated potato failed to mix with the meat, standing out visually and texturally. Though not visually distinct, mashed pinto beans made the loaf taste like it needed taco chips and salsa.

After tasting all the meat loaves, we realized that a good binder should help with texture but not provide distinct flavor. Cracker crumbs, quick-cooking oatmeal, and fresh bread crumbs ended up fitting these criteria.

Just as we found that we liked the less dis-tinctly flavored fillers, so we preferred sautéed—not raw—onions and garlic in the meat mix. Because the meat loaf only cooks to an internal temperature of 160 degrees, raw onions never fully cook. Sautéing the vegetables is a five-minute detour well worth the time.

Dairy Products Moisten Best

Meat loaves need some added liquid to moisten the filler. Without it, the filler robs from the meat, making the loaf dry. As with the fillers, we ran across a host of meat loaf moisteners and tried as many as made sense.

Tomato sauce made the loaf taste like a meatball with sauce. We liked the flavor of ketchup, but ultimately decided that we preferred it baked on top rather than inside.

Beer and wine do not make ideal meat moisteners either. The meat doesn't cook long enough or to a high enough internal temperature to burn the alcohol off, so the meat ends up with a distinctly raw alcohol taste.

As with many other aspects of this home-cooked favorite, we found that there is a good reason that the majority of meat loaf recipes call for some form of dairy product for the liquid—it's the best choice. We tried half-and-half, milk, sour cream, yogurt, skim and whole evaporated milk, and even cottage cheese. Whole milk and plain yogurt ended up as our liquids of choice, with the yogurt offering a complementary subtle tang to the rich beef.

Free-Form or in the Pan

Cooks who don't like a crusty exterior on their meat loaf usually prefer to bake it in a loaf pan. We found that the high-sided standard loaf pan, however, causes the meat to stew rather than bake. Also, for those who like a glazed top, there is another disadvantage: The enclosed pan allows the meat juices to bubble up from the sides to dilute and destroy the glaze. Similarly, bacon placed on top of the meat loaf curls and doesn't properly attach to the loaf, and if tucked inside the pan, the bacon never crisps.

For all these reasons, we recommend that you not use a standard loaf pan. If you prefer a crustless, soft-sided meat loaf, you should invest in a meat loaf pan with a perforated bottom and accompanying drip pan. *See* Sources and Resources, page 32, for more information. The enclosed pan keeps the meat soft while the perforated bottom allows the drippings to flow to the pan below. While still not ideal for a crispy bacon top, it at least saves a glaze from destruction.

We ultimately found that baking a meat loaf free-form in a shallow baking pan gave us the results we wanted. The top and sides of the loaf brown nicely, and as an additional advantage, basting sauces, like the brown sugar–ketchup one

we developed (*see* recipe, below), glaze the entire loaf, not just the top. Bacon, too, covers the whole loaf. And because its drippings also fall into the pan, the bacon crisps up nicely. Incidentally, bacon arranged crosswise and overlapping slightly (*see* illustration 1, below) adheres best and slices easier. Tuck only the bacon tip end under the loaf so that as much of the strip as possible will crisp up during baking.

BACON-WRAPPED MEAT LOAF WITH BROWN SUGAR–KETCHUP GLAZE
Serves 6 to 8

If you like, you can omit the bacon topping from the loaf. In this case, brush on half the glaze before baking and the other half during the last fifteen minutes of baking. If you choose not to special-order the mix of meat below, we recommend the standard meat loaf mix of equal parts beef, pork, and veal, available at most grocery stores.

Brown Sugar–Ketchup Glaze
- ½ cup ketchup or chili sauce
- 4 tablespoons brown sugar
- 4 teaspoons cider or white vinegar

Meat Loaf
- 2 teaspoons oil
- 1 medium onion, chopped medium
- 2 garlic cloves, minced
- 2 large eggs
- ½ teaspoon dried thyme leaves
- 1 teaspoon salt
- ½ teaspoon ground black pepper
- 2 teaspoons Dijon mustard
- 2 teaspoons Worcestershire sauce
- ¼ teaspoon hot red pepper sauce
- ½ cup whole milk or plain yogurt
- 2 pounds meat loaf mix (50 percent ground chuck, 25 percent ground pork, 25 percent ground veal)
- ⅔ cup crushed saltine crackers (about 16) or quick oatmeal or 1 ⅓ cups fresh bread crumbs
- ⅓ cup minced fresh parsley leaves

6–8 ounces thin-sliced bacon (8 to 12 slices, depending on loaf shape)

1. *For the glaze:* Mix all ingredients in small saucepan; set aside.

2. *For the meat loaf:* Heat oven to 350 degrees. Heat oil in medium skillet. Add onion and garlic; sauté until softened, about 5 minutes. Set aside to cool while preparing remaining ingredients.

3. Mix eggs with thyme, salt, pepper, mustard, Worcestershire sauce, pepper sauce, and milk or yogurt. Add egg mixture to meat in large bowl along with crackers, parsley, and cooked onion and garlic; mix with fork until evenly blended and meat mixture does not stick to bowl. (If mixture sticks, add additional milk or yogurt, a couple tablespoons at a time until mix no longer sticks.)

4. Turn meat mixture onto work surface. With wet hands, pat mixture into approximately 9-by-5-inch loaf shape. Place on foil-lined (for easy cleanup) shallow baking pan. Brush with half the glaze, then arrange bacon slices, crosswise, over loaf, overlapping slightly and tucking only bacon tip ends under loaf (*see* illustration 1, below).

5. Bake loaf until bacon is crisp and loaf registers 160 degrees, about 1 hour. Cool at least 20 minutes. Simmer remaining glaze over medium heat until thickened slightly. Slice meat loaf and serve with extra glaze passed separately.

LOAF PAN VARIATION FOR MEAT LOAF

Follow instructions for Bacon-Wrapped Meat Loaf with Brown Sugar–Ketchup Glaze, omitting bacon. Turn meat mixture into meat loaf pan with perforated bottom, fitted with drip pan (illustration 2). Use fork to pull mixture from pan sides to prohibit glaze from dripping into oven (illustration 3). Brush with one-quarter of glaze. Bake until glaze is set, about 45 minutes. Top with another one-quarter of glaze; continue to bake until second coat has set and loaf registers 160 degrees, about 15 minutes longer. Cool at least 20 minutes. Simmer remaining glaze over medium heat until thickened slightly. Slice meat loaf and serve with extra glaze passed separately. ∎

FORMING THE LOAF

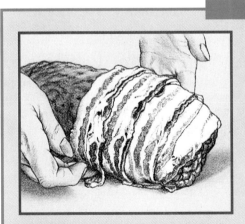

1. For a free-form loaf, lay the bacon strips crosswise over the loaf and overlapping slightly, tucking bacon ends underneath.

2. A loaf pan with a perforated bottom keeps the meat from stewing in the pan.

3. If using a perforated loaf pan, use a fork to pull the mixture away from the pan sides.

Pie Pastry Revisited

Suggestions from our readers sent us back into the kitchen to try varied additions to traditional American pie pastry.

∼ BY CHRISTOPHER KIMBALL WITH EVA KATZ ∼

In our September/October 1994 issue, I wrote a story entitled "Perfect Pie Crust," which explored the best, and most foolproof, method for making this common but often troublesome recipe. After extensive testing, the answer was clear: Use a high proportion of fat for good texture, including both butter and vegetable shortening for the optimal mix of flavor (from the butter) and flakiness (from the shortening). However, many readers swear by other methods, very often learned at their mother's knee and tested over years of repetition. In an effort to satisfy their queries—and to see if we might learn a new trick or two—we compiled the suggestions and headed toward the test kitchen.

We started with the most interesting suggestions, those that incorporated an unusual ingredient.

First we tested recipes that used dairy products, including cream cheese, milk, and sour cream. The crust made with cream cheese did have a sour tang to it, but it was also quite tough and, without any butter, rather flavorless; one taster said it reminded him of diner-style crusts. Pie pastry made with milk was also a failure, giving the crust a sandy texture.

The first recipe we tried that used added sour cream gave us a crust that was very flaky, if still a bit tough; it was a bit like a cheap bakery croissant. However, I remembered a wonderful recipe from Richard Sax's *Cooking Great Meals Every Day* (Random House, 1982) that used only two tablespoons of sour cream but also included six tablespoons of butter and four tablespoons of vegetable shortening (to one and one-half cups of flour)—versus the whopping one-third cup of sour cream and paltry one-quarter cup of butter used in our test recipe. The Sax version was substantially better. In fact, it was so good that we have reprinted our version below. It still lacked flavor when compared to our master recipe, but the light, puffy texture was so delectable that it deserves an honorable mention.

We then moved on to some other unusual ingredients, from vegetable oil to vinegar to hot water.

Vegetable oil was a disaster as a pastry ingredient. The dough proved impossible to roll out, and the resulting crust, which fell apart when we tried to work with it, was both greasy and utterly tasteless. (From reading our mail, however, I know that there is a small but hard-core group of vegetable oil pastry crust enthusiasts. For those of you in that camp, please send us explicit recipe directions, and we promise to test them.)

One reader had suggested using vinegar, so we added one teaspoon of raspberry vinegar, and the crust tasted, well, like vinegar. Not a pleasant vinegar taste, either, but a particularly unpleasant off taste. Using hot water instead of cold had been suggested by more than one reader, so we tried that, too, with unexpected results. Two of the tasters immediately identified the texture and flavor as being close to a saltine! The crust turned out hard and crackerlike, and shattered when cut.

Holding an Edge

A number of readers had also written that my master recipe did not hold an edge well. This is true. The high proportion of fat to flour (I use one part fat to two parts flour; many recipes use much lower ratios, down to one part fat to five parts flour) provides terrific flavor and texture, but it also softens the edge, resulting in a slightly "melted" look. In a series of tests, we reduced the amount of butter and shortening to the point at which the edge held well and the crust remained still reasonably tender and tasty. That recipe is offered below as the Firm Crust Variation. However, if taste and texture are your main concerns, stick with the master recipe.

I also wanted to find out if the processing method affects the quality of the edging. We tried overprocessing the shortening and the flour under the theory that well-coated flour will shrink less when baked. In fact, it seemed to shrink even more than when some of the butter was still in pea-sized pieces. One answer to this conundrum is that butter, an important ingredient in the master recipe, contains water, which was being worked into the flour more thoroughly during the overprocessing. This interaction may have created more gluten development, which would result in additional shrinkage. (Gluten is a protein, and when protein is cooked, it shrinks.) We did find, however, that the longer the crust is refrigerated or even frozen before baking, the better. This chilling provides sufficient time for the dough to hydrate evenly, for the relatively small amount of gluten to relax, and for the shortening to firm up, all of which are important to a superior crust. (In a cold refrigerator, thirty minutes is sufficient time for hydration. If you leave the dough longer, it should be warmed at room temperature for a few minutes so that it is pliable enough for rolling.)

So in the final analysis, two new recipes did come from our testing; I have also included the original master recipe for reference.

MASTER RECIPE FOR AMERICAN PIE DOUGH
For an 8- or 9-inch single pie shell

- 1 ¼ cups all-purpose flour, plus extra for dusting dough
- ½ teaspoon salt
- 1 tablespoon sugar
- 6 tablespoons chilled unsalted butter, cut into ¼-inch pieces
- 4 tablespoons chilled all-vegetable shortening
- 3–4 tablespoons ice water

1. Mix flour, salt, and sugar in food processor fitted with steel blade. Scatter butter pieces over flour mixture, tossing to coat butter with a little of the flour. Cut butter into flour with five 1-second pulses. Add shortening and continue cutting in until flour is pale yellow and resembles coarse cornmeal, with butter bits no larger than small peas, about four more 1-second pulses. Turn mixture into medium bowl.

2. Sprinkle 3 tablespoons ice water over mixture. With blade of rubber spatula, use folding motion to mix. Press down on dough with broad side of spatula until dough sticks together, adding up to 1 tablespoon more ice water if it will not come together. Shape into ball with hands, then flatten into 4-inch-wide disk. Dust lightly with flour, wrap in plastic, and refrigerate at least 30 minutes before rolling.

SOUR CREAM VARIATION FOR AMERICAN PIE DOUGH

This recipe was adapted from Richard Sax's *Cooking Great Meals Every Day*.

Follow directions for master recipe, substituting 2 tablespoons sour cream for an equal amount of water and reduce butter to 5 tablespoons and shortening to 3 tablespoons.

FIRM CRUST VARIATION FOR AMERICAN PIE DOUGH

This crust has less flavor and a firmer texture than the master recipe, but decorative edging will hold up nicely in the oven (*see* "Easy Decorative Pie Edgings," page 16, for sixteen techniques).

Follow master recipe directions, using just 4 tablespoons butter and 3 tablespoons shortening. ∎

Simple Stovetop Rice Pudding

Highlight the rice by cooking it in water first and eliminating extra ingredients.

~ BY ADAM RIED WITH EVA KATZ ~

At its best, rice pudding is simple, lightly sweet, and tastes of its primary component: rice. At its worst, the rice flavor is lost to cloying sweetness, condensed dairy, and a pasty, leaden consistency. Tired of groutlike puddings, we embarked on the pursuit of a really wonderful rice pudding, one that would cushion the sharp edges of a bad day rather than hold our bathroom tiles in place.

Right away we agreed on the qualities of the ideal candidate: intact, tender grains bound loosely in a subtly sweet, milky sauce. We were looking for a straightforward stovetop rice pudding, in which both the texture and flavor of the primary ingredient would stand out.

The Medium and the Method

We decided to check out the cooking medium and method first. For our first experiment, we prepared and tasted eight existing recipes for rice pudding, each using a different combination of water, milk, and cream and each with varying ratios of rice to liquid. This tasting revealed that cooking the rice in milk or cream obscured the rice flavor while a cooking medium of water emphasized it. The most appealing balance of rice flavor and satisfying, but not too rich, consistency derived from cooking the rice in two cups of water until it was all absorbed, then adding equal parts (two and one-half cups each) of whole milk

and half-and-half to make the pudding. The whole milk alone made the pudding too thin, but the milk and half-and-half together imparted just the right degree of richness. Eggs, butter, whipped cream, and heavy cream—on their own or in combination—overpowered the flavor of the rice.

We also tried a couple of variations in the cooking method, such as covering the pot or not, and using a double boiler. The double boiler lengthened the cooking time by twenty-five minutes and turned out a pudding that was gummy and too sweet. By far the best results came from cooking the rice and water in a covered pot first, followed by simmering the cooked rice uncovered in the dairy mixture. The texture of this pudding was just what we wanted—distinct, tender grains in a smooth sauce that tasted of milk rather than reduced cream. We found we could cut ten minutes off the total cooking time by simmering the rice in the water and dairy mixture together, rather than sequentially, but this approach sacrificed the texture of the grains and resulted in a pudding that our tasters rated overly dense and sweet.

Rating Rices

Now it was time to try different kinds of rice. We learned from the USA Rice Council in Houston that short-grain rice is generally not sold on the retail level, so we tested the readily available varieties: supermarket brands of long- and medium-grain white (such as Goya, which distributes both of these types nationally), arborio (a superstarchy Italian medium-grain white used to make risotto), and basmati (an aromatic long-grain white).

All rice contains two types of starch, called amylose and amylopectin, but they are present in different concentrations. Arborio, with its high level of amylopectin, made a stiff, gritty pudding. On the other end of the starch scale, long-grain rice, which is high in amylose starch, cooked up separate and fluffy. But the puddings made with long-grain rice were a little too thin for our liking (although not objectionable), while the flavor of the basmati was too perfumy, overwhelming the milk. Medium-grain rice, which has a high proportion of amylopectin (but less than short-grain), cooked up a little moister and stickier than long-grain. This type proved ideal for our rice pudding, which turned out creamy-textured and tasting dis-

tinctly of rice and milk. As a final test, we made a pudding with rice that had been refrigerated overnight. Unfortunately, the result was liquidy and grainy without discernible rice flavor.

SIMPLE STOVETOP RICE PUDDING
Serves 6 to 8

We prefer pudding made from medium-grain rice, but long-grain is perfectly acceptable if that's what you happen to have on hand.

- ¼ teaspoon salt
- 1 cup medium- or long-grain rice
- 2 ½ cups whole milk
- 2 ½ cups half-and-half
- ⅔ cup sugar
- 1 ¼ teaspoons vanilla extract

1. Bring 2 cups water to boil in large, heavy-bottomed pot (at least 3 quarts) or small soup kettle (4 to 5 quarts). Stir in salt and rice; cover and simmer over low heat, stirring once or twice until water is almost fully absorbed, 15 to 20 minutes.

2. Add milk, half-and-half and sugar. Increase heat to medium-high to bring to simmer, then reduce heat to maintain simmer. Cook uncovered, stirring frequently, until mixture starts to thicken, about 30 minutes. Reduce heat to low and continue to cook, stirring every couple of minutes to prevent sticking and scorching, until a spoon is just able to stand up in the pudding, about 15 minutes longer.

3. Remove from heat and stir in vanilla extract. Cool and serve at room temperature or chilled. (Can be covered with plastic wrap on surface of pudding and then refrigerated up to 2 days.)

RICE PUDDING WITH ORANGE AND TOASTED ALMONDS

Follow recipe for Simple Stovetop Rice Pudding, adding ⅓ cup slivered almonds that have been toasted until just golden and fragrant, stirring frequently, in small heavy skillet over medium heat (4 to 5 minutes), and 2 teaspoons grated orange zest along with vanilla extract.

RICE PUDDING WITH CINNAMON AND DRIED FRUIT

Follow recipe for Simple Stovetop Rice Pudding, adding ½ cup dried fruit (such as raisins, cranberries, cherries, or chopped prunes or apricots) and 1 teaspoon ground cinnamon along with vanilla extract. ∎

Rice pudding continues to thicken as it cools, so pull it off the heat when a spoon is just able to stand up in it.

Extra-Virgin Olive Oils Prove Uniformly Good

Among drizzling oils differences are subtle and quality is high. Surprisingly, our panel found no relation between price and value.

⤳ BY JACK BISHOP ⤳

"Italians say wine is a fact, but olive oil is an opinion." This axiom was offered up by one of the most experienced panelists after our grueling tasting of extra-virgin olive oils. I have run dozens of tastings for this magazine and have never finished with less conclusive information. As this panelist's proverb indicates, olive oil is very hard to taste-test.

My goal for this tasting seemed simple. Given the hundreds of extra-virgin olive oils (defined by European law as unflawed oils with an acidity of less than 1 percent) on the market, how does one choose a brand? By region? By price? Can supermarket oils, usually priced at around $10 per liter, compete with boutique oils often priced at $50 or more a liter?

My first task was to assemble the field. I wanted to include the three major supermarket brands from Italy—Berio and Bertolli as well as Colavita, which won the tasting of pure and extra-virgin oils the magazine ran back in 1992 (see "Taste-Testing Olive Oils," Charter Issue). To choose from among the many boutique brands, I turned to three leading gourmet stores located in different parts of the country and known for their outstanding selection of oils.

I asked Dean & DeLuca in New York, Zingerman's in Ann Arbor, Michigan, and Corti Brothers in Sacramento, California, to send me their favorite oils. All three stores sell oils by mail to consumers (see Sources and Resources, page 32, for more information). Because olive oil loses much of its flavor after eighteen months or so in the bottle, I asked for oils from the 1995 harvest, which took place late last fall, and made sure to avoid 1994 oils, which were approaching the end of their shelf life.

Some twenty-three oils ranging in price from $10 to $84 a liter eventually arrived at my door. A pretasting was held to narrow the field to twelve. Almost all of the oils were quite good, so we kept the cheaper oils and decided to go for regional balance when selecting among the more expensive brands. The final field consisted of one Spanish oil, three from California, and the remainder from Italy. Among the Italian oils, three were supermarket brands (which are bottled in Italy but are often made with olives from various locations), two were from Tuscany, two from Sicily, and one from Liguria.

There are a number of factors that can affect the quality of an oil. A representative of MICO, a well-regarded, independent olive oil association based in Italy, told me that the maturity of the olives (riper olives yield a gentler oil while younger olives produce spiciness), the extraction system, and the type of olives are most important. The method and length of storage and harvesting are lesser influences.

The Tasting

With this in mind, we asked nine olive oil aficionados to evaluate twelve oils based on several industry criteria. Color, which ranges from golden to green, indicates the type of olives and their ripeness, but is not really a gauge of quality. As one expert told me, "color is only important for the imagination." Clarity reveals whether the oil has been filtered. Because olive particles may hasten rancidity, filtered oils tend to last longer than unfiltered ones. We were tasting all young oils, so clarity did not seem to affect flavor.

Aroma is an especially important way to judge olive oil. To assess this factor, samples were poured into small plastic cups, which tasters covered with their hands in order to warm the oils slightly and to trap aromas. After smelling each oil several times, tasters poured a little onto their tongues and drew air into their mouths to spray the droplets over the palate.

As they tasted, our panel members tried to identify flavor characteristics. Experts describe an oil in terms of other flavors or aromas, including grass, herbs, artichokes, tomatoes, apples, almonds, and flowers. In addition, our tasters focused on fruitiness (how olive-y did the oil taste?) and spiciness (did the oil have a peppery quality and if so, how long did it pinch in the throat?).

Because we were tasting young oils, we expected spiciness to be prevalent. With time, this aspect can fade. In fact, several very spicy oils elicited mixed support from the panel, but everyone agreed that in time these oils may be superb.

The Results

After the blind tasting, we asked panelists to rank the oils. From past experience, I have found that a few entries earn top marks from most panelists and a few entries receive no top marks at all. The remaining entries usually get mixed reviews. In

this tasting, one oil was the clear favorite, but the remaining oils, even those at the bottom of the chart on page 27, each had their ardent supporters. There were no bad oils in the bunch, just one stellar oil and a lot of difference of opinion.

I was even more intrigued when I sat down and read the tasting sheets filled out by our panelists. Usually, I see the same adjectives being used over and over again to describe individual entries. For many of the oils we tasted, there was no such overlap. One oil was described as "grassy and gentle" by one taster, "spicy and fruity" by another, and "like tomatoes" by a third.

With hundreds of volatile compounds, it is apparent that different palates were detecting different elements in the oils. The absence of defects (all extra-virgin oils must go through a rigorous independent tasting process that eliminates flawed samples) makes it hard to get a handle on these good oils. In my experience, tasters tend to latch on to obvious defects or peculiarities in whatever product they are tasting. But in this case, they had to describe complex positive attributes that are difficult to put into words.

So what does this mean for the consumer? Of the three supermarket oils, two finished at the bottom of the rankings. But each had a number of vocal supporters, and they certainly were able to compete with the rest of the field. (Incidentally, the fact that Colavita finished last in this field shows the superiority of extra-virgin oils over the mixed field of extra-virgin, pure, and light olive oils we tested four years ago, when Colavita ranked first.) The third supermarket oil, Berio, finished in fourth place and appeared on all but one taster's list of favorite oils. It did not capture any top votes, but Berio received uniform (if modest) praise from our panel.

As for price, the most expensive oil in the tasting (Castello di Cacchiano, a Tuscan oil that costs $84 a liter) finished just above the bottom two supermarket oils, both of which cost $10 a liter.

However, the clear favorite, Tenuta di Valgiano, also comes from Tuscany and is quite expensive. At $48 a liter, it's hardly a bargain.

So what's my advice? Buy what you like. It may sound like a cop-out, but as long as the label says extra-virgin, you can be assured that the oil will deliver a certain level of quality.

This advice was also supported by the second part of the tasting. After we had ranked the oils, panelists were asked to taste each oil with three different dishes: tomato, mozzarella, and basil salad; grilled zucchini; and steamed halibut.

Panelists agreed that subtle differences in the oils evaporated on the zucchini (the caramelized grill flavor overpowered nuances in the oils). The cheese (but not the tomatoes) and especially the steamed fish were better foils for the oils but still proved to be quite a distraction.

When drizzled onto food, an oil that seemed quite spicy tasted much like an oil that was originally described as mild and gentle. The lack of clear results in the food and oil pairings further suggests that the selection of a particular extra-virgin oil is not especially crucial. ∎

RATING EXTRA-VIRGIN OLIVE OILS

For our tasting, twelve extra-virgin olive oils were tasted blind at The Library restaurant at the Regency Hotel in New York. The oils are listed in order of preference based on scores awarded by our judges. The top oil was the clear favorite of the panel. The remaining oils were generally well liked and the scoring was quite close.

Oils were poured into small glasses and then sampled as is. Tasters had access to water and bread. The locations listed after the oils refer to the bottling sites listed on labels. Prices indicate what we paid either from the mail-order companies listed in "Sources and Resources" on page 32, or in New York supermarkets.

In addition to the author, the panel included

eight other experts: two *Cook's Illustrated* editors (Mark Bittman and Stephanie Lyness); food writer and teacher Katherine Alford; cookbook author Anna Teresa Callen; Giorgio DeLuca, co-owner of Dean & DeLuca; food writer Cara De Silva; baking teacher and cookbook author Nick Malgieri; and cookbook author Michele Scicolone.

RECOMMENDED OILS

These oils were liked by the panel. Oils at the top of this list received more votes than the last few oils, but the differences were not as sharp as in most tastings.

Roi Olio Extra Vergine d'Oliva (Badalucco, Italy), $27 for 1 liter bottle. This Ligurian oil has a light yellow color and is "cloudy" or "slightly murky." The aroma is quite vivid and elicited a variety of descriptions: "very olive-y," "fruity," "almost like peaches or berries," and "herbal." Again, tasters thought this oil was interesting and "lively" without being overpowering.

Lérida Extra Virgin Olive Oil (Sarocca de Lérida, Spain), $28.50 for 1 liter bottle. This yellowish, clear oil has "a nice olive nose." Its flavor is more "subtle" than others, but tasters responded to the fruit and low spice. "Very gentle with nice olives and herbal notes." A few detractors thought it to be "somewhat one-dimensional."

Filippo Berio Extra Virgin Olive Oil (Lucca, Italy), $7.59 for 750 ml bottle. This readily available supermarket oil was the real shocker of the tasting. The bright green oil has a "good olive smell but not much else." The "muted" aroma gives way to a pleasant flavor that was described as "grassy" and "a bit peppery." A "familiar," "quite pleasant" choice that did not receive any top votes but scored decently with every taster, bringing it up into the top rank, well above several extra-virgin oils that are far more expensive.

Consorzio Extra Virgin Olive Oil (Napa, California), $10 for 375 ml bottle. This light-colored, cloudy oil comes from chef Michael Chiarello and his company Napa Valley Kitchens. The aroma is "very fruity," or "almost like berries," with a good balance of fruit and spice. Several tasters commented on the "round," "grassy" flavor.

Stutz California Extra Virgin Olive Oil (Berkeley, California), $14.95 for 750 ml bottle. This light yellow oil has a very strong olive nose ("smells very ripe") with some hints of "mustiness." The flavor really divided the panel. Some tasters described this oil as "odd" or "not enough olives" while others liked the "artichoke quality" and "lighter" olive notes.

Ravidà Olio Extravergine di Oliva (Menfi, Italy), $25 for 750 ml bottle. This light green Sicilian oil has an "unbelievable" aroma, with strong olive, spice, grass, and herb notes. The flavor, however, was "too intense" for most tasters. As one panelist wrote, "way too much pinch and not enough else." Several thought this oil showed promise and might soften with time.

Verdesco California Extra Virgin Olive Oil (Modesto, California), $7.99 for 375 ml bottle. This golden oil has a "fruity" nose that was liked by most tasters, with remarks like "lovely olive aroma." Many tasters detected "nutty" or "buttery" notes while others picked up "artichokes." A "simple, not overly complex" oil that many liked but some found "too mild," an opinion that lowered its rank.

Barbera Frantoia Extra Virgin Olive Oil (Palermo, Italy), $19.95 for 1 liter bottle. This Sicilian oil is bright green and a bit cloudy. The aroma is very "grassy" or "almost sweet," with two panelists picking up "minty" notes. The flavor was described as "full" and "round" by panelists who liked this oil and "one-dimensional" and "sort of tepid" by others. An aromatic oil that's also fairly delicate.

Castello di Cacchiano Terre del Chianti Classico Olio Extra Vergine di Oliva (Gaiole, Italy), $42 for 500 ml bottle. The most expensive oil in the tasting comes from the area in Tuscany that also produces fine Chianti wines. All but a few tasters found this green oil with a "strong nose" to be "too peppery" and "too bitter." Again, time may smooth out the rough edges.

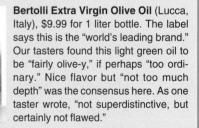

Bertolli Extra Virgin Olive Oil (Lucca, Italy), $9.99 for 1 liter bottle. The label says this is the "world's leading brand." Our tasters found this light green oil to be "fairly olive-y," if perhaps "too ordinary." Nice flavor but "not too much depth" was the consensus here. As one taster wrote, "not superdistinctive, but certainly not flawed."

Colavita Extra Virgin Olive Oil (Campobasso, Italy), $9.79 for 1 liter bottle. The third supermarket brand in the tasting is light green in color and has a "pungent olive aroma." The flavor was deemed "flat" or "decent but nothing special." Another taster thought it was "bland and neutral, but fine for cooking." A case where tasting did not live up to smelling.

Multifeatured Electronic Timers Win Testing

Forget about dial timers. Newer multifunction electronic models win big in kitchen test.

∼ BY STEPHANIE LYNESS WITH JACK BISHOP ∼

Kitchen timers are one of those essential tools that have mostly been taken for granted. Like oven thermometers, we buy them more or less on impulse, with the idea that they're all more or less alike, so we might as well just buy one as another.

To find out if this was actually the case, we examined fifteen timers—seven dial and eight electronic—to find out what each did, whether they all performed as promised, and if there were any out there that we really loved. What we found was that there are indeed differences among timers, and the proper model can make a difference in efficiency.

Setting the Ground Rules
Our first step was to come up with a list of what we felt were important features in a timer.

The obvious first requirement was that the timers keep time accurately. This point may be argued: We actually had to scratch our heads a bit to think of foods (notably eggs) that might suffer from even thirty seconds of over- or undercooking. But still, these are timers. At any rate, in the end, all of the timers performed adequately. Even the dial timers, slightly less accurate than the electronic if only because they are hard to set precisely, were accurate to within fifteen seconds.

In addition to accuracy, there are a number of basic "ease of use" aspects to timers. These aspects fall mostly in the area of avoiding what seem like unnecessary difficulties. If you can't set the timer because the directions are badly written or require you to hold down two buttons while manipulating a third, or the display is small or badly lit, who cares how many brilliant things it does? So we checked the electronic timers for these factors.

As it turned out, none of the timers were particularly difficult to figure out or to work with, even for the digitally impaired. We downgraded those with small displays, though, because they were harder to read, particularly when we were passing the stove in a hurry and just wanted to glance at the timer to see how long before something needed to be removed from the oven.

We also examined the timers for several features that we consider practical. First, it's important that timers show seconds as well as minutes so that the cook can accurately and easily judge how much time remains. Second, because every now and then we cook some dish that requires long, slow cooking, we gave higher ratings to timers that ran for several hours without a need for resetting. We also preferred models that had the capacity to time more than one food at a time,

---

RATING ELECTRONIC KITCHEN TIMERS

Eight electronic timers from six different companies were tested for this article and judged on the basis of the following criteria. West Bend sells an additional single timer with smaller buttons; we chose the model below because it was exactly the same with larger buttons.

Price: Retail prices from New York City and Boston kitchen stores and mail-order catalogs.

Maximum Time: We felt that two of the most important features of an electronic timer (distinguishing it from a dial timer) are that it time foods that cook for several hours and display seconds as well as minutes. The seconds display is crucial for professional cooks or for home cooks timing eggs or other items requiring precision. Therefore, timers that counted over one hundred minutes and displayed seconds were rated more highly than those that didn't.

Number of Timers: It seemed to us that if you're going to buy a timer, you

might as well buy one that can time more than one dish at the same time.

Counts Up After Beep Sounds: All of the rated timers count down from the programmed time to zero. In addition, timers with this feature continue counting back up after the programmed time has been reached. This feature is not only very desirable for recipe development and testing, but if you miss the beep, you'll see how long the food has cooked past the set time.

Interrupt: This feature allows the cook to stop the timer to interrupt cooking, and then start it again. We felt that this was a useful feature in case you need to stop timing to check doneness or add an ingredient.

Clock: A timer that also functions independently as a clock is not common. But if your stove doesn't have a built-in clock, it proves very handy.

Memory: If you hit start again after the bell sounds, the timer begins timing from the last programmed time. We couldn't think of many situations in which this would be necessary, so it didn't carry much weight in the rating.

NAME	PRICE	MAXIMUM TIME	NUMBER OF TIMERS	COUNTS UP AFTER TIME	INTERRUPT	CLOCK	MEMORY
West Bend Clock/Double Electronic Timer Model #40031x	$16.98	24 hours	2	yes	yes	yes	yes
West Bend Timer Model #40030	$10.98	100 minutes	1	no	yes	no	yes
Polder Cooking Thermometer/Timer	$29.95	24 hours	1 plus meat thermometer	yes	yes	no	yes
West Bend Electronic Triple Timer Model #40032	$37.95	10 hours	3	no	no	no	no
EK Digital Timer	$22	100 minutes	1	no	yes	no	yes
Terraillon Electronic Micro-Timer Model #T40750	$14.75	100 minutes	1	no	yes	no	yes
Cooper Chef's Timer-Stopwatch	$18.75	100 minutes	1	no	yes	no	yes
Time Check Big Digit Timer Model #TM4	$17	20 hours	1	no	yes	no	no

West Bend Clock/Double Timer: Our favorite, reasonably priced model does everything we want: times up to twenty-four hours, counts down and up, times two foods at the same time, and serves as a clock as well as a timer.

Polder Thermometer/ Timer: High-tech design single timer counts down and up and does double duty as a meat thermometer! Sexy idea, but keep in mind that you can buy the winning model and an instant-read thermometer for the same or less money.

EK Digital: Expensive single timer boasts a sleek design but small display and is easy to knock over while setting.

Cooper Chef's Timer: Very lightweight single timer hangs around the neck for those who want to carry the timer with them. Costs more money than you need to spend.

West Bend Timer Model #40030: Solid if unexciting second-place winner is an inexpensive single timer, and times minutes and seconds, but for an extra $6, why not buy the winning West Bend Double?

West Bend Triple Timer: Very expensive timer counts down with three independent timers. Open the package to find that you must spring for the battery on your own. We weren't happy with this timer; it only rated this highly because, as advertised, it does time three foods at once. But for $4 less you can buy two of the winning timers and get its extra features as well.

Terraillon Micro-Timer: Small, cheesy-feeling, single timer has a small display; for just a bit more you could buy the winning West Bend.

Time Check Big Digit: Large display single timer doesn't display seconds but times up to twenty hours.

given that most of us cook more than one dish at a time. We also thought it useful to be able to interrupt the countdown (to remove the pan from the stove to add an ingredient, for example) and then start it up again. Finally, we looked for timers that continue timing after the buzzer has sounded. If the cook can't get to the stove right away, this feature lets him or her know how long past ideal the food has cooked.

Our final tests were for durability. Some cooks grumble that their electronic timers fail after only a year. So we dropped all the timers onto a hard counter from a six-inch height and then into a bowl of water to see if any survived.

The Big Split: Dial Versus Electronic
Once most of the timers had adequately satisfied our initial basic performance tests of accuracy and ease of use, it became evident that the rating would break on the issues of features and durability. We very quickly determined that dial timers couldn't hope to compete with the multifeatured electronic timers in the features department, so we decided to rate only the electronic models in the chart on page 28 (see "Dial Timers," right, for more information on that category).

It is important to note, though, that the dial timers outperformed the electronics in one area: durability. All of the dial timers, seemingly indestructible, passed both drop and water tests. The electronic models did well in the drop test but failed miserably when dipped into a bowl of water. The LED displays either went blank or behaved skittishly for about twenty-four hours until they dried out. (That said, all of the electronic timers worked perfectly once again after having had an opportunity to dry out.)

Electronic Models
Substantial differences manifested themselves among the electronic models. While most were single timers, one had the capability to time two foods at the same time, and another three. One combined a timer with a meat thermometer (it really worked). Maximum times ranged from one hundred minutes to twenty-four hours. Most had the "interrupt" feature we were after. We were stumped as to why, but six out of the eight timers also had a "memory" capability, meaning that if you pressed start again after the bell sounded, the timer would automatically start timing from the last programmed time. Finally, while all timers counted down, only two satisfied us by counting up again after the beep sounded.

The Results
Only one timer, the West Bend Clock/Double Timer, passed performance tests and had all of the functions we were looking for and then some. This model comes equipped with two timers, an easy-to-read display, long timing capability, and the ability to count up after the buzzer sounds. In addition to all that, it is also a clock. The simpler West Bend Model #40030 won second place because it features a large, easy-reading display and stays solidly on the counter while being manipulated (other lighter-weight models slid easily) for a very good price. The Polder single timer won third place because it times up to twenty-four hours, counts up after the buzzer sounds, and offers the bonus of an attached meat thermometer. The triple timer rated only fourth place because it costs so much for what it is, the battery is a bear to insert, and we were outraged that the battery is not included. The Big Digit rated last because it doesn't show seconds.

The remaining electronic timers, little different from each other, were rated on design. The Cooper was downgraded, as we didn't buy the logic of carrying the timer around our necks. ∎

DIAL TIMERS

These models all performed about the same; the only difference is in design. Two were marginally more difficult to set accurately (only the first fifteen minutes on the Terraillon Clip are marked individually, with the remaining forty-five minutes marked in increments of five; the minute marks on the EK dial sit about one-half inch below the raised, stationary mark at the top so that you need to eyeball the correspondence). In terms of setting the dial timers, all must be turned past the fifteen-minute mark and then set to the desired time. Our favorites were the Bodum and the EK for their sleek, sexy design.

To our thinking, the only advantage these timers have over the electronic models is that they're sturdy. They're not much, if at all, cheaper. If durability is important and you can do without the precision and longer timing offered by an electronic timer, you may be happy with one of these, clockwise from bottom left: Bodum ($9.95), EK ($14), Acme Apple Shape Model #92500 ($8.89), Lux Long Ring Minute Minder ($16.95), Sunbeam 60 Minute ($8.99), Terraillon Clip ($10.95), and Terraillon Cordon 60' ($17). —S.L. and J.B.

Acceptable Cheap Reds

Think cheap reds are undrinkable? Not always.

～ BY MARK BITTMAN ～

Making great wine takes nearly perfect grapes, which are in themselves a notable combination of hard work and good fortune. It takes skill, experience, the right equipment, labor, and even talent. And it takes time.

Making wine destined for sale to people on a tight budget forbids the use of the first and last of these ingredients—wonderful fruit and loads of time—which, most experienced winemakers would argue, are the most important. Great grapes cost much more than cheap ones, and in winemaking as in anything else, time is money. If you tie up your investment by aging wine in vats or bottles, you have less money to spend elsewhere.

In short, it is literally impossible to make great wine and sell it for five dollars a bottle. The question then is this: Can you make *decent* wine at that price? And the answer: Yes. But evidently it isn't easy.

The process of making white wine is relatively uncomplicated, and consumer expectations of inexpensive white wine are low. To make simple white wine, you remove the stems from grapes—they may be white or red—crush the grapes, and immediately strain out the juice. You ferment the juice and bottle it (naturally, making better white wine requires more steps). If it tastes clean (with no off odors or tastes) and refreshing, you have a potentially successful product.

But making even the most basic red wine takes an extra step or two. To make simple red wine, red grapes are crushed with their skins (and sometimes stems), then allowed to ferment with the skins. At that point, the juice is drained off, fermentation is completed, and the wine is bottled.

Two snags in this process make the successful production of cheap red wine a highly challenging process. First of all, while fermenting with the skins makes the resulting juice more complex and full of desirable flavor, it can ultimately also produce undesirable flavors. The other snag is that consumers expect red wine to taste like something distinctive: You can't just produce an inoffensive, nearly tasteless beverage and expect anyone to buy it more than once.

We knew all of this going into our tasting of very inexpensive red wines, in which no wine cost more than $6 per 750 ml (a magnum) and some came in at considerably less. Still, most of the tasters, who'd had considerable experience with near cheap reds, were looking forward to the tasting because they believed, as did I, that winemaking had advanced to the point where we'd find some hidden gems even among these minimally priced offerings.

Although most of our panel members expressed profound distaste with most of the wines, there were some winners. A cabernet from Sebastiani was ranked in the top seven by all the tasters but one, and was even called "pleasant" by a couple of tasters. Tied for second were a Chianti from Melini and a cabernet from Robert Mondavi's Woodbridge, California, winery. These red wines, too, garnered mostly positive comments. After that, however, it was pretty much downhill. ∎

BLIND TASTING RESULTS

As usual, the wines in our tasting were judged by a panel made up of both wine professionals and amateur wine lovers. In the judging seven points were awarded for each first-place vote; six for second; five for third; and so on. Prices reflect typical discounts; they will vary from one region to another (our wines were purchased in the Northeast). In this tasting, Recommended wines received predominantly positive comments; "Worth a Shot" wines had a few positive comments; and Not Recommended wines had no or almost no positive comments.

NOTE: Prices are for 1.5 liter bottles.

RECOMMENDED

N.V. August Sebastiani California Cabernet, $10. Solid entry that was given at least grudging respect by all but one taster. Comments on this red ranged from "fruity and balanced" to "better than drinkable."

1994 Melini "Borghi d'Elsa" Chianti, $12. Two experienced tasters picked this as a Chianti, so at least it has identity. "More than decent," "almost appealing," and "decent after it sits in the glass" was the general consensus.

1993 Mondavi (Woodbridge) Barrel Aged California Cabernet, $12. Although some thought this wine "vapid," a couple of tasters expressed enthusiasm, along the lines of "darker, more flavorful," and "actually quite nice."

WORTH A SHOT... MAYBE

1994 Fetzer Valley Oaks Cabernet (California), $11. From one of the leaders in inexpensive varietals. Some tasters found "some character here," but others found it "dry" and "tasteless." To sum up, "lots of oak, little fruit."

N.V. George Duboeuf Vin de Table Francais, $7. Note the price, which, for even a magnum of any real wine, is amazing. Depending on whether you find this "spicy" and "not bad" or "caustic and sour," it may be the cheap wine for you.

1993 Bolla Valpolicella (Italy), $12. Twenty years ago, it was deemed the standard in cheap red wines. Now, "simple, extremely light, and halfway decent," according to more than one taster. Other tasters hated it.

1994 Monterey Vineyards Languedoc Merlot, $12. Here's a twist: An established California winery making wine from juice made from French grapes. The results are mixed: More found it "tannic" and "sour" than "rich and ripe."

1993 Glen Ellen Proprietor's Reserve California Merlot, $12. Many found this wine "drinkable." Some thought it "overly sweet."

1994 Concha y Toro Rapel Valley Cabernet/Merlot (Chile), $7. Note the price. Most agreed that this wine was "not bad."

N.V. Carlo Rossi Burgundy (California), $5.49. Note the price. Although it barely squeaked into this category, this wine was closer to those selections above it than to those that were below it. Some people hated it, and all agreed that it was "off-dry," but two or three tasters included "nice" or "pleasant" in their comments.

NOT RECOMMENDED

1994 Dulong Côtes du Roussillon (France), $9.

1994 Mondavi Napa Valley Cabernet, $11.

1994 Cedar Creek S.E. Australian Cabernet, "Bin 99," $10.

1992 Mouton Cadet Bordeaux, $10.

Book Reviews

Mediterranean cuisine has been one of the biggest recent trends in American cooking. It has spawned literally hundreds of cookbooks, some wonderful and others of little use to an American home cook. These four are among the best of the most recent crop.

Red, White, and Greens
Faith Willinger
HarperCollins, $25

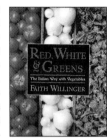

Faith Willinger, who has lived for years in Florence, Italy, has put together an encyclopedic guide to cooking vegetables in the Italian manner. On all counts it is a winner. We tested some twenty recipes from this book, and they were universally well received—easy to make, delicious, and innovative without being too eclectic. A yellow pepper soup, for instance, was great and easy enough for midweek cooking; fennel-spiced figs were delicious, original, and mindlessly easy to prepare (we made them while watching a video); "overstewed" green beans were excellent and the directions were exemplary; and a monkfish roasted on a bed of thinly sliced potatoes made its own rich sauce (the starch from the potatoes provided the thickener). A few less than stellar recipes still seemed deserving of a second try, including a bread salad recipe that could have used a more precise ingredient list and a "new wave" carbonara pasta dish that suggests heating the mixture to 160 degrees for safety reasons, which resulted in scrambled eggs. Despite these minor missteps, Willinger's book offers a fresh blend of solid instruction and very appealing recipes that makes it a must-buy.

Salse di Pomodoro
Julia della Croce
Chronicle, $14.95

As prepared in most American kitchens, tomato sauce is a bit like salad dressing: Most of us don't follow a recipe, we are unaware of the possibilities, and we are therefore condemned to a second-rate outcome. In *Salse di Pomodoro*, della Croce sets out to remedy this situation. She does so both by exposing home cooks to a wide range of flavoring ingredients for tomato sauce, such as squid, shrimp, pork chops, roasted bones, giblets, and vegetables, and by making us rethink the basics through a discussion of pastes versus purees and uncooked versus cooked sauces. Most of the recipes we tested received high marks for their flavor, but some of the instructions needed tweaking. In one sauce flavored with squid, for example, the squid gave off a good one-third cup of liquid when seared, an unexpected outcome that diluted the sauce. I would also have liked della Croce to be more definitive on the subject of brands of canned tomatoes (which does she use?) and the differences among styles (crushed, in puree, and in juice). But for the most part, this book fulfills its promise admirably, providing excellent recipes and fresh ideas to convert a tired culinary standby into something special.

Mediterranean Hot
Aglaia Kremezi
Artisan, $19.95

This book is a very personal and eclectic collection of zesty Mediterranean recipes from its author, Aglaia Kremezi. Some recipes included in this handsome volume, such as Ethiopian Lamb & Red Lentil Stew, seem naturally robust. Others, however, seem converted to spiciness by the mere addition of a dash of green chiles, Aleppo pepper, and/or red pepper pastes. I am not quite sure what to make of, for example, hot-and-spicy versions of focaccia, hummus, or pesto; it feels to me as if they have undergone vigorous conversions to spiciness by means of a shotgun pairing with a bit of capsicum. In the test kitchen, our best results came from recipes that did not only depend on a teaspoon or two of hot peppers to make them robust. The Tuna Fillets Marinated in Vinegar & Pepper was easy to make and delicious, as were the Green Beans with Garlic, Chili, Vinegar, Caraway & Cilantro, a simple but very effective combination, and the Cold Almond & Garlic Soup, which showcased the clear flavors of garlic, ginger, and sherry vinegar. Other recipes were mixed, including a chicken tagine that was good but overwhelmed by too many preserved lemons, and a delicious couscous that took a whopping three hours of preparation time and might have been better without the addition of chiles. The North African Zucchini Salad was virtually inedible (the flavors were odd, and the zucchini skins resisted mashing even though the interior was thoroughly cooked); a lamb tagine had too many figs for our taste (two pounds of figs to three pounds of meat) although the spice mixture was very nice; and a traditional Italian dessert—a cream cheese tart with dried fruit, pine nuts, and a sprinkling of black pepper—was authentic but not very good (the pastry is made with olive oil, which results in a hard, crisp, relatively tasteless container). But if you are willing to sort through a personal collection of favorite recipes—some authentic and some hybrids—and if you can handle less than explicit recipe instructions, you will be rewarded with some gems that make the effort worthwhile.

La Vera Cucina
Carlo Middione
Simon & Schuster, $35

In *La Vera Cucina*, Carlo Middione accomplishes what he sets out to do: provide an American audience with authentic recipes from the homes and farms of Italy. As he notes in his introduction, he is not a reporter documenting a foreign culture—he has lived these recipes, albeit in Buffalo, New York, where he grew up in a tightly knit immigrant community that had not yet been immersed in the American melting pot. The question is, How well do these recipes adapt to the American kitchen and to American cooks? The recipes we tested pretty much tell the story. A beef salad with a "salmoriglio" sauce, which is a Sicilian lemon vinaigrette, was outstanding. In this recipe, rump roast is simmered in water and vegetables (which makes a stock that can be used in other dishes), sliced or shredded into small pieces, and then served with the sauce—delicious, authentic, and easy to prepare. A potato and cheese soufflé, however, was less successful. The base was much too thick, which made folding in the egg whites virtually impossible, resulting in a heavy, thick pudding rather than a soufflé. Other recipes followed suit. A rustic cake was full of flavor and so easy that we made two in under an hour, yet when we made a fried pasta dish with spinach, the pasta stuck to the skillet. In short, Carlo Middione is the real thing—his first book, *The Food of Southern Italy* (William Morrow, 1987), is a classic, and so are his recipes. However, what works on an Italian farm doesn't necessarily translate well to American kitchens. If you are hungry for authentic Italian home-style recipes, we can strongly recommend this book, as long as you keep in mind that some of Middione's recipes have made the trip in better condition than others. ∎

—*Christopher Kimball*

Sources and Resources

Most of the ingredients and materials necessary for the recipes in this issue are available at your local supermarket, gourmet store, or kitchen supply shop. The following are mail-order sources for particular items. Prices listed below were current at press time and do not include shipping or handling unless otherwise indicated. We suggest that you contact companies directly to confirm up-to-date prices and availability.

KITCHEN TIMERS

Two West Bend timers, the Model 40031x Clock/Double Electronic Timer for $16.98 and the Model 40030 Timer for $10.98, were rated first and second in the testing on page 28. To locate the nearest retailer of West Bend timers, call West Bend customer service at 414-334-2311.

TIME AND BEYOND

Timing is but one of the talents of the third-place winner in the timer testing. With a unique, high-tech design, the Polder Cooking Thermometer/Timer combines an electronic timer with an electronic thermometer for testing the doneness of meat and bread. A thirty-six-inch metal cord connects the probe, which has been stuck into the cooking item, with the thermometer/timer, into which you have programmed the desired finish temperature. The alarm will sound when the food reaches the preset temperature. The Polder Cooking Thermometer/Timer is available for $29.95 from the King Arthur Flour Baker's Catalogue (P.O. Box 876, Norwich, VT 05055-0876; 800-827-6836).

THE KITCHEN WHIZ

Along with the kitchen timers, we also tested the Kitchen Whiz "Food Preparation/Conversion Computer." Developed at the Massachusetts Institute of Technology (M.I.T.), the Kitchen Whiz works as timer, clock, calculator, and kitchen mathematical converter. It converts weights, volumes, and lengths from American to metric and vice versa, and tempera-tures from centigrade to Fahrenheit and back. It will also increase and decrease recipes for easy halving, doubling, and so forth. The King Arthur Flour Baker's Catalogue (800-827-6836) sells the Kitchen Whiz for $30.25.

EXTRA-VIRGIN OLIVE OILS

If you know which flavors and qualities you prefer in a drizzling olive oil, you can rely on the guidance—as we did to assemble our field of contestants in the testing on page 26—of three mail-order specialty food businesses whose staffs are knowledgeable and passionate about olive oil. In fact, between them, Zingerman's Delicatessen, Dean & DeLuca, and Corti Brothers sell well over one hundred 1995 harvest olive oils. Our first- and second-choice oils, Tenuta di Valgiano Olio Extra Vergine di Oliva (Lucca, Italy; $24 for a 500 ml bottle) and Roi Olio Extra Vergine d'Oliva (Badalucco, Italy; $27 for a 1 liter bottle), were purchased from Zingerman's Delicatessen (422 Detroit Street, Ann Arbor, MI 48104; 313-769-1625). The oils that came in third, sixth, and ninth, Lérida Extra Virgin Olive Oil (Sarocca de Lérida, Spain; $28.50 for a 1 liter bottle), Stutz California Extra Virgin Olive Oil (Berkeley, California; $14.95 for a 750 ml bottle), and Barbera Frantoia Extra Virgin Olive Oil (Palermo, Italy; $19.95 for a 1 liter bottle), came from Dean & DeLuca (560 Broadway, New York, NY 10012; 800-221-7714). The oils that were rated fifth and eighth, Consorzio Extra Virgin Olive Oil (Napa, California; $10 for a 375 ml bottle) and Verdesco California Extra Virgin Olive Oil (Modesto, California; $7.99 for a 375 ml bottle), came from Corti Brothers (5810 Folsom Boulevard, Sacramento, CA 95819; 916-736-3803 or 800-509-3663).

FLAVORED VINEGARS

With all this talk of olive oil, it seems natural to mention vinegar in the same breath. Lately we have been enjoying the Consorzio line of flavored vinegars called "vignettes." The brainchild of chef Michael Chiarello of the restaurant Tra Vigne in St. Helena, California, each vignette is composed essentially of a puree of the primary sweet or savory flavoring agent, enhanced with herbs and spices and mixed with champagne vinegar. The result is rich, thick, and intensely flavored, with a consistency more like a vinegar-flavored puree than the clear, liquid, infused vinegar in our mind's eye. The savory vignettes, among them Mustard Seed, Roasted Garlic, and Tomato, make great pan sauces and pair well with the drizzling oils from our tasting article on page 26. The fruit-flavored vignettes, including Mango, Raspberry, and Passion Fruit, are more sweet than tart. Use them in pan sauces, salsas, drinks, fruit salad, and dessert sauces. The fruit-flavored vignettes are also great in vinaigrette dressings, though you should steer clear of the drizzling oils for these because the oils' strong flavors would not complement these sweet vinegars. Along with a line of flavored olive oils and other specialty products, Consorzio vignettes are available by mail order for $5 per 375 ml bottle from Napa Valley Kitchens (4 Financial Plaza, Napa, CA 94558; 800-288-1089).

THE REAL McCOY: AN AMERICAN BEAN POT

While we found that a stoneware bean pot is not absolutely necessary to prepare the Boston baked beans from the story on page 14, these pots do offer unparalleled authenticity, ambiance, and Americana. Ironically, though, many examples of this classic American bean pot on the market today are manufactured in the Far East! Not so the pots sold by La Cuisine, The Cook's Resource (323 Cameron Street, Alexandria, VA 22314; 800-521-1176). Manufactured in the Midwest by Western Stoneware since the late 1800s, these pots feature a narrow neck to help retain moisture over long baking periods and are safe for use in conventional, convection, and microwave ovens. The pots are glazed in the original two-tone brown color scheme, and they come in three sizes: five-and-one-half cups for $23, five pints for $30, and four quarts for $38.

MEAT LOAF PAN

Free-form or baked in a pan? That was one of the many questions about meat loaf we investigated for the story on page 22. These baking methods produce different styles of meat loaf, and we concluded that if you prefer a crustless, soft-sided meat loaf, you should avoid using a standard loaf pan in which the meat stews rather than bakes. Instead, we suggest that you invest in a specially designed meat loaf pan with a perforated bottom that fits into an accompanying drip pan. As the meat cooks, the drippings flow to the pan below rather than bubbling up the sides. The Chef's Catalog (3215 Commercial Avenue, Northbrook, IL 60062; 800-338-3232) sells just such a meat loaf pan by Chicago Metallic. The pan measures eight-and-one-half inches long by five inches wide, has a Silverstone nonstick coating, and costs $12.99.

COOLING RACKS

Practically every baked item that emerges from the oven has to be cooled on a wire rack. For the oven-dried tomatoes from the story on page 20, it is just the reverse case: They are gently heated on a wire rack in the oven. Either way, a good strong rack is essential equipment. Flimsy racks with widely spaced rungs that bend under pressure from a heavy pan or that let cookies fall through should be avoided. We prefer the firmly welded, chromed cooling and icing racks used by commercial bakeries. The Sur La Table catalog (410 Terry Avenue North, Seattle, WA 98109; 800-243-0852) sells a set of two racks with tightly woven grids that will keep even the smallest cookies, not to mention tomatoes, in place. One rack is ten inches by eighteen inches, the other sixteen inches by twenty-four inches. Both racks are supported by long chrome bars that keep the mesh grid from sagging. The set of two racks costs $28.95. ∎

ASSORTED BRUSCHETTA
page 8

BOSTON BAKED BEANS
page 15

**CREAM-BRAISED CABBAGE WITH
LEMON AND SHALLOTS**
page 9

MUFFULETTA
page 21

ASSORTED MACAROONS
page 6

CHOCOLATE SOUFFLÉ
page 19

Arugula Salad with Grilled Figs and Roasted Pepper Vinaigrette

In small bowl, mix ½ cup olive oil, 1½ tablespoons each of red wine vinegar and balsamic vinegar, 1 medium minced garlic clove, 1 large roasted and diced red pepper, and ⅓ cup roughly chopped fresh basil leaves with salt and ground black pepper to taste; set aside. Rub 10 halved figs lightly with vegetable oil and sprinkle with salt and ground black pepper; grill over medium-hot fire, along with 16 thinly-sliced pieces of prosciutto, until lightly browned, about 1 minute per side for both figs and prosciutto. Place 8 cups arugula in large bowl; add enough vinaigrette to moisten greens and toss to coat. Place greens on serving platter and arrange figs, prosciutto, and ½ pound provolone cheese, cut into thick strips, over greens. Drizzle with remaining vinaigrette and serve immediately.

Serves 8

COOK'S
ILLUSTRATED

Best Holiday Cookies

Light, Buttery Cookies
That Don't Fall Apart

No-Cream
Cream Soups

Rich, Creamy Vegetable
Soup Without the Cream

How to Cook
a Country Ham

Getting More Flavor
With Less Salt

Rating Espresso
Machines

Do Affordable Ones
Really Work?

CLASSIC TRIFLE

PERFECT BAKED
SWEET POTATOES

MAKE-AHEAD TURKEY GRAVY

HOW TO COOK
GREEN BEANS

$4.00 U.S./$4.95 CANADA

Table of Contents

NOVEMBER/DECEMBER 1996

NUMBER TWENTY-THREE

"Fall Flavors"

ILLUSTRATION BY
BRENT WATKINSON

**"Cranberry-Pear Salsa
in Pear Shells"**

from *Pears*
(Chronicle, 1996)
by Linda West Eckhardt

ILLUSTRATION BY
VINCENT McINDOE

COOK'S
ILLUSTRATED

Publisher and Editor CHRISTOPHER KIMBALL

Executive Editor PAM ANDERSON

Senior Editor JOHN WILLOUGHBY

Senior Writer JACK BISHOP

Associate Editor ADAM RIED

Consulting Editors MARK BITTMAN
STEPHANIE LYNESS

Editorial Assistant ELIZABETH CAMERON

Test Cooks MELISSA HAMILTON
EVA KATZ

Art Director ANNE MURDOCK

Food Stylist MARIE PIRAINO

Special Projects Designer AMY KLEE

Managing Editor KEITH POWERS

Editorial Prod. Manager SHEILA DATZ

Copy Editor GARY PFITZER

Marketing Director ADRIENNE KIMBALL

Vice President Circulation CAROLYN ADAMS

Fulfillment Manager JAMIE AYER

Circulation Coordinator JONATHAN VENIER

Vice Pres. Prod. & Technology JAMES MCCORMACK

Advertising Prod. Manager PAMELA SLATTERY

Systems Administrator MICAH BENSON

Production Artist KEVIN MOELLER

Advertising Prod. Assistant DANIEL FREY

Editorial Prod. Assistant ROBERT PARSONS

Vice President JEFFREY FEINGOLD

Controller LISA A. CARULLO

Accounting Assistant MANDY SHITO

Office Manager TONYA ESTEY

Special Projects FERN BERMAN

Cook's Illustrated (ISSN 1068-2821) is published bimonthly by Boston Common Press Limited Partnership, 17 Station Street, P.O. Box 569, Brookline, MA 02147-0569. Copyright 1996 Boston Common Press Limited Partnership. Periodical postage paid at Boston, MA, and additional mailing offices. USPS #012487. For list rental information, please contact List Services Corporation, 6 Trowbridge Drive, P.O. Box 516, Bethel, CT 06801; (203) 743-2600, FAX (203) 743-0589. Editorial office: 17 Station Street, P.O. Box 569, Brookline, MA 02147-0569; (617) 232-1000, FAX 617) 232-1572. Editorial contributions should be sent to: Editor, Cook's Illustrated. We cannot assume responsibility for manuscripts submitted to us. Submissions will be returned only if accompanied by a large self-addressed stamped envelope. Subscription rates: $24.95 for one year; $45 for two years; $65 for three years. (Canada: add $6 per year; all other countries: add $12 per year.) Postmaster: Send all new orders, subscription inquiries, and change of address notices to Cook's Illustrated, P.O. Box 7444, Red Oak, IA 51591-0444. Single copies: $4 in U.S., $4.95 in Canada and other countries. Back issues available for $5 each. PRINTED IN THE U.S.A.

EDITORIAL

BETWEEN THE BREAD AND THE BUTTER

One Saturday morning last winter, I was holed up in our guest bedroom/office, hunched over the portable computer, my head stuffed full of things undone, when I looked up and saw the sky clearing, the large, bare maple tree that my wife and I had planted ten years ago just starting to throw a wispy shadow on the deep drifts of snow that had recently covered up the wet January thaw. I shut down the computer, grabbed thick gray socks and my old fawn-colored work boots, and headed toward the back porch.

CHRISTOPHER KIMBALL

For many, winter in Vermont is about downhill or cross-country skiing, but for me it has always been about snowshoeing. It's one of the few outdoor sports that has yet to be discovered by glossy magazines, it requires no special apparel or lift tickets, and it's best done alone, thus well suited to the New England character. So I strapped on my Sherpa Snow-Claws, which are narrow and designed for climbing steep, icy slopes, and set out up our mountain.

As I started up the old logging road, I was still mentally back at the computer, worrying over unfinished projects. But the sky had now completely cleared, turning a pure, soft winter blue, and I started to focus on the sound of the snowshoes making a rhythmic whuff and scrunch as they settled through the deep snow and the "ha" and "sa" of breathing in and out. With a thick wool cap down over my ears, the sound of my own breathing cleared my mind wonderfully, an icy tonic like the aching shock of jumping into a Vermont pond in August, fed by the trickle of a fern-scented mountain stream. As I moved through stands of hickory, sugar maple, red maple, white and black birch, dying chestnuts, and the occasional large oak missed by Greg Squires, a local logger, I picked up the pace, in full gear, moving quickly up the last incline, and then came out on top of the world. In a small clearing at the peak, I could see the large chain of the Adirondacks, the open, windswept hayfields of New York State, and feel the cold wind on my forehead, stinging but refreshing from the hot climb. There was nothing else in that moment except the wind, the snow, and my breath.

It should be noted that it's not much of a trick to feel the infinite on top of a mountain on a cold, sunny January day; it's finding the infinite in the everyday that proves more difficult. Of course, our eighteen-month-old son, like any other young child, has no trouble with this. Given a moment's inattention, he makes a lurching escape down the driveway to the brook, followed closely by a frantic parent, where he enthusiastically pitches rocks into the knee-deep water just down from the culvert. This is an all-consuming proposition, one that seemingly has no limits. After a full hour of this activity, he has just warmed up to the task at hand. He is totally living the moment, the past and future having no meaning whatever.

Although in recent months I have taken to pitching rocks along with my son, I have always found the kitchen a good place to focus the mind. As Steven Lewis notes in *Zen and The Art of Fatherhood*, it is between the bread and the butter that the great moments of life are lived, where enjoying a meal is an end in itself, where the little bits and pieces of daily life are all-encompassing, pushing out the past and future. I would add that chopping onions, sautéing stew meat, or rolling out pie dough are all handy for shutting down our inner conversations. I am always too worried about burning garlic or overcooking custard to give a moment's thought to the meaning of existence. Perhaps, in an odd way, that is when we come closest to really living: when we are consumed with the present, unaware of a greater context.

After supper in the summer, our family always takes a walk to watch the bees floating down into the hive, or into the upper fields to check on the berry crop, or across the road to visit the local cemetery to read the inscriptions. The one that I most cherish (other than old Fred Woodcock's tombstone, which features a carved likeness of a can of Pabst Blue Ribbon beer and a plate of doughnuts) was written by Urana Sulliff, wife of John, who died in 1835. As was the custom in the nineteenth century, she sends a stern warning from beyond the grave. She notes that she was "once beloved like you" and asks us to stop to "take another view" and then ends her plea with these words: "No longer then on future time rely, improve the present and prepare to die." Harsh words? Perhaps. But in this holiday season toward the end of this second millennium, I am happy to be present and accounted for in the kitchen, merrily engaged in our family's seasonal culinary rituals, knowing that my short time on this earth is well spent between the bread and the butter. ■

Notes from Readers

CASTOR SUGAR

The manual for the Krups La Glacière, which was noted in the Sources and Resources page of the May/June 1996 issue, lists castor sugar as an ingredient. What is this?

NICOLE MICHAELS
Brooklyn, NY

Castor sugar is essentially the British equivalent of American superfine granulated sugar. Its name comes from the shaker used in Britain to dispense this fine sugar.

There are many types of refined, white, granulated sugar, which vary according to the size of the crystals. According to representatives from The Sugar Association in Washington, D.C., the coarsest is *strong sugar*, which has exceptionally large granules that resist changes in color and chemical composition at high temperatures. A second type of large crystal sugar is *sanding sugar*. Because these large crystals reflect light and therefore appear to sparkle, they are widely used in the confectionery industry, most often sprinkled on top of baked goods. Supermarket sugar of the type most often used in home food preparation is called *regular granulated*, referred to in the food processing industry as *fine* or *extra fine sugar*. The next finest granulation is *fruit sugar*, which is found naturally in fruit as fructose. When processed for commercial use in products such as dry gelatin and pudding dessert and drink mixes, fruit sugar crystals are more uniform in size than regular sugar crystals, so they remain evenly distributed in dry mixes, with no separation and settling of smaller crystals to the bottom of the batch. The crystals of *bakers special sugar* are finer yet. As the name suggests, this granulation was developed specially for the baking industry. The finest of all the granulated sugars is *superfine*, which is also sometimes called *ultrafine* or *bar sugar*. It dissolves quickly, so it is used to sweeten beverages and fruit, as well as meringues and very fine-textured cakes. This is the crystal size to which castor sugar, with the variant spelling caster, is most similar.

MORE DETAILS ON CLABBERED MILK

In the Notes from Readers section of your July/August 1996 issue, you included a letter from Levenia Keleman asking about clabber. Your response covered it very well with the exception that when clabber was an important homemade ingredient, milk was not only unpasteurized, it was also unhomogenized. The process was to first skim off all or most of the cream, then cover the remaining milk and keep it at room temperature overnight. By then the milk had solidified into curds separate from the whey, which was drained off. The resulting curds (clabber) were stirred to arrive at the consistency desired by the particular person—some liked it globular, others fine like coarse buttermilk.

In making clabber, whole unhomogenized milk makes gelatin-type curds that shake when tapped. Homogenized milk makes fine, granular curds with very little separation of whey. In other words, homogenizing messes up the process of clabber.

BILL MORAN
San Diego, TX

You make an excellent point that we should have made clearer. We did mention that real clabber, which is a soured, thickened milk product, was originally made from raw milk, and thus connotes unpasteurized and unhomogenized. However, we went on to briefly discuss pasteurization, which reduces the number of enzymes and bacteria in milk, but we did not concentrate on homogenization. Homogenization helps emulsify milk by decreasing the size of its natural fat globules. The milk is forced through a tiny nozzle at extremely high pressure onto a hard surface, which breaks down the fat globules into uniform particles roughly one-quarter of their original size. In the process, the fat becomes more evenly dispersed throughout the liquid. The broken down and redistributed fat globules will not rise to the top of the liquid to form the thick, cream layer present in raw milk. Neither are they large enough to aggregate into the large curds you know from the clabber of your youth. Our best effort at making clabber from homogenized milk—we have no source for raw milk nearby—resulted in a consistency only slightly thicker than buttermilk.

A PIECE OF CAKE

I was hoping you could settle a debate I've been having with my fiancé over how to cut a cake. I say to get a smooth, clean, well-defined cut, you must do the following: Use a very warm, sharp, straight-edged knife. To heat the knife, either run it under hot water or let it stand in a glass of hot water for a few moments. Take the hot knife out of the water and dry it before cutting. After each cut, wipe the knife clean, stick it in hot water, dry it, and cut again. My fiancé says that it doesn't matter if the knife is serrated or straight-edged, warm or cold.

CHRISTINE ONDRUS
Beverly Hills, CA

Unfortunately, we cannot settle your debate conclusively. We called a dozen highly reputed local bakeries to ask their advice, and they were split right down the middle: Six of them favored serrated knives, and the other six use straight-edged blades! You do have one leg up on your fiancé, though, on the point of heating the knife blade. This was suggested by every baker with whom we spoke. Also, whichever knife you choose, make sure the blade is as thin as possible.

We tested both types of blade, slice for slice, on a couple of frosted layer cakes in our test kitchen. For us, the serrated edge with small, compact teeth (as opposed to a bread knife with wider teeth), wiped clean after every cut with a hot, damp towel, was more successful. We also noted that room temperature cakes sliced more neatly than refrigerated cakes. When you reach the bottom of the cake, wiggle the blade gently to ensure that the slice is free from the rest of the cake and then pull the blade out toward you. If you lift the blade up through the cut, you'll probably get crumbs all over the icing. For really moist, dense cakes such as cheesecake, we prefer to use dental floss for slicing.

CUTTING ANOTHER CAKE

I learned the following tip for cutting angel food cake from my mom: Use a serrated knife and wet the blade before each cut. The piece of cake does not shred or crumb, and the knife stays clean. Use a slicing motion just as you would when slicing a roast.

MARYANNE COELLN
Richardson, TX

We tried your method using a moistened serrated knife, and it worked like a charm. The slices were practically crumb-free, and much neater than those cut with a traditional angel food cake cutter, which looks a bit like a rake, with three-inch-long, blunt tines designed to gently tear the slice from the rest of the cake. Just make sure that the water on the blade is minimal so that the cake slices do not become soggy.

THREE GREAT BAKING SHORTCUTS

If you make a particular baked good frequently, try mixing together an extra batch or two of the dry ingredients and freezing them in a zipper-lock bag. This saves time for all recipes, but I find it especially helpful in making breads that call for more than one kind of flour—no more lugging out of three or four flour bags each time.

MICHAEL FELDMAN
Hendersonville, NC

I hate to waste a whole egg making an egg wash for scones or other baked items that require them. Instead, I use the leftovers from the container in which I mixed the liquid ingredients. I always mix all the dry ingredients first, and then the liquid ingredients (usually egg, milk, vanilla extract, etc.) separately, finally adding the liquids to the dry blend to mix up the dough or batter. Any residue left in the liquid ingredients container, mixed with a little water, makes a great egg wash to brush over the scones or bread.

PHAEDRA HISE
Somerville, MA

*D*on't throw away butter or margarine wrappers after finishing the stick. I keep the wrappers in a container in the refrigerator and use them to grease baking pans easily and without mess or waste.

S. YATES
Franz Josef, New Zealand

DEEP-FRYING METHOD

*I*n your July/August 1996 issue, you propose a recipe for french fries that uses two quarts of peanut oil heated in a large open pot. In your charter issue you tested electric deep fryers and suggested that the use of these machines was superior to open-pot deep frying in that the amount of oil was smaller and the temperature control more effective. Can the perfect french fries be reproduced in the electric fryer? Will the fryer maintain a consistent temperature as low as 325 degrees for the first frying?

VICTOR ROSTROW
Alexandria, VA

We are indeed fans of the electric fryer for the reasons you point out—reduced oil use, temperature control, and ease of cleaning—and it was mentioned as an option in the french fries recipe. We use a DeLonghi Roto-Fryer Model D-20, which along with a less expensive variation, the Model D-17, is the current version of the winner of the electric fryer testing in our charter issue back in 1992. The Roto-Fryer produces fantastic french fries with minimal effort. With a temperature range from 300 to 370 degrees, the Roto-Fryer handles easily and fairly accurately, according to our testing, the 325-degree initial frying. Despite its benefits, though, we included the open-pot option in the french fries recipe because not everyone owns an electric fryer, and we were able to make great fries in the open pot.

GRAPESEED OIL

*I*n the same letter as above, Mr. Rostrow also commented: *I generally use grapeseed oil for initial sautéing of meats and fish, but I have found it only in small (250 ml) containers. Is there a source for grapeseed oil in bulk, or at least in liter bottles? Would grapeseed oil (with the addition of strained bacon grease) be an*

acceptable substitute for peanut oil in the fries recipe?

With regard to mouth feel, grapeseed oil works well in the french fries recipe. Compared to peanut oil, though, grapeseed oil has a much fainter taste. Therefore, it flavors the potatoes less than the peanut oil, which is fine if you favor a stronger potato flavor in your fries. Another issue is the expense of the oil. According to Robert Reeves, President of the Institute of Shortening and Edible Oils, grapeseed oil is expensive and generally sold only in small bottles because most of the products available in the United States are imported from winemaking countries such as France and Italy. Grapeseed oil is, as its name zimplies, extracted by a solvent treatment from grape seeds. As noted, the oil's flavor tends to be bland and its smoke point, like most other cooking oils, is well above 400 degrees, a temperature that most likely will not be reached in a home kitchen. For information on ordering grapeseed oil, *see* Sources and Resources on page 32.

CLARIFYING BROTH

I really enjoyed the article "Quick Homemade Chicken Soup" in the March/April 1996 issue. A Chinese method of preparing a "remarkably clear" chicken broth by first blanching and then simmering chicken was mentioned. It is my understanding that clear broths, chicken or beef, are highly valued in Asian cooking in general. I have had a problem when preparing beef broth. If it is boiled too hard, it turns cloudy. Is there any way to rescue broth that has turned cloudy? I have tried filtering it, but it remains cloudy.

BRAD GILCHRIST
Iowa City, IA

In a sense, you've already hit the nail on the head. Along with faithfully skimming the scum from the surface, one of the most important steps you can take to help prevent your broth from turning cloudy in the first place is to make sure that it

simmers rather than boils. Not only will boiling churn fat and food particles back into the stock so that they will not rise to the top to be skimmed off, but, as our food science consultant Shirley Corriher explains, vigorous boiling also forms an emulsion in the stock that incorporates tiny fat particles into the liquid. Such stocks may never clarify.

In most cases, we simply filter stock by ladling it carefully through a strainer lined with a triple layer of clean, damp cheesecloth. Ladling works better than pouring the stock because fewer food particles are disturbed in the process. To further clarify stock so it all but sparkles, such as for consommé, we have adapted from Jacques Pepin's *The Art of Cooking* (Knopf, 1987) the classic method of adding egg whites and shells and extra greens. For every quart of stock to be clarified, mix together the white and shell of one egg and three-quarters cup of coarsely chopped parsley stems and leaves. Starting with thoroughly strained, defatted, and chilled stock, heat it very slowly until it is lukewarm and stir in the egg and parsley mixture. Increase the heat to medium high and cook, stirring frequently, until the stock begins to boil. The stock will become increasingly muddy-looking on its way to the boil because the proteins in the egg white are beginning to unwind. As the protein molecules continue to unwind, they will bump into each other and make a complex mesh that, as it tightens, traps the minute particles floating in the stock that cause cloudiness while allowing the liquid to slip through. The parsley provides extra surfaces onto which the particles can cling. The mesh will rise to the surface, forming a frothy crust roughly an inch thick. At this point, reduce the heat to very low and use a ladle to punch a small hole in the crust through which you can look to make sure that the liquid beneath is simmering, and not boiling. If the liquid boils at this stage, the egg white might congeal too fast and the clarification will fail. Continue simmering for about twenty minutes, and remove the pot from the burner to cool for at least fifteen minutes. When the stock is cool, repeat the original filtering process by ladling the liquid out of the pot and into a strainer lined with a triple thickness of clean, damp cheesecloth. ■

WHAT IS IT?

*M*y brother loves to test my knowledge of cooking. He brought these weird little tongs back from a recent trip to New York, but won't share their real purpose and challenged me to find out. They are about five-and-a-half inches long and the ends, which are wider than the arms, are perforated. Can you tell me what they're for?

EMMA KILEY
Ketchum, ID

Your brother brought you a tea bag squeezer. After steeping the tea, the squeezer—also called tea tongs—is used to lift the tea bag out of the pot or cup and, using the flat, rectangular, perforated area, efficiently squeeze out the last drops of liquid. In front of company, this procedure would certainly be neater than smooshing the tea bag into a spoon with your fingers or wrapping the tea bag string around the dripping bag. Generally made of stainless steel, tea bag squeezers can be mail-ordered from Utilities (393 Commercial Street, Provincetown, MA 02657; 508-487-6800). The squeezer costs $2.95, plus shipping and handling.

Quick Tips

To prevent milk from boiling over when heating it on the stove, try this tip from Pam Baron of Los Altos, California.

1. Rub butter along the top edge and inside lip of the pan.

2. Even if the milk does foam up in the pan, it will stop when it hits the butter.

CLEANING UP AFTER BREADMAKING

Cleaning up hands, workbowl, and kneading surface after breadmaking can be a pain. A scrubbing pad is most effective for removing the dough, but the dough tends to stick to the pad so it has to be discarded. Shelly Stephan of Mission Viejo, California, suggests doing dough cleanup with a square of the plastic mesh used to package shallots, onions, potatoes, and so forth, which can then simply be thrown away.

PROOFING BREAD

Lois McAlpine of West Newton, Pennsylvania, finds the microwave to be perfect for proofing bread. To do so, she heats a measuring cup of water in the microwave to boiling point, then shuts off the microwave and places the dough inside. The preheated water keeps the dough at a warm temperature while it proofs in a moist and draft-free environment. This method works well regardless of the ambient humidity.

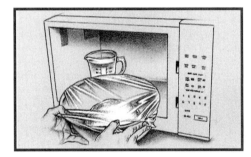

CLEANING THE TRIFLE BOWL

When you make the trifle on page 8, the finished dish is spectacular. Its appearance can be marred, though, by fingerprints or smears on the sides of the bowl. To clean the bowl after assembling the dessert, follow the suggestion of author Stephen Schmidt: Firmly cover the top of the bowl with plastic wrap to protect the trifle, clean the sides of the bowl with glass cleaner, then remove the plastic wrap.

STABILIZING STUFFED CHICKEN BREASTS

While making Chicken Kiev, Warren Orloff of Upper Arlington, Ohio, discovered this ingenious method for holding stuffed chicken breasts together.

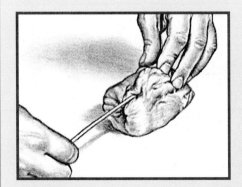

1. Stuff the breast, then pin it together by pushing an uncooked spaghetti noodle through the meat.

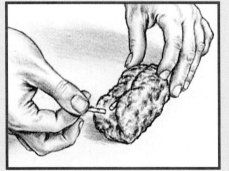

2. After the breast has been cooked, break off the blackened end of the noodle; the part that remains inside the chicken will have cooked through in the chicken juices and will not interfere with the taste of the chicken.

LIFTING HOT LIDS

Faith Lang of Troy, New Hampshire, and Carolyn Tumbleson of Murfreesboro, Tennessee, had the same tip for lifting hot lids.

Rather than burning fingers or reaching for a pot holder every time they want to lift the lids, both of these cooks wedge wine corks under the handles of the lids. The corks stay cool when the lids get hot, so the lids can be lifted safely.

ILLUSTRATIONS BY ALAN WITSCHONKE

REMOVING CAKE FROM A BUNDT PAN

Tammie Warnke Dufrene of Baton Rouge, Louisiana, has developed this surefire method to keep the tender crust of her prizewinning pound cake from sticking to the Bundt pan.

1. Just before the cake is through baking, place a folded bathroom towel in the sink and saturate it with steaming hot water.

2. When the cake comes out of the oven, immediately set the it on top of the towel, pan side down, and leave it for ten seconds.

3. Immediately invert the cake onto a cooling rack. The cake will come out clean and whole without sticking.

REMOVING DRUMSTICK TENDONS

To make turkey drumsticks more tender and more pleasant to eat, Ter DePuy of Volcano, Hawaii, suggests removing the drumstick tendons, which turn bonelike during roasting.

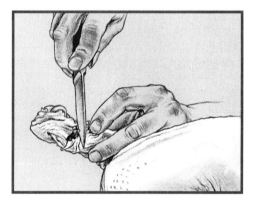

1. Before roasting, slice through the skin about one inch from the bottom of the drumstick to provide access to the tendons.

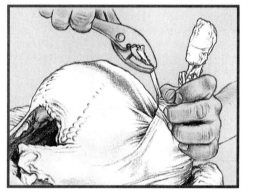

2. Using a clean pair of pliers, grasp the exposed white tendons firmly and pull away from the bone.

INGENIOUS RECIPE HOLDER

Carol Alexander of Park Ridge, New Jersey, slips one or more recipe cards into a five-by-seven-inch freestanding Lucite picture frame, which slants backward slightly for easier reading and also keeps the cards free from splatters during cooking.

HOLDING A BOWL STEADY

When you need to pour with one hand and whisk with another, here's a way to hold your bowl steady.

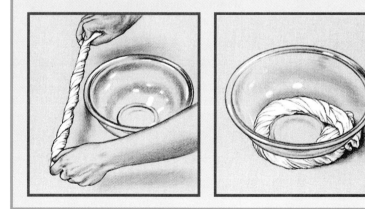

1. Wet a kitchen towel, grasp it by both ends, and wring it until it is tightly twisted.

2. Place the bowl on the counter, then wrap the towel around the base of the bowl.

3. The bowl will stay steady as you whisk and pour.

Thanks to our readers for Quick Tips: The editors of *Cook's Illustrated* would like to thank all of the readers who have sent us their quick tips. We have enjoyed reading every one of them and have learned a lot. Keep them coming. We will provide a one-year complimentary subscription for each quick tip that we print. Send a description of your special technique to *Cook's Illustrated*, P.O. Box 569, Brookline Village, MA 02147-0569. Please write "Attention: Quick Tips" on the envelope and include your name, address, and daytime phone number. Unfortunately, we can only acknowledge receipt of tips that will be printed in the magazine. In case the same tip is received from two readers, the one postmarked first will be selected. Also, be sure to let us know what particular cooking problems you would like us to investigate in upcoming issues.

Two Good Ways to Cook Green Beans

Boil or braise depending on the beans' age and toughness.

∼ BY JACK BISHOP ∼

When it comes to holiday side dishes, many cooks avoid green beans. It may be that, like me, they are haunted by memories of an awful green bean casserole. Just thinking of those mushy green beans floating in a pool of canned cream of mushroom soup and topped with fried onion rings (from a can, of course) makes me shudder.

But there is no reason to blame the beans for this recipe disaster. Although a summer crop, green beans grown in warm climates are available in U.S. markets year-round. While other holiday vegetables may have a hard time pleasing a crowd (I'm thinking of brussels sprouts), green beans are generally welcomed by all.

The trick, though, is to figure out how to cook them. In the past, I have prepared green beans two ways—either cook/then flavor or flavor and cook simultaneously. After researching recipes in dozens of cookbooks, I found that this distinction was fairly uniform. My goal for this piece was to test the variables and devise two master techniques for cooking green beans.

Cook, Then Flavor

For this first method, green beans are boiled or steamed and then sautéed or simply dressed with flavorful ingredients. Sounds simple (and it is), but I still had questions. Is boiling better than steaming? Should beans be cut (either into pieces or lengthwise) before cooking? Should salt be added to the water? How long should beans cook? Should they be refreshed in cold water?

After a number of experiments with boiling and steaming, I came to prefer boiling for several reasons. Steaming takes twice as long as boiling, and when steaming a pound or more of beans I found it necessary to turn them during cooking because those at the bottom were cooking faster than those at the top of the pile. Finally, boiling cooks each bean more evenly; steamed beans are often tender on the outside but raw-tasting in the middle.

Just as important, boiling permits the addition of salt during cooking. The beans need additional salting after they are drained, but adding salt during cooking results in more even seasoning because the salt has time to be absorbed into the beans.

As for preparation, I prefer to tip the tops and tails with my fingers (*see* illustration, page 7) but leave the beans whole otherwise. Cutting the beans into shorter lengths exposes the tender flesh to too much heat. Because the skin cooks more slowly than this exposed flesh, the inside of the beans tends to become mushy. I also am not enthusiastic about "frenching" (*see* "Do the French Really Do It?" page 7).

Another batch of tests centered around refreshing the beans in cold water. I found that this "tip" advocated by many cookbook authors makes the bean soggy-tasting. If you want to use the beans later and stop the cooking process, I would suggest spreading the beans out over a baking sheet, an idea I picked up from Alice Waters' *Chez Panisse Vegetables* (HarperCollins, 1996). The beans cool off fairly quickly and do not soften further.

Boiling times vary greatly in the sources I consulted. One respected Italian cookbook author recommends cooking green beans for twenty to twenty-five minutes. Another suggests one and one-half minutes. Could they be writing about the same vegetable?

I found that the freshness and thickness of the beans greatly affects cooking time. Really fresh, thin beans, not much thicker than a strand of linguine, may be done in as little as two minutes. Most beans in the supermarket, though, have traveled some distance and are considerably thicker. Due to their age and size, they need five to six minutes to become tender. I don't like mushy green beans, but beans that are too crisp or raw-tasting are likewise unappealing.

After boiling and prompt draining, beans may be flavored in two ways. They can be "dressed" (drizzled with a flavorful oil or vinaigrette) or quickly sautéed. If dressing the beans, do so when they are hot for maximum absorption. Beans that will be sautéed can be set aside at room temperature for a few hours. Whether dressing or sautéeing beans, use very flavorful ingredients—a drizzle of walnut oil and the addition of toasted walnuts and tarragon, for example, or a quick sauté with onions that have been browned in bacon fat.

Flavor During Cooking

This second method for preparing green beans is slower than the first, but allows the beans to absorb flavors as they cook. Tomatoes, cream, or stock can be used as a braising liquid. While the principle is quite simple, I did have a few questions. Could the bright green color be preserved by blanching the beans before braising? And what kind of heat was best—long and slow or fast and furious? Also, how long should the beans be braised so they pick up a good amount of flavor from the braising liquid but still keep some of their original color and texture?

After several attempts at blanching beans before braising (for thirty seconds, one minute, and two minutes), I realized this path was going nowhere. Even short blanching reduced braising time dramatically so the beans didn't spend enough time in the braising pan to pick up flavors. More importantly, blanching before braising failed to keep the color bright; no matter what I tried, the color of the braised beans faded to an olive green.

As for the cooking time, I found that the beans need at least fifteen or twenty minutes to pick up enough flavor to make this method worthwhile. More time (like forty-five minutes) added little in terms in flavor but did hurt both color and texture.

Age Determines Method

As I continued to experiment, I began to realize that the choice between these two distinct methods should be made on the basis of the beans that you are cooking. Really fresh beans are best boiled and seasoned, retaining much of their flavor and texture. But older, tougher beans benefit from slow cooking in a covered pan. The beans will lose some color, but they pick up wonderful flavors from the braising medium.

Very fresh, young green beans are best when boiled, but braising is the best cooking method for older beans.

Natural variations in the size and quality of the beans make a real difference, so it's worthwhile to keep a few points in mind while shopping. A green bean is a legume that is harvested when the pod is tender and the seeds are immature. However, there are times when the beans are harvested too late. Very thick pods swollen with not-so-immature seeds should be avoided. They do not possess the gentle sweetness I associate with good green beans and can remain tough and chewy after cooking. Also, spend some time choosing pods that are fairly uniform in size. Thickness determines cooking time, so this is important.

The two cooking methods outlined above can be used with regular green beans. Haricots verts—very thin green beans sometimes available at this time of the year but commonly seen in the summer—should be boiled and then flavored. Two to three minutes in boiling water will make these beans tender. The sweet flavor and delicate texture of these beans makes them ill-suited to braising.

GREEN BEANS WITH TOASTED WALNUTS AND TARRAGON
Serves 4 to 6

Green beans are boiled and then tossed with toasted walnuts, tarragon, and walnut oil. Basil or parsley may be used as a substitute.

 ¼ cup chopped walnuts, toasted
    and chopped coarse
 1½ tablespoons minced fresh tarragon
    leaves
 1 pound green beans, ends snapped off
    Salt
 1½ tablespoons walnut oil
    Ground black pepper

1. Bring 2½ quarts of water to boil in large saucepan. Place toasted nuts and tarragon in large serving bowl and set aside.

2. Add green beans and 1 teaspoon salt to boiling water. Cook until tender, about 5 minutes. Drain beans and add to bowl with nuts and tarragon.

3. Drizzle oil over beans and toss gently to coat evenly. Sprinkle with salt and pepper to taste and serve immediately.

GREEN BEANS WITH BACON AND ONION
Serves 4 to 6

This rich dish is a nice addition to a holiday table. If you like, substitute pancetta for the bacon.

 1 pound green beans, ends snapped off
    Salt
 4 strips bacon, cut into ½-inch pieces
 1 medium onion, minced
 3 tablespoons minced fresh parsley leaves
    Ground black pepper

1. Bring 2½ quarts of water to boil in large saucepan. Add green beans and 1 teaspoon salt. Cook beans until tender, about 5 minutes. Drain and set aside for up to several hours.

2. Fry bacon over medium heat in large skillet until crisp. Remove bacon from pan with slotted spoon; drain on paper towels. Remove all but 2 tablespoons bacon fat from pan. Add onion to fat in skillet; sauté until softened and golden, about 5 minutes.

3. Add beans and parsley to pan. Toss to heat through for 1 to 2 minutes. Crumble bacon over pan, season with salt and pepper to taste, and serve immediately.

GREEN BEANS BRAISED IN TOMATOES
Serves 4 to 6

This Italian recipe uses a simple tomato sauce flavored with onions and garlic as the braising medium. Add the parsley (or basil) at the end of cooking for extra color.

 2 tablespoons olive oil
 1 small onion, diced
 2 medium garlic cloves, minced
 1 cup chopped canned tomatoes
 1 pound green beans, ends
    snapped off
    Salt and ground black pepper
 2 tablespoons minced fresh parsley leaves

1. Heat oil in large sauté pan over medium heat. Add onion; cook until softened, about 5 minutes. Add garlic and continue cooking another minute. Add tomatoes; simmer until juices thicken slightly, about 5 minutes.

2. Add green beans, ¼ teaspoon salt, and a few grindings of pepper to pan. Stir well, cover, and cook, stirring occasionally, until beans are tender but still offer some resistance to the bite, about 20 minutes. Stir in parsley and adjust seasonings. Serve immediately.

GREEN BEANS AND MUSHROOMS BRAISED IN CREAM
Serves 4 to 6

This recipe takes the flavors in the tired green bean casserole and gives them new lift.

 2 tablespoons unsalted butter
 1 tablespoon vegetable oil
 4 medium shallots, peeled and sliced
    thin crosswise
 ½ pound domestic mushrooms, wiped
    clean, stems trimmed, and quartered
 1 pound green beans, ends snapped off
 ⅔ cup heavy cream
 2 teaspoons juice from small lemon
 1½ teaspoons minced fresh thyme
    leaves
    Salt and ground black pepper

1. Heat butter and oil over medium-high heat in large sauté pan. Add shallots; sauté until golden brown and crisp, about 7 minutes. Transfer with slotted spoon to paper towel–lined plate; set aside.

2. In same pan, bring mushrooms, green beans,

cream, lemon juice, and thyme to strong simmer; season to taste with salt and pepper. Reduce heat to low; cover and simmer, stirring occasionally, until beans are tender but still offer some resistance to the bite, 15 to 20 minutes.

3. Remove cover; simmer briskly to thicken cream if necessary. Adjust seasonings and transfer beans to large serving bowl. Garnish with fried shallots and serve immediately. ■

Do the French Really Do It?

As best I can tell, "frenching" (cutting thick beans in half lengthwise) is supposed to turn thick green beans into delicate haricots verts. Or at least several cookbooks mention "frenching" as a method of making haricots verts at half the price.

To do this, each bean must be sliced lengthwise with a small knife or with a gadget like the Bean Slicer (see photograph, below). A knife is very tedious for this task and self-inflicted wounds are a real possibility. A Bean Slicer works better, but I must say I don't get the point.

The Bean Slicer has a sharp stationary blade in the top loop for cutting the top and tail of the bean. However, each bean must be inserted, one at a time, into the loop and forced down against the blade to remove the end. It's faster to squeeze off the top and tail with your fingers, as shown above.

For frenching, each bean must be inserted into the funnel-like hole and then forced through several sharp blades, which yield several (not two) thin strips per green bean. Although this method beats working with a knife, the Bean Slicer doesn't make a real haricot vert.

The pods on real haricots verts completely encase the flesh and prevent the insides from overcooking. "Frenched" beans will always cook unevenly because the slower-to-soften skin and flesh are both exposed. — J.B.

Classic Trifle

For perfect texture, taste, and appearance, bake your custard in a very shallow dish and use small squares of relatively firm sponge cake.

∼ BY STEPHEN SCHMIDT ∼

Most Americans think of trifle as a dessert of Victorian England. In fact, trifle is older than that, and American hostesses of the 1850s would have been very surprised to hear the dessert described as English, for they made trifle nearly as often as they made any other fancy dessert.

Still, the kind of trifle made in England during Victoria's long reign, which stretched from 1837 to her death in 1901, is indeed glorious, and so we are justified in calling it classic. Victorian trifle is composed of three or more layers of sherry-moistened sponge cake, each dotted with tiny almond cookies and fresh berries or dabs of jam and spread with a rich custard. The top is crowned with rosettes of lemon-scented whipped cream, then adorned with fresh or candied flowers.

The texture of this celebratory dish is delicate and creamy, never heavy or wet, and the flavor is a subtle balance of tart fruit, slightly astringent wine, toasty almonds, and suave, eggy custard. I adore classic Victorian trifle and have been making it for years, so I was delighted to have the opportunity to experiment with and refine my recipe.

Two issues were already settled in my mind before I began: the fruit and the topping. I decided long ago that I preferred to make trifle with fresh berries rather than jam, which is simply too sweet. As for the topping, I had unearthed the perfect recipe some years back in a nineteenth-century cookbook. Called "whipped syllabub" by cooks of the day, the topping is actually a clabber of heavy cream, lemon juice, and wine that is beaten until stiff. It is rich yet also tart and refreshing, the perfect foil for the layers of custard and cake.

The little almond cookies that are so indispensable to a classic trifle had always been a thorn in my side. Victorian cooks could buy miniature macaroons called ratafias (ra-tuh-FEE-uhs). I had always used amaretti in lieu of these vanished cookies, but I had found them lacking in flavor and prone to dissolving to a mush in the custard. Because I had just finished a piece on macaroons for *Cook's Illustrated*, I was feeling confident that I could work up a quick, simple recipe for miniature almond cookies without much sweat, and I did, in just two tries. I still might resort to amaretti or commercial macaroons if I found myself pressed for time, but my homemade cookies are really much better.

A Thick and Creamy Custard

Now I was ready to tackle a more difficult problem: the custard. I had long been unhappy with my custard because it tended to run, obscuring the carefully constructed layers of cake and berries that should be visible from the sides of the deep, glass trifle dish. I made my custard on the stove, so it was really a custard sauce or crème anglaise. I used a dozen egg yolks, two cups of milk, one cup of cream, and one cup of sugar. As custard sauces go, this one was very thick, but evidently it was not thick enough. What to do?

I knew four ways to make a custard sauce thicker: increase the egg yolks, increase the amount of cream in relation to milk, decrease the sugar, or add a binder such as gelatin, flour, or cornstarch. Because the custard already tasted quite eggy, I was not about to add more yolks, but I did faithfully

try variation after variation of the other three possible solutions. I halved the milk, doubled the cream, decreased the sugar by one-fourth, added gelatin, tried thickening with cornstarch, decreased the amount of starch, and on and on. But nothing gave me the thick, rich custard I was looking for.

Next, taking a cue from *The Virginia Housewife*, a cookbook published in 1824, I tried cooking the custard in a double boiler as well as in a Pyrex measuring bowl set directly in simmering water. This time I had gone too far—I ended up with a custard that was so thick that when I tried spreading it on a piece of sponge cake, it separated into curdish bits.

There was only one alternative left: I was going to have to bake the custard. This, though, proved more easily said than done. I made a custard according to my original formula and baked it at 300 degrees in a two-quart soufflé dish set in a water bath. Unfortunately, by the time the center had thickened, the outside was sliceably stiff. Somehow I needed to encourage the entire custard to heat at a uniform rate so that it would set into a smooth, soft, spreadable cream from the edge of the dish to the center.

After deliberating for a day or two, I hit upon the strategy of baking the custard in a very shallow layer so that the center would cook by heat conducted through the bottom of the dish as well as through the sides. A ten-inch cake pan proved not quite shallow (and perhaps not quite heavy) enough (the custard still solidified around the rim), but a thirteen-by-nine-inch glass baking dish worked perfectly. I obtained a thick, glossy, completely smooth custard with precisely the same consistency as homemade mayonnaise.

Stiffening the Cake

Once I had finally fixed the custard, I turned my attention to the cake. Like many other contemporary bakers, I had always constructed my trifle with genoise, but I wondered if this was the right choice. When moistened with sherry and custard, my genoise became a little limp and pasty. Rose Beranbaum, whose own ethereal genoise was featured in the December 1995 issue of this magazine, explains in *The Cake Bible* (Morrow, 1988) that genoise is less capable of absorbing moisture than drier, sturdier types of sponge cake such as Savoy cake or biscuit. Because Savoy cake is, in fact, the cake called for in the nineteenth-century trifle recipes, I gave it a try, and I found the improvement stunning. Instead of dissolving, the cake remained springy and slightly chewy, a tender sponge saturated with sherry, berry juice, and custard.

Cutting the sponge cake into small squares helps to create a trifle with a dazzling appearance.

Having firmed up the custard and stiffened the cake, I had now arrived at a more attractive and better-textured trifle than the one with which I had begun. But the trifle was still not quite the showy masterpiece that I thought it should be, especially given all the work involved. Using a nonrunny custard, I had succeeded in making the layers of cake, berries, and custard distinct, but the layers, now that they were plainly visible, seemed haphazard, lacking a sense of design.

After much fiddling, I devised a plan. I cut the sponge sheet in little squares and arranged a third of the squares on their ends on the bottom of the dish so that they looked like rows of fallen dominoes. I tucked berries between the squares, then scattered additional berries and almond cookies over the top of the cake, drizzled on a bit of berry puree, and finally laid on a thick blanket of custard. I repeated the whole procedure twice more to make two additional layers, then piped on the topping and applied a decoration of berries and candied violets. The trifle was no longer merely pretty. It dazzled.

FOR STEP-BY-STEP RECIPE, *SEE* ILLUSTRATIONS 1 TO 10, PAGE 10.

SPONGE SHEET CAKE
Makes one 18-by-11-inch cake
A sixteen-by-twelve-inch half sheet pan can be used in place of the jelly roll pan called for in this recipe.

    6   large eggs, separated
    ½   teaspoon cream
            of tartar
    ½   teaspoon salt
    ½   cup plus 3 tablespoons sugar
    1   teaspoon vanilla extract
    2   tablespoons hot water
    1   cup plain cake flour
            (measure by dip-and-sweep method)

1. Adjust oven rack to center position and heat oven to 350 degrees. Lightly grease 18-by-11-inch jelly roll pan. Line pan bottom and sides with waxed paper, allowing 1-inch overhang on each end. Do not grease paper.
2. Place egg whites in bowl of electric mixer; bring to warm room temperature over pan of hot water. Remove whites from pan of hot water and whip whites at medium speed until foamy. Add cream of tartar and salt, increase mixer speed to medium-high, and beat whites to soft but definite peaks. Slowly sprinkle on 3 tablespoons sugar; continue to beat until whites are shiny and very thick, 3 to 4 minutes. Scrape whites into wide 4-quart mixing bowl; set aside.
3. Without washing bowl or whisk attachment, add yolks to bowl; bring to warm room temperature over pan of hot water. Add vanilla and hot water; beat at high speed 1 minute. Slowly add remaining ½ cup sugar; beat until mixture is pale, shiny, and almost as thick as marshmallow cream, 4 to 5 minutes longer.
4. Scrape yolk mixture over egg whites; gently fold with rubber spatula until about two-thirds mixed. Sift flour over egg mixture; gently fold until flour is completely incorporated. Spread batter in prepared pan, running it up to edges and smoothing top with rubber spatula. Bake until cake top is lightly browned and center springs back when gently pressed, 12 to 15 minutes. Follow instructions in steps 1 and 2 for "How to Make a Trifle," page 10, in order to remove cake from pan.

ALMOND COOKIES
Makes 36 marble-size cookies

        Grease and flour for
            cookie sheet
    1   scant cup (4 ounces)
            blanched slivered
            almonds
    ¼   cup sugar
    2   tablespoons beaten egg
            (½ large egg)
    ½   teaspoon almond extract

1. Adjust oven rack to center position and heat oven to 350 degrees. Grease, then flour cookie sheet; tap off excess flour.
2. Finely grind almonds in food processor fitted with metal blade, about 1 minute. Add sugar; grind 15 seconds longer. Add egg and extract; process until mixture forms stiff dough that clumps around blade, 15 to 20 seconds longer.
3. Pinch off thirty-six raspberry-size pieces of dough, then roll each into smooth ball. Arrange balls ½ inch apart on prepared sheet. Bake until very lightly browned, 12 to 15 minutes. Let cool completely on sheet, then scrape free with metal spatula. (Can be stored in tightly covered container 1 week.)

FRESH RASPBERRY PUREE
Makes 1 cup

    2   cups raspberries
    3   tablespoons sugar

Puree berries and sugar in blender or food processor fitted with metal blade. Strain through fine sieve, pressing on solids to release juice; discard seeds. (Can be covered and refrigerated 1 day.)

RICH BAKED CUSTARD
Makes one 13-by-9-inch dish

    12 large egg yolks
    1   cup sugar
    ½   teaspoon freshly grated nutmeg
    2   cups milk
    1   cup heavy cream
    ¼   cup brandy or Cognac

1. Adjust oven rack to center position and heat oven to 300 degrees. Line pan bottom of large deep roasting pan with kitchen towel. Set Pyrex baking dish in roasting pan. Bring large kettle of water to boil.
2. Whisk yolks, sugar, and nutmeg in large mixing bowl. Meanwhile, bring milk and cream to gentle simmer in large saucepan, stirring frequently to prevent boiling over. Slowly whisk milk mixture into yolks; stir in brandy or Cognac. Set roasting pan in oven; pour custard into baking dish. Pour enough boiling water into roasting pan to reach mixture's height. Cover roasting pan with heavy-duty foil.
3. Bake custard until spoonful taken from center is texture of soft yogurt, 45 to 55 minutes. Remove custard from oven; let cool to tepid in water bath. Remove dish from water bath, cover with plastic wrap, and refrigerate custard until completely cold. (Can be refrigerated overnight.)

The Science of Custard

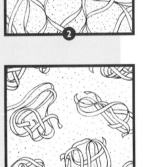

When eggs are raw, various bonds hold the individual protein molecules in separate, tightly wound bundles (*see* illustration 1, right). Heat breaks the bonds, causing the proteins to break out of their bundles and unwind into free-floating, flat strands, which then bump into one another and stick together (illustration 2). It is primarily this bonding of the egg proteins that causes custard to thicken as it is heated. Temperature is the crucial factor in this process. So long as the custard is maintained at a relatively low temperature, the egg bonds remain loose and relaxed and the custard stays smooth. But once custard approaches the boiling point, the egg proteins fuse so tightly that they harden into lumps and squeeze out all the liquid that is held between them (illustration 3). This situation, of course, is the sad, watery-lumpy mess that we call "curdled" custard.

It is easy to see why a stovetop custard, that is, a custard sauce or crème anglaise, can never become as thick as a baked custard. A stovetop custard must be stirred constantly as it heats or else it will curdle along the bottom of the pan where the heat is most intense. But stirring also disrupts the bonding of the egg proteins, and thus a stovetop custard can never set as firmly as a baked custard, which cooks undisturbed.

LEMON WHIPPED CREAM
Makes about 1 quart

Because the lemon zest needs time to infuse the cream, be sure to prepare this lemon cream mixture at least twelve hours and up to thirty-six hours before you intend to use it. This topping is less likely to break down than ordinary whipped cream, but it will begin to thin out if overbeaten.

   3 medium lemons, washed with warm
       water and dried
  ½ cup sugar
  2 cups heavy cream
  2 tablespoons cream sherry

1. Remove lemon zest with vegetable peeler. Squeeze, then strain enough juice from lemons to make ½ cup.

2. Finely grind zest with sugar in food processor fitted with metal blade, about 2 minutes. With machine running, gradually dribble in lemon juice. Scrape mixture into large airtight container. Stir in cream and sherry; cover tightly and refrigerate until mixture is thick and lemon-flavored, at least 12 hours. (Can be refrigerated up to 36 hours.)

3. Strain topping through fine-mesh sieve into bowl of electric mixer, pressing on zest to release cream. Whip cream to stiff peaks on medium-high. ∎

Stephen Schmidt is a cooking teacher, regular contributor to *Cook's Illustrated*, and author of the forthcoming *Dessert America* (Morrow).

How to Make a Trifle

YOU WILL NEED:

1 recipe Sponge Sheet Cake (page 9)
¾ cup cream Sherry
3 cups raspberries plus extra for garnish
1 recipe Almond Cookies (page 9)
⅓ cup Amaretto
1 recipe Fresh Raspberry Puree (page 9)
1 recipe Rich Baked Custard (page 9)
1 recipe Lemon Whipped Cream (above)
   Candied violets or small fresh edible
    flowers (optional)

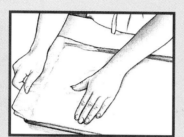

1. Immediately after baking Sponge Sheet Cake (see recipe, page 9), free the cake edges from the pan sides with a knife and smooth a sheet of waxed paper over the cake top.

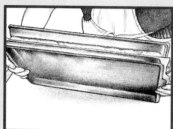

2. Place another sheet pan or cookie sheet on top of the cake. Flip over as shown, then lift off the baking pan.

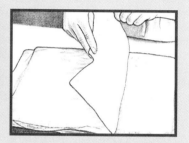

3. Let the cake cool completely, then gently peel the waxed paper off the cake bottom, removing the bottom crust. Flip the cake, top side up, then peel off the second sheet of waxed paper, removing the top crust. (Can be wrapped in plastic, then in foil, and refrigerated for 1 day.)

4. Brush the cake evenly with ¾ cup of cream sherry; let it stand 10 minutes.

5. Using a serrated knife, cut the cake into six lengthwise and eight crosswise strips to yield forty-eight approximate 2-inch squares.

6. Arrange sixteen cake squares, fallen domino-style, around the bottom of a 14- to 16-cup footed glass trifle dish, placing twelve to thirteen in a ring against the dish wall and the remaining squares in the center.

7. Tuck two to three raspberries between the outer cake squares, using about ⅓ cup berries total. Scatter about ⅔ cup raspberries over the top of the inner cake squares. Dip twelve almond cookies (recipe, page 9, or substitute store-bought) into Amaretto for 1 second, using about 5 teaspoons Amaretto total, then place them on top of the outer cake squares as well.

8. Drizzle ⅓ cup of Fresh Raspberry Puree (recipe, page 9) over the cake and cookies. Finally, spread one-third of Rich Baked Custard (recipe, page 9) over the layer, coming to within ½ inch of the edge. Repeat steps 7 and 8 twice more to make a total of three layers. Cover the bowl with plastic wrap and refrigerate it for at least 12 but not more than 36 hours.)

9. No more than 8 hours before serving, fill a large pastry bag fitted with a ¾-inch fluted tip with Lemon Whipped Cream (recipe, above). Pipe large, 2- to 3-inch-high rosettes over the trifle top. Pipe any remaining cream into tiny rosettes to fill in between the larger rosettes.

10. Garnish the trifle with additional berries and candied violets or fresh flowers if you like. Serve.

ILLUSTRATIONS BY WENDY WRAY

The Best Baked Sweet Potato

For moist flesh and soft, lightly caramelized skin, oil before baking, place on the middle rack in a 400-degree oven, and never turn during baking.

⁓ BY STEPHANA BOTTOM ⁓

Sweet potatoes have been hiding under the bushel basket of holiday meals long enough. They have wonderful flavor and they're available all year, so why not bake and eat one anytime, just like a potato?

I believe we should do just that, so I set out to find the best way to bake sweet potatoes. I was looking for evenly cooked, moist flesh and softened, slightly caramelized, delicious skin. In trying to reach this goal, I considered and tested twenty-three individual variables.

Oven variables included temperature, rack level, and whether a baking sheet worked better than just laying the potatoes on the oven rack. I found that the best oven temperature was 400 degrees. Lower temperatures took longer with no improvement while higher temperatures left burned spots on the bottom of the potatoes. Similarly, the best rack position was the center. Placing the rack either higher or lower resulted in blackening of the potatoes' thin skins. When I placed the potatoes directly on the rack, sticky juice oozed straight down and burned, so I use a flat baking sheet lined with foil.

I also tested oven tricks like placing the potatoes on unglazed oven tiles and beds of rock salt, but neither proved productive. I even tried cooking the potatoes halfway in the microwave and then transferring them to the oven, but the skin did not soften and there was no caramelization. I also tried baking the potatoes wrapped in foil, which turned out to be just what I suspected—a school cafeteria abomination that holds heat in soggy, overbaked potatoes.

I also did a number of tests to find the best way to deal with the skin, which is thin and very delicious when cooked properly. Uncoated skin stayed tough and unappealing, but coating it with butter tended to cause burning. Lightly rubbing with fresh vegetable or olive oil, though, softened the skin just the right amount.

Piercing the skin, I found, was essential to prevent the infamous exploding potato. But my big payoff in the search for tasty skin was the discovery that you should not turn the potatoes during baking. This method resulted in perfectly browned bottom skin, beautifully caramelized.

Mysteries Unfolded

You might also want to pay some attention to the type of sweet potato you buy. Sweet potatoes, often mislabeled as "yams" in grocery stores, come in two very distinct types, dry and moist. Endless varieties allow for confusion with sizes and shapes, but the most basic rule is that dry sweet potatoes have white to yellow flesh while moist ones have varying deep shades of orange.

Dry sweet potatoes are slightly sweet and, because they have a relatively high starch content also somewhat mealy. Moist sweet potatoes have a higher sugar content, and are dense, watery, and more easily caramelized.

Whatever the variety, most commercially grown sweet potatoes are harvested in the fall. They are then transferred to ventilated curing rooms where, for a period of days, high heat and humidity levels allow cuts and bruises from harvesting to heal. In this controlled environment, starches begin converting to sugar, so that a cured sweet potato is literally sweeter than a freshly harvested one.

Once you get the sweet potatoes home, do not wash them until you are ready to use them because this exposes the vulnerable skin and causes them to go bad more quickly. Refrigeration is also a no-no; it causes the core of the potato to gradually change texture until it resembles a soft, damp cork. The best storage is a dark, well-ventilated spot, out of plastic bags.

BAKED SWEET POTATOES
Serves 4

These recipes are for the moist, orange-fleshed varieties of sweet potatoes; drier white-fleshed types take longer to bake and require larger amounts of fat and/or liquid to counteract their drier texture. You can cook up to six potatoes at one time without altering the cooking time. Buying potatoes of the same size is a good idea because it standardizes cooking time.

- 4 medium sweet potatoes (about 2 pounds), washed, dried, and lightly pricked with fork in 3 places
- 2 tablespoons oil, vegetable or olive Salt and ground black pepper Unsalted butter

1. Adjust oven rack to center position and heat oven to 400 degrees. Rub potatoes with oil, then arrange on foil-lined baking sheet as far apart as possible.

2. Bake until knife tip slips easily into potato center, 40 to 50 minutes. Slit each potato lengthwise; using kitchen towel, hold ends and squeeze together slightly until soft flesh mounds up. Season to taste with salt and plenty of pepper. Dot with butter to taste and serve.

SAVORY MASHED SWEET POTATOES
Serves 4

Follow recipe for Baked Sweet Potatoes, peeling, then mashing them in medium bowl with potato masher. (For smooth, silky-textured puree, use ricer or food mill.) Stir in 5 tablespoons butter. Season with salt and plenty of pepper. ∎

Stephana Bottom, a food writer, editor, and cook, is developing recipes for a book on food and health.

Don't check sweet potatoes for doneness by pushing on the sides, because the core can still be hard even when the sides give a bit. A knife slipped into the potato works best.

How to Cook a Country Ham

We find that only older hams need to be soaked before cooking and that baking and simmering yield delicious but very different results.

∼ BY SARAH FRITSCHNER AND JOE CASTRO ∼

Being raised in the South, we thought cooking a country ham was pretty straightforward. It isn't. For every Southern cook, it seems, there's a different way to prepare a country ham.

Some cooks bake a country ham as they would a standard ham; others simmer it in a tremendous pot. Some soak their ham overnight, others for as long as three days. Some people add vinegar or brown sugar to the soaking water. We even found a recipe that required both of those, with a final treatment in Coca-Cola.

We set out to find the best way to cook a whole country ham for a holiday buffet or meal. Our testing focused on the soaking and cooking method, the goal being a tender ham that could be sliced thin and mounded on small sandwich buns. Northerners may want to use biscuits, but where we come from it's soft, squishy buns.

To Soak or Not to Soak

Many people believe that soaking a ham is essential to its final edibility. The theory is that soaking causes the meat to lose some of the salt with which it was cured, as the salt naturally moves from places of greater concentration (in the ham) to places of lesser concentration (the soaking water). As salt migrates out of the ham, water replaces some of it, a process that helps soften the ham's texture and prevent excessive dryness.

Our testing supported this theory, but also showed that the process doesn't happen as quickly as you might think. When we cooked a year-old ham that had been soaked for twelve hours, we found no difference in texture or saltiness when compared to a similar ham that had not been soaked at all. Even a ham that had soaked an entire twenty-four hours had little difference in texture. Only when we had soaked a year-old ham for a full thirty-six hours did the texture of the finished ham change—and we thought improve. The ham still had plenty of flavor, but it was a bit less dry and a little less salty.

We also found that the age of a ham is the most important factor in determining whether to soak or not to soak. High-tech younger hams, which have lost less moisture during curing (see "Aged Country Hams Win Tasting," page 26, for more information) do not need to be soaked. Our guidelines for soaking, then, are as follows: For hams aged under six months, skip soaking; for hams aged six months to a year, soak for thirty-six hours; and for hams aged more than a year, soak for three days, changing the water every day.

What doesn't seem to improve hams is adding ingredients to the soaking liquid. In fact, adding sugar (or Coke) to the liquid might slow down the seeping of salt into the water, as sugar would tend to equalize the osmotic pressure. And if you are trying for a milder ham or a sweeter ham, you won't get it by adding a cup of sugar (or a liter of Coke) to the soaking water. White vinegar, which some old cookbooks say will balance the salt much like sugar, had no affect.

A Baking Surprise

With the soaking issue under control, we moved on to cooking. We thought there would be no surer way to ruin a ham than to stick it in the oven. But we were wrong.

We discovered this when we prepared a dozen hams, some baked by various methods and others simmered by various methods, for a group of ham lovers and novices. We had expected one of the simmered hams to be the clear favorite, so we were surprised to see part of our crowd lingering around a ham baked over aromatics. As it turned out, novices gave this baked ham low scores, but it was the clear favorite of those who had grown up eating country ham and love its strong, salty flavors. These folks ate helping after helping.

It's not traditional to cook country ham with aromatics, but because other meats are often roasted with vegetables, we had thought it worth a try.

So the winning baked ham had been set on a "rack" built of crisscrossed carrots and celery and seasoned with a lot of onions and fresh rosemary. About thirty minutes before the ham was finished cooking, we skinned it, removed all but a thin layer of fat, brushed it with sorghum—sweeter and less harsh than molasses, easier to spread than brown sugar—then finished baking it.

The ham baked this way was rather dry and salty, but the aromatics seasoned it unbelievably well and the sweet sorghum predictably added a wonderful foil to the saltiness of the ham. So baking a ham over aromatics is our top choice if you want to serve a ham warm. When cut, juices actually ooze out of this ham. But be aware that it has some complications: The bone makes it trickier to carve than a simmered and boned ham, and the strong flavor may only appeal to real country ham fans.

Simmer for Tenderness and Mildness

A more universally acceptable way to prepare a country ham is to simmer it. Simmering adds a touch of moisture that many people believe the ham needs, and makes it much easier to remove the ham bone for more convenient serving. A simmered ham is also firmer than a baked ham, with a texture akin to cold cuts, and is less likely to fall apart into small pieces when sliced. Our most important finding, though, was that the milder, less salty flavor of simmered hams appeals to a greater range of tastes. Because this is an important consideration for holiday meals or buffets, we believe simmering to be the best all-purpose cooking method for a country ham.

But what's the best simmering method? We tried all kinds of variations—simmering ham a set time according to its weight, bringing it to a boil then roasting it in water in the oven, simmering it on top of the stove, bringing it to a boil then wrapping it in blankets (something my family did on the theory that insulating the ham allowed it to cook more slowly)—and the method we ended up liking the best is cooking at the barest simmer on the stove. The gentle heat cooks the ham much more evenly than boiling.

As for telling when the ham is done, fifteen minutes per pound is a good guess. For more accuracy, use an instant-read thermometer. At 140 degrees, a simmered ham is moist and tender. Traditionalists, who like their meat a little less juicy, may want to cook the ham to 155 or even 160 degrees. The same numbers hold true for baking.

SIMMERED COUNTRY HAM
Serves 30

Any size ham can be adapted to this recipe; just adjust the cooking time depending on the ham size. Bits of leftover ham can be mixed with cream cheese for a sandwich spread or ground to make deviled-style ham. Kale, cauliflower, spinach, or cabbage flavored with country ham can be tossed with pasta or risotto. Use the hock to flavor a big pot of bean soup.

- 1 country ham, 14 to 15 pounds
- 3 medium carrots, cut into large chunks
- 3 ribs celery, cut into large chunks
- 2 medium onions, cut into large chunks
  Several sprigs fresh rosemary or thyme

1. Following illustration 1, page 13, scrub mold from ham if necessary.

2. Following illustration 2, saw hock off ham so that it will easily fit into big stockpot.

3. Place ham in stockpot and cover with water. Soak ham, changing water at least daily, to release salt and rehydrate ham, about 36 hours for hams

Dealing with a Country Ham

TO PREPARE FOR COOKING

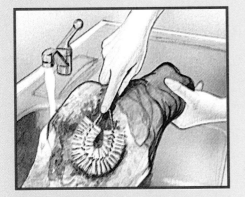

1. If using an older ham, scrub mold off with a vegetable scrubbing brush under running water. (Hams that have been aged for 6 months to 1 year should have been soaked for 36 hours; those aged over 1 year should have been soaked for 3 days.)

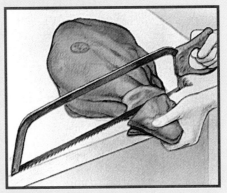

2. Use a hack saw to remove the hock, so that the ham fits more easily into a large stockpot. (This can also be done by your butcher.) It is not necessary to remove the hock if baking the ham.

TO BONE A SIMMERED HAM

3. Remove skin and most but not all of fat from cooked ham by running fingertips underneath skin and peeling it away. Use knife at the end to trim excess fat.

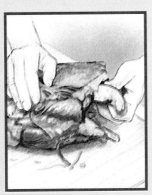

4. Starting at the hip end, reach in and pull out small bones. Once small bones have been removed, find the large hip bone running through the ham.

5. Make a slit down ham running parallel to the large hip bone. Open up the ham, grab the hip bone, and twist to pull it out; use a boning knife to help free bone if necessary. Once the hip bone is removed, trim very dark tough pieces of meat (especially present in older hams) and gristle from ham exterior and interior.

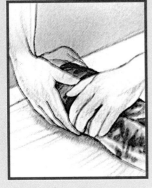

6. Roll the ham back up, pressing any little chunks that have fallen off back into the ham. For easy carving, wrap ham as tight as you can in clear plastic wrap.

7. Set ham in a large bowl with a plate on top. Weight it down with a brick or cans. Refrigerate at least eight hours, or up to two weeks.

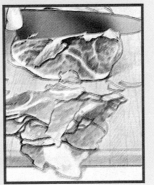

8. Slice ham as thin as possible. The older the ham, the more jerky-like chunks that may be too leathery to eat, but are great for flavoring a pot of greens, beans, or soup.

---

aged 6 to 12 months and 3 days for hams aged over a year. Hams aged less than 6 months do not need to be soaked.

4. Drain ham; discard soaking water. Place ham, carrots, celery, onions, and herbs in same pot; cover with water. Bring water to boil over medium-high heat. Reduce heat to barest simmer. Simmer until meat thermometer registers 140 degrees or knife inserted into thickest part of ham slips out easily, 3½ to 4 hours. (For a firmer-fleshed ham, cook to internal temperature of 155 to 160 degrees.) Turn off heat; cool ham to room temperature in cooking liquid. Remove ham from water; discard aromatics. (Ham broth can be refrigerated or frozen and used for cooking greens, rice, or soup.)

5. Following illustration 3, remove skin and most but not all fat from cooked ham by running fingertips underneath skin and peeling it away. Use knife at the end to trim excess fat.

6. Following illustrations 4 through 7, bone ham, wrap in plastic wrap, weight it down, and refrigerate.

7. Following illustration 8, slice ham as thin as possible. Serve with soft rolls or biscuits. (Leftovers can be wrapped in plastic wrap and frozen up to 3 months.)

....

SORGHUM-GLAZED BAKED COUNTRY HAM

For a nicer presentation, you may decide not to remove the hock. To soak a hock-on ham, we found a clean garbage can lined with a heavy-duty trash bag to be an ideal soaking vessel.

1. Follow steps 1, 2, and 3 in Simmered Country Ham recipe, starting on previous page (step 2 is optional for baked ham).

2. Bring large kettle of water to boil. Adjust oven rack to low position and heat oven to 325 degrees. Drain ham; discard soaking water. Cover bottom of roasting pan with large piece of foil (the foil should be long enough to form tent over ham). Build grid with carrots and celery, tucking onion chunks and herbs between them. Set ham over vegetable bed, fat side up. Place pan in oven. Pour boiling water halfway up pan sides; pull foil around ham, forming loose tent. Bake until meat thermometer inserted into thickest part of ham registers 125 to 130 degrees, 2½ to 3 hours.

3. Remove from oven (cool ham slightly if necessary). Carefully remove skin with knife, leaving ¼-inch layer of fat. Score fat into diamonds, if desired, then brush with ½ cup sorghum or rub with ½ cup brown sugar. Remove vegetables and cooking liquid from roasting pan, return ham to pan; bake to internal temperature of 140 to 155 degrees (depending on desired crispiness), 30 minutes to 1 hour longer. Cool slightly, carve into thin slices, and serve. ∎

Sarah Fritschner is author of the *Express Lane Cookbook* (Chapters, 1995) and the *Vegetarian Express Lane* (Chapters, 1996). **Joe Castro** is chef at the English Grill in Louisville, Kentucky.

The Key to Cooking Mussels

Buy in season, steam in a flavorful broth, and to avoid grit, buy a rope-cultured product or Great Eastern bottom-cultivated mussels.

~ BY STEPHANIE LYNESS ~

I used to teach a class on how to cook mussels. The wild mussels came in muddy, and three of my ten students were out of commission for most of the class scrubbing, debearding, poking, and rinsing. Sometimes I loved the finished dish, but more often I didn't. Despite all that work, the broth was often gritty, and the mussels sometimes tasted funky. I've never considered myself a mussel enthusiast.

Last February I tested a mussel recipe for a book review in this magazine. With little enthusiasm I cooked up tightly closed, debearded, farmed mussels from Canada that were so clean they hardly needed rinsing. Sweet and grit-free. I was wild about them. I think I ate all four pounds that day. But in May, I cooked the same recipe with the same type of mussel, many of which were gaping when I bought them. They tasted like my beachfront backyard smells on a sweltering day at low tide. Thank God I didn't have guests.

So I set out to uncover the story on these critters. How could I reliably ensure tasty mussels? Why are some clean and some not? What's the story on the gapers? And is steaming still the best way to cook them? In the end, much of my answer was related to seasonality and techniques of mussel production.

Grit from Method of Growth

The way a mussel is produced directly impacts the amount of grit it holds and how time-consuming it is to clean.

In Canada, New Zealand, Maine, California, and Washington State (and in other parts of the world), mussels are cultivated by an aquaculture technique known as rope culture. Mussel spat (mussel babies) are attached to nylon tubes and then suspended either from lines held up by floats or from floating rafts. All species of rope-cultured mussels I tested were grit-free. Rope culturing is labor-intensive and you pay for it: Rope-cultured mussels are usually at least twice as expensive as wild mussels.

Rope-cultured Blue mussels from Prince Edward Island in Canada are the darlings of the mussel industry. They are tiny and startlingly uniform in size with especially pristine, shiny, thin shells. Debearded at the plant on a *debysser*, the mussels have no beards and can simply be rinsed.

Bottom culture, on the other hand, is a type of aquaculture in which mussel seed is distributed over an area of leased ocean bottom and allowed to grow. The mussels grow more quickly than in the wild because they're seeded more thinly and so don't have to fight for food. These mussels are harvested with a mesh dredge and then are allegedly purged in controlled saltwater tanks for twelve to twenty-four hours to clean them of grit and sand. Tests of mussels sold by two producers of bottom culture yielded very different results: Maine-based Great Eastern mussels were only a speck of grit away from perfectly clean while another East coast producer's mussels were unpleasantly crunchy. Happily, Great Eastern is a large producer and sells its product in clearly marked bags to many large supermarket chains. Great Eastern mussels should cost about the same as Atlantic rope-cultured mussels.

Wild mussels are commercially harvested by dredging. They're cheap because so little labor is required, but quality is variable. Wild Blue mussels can be recognized by the silverish-gray cast of the shells—a result of abrasion from tides and currents. The shells are noticeably thicker than their cultured counterparts, are also muddy, and hold a lot of grit. Many people I respect swear by their taste, but I've found no successful way to purge them before cooking . It was not for lack of trying. I tried soaking in cold water for two hours, soaking in running cold water for two hours, soaking in water with flour in it for two hours, scrubbing and rinsing in five changes of water. NONE of these techniques worked. You'll need to rinse the mussels and strain the cooking liquid if you choose wild mussels. Personally, I no longer buy them.

Cooking and Cleaning Mussels

But, aside from grit content, what makes some mussels sweet and others nasty? In brief, those unappetizing mussels I bought in May were bitter and gaping because it was spawning season (*see* "Why Do Mussels Gape?" below). Once I got hold of some mussels that weren't spawning, I ran some cooking tests. I compared steaming in an aromatic wine broth to steaming over the same broth. I also tried cooking the mussels without embellishment in the oven and on top of the stove, and sautéing in a little oil.

Why Do Mussels Gape?

According to Kurt Johnson, who has a Masters in Fisheries Biology and is a shellfish producer in Washington State, mussels open and close naturally when submerged in the waters of their natural habitat. Take them out of the water and they close their shells tightly to resist dehydration. But once harvested, mussels can only hang on so long. Eventually, depending on how they're handled, they weaken and gape. Gaping makes them dehydrate, causing them to gape more, dehydrate more, and eventually to die. So there's a simple rule for the consumer. If you see more than just a few mussels in a batch gaping, don't buy and do complain: The mussels are almost certainly tired, may be old or badly handled, and certainly are not as tasty as they should be.

All live shellfish, including mussels, are required to carry a tag noting where and when the shellfish were harvested. Retailers are required to hold onto these tags for ninety days so that any incidence of shellfish-borne sickness can be traced to the home bed. If you have questions about the age of mussels, ask to see the tag.

Gaping may also indicate that mussels are spawning. Mussels spawn at a particular time of year depending on a number of factors including location, water temperature, and species. In preparation for spawning, the mussel converts part of its stored glycogen (a form of sugar molecule that makes the flesh sweet) into gametes, which taste bitter. Spawning also stresses the mussel, reducing shelf life, and shrinks the meat. It takes two to eight weeks for the animal to recover. Therefore, during this period, mussels not only gape, but their meat is small and tastes bitter.

To complicate matters, mussels are what are called "dribble spawners." They may spawn a bit one week, stop, and spawn a little more the next. Or they may spawn in May, recover in June, and spawn again in July. Producers manage this by shifting mussel beds as the animals begin to spawn. After several pounds of disappointing mussels, my advice is to stay away from gaping mussels and be particularly watchful during spawning season. If necessary, switch to a different species of mussel (see "Mussel Primer," page 15).—S.L.

Mussel Primer

I tested three species of mussel for this piece. I don't include here two others, the native Puget Sound blue mussel (*Mytilus trossulus*), sometimes marketed as the Penn Cove mussel, and the California mussel (*Mytilus californianus*) because production of these two species is so small that the mussels are only available locally.—S.L.

The **NORTH ATLANTIC BLUE MUSSEL** (*Mytilus edulis*), with the largest production in North America, is the blue-black–shelled mussel that is most familiar to American cooks. Depending on where and how it's produced, there is a marked difference in size, how the mussel looks, and how much cleaning it needs. On the Atlantic coast, the spawning and recovery period for the Blue mussel is roughly between May and July.

The **"MEDITERRANEAN" MUSSEL** (*Mytilus galloprovincialis*) also has a blue-black shell, broader than that of the Blue mussel. It's marketed at a length of about three inches. Dubbed the Mediterranean mussel because the species grows naturally in that region, this mussel is being rope-cultured from rafts in California and Washington State. The mussels are absolutely free of grit, and the beards pull out more easily than on other species. On the Pacific coast, the Mediterranean mussel spawns roughly between February and the end of May.

The **NEW ZEALAND GREENSHELL MUSSEL** (*Perna canaliculus*) is rope-cultured on long lines. It's easily distinguished by its large (three-and-one-half- to four-inch) greenish shells. It's very clean, but the beards are a bear to pull out. It's difficult to identify a spawning season for the Greenshell mussel because mussels grown in different areas of New Zealand spawn at different times of year. For mussels exported live to the United States, the spawning season is likely to be July to September. That said, given the different spawning cycles, it also seems likely that New Zealand exporters can deal in good-quality mussels year-round.

The essential taste difference between the four techniques is that when mussels are roasted, sautéed, or steamed over broth, they steam in their own juices and taste of pure mussel. Mussels steamed in the broth pick up its aromatic flavor. For me, this is a case where more is better: I prefer the way the broth-soaked mussels taste. I use two cups of wine (a lot more than you need to steam open the mussels) to four pounds of mussels because the broth, soaked into bread or rice, is so good I want a lot of it.

A few refinements: Garlic in the broth balances and enriches the flavor of the mussels. Simmering the broth for three minutes before adding the mussels beefs up the flavor. I've found that larger mussels need to cook a few minutes after they open to firm up. But it all evens out somehow if you simply cook until all the mussels open.

Depending on how dirty they look, mussels should be rinsed, then scraped or scrubbed with a scratchy pad or scrub brush. If there is a beard, pull it out with the back of a knife so that none is left inside the mussel. I found that a quick way to test a "gaper" is to run the open mouth under cold water. If it closes, I'll cook it. If not, it's dead, and I throw it out. (I found this to be just as effective and much faster than the traditional test of sticking a knife into the opened mussel to see if it closes.) Rapid bacterial growth makes dead shellfish dangerous to eat.

Storing Mussels

In the industry, mussels are stored spread out over or under ice to retard bacterial growth and dehydration that kills the mussels. That's great in a fish store, but I wanted to see if there was an easier way. I found that if fresh, mussels will stay closed and alive in a bowl in the refrigerator for three days, whether covered with a damp towel or not.

I had also heard that mussels should be debearded at the last minute because the pulling action of debearding kills the animal. So I bearded one batch and re-frigerated them. After twenty-four hours they were all still alive; fifty percent had died by a day later.

Clearly, if the mussels are in good shape when you buy them, they'll last at least three days in the refrigerator without much protection. As with all seafood, however, time doesn't improve the flavor. There isn't any problem debearding them several hours before cooking, if that's convenient.

MASTER RECIPE FOR MUSSELS STEAMED IN WHITE WINE
Serves 4

2 cups white wine
½ cup minced shallots
4 medium garlic cloves, minced
½ cup chopped fresh parsley leaves
1 bay leaf
4 pounds mussels, cleaned and debearded
4 tablespoons unsalted butter

1. Bring wine, shallots, garlic, parsley, and bay leaf to simmer in large pot; continue to simmer to blend flavors, about 3 minutes. Increase heat to high. Add mussels; cover and cook, stirring twice, until mussels open, 4 to 8 minutes, depending on pot and mussel size.

2. Remove mussels from liquid, twist off and discard top shells, and put in large serving bowl. Meanwhile, swirl butter into pan liquid to make emulsified sauce. Pour broth over mussels and serve immediately with warm bread or rice.

MUSSELS STEAMED IN WHITE WINE WITH CURRY AND BASIL

Follow Master Recipe for Mussels Steamed in White Wine, adding 1 teaspoon Madras curry powder to simmering liquid and reducing parsley to 2 tablespoons. Right before swirling in butter, stir in 2 tablespoons each chopped fresh cilantro and basil leaves.

MUSSELS STEAMED IN WHITE WINE WITH TOMATO AND BASIL

This recipe is adapted from Jim Peterson's *Fish and Shellfish* (Morrow, 1996). Serve these tomato-bathed mussels over one pound of cooked, drained cappellini.

Follow Master Recipe for Mussels Steamed in White Wine, decreasing wine quantity from 2 cups to 1 cup and substituting basil for parsley. Once mussels have been removed from broth, add 2 cups crushed tomatoes along with ¼ cup olive oil in place of butter; simmer until reduced to sauce consistency, about 10 minutes. Season to taste with salt and pepper. Return mussels, whose top shells have been removed, into the reduced sauce. Serve.

STEAMED MUSSELS WITH ASIAN FLAVORS

This recipe is adapted from one by Mark Bittman, the author of *Fish* (MacMillan, 1995).

Follow Master Recipe for Mussels Steamed in White Wine. Omit ingredients list, except mussels. Rather, steam mussels in 1 cup chicken stock, 2 tablespoons soy or fish sauce, 2 teaspoons vinegar (preferably rice), ⅛ teaspoon cayenne pepper, 2 tablespoons minced fresh gingerroot, 2 minced garlic cloves, 4 minced scallions (green and white parts, and 2 tablespoons minced lime zest (optional). Garnish with 2 tablespoons chopped fresh cilantro leaves, 2 tablespoons minced chives or finely minced scallions, and lime quarters. Do not swirl in butter. ■

Freestyle Cookie Decorating

~ BY PAM ANDERSON AND KAREN TACK ~

You don't need a rolling pin, cookie cutters, or specialty decorations to make attractive and interesting-looking cookies for the holidays. We came up with these shapes using gadgets that we found in our kitchen. Look around your kitchen and come up with your own cookie decoraters. The recipe for Multipurpose Butter Cookie Dough on page 19 of this issue is ideal for these decorated cookies. To shape the dough into cookie rounds prior to decorating, follow the illustrations on page 20.

FLORAL DESIGN

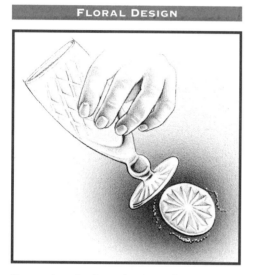

Press a glass that has a decorative bottom onto the flattened dough rounds.

WAFFLE TEXTURE

Use the small-textured prongs of a metal meat mallet to give the dough a fine waffle texture.

GROOVED LOOK

Imprint the dough rounds with a wooden meat mallet that has grooves running in only one direction.

DIAMOND CUT

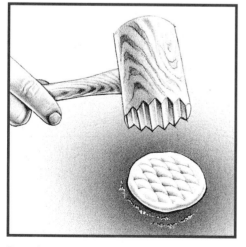

For a diamond cut, press the same meat mallet into the dough rounds diagonal to the original position.

SUBTLE GROOVES

Use a butter paddle for more subtle grooves.

POLKA-DOT EFFECT

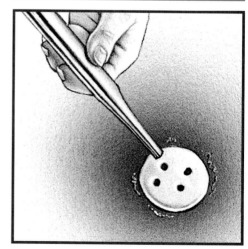

Cut out tiny circles from the cookie dough rounds with a bulb baster. Squeeze the bulb to release the dough.

ILLUSTRATIONS BY HARRY DAVIS

TAILORED CROSSHATCH

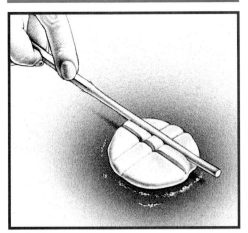

Press chopsticks into the dough at perpendicular angles for a crosshatch look.

SCALED EFFECT

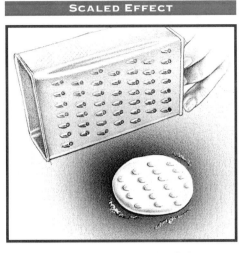

Press with the coarse-grating side of a box grater for a scaled effect.

RICRAC DESIGN

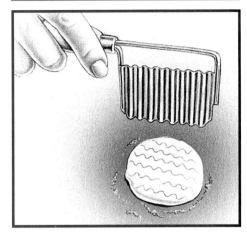

Use a vegetable crinkle cutter for a ricrac design.

STAR PATTERN

With the tip facing in and the pointed side up, press a church key around the center of the dough rounds to make a starlike pattern.

CRIMPED EDGE

Use a fork to crimp around the edge of the dough rounds.

QUILTED LOOK

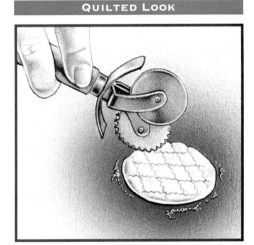

Lightly run a fluted pastry wheel over the surface of the cookie dough for a quilted look.

WAVY PLEATS

Use a cake server to create a wavy, pleated effect.

GEOMETRIC DESIGN

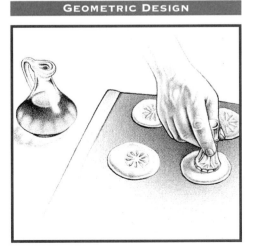

Imprint designs from the decorative top of a cruet or decanter.

ZIGZAG LOOK

Use a cake comb for a zigzag effect.

All-Purpose Holiday Cookies

For a durable cookie that's crisp, light, and buttery, skip the leavener and use bleached flour, superfine sugar, and an extra yolk.

∼ BY PAM ANDERSON WITH KAREN TACK ∼

Each year, most food magazines do the obligatory decorated cookie story. To rekindle interest, there's a different take each year—usually trendy shapes or the latest decorating techniques.

Although I'm attracted to these centerfold cookies as much as the next baker, I find they're more fun to think about than to actually make. One year, I mindlessly followed a magazine recipe, tracing and cutting cardboard patterns for seven consecutively smaller stars. The resulting cookies were to be stacked together and tied with a ribbon. I could have made seven dozen simple, beautiful cookies in the time it took me to cut out and bake one set of those stars. A few experiences like that, and I've gotten my priorities straight. On a leisurely afternoon, I want to crank out several dozen impressive-looking cookies that taste even better than they look.

To do that, though, you have to start with a rolled cookie dough that's just right, so I set out to develop just such a dough. In defining the ideal rolled cookie, I felt a little like cooking colleague and friend Stephen Schmidt in his attempts to achieve seemingly contradictory textures within the same cake (*see* "The Best Pound Cake," May/June 1994). He was eventually successful in developing a pound cake that was at once moist, soft, dense, light, and rich. Similarly, I wanted a cookie that was at once crisp and tender, light and sturdy. As if that weren't enough, I also wanted a clear, buttery flavor. Was it possible to have all of these characteristics in the same cookie? Ingredients like cornstarch can tenderize cookies but also have the potential to make them fragile. Egg whites and sugar crispen cookies, but too much of these ingredients and the cookies bake up brittle and hard. Leaveners like baking powder and soda can lighten cookies, but their distinct metallic taste can also muddy flavors. Developing such a demanding recipe was like walking a culinary tightrope.

Keep It Simple

Despite the many differences among rolled cookie recipes, we found that most have the same basic ingredients: flour, sugar, fat, egg, and vanilla. Of course, there are still significant differences. Some recipes use less egg and compensate with milk, cream, or sour cream. Others add chemical leaveners to lighten the cookies. And the basic ingredients certainly vary. What kind of flour should be used? Is granulated or confectioners' sugar better? Is the best cookie made with butter, shortening, oil, or from a combination of some sort?

In order to understand the role of each of these many possible ingredients, we developed a composite formula, based on a review of scores of cookie recipes, to use in our testing. The recipe was as follows:

> ¾ cup flour
> ¼ cup sugar
> ¼ cup unsalted
>   butter
> 1 large egg yolk
> ½ teaspoon vanilla
>   extract
>   Pinch of salt

With the basic recipe in hand, we proceeded to substitute different flours, sugars, fats, and egg parts as well as to vary the quantities of each. Following the formula, we also made doughs with different leaveners as well as with milk, cream, and sour cream standing in for part of the egg. Curious about whether fresh vanilla bean might make a more flavorful cookie, we scraped flecks of vanilla into a batch. Finally, in an attempt to lighten the cookies without chemical leaveners, we tried cutting butter into flour rather than creaming it with the sugar. The melting butter bits, we speculated, would create space between the set flour, creating a lighter, crisper cookie without a leavener lift.

From these initial tests, we learned that our original formula wasn't far off the mark. Although the recipe did need refining, none of the extra ingredients we had added were necessary.

Using cake flour, adding cornstarch for part of the flour, and relying on smaller quantities of flour all made the cookies too tender and fragile as did substituting confectioners' sugar for granulated sugar. Cookies made with shortening and oil were sandy-textured and lacked flavor.

Although baking powder and soda helped lighten the cookies, we found their distinct flavors too distracting. Using half of a whole egg, rather than just the yolk, made the cookies brittle rather than crisp. Adding milk and cream for part of the egg made moist, difficult doughs, and the resulting cookies tasted hard and stale, while sour cream neither helped nor hurt the outcome. Cookies flecked with fresh vanilla bean looked promising, but the flavor was absolutely imperceptible in the finished cookies. Finally, cutting the butter into the flour resulted in cookies with a nice texture but a disastrous, pocked appearance as if they had a rash.

Bleached Flour Makes Better Cookies

We did make one real discovery during this testing, though, and it was one that came as a surprise. Working on various baking articles over the past few years, we've seen firsthand the dramatic differences in flours. Clearly, cake flour doesn't make a good rustic country loaf, and bread flour doesn't make a tender buttermilk biscuit. We never expected there would be a noticeable difference, however, between cookies made with bleached and unbleached flours.

I'm not even sure what prompted us to test cookies made with unbleached and bleached all-

After rolling out the dough or shaping it into individual rounds, decorate with everyday kitchen tools as shown on pages 16 and 17.

purpose flours. Perhaps I had seen recipes specifically calling for one or the other. In any case, we were surprised at the very perceptible difference in taste and texture between the two cookies in a side-by-side tasting. Without a doubt, we both preferred the buttery-flavored, lighter-textured cookie made with Gold Medal bleached flour as opposed to the cookie made with Gold Medal unbleached flour.

This was so unexpected that we thought our experience was a fluke. As it turns out, though, we were not the first to notice the differences between bleached and unbleached flour in cookies. In a *Washington Post* article entitled "The Bottom Line: Putting Flours to the Taste Test" (December 6, 1995), Carole Sugarman and Stephanie Sedgwick had come to the same conclusion. According to Sugarman, cookies made with bleached flour were "much lighter and had a much better butter flavor. The unbleached flour produced a chewier, denser and tougher cookie that was not nearly as butter-tasting. Ditto," she adds, for pie crust.

For further explanation of this phenomenon, we turned to Atlanta-based food scientist Shirley Corriher, who offered explanations for the better texture and flavor of the cookie made with bleached flour. First, bleaching agents slightly modify the protein in flour, producing a more elastic gluten, which in turn results in a more tender texture. As for the flavor difference, Corriher speculates that during the bleaching process elements in raw (or unbleached) flour are converted to other compounds that simply taste better. Our tasting confirmed her speculation. The cookies made with unbleached flour had a raw cereal, wheaty undertone. The cookies made with bleached flour, on the other hand, tasted buttery, fresh, with a more delicate flavor.

Refining the Formula

Now that we felt sure we were using just the right ingredients in the right proportion, we needed to make sure that the recipe could easily be multiplied to produce a big batch of cookies.

We quadrupled the recipe, using three cups of flour, one cup of sugar, one cup of butter, two teaspoons of vanilla extract, and one-quarter of teaspoon salt. We did change the egg. In the original formula, one egg yolk made sense because half an egg delivered brittle cookies. Working in larger quantities allowed us to try a whole egg plus two yolks rather than four yolks.

Right off, we found that cookies made with three cups of flour tasted dry and not very buttery. To solve this problem, we reduced the flour by one-half cup, eliminating one of the two yolks to compensate for the loss of dry ingredients. Since the dough seemed wet enough with just one whole egg, we didn't add the remaining extra yolk. The flavor of these reduced-flour cookies was excellent because the reduced amount of flour intensified the buttery flavor. Once again, though, we found that whole egg alone makes brittle, hard cookies. Adding the egg yolk back into the cookie made it more tender without making it too wet,

and increasing the salt to one-half teaspoon balanced the relatively high sugar quantity. Cookies with even two tablespoons less sugar threw off that tender/crisp texture and accentuated the flouriness.

As we described our cookie recipe to friend and colleague Gail Nagele-Hopkins, she told us about her grandmother's rolled cookie recipe, which called for superfine sugar. Using the food processor, we turned granulated sugar into superfine and made a batch of cookies. This finer-grained sugar quite naturally gave the cookies a lightness and fineness of texture that we liked better.

A generous amount of butter guaranteed rich flavor. The extra yolk saved the cookies from brittleness. The superfine sugar made the cookies light and tender, but unlike cornstarch or confectioners' sugar, kept them durable and sturdy. We like this cookie recipe. No gimmicks. Just simple ingredients in the right proportions.

MULTIPURPOSE BUTTER COOKIE DOUGH
Makes about 7 dozen 2½ inch cookies rolled to ⅛-inch thick (rerolling only once)
We found that dough rolled three times does indeed bake into a tougher cookie. So get as many

dough shapes as you can out of each sheet, and donate dough that's been rolled more than twice to someone who needs rolling practice. Or following the illustrations on page 20, form the cookie dough into balls and flatten them with a round meat mallet or flat glass bottom.

½ pound (2 sticks) unsalted butter, at cool room temperature
1 cup granulated sugar, processed in food processor for 30 seconds, or superfine sugar
½ teaspoon salt
1 whole egg plus 1 yolk
2 teaspoons vanilla extract
2½ cups bleached all-purpose flour, plus extra for work surface

1. Cream butter, sugar, and salt in workbowl of electric mixer at medium speed until light and fluffy. Add yolk, beat well then add whole egg and vanilla; continue beating until well incorporated. Add flour; beat over low speed until flour is just mixed. Divide dough in half and wrap in plastic wrap. Refrigerate until firm, at least 1 hour. (Can be refrigerated up to 2 days or double-wrapped and frozen 1 month.)
2. Adjust oven racks to upper and lower middle

Making Marble Cookies

First, mix two ounces of melted and cooled semi- or bittersweet chocolate into one-quarter recipe of Butter Cookie Dough. Then:

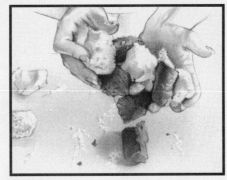

1. Divide chocolate dough into six portions. Press into remaining three-quarter recipe of butter dough.

2. Knead doughs together to create a marbled effect.

3. Roll out the combined dough in the usual fashion.

4. The dough rounds will have a delicate marbled appearance.

Shaping Cookie Rounds Without a Rolling Pin

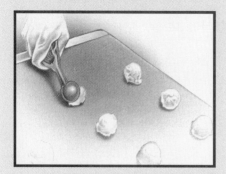

1. Scoop the cookie dough into 1-tablespoon balls with a small ice cream scoop.

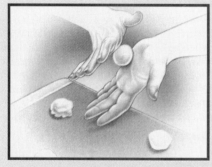

2. Roll each portion into a smooth ball and place 2 inches apart on a parchment-lined cookie sheet.

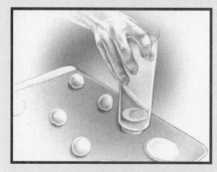

3. Flatten each dough ball to a thickness of about ⅛ inch with a smooth, round, flour-coated glass bottom.

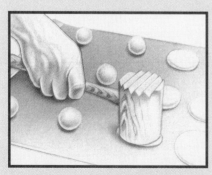

4. Alternatively, flatten the dough balls with the smooth side of a flour-coated meat mallet.

positions. Heat oven to 375 degrees. Remove one disk of dough from refrigerator and cut in half. Return unused portion of dough to refrigerator.

3. Follow steps 1 through 4 (left) or lightly flour work surface; roll dough to ⅛-inch thick, using offset spatula to loosen dough. Sprinkle surface lightly with flour as needed to keep dough from sticking.

4. Cut or form dough into desired shape. Place dough shapes ½-inch apart on parchment-lined cookie sheet. Bake, rotating cookie sheets halfway through baking if necessary, until evenly golden brown, 6 to 8 minutes.

5. Use thin-bladed spatula to immediately transfer cookies to cooling rack. Cool to room temperature. Repeat rolling, cutting, and baking remaining dough. Decorate cooled cookies, if desired, and transfer to airtight container (can be stored up to 3 weeks).

CORNMEAL-CITRUS COOKIES
Follow master recipe for Multipurpose Butter Cookie Dough, adding 1 teaspoon finely grated lemon or orange zest to creamed butter, sugar, and salt and substituting 1 cup fine cornmeal for 1 cup of the flour.

CHOCOLATE-CINNAMON COOKIES
Follow master recipe, adding 1 ounce melted and cooled, unsweetened chocolate to creamed butter, sugar, and salt. Substitute ¼ cup cocoa for ¼ cup of the flour and mix in ¼ teaspoon cinnamon to flour-cocoa mixture.

LEMON BUTTER COOKIES
Follow master recipe, adding 2 teaspoons finely grated lemon zest to creamed butter, sugar, and salt.

LEMON–POPPY SEED COOKIES
Follow master recipe, adding 2 teaspoons finely grated lemon zest to creamed butter, sugar, and salt, and stirring in 2 tablespoons poppy seeds to finished dough.

ORANGE BUTTER COOKIES
Follow master recipe, adding 1 teaspoon finely grated orange zest to creamed butter, sugar, and salt.

ORANGE-NUT COOKIES
Follow master recipe, adding 1 teaspoon finely grated orange zest and 1 cup finely ground walnuts, pecans, or hazelnuts to creamed butter, sugar, and salt.

SPICE COOKIES
Follow master recipe, substituting 1 cup light brown sugar for granulated sugar and adding ¾ teaspoon ground cinnamon, ½ teaspoon ground ginger, ¼ teaspoon ground nutmeg, ¼ teaspoon ground allspice, and ⅛ teaspoon ground cloves to flour.

COCONUT COOKIES
Follow master recipe, stirring 1 cup toasted, flaked, sweetened coconut into finished batter.

GINGER COOKIES
Follow master recipe, adding 1 teaspoon ground ginger to flour and stirring 6 tablespoons finely minced candied ginger into finished dough.

BUTTERSCOTCH COOKIES
Follow master recipe, substituting 1 cup packed light brown sugar for granulated sugar.

RAISIN-SPICE COOKIES
Follow recipe for Spice Cookies, stirring ½ cup finely minced raisins or ½ cup currants into finished batter.

PEANUT BUTTER COOKIES
Because of the extra fat from the peanut butter, these cookies have a sandier, melt-in-your-mouth texture. Follow master recipe, creaming ⅔ cup peanut butter with butter, sugar, and salt.

LEMON, ORANGE, OR PLAIN GLAZE
Makes about ¾ cup
Spread the glaze on each cookie with a knife or drizzle the glaze on the cookies with the tines of a fork or a pastry bag fitted with a writing tip. If you decide to color the glaze, cut back a bit on the liquid unless using color pastes.

  1 cup confectioners' sugar
5–6 teaspoons lemon or orange juice or milk

Mix sugar and liquid in small bowl, adding just enough liquid to make spreadable or pourable glaze. Use immediately or cover with sheet of plastic wrap directly on surface of glaze to keep it from hardening.

ALL-PURPOSE CHOCOLATE GLAZE AND FROSTING
Makes ½ cup
Dip cookie tops in this glaze or drizzle the glaze onto the cookies with the tines of a fork or a pastry bag fitted with a writing tip. Because the glaze hardens as it cools, you may need to warm it several times during decorating.

  4 ounces bittersweet or semisweet
      chocolate
  4 tablespoons butter
  1 tablespoon corn syrup

Melt chocolate and butter in medium bowl set over pan of almost simmering water. Stir in corn syrup. Proceed with decorating. ∎

Winter Fruit Salads

Winter fruits combine with other ingredients to make substantial, flavorful salads.

~ BY KATE ELDRED ~

In summer, when fruits of all kinds are available, ripe and ready to eat, putting together a wonderful fruit salad is a breeze. In the winter, though, when the produce bins offer fewer choices, keeping fresh fruit on the table can be a challenge. Fortunately, the fruit that is available in the dark, cold season combines well with other ingredients to make substantial salads with many well-defined flavors. From the acid tang of citrus to the mellow smoothness of pears and the satisfying crunchiness of apples, these fruits will add variety as well as healthfulness to any winter table.

CITRUS SALAD WITH BITTER GREENS AND PARMESAN SHAVINGS
Serves 4

This slightly tart dish makes a refreshing appetizer before a relatively high-fat meat like roast pork, duck, or goose.

- ½ small red onion, diced fine
- 2 tablespoons red wine vinegar
- ⅓ cup olive oil
  Salt and ground black pepper
- 4 cups watercress, rinsed and large stems trimmed
- 2 heads Belgian endive, cut into 2-inch pieces
- 1 large orange, peeled and sectioned, juice reserved
- 1 large grapefruit, peeled and sectioned, juice reserved
- 2 tablespoons chopped fresh parsley leaves
  Shavings from Parmesan cheese block

1. Mix onion and vinegar in small bowl; let stand 30 minutes. Whisk olive oil into onion mixture; season to taste with salt and pepper.
2. Mix watercress and endive in medium bowl. Add fruit and juices, onion mixture, and parsley; toss to coat. Divide among four salad plates; garnish with cheese shavings and serve immediately.

GRAPE AND FETA SALAD WITH ROSEMARY
Serves 4

With wine and crusty bread, this makes a wonderful luncheon dish. If fresh rosemary is unavailable, substitute fresh mint, not dried rosemary.

- ⅓ pound mild feta cheese, crumbled coarse
- ½ pound black grapes, halved and seeded if necessary
- 2 teaspoons minced fresh rosemary
- 2 tablespoons olive oil
  Salt and ground black pepper
- 1½ quarts mesclun, rinsed and dried
- 1 tablespoon raspberry vinegar

1. Mix cheese, grapes, and rosemary in medium bowl. Add oil; toss to coat. Sprinkle generously with pepper.
2. Toss mesclun with vinegar in medium bowl. Season to taste with salt. Arrange on large serving platter or individual plates. Top with cheese mixture and serve.

PEAR SALAD WITH ARUGULA, WALNUTS, AND GORGONZOLA
Serves 4

Watercress and stilton can stand in for the arugula and gorgonzola in this recipe.

- 2 large, ripe but firm red pears, each halved, cored, and cut into 12 wedges
- 3 tablespoons juice from one lemon
- ¼ cup canola or vegetable oil
- 2 tablespoons walnut oil
  Salt and ground black pepper
- 1½ quarts arugula, stemmed, rinsed, and dried
- 3 ounces gorgonzola cheese, crumbled
- ½ cup walnuts, toasted and chopped coarse

1. Toss pear wedges with 1 tablespoon lemon juice in medium bowl; set aside.
2. In small bowl, slowly whisk oils into 2 remaining tablespoons lemon juice to make vinaigrette; season to taste with salt and pepper.
3. Toss arugula with vinaigrette. Place a portion of dressed greens on each plate. Arrange pears over greens, sprinkle with cheese, walnuts, and a generous grind of pepper. Serve immediately.

APPLE-CRANBERRY SALAD WITH CREAMY LEMON VINAIGRETTE
Serves 4

If you are unable to get dried cranberries for this recipe, you can simply substitute raisins.

- 2 Granny Smith apples, halved, cored, and cut into ¾-inch chunks
- 2 tablespoons juice and ½ teaspoon zest from small lemon
- 3 tablespoons canola or vegetable oil
- 2 tablespoons heavy cream
  Salt and ground black pepper
- 1 large celery stalk, sliced thin crosswise
- 3 tablespoons dried cranberries
- ¼ cup walnuts, toasted and chopped coarse
- 1 large head Boston lettuce, leaves separated, rinsed, and dried

1. Toss apples in 1 tablespoon lemon juice in medium bowl; set aside.
2. In small bowl, add remaining tablespoon lemon juice and zest; whisk in oil, then cream. Season to taste with salt and pepper.
3. Add celery, cranberries, and walnuts to apples. Drizzle dressing over fruit mixture; toss to coat. Place a large leaf or two of lettuce onto each plate. Spoon portion of salad onto each bed of lettuce and serve immediately.

APPLE-BEET SALAD WITH CREAMY DILL DRESSING
Serves 4

Dress the salad after it has been individually plated. If not, the dressing turns an unappetizing pale pink. Jarred pickled beets can be substituted for the fresh beets in this recipe.

- 3 tablespoons red wine vinegar
- 3 medium beets, steamed, peeled, and julienned
- ¼ cup plain yogurt
- ¼ cup mayonnaise
- 1 small garlic clove, minced
- 1 tablespoon minced fresh dill leaves
  Salt and ground black pepper
- ½ small lemon
- 2 tart apples, preferably Granny Smith, halved, cored, and cut into ⅛-inch slices
- 1½ quarts mixed mild greens, such as romaine, Boston, or leaf lettuce
- ¼ cup toasted pecans, chopped coarse

1. Drizzle vinegar over beets; refrigerate overnight.
2. Mix yogurt, mayonnaise, garlic, and dill in small bowl. Season to taste with salt, if necessary, and pepper to taste; set aside.
3. Squeeze lemon juice over apple slices. Place greens on platter or individual plates. Arrange apple slices and julienned beets over the greens; top with toasted pecans. Drizzle salad with dressing and serve. Or serve salad and pass dressing separately. ■

Kate Eldred is a physical geographer and freelance food writer.

No-Cream Cream Soups

For vegetable soups with fresher flavor, use a high proportion of vegetables, cook them in stock, and then enrich with milk.

∾ BY PHILLIS M. CAREY ∾

This creamy soup is thickened not with a starch, but with the vegetables themselves.

I enjoy the smooth, silky texture of creamed vegetable soups, but I often find the flavor to be lacking. The dairy elements (usually lots of butter and cream) mask the taste of the vegetables. Instead of an intense carrot flavor in a creamy base, for example, I usually taste cream with carrots in the background.

I wanted to see if there was a way to make a pureed soup that tasted more like vegetables. I wanted a creamy carrot soup reminiscent of the sweetest carrots, a broccoli soup that really had the flavor of broccoli. However, I was not willing to sacrifice anything in terms of consistency. Pureed vegetable soups must be silky. Otherwise there is no point in pureeing them.

Cream soups usually begin one of two ways. The first method calls for making a white sauce (flour cooked in butter and lightened with milk or cream) and then adding vegetables and more cream. In addition to the dairy products, the vegetables must compete with the flour, which can sometimes give these soups a gummy or starchy quality. I had to find another way. So I began a series of tests using carrots. Once I had developed a workable technique, I figured I could try some other vegetables.

I started out by experimenting with other starches (cornstarch and potato starch) but found

the results to be similar to soups made with flour. The texture was still too thick and gummy and the vegetables were not the primary flavor. I had also seen recipes using potatoes or rice as thickeners, usually cooked right along with the vegetables in broth. When I tried this, though, the potatoes and rice detracted from the carrot flavor and caused the color of the soup to fade.

A second classic technique for making cream soups begins by sautéing vegetables, adding some broth and seasonings, and finally adding cream, which is then cooked down to create the proper texture. I found that the elimination of the starch improved the texture of the soup, but the dairy component still dominated. I liked the idea of starting with the vegetables, though it seemed to me that the best idea might be to use a larger quantity of vegetables and puree them for texture.

So I increased the amount of vegetables I had been using. Most of the recipes I had consulted used equal amounts of vegetables and liquid, or in some cases slightly more liquid than vegetables. I decided to alter this ratio in a big way and cook four cups of carrots in two cups of stock. I figured I would get more vegetable flavor and could use the vegetables themselves as a thickener.

This change resulted in an immediate improvement. By the time the vegetables were cooked, the mixture was thick enough to create a puree with good body. In fact, the pureed carrots and broth were actually a little too thick. Instead of adding cream to the vegetables as they cooked, I now needed to add cream to the blender to thin out the pureed carrots.

I used about one cup of cream to get the right consistency, but this amount added too much dairy fat for my taste so I tried substituting half-and-half as well as whole and lowfat milk. I found that whole milk provided just the right amount of dairy fat to improve the texture, giving smoothness and a creamy mouth feel without blocking out the carrot flavor. Using skim milk or 2 percent milk was like adding more broth and not satisfying at all. Half-and-half was good, but a tad too rich.

I still wondered about this result and thought maybe I could use more stock earlier in the recipe so that I would need less cream or other liquid to thin out the vegetable puree. This tack failed. I increased the stock by two-thirds of a cup and then used just one-third of a cup of cream. The original version with less stock and more milk tasted better. I then thought about using somewhat fewer carrots so the puree would not be so thick and might require less dairy. Again, this failed. Reducing the carrots made a soup with less carrot flavor. The ratio of four parts carrots to two parts stock and one part milk was right on the money.

Adding Flavor Refinements

Now I was ready to work on flavor refinements, and I had a basic technique in hand. I planned to briefly sauté the aromatics (I was using onion) in a little fat, add some wine for flavor, and then cook the diced vegetables in stock. When the vegetables were tender, I would puree them and whatever stock had not been absorbed by the vegetables and milk to create a soup with good body and strong vegetable flavor.

A few questions still remained, however. First I wanted to find out which fat was best. I experimented with butter, olive oil, and vegetable oil and found that butter was my favorite, but that the differences were fairly subtle. If you intend to serve any of these soups cold, use oil because it will not congeal when chilled like butter.

I had used a medium onion in my testing and decided to try increasing and decreasing the amount. A single minced onion provided some sweetness and subtle flavor when sautéed, but more onions made the soup oniony. I tried shallots and leeks and found that either could be used in place of the onion. I think the leeks work especially well with potatoes and that shallots add a nice touch to the carrot soup, but any of the three alliums are fine in any recipe.

In my basic recipe, I was adding two tablespoons of sherry after the onion was sautéed. My theory was that the sherry would give the carrots a little boost. I tried varying the amount of sherry and also tried replacing it with white wine and omitting it altogether. The wine worked fine, but more than two tablespoons of alcohol is too acidic for this amount of soup. When made without any sherry or wine, on the other hand, the soup was a little flat. It's a refinement, but if you have some sherry or white wine on hand, add it.

I used homemade chicken stock for most of my

Which Tool Is Best for Pureeing?

Given the many choices, I wondered which kitchen tool was the best for pureeing vegetable soups. The texture of a pureed soup should be as smooth and creamy as possible. With this in mind, I tried pureeing the master recipe in a food mill, a food processor, a handheld immersion blender, and a regular countertop blender.

Forget using the food mill for this purpose. I used my Italian mill and tried all three blades (coarse, medium, and fine). In each case, the liquid ran right through the blade as I churned and churned only to produce baby food of varying textures. The liquid and pureed solids were separated and could not be combined with a whisk. A food processor or blender could do the job, but what's the point?

The food processor does a decent job of pureeing, but some small bits of vegetables can be trapped under the blade and remain unchopped. Even more troubling is the tendency of a food processor to leak hot liquid. Fill the workbowl more than halfway and you are likely to see liquid running down the side of the food processor base. Even small quantities of soup must be pureed in batches, and that's a hassle.

The immersion blender has more appeal since this tool can be brought directly to the pot and there is no ladling of hot ingredients. However, I found that this kind of blender also leaves some chunks behind. If you don't mind a few lumps, use an immersion blender, but it's not my first choice for perfectly smooth pureed soups.

So what is my first choice? A standard blender. As long as a little headroom is left at the top of the blender, there is never any leaking, and the blade on the blender does an excellent job with soups because it pulls ingredients down from the top of the container. No stray bits go untouched by the blade. The recipes below can be pureed in a single batch in a standard seven-cup blender.—P.M.C.

---

initial tests. I also liked the results with homemade vegetable stock. I then tried reduced-sodium canned chicken broth as well as canned vegetable broth. Both are acceptable, but not my first choice.

Finally, I wondered if some spices and/or herbs could be used to enhance the flavor of various vegetables. I found that spices are best cooked right along with the vegetables (for example, nutmeg is a nice enhancement for carrot soup) while fresh herbs can be used as a garnish. The recipes below offer some suggestions, but feel free to create your own combinations.

Beyond Carrots

Now that I had successfully developed a bright orange carrot soup that tasted like good, sweet carrots, I wondered which other vegetables might take to this technique. After much trial and error, I found that vegetables with a relatively low water content worked best. Broccoli, butternut squash, cauliflower, and potatoes all yielded thick, creamy soups when prepared according to the master recipe. I found it necessary to adjust the amount of milk added at the end (very starchy potatoes needed more milk than broccoli, for example), but the recipe was easy enough to adapt.

Watery vegetables, however, refused to work. Mushrooms, for instance, don't have enough fiber and bulk to work as their own thickening agent. Spinach and asparagus are also poor candidates for this technique, which works best with tubers, roots, and hearty winter vegetables.

PUREED CARROT SOUP WITH NUTMEG
(Master recipe for pureed vegetable soup)
Serves 4 to 6

Either chicken or vegetable stock can be used in this recipe. Canned broths may be used, if desired.

Add enough water to one 14.5-ounce can to make the necessary two cups.

- 2 tablespoons unsalted butter, olive oil, or vegetable oil
- 1 medium onion, 3 medium shallots, or 1 medium leek (white and light green parts only), chopped
- 2 tablespoons dry sherry or white wine
- 1½ pounds (about 8 medium) carrots, peeled, halved lengthwise, and sliced thin (about 4 cups)
- 2 cups chicken or vegetable stock
- 1 teaspoon salt
  Ground white pepper
  Pinch freshly grated nutmeg
- 1–1¼ cups whole milk
- 2 teaspoons minced fresh tarragon, mint, chive, or parsley leaves

1. Heat butter or oil in large saucepan over medium-high heat. Add onion; sauté until golden, about 5 minutes. Add sherry and carrots; stir-cook until sherry evaporates, about 30 seconds.

2. Add stock, salt, pepper to taste, and nutmeg to saucepan; bring to boil. Reduce heat to simmer; cover and cook until carrots are tender, about 20 minutes.

3. Ladle carrot mixture into blender. Add 1 cup milk; blend until very smooth. Return soup to saucepan; cook over low heat until warmed through. If soup is too thick, stir in additional milk to thin consistency. Adjust seasonings. (Soup can be refrigerated for 3 days and reheated just before serving.)

4. Ladle soup into individual bowls. Garnish with minced herb and serve immediately.

PUREED BROCCOLI SOUP WITH BASIL

Follow recipe for Pureed Carrot Soup with Nutmeg, replacing carrots with 2 pounds broccoli, stalks discarded and florets cut into bite-sized pieces to yield 5 cups. Omit nutmeg and cook broccoli until tender, about 10 minutes. Thin with ½ to ¾ cup milk and garnish soup with 2 tablespoons minced fresh basil leaves.

PUREED BUTTERNUT SQUASH SOUP WITH GINGER

Follow recipe for Pureed Carrot Soup with Nutmeg, replacing carrots with 1 medium butternut squash (about 2½ pounds), which has been halved, seeded, peeled, and cut into ½-inch cubes to yield 5 cups. Substitute 1 teaspoon ground ginger for nutmeg and cook squash until tender, about 15 minutes. Thin with ¾ to 1 cup milk and garnish with minced fresh chives or parsley.

PUREED CAULIFLOWER SOUP WITH CORIANDER

Follow recipe for Pureed Carrot Soup with Nutmeg, replacing carrots with 1 medium head cauliflower (about 2 pounds), stems discarded and florets cut into bite-sized pieces to yield 5 cups. Replace nutmeg with 1 teaspoon ground coriander and cook cauliflower until tender, about 12 minutes. Thin with ½ to ¾ cup milk and garnish with minced chives or parsley.

CREAMY POTATO SOUP WITH CHIVES

Follow master recipe, replacing carrots with 2 large baking potatoes (about 1½ pounds), peeled and cut into ½-inch dice to yield 4 cups. Omit nutmeg and cook potatoes until very tender, about 20 minutes. Thin with 1 to 1¼ cups milk and garnish with minced chives. ∎

Phillis M. Carey is a cooking instructor and freelance writer based in San Diego.

Make-Ahead Pan Gravy

To minimize hassle while maximizing flavor, use a dark roux as thickener, reduce the sauce in advance, and enrich it with concentrated pan drippings.

∾ BY CHARLOTTE BRUCE HARVEY ∾

To a traditionalist, the thought of a gravy-less Thanksgiving dinner is culinary heresy. Good gravy is no mere condiment; it's the tie that binds. But too often gravy is a last minute affair, thrown together without much advance preparation or thought. Many of us have experienced the result: either dull, greasy gravy or thin, acidic pan juices that are one-dimensional, lacking the body and stature that we expect from a good American gravy.

So I set out to produce a rich, complex sauce with as much advance preparation as possible to avoid that last minute time pressure, when space is at a premium and potatoes need to be mashed, turkey sliced, water goblets filled, and candles lit.

I began my tests by experimenting with thickeners. In a blind taste test I tried four different options including cornstarch, beurre manié (a paste made from equal parts by weight of wheat flour and butter), and two flour-based roux, one regular (a mixture of melted butter and flour stirred together over heat) and one dark (in which the butter-flour paste is cooked until it is dark brown).

Although most tasters were pretty sure before the tasting began that the cornstarch-thickened gravy would have inferior texture and flavor, it actually turned out to be quite good. Admittedly, it was a bit thinner in body and more acidic in flavor than the roux-based sauces, but it was acceptable. Personally, I also disliked its glossy sheen and translucence, which looked artificial to me, but those qualities did not bother other tasters.

Overall, though, the dark roux proved the best thickener. It added a subtle depth and complexity to the sauce not found with the other options. It can also be made ahead of time, a slight advantage because the other methods require last minute whisking.

To this dark roux, I added turkey stock made from the neck and giblets. Cooking the sauce over low heat for a half hour or more helped develop the flavor, but the resulting gravy was still pale and lacked punch. I then tried using a bulb baster to remove fat from the roasting turkey and using this as the base for the roux, instead of the butter. This tasted fine but was not an improvement over the butter version. I soon discovered, however, that the trick was to take this basic brown sauce—prethickened—and enrich it with pan drippings.

Pan drippings are the source of gravy's allure and also its difficulties. That gorgeous mahogany-colored goo that congeals at the bottom of a roasting pan is one of the best-tasting things on earth, a carnivore's ambrosia. But I found that to get dark brown pan drippings with a complex range of flavors, you need to roast your turkey over aromatic vegetables: a chopped onion, a couple of carrots, and bunches of fresh rosemary and thyme. I also found it necessary to keep an eye on the pan, adding water or stock whenever things start looking too dry.

When one of my test turkeys, roasted at a low oven temperature, produced drippings that were too pale, I discovered another technique for intensifying the gravy flavor. I poured off almost all the fat and liquid, then placed the pan back over two hot burners. After smashing the vegetables with a wooden spoon, I proceeded to reduce the drippings until they carmelized, developing color and a gooey consistency.

To deglaze the pan, I tried several approaches, all designed to add to the drippings missing dimensions of flavor. Dry sherry and Madeira are both traditional in giblet gravy, and their sugars, alcoholic bite, and rich, full body complemented the slight bitterness of the turkey organs in the giblets. These wines made complex, meaty gravies, as did port wine for the same reason. But then I deglazed one pan, in which I had included garlic and herbs, with leftover, flat, birthday champagne. I thought I'd discovered heaven. The extra acidity of the champagne and the herbs gave the sauce a heady, almost lemony flavor, both light and sharp. Five-dollar dry Chilean chardonnay proved a reasonable substitute. Although I know people who favor Cognac in turkey gravy, it does not make me sing; I prefer it with red meat or in unthickened chicken sauces.

After deglazing the pan and simmering off the alcohol, I strained the resulting wine sauce into the roux, smashing the remaining herbs and vegetables with a wooden spoon to wring the taste out of them. The result was worth the effort. After a quick simmer, and an adjustment of the seasonings, I had an intense, rich sauce that had the familiarity and comfort of traditional American gravy but hinted at the sophistication of a fine French brown sauce.

BEST TURKEY GIBLET GRAVY
Makes about 1½ quarts

1 tablespoon vegetable oil
  Wing tips, neck, and giblets (except liver) from one turkey
1 onion chopped, including skin
1½ quarts homemade chicken stock or 1 quart canned low-salt chicken broth plus 2 cups water
4 thyme branches
8 parsley stems
  Salt and ground black pepper
3 tablespoons unsalted butter
¼ cup flour
1 roasting pan full of caramelized meat drippings, onions, carrots, garlic heads, and herbs
1 cup dry or sparkling white wine

1. Heat oil in soup kettle; add giblets, wing tips, wings, and neck, then sauté until golden and fragrant, about 5 minutes. Add onion; continue to sauté until softened, 3 to 4 minutes longer. Reduce heat to low; cover and cook until turkey and onions release their juices, about 20 minutes. Add stock, bring to boil, then lower heat. Add herbs (and salt if necessary). Simmer, skimming any scum that may rise to surface, until broth is rich and flavorful, about 30 minutes. Strain broth (you should have about 5 cups) and reserve neck, heart, and gizzard. Once cool enough to handle, shred meat off neck, remove gristle from gizzard, then dice reserved heart and gizzard. Refrigerate meat and broth until ready to use.

2. Melt butter in a large, heavy-bottomed saucepan over medium-low heat. Vigorously whisk in flour (the roux will froth and then thin out again). Cook slowly, stirring fairly constantly, until nutty brown and fragrant, 10 to 15 minutes. (Return turkey broth to simmer.)

3. Vigorously whisk 1 quart hot broth into roux. Bring to a boil, then continue to simmer until gravy is lightly thickened and very flavorful, about 30 minutes. Set aside until ready to finish with pan juices and wine.

4. When turkey is cooked, remove from roasting pan, then spoon out as much fat as possible, leaving caramelized herbs and vegetables. Place roasting pan over medium-high heat and mash vegetables with wooden spoon (if drippings are not a dark brown, cook, stirring constantly, until they caramelize).

5. Return gravy to simmer. Add wine to pan of caramelized vegetables, scraping up browned bits with wooden spoon and boiling until reduced by about half. Add remaining 1 cup of broth, then strain pan juices into hot gravy, pressing as much juice as possible out of vegetables with wooden spoon. Stir reserved meat into gravy; return to boil. Adjust seasonings and serve. ∎

Charlotte Bruce Harvey is a Boston-based free-lance writer.

Southern Spoon Bread

For light, tender spoon bread, choose fine-grind cornmeal and use beaten egg whites instead of baking powder for lift.

~ BY CYNTHIA HIZER ~

To make a spoon bread, you must first whisk cornmeal into a simmering liquid and let it thicken into a "mush," as though you were cooking oatmeal or farina. To the cooled mush you add eggs, salt, butter, and other ingredients. The mixture is poured into a baking dish and baked for thirty-five to forty-five minutes. The resulting dish should be light as air with a tender, rich crumb. Nothing about the dish is rough or rustic. As with many historic dishes, however, ingredients and cooking techniques vary enormously. To find the spoon bread recipe that I liked best, I started by figuring out the best way to make the initial corn mush.

The proportion of liquid to solids differed wildly in the recipes I consulted; just by looking I couldn't see any rules gelling. After trying various ratios, I eventually settled on a medium-thick batter using three cups liquid to one cup cornmeal. Heavier mushes made it harder to incorporate beaten egg whites and retain their lightness while lighter versions simply did not gel adequately.

The act of stirring cornmeal into simmering milk can be tricky; if you don't do it properly, the meal can separate from the liquid and turn into a bunch of lumps rather than a smooth mush. Plenty of recipes call for the use of a double boiler to avoid lumping, but my suggestion is to turn off the phone and focus on the job at hand. Start whisking like crazy and don't stop until the mush is thickened, two to four minutes. It's not much of a time investment when you consider the alternative: twenty to thirty minutes of gentle stirring in a double boiler. Keep the cooking temperature low rather than high because you want the cornmeal to soften as it cooks.

The microwave oven also makes a superb mush, with no lumps and only a single stirring. The cooking time was longer than on the stovetop, however; five minutes on medium power worked the best with a stop halfway through to stir. Also, if you're going to use the microwave, it works best to cover the container with plastic wrap.

Other Ingredients

Having settled on the mush-making method, I moved on to consider the individual ingredients of the dish. Plenty of people (even Southerners) prefer a spoon bread made with mostly water and a little milk stirred in. This produces a moist bread, but surely not a rich one. For me, spoon bread made with water is like cornbread made with water: lean. Because spoon bread is a special meal dish, I prefer to splurge on the real article, and cut fat and calories some place else. Half-

and-half was my favorite, supplying just the right amount of richness; cream provided too much, and milk not quite enough.

The oldest recipes for spoon bread call for whole eggs, not separated, but in later recipes the eggs are separated and beaten to produce a light, high soufflé. Now we are beginning to see inroads to that procedure, with chemical leaveners compensating for the work eggs used to do. After tasting several dozen spoon breads made with simple ingredients, I found those made with baking powder or soda jumped out on my tongue because I could taste the chemicals so readily. I'll stick with beaten whites for my leavening.

Finally I considered the important question of what type of cornmeal to use. Yellow corn is more common in the North, and Southerners choose white for the same reason. Both are available in national brands (white from Hodgson Mill, yellow from Quaker). I tried both with an open mind and found that both were fine, the major difference being that the white produced a bread that was slightly milder in flavor.

A more important variation, however, came with grinds. In the South, white cornmeal is available in both medium and fine grinds. I prefer a fine grind because it produces a considerably smoother texture. In my many bakings, I continued to go back to the fine grind every time, as the bread was velvety smooth. If you can't get fine grind in your local store, it's no problem. You can approximate a fine grind by putting a medium-grind cornmeal in the food processor or even better, in the blender. The processing will take several minutes, but eventually you will have little clouds of powder-fine meal in the bottom of the bowl.

....

SOUTHERN SPOON BREAD
Serves 6 to 8

A standard eight-inch soufflé dish works beautifully, but any straight-sided, heavy pan will work, even an iron skillet. Because the spoon bread soon falls from its spectacular height, serve it as quickly as possible; even in its deflated state, though, spoon bread still tastes delicious. Serve leftovers with maple or cane syrup.

- 3 cups half-and-half
- 1 teaspoon salt
- 1 cup fine-ground white or yellow cornmeal

2–3 tablespoons unsalted butter, plus extra for soufflé dish
3 large eggs, warmed to room temperature, then separated

1. Heat oven to 350 degrees. Butter a 1½-quart soufflé dish.
2. Bring half-and-half and salt to simmer in large, heavy saucepan. Reduce heat to low. Slowly whisk in cornmeal. Continue whisking until cornmeal thickens and develops satin sheen, 2 to 4 minutes. Turn off heat and stir in butter; set mush aside.
3. Whisk yolks and 1 to 2 teaspoons water together in small bowl until lemon-colored and very frothy. Stir them into cooled mush, a little at a time to keep yolks from cooking. Beat egg whites to stiff but not dry peaks; gently fold them into mush mixture.
4. Pour mixture into buttered soufflé dish. Bake in oven until spoon bread is golden brown and risen above dish rim, about 45 minutes. Serve immediately.

....

SPOON BREAD WITH CHEDDAR CHEESE
Serves 6 to 8

Follow recipe for Classic Spoon Bread, stirring 1 cup (2 ounces) grated sharp cheddar cheese along with the butter. ∎

Cynthia Hizer is an organic farmer and food columnist for the *Atlanta Journal and Constitution.*

Aged Country Ham Wins Tasting, But Young Hams Also Do Well

A full-flavored ham aged over one year wins top honors, while new-style, fast-aged hams deliver less salt and milder flavor.

∼ BY SARAH FRITSCHNER ∼

Like grapes, fresh pork can be processed several ways with widely varying results. The person who cures a ham can be a technician or an artist. Industry and the U.S. Department of Agriculture encourage the former because it's easier to control: Ham makers can hang a ham in a metal room, turn down the heat to mimic winter, turn up the heat to mimic summer, keep the proper temperature records, and ship the ham to the supermarket on the day promised.

Connoisseurs prefer the artist, who may raise the hogs himself (though most ham producers of any size buy from a packing house). He invariably will kill the hogs in winter so the cold winter temperatures preserve the meat until it has lost enough moisture to ensure its long-term storage capabilities. These processors let the ham age through "summer sweats" until it is at least nine months old because they know that not just temperature and humidity, but time and nature do for meat the same thing they do for grape juice and Levi's jeans—inexplicably improve it.

With all this in mind, we rounded up an expert panel to taste country hams sold by mail. Ham enthusiasts will drive the back roads of Western Kentucky or North Carolina looking for a promising lead on a home-cured country ham. But the rest of us mortals have to order a ham by mail and would like some direction in doing so. Some mail-order firms can turn out hams in less than three months and might sell ten thousand a day; others take fifteen months to cure a ham and might not sell ten thousand a year. We ordered ten hams to see if we could tell which was which, and how that knowledge might affect our purchasing decisions.

Our tasting revealed two different styles of country ham with obvious differences between them. Those that were aged a year or more were more intensely flavored, with more of the complex overtones characteristic or aged foods. Because aging makes the meat rosier, the flesh of these older hams was denser and prettier, and the salt levels were usually balanced by the deep meat flavors achieved through aging. Hams aged a short time, on the other hand, were moister and tasted more like straight pork, with less complicated flavors. The extreme ends of the spectrum were very different hams, and though there were hams that fell in between (a Smithfield, for instance), it's wise to ask how long the hams have been aged before you buy one. That way you'll be more prepared for what you're going to receive.

The Importance of Aging

Country hams are quite narrowly defined. To begin with, a country ham must be made from the hind quarter of the hog, including both the leg and shank bones. The meat is buried in salt or a mixture of salt, sugar, and spices for about five weeks. This is the dry-curing period. During this time the meat must lose at least 18 percent of its fresh weight to qualify for the name "country ham." Many older hams lose up to 25 percent. A country ham must also contain at least 4 percent salt, and those that are cured without nitrates or nitrites must contain a little more than that. The ham must also be aged to ensure it is free of trichina parasites.

That's the official definition. A Smithfield ham, the most famous country ham, is somewhat more specific: a dry-cured ham that is aged for a minimum of six months in the Tidewater town of Smithfield, Virginia. The "Smithfield" moniker is useful to consumers because it guarantees that a ham has been aged six months. Because many experts believe country hams should be aged a minimum of nine months, buying a Smithfield ham guarantees you're most of the way there. But as we shall see, it doesn't necessarily guarantee that you're buying the best country ham.

The official definition of country ham tells you many things. It tells you a country ham will be saltier and drier than what a Southerner might call a "city ham" and what other consumers just call ham. City hams are the same cut of meat processed in a wet cure (brine) and then usually simply smoked and not aged. Dry curing makes a country ham less juicy, and aging gives it a stronger flavor.

But the term "country ham" allows for plenty of variation. Country ham aged for shorter periods will be milder and moister, longer-aged hams stronger and drier. But even within the extremes of taste and texture, between the mass producer and the small-scale farmer, there are hundreds of choices and factors that can affect the final quality of the ham. It can be smoked a short time in really dense smoke or several weeks in smoke that isn't so dense; the woods can differ; the ham sizes might differ (which affects their rate of dehydration and therefore affects the aging process); the temperature and humidity during aging are also factors.

As a country ham buyer, you should ask the producer how long the ham has been aged. Any less than six months will yield a gentler piece of meat. After you've determined aging, other flavor factors will be less reliable. Like wine, ham flavors depend on the nature of the raw ingredients and the weather as well as on the skill of the maker. A ham from the same house may differ from year to year, sometimes from ham to ham. Two nine-month hams from different processors can taste almost the same or be totally dissimilar.

Choosing the Right Ham

Good country ham, like good wine, is a matter of taste. A novice might prefer a flavor that's non-threatening, uncomplicated, and easy to like. With experience you get pickier; layers of flavor and quirkiness appeal to you, and you learn to recognize and appreciate the art that went into the product.

In this tasting, we learned that a great ham is a great ham no matter who you are. Yankees and traditionalist Southerners, novices and gourmands alike all gravitated to one ham—a ham cured more by art than by science for fifteen months in small batches in the central Kentucky town of Bremen. This Gatton country ham had a recognizable "cheesiness," firm texture, and dark color. In addition, it had the characteristic white flecks in the flesh that signify long aging. These white flecks, which look like fine grains of salt, are crystallized proteins that have precipitated out of the ham due to extensive dehydration and long aging. Although the Gatton ham was characteristically salty, it wasn't overwhelmingly so—a fine line that often separates good hams from great hams.

Southern food experts will snort that choosing a milder, "quick-cure" ham is the culinary equivalent of Muzak. They argue that it isn't "the real thing" and that the growing sales of quick-cure hams endanger the very integrity of indigenous American cuisine, giving up ground to the assembly-line mentality of commercially processed food.

But our tasters agreed that most quick-cure hams aren't bad food. Rather than characterizing the hams as insipid and uninspired, it's more accurate to compare them to the simple and pleasing melodies of *Help!* which, in time, leads to an appreciation of the more complex *Sgt. Pepper's Lonely Hearts Club Band*. The tragedy to indigenous cuisine is not that these milder hams are produced, but that there isn't ample opportunity to taste the longer-aged hams over and over. That way, modern consumers could, like their ancestors, learn over time to enjoy the hams with more idiosyncrasies and, almost inevitably, eventually come to appreciate them for their more complex flavors.

Be that as it may, ham novices would do well to start with Stadler's, a short-cure, mass-produced ham from North Carolina. The flesh is moister than Gatton hams or any of our older hams, the flavor is not too assertive, the smoke isn't overwhelming. Yet it has a characteristic muskiness that makes it a good "beginner's" country ham. Any of the hams we rated "satisfactory" are comparable—good beginner hams that you could feel confident putting on your holiday buffet, the kind that will please all the people all the time.

Gwaltney can be credited with most of the reputation of Smithfield hams. Though these hams are mass-produced, they are by definition at least six months old, so they have a little more flavor than a ninety-day ham, are a little drier, and can be considered a decent "in-between" ham. They are a good choice for those who want to experiment with stronger flavors but who don't have a lot of experience with country ham.

Of course, food ratings can also be misleading. If a winner is selected from a list of averages, strong likes and dislikes are naturally discarded. For that reason, we list Finchville hams among our "recommended" hams. A couple of our tasters liked it best, but another said the salt nearly burned his mouth. One commented that it would have been a favorite had it been soaked longer. The ham is characteristic of old, dry, aged hams and will probably be appreciated best by those who love old hams. The hams from S. Wallace Edwards and Gatton are just as complex if perhaps less controversial. ■

Sarah Fritschner is the food editor of the *Louisville Courier-Journal* and the author of *The Express Lane Cookbook* (Chapters, 1995) and *The Vegetarian Express Lane* (Chapters, 1996).

Ten hams from the Southeastern United States were compared in our tasting: three from Kentucky, three from Virginia, three from North Carolina, and one from Tennessee. They represented all types of cure, from a fifteen-month cure at ambient temperatures to ones that had been quick-aged a minimum amount of time in an artificially controlled atmosphere. Hams were simmered without aromatics (to keep distractions to a minimum) and then sliced twelve pieces to the inch and sampled at room temperature. Prices include shipping unless otherwise noted below. Curing times are approximate and will vary slightly depending on the time of year.

In addition to the author, our panel included sausage maker Bruce Aidells; author and meat expert Merle Ellis; Robin Kline of the Pork Producers Association; Russ Parsons, managing editor of the food section for the *Los Angeles Times*; Richard Reynolds, executive chef at the Restaurant School in Philadelphia; and Christopher Kimball, Pam Anderson, and Stephanie Lyness from the *Cook's Illustrated* editorial staff.

RECOMMENDED HAMS
These hams were judged to be quite good.

S. Wallace Edwards & Sons Wigwam Ham (Surry, Virginia; 800-222-4267), $60 plus shipping for a 15-to-16 pound ham, cured twelve months. This ham was salty but not overly so, and had a strong "old" flavor with good smokiness, a jerky texture, and the peppered exterior typical of Virginia hams. It got lots of high marks.

Finchville Farms Country Ham (Finchville, Kentucky; 502-834-7952), $55 for 13-to-15 pound ham, cured fifteen months. The most controversial ham received very high marks from some tasters and very low marks from others. Described by some as "beautiful mahogany" with "good tang" and "musty" flavor, it was way too salty and strong for most people. One suggested that it be soaked longer before cooking. Recommended for those who like strong hams.

Gwaltney Genuine Smithfield Ham (Smithfield, Virginia; 800-292-2773), $49 plus shipping for a 12-to-16 pound ham, cured at least six months. A beautiful ham with a silky texture and great, musky aroma. It was characteristically salty with lots of cheesy tones as well.

Stadler's Country Ham (Elon College, North Carolina; 910-584-1396), $40 for a 13-to-15 pound ham, cured at least three months. With light smokiness, medium salt, and almost no aroma, this ham has a balanced finish that doesn't bowl you over. It was described as the "best of the mild hams." Recommended for beginners.

SATISFACTORY HAMS
These hams were judged to be fine, but nothing special.

Johnston County Country Ham (Smithfield, North Carolina; 919-934-8054), $2.39 per pound plus shipping, cured about five months. Described as a "little sour" and "tangy," this ham was very mild. A middle-of-the-road ham that elicited no strong comments.

Craver's Whole Country Ham (Winston-Salem, North Carolina; 910-724-5508), $31.64 plus shipping for a 14-to-16 pound ham, cured seven to eight months. One taster liked this ham, but others described it as "young" and "bland."

Mar-Tenn Country Ham (Martin, Tennessee; 901-587-3803), $32.58 plus shipping for a 14-pound ham, cured about six months. Tasters were unenthusiastic, saying it had a "generic ham taste" that was "very, very mild."

Harper's Country Ham (Clinton, Kentucky; 502-653-2081), $46.95 plus shipping for a 14-to-15 pound ham, cured about six months. More like a good city ham, with little salt or aged flavor. A good ham but would disappoint people searching for aged muskiness.

NOT RECOMMENDED HAM
Only one ham received uniformly negative remarks.

V.W. Joyner Smithfield Collection Ham (Smithfield, Virginia; 804-357-2161), $50 for a 13-to-15 pound ham, cured six to nine months. Heavy smoke and excessive salt did not hide off-flavors one panelist described as "rancid."

Do Espresso Machines Under $200 Really Work?

Like computers, the price of espresso machines has dropped as quality has risen. We found several models under $200 that are quite good.

∽ BY JACK BISHOP ∽

Three years ago I tested espresso machines for this magazine and was underwhelmed. My goal then was to find machines that were reasonably priced but could still compare with pricier models.

There are three types of espresso machines, distinguished by the method they use to force hot water through the coffee grounds: a manual pump, an electric pump, or steam pressure. In my experience, machines that work by steam pressure cannot generate enough power to produce real espresso. They are very cheap but useless. I have used a very expensive manual pump machine for many years, but figuring that most people don't really want to spend a week's salary on a device to make coffee, I decided to restrict the field to less expensive electric pump machines. Three years ago, I was able to find only five electric pump models that were priced under $225. Several of them were fine, but nothing like my machine, which acted as a kind of gold standard during my testing.

That's all changed. Espresso machines are hot items, and manufacturers have increased quality while slashing prices. This time around, I set a limit of $200 and found eleven machines. Of these, four turned out to be well-made, in the same league (although not as good) as my more expensive machine. There was some bad news. The three really cheap machines (priced under $110) fell to the bottom of the rankings. But take heart, $150 now buys a good espresso machine.

Selecting a Machine

An espresso machine only needs to accomplish two tasks—make espresso and froth milk for cappuccino and latte. But the espresso must be really hot with an intense, rounded flavor, and a thick layer of light brown foam (called crema) must float on top. The crema is crucial because it adds smoothness and creaminess—without it, espresso is just strong coffee. As for steaming milk, the wand should be able to double (at the very least) the volume of the milk, without scorching or leaving it tepid.

Last time around, the machines I tested produced decent espresso, but the frothing ranged from fair to abysmal. They lacked the power of more expensive models and could not produce as much pressure. After testing eleven machines for this article, it's clear to me that manufacturers

RATING ESPRESSO MACHINES

Ten espresso machines were tested and evaluated based on the following criteria. They are listed in order of preference.

Price: Refers to retail prices paid at stores listed in Sources and Resources on page 32 and does not include shipping.

Tank Capacity: All models come with a removable plastic tank. Larger tanks are nice, but only practical for people who make a lot of espresso since water should be used up (or changed) every few days.

Espresso Quality: Two types of beans were ground and then used to make one and two cups of espresso several times. Crema production (the foamy, butterscotch-colored layer on top) was the most important factor here.

Frothing Ability: One-half cup of whole milk was frothed several times and measured. Good machines were able to create volume (at least one cup plus foam) as well as density. Top choices heated the milk thoroughly without any scorching.

GOOD   FAIR   POOR

ESPRESSO MACHINE	PRICE	TANK CAPACITY	ESPRESSO QUALITY	FROTHING ABILITY
Krups Novo 2000 Plus	$200	41 ounces	Good	Good
Briel Estoril ES-33	$150	62 ounces	Good	Good
Estro 410	$189	48 ounces	Good	Good
La Pavoni Espresso Si PA-16	$160	30 ounces	Good	Good
Buon Caffè 330	$199	48 ounces	Good	Fair
Buon Caffè 320	$169	34 ounces	Fair	Good
Briel Vilamoura ES-16	$109	60 ounces	Fair	Good
Salton Cappuccino Dolce PE-70	$100	60 ounces	Fair	Poor
DeLonghi Caffè Rialto BAR-19	$130	40 ounces	Fair	Good
DeLonghi Caffè Treviso Bar-14	$100	36 ounces	Poor	Good

have improved the frothing ability in inexpensive pump models. But even more important, many machines are now more user-friendly.

I gave my mother an inexpensive espresso machine several years ago. It requires the skill and patience of a trained Starbucks barista to operate. My mother would rather avoid the fuss and gets her latte on the way to work. Mom, manufacturers have heard your complaints and removed much of the guesswork.

Some examples. Many machines now come with a crema-enhancing device. Either built into the bottom of the filter basket (as with the top-rated Krups and second-rated Briel Estoril) or used as an insert under the basket (this diminishes the value of this feature since the insert can be mis-used or misplaced), these devices form a narrower channel for the coffee to go through; this has the

effect of intensifying the pressure and thereby increasing the amount of crema that is produced. You still need to get the coffee ground finely and then lightly tamp it into the filter basket, but these devices compensate for minor errors and allow the novice to turn out good espresso on the first try.

In some models (including the third-rated Estro and fourth-rated Pavoni), the basket is no longer a separate piece and is welded right into the filter holder. Again, fewer parts to lose and this setup produces more pressure and gets more crema out of the coffee.

The Estro and Pavoni also allow pressure to build in the brew head before the water is released into the filter basket. The Estro automatically releases the water after five or six seconds. The Pavoni requires the user to listen for the pressure to build and then to turn the handle on the filter

BEST MACHINE
Krups Novo 2000 Plus: Crema sieves integrated into one- and two-cup filter baskets really work. Filter holder is easier than most to get into place and clicks when correct position is reached. Automatic frothing (no dial to turn) is slow but yields greatest volume. Warming plate is nice feature but only gets hot enough after several uses.

BEST BUY
Briel Estoril: Single-filter basket with built-in "crema master" works well as long as basket is not filled to rim. Use one and three-quarter scoops for two cups of espresso; otherwise filter holder will not lock into place. Excellent frothing with factory-issue steaming wand, plus automated "Quick Froth Cappuccino" attachment that is great for novices.

Estro 410: Excellent espresso with built-in filter basket and automatic function that builds pressure before releasing water into grounds. Steaming wand does not produce tremendous volume but delivers good density.

La Pavoni Espresso: Similar design to Estro but pressure-building function is not automatic and handle on filter holder must be turned to release water into basket. Steaming wand creates plenty of volume but not quite as much heat as other top units.

Buon Caffè 330: Super crema production with good but not great frothing that requires practice and patience. Dials are hard to understand and manual is just as misleading.

Buon Caffè 320: Decent espresso although crema insert (which is not mentioned in manual) does not work. Fast and strong frothing. A bit messier than other machines.

Briel Vilamoura: Like the Estoril, this machine froths milk with ease. However, espresso is only so-so, and cord placement is too close to water tank. Very compact.

Salton Cappuccino Dolce: Good espresso with crema disc and two-cup basket, but frothing produces too many bubbles and not enough heat.

DeLonghi Caffè Rialto: Decent espresso but foaming is temperamental and machine feels very flimsy.

DeLonghi Caffè Treviso: No crema and machine vibrates so much that cups move out of position.

Some Conclusions

Besides being more user-friendly, the top four machines also produced excellent espresso and steamed milk on the first as well as subsequent attempts. Priced at $200 and under, these machines offer an excellent value. The next three machines (the two by Buon Caffè and the Briel Vilamoura) can turn out decent espresso and steamed milk but are more temperamental. Design flaws also prevent me from giving them my endorsement. As for the Salton and two DeLonghis, the price is right, but because I had trouble getting these problematic machines to perform basic tasks, I recommend that you steer clear of them. ∎

Espresso Without the Mess

Even the best machines can't eliminate the mess. Just ask my wife. I grind my own beans (and you should, too), but no grinder does this neatly (*see* our January/February 1995 issue for a rating of grinders). I then spoon the grounds into the filter basket and tamp, making more of a mess. By the time I'm done, my wife is usually threatening to throw my whole setup in the trash.

The Krups Nespresso System 986 ($199.99) was designed for folks who like good espresso and cappuccino but can't stand the mess and want to eliminate all guesswork. The machine, which is built by Krups, uses vacuum-sealed pods of already ground coffee (from food giant Nestlé). Just pop a pod into the filter basket, turn on the pump, and out comes espresso. The model I tested also does a great job of frothing milk.

The machine is sold with twenty pods, each capable of making a single espresso. Users must purchase more pods (available at stores or by mail from the Nespresso Club; see Sources page 32 for more information) and have a choice of seven blends. This system is not cheap (ten pods cost $4.50 plus shipping as opposed to about $1.50 worth of fresh beans to turn out an equal amount of espresso), but can you really put a price on marital bliss?—*J.B.*

holder to release the water. Although the Pavoni can be mastered and turns out excellent espresso, the Estro is easier to use.

As for frothing, I have heard plenty of complaints from friends: scorched milk, no increase in volume, milk that was lukewarm after frothing. While some models still have weak frothers, the top models are all able to double or triple the volume of the milk.

Some of the top models also take the guesswork out of steaming milk. There are no knobs to turn on the Krups and therefore no doubts about how far to open it. The steaming wand works automatically although more slowly than the wand on other machines. Briel simplifies steaming even further by including a "Quick Froth Cappuccino" attachment with their machines. Simply remove the steaming wand and slide the steaming duct into this attachment. Pour milk into the attachment, press a button, and wait a few seconds for perfectly frothed milk to pour into a cup below.

Tasting True Champagnes

Nonvintage Champagnes are consistently wonderful, if more expensive than sparkling wines from other regions. Although you can't go wrong, we pick the best.

~ BY MARK BITTMAN ~

All sparkling wines that bear the name Champagne—legitimately at least—are made by the *méthode champenoise* (described in some detail in our November/December 1995 issue) and hail from France's northernmost winemaking region: Champagne.

Although many countries have venerable traditions of making sparkling wine—especially Italy and Spain but also others including, in recent years, the United States—the French product has long been considered the best. So much so that its name became generic. Strictly speaking, Spanish sparkling wines are called *cavas*, and Italian *prosecco*, but one might just as easily order Spanish or Italian "champagne."

American sparklers, which have no traditional name, are often called champagne even though they are no more so than American pinot noir is a Burgundy. Nevertheless, as we have demonstrated in tastings of sparkling wines in previous years, some American sparkling wines have become very good. They've also become pricey, whereas the price of the French article has stabilized in recent years to the point where almost every good basic Champagne costs less than $30, and some far less—as little as $20 in highly competitive markets. By most people's standards, of course, this is still far from cheap and, generally speaking, Champagne remains more expensive than California sparklers.

But at holiday time, when celebrations and budget busting are the rule, there is good reason to consider these wines, especially since the results of our tasting indicate that there is not a loser in the bunch. (Although some wines finished well down on the list because of our objective scoring system, even those wines had predominantly positive comments from the tasting panel.)

The wines under consideration are the standard, nonvintage brut (the driest) blends of the well-known French Champagne houses, such as Veuve Cliquot, Bollinger, Taittinger, Mumm, Moët, and so on. These houses buy the best grapes (many growers in Champagne, as in others areas of France, have tiny plots and sell their grapes to producers) and treat them right. With these grapes—chardonnay, pinot noir, and meunier —each house makes a proprietary *cuvée*, a blend of many wines from different vintages in different proportions. Anyone can employ the *méthode champenoise* to make sparkling wine, but only the winemakers of Champagne have a two-hundred-year-plus tradition of employing this blending process, all-important in determining the quality of Champagne.

The goal for nonvintage wines is to have a consistent *cuvée*, a wine that tastes almost the same from year to year. And as devoted Champagne drinkers know, each house has its own style, so each *cuvée* is different and consistent. Bollinger, for example, makes a very full-bodied, powerful wine while Taittinger is much more delicate. Each has its fans, and in digesting the results of our tasting, bear in mind that in this instance the differences among the winners may say even less than usual about the quality of the Champagnes, which were all well-made, sound wines, than they say about the preferences of our panel.

One great thing about nonvintage Champagne is that if you find a brand that you like, you can stick with it, with the assurance that it will change very little, if at all, from year to year. For that reason, many veteran Champagne lovers prefer nonvintage to the costlier and less consistent vintage Champagnes. ∎

BLIND TASTING RESULTS

As usual, the wines in our tasting—held at Chamard Vineyards in Clinton, Connecticut—were judged by a panel made up of both wine professionals and amateur wine lovers. In the judging, seven points were awarded for each first-place vote; six for second; five for third; and so on. The wines, which were all nonvintage, brut Champagnes, were all purchased in the Northeast; prices will vary considerably throughout the country. List prices for most Champagnes are in the $30 to $40 range, but they are almost always heavily discounted.

Within each category, wines are listed based on the number of points scored. Highly Recommended wines received few or no negative comments; Recommended wines had predominantly positive comments. The wines in the "Recommended with Reservations" category also had predominantly positive comments but were not ranked as highly by the tasters.

VERY HIGHLY RECOMMENDED

Charles Heidsieck, $30. Out of ten tasters, five ranked this in first place and three in second. "Rich nose," "full-flavored," "very classy," "great range of flavors." A stunning wine.

HIGHLY RECOMMENDED

Laurent-Perrier, $28. A distant but strong second. "Complex," "yum, yum," "almost sweet but with complexity to carry it." Strong showing for a less well-known Champagne.

Deutz, $25. "Super flavorful" and "clean," if a bit "heavy-handed." Big wine with a following.

Mumm Cordon Rouge, $25 (sometimes can be found for $20). "Sweet, elegant, and fruity." "On second tasting," wrote one taster, "this is PURE."

RECOMMENDED

Ayala, $20. Dark horse, from a little-known house whose wines are always good and priced a bit under the others. "Quality and finesse," "full-flavored," but "not much stuffing."

Taittinger, $27. "Light," "elegant," and "a little sweet"; "lacking a great finish."

RECOMMENDED WITH RESERVATIONS

Pol Roger, $25. "Distinctively chardonnay," "light and elegant," but "some off-flavors" and "not dry enough."

Perrier-Jouet, $23. "More toast, less fruit," a style some people liked. Some found it "not as clean" as other wines.

Piper Heidsieck, $25. "Very flavorful," but more than one taster found it "too dry," "austere," or "sour."

Veuve Cliquot Ponsardin, $30. "A lovely wine, tasting of fruit and toast" that was evidently "too sweet" to garner many votes.

Moët et Chandon, $25. "Lots of wood and fruit," thought some, but others found it "not so clean."

Bollinger, $27. A heavy wine you either like or hate: "Biggest nose, very dry, great stuff." "Strong nose, heavy fruit, not clean."

Roederer, $27. Another big wine: "Rich flavors," "very nice," but "very heavy" and "not clean."

Pommery, $23. The general high quality of the wines in this tasting can be summed up by this: A wine that more than one taster found "pleasantly sweet," "creamy," or "high-quality" got almost no votes in the ranking.

Book Reviews

Four-Star Desserts
Emily Luchetti
HarperCollins, $32.50

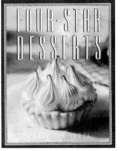

From the title of this worthy book, one might expect the usual repertoire of restaurant recipes, designed exclusively for execution by a cadre of skilled pastry chefs. After all, Emily Luchetti is the former pastry chef at Stars Restaurant in San Francisco and also author of *Stars Desserts* (HarperCollins, 1991).

To our surprise, however, this collection of fresh, interesting desserts is rarely ornate and almost always delivers reliable, easy-to-follow recipes. Rather elaborate confections, such as Eclairs with Pear Pastry Cream, are nicely balanced with the simplest of recipes, such as Caramel Strawberries, which contain a mere handful of everyday ingredients. I also noted a refreshing tone of common sense and culinary moderation. Luchetti notes in the introduction, for example, "The addition of mint leaves . . . should be limited to a dessert that has mint in it." Not front page news, perhaps, but a welcome sentiment nonetheless.

The desserts we made from this book were almost uniformly pleasing. Goat Cheese Cake with Mixed Berries was simple to prepare, contained a pleasing counterpoint of lemon zest, and was quite good with the fresh blackberries and raspberries called for as a simple topping. Bing Cherry Dumplings were also good. (One caveat: The recipe calls for individual muffin cups, a piece of cookware that few have on hand; I had to make do with a regular muffin tin, which has cups that are a bit small for the recipe.) I was initially skeptical about the dough, which is made from cream cheese and enough butter to slow down Carl Lewis, but it was very good although a truly decadent construct. The bottoms of the dumplings were soggy, but this was neither unpleasant nor necessarily unintended. The Strawberry Gratin, nothing more than quartered strawberries topped with sour cream, half-and-half, and brown sugar and then placed under the broiler to melt the sugar, was outstanding. So good, in fact, that we made it twice more, substituting blueberries and thin-sliced nectarines for the strawberries. Guests invariably asked for the recipe. Raspberry Lemon Buttermilk Pie was also easy to make, a hit at two separate dinner parties given by one of our editors, but a fairly deep nine-inch pie plate was required to handle the full five cups of filling.

I could list many other recipes from this book

that our editors tested and liked. In fact, the only clear loser was Plum Biscuits, which had little plum flavor (they needed more sugar), had a strange sour flavor from the cream cheese, and never completely cooked inside, even when put back into the oven. These biscuits were sodden with fat but without the benefit of mouth-filling flavor.

This leads us to the book's one small blemish, which is that the author is fearless about fat, often starting off a recipe with two sticks of softened butter or eight ounces of cream cheese. At a restaurant, one is in the mood to enjoy a bit of sin, and as we all know, ignorance is bliss. But when faced with a list of recipe ingredients, reality often gives us pause. *Cook's Illustrated* is no health publication, but we do believe that calories should be worth the ride. For the most part, Luchetti delivers handsomely; upon occasion, however, a lighter, more frugal hand in the dairy case would be welcome.

That being said, Luchetti delivers an original, reliable collection of dessert recipes, most of which are within the sights of the home cook. In addition, the proportion of winning recipes is unusually high—only two of the nine recipes tested were problematic. This batting percentage, paired with her originality, makes this an excellent choice for the holidays or any other time of year.

—*Christopher Kimball*

Fresh & Fast
Marie Simmons
Chapters Publishing, $29.95

Modern lifestyles and sophisticated appetites have been building up a demand for this kind of book for decades. Marie Simmons has succeeded with a book of quick recipes, where others have failed, for several reasons: She has a genuine palate (Italian), a commitment to seasonal ingredients (notably late summer's), and the character to keep things simple. Crucially, she knows that quick recipes still require good techniques, so it's all right if it takes longer to read the explanation than it does to make the recipe. Many such books are dishonest about preparation times; Simmons restores credibility by opening up her "fast" cuisine to forty-five minutes, with many good recipes for "When you have more time."

Our favorite recipes were simple composed salads. Swordfish, Potato, and Celery Salad with Lemon and Parsley, for instance, had flavor way beyond the sum of its parts. Warm Lentil and New Potato Salad multiplied the virtues of potatoes

and lentils with a quality vinaigrette dressing. Spinach, Shrimp, and Warm New Potato Salad played off a white wine dressing. Not only are these fresh and fast, they also hold well if a family "eats in shifts."

Simmons has a very fine hand with pasta, specifying shapes to go with vegetables cut in certain ways. The results were extremely convincing in her family recipe of chickpeas and shells as well as in Pasta e Ceci and the ultrafast yet complex Pasta with Arugula, Olives, and Fresh Tomatoes.

An advantage to the mostly Italian flavorings is that dishes mix and match with each other well, and the author has a real command of the seasonings. Obvious and easy, even familiar dishes jump to new levels for her. For example, everyone has a recipe for marinating black olives, but not one as amazing as her orange-and-fennel-flavored olives, good to the last drop of oil. Simmons' doctoring also raises Fresh Goat Cheese with Basil and Lemon, Famous Lemon and Basil Chicken, and even sweetened ricotta—the stuff inside cannoli—to new heights. Oven-roasted Carrots with Lemon and Olives come out tart and tangy, like an unfamiliar fruit. Curried Carrot Soup uses buttermilk and a touch of cumin to suggest a basic but hitherto unknown vegetable. Grilled Cumin-Marinated Swordfish is so subtly good people will ask about your fish dealer instead of "What's the herb in this?"

Simmons' Rich Chocolate Pudding is almost the same cornstarch pudding recipe as in *Joy of Cooking*, but by cutting the cornstarch and tripling the chocolate, she is able to eliminate the double boiler and other fussy techniques to make a twenty-minute pudding that eclipses anything out of a box.

A couple of dishes were duds for us. Both the Chilled Fresh Corn and Buttermilk Chowder with Shrimp and the Quick-Chilled Cumin-Scented Fresh Tomato and Corn Soup rely on raw, fresh sweet corn, and July corn left a barn-sized hole in the taste. These dishes also push the envelope on preparation time and mess up quite a few pots. The former, for example, uses both a food processor (twice) and a food mill plus several bowls. Dishwashing times ought to be included.

Cook's Illustrated editors tried a lot more recipes than usual in this book. There was a very high percentage of hits, and most of the misses required only one adjustment, for example, less hot pepper in Umberto's Oranges, spreading out the chicken pieces in Famous Lemon and Basil Chicken, or chopping rather than squeezing garlic in a number of recipes.

In short, I cannot think of a more encouraging and rewarding first cookbook for those just starting out in the kitchen. And this is the only cookbook you need to take on summer vacation—which is what a lot of us did. ■

—*Mark Zanger*

Sources and Resources

Most of the ingredients and materials necessary for the recipes in this issue are available at your local supermarket, gourmet store, or kitchen supply shop. The following are mail-order sources for particular items. Prices listed below were current at press time and do not include shipping or handling unless otherwise indicated. We suggest that you contact companies directly to confirm up-to-date prices and availability.

ESPRESSO MACHINES

As a group, the espresso machines tested in the story on page 28 perform far better than those we reviewed in 1993. Among the ten machines tested in this go-around, four stood out for their superior milk frothing ability and the excellent espresso they produced. Our top-rated machine, the Krups Nova 2000, is available at the promotional price of $199.95 at Macy's, Bloomingdales, and The Bon Marché. For additional sources, where the machine may be sold for slightly more, call the Krups Customer Service Department (800-526-5377). Available by mail order from Zabar's (2245 Broadway at 80th Street, New York, NY 10024; 212-787-2000) are the second-rated Briel Estoril ES-33 espresso maker for $150 and the fourth-rated La Pavoni Espresso Si PA-16 for $160. The Estro 410, which rated third, can be bought for $189 from the Starbucks Coffee Company Catalog (2203 Airport Way South, P.O. Box 34510, Seattle, WA 98124-1510; 800-782-7282).

NESPRESSO

In addition to the espresso machines rated in the article on page 28, we also experimented with the new Nespresso system. A collaboration between Krups and Nestlé, the Nespresso system uses coffee capsules that contain enough premeasured, roasted, ground coffee for one cup of espresso. The capsules are used in place of coffee beans that you have to grind and measure yourself. The Nespresso Club (214 East 52nd Street, New York, NY 10022-6201; 800-562-1465) sells by mail the coffee capsules, which come with seven different blends, in packages of ten for $4.50 per package. Also available through the Nespresso Club are the machines themselves. We tried the model 986, which costs $199.99.

TRIFLE BOWL

Given its ten-step assembly process, the classic trifle from the story on page 8 should be equal parts celebratory dessert and architectural achievement. Choosing the correct vessel—a tall, footed, clear glass trifle bowl—is essential to display the intricate layers of cake, berries, and custard. The Crate & Barrel Catalogue (P.O. Box 9059, Wheeling, IL 60090-9050; 800-323-5461) sells a handblown Polish trifle bowl for $24.95. The bowl has a wide base for good support; high, straight sides to show off the contents within; and a capacity of just over three quarts.

CANDIED VIOLETS

If you have a yen to be a little fancy this holiday, consider following author Stephen Schmidt's lead and decorating your trifle (see page 8) with some crystallized violets. These sugared blooms, which are imported from France, are an incredibly easy way to finish the trifle, or other desserts such as cakes, tarts, or ice cream, with a professional look. Among the many specialty confections available from the catalog of Sweet Celebrations Inc., known formerly as Maid of Scandinavia (P.O. Box 39426, Edina, MN 55439-0426; 800-328-6722), are candied violets ($6.39 for a two-ounce package), candied rose petals ($7.65 for a two-ounce package), and candied mint leaves ($5.99 for a two-ounce package).

FRESH RASPBERRIES

Finding fresh berries during the winter season can be a spotty proposition, but the trifle from the article on page 8 just would not be the same with frozen ones. June and September are the two peaks for the domestic raspberry crop, of which the majority comes from the Pacific Northwest, Michigan, and New York. But thanks to climate-controlled packaging and quick transportation, some berries are now exported to the United States during our winter months from countries such as Chile and New Zealand (where, below the equator, it is summer). Imported raspberries and strawberries are available by mail order from Indian Rock Produce (530 California Road, Box 317, Quakerstown, PA 18951; 800-882-0512). Prices for the winter berries had not been finalized by our press time, so call Indian Rock for information on pricing and ordering.

MAIL-ORDER CORNMEAL

As we found in the story on page 25, one key to making great spoon bread, with its characteristic mild flavor and smooth texture, is to use finely ground cornmeal, either white or yellow. The author of the story recommends two Southern mills whose products are available by mail order. The products of Logan Turnpike Mill (3485 Gainesville Highway, Blairsville, GA 30512; 800-84-GRITS), from the finely ground cornmeal ($3.50 for a five-pound bag) to coarse "speckled" grits, are all ground from fresh, local corn. Also excellent is the finely ground cornmeal from J.T. Pollard Mill (Route 2, Box 144, Hartford, AL 36344; 334-588-3391), which sells for $2 per five-pound bag. We also like the high-quality fine-ground cornmeal available from Gray's Grist Mills (Box 422, Adamsville, RI 02801; 508-636-6075), which sells a 28-ounce bag for $9.95.

GRAIN STORAGE CONTAINERS

Artisan-produced stone- and water-ground grains, such as the cornmeals listed above, pack so much flavor because they retain much of the germ and with it, the flavorful oil of the grain. The high oil content has a downside, though, in that these meals go rancid far more quickly than the degerminated supermarket varieties to which preservatives have been added. Proper storage of the grains, refrigerated or frozen in airtight containers, will help maximize freshness and shelf life. The King Arthur Flour Baker's Catalogue (P.O. Box 876, Norwich, VT 05055-0876; 800-827-6836) sells heavy-duty, air-tight, locking, acrylic containers, called ClickClacks, which are ideal for the job. ClickClack canisters are available in four sizes: eight-ounce for $7.25; one-pound for $7.85; two-pound for $10.50; and five-pound for $15.75.

GRAPESEED OIL

Reader Victor Rostrow points out in Notes from Readers on page 3 that grapeseed oil is yet another choice among the many culinary oils. Considered a specialty oil that is not widely used in this country, grapeseed oil is particularly light in both taste and color and is said to have numerous health benefits. Cuisine Perel, a California-based supplier, sells grapeseed oil in 12.7-ounce bottles by mail order under its own label. The grapeseed oil is available either unflavored for $4.90 per bottle or $54 per case of twelve bottles, or infused with flavors such as roasted garlic, basil and garlic, ginger and garlic, rosemary, chile, or citrus and cilantro for $6.50 per bottle or $66 per case of twelve bottles. For ordering information, send a self-addressed stamped envelope to Cuisine Perel, 3100 Kerner Boulevard, San Rafael, CA 94901.

FRESH PHYLLO

Since developing the "Fearless Phyllo" story that ran in the November/December issue last year, we have discovered a mail-order source for fresh, never-frozen phyllo dough. The Fillo Factory Inc. (56 Cortland Avenue, Dumont, NJ 07628; 800-OK-FILLO) sells fresh phyllo dough in one-pound packages for $2.45, in one-half–pound packages for $1.49, and in preformed pastry shells for $3.79 for a box of six large shells and $2.99 for a box of fifteen small shells. Difficulties with tearing phyllo sheets, which occur often with frozen and then thawed dough, are almost nonexistent with this fresh, pliant phyllo. We made pastries in a number of shapes and two huge trays of baklava and managed to lose only a single sheet. ∎

COUNTRY HAM page 12
WITH GREEN BEANS AND
MUSHROOMS BRAISED IN CREAM page 7

SOUTHERN SPOON BREAD
page 25

CITRUS SALAD WITH BITTER GREENS
AND PARMESAN SHAVINGS
page 21

RECIPE INDEX

ASSORTED HOLIDAY COOKIES
page 19

CLASSIC TRIFLE
page 9

STEAMED MUSSELS
WITH ASIAN FLAVORS
page 15

Cranberry-Pear Salsa in Pear Shells

Place 1 cup cranberries, ½ medium seeded and stemmed jalapeño, and ¼ cup sugar in food processor fitted with steel blade; pulse five or six times to roughly chop. Transfer to small bowl; refrigerate 1 hour. Scoop flesh out of 2 Seckel pears (or pear of choice) that have been halved and cored, leaving ¼-inch-thick shell. Chop pear flesh coarse and add it to cranberry mixture; stir in 1 teaspoon white wine vinegar. Fill pears with cranberry mixture and serve with roast turkey or baked ham.

Serves 4